God's Treasured Possession

A Welwyn Commentary
on Deuteronomy

Andrew Stewart

 Books

EP BOOKS
Faverdale North
Darlington
DL3 0PH, England

web: www.epbooks.org
e-mail: sales@epbooks.org

EP BOOKS are distributed in the USA by:
JPL Distribution
3741 Linden Avenue Southeast,
Grand Rapids, MI 49548

e-mail: orders@jpldistribution.com
Tel: 877.683.6935

First published 2013

British Library Cataloguing in Publication Data available
ISBN : 978 085234 8178

Printed and bound in the UK by MPG

I would like to dedicate this commentary to my wife, Katie, and to thank her for her love and support over the past fifteen years. For most of that time I have been studying, preaching, teaching and writing about Deuteronomy. I hope this anniversary present will be a suitable acknowledgment of your patience over those years.

Contents

Author's Preface

One of the first things I urge a new believer to do is to read the whole Bible. Sometimes they come back and say, "The Bible is such a big book, where do I start?" In response I usually quote Fraulein Maria and say, "Just start at the very beginning, a very good place to start." These intrepid students of God's Word get off to a flying start as they read about God's mighty work of creation and his wonderful promises to Abraham. Then they are gripped by the drama of Joseph and the Exodus. But then they come to the laws of Israel. Often they grow weary and give up somewhere between the middle of Exodus and the end of Numbers. This is a great pity, for many reasons, not the least of which is that they miss out on reading Deuteronomy.

The book of Deuteronomy consists of a series of sermons preached by Moses on the plains of Moab, as the Israelites came towards the end of four decades of wandering in the wilderness and just before Moses handed over the leadership of God's people to Joshua. In these sermons he summarised Israel's history and he expounded Israel's laws. But this is more than history and regulations. Deuteronomy is a work of mature theology. It is the product of a lifetime of listening to and learning about the God of Israel. Along the way Moses has experienced failure and frustration, but he has been able to learn through these experiences. As he listened and learned he thought deeply about God's plan for Israel. He helps us to make sense of what we read in the first books of the Old Testament.

The theology of Deuteronomy is theology of grace. The majestic and holy Creator has chosen a nation of sinners – and Moses was one of them – to be his very own people and to enjoy his blessing.

They have become God's "treasured possession." God wants the very best for them. So, after redeeming them from slavery, he gave them laws to mould them into an ideal community which would reflect his holy character before the watching nations of the world.

This process of spiritual and moral transformation would be a lengthy, and at times painful, process because the people of Israel were steeped in sin. The cruelty and barbarity of the ancient world – much of it taking place in the name of false religion – shocks even modern sinners. Although the people of Israel were being redeemed out of this wicked world, they kept falling back into the evil from which God sought to deliver them. Over and over again they failed in their calling to be a beacon of hope for that fallen world.

The hope that God's holy people would bring light into a dark world, which is one of the guiding themes in Deuteronomy, set the agenda for the rest of the Old Testament. Sadly, it almost disappeared during the dark days of the Judges. It regained new impetus with the inauguration of the Monarchy. As the high hopes of those who longed for the righteous king turned into bitter disappointment, the prophets of Israel preached the message of Deuteronomy with fresh hope and vigour.

Then, with the coming of the Lord Jesus, arrived the day when God redeemed his elect people in all nations through the sacrifice and death of his own dear Son. Jesus Christ was identified as the King and Prophet to whom Moses had looked and his followers were identified as a new Israel. Peter describes them as "as chosen people, a royal priesthood, a holy nation, a people belonging to God, that you may declare the praises of him who called you out of darkness into his glorious light." (1 Peter 2:9) Paul describes the goal of our Lord's ministry in Titus 2:14. He "gave himself to redeem us from all wickedness and to purify for himself a people that are his very own, eager to do what is good." In Philippians 2:14-5 Paul addressed this challenge to the Church, "Do everything without complaining and arguing so that you may become blameless and pure, children without fault in a crooked and depraved generation, in which you shine like stars as you hold out the word of life."

When we read Deuteronomy we read how the eternal God sought to accomplish these same goals more than a millennium before the birth of our Lord. It is true that they cannot be accomplished apart from the redemptive work of Jesus Christ. However, through this portion of sacred Scripture God assures his chosen people that they are precious to him and reminds them of their high calling. That is why we need to read the book of Deuteronomy and reflect deeply on the kind of community we – "God's treasured possession" - are called to be.

And finally, I would like to thank those who have studied the book of Deuteronomy with me and in so doing have helped me learn and apply its message. Over the past ten years I have preached three different series of sermons (first on the book as a whole and then on specific themes and passages) on Deuteronomy from the pulpit of the Reformed Presbyterian Church in Geelong. I am grateful to the members of the congregation for their forbearance and their responses. The maps included in this commentary have been prepared by Andrew Barkley, a member of this congregation, and I would want to acknowledge his skill and help in this area.

Then in September 2004 I had the opportunity to teach a series of classes on Deuteronomy at the Kobe Theological Hall of the Reformed Presbyterian Churches in Japan. This challenged me to apply the message of Deuteronomy afresh in a context where the sins of idolatry are very visible. As this commentary goes to publication may the timeless message of God's servant Moses find fresh application in the lives of God's people for we are still called to keep ourselves from idols.

January 2013
Geelong
Australia

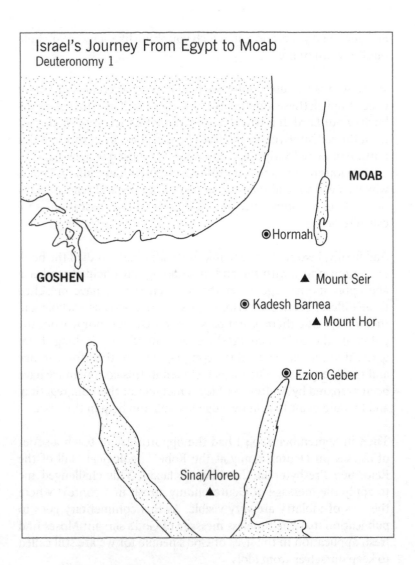

Israel's Journey From Egypt to Moab
Deuteronomy 1

MOAB

⊙Hormah

GOSHEN

▲ Mount Seir

⊙ Kadesh Barnea

▲ Mount Hor

⊙ Ezion Geber

Sinai/Horeb
▲

Chapter 1
The importance of obedience

Please read Deuteronomy 1:1-46

Works of literature can be slotted into several different categories. The various types of prose writing include novels, short stories, essays, biographies, histories, journals, letters, speeches and sermons. I can vividly remember my English literature teacher at school listing these genres and placing the sermon last in his list because, he claimed, 'This is the most boring of all and no-one in their right mind would want to read them.' This, all too frequently, is the view that people (even professing Christians) have of sermons. However, the very fact that you are reading this commentary shows that you have some desire to read a sermon. The book of Deuteronomy can best be described as a sermon, or a series of sermons, and the Holy Spirit has included it in the Bible for our blessing.

Setting the scene (1:1-4)

Deuteronomy records the sermons which Moses preached on the plains of Moab, east of the River Jordan, just before the people of Israel entered the land of Canaan. *'These are the words Moses spoke to all Israel in the desert east of the Jordan'* (1:1). Similar words of introduction are found in 4:44-45 and 29:1, and it is commonly recognised that the three main sections or sermons of Deuteronomy are 1:1 – 4:43, 4:44 – 28:68 and 29:1 – 30:20.

The sermons in Deuteronomy were preached '*in the fortieth year*' after the people of Israel had left Egypt (1:3). They had defeated the Amorite kingdoms to the east of the River Jordan (1:4) and were about to enter the promised land of Canaan. This was an unusual approach, but they had come to this point because of their stubborn refusal, forty years earlier, to enter the land at Kadesh Barnea. Moses notes that '*it takes eleven days to go from Horeb to Kadesh Barnea by the Mount Seir road*' (1:2); yet it took the Israelites forty years to arrive at the borders of the promised land. Thirty-eight of those forty years had been spent wandering in the wilderness. Those years of wandering were about to come to an end. The people of Israel were about to leave the wilderness and make the land of Canaan their home.

In 1:1 – 4:43 Moses traces the events that brought the Israelites to the borders of the promised land. Then in 4:44 – 26:19 he sets out the law code which was to govern the way they would live in the promised land. The historical narrative explains the importance of the law code. The people of Israel were the Lord's people and they were about to take possession of the land which God had promised them. This was a task which would require military discipline and dedication for, as the redeemed people of Jehovah, they were also the Lord's army.

One of the first lessons an army recruit must learn when he enters military service is the importance of following orders. Lives, and even battles, may be lost if soldiers decide that they can ignore the orders of their commanding officers. Sometimes the commanding officer gives out difficult orders, but a soldier must obey. This is a mindset that needs to be cultivated, and it was not something that came naturally to the people of Israel. Many of us might say the same about ourselves. It often takes a lifetime of disciplined obedience, walking with God and feeding upon his word, to learn to be a soldier in his army (see 2 Tim. 2:3). The book of Deuteronomy has many lessons to teach us in this regard, for it is a training manual in godly living. In it we see how Moses trained the Israelites to live as God's people in God's land. In this opening chapter we are introduced to God's people and the task that lay before them.

A nation under God (1:5-8)

Moses began his sermon by reminding Israel of the events that had taken place at Horeb (or Sinai as it is better known) shortly after the exodus. 'The LORD our God said to us at Horeb...' (1:6). Horeb was the mountain where God entered into a covenant with the family of Jacob, thus transforming it from a family of tribes into a nation. Moses repeatedly reminds the Israelites of this foundational event because it defined the character of their nation. They are a nation in covenant with God and this is the thread which runs through Deuteronomy.

The purpose of the national gathering in Moab was to renew that covenant before advancing into the promised land. The Israelites would again renew that covenant after they had entered into the land (see 27:1-7). Recent studies have shown that written covenants or treaties were commonly used at the time of Moses to regulate the relationship between a conquering king and his subject people. These treaties had standard features (there was a preamble, a historical prologue, an exposition of the obligations, a witness clause, and a list of sanctions; a memorial was erected, an oath was taken and the witnesses were identified). Some of these are found in Deuteronomy.

The reason for this similarity with secular treaties of loyalty is obvious For many years the Israelites had been slaves of Pharaoh, king of Egypt, yet God had heard their cries for help and liberated them from the tyranny of this earthly king so that they might become his people. In this new relationship the Israelites were to enjoy freedom from slavery and oppression. Yet they were not without a sovereign, for God was their king and they were his subject people. This new relationship was ratified at a formal ceremony at Horeb when God came down upon the mountain and gave his law. He declared that he had chosen Israel out of all the nations on the earth to be his favoured nation. In response, Israel was to serve only Jehovah as their God; and in his law Jehovah set out exactly what he required of them.

Moses' purpose was not simply to revisit the past and contemplate the great events which had taken place at Horeb. It had not been God's desire that the Israelites stay at Horeb to worship him in isolation in the wilderness. Moses reminds the Israelites of God's direction in 1:6-7:

> *You have stayed long enough at this mountain. Break camp and advance into the hill country of the Amorites; go to all the neighbouring peoples in the Arabah, in the mountains, in the western foothills, in the Negev, and along the coast, to the land of the Canaanites and to Lebanon, as far as the great river, the Euphrates.*

God wanted them to possess the promised land, and this is the first of many wonderful descriptions of the land which God had promised to Abraham's descendants.

At Horeb God repeated the promise which he had made many hundreds of years earlier to Abraham that his descendants would possess the land in which he then lived as a stranger. '*Go in and take possession of the land that the LORD swore he would give to your fathers – to Abraham, Isaac and Jacob - and to their descendants after them*' (1:8). The key words in this promise are the words *give* and *land*.

The importance of obedience

Notice how the verb *to give* is used twice in 1:8. First of all it describes what God had already done. *'See, I have given you this land.'* He had already made over the title deed to the Israelites. The land was theirs. The only problem was that the Canaanites were squatting on it. To remedy this problem God promised that he would give the Israelites actual possession of the land. 'Go in and take possession of the land that the LORD swore he would give to your fathers.' What God has promised to give, he will in fact give.

This gives us an insight into the character of God. He is a giving God. Without their asking or desiring, God had given this good land to Israel. Moreover he gave it freely. This is true not just of the promised land, but of every gift that God gives. 'Every good and perfect gift is from above...' (James 1:17). We see the greatest manifestation of God's goodness in his gift of salvation in Christ. 'God so loved the world that he gave his one and only Son...' (John 3:16). The gospel itself is possible only because God is a giver.

God's promised gift was the *land* of Canaan. It is described in 1:7. The scene which Moses set before his hearers is breathtaking. We will return to this amazing panorama later in 11:24, 33:6-25 and 34:1-4. Just as the snow-capped mountains and beautiful valleys of New Zealand provided a spectacular setting for Peter Jackson's production of *The Lord of the Rings,* so the hills, valleys and plans of Canaan provide the backdrop for Deuteronomy. They were set before the people of Israel to whet their appetite for God's promised blessing. This promise reaches its ultimate fulfilment in a Messianic king who 'will rule from sea to sea and from the River to the ends of the earth' (Ps. 72:8).

Along with God's blessing came a challenge. *'Break camp and advance into the hill country of the Amorites... Go and take possession of the land.'* The Israelites were not simply to admire the land and rejoice in their privileged status. They were to take the land. When God said 'Go', they were to move forward. They were to leave the spiritual mountain-top at Sinai and move forward into difficult terrain where they would face hostile nations. Many of us enjoy times of spiritual blessing when we can withdraw from the business of the world for prayer and meditation upon God's word. Yet we must leave these and go into the spiritual battlefield to serve our Saviour and preach his gospel. We go at God's command with his promise. 'Therefore go and make disciples of all nations... And surely I am with you always, to the very end of the age' (Matt. 28:18-20).

A nation organised under leaders (1:9-18)

God kept the promise he had given to Abraham in Genesis 15:5: 'Look up at the heavens and count the stars - if indeed you can count them... So shall your offspring be.' By the time that Abraham's descendants reached the borders of the promised land they had become a large nation. This blessing brought new challenges for Moses. In 1:9-10 Moses said to the Israelites, *'You are too heavy a burden for me to carry alone. The LORD your God has increased your numbers so that today you are as many as the stars in the sky.'* This was not a complaint, for Moses wanted even more of God's blessing. *'May the LORD, the God of your fathers, increase you a thousand times and bless you as he has promised'* (1:11). However, he recognised that the task of leading this multitude was more than he could bear on his own. *'How can I bear your problems and your burdens and your disputes all by myself?'* (1:12; see also Paul's words in 2 Cor. 3:5).

At the time of the exodus Moses' father-in-law, Jethro, could see that he was being overwhelmed by his workload and advised him to appoint deputies (see Exod. 18:1-26). At that time Moses put the suggestion to the people and they agreed with him (1:13-14). *"'Choose some wise, understanding and respected men from each of your tribes, and I will set them over you." You answered me,*

The importance of obedience

"What you propose to do is good."' As a result, commanders were appointed over the units of fighting men (1:15) and judges were appointed to hear disputes (1:16). Moses' role was as an appeal judge for 'hard' cases. However, God was the ultimate judge over all, *'... for judgment belongs to God'* (1:17).

Two features of this new administrative system have implications for us today. First of all, *these men had authority over the people.* Moses told the Israelites in 1:15, *'So I took the leading men of your tribes... and appointed them to have authority over you.'* Although Moses made the appointment and they were answerable to Moses, ultimately they received their authority from God. Moses, too, was a servant of God who had been appointed to rule God's people. Later, in the law code at the heart of Deuteronomy, Moses will have much more to say about the important work of civil rulers such as elders, judges and kings. All these public servants do their work for God, and the people must be subject to them as unto the Lord. This is what the apostle Paul tells us in Romans 13:1: 'Everyone must submit himself to the governing authorities, for there is no authority except that which God has established. The authorities that exist have been established by God.'

The second point to notice about Moses' charge to the leaders of the Israelites is that *these men have a responsibility to rule the people well.* According to Moses they were to be *'wise and respected men'* (see 1:13, 15). They were to listen to cases *'fairly'* (1:16). In particular, they were not to *'show partiality in judging'* (1:17). True justice is meant to be blind, in that it does not look at the face of those who come to court seeking a resolution of their dispute. Justice does not look at a person's social status, bank balance, skin colour or family connections, whereas partiality shows favour to some on account of these things. In Deuteronomy 16:18-20 Moses will apply this principle more broadly.

Sadly, today the evils of corruption, nepotism and bribery are rife in many countries and they cause immense social problems. The cost of basic services is often grossly inflated because officials line their pockets with bribes. This is a perennial problem, and many centuries later James 2:1-4 described corrupt officials as 'judges with evil thoughts'. They have more regard for men who offer rewards than they have for God, who seeks righteous conduct in every area of life. They forget that they are answerable to the Judge of all.

A nation under orders (1:19-46)

The importance of following God's orders became apparent when Israel went to take possession of the promised land. Moses reminds them of their first, unsuccessful, attempt to enter the promised land at Kadesh Barnea.

a. God's goodness was confirmed (1:19-25)
By following God's direction, the people of Israel came to the land that had been promised to Abraham. God had told Moses that the land was 'a good and spacious land, a land flowing with milk and honey' (Exod. 3:8). However, before going into the land the people sought a report: *'Then all of you came to me and said, "Let us send men ahead to spy out the land for us and bring back a report about the route we are to take and the towns we will come to"'* (1:22). They gave some very sensible reasons for seeking information about the land of Canaan. However, was there a hint of reluctance in their actions? Were they unsure that the land really was as good as God had said? Why did they want a second opinion?

In Deuteronomy this spying expedition is presented as an idea coming from the people, while in Numbers 13:1 it is presented as the Lord's command to Moses. These accounts are easily reconciled if we understand the Lord to be sovereignly directing both the desires of the people and the actions of Moses. Of course, not everything the people desired was pleasing to God or Moses; but in this instance the people's desire was good (1:23). *'The idea seemed good to me; so I selected twelve of you...'* The report which the spies brought back to the people confirmed that the Lord had indeed brought them to a good land. *'Taking with them some of the fruit of the land, they brought it down to us and reported, "It is a good land that the Lord our God is giving us"'* (1:25). The people need not have doubted the Lord's goodness or his abundant provision.

b. The people were paralysed by fear (1:26-33)
In spite of all the good things that the twelve spies had seen in the land, their report emphasised the difficulties which lay before the Israelites. Ten of the spies warned against entering the land because the people of the land were strong and their cities were well fortified. *'The people are stronger and taller than we are; the cities are large, with walls up to the sky. We even saw the Anakites there'* (1:28). The mere mention of the Anakites was enough to terrify anyone. The Anakites were a fearsome race of giant warriors whose reputation made other nations quake (see 9:2). Yet there was no need to fear because, as Moses pointed out, *'The LORD your God, who is going before you, will fight for you...'* (1:29-31). Even the Anakites would be driven out (see Josh. 11:21-22; 14:12; 15:14) and their fortified cities would fall to the Israelites.

At this stage the Israelites were unwilling to believe that, with God's help, they were able to drive out the Canaanite inhabitants of the land. The report of the ten spies unnerved the people. In spite of Moses' appeal (1:29-31) they refused to go into the promised land.

> *Then I said to you, 'Do not be terrified; do not be afraid of them. The LORD your God, who is going before you, will fight for you, as he did for you in Egypt, before your very eyes,*

and in the desert. There you saw how the LORD your God carried you, as a father carries his son, all the way you went until you reached this place.'

Their fear was a failure to trust God. *'In spite of this you did not trust in the LORD your God'* (1:32).

Fear is a powerful emotion with disastrous consequences, as F.D. Roosevelt recognised during the depression years of the 1930s when he told the American people that all they had to fear was fear itself. These verses show the spiritual consequences of fear. Fear can so fill our minds that we lose sight of all hope. Our focus on the darkness can be so intense that we do not see the light. When we do not look to the Lord or rely on him we lack the strength which he supplies to those who trust in him. The fear which blinds us may be a fear of Satan or of evil men; a fear of illness, pain or death; a fear of failure and condemnation by God. Peter was afraid of the wind and the waves and when he turned his focus from Christ to them he sank into the waters (Matt. 14:30). The antidote to paralysing fear is the faith that looks to God, listens to his word, and remembers what he has done.

> When 1 am afraid,
> 1 will trust in you.
> In God whose word 1 praise,
> in God 1 trust; 1 will not be afraid.
> What can mortal man do to me? (Ps. 56:3-4)

c. The Lord refused admission to the promised land (1:34-40)

God was angry with the people because of their disobedience and unbelief. He was angry with the spies (excepting only Joshua and Caleb, who urged the people to trust the Lord, see 1:36, 38). He was also angry with the whole generation of Israelites that followed their lead. *'Not a man of this evil generation shall see the good land 1 swore to your forefathers'* (1:35). Instead, their children, who had not participated in their sinful decision (*'the little ones... who do not yet know good from bad'*), would enter the land (1:39).

The Lord God was also angry with Moses. *'Because of you the LORD became angry with me and said, "You shall not enter it* [the promised land] *either"'* (1:37). In Numbers 20:12 we read that Moses was not permitted to enter the promised land because of a later incident when Moses struck the rock rather than speaking to it. Moses refers to this explanation in 32:51-52. Clearly there were multiple reasons why Moses was denied entry into the promised land. Both his own sin and the sin of the people lay behind God's refusal. Sin is complicated and messy. It weaves a tangled web which ensnares both those who sin and others. Its implications reach farther than we imagine and affect people in ways we do not expect. However, God is always just and compassionate in his dealings with us.

d. The people added to their sinfulness by rejecting their punishment (1:41-46)
As the Israelites faced the prospect of retracing their steps through the desert and back to the Red Sea, the stupidity of their actions dawned on them. They changed their minds and decided that they would like to take possession of the promised land after all. *'Then you replied, "We have sinned against the LORD. We will go up and fight, as the LORD our God commanded us"'* (1:41a). Without waiting for God's response, they put on their weapons and set off to attack the Canaanites, *'thinking it easy to go up into the hill country'* (1:41b).

By this time it was too late. Moses warned the people of Israel that the Lord would not go with them (1:42-33) and, as a result, they would be an easy prey for the Amorites. *'You will be defeated by your enemies...'* The Lord's warning came true and Moses reminded them of the tragic consequences of their disobedience. *'The Amorites who lived in those hills came out against you; they chased you like a swarm of bees and beat you down from Seir all the way to Hormah'* (1:42, 44). When they cried out to God, *'he paid no attention to your weeping and turned a deaf ear to you'* (1:45). For a time the Lord withdrew his face from them, and they languished in the desert of Kadesh for *'many days'* (1:46). Like sailors stranded on a desert island they were lost and hopeless, but they had lessons to learn from this experience.

The Israelites were doubly punished (they missed out on the blessings of the promised land and they suffered defeat at the hands of their enemies) because of their double disobedience (they refused to go in when the Lord told them and they went in when the Lord told them to go back to the Red Sea). Their punishment was especially severe because their sins were hidden under a mask of piety. First of all we see the sin of *false repentance.* The Israelites confessed that they had done wrong; but they refused to submit themselves to God's leading in the future. To this they also added the sin of *arrogant presumption.* They expected God to be thankful for their delayed obedience and bless them as though their sin had never happened. They showed no evidence of true sorrow for their sin because they had no understanding of the sinfulness of their actions. If God had blessed them with an easy victory at this point their sinful way of thinking would have continued unchallenged.

Living under God's lordship means *learning to grieve over sin.* When it dawned on the Israelites that they had foolishly rejected the land of the covenant and that they faced another long period in the desert, they must have been bitterly disappointed. As they thought of the privations which lay ahead of them they were truly sorry that they had been so foolish, yet their disappointment was not the same as true repentance. It was essentially selfish. It is not to be confused with true sorrow for sin which leads to repentance. It is all too easy for us to say that we are sorry for our sin when we see the consequences of our sins staring us in the face; but true repentance grieves over the dishonour which our disobedience causes to God as well as the disappointment which we bear.

Living under God's lordship also means *resolving to accept that God's chastisements are just.* Even though the eternal consequences of sin are removed forever by the atoning work of Christ, God's redeemed people may still suffer temporal and temporary consequences of sin while on earth. One whole generation was condemned to wander in the wilderness because of its rebelliousness. Their words in 1:41 may sound pious and well-intentioned. *'Then you replied, "We have sinned against the LORD. We will go up and fight, as the LORD our God commanded us." So every one of you put on his weapons, thinking it easy to go up into the hill country.'* They were, however, deeply defiant. Rather than learning from their failure, they dug in their heels and refused to bear God's chastisement.

There are important lessons which Christians today can learn through disappointment and failure. These chastisements may take many different forms - illness, unemployment, financial ruin and the loss of peace of mind. Yet we know that all these proceed from the sovereign providence of God. In response we are to ask, 'What might God be teaching us? Where might we have sinned? How might God be calling us to repentance?' For the Israelites, true repentance meant accepting the disappointing prospect of many more years in the desert. For us it means following our repentance with a new resolve to do the will of our Father in heaven.

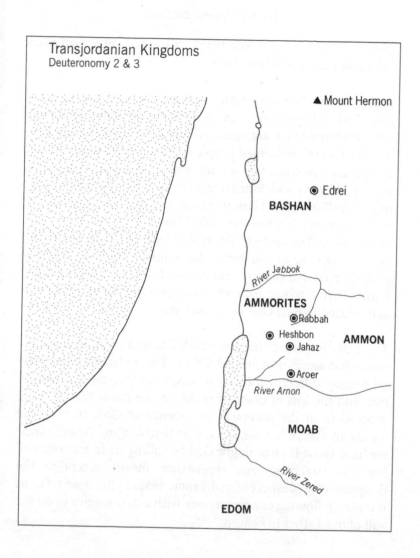

Transjordanian Kingdoms
Deuteronomy 2 & 3

▲ Mount Hermon

◉ Edrei

BASHAN

River Jabbok

AMMORITES

◉ Rabbah

◉ Heshbon
◉ Jahaz

AMMON

◉ Aroer
River Arnon

MOAB

River Zered

EDOM

Chapter 2
Back from the wilderness

Please read Deuteronomy 2: 1-37

Deuteronomy is a sermon explaining the grace of God to sinners. Sometimes this fact gets overlooked amidst the details of Israel's history and laws and we miss the great message of Deuteronomy, which is that God is a gracious Saviour who will never forsake his chosen people. Even when the Israelites stubbornly refused to enter the promised land (1:26), and then presumptuously went up to take possession of the land (1:43), the Lord did not abandon them.

In Deuteronomy 2 Moses describes how the Lord remained with Israel when they returned to the desert (2:1-3, 7, 14-15); while they travelled towards the promised land (2:4-23); and as they went into battle (2:24-37).

In the desert (2:1-3, 7, 14-15)

In the desert they learned to accept God's chastisements. '*Then we turned back and set out toward the desert along the route to the Red Sea, as the LORD had directed me.*' Through Moses, the Lord directed the next steps of the Israelites. His directions were exactly what he had told the Israelites to do in 1:40 following their rebellion at Kadesh. At that time they were not willing to go up against the Canaanites; nor were they willing to return to the wilderness. On both counts they were stubbornly disobedient. Numbers 20:14-21 records how they tried to travel through Edomite territory to find another entry point into the promised land. However, the Edomites 'refused to let them go through their territory' and 'Israel turned away from them'. This incident is not to be confused with the events of Deuteronomy 2:8 (which took place thirty-eight years later) when the Israelites passed *alongside* Edomite territory. This earlier encounter with the Edomites compelled the Israelites to fall into line with God's command in Deuteronomy 1:40.

The Israelites went back along the road they had travelled and returned to the wilderness for thirty-eight long years. In 2:1b it is referred to as *'the hill country of Seir'*. Seir is another name for Edom, although, in this verse, it is unlikely to refer to the heartland of the Edomites. More probably it refers to the hilly desert area to the south, between Edom and the Red Sea.

Israel's time in the wilderness is described in 2:14-15 as a time of painful chastening. By the time it had come to an end, *'that entire generation of fighting men had perished from the camp, as the LORD had sworn to them'*. God had warned in 1:35 that this would happen, and it did. As the book of Deuteronomy unfolds we will see that God's promises are a two-edged sword. As well as promising blessing to those who love and serve him, God promises cursing for those who rebel and disobey him. Both sets of consequences are underwritten by the faithfulness of God.

Moses describes the vehemence of God's opposition to those who rebelled against him at Kadesh in 2:15: *'The LORD's hand was against them until he had completely eliminated them from the camp.'* To indicate God's purpose Moses used the Hebrew verb *hamam*, which means to crush, trouble or vex. God did not simply wait for this generation to die, but he actively rooted them out of the camp and ensured that they died under God's chastisement. This reminds us of the awesome truth that there is no peace for those who rebel against God.

> But the wicked are like the tossing sea, which cannot rest, whose waves cast up mire and mud.
> 'There is no peace,' says my God, 'for the wicked.'
> (Isa. 57:20-21)

In spite of the anger which he directed towards those who sinned at Kadesh, God did not abandon the nation as a whole. Israel was his chosen nation and he blessed them even during those difficult years. Moses was able to look back over the thirty-eight years in the desert and see God's goodness: *'The LORD your God has blessed you in all the work of your hands. He has watched over your journey through this vast desert ... you have not lacked anything'* (2:7). God provided for their material needs in a most amazing way and later, in Deuteronomy 29:5, he told them: 'During the forty years that I led you through the desert, your clothes did not wear out, nor did the sandals on your feet.'

Israel's greatest blessing during those years was God's presence (*'the LORD your God has been with you'*) and his watchful care (*'He has watched over your journey'*). Because of God's blessing the people lacked nothing. This is not to say that they had many earthly treasures. There must have been many times when the Israelites cast their minds back to the riches of Egypt and wished that they could have had some delicacy that was unavailable in the desert. No doubt there were many things they had to do without. However they lacked no good thing. Even in the wilderness God spread his table for them (see Ps. 78:15-16, 23-29). God does the same for his people today.

We sometimes go through 'wilderness times' when calamity comes upon us because of our folly; yet even in the midst those times God cares for us and preserves us from disaster. God does not leave his people without help and encouragement, and most certainly God does not abandon them. He is with us always, even though his rod may be painful.

Thankfully, God's chastening does not continue forever. Israel's time in the wilderness came to an end because God looked upon her in mercy. *'Then the LORD said to me, "You have made your way around this hill country long enough; now turn north."'* From now on their travels would take them towards the entry point into the promised land of Canaan, on the plains of Moab. God took no pleasure in the hardships of his people, and kept them in the wilderness not a moment longer than was necessary for their good. This reminds us that God delights in mercy and does not hold on to his anger forever. When he chastens us today, he does so only to bring us back to an even closer relationship with himself. His anger is real and his chastening may be painful, but on account of the atoning work of the Lord Jesus it comes to an end. 'I will not accuse for ever, nor will I always be angry' (Isa. 57:16). 'He will not always accuse, nor will he harbour his anger forever' (Ps. 103:9). 'For his anger lasts only a moment, but his favour lasts a lifetime' (Ps. 30:5).

En route to the promised land (2:4-23)

In 2:4-19 Moses recorded how God charted the journey they would take from the southern desert into the more fertile and densely populated lands east of the Jordan. They would cease to be nomads and would become an army moving towards the land which they would possess as an inheritance from the Lord. Along the way they would pass through, or around, a series of hostile kingdoms. In 2:4-23 Moses describes the three nations whose territory they would not invade: the Edomites (2:4-6, 8a), the Moabites (2:8b-9, 16-18) and the Ammonites (2:19).

God made three statements about each of these nations. First of all, he gave a *command* – do not provoke them or engage them in war. Secondly, God made a *statement* – their land will not be given to Israel. Thirdly, God gave an *explanation* – he would not give their land to Israel because he had already given it to those nations as their inheritance. Interspersed through this section are historical footnotes referring to the former inhabitants of these lands and how the Lord ejected them before the Edomites, Moabites and Ammonites (see 2:10-12, 20-23).

This record raises the question: why were these three nations spared when other nations were not? We know that God does good even to godless people (see Matt. 5:45). However, in just a few verses, we will read that no mercy was shown to the godless Amorites. Why this discrepancy in God's dealing with the nations east of the Jordan?

The Edomites, Moabites and Ammonites were 'cousins' of the Israelites. The Edomites were the descendants of Esau, the twin brother of Jacob. The Moabites and Ammonites were descended from Lot (the nephew of Abraham) through his two daughters after they had fled the destruction of Sodom. The unsavoury story of how the fathers of these two nations were conceived is found in Genesis 19:30-38.

The Edomites, Moabites and Ammonites grew into wicked nations and became bitter enemies of the people of Israel. We find examples of the hostility of this terrible trio in 1 Samuel 14:47, 2 Samuel 8:12, 2 Chronicles 20:10-11 and Psalm 83:5-8. In spite of this they remained offshoots from the same stock. They had godly ancestors. Lot is described as a righteous man in 2 Peter 2:7. The Edomites had the patriarchs Abraham and Isaac as their forebears and they gain a mention in the history of Abraham's descendants in 1 Chronicles 1:35-54. Thus God distinguished these nations from other Gentile nations. In

29

God's treasured possession

Deuteronomy 23:7 God commanded, 'Do not abhor an Edomite, for he is your brother'. Even if God did not redeem these nations or enter into a covenant them he showed mercy to these outer branches of the family of Abraham for the sake of their godly ancestors.

Godly parents and grandparents leave a legacy that brings blessing to their descendants for many generations. Even after those children have turned away from God, many common blessings remain as a testimony to God's goodness to those who love him. That legacy can be seen even amongst those who have abandoned the faith of their parents or grandparents, but who continue to enjoy remarkable natural talents and material blessings. History records many instances of 'sons of the manse' who went on to make their mark in the fields of politics, science or sport because of the disciplines which they learned from godly parents. On a wider canvas, history also records how nations with a Christian heritage develop habits of honesty, diligence and respect for the law which then establish the conditions necessary for higher than average levels of peace and prosperity. These are blessings from God which even the ungodly enjoy. Sadly, many people who enjoy these blessings give no thought to the God who has blessed them.

Another principle illustrated in these verses is that of God's sovereignty over all the earth. The Lord warned Israel not to seek conflict with the Edomites (2:5), the Moabites (2:9) or the Ammonites (2:19), not because these nations were too strong for him, but because God had allocated their lands to them. God could easily have conquered all of these nations and given their land to Israel. Already God had taken these lands from other nations and given them to the Edomites, Moabites and Ammonites (see 2:10-12, 20-23). One of these nations, the Rephaites (see 2:11, 20), was reputed to be giants. *They were a people strong and numerous, and as tall as the Anakites.* However, *The LORD destroyed them.*

For his own purposes the Lord chose to cast out the Emites and give their land to the Moabites (2:10-11). Likewise he cast out the Horites in favour of the Edomites (2:12, 22), and the Zamzummites in favour of the Ammonites (2:20-21). All this land belonged to Jehovah and he chose to give it to the Edomites, Moabites and Ammonites as their possession or inheritance. *'I have given Esau the hill country of Seir as his own... I have given Ar to the descendants of Lot as a possession... I have given it as a possession to the descendants of Lot'* (2:5, 9, 19). *'Possession'* comes from a word family which is commonly used in Deuteronomy to describe Israel's exclusive enjoyment of the land as a gift from God (see 2:12; 3:20). Yet here it describes the land given to the Edomites, Moabites and Ammonites. In 2:23 Moses refers to others who were dispossessed of their land: *'And as for the Avvites who lived in villages as far as Gaza, the Caphtorites coming out from Caphtor destroyed them and settled in their place.'* Afterwards the Caphtorites were removed from this land so that the Israelites might possess it.

The lesson which Moses wanted the Israelites to learn was that all the earth belongs to Jehovah. It does not belong to the people who happen to possess it at any given time. It did not belong to the Edomites, nor even to the Israelites or to any other nation. It belongs to Jehovah and he apportions it to whomsoever he will. He takes from one nation and gives to another. He establishes the boundaries between nations. Moses will make this point more explicitly in Deuteronomy 32:8: 'When the Most High gave the nations their inheritance, when he divided all mankind, he set up boundaries for the peoples'. This prerogative does not belong to any other god. The gods of the Canaanites had not given those nations their land. The God of Israel had given it to them, and he would take it from them when he saw fit.

This is a reminder to us all that the God who gives good things is also the God who takes them away. The God of Israel had the authority to remove the Edomites, Moabites and Ammonites from their possession whenever he saw fit. In due time he did remove them! More ominously, the Lord could equally well remove the Israelites from the land which he had given them as a possession. This is the warning of the covenant to which Moses will return later in Deuteronomy.

We too are reminded not to grow complacent in our enjoyment of the earthly and material blessings which God has given us. After he so tragically lost all his earthly possessions Job reminded himself that they had come from God in the first place.

Naked I came from my mother's womb,
and naked I will depart.
The LORD gave and the LORD has taken away;
may the name of the LORD be praised.
(Job 1:21)

Our Lord told the parable of a rich man, whose soul delighted in his abundant harvest. 'But God said to him, "You fool! This very night your life will be demanded from you. Then who will get what you have prepared for yourself?" This is how it will be with anyone who stores up things for himself but is not rich toward God' (Luke 12:20-21).

Into battle (2:24-37)

At last God brought the Israelites to the land which he had planned to give them. This was the land of the Amorites. It lay to the east of the River Jordan, reaching from the Arnon Gorge in the south as far as the mountains of Lebanon in the north. Its conquest and division is described in two stages in Deuteronomy 2:24-3:20. The first stage was the conquest of Sihon, king of Heshbon (2:24-37). His kingdom stretched from the Arnon to the hills of Gilead. The conquest of this land gave Israel a first taste of the battles which lay before her in Canaan.

It also gave her a first taste of the blessings of possessing a homeland of her own.

God's charge (2:24-25)
God started to give directions to his people in 2:4, and continued in that vein through 2:9, 13 and 18. Those directions continue in 2:24. *'Set out now and cross the Arnon Gorge. See, I have given into your hand Sihon the Amorite, king of Heshbon, and his country. Begin to take possession of it and engage him in battle.'* This was the first step towards the realisation of what God had promised many years earlier to Abraham. The conquest of Canaan commenced when the Israelites took control of its eastern approaches. It was a small step, but an important one because it cut off the possibility of these eastern nations coming to the aid of their Canaanite kinsmen and so trapping the Israelites in a pincer movement. This gradual approach to taking possession of the promised land was a very deliberate part of God's strategy (see 7:22). God's plans are accomplished as his people fight many small battles, realising that the really decisive battle has been fought and won by God himself.

God followed this battle call with an assurance of ultimate victory which rested upon his sovereign decree. *'See, I have given into your hand Sihon the Amorite... This very day I will begin to put the terror and fear of you on all the nations under heaven. They will hear reports of you and will tremble and be in anguish because of you.'* The Amorites were as good as defeated and the land was as good as Israel's because God had spoken the word. This did not relieve them of the responsibility of going forward in faith, but it did strengthen their resolve as they went forward in faith.

God knows that his people often face violent opposition and need to be reassured. At a crucial stage in his ministry in Corinth, the apostle Paul received words of reassurance in a vision (see Acts 18:9-10). Only a handful of people had believed the gospel, and the enemies of the gospel threatened to bring his ministry to an end, but the Lord appeared to Paul and said: 'Do not be afraid; keep on speaking, do not be silent. For I am with you, and no-one is going to attack and harm you, because I have many people in this city.' Even though they had not believed, their conversion was a certainty. Nothing is more certain than what God has decreed and promised. We are to live as soldiers who are fighting a battle that we cannot lose.

Moses' strategy (2:26-29)
Moses sought a peaceful passage through Sihon's territory and he made his purposes clear in a letter. *'Let us pass through your country. We will stay on the main road; we will not turn aside to the right or to the left."* In all probability 'the main road' refers to the historic Kings' Highway (see Num. 21:22) which, even today, is a major route between Amman and Aqaba. In Moses' day it provided the most direct route to the point from which the Israelites would cross the River Jordan into Canaan. See 2:29: *'...until we cross the Jordan into the land the LORD our God is giving us'.* In spite of God's promise in 2:24-25, Moses tried to pass through Amorite territory en route to the promised land, rather than take the area by conquest. Moses demonstrated his peaceful intent by offering to pay for everything that the Israelites would use along the way. *'Sell us food to eat and water to drink for their price in silver.'* His request for peaceful passage was sincere and credible, for in 2:29a he was able to point to Israel's dealings with the Edomites and Moabites to confirm their good faith.

Moses' peaceful strategy was not an act of cowardice or disobedience, in which he sought to avoid the inevitable conflict with the Amorites. It was an act of mercy on the part of God. God gave Sihon the opportunity to co-operate with his purposes, just as he gave Pharaoh the opportunity to let the Israelites leave Egypt in peace; but sadly (for Sihon and his kingdom) Moses' request for a peaceful passage received a hostile response. God's people must expect to face hostility and conflict as they live in a fallen world – yet we are not to seek it. The Lord Jesus instructed his disciples to be 'as shrewd as snakes and as innocent as doves' (Matt. 10:16). He rebuked Peter when he took his sword to fight off those who came to arrest him. 'Put your sword away! Shall I not drink the cup the Father has given me?' (John 18:11). Peace-making is to be a priority for Christians (see Matt. 5:9, James 3:18). We are to seek peace, yet prepare ourselves to face hostility when, in God's providence, it comes.

Sihon's belligerence (2:30-33)

Sihon responded to Moses' peaceable letter by preparing for war. *'But Sihon king of Heshbon refused to let us pass through.'* Moses explained what lay behind Sihon's hostile response: *'for the LORD your God had made his spirit stubborn and his heart obstinate in order to give him into your hands'.* The hardening of Sihon's heart is similar to that of Pharaoh when he refused to let the people of Israel leave Egypt. God told Moses that he would harden Pharaoh's heart (Exod. 4:21; 7:3); but Pharaoh also hardened his own heart (Exod. 8:15, 32); and then God confirmed Pharaoh's stubbornness by hardening his heart again (Exod. 9:12). Thus even the intransigence of an evil man brought about God's holy will. The apostle Paul tells us that this happened in order to demonstrate God's power and justice (see Rom. 9:17-18).

Similarly, it was God's will that Sihon start the war that would spell his own destruction. That war and its consequences are described in 2:32-33. *'When Sihon and all his army came out to meet us in battle at Jahaz, the LORD our God delivered him over to us and we struck him down together with his sons and his whole army.'* Sihon's hostility towards the people of God led to the destruction of his kingdom, just as God had decreed. No-one can say that God acted unfairly in the way he brought about

Sihon's downfall, for Sihon picked this fight for himself. Here we have an example of divine sovereignty and human free will existing and operating together.

Nestled between Moses' description of Sihon's belligerence in 2:30 and 2:32-33 – and therefore in a position of emphasis – is God's message of encouragement for Moses and the Israelites in 2:31. *'See, I have begun to deliver Sihon and his country over to you. Now begin to conquer and possess the land.'* God assured them that, even though they did not seek the battle which lay ahead of them, he would be with them and give them the victory. They could enter the battle with confidence, for they had not picked a fight presumptuously. Note the contrast between the way they went out to fight Sihon and the way they went out to fight the Canaanites in 1:43-44. Presumption then was the path to disaster, while their approach at this point is one of humble reliance upon God. They sought peace, but were prepared to fight if that was what God wanted them to do.

The hostility which Christians face today is not to be met with violence, but there are times when truth is under attack and we must 'contend for the faith that was once for all entrusted to the saints' (Jude 3). When those times come we are to contend, not belligerently, but confidently and out of love for God, his truth and even our enemies (Matt. 5:44-45).

Israel's victory (2:34-37)
The extent of Sihon's defeat is described in these verses. *'At that time we took all his towns and completely destroyed them – men, women and children... The LORD our God gave us all of them.'* Israel's victory over Sihon's kingdom was total victory. The territory which Israel conquered is described in 2:36: *'from Aroer on the rim of the Arnon Gorge, and from the town in the gorge, even as far as Gilead, not one town was too strong for us.'* At Kadesh Barnea the Israelites refused to enter the land of Canaan because the Canaanite towns were fortified and they feared that

these would be too strong for them (1:28). .... implied rebuke to the unbelief of that generation. With God's help the towns east of the Jordan fell to the Israelites. 'The Lord our God gave us all of them.' The same Lord would also give them possession of the towns west of the Jordan.

When we face our own struggles against sin and temptation it is good to remember the victories which God has already given us, and to meditate on the power of God which is manifest in them. David praised God when he thought of God's power.

> Praise be to the LORD my Rock,
> who trains my hands for war,
> my fingers for battle.
> He is my loving God and my fortress,
> my stronghold and my deliverer,
> my shield, in whom I take refuge,
> who subdues peoples under me.
> (Ps. 144:1-2)

When the apostle Paul faced the twin enemies of sin and death, he rejoiced in the resurrection victory of our Lord. 'But thanks be to God! He gives us the victory through our Lord Jesus Christ' (1 Cor. 15:57). In Romans 8:37 he assures believers that 'we are more than conquerors through him who loved us'.

It is appropriate to draw spiritual lessons from the events of these verses because the Israelites were not mindless marauders, plundering the towns and countryside of Heshbon. They were soldiers of God, engaged in a holy war to establish the kingdom of Jehovah. Two aspects of the narrative point to the role which they played in God's wider purposes.

First of all, *they devoted the towns they captured to the Lord* (2:34). *'At that time we took all his towns and completely destroyed them.'* The phrase 'completely destroyed' translates the Hebrew verb *herem*, which means 'to devote to Jehovah by means of destruction'. Destruction was not mindless vandalism, but purposeful consecration. In this case God allowed the Israelites to keep the livestock for their own use (2:35), but in other cases he did not (see Josh. 6:17-19). The Amorite population was to be removed from the land they had once occupied because it was being made ready for new inhabitants who worshipped the Lord. Thus the land was to be wholly devoted to Jehovah. This was what Zechariah foresaw when he foretold a day when 'HOLY TO THE LORD will be inscribed on the bells of the horses, and the cooking pots in the Lord's house....And on that day there will no longer be a Canaanite in the house of the LORD Almighty' (Zech. 14:20-21).

Secondly, *they took only the land which had been allocated to them by the Lord* (2:37). *'But in accordance with the command of the LORD our God, you did not encroach on any of the land of the Ammonites.'* They were to take only the land which God had promised them. This land they were to settle and subdue; and gradually they were to establish a community which would show the world what it means to live as the redeemed people of God. They were not to take more land than they could subdue at that time. In due time the day would come when God's covenant with Israel would bring blessings to the whole world, but in the meantime God's mercies were to be unfolded upon a smaller stage. Ultimately, however, every enemy and every inch of enemy territory will be brought into subjection to the King of kings, who will hand everything over to God the Father, so that 'God may be all in all' (see 1 Cor. 15:25-28).

Chapter 3
A foretaste of better things

Please read Deuteronomy 3: 1-29

After the allied victory at El Alamein, a significant turning point in the Second World War, Winston Churchill made the sobering observation, 'This is not the end. This is not even the beginning of the end. It is, perhaps, the end of the beginning.' The same assessment might have been made of the Israelite conquest of the territories east of the River Jordan, recorded in Deuteronomy 2 and 3. The people of Israel had not yet entered the promised land of Canaan, let alone conquered it. The story of that conquest will be told in the book of Joshua. However, by the end of chapter 3 we see the Israelites encamped on the plains of Moab *'in the valley near Beth Peor'*, poised to enter the promised land from the east.

Ahead of the Israelites lie many battles, both military and spiritual. As they go into battle their faith will be severely tested and, on occasions, found to be wanting. In preparation for these testing times Moses called the nation of Israel to renew its covenant with Jehovah. Moses' summary of Israel's journey from Egypt to Moab which we find in Deuteronomy 1-3 was an historical introduction to this act of spiritual renewal which prepared the Israelites to take possession of the land promised by God to their forefathers. Moses had much to tell the Israelites about God and his faithfulness. The land they would conquer had been promised by God and it was a guaranteed inheritance. Already they had received a foretaste of what was to come. Moses reminded them of that fact as he completed his account of the conquest of the Amorite kingdoms east of the Jordan. The conquest of Sihon and his kingdom is recounted in 2:24-37; and in 3:1-7 we come to the conquest of Og and his kingdom in Bashan.

A foretaste of victory (3:1-7)

By this stage Israel's military advance has built up some momentum and conflict with Og and his kingdom is inevitable. *'Next we turned and went up along the road toward Bashan, and Og king of Bashan with his whole army marched out to meet us in battle'* (3:1). There was no opportunity to seek a peaceful way through Og's territory, as Moses had sought in 2:26 when the Israelites approached the boundaries of Heshbon. King Og and his armies were already mobilised and marching towards the Israelites. The Israelites must either fight or die. Having won a resounding victory over the southern Amorites, the Israelites too were ready for battle. Conflict between Israel and the northern Amorites was inevitable.

As the Israelites went into battle God spoke to encourage them. *'Do not be afraid of him, for I have handed him over to you with his whole army and his land. Do to him what you did to Sihon king of the Amorites, who reigned in Heshbon'* (3:2). Just as God gave words of encouragement to the Israelites as they went into battle against Sihon and his army, so God again told the Israelites that he would give them victory. He encouraged them not to be afraid as they advanced, for he had decreed the destruction of Og's armies and his kingdom. 'I have handed him over to you with his whole army and his land.' On the battlefield they will observe the unfolding of plans which God had made in eternity. In God's mind, the battle is already won and the land is already theirs, because he has decreed it. Yet the Israelites had a vitally important task to perform, for through them God would win the victory. Hence the exhortation, 'Do to him what you did to Sihon king of the Amorites, who reigned in Heshbon.'

Just as God had said, so the Israelites were victorious. The account in 3:3-7 highlights the parallels between the defeat of Og and the conquest of his kingdom and the defeat of Sihon in 2:24-37.

Og's army was completely destroyed. *'So the LORD our God also gave into our hands Og king of Bashan and all his army. We struck him down, leaving no survivors'* (3:3; compare 2:32-33).

Og's fortified cities were taken. *'At that time we took all his cities. There was not one of the sixty cities that we did not take from them'* (3:4-5; compare 2:34, 36).

Og's land was consecrated to the Lord. 'We completely destroyed them, as we had done with Sihon king of Heshbon' (3:6). The significant Hebrew verb *herem* is used to describe the destruction of Og and his kingdom. By fire and sword the evil influence of the idolatrous inhabitants of the land was removed and the land itself was dedicated to the Lord. Compare 2:34.

Og's wealth was taken. 'But all the livestock and the plunder from their cities we carried off for ourselves' (3:7). In this way the wealth of the heathen nations was given into the hands of God's people, and thus brought into the sphere of God's earthly rule. Compare 2:35.

By highlighting the parallels between the conquest of Bashan and the conquest of Heshbon, Moses emphasised *the continuity of God's purposes*. Israel's victory over Sihon was not a chance occurrence, but an expression of God's determined purpose. God would give many, many more victories to his people in the coming years. What had been commenced with the conquest of Heshbon was brought to completion in the conquest of Bashan. Taken together, these conquests provide a foretaste of victories to come.

As Moses recounted the story of these victories, he highlighted *the controlling power of God's word*. God had decreed that Og would be defeated and that Israel would win the battle. If God had not spoken, the Israelites would not have known what God had planned to do; but when God spoke through Moses, his word was able to direct their actions and reassure their hearts. We know that God's secret decrees direct the flow of history, but it was 'the things revealed' (see Deut. 29:29) that guided Israel's conduct. God's promises and exhortations spurred the Israelites to fight courageously and, ultimately, victoriously against the Amorites. God's word turned the course of these battles.

We also know that God has decreed that his Son will win a mighty victory over the great enemy himself. God told Eve that 'your offspring... will crush (his) head' (Gen. 3:15). The enemy we face is Satan; and his instruments for controlling our lives are sin and death. We can take heart from the fact that God has decreed his downfall. 'The God of peace will soon crush Satan under your feet' (Rom. 16:20). 'In all these things we are more than conquerors through him who loved us' (Rom. 8:37). 'But thanks be to God! He gives us the victory through our Lord Jesus Christ' (1 Cor. 15:57). God has placed his word, like a sword, into our hands so that we might overcome Satan on the spiritual battlefield.

A foretaste of the land (3:8-17)

After recounting the defeat of *'these two kings of the Amorites'* (3:8), Moses pauses to take stock of what had been accomplished by the events described in 2:24-3:7. *'So at that time we took from these two kings of the Amorites the territory east of the Jordan, from the Arnon Gorge as far as Mount Hermon... We took all the towns on the plateau, and all Gilead, and all Bashan as far as Salecah and Edrei, towns of Og's kingdom in Bashan.'* Israel now controlled a large swathe of territory east of the Jordan, from which they could now safely launch a major assault on the land of Canaan.

Moses describes *the dimensions* of the land east of the Jordan in 3:8-11. It lay between two distinctive landmarks, the Arnon Gorge in the south and Mount Hermon in the north. These were the northern and southern limits of the Transjordan inheritance. Between them lay the tablelands of Bashan and Gilead (see 3:10). These upland areas were famed for their forests and rich grazing (see Isa. 2:13; Ezek. 27:6; Deut. 32:13-14; Micah 7:14). The eastern limits of the plateau were marked by the towns of Salecah and Edrei.

A passing comment is made in 3:9 on the various names given to Mount Hermon. The Sidonians (who lived to the west near the coast) called it Sirion, while the Amorites (who had just been conquered) called it Senir. The name Hermon was Israelite in origin and it is theologically significant. Conquerors often rename the places they conquer, and the name Hermon comes from the important Hebrew verb *herem*. This was used in the Old Testament to describe the total destruction of Canaanite cities and communities as a means of consecrating the land to Jehovah. In Judges 3:3 this important mountain peak was called Mount Baal Hermon, and this may indicate that had been a centre for pagan rituals as well as a home for pagan nations. However, the use of the simple name Hermon in 3:8-9 and subsequently by the Israelites (see Ps. 42:6; 133:3) may well indicate their belief that the promised land was to be a holy land.

Throughout Deuteronomy there is a strong link between the promised land and the chosen people. Both land and people have been devoted to the Lord and both are to be holy. The land can only be considered holy when the people living in it worship and serve God. God sent the armies of Israel into the land to purge it of idols. The complete victory described in these verses is a prelude to the victory of the living God over idols and the victory of righteousness over wickedness. That is a battle which God's people continue to wage in every era, and our goal remains complete victory (see Heb. 12:14-15).

There is another interesting historical footnote in 3:11, this time about King Og. '*Only Og king of Bashan was left of the remnant of the Rephaites. His bed was made of iron and was more than thirteen feet long and six feet wide. It is still in Rabbah of the Ammonites.*' The Rephaites were a race of people who lived in Canaan before the Israelite conquest. In 2:20-21 they were compared to the Anakites, a race of people known and feared for their great size. The Hebrew word for Rephaites has been translated as 'giants' in the Septuagint and some English translations. Like the rest of his race, Og seems to have been a large man, a man to be reckoned with. Even his bed was enormous. The Hebrew word translated 'bed' in 3:11 is *eres* or 'resting-place'. If it describes the couch on which he slept, it suggests that he was a man of gigantic physical proportions. However, some have suggested that the verse describes Og's final resting-place – that is, the tomb or sarcophagus he had built for himself. In this case it indicates the size of his ego. Although Og was a formidable foe, he was soon cut down to size by an even mightier King, and his land give to the subjects of Jehovah.

The Rephaites were known to Abraham (see Gen. 15:20). They were one of the nations amongst whom Abraham lived in the land of Canaan, but God promised that he would give their land to Abraham's descendants. That promise had come to fulfilment now that God had cut down Og, the last of the Rephaites. Formidable foes they may have been, but even the Rephaites fell before the might of Jehovah.

Moses describes *the division* of the land east of the Jordan in 3:12-17. It was *'the land that we took over'* or, more literally, 'the land we inherited' (3:12). The verb which Moses used is *yarash* and it means 'to possess as an inheritance'. It can also mean 'to dispossess'. Before the Israelites could possess the land, the original inhabitants must be removed. This happened because Jehovah, the Lord of all the earth, had decided to take the land from the Amorites and give it to the Israelites. There is nothing arbitrary or unfair about God's actions, for the earth is his (Ps. 24:1) and he distributes it amongst the nations according to his wisdom and mercy. He does what will best advance his perfect will and his righteous rule on earth.

Not only did Jehovah allocate this land to the people of Israel, he allocated it to particular groups within Israel.

> *Of the land that we took over at that time, I gave the Reubenites and the Gadites the territory north of Aroer by the Arnon Gorge, including half the hill country of Gilead, together with its towns. The rest of Gilead and also all of Bashan, the kingdom of Og, I gave to the half tribe of Manasseh.* (3:12-13)

Two whole tribes (Reuben and Gad) and the half tribe of Manasseh were given their inheritance east of the Jordan and the boundaries of their inheritance are sketched out in general terms. Even sub-groups within these tribes – the descendants of Jair and Makir - are singled out for mention in 3:14-15. The boundaries of their inheritance were set out and recorded by Moses.

The remaining nine and a half tribes received their inheritance later, after the conquest of Canaan (see Josh. 14-21). In this small-scale division we get a foretaste of that much larger distribution of the promised land when, through Moses, God distributed to each tribe exactly the portion of land that he wanted them to have. Their tribal territories were precisely defined and their boundaries were marked out on a map for all to see. This was a demonstration of God's sovereignty and his goodness. Yet four times in these verses Moses used the expression 'I gave'. Moses was not the ultimate source of this blessing, but the servant through whom Jehovah distributed his gift amongst his people. *Give* is a very significant word in Deuteronomy, and it was God who did the giving.

After receiving their inheritance, the tribes of Reuben, Gad and eastern Manasseh were better able to appreciate God's goodness because they actually possessed the land. After many years of waiting and longing, they were able to see the promised inheritance with their own eyes and touch it with their own hands. In the middle years of the nineteenth century many people were drawn to the 'wild west' of North America by the promise of land. Yet their hopes were only dreams until they were able to stake their claim and farm their own parcel of land. There, east of the Jordan, and later in the land of Canaan, the dreams of God's covenant people became a tangible reality. God's goodness became so real that the Israelites could touch it.

The promises of God, which find their ultimate fulfilment in the gospel of Jesus Christ, far excel these promises of a homeland for Israel. God promises to those who believe in his Son a place in his heavenly kingdom. 'Blessed are the poor in spirit, for theirs is the kingdom of heaven' (Matt. 5:3). The blessings of this kingdom are no less real than those inherited by the Israelites. We read of God's people being able to taste the goodness of God (Ps. 34:8; 1 Peter 2:3) and even smell 'the fragrance of life' (2 Cor. 2:16). John describes his vivid experience of God's blessing in the person of His Son. 'That which was from the beginning, which we have heard, which we have seen with our eyes, which we have looked at and our hands have touched—this we proclaim concerning the Word of life' (1 John 1:1). God's blessings in Christ are even more real and vivid than the good land which God gave to Israel in the days of Moses and Joshua.

A foretaste of rest (3:18-20)

Moses told the Israelites that God had given them land so that they might '*take possession of it*' and enjoy it. As well as providing for their material needs the land was a place of rest for the people of God. There they would enjoy rest from slavery (which had been their lot in Egypt) and from the physical trials of their journey through the wilderness. They looked forward to rest from warfare after they had defeated their enemies and taken possession of the land. They also looked forward to spiritual rest when they would be delivered from bondage to idols and set free to worship Jehovah.

The nine and a half tribes whose inheritance lay beyond the Jordan in Canaan were given a very brief glimpse of what that rest would be like when the tribes of Reuben, Gad and eastern Manasseh were allocated their inheritance east of the Jordan. Before they could relax and enjoy that rest they must enter the promised land and take possession of it, and the fighting men of Reuben, Gad and eastern Manasseh would go with them. Moses addressed those two and a half tribes: '*All your able-bodied men, armed for battle, must cross over ahead of your brother Israelites*'. Only the women and children and livestock were allowed to remain with their newly acquired inheritance (3:19). It must have been with heavy hearts that these men left their families behind in the land that they had so recently conquered. It must have been an unsettled place for their women and children, as the remnants of the Amorites hid in the hills and caves seeking an opportunity to exact revenge. The rest they longed for was not to be enjoyed just yet. Only when the nine and a half tribes were able to enjoy their rest would the fighting men from Reuben, Gad and eastern Manasseh be allowed to return to

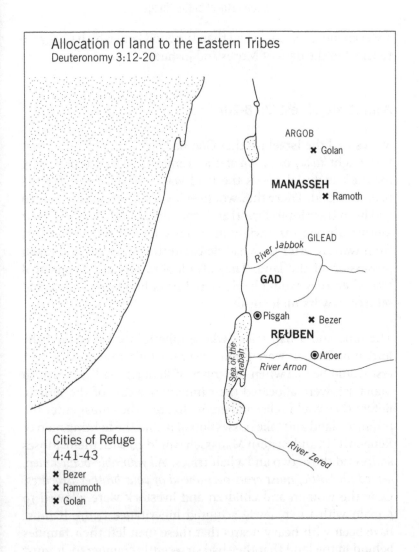

Allocation of land to the Eastern Tribes
Deuteronomy 3:12-20

ARGOB

✖ Golan

MANASSEH

✖ Ramoth

River Jabbok   GILEAD

GAD

◉ Pisgah   ✖ Bezer

REUBEN

◉ Aroer

Sea of the Arabah

River Arnon

River Zered

Cities of Refuge
4:41-43

✖ Bezer
✖ Rammoth
✖ Golan

their inheritance and enjoy peace: *'After that, each of you may go back to the possession I have given you'* (3:20).

God's desire for Israel was that the whole nation should enjoy peace together. Each tribe and each family was to look out not only for its own interests, but for the good of all. (See how the apostle Paul gave similar counsel to the believers in Philippi, Phil. 2:4.) When everyone had peace then all could rest together. The Israelites stood or fell together, for they were one nation, and their unity was a source of strength.

Moses's command to the two and a half tribes anticipates the New Testament doctrine of the church, for the church is 'the Israel of God' (Gal. 6:16) and it functions like a body. When one part of the body suffers, every part is afflicted. Christians who enjoy peace and prosperity cannot rest easily while their brothers and sisters face persecution or temptation or illness or spiritual warfare. When our brother or sister struggles we do not watch from the side-lines or leave them to fight alone; rather we 'carry each other's burdens' (Gal. 6:2) and we 'mourn with those who mourn' (Rom. 12:15), for we are members of the body of Christ (1 Cor. 12:12-21).

It would be many years before the people of Israel would enjoy perfect peace in the land of Canaan. Under Joshua's leadership, the nine and a half tribes eventually received their inheritance. Then Joshua blessed the two and a half tribes, and sent them back to their lands and families with these words: 'Now that the LORD your God has given your brothers rest as he promised, return to your homes in the land that Moses the servant of the LORD gave you on the other side of the Jordan' (Josh. 22:4). Yet even after 'major conflict' came to an end, the Canaanites continued to be a thorn in the flesh of the Israelites. However, 'rest', or peaceful possession of the promised land, remained God's promise.

In 3:20 we note two important aspects of this rest. First of all, rest is a *blessing bestowed by God*. Every blessing is a gift from God, so ultimately *'the Lord gives rest'*. Then secondly, rest *follows conflict and struggle*. God's people will face hostility and fight spiritual battles. We should not expect to be draft-dodgers in the battles of God's kingdom. The Lord Jesus faced hostility during his earthly life and he told his followers that if they would follow him, they must be ready to take up a cross and to lay down their lives for the sake of his kingdom (Mark 8:34-35). When he faced hostility, Jesus was strengthened by the prospect of the rest that would follow. He 'endured the cross, scorning its shame' because of the 'joy set before him' and then he 'sat down at the right hand of the throne of God' (Heb. 12:2). We are encouraged to do the same. 'Let us fix our eyes on Jesus, the author and perfecter of our faith.' We are also helped by the, admittedly imperfect, example of the Israelites, who endured hardship as those who looked forward to a better kingdom.

Rest is a very significant thread woven through the Scriptures. After God created the world, he rested and enjoyed his creation (Gen. 2:2; Exod. 20:11). Not only did God cease from his work of creation; he also enjoyed the beauty of his perfect creation and he set apart a day in which mankind could join him in the enjoyment of rest. Although this rest was shattered by Adam's sin, God redeemed his chosen people and brought them into the promised land so that they might have that rest restored to them (Deut. 12:10). The essence of spiritual rest is the enjoyment of God's presence. God's promise to Moses was, 'My Presence will go with you and I will give you rest' (Exod. 33:14). God's presence is essential to the enjoyment of rest. The psalmist exclaims,

My soul finds rest in God alone;
my salvation comes from him...
Find rest, O my soul, in God alone;
my hope comes from him.
(Ps. 62:1, 5)

It comes as no surprise that in the New Testament 'rest' is used to describe the blessings of salvation which are offered in the gospel. Jesus himself said, 'Come to me, all you who are weary and burdened, and I will give you rest' (Matt. 11:28). The writer to the Hebrews emphasises the superiority of the rest which Jesus offered over the rest into which Moses and Joshua led the Israelites. 'If Joshua had given them rest, God would not have spoken later about another day. There remains then a Sabbath-rest for the people of God' (Heb. 4:8-9). Yet this New Testament writer draws valuable lessons from those Old Testament passages which urged the Israelites to obey God and enter his rest. Quoting from Psalm 95 ('Today, if you hear his voice, do not harden your hearts as you did in the rebellion... So I declared on oath in my anger, "They shall never enter my rest"'), the writer to the Hebrews continued, 'Therefore, since the promise of entering God's rest still stands, let us be careful that none of you be found to have fallen short of it' (Heb. 4:1).

A foretaste but not fulfilment (3:21-29)

These verses highlight a painful problem for Moses. He had led the people of Israel to the borders of the promised land, but he himself would never go into it. He saw God's mighty hand at work and he received a foretaste of the promised inheritance, but he was not permitted to see the fulfilment of God's promises in the land of Canaan. That was a bittersweet experience.

In 3:21-22 *Moses addressed Joshua*, his divinely appointed successor, to remind him of the victories which God had given to the Israelites east of the Jordan. *'You have seen with your own eyes all that the LORD your God has done to these two kings.'* Their defeat was only 'the end of the beginning', but it gave Joshua the confidence to believe that God would give Israel even greater victories when they entered the lands of the Canaanites west of the Jordan. *'The LORD will do the same to all the kingdoms over there where you are going.'*

In 3:23-25 Moses made a very understandable request to God. *'O Sovereign LORD, you have begun to show to your servant your greatness and your strong hand ... Let me go over and see the good land.'* Moses had been given the foretaste, but he also wanted the full taste. That was understandable, but it was not what God had planned.

In 3:26-27 Moses recorded God's negative response to his plea. *'But because of you the LORD was angry with me and would not listen to me. "That is enough," the LORD said. "Do not speak to me any more about this matter."'* God refused to let Moses enter the promised land, but allowed him to see the whole land from the top of Pisgah. *'Go up to the top of Pisgah and look west and north and south and east. Look at the land with your own eyes, since you are not going to cross this Jordan'* (3:27). Moses was allowed one final look into the promised land just before he died. This is recorded more fully in Deuteronomy 34. God's mind was made up and he told Moses not to raise the matter again. This was one situation where persistence in prayer would have been displeasing to God, because we are not to seek outcomes that are clearly contrary to God's revealed plans.

Moses blamed the Israelites for God's stern pronouncement. It was because of their rebelliousness at Meribah that Moses would not be allowed to enter the promised land, for there they grumbled against God. Moses himself was not without fault at Meribah, as we are told in Numbers 20:12 and also in Deuteronomy 32:51. Yet the emphasis here falls upon the guilt of the nation as a whole, and the consequences which fell upon Moses. See also Deuteronomy 1:37; 4:21; Psalm 106:32-33. Here is an example of one man suffering the consequences of his people's sins.

A foretaste of better things

In 3:28 *Moses encouraged Joshua*. '*But commission Joshua, and encourage and strengthen him, for he will lead this people across and will cause them to inherit the land that you will see*' (3:28). Although Moses would not enter the promised land, Joshua would; and Moses was instructed to draw consolation from this. He was to rejoice in the promises made to his younger colleague and successor, just as King David rejoiced in God's promise that his son would build the temple that he had not been allowed to build (see 2 Sam. 7:18-29). God will not allow Moses to wallow in self-pity, but instructs him to encourage and strengthen Joshua. Moses' words of encouragement are recorded in Deuteronomy 31:7-8, when Moses and Joshua presented themselves before the Lord at the Tent of Meeting shortly before Moses' death.

This final section of the chapter opens and closes with an encouragement to Joshua to open his eyes and 'see' what God had in store for the Israelites in the promised land. This was good news for Joshua, but not for Moses. His words of encouragement for Joshua serve to emphasise the pain of Moses' disappointment in 3:23-27. His intense desire ran into the brick wall of God's rebuke. Moses' disappointment sheds light on three important matters.

First of all, it sheds light on *the purpose of the book of Deuteronomy*. References to Moses' disappointment are clustered in the introductory historical narrative (chapters 1 – 3) and the concluding section (chapters 31 – 34). These chapters have been called the 'outer shell' of Deuteronomy. They demonstrate the need for one who would succeed Moses and lead the Israelites after his death. Between these opening and closing sections is the core message of Deuteronomy – the law code which teaches how God's redeemed people are to live in the promised land. This was Moses' legacy for Joshua and God's training manual for the Israelites who were about to enter the land. Their revered law-giver would not go with them, but 'the book of the law' would.

Secondly, it sheds light on *the mediatorial role of Moses* in Deuteronomy. We have seen that the reasons for Moses' exclusion from the land were complex, including both his own sin and the sin of the people. Even his responses to the sins of the people added to his guilt. Yet the fact remains that God's anger rested upon Moses because of the actions of the people. This surely reminds us of the Lord Jesus Christ, who was excluded from communion with his Father during the dreadful hours of his passion on the cross. 'My God, My God, why have you forsaken me?' (Matt. 27:46). His agony is inexplicable, until we come to realise that he was a substitute for sinners (see Isa. 53:4-6; Rom. 4:25a). The outstanding difference between Moses and our Lord is that, while Moses was partly to blame, our Lord had done nothing worthy of punishment. 'God made him who had no sin to be sin for us so that in him we might become the righteousness of God' (2 Cor. 5:21).

Thirdly, it *represents the grief of God's people* in every age. Moses grieved because he had set his heart on the promised land, but was not allowed to enter it. He saw it, but only from a distance, and he would never enjoy its ripe fruit. Believers are those who have set their minds on things above where Christ is seated at the right hand of God, and not upon earthly things (Col. 3:2). They are 'longing for a better country – a heavenly one' (Heb. 11:16). In the meantime they suffer pain, shed tears, and experience grief as they look forward to a world where there will be neither pain, nor tears, nor sadness. What a wonderful place heaven will be, yet none of us has seen it with our own eyes!

Edward Payson was a Christian minister who died in 1827 with a clear view of better things before him. He described what he saw. 'The celestial city is full in my view. Its glories beam upon me, its breezes fan me ... and its spirit is breathed into my heart. Nothing separates me from it but the river of death ... that may be crossed at a single step, whenever God shall give permission.'

A foretaste of better things

Praise God that he helps us through times of difficulty and disappointment by showing us the beauty of the land into which he will take his beloved people.

Chapter 4
The purpose of God's law

Please read Deuteronomy 4: 1-43

There are two things which a preacher will seek to convey to his hearers in every sermon: the truths which God has revealed in his word, and the ways in which we are to apply them to our lives. This reflects the twofold message of the Bible itself. In answer to the question, 'What do the Scriptures principally teach?' the *Westminster Shorter Catechism* replies, 'The Scriptures principally teach what man is to believe concerning God, and what duty God requires of man' (answer 3). Sometimes this twofold aim is described in grammatical terms. Doctrine is stated in the indicative mood, while application is presented in the imperative. We see this pattern in many of Paul's letters, which begin with teaching and end with exhortation. Often a strategically placed "therefore" indicates when his emphasis shifts from doctrine to application.

We can also see this pattern in the book of Deuteronomy, which records the sermons which were preached by Moses when the Israelites gathered on the plains of Moab to renew their covenant with Jehovah as they made ready to enter into the land of Canaan. The first of these sermons is found in chapters 1 – 4. The historical prologue in chapters 1 – 3 sets out what God had done for Israel, as he led them from Horeb to the plains of Moab. However, in chapter 4 Moses moves from history to law;

from what God had done, to what they were to do; from God's mighty actions on their behalf, to their grateful response when they would enter the land which they were about to possess. Moses exhorted them to hear the law of God. *'Hear now, O Israel, the decrees and laws which I am about to teach you...'* (4:1). Moses' teaching in the verses which follow is characterised by the imperative mood.

Many critical scholars have found it hard to accept that the narrative in chapters 1-3 and the exhortation of chapter 4 belong together. They pose a range of theories to explain how the text as we have it before us evolved by a process of cutting and pasting together different traditions in Israel. Ingenious though these theories may be, they create tension where there is harmony and they overlook a very important reason why Moses would want to conclude his account of Israel's progress thus far with an exhortation to serve God faithfully. Israel's journey from Horeb brought the Israelites to Beth Peor, in the plains of Moab, overlooking the promised land (3:29). At Beth Peor their journey almost came to a tragic end (see Num. 25). There, the Israelites joined with the Moabites in their idolatry and sexual immorality and, but for the righteous actions of Phinehas, the whole nation might have perished under God's anger. With these tragic events fresh in his mind, Moses called the people to renounce idolatry and recommit themselves to Jehovah. He reminded them of the things that they had seen and heard at Horeb, the point of departure for their journey through the wilderness.

Deuteronomy 4 is a wonderful climax to Moses' first sermon. Figuratively and theologically it took the Israelites back to Horeb and impressed on them the importance of total faithfulness to their covenant Lord. As Moses reaches the theological climax of this first Deuteronomic sermon, his preaching becomes more urgent; his message becomes more explicit; his style becomes more sublime; and the majesty of Jehovah is more clearly impressed on the consciences of his hearers. Israel has been richly blessed by God and now Moses draws out the implications.

Hear and obey God's words (4:1-14)

In 4:1-2 Moses called the Israelites to *hear and obey*. *'Hear now, O Israel, the decrees and laws I am about to teach you ... keep the commands of the LORD your God that I give you.'* These commands gave clear and precise applications of the covenant principle. The *'decrees and laws'* are like the case law that judges build up over many years as they seek to apply broad legal principles to many specific situations. They are detailed and practical, as we shall see when we come to the law code of chapters 12-26. Godliness is to be lived out in everyday situations. Moses urged the people to hear these specific applications and follow them.

These commands were the condition of covenant blessing. *'Follow them so that you may live and may go in and take possession of the land that the LORD, the God of your fathers, is giving you.'* The nation of Israel had already promised to serve and obey God (see Exod. 24:1-8). They, in turn, expected that God would keep his promise and lead them into the promised land. Of that, there was no doubt. The only question was whether the people of Israel would keep their promise and continue to obey their Lord. The obedience that God sought was not tokenistic. He sought faithful following, not occasional or symbolic acts of obedience. If they followed God faithfully, they would be assured of the land as their inheritance. If they were unfaithful, the consequences would be disastrous.

God's laws were to be received and obeyed in their entirety. *'Do not add to what I command you and do not subtract from it.'* Recent studies of ancient treaties have shed some light on these words. Kings who made a treaty with a conquered people would write out their terms for both parties to keep in a sacred place. In the terms of the treaty there would often be a clause stating that the treaty could not be altered. The covenant between God and his people was the result of God's mercy not negotiation. For that very reason every word that proceeded from God's mouth was precious and ought to be treasured (see Ps. 19:10; Prov. 30:5). God's people were to hear God's words and obey them. A similar warning is found in Revelation 22:18-19, strategically placed at the conclusion of the last book in the canon of Scripture. This warning applies to us today as we hold the completed Bible in our hands.

Moses' opening exhortation has some important lessons for all of us who hear God's word. Moses calls for *active listening* to God's word. Many people today learn bad habits of listening from the stream of sound which comes from our television sets and iPods. They hear sounds with their ears, but they do not absorb the message with their minds. It is so easy simply to switch off because we are constantly bombarded with information. We become passive recipients rather than active enquirers. By contrast, we need to cultivate habits of active listening as we hold the Bible in our hands and as we hear God's word read and preached. We need to sit up (physically and metaphorically) and get our minds engaged in the process of listening to the most important message we will ever hear.

Moses also encouraged the people to be *obedient hearers* of God's word. In many congregations today there are people who love to hear a good sermon. In fact, they will move from church to church to hear the kind of preaching that they like. They analyse what they hear, comparing one sermon with another, but that is all they do. They do not expect to be challenged, much less changed, by what they hear. The outcome of their hearing is personal satisfaction rather than sanctification.

The purpose of God's law

In 4:3-4 Moses outlined the *consequences of obedience and disobedience*. He reminded them of what they saw at Baal Peor (sometimes called Beth Peor, as in 3:29) in the plains of Moab. This was a centre for pagan worship among the Moabites, who invited the Israelites to join with them in their sexually explicit pagan rituals (see Num. 25:1-18). Many Israelites joined them. On account of this the Lord was angry and sent a plague upon the Israelites. Only when Phinehas intervened, by putting to death an Israelite man and his Moabite consort, did the plague subside. Painful as the remedy was the outcome was positive. *'The Lord your God destroyed from among you everyone who followed the Baal of Peor'* (4:3). A destructive cancer was removed and Moses was able to address words of encouragement to those who remained. *'All of you who held fast to the Lord your God are still alive today.'* They were alive because they had resisted the temptation to engage in idolatry. Moses commended them for their faithfulness, yet he exhorted them never to rest on their laurels.

In 4:5-8 Moses describes the people of Israel as *a light to the nations.*

> *See, I have taught you decrees and laws as the Lord my God commanded me ... Observe them carefully for this will show your wisdom and understanding to the nations, who will hear about all these decrees and say, 'Surely this great nation is a wise and understanding people' (4:5-6).*

When the Israelites heard and obeyed God's laws, the surrounding nations would see their obedience and draw conclusions. In particular, Israel's national life was to bear witness to two truths.

First of all, Israel's national life would testify to *the superiority of God's wisdom*. When the Gentile nations asked *'What other nation is so great as to have such righteous decrees and laws?'* they were passing comment on the wisdom that God had given his people and not on any wisdom that was inherent in them. God's wisdom is not like the wisdom of this world. See 1 Corinthians 1:25. It is not abstract, but eminently practical. It is not content to secure the end by any means available. It is righteous wisdom. It manifests itself in moral principles and judicial applications which display a deep understanding of human nature and communal behaviour. In ancient times impressive legal systems were developed in Mesopotamia and Egypt. Even today their legal texts are read with great respect for the ways in which they strove after fairness. Yet no other nation had a legal system which reflected the wisdom and righteousness of God in such minute detail.

Secondly Israel's national life would testify to *the nearness of God to his people*. *'What other nation is so great as to have their gods near them the way the LORD our God is near us whenever we pray to him?'* Israel's greatness was not political (except for a short time during the reigns of Solomon and other kings) but spiritual. Israel was greatly blessed, for Jehovah, her Lord, had spoken to her at Sinai and confirmed his covenant with her. God had come so near to them that they felt afraid and uncomfortable (see Exod. 20:18-19). Nevertheless, it was a great blessing that God should come so near to them. God's word was a reminder that God had come close enough for them to hear his voice.

Not only were the Israelites able to hear God's voice, they were invited to respond in prayer. When they prayed to God they could be sure that he had heard them (see Ps. 4:3; Micah 7:7). This was a blessing which the servants of false gods could never enjoy (see Ps. 135:15-17). In the time of King Ahab, the prophets of Baal cried out to their god but received no response. When Elijah prayed, God heard and answered and everyone could see that 'the LORD–he is God' (see 1 Kings 18:26-39).

The purpose of God's law

Today, nearness to God is freely offered to people from every nation through the redeeming work of God's Son, the Lord Jesus Christ. 'Now in Christ Jesus you who were far away have been brought near through the blood of Christ. For he himself is our peace... He came and preached peace to you who were far away and peace to those who were near. For through him we both have access to the Father by the one Spirit' (Eph. 2:13-18). See also Hebrews 10:19-22; James 4:8.

Moses reminded the Israelites that there was a place in God's plan of salvation for the nations as well. Even though God would drive the Gentile nations from the land of Canaan, he had a message for the Gentiles and the nation of Israel was to be his messenger. Israel was to 'show... wisdom and understanding to the nations'. When the nations saw Israel, they were to see a message of hope for every nation being enacted amongst God's people in God's land. This is a reminder that when God chose Abraham to be his servant he promised, 'I will bless those who bless you and whoever curses you I will curse; and all peoples on earth will be blessed through you' (Gen. 12:3). This promise of blessing for the nations echoes through the Old Testament Scriptures (see Ps. 67:3-5; 72:17; Isa. 49:6; 51:4; Jonah 4:10). Sadly, Israel was not the light that God had called her to be. Israel's failure prompts us to ask whether the witness of the church today is any more effective?

In 4:9-14 Moses reminded them of *what they had seen and heard at Sinai* – here called Horeb. '*Remember the day you stood before the LORD your God at Horeb...*' (4:10). The scene had been breathtaking. '*You came near and stood at the foot of the mountain while it blazed with fire to the very heavens, with black clouds and deep darkness*' (4:11). Yet they did not see God on the mountain. '*The LORD spoke to you out of the fire. You heard the sound of words but saw no form; there was only a voice*' (4:12). The point to note is that God revealed himself in audible words, rather than visible images. This was to have profound implications for the piety of his people and the ministry of his servants. Theirs was to be a ministry of the word, and the piety of the Israelites placed a premium on hearing and obeying God's word.

The Ten Commandments were the authoritative summary of what God had said to the people of Israel at Horeb. According to 4:13 they capture the essence of God's covenant relationship with Israel. *'He declared to you his covenant, the Ten Commandments, which he commanded you to follow and then wrote them on two stone tablets.'* See also Exodus 34:28. They were given to the redeemed people of God (Exod. 20:2) to show how redeemed people ought to live. They were the people's response to God's merciful deliverance. Moses' account of the events at Horeb highlights the importance of the summary of the law in the Ten Commandments. This is covenant law. It had two important uses in the lives of God's people.

God's commands were *an aid to the people generally*, helping them to remember God's covenant with them. *'Only be careful, and watch yourselves closely so that you do not forget the things your eyes have seen or let them slip from your heart as long as you live'* (4:9). The exhortation to watchfulness is repeated in 4:15, where the people were warned against idolatry; and in 4:23, where the people were warned not to forget their covenant with God. Moses knew that mountain-top experiences very quickly pass into history and sinful habits quickly reassert themselves. He knew too that the Ten Commandments were short, simple stipulations that were eminently memorable. They taught the people about the holiness of God and they taught the people about themselves, showing how far they fell short of God's perfect standards. Yet God made a covenant to save such people, and the commandments were a token of that covenant.

God's commands were also *an aid to parents*, helping them to train their children in God's ways. *'Teach them to your children and to their children after them'* (4:9). One way of ensuring that

Israel did not forget her covenant with God was to nurture godly families where parents taught their children from God's law. At Horeb God had said, *'Assemble the people before me to hear my words so that they may learn to revere me as long as they live in the land and may teach them to their children... And the LORD directed me at that time to teach you the decrees and laws you are to follow in the land that you are crossing the Jordan to possess'* (4:10, 14). That is why Moses taught the parents and then exhorted them to teach their children. Likewise, Christian nurture begins in the home, with parents who strive to live lives of consistent obedience before God. An extensive programme of children's activities in the church will have little effect if children see that their parents do not honour God by obeying his law.

Reject idolatry (4:15-31)

In this central section of Deuteronomy 4, Moses moves from general exhortation to specific application. In 4:15-16a he returns to the observation found in 4:12 that the Israelites had seen no form at Horeb, but simply heard the words of God. He repeats the exhortation found in 4:9 to watch themselves lest they forget what they heard. *'You saw no form of any kind the day the LORD spoke to you at Horeb out of the fire. Therefore watch yourselves very carefully, so that you do not become corrupt and make for yourself an idol, an image of any shape...'* Idolatry was the besetting sin of Israel from the time they entered into the promised land until the exile.

In 4:16b-19 Moses anticipates the various forms that their idolatry would take. Sometimes they worshipped man-made images, *'formed like a man or a woman, or like any animal on earth or any bird that flies in the air, or like any creature that moves along the ground or any fish in the waters below'*. These artistic creations were intended to make some statement about the divine being. The commonly used image of a bull, for instance, was intended to convey the impression of brute strength or masculine fertility. At other times the Israelites turned to objects in the natural world that had been created by God and made them their gods. That is described in 4:19: *'And when you look up to the sky and see the sun, the moon and the stars – all the heavenly array – do not be enticed into bowing down to them and worshipping things the LORD your God has apportioned to all the nations under heaven.'*

To the ancients these heavenly bodies seemed to have a powerful influence over the rhythms of human life. They governed day and night, the tides and the seasons. The sun provided light and warmth and made the land fruitful. For these reasons the heavenly bodies were worshipped. Anticipating these temptations, Moses tells the Israelites that Jehovah holds them and all creation in his hands. What they see in the heavens above and the earth around them are the *'things that the Lord your God has apportioned to all the nations under heaven'.* Our Lord taught this in his Sermon on the Mount: 'He causes the sun to rise on the evil and the good' and through its influence 'sends rain on the righteous and the unrighteous' (Matt. 5:45). All nations ought to worship Jehovah, and Israel is not to be 'enticed into bowing down' to the false gods of the nations. How foolish to worship to worship the creature rather than the Creator!

Both forms of idolatry have a common feature, in that they seek to make the object of human worship visible to the eye. Herein lies the attractiveness of idolatry. Many people find it hard to think about, let alone worship, a god they cannot see. Yet Jehovah cannot be seen, for he is a Spirit (see John 4:24). Nor can Jehovah be depicted by any man-made object. Even the heavenly bodies, whose splendour declares the glory of God (see Ps. 19:1) cannot depict God, for dead objects cannot depict the living God. Only the Lord Jesus can rightly be called 'the image of the invisible God' (Col. 1:15).

Another reason why God forbade idolatry was because Israel had been redeemed out of the land of Egypt, a land infested with idols. *'But as for you, the LORD took you and brought you out of the iron-smelting furnace, out of Egypt, to be the people of his inheritance, as you now are'* (4:20). Here Moses compares Israel's deliverance to the process of extracting metal from ore. In order to extract the iron, the rock must first be crushed and heated to a very high temperature. During this process the molten metal runs off and leaves the impurities behind. The crushing and the heat represent the suffering of the people of Israel as they toiled under the Egyptian sun and the cruelty of their slave-drivers. Yet God had a gracious purpose in their trials. He wanted to deliver them from Egyptian idols as well as from Egyptian cruelty. He wanted to deliver them from the false gods that enslaved the nations. That is why God wanted to purify the land of Canaan from its idols so that the Israelites might live as a nation devoted to Jehovah.

Modern idols may be very different from those of the ancient Israelites. People today make idols of their superstars, their careers, their egos and their ideologies. Some who profess to be Christians make idols of the 'saints' or the virgin Mary. Sadly, too, we are seeing a resurgence of modern paganism, which idolises Gaia or 'mother earth'. This modern idolatry is just as sinful as its ancient predecessors. It robs God of his glory. It distracts many people from the truth of the gospel and fills their minds with inadequate thoughts about the true and living God.

A warning from personal experience (4:21-24)

These verses seem to follow rather awkwardly from Moses warning against idolatry. They describe the Lord's anger against Moses. *'The LORD was angry with me because of you, and he solemnly swore that I would not cross the Jordan and enter the good land the LORD is giving you as your inheritance'* (4:21). We should not conclude that God was angry with Moses on account of any idolatrous act. There is no evidence in the Scriptures that Moses was an idolater, but he was a sinner! One sin in particular is recorded in Numbers 20:1-12, which describes how Moses struck a rock in the wilderness to bring forth water for the thankless Israelites. God had not commanded Moses to strike the rock, only to speak to it. Because of his rashness, Moses was not permitted to enter the promised land.

Here in 4:21 (as well as in 1:37 and 3:26) Moses emphasises the culpability of the people. Their constant murmuring was the occasion of his lapse. Yet, while the nation of Israel would enter the promised land, Moses would not. '*I will die in this land; I will not cross the Jordan; but you are about to cross over and take possession of that good land*' (4:22). Why did God deal with Moses in this way; and why did Moses raise the memory of this sad and painful incident at this point in his sermon? Surely, it is because Moses was a representative figure. He represented the people of Israel before God and he bore the consequences of their sin. He bore God's anger and in this regard he was a pointer to Christ.

Moses' purpose in recounting this unhappy incident was also to show that God takes unbelief and disobedience very seriously. Moses' punishment was a conspicuous demonstration of this principle. If he was prevented from entering the promised land because of their sin of grumbling (as well as his own sin of rashness), what would become of those who committed idolatry in the land? The answer that Moses gives in the following verses is that the Israelites too will be removed from the land if they fall into idolatry. So Moses' personal experience added force to the warning of 4:23-24: '*Be careful not to forget the covenant of the LORD your God that he made with you; do not make for yourselves an idol in the form of anything the LORD your God has forbidden. For the LORD your God is a consuming fire, a jealous God*' (4:23-24).

Because Jehovah is *'a consuming fire'* he must punish sin. This is not a primitive religious superstition which need not trouble enlightened people in a modern age. The writer to the Hebrews points out the superiority of Christ to all the great figures of the Old Testament and the superiority of Christianity over Judaism. However, the God who speaks and acts in the person of Jesus Christ is the very same God whom Moses proclaims in these verses. *'For our God is a consuming fire,'* the writer to the Hebrews tells us in Hebrews 12:29. Our sin must be punished – either in the person of Christ upon the cross or through the eternal punishment of those who will not turn from their sin and trust Christ as their Saviour. Hence the gospel of Jesus Christ calls sinners to turn from idols who cannot save to the only Saviour who can (see 1 Cor. 10:14; 1 Thess. 1:9).

Warnings about the exile (4:25-31)

Moses develops and expands his warning in 4:25-31. *'After you have had children and grandchildren and have lived in the land a long time – if you then become corrupt and make any kind of idol...'* (4:25). Moses spoke as a prophet foretelling Israel's sins and God's response. He was also a preacher who pulled out all the stops in his efforts to persuade the Israelites to renounce idolatry and all that went with it. *'I call heaven and earth as witnesses against you this day that you will quickly perish from the land that you are crossing the Jordan to possess. You will not live there long but will certainly be destroyed. The LORD will scatter you among the peoples'* (4:26-27).

Some critical commentators have argued that these verses were written in the late seventh century BC (when the threat of exile hung like a dark cloud over Judah) or later (when the exile was a tragic reality). We should not, however, be surprised that God might reveal, through Moses, what he planned to do in the distant future. God's foreknowledge distinguishes him from false gods (Isa. 41:21-26). Moreover, the threat of expulsion from the land was implicit in the nature of God's covenant with Israel. The land of Canaan was the sphere within which the covenant operated. There God blessed his people. There, too, the people expressed their whole-hearted loyalty to God. There was simply no room for idolatry in the promised land, just as there is no room for an adulterous partner in a family home. Something has to go. In this case it would be Israel.

In a dramatic flourish Moses called 'heaven and earth' as witnesses to remind them that they had been warned. Moses will do the same in his climactic appeal in 30:19 (see also 32:1), where he appeals to the Israelites to 'choose life' and love the Lord. Here, Moses appeals to them to flee from destruction. If they worship idols they will 'quickly perish from the land'. Although not every Israelite would die, their numbers would be greatly reduced (4:27); and in the land of their exile they will 'worship man-made gods of wood and stone, which cannot see or hear or eat or smell' (4:28). To serve a dead idol is a form of spiritual death, from which only a powerful and sovereign God could rescue them. Jehovah is such a God! See Ephesians 2:1-5.

In 4:29-31 Moses sets forth to the great theme of Deuteronomy – the mercy which Israel's covenant-keeping Lord will bestow upon his people when every other hope of deliverance has vanished. The threat of exile was not God's last word to his people. Moses addresses those who will go into exile with a promise: 'But if from there you seek the LORD your God, you will find him if you look for him with all your heart and with all your soul. When you are in distress and all these things have happened to you, then in later days you will return to the LORD your God and obey him.' This was a twofold promise.

First of all, it was a promise *that Israel would cry out to him* in their distress. Distressing experiences do not always lead people to cry out to God. Often they embitter and harden sinful people so that they turn even further away from God. It was the sad observation of the Old Testament prophets that the people of Israel often preferred to rely on their own strength or seek help from other nations, rather than repent and turn to God. King Ahaz refused God's offer of a sign of deliverance and tried the patience of God and his servant Isaiah (see Isa. 7:10-13). Hosea observed this stubborn trait in the northern kingdom of Israel (see Hosea 7:7, 10, 13-14). It soon became clear that invasion and exile alone would not draw the Israelites to repentance. A work of God within their hearts was required. That is what Moses foretells in 30:6: 'The LORD your God will circumcise your hearts ... so that you may love him with all your heart and with all your soul and live.' This is sovereign grace. This comes before sinners turn to God and it draws them to God. God promised then that he would draw sinful Israel to himself; and he promises today that he will draw men and women to seek him (see John 6:44).

This is also a promise *that God would listen attentively* to those who seek him. Psalm 137:1 describes how the exiles of Israel would sit by the rivers of Babylon and weep as they remembered Zion. They would also remember God's promises to Moses and cry out to their covenant Lord. God would hear their weeping and answer their cry. God would restore their nation and bring them again to the land of promise. The unfolding history of the Old Testament is the story of God's covenant faithfulness. The hopes of Israel over the centuries rest on these foundational promises given to Moses by Jehovah and preached to Israel on the plains of Moab. *'For the LORD your God is a merciful God; he will not abandon or destroy you or forget the covenant with your forefathers, which he confirmed to them by oath.'*

We find this twofold promise echoed in the words of our Lord in John 6:37. 'All that the Father gives me will come to me, and whoever comes to me I will never drive away.' God has his people and they will come, for he will draw them. Moreover those who hear the word of God are called to take a conscious step of faith. These two truths complement each other. Whether preached by Moses or by Jesus or any of his followers, the promise of the gospel rests on the same foundation – the covenant promises of God.

> Because God wanted to make the unchanging nature of his purpose very clear to the heirs of what was promised, he confirmed it with an oath. God did this so that, by two unchangeable things in which it is impossible for God to lie, we who have fled to take hold of the hope offered to us may be greatly encouraged. We have this hope as an anchor for the soul, firm and secure. It enters the inner sanctuary behind the curtain, where Jesus, who went before us, has entered on our behalf. He has become a high priest forever, in the order of Melchizedek (Heb. 6:17-20).

Marvel at what God has done (4:32-40)

As Moses looked back over Israel's years in the wilderness, he was amazed at what God had done for Israel. In these verses he sought to instil that sense of wonder into the hearts of his hearers. He urged them to ask questions about their nation's history. *'Ask now about the former days, long before your time, from the day God created man on earth; ask from one end of the heavens to the other. Has anything so great as this ever happened, or has anything like it ever been heard of?'* All history is 'his story' in the sense that it is the story of God accomplishing his purposes. The history of Israel, however, is the story of redemption. God's salvation is rooted in the history of Israel, and for that reason it has much to say to us.

Asking the right questions is an important skill to learn; and in 4:33 Moses supplied a question which would help the Israelites to tease out what was really important in God's dealings with them.

The purpose of God's law

Has any other people heard the voice of God speaking out of fire, as you have, and lived? Has any god ever tried to take for himself one nation out of another nation, by testings, by miraculous signs and wonders, by war, by a mighty hand and an outstretched arm, or by great and awesome deeds, like all the things the LORD your God did for you in Egypt before your very eyes?

Moses' question was a backward look at a series of events; the Exodus, the giving of the law at Sinai, and many battles with desert tribes. These events were an amazing display of God's power and mercy.

Is there any parallel in human history? The answer, obviously, is 'No!' Moses, however, did not answer his question directly. It was a rhetorical question designed to provoke his hearers to think about their experiences and ask questions of their own. Moses wanted the Israelites to pause and reflect upon these things. Just like many people today, the Israelites were prone to lose sight of God's goodness to them. They were quick to grumble when they ran out of food and water, because they forgot how mightily God had rescued them from slavery in Egypt and preserved their lives as they travelled though the hostile wilderness.

Moses drew his hearers' attention to Jehovah's most important characteristic. *'You were shown these things so that you might know that the LORD is God; besides him there is no other.'* This is a truth to which Moses will return many times in Deuteronomy: see 4:39; 6:4-5; 32:39; 33:26. It is the foundation stone of true religion in the Old Testament. Moreover, the nation of Israel enjoyed a unique relationship with this unique God, and Moses highlights two unique features of that relationship.

Firstly, *God spoke to them from heaven. 'From heaven he made you hear his voice to discipline you...'* God's words revealed what men could never discover by enquiry or speculation; what the apostle Paul described as 'inexpressible things' in 2 Corinthians 12:4. These are truths that come from God in heaven and they are revealed so that men might seek God and follow him. Revelation is never given to satisfy our idle curiosity but to lead us to salvation and nurture us in holiness.

Secondly, *God loved the nation of Israel*. *'Because he loved your forefathers and chose their descendants after them, he brought you out of Egypt by his Presence and his great strength.'* Other nations might seek favours from their gods, but none could be sure of their affection. Certainly none of Israel's neighbouring nations expected their gods to love them with an undying love. Yet that is the love that God bore to his chosen people (see Jer. 31:3; Mal. 1:2). This, too, is the love that God promises to those who are in Christ (see Rom. 8:38-39).

And so in 4:39-40 Moses urged his hearers to respond to these truths about Jehovah and his covenant with Israel.

> *Acknowledge and take to heart this day that the LORD is God in heaven above and earth below. There is no other. Keep his decrees and commands, which I am giving you today, so that it may go well with you and your children after you and that you may live long in the land the LORD your God gives you for all time.*

This is a call to action, to worship and to obedience. Moses proclaims these truths about God so that they might dwell deeply in the hearts of his people, and so that the Israelites might live as a holy nation for many years in the land of Canaan.

It ought to amaze us that God should choose any nation to be his own people. Israel was not chosen for its special role in the story of redemption because it was particularly useful or attractive to God. Yet God chose her and blessed her and Moses called her to remember her calling and election. It ought to be just as amazing to us that God should set his love on sinful people and call them into his family. Yet, through the redemptive work of Jesus Christ, that is exactly what he has done (see Rom. 5:6-8). He has even prepared a home in heaven for believers, just as he prepared a home for his people in the promised land. As a result we ought to be very eager to make our calling and election sure by living godly and fruitful lives (see 2 Peter 1:10). 'For if you do these things, you will never fall, and you will receive a rich welcome into the eternal kingdom of our Lord and Saviour Jesus Christ' (2 Peter 1:10b-11).

The cities of refuge (4:41-43)

At the conclusion of Moses' first covenant-renewal sermon and just before the beginning of his second main address, the narrative records how *'Moses set aside three cities east of the Jordan'* as cities of refuge. Cities like these were eventually to be set up throughout the land of Israel for those who had killed unintentionally and were not to be punished as murderers with the death penalty. This feature of Israel's criminal justice system is described in principle in Exodus 21:13 and Numbers 35:9-29, and is summarised here in 4:42. *'Anyone who had killed a person could flee if he had unintentionally killed his neighbour without malice aforethought. He could flee into one of these cities and save his life.'*

Although the principle had been promulgated at Sinai, the system could only be established in practice when Israel took possession of the land. With the land east of the Jordan now within their control they were in a position to begin implementing this system, even if only partially. Three cities in the recently captured territories east of the River Jordan were designated as places of refuge (4:41). They are listed in 4:43: *'The cities were these: Bezer in the desert plateau, for the Reubenites;*

God's treasured possession

Ramoth in Gilead, for the Gadites; and Golan in Bashan, for the Manassites.' In each of the three tribal territories east of the Jordan (Reuben, Gad and eastern Manasseh) one city was set aside as a city of refuge for the people of that area. In time, the other tribes would have their cities of refuge (see Josh. 20:7).

These details about Israel's criminal justice system may seem out of place, coming as a footnote to Moses' sermon on God's mercy. Yet even this historical footnote serves as a reminder that God has shown his mercy to his people by giving them a homeland. Now God's mercy was to be reflected in the way in which his people administered criminal justice in the land which the Lord had given them. These verses remind the reader that God's promises were already coming to fruition. God had already given his people a portion of the land. They were already in the process of establishing a new kind of society which was leavened by grace and truth, righteousness and mercy.

As Christians we pray, 'Your kingdom come' in the expectation 'that Satan's kingdom may be destroyed; and that the kingdom of grace may be advanced... and that the kingdom of glory may be hastened' (*Westminster Shorter Catechism*, answer 102). These are future events, but the kingdom of God does not lie exclusively in the exclusively in the future. Jesus Christ is already king, for all authority in heaven and earth has been given to him (Matt. 28:18). While many people and nations refuse to submit to his rule, his kingdom on earth is a present reality. From a small beginning it has grown over the centuries and its influence will fill the world. Kingdoms that are now hostile to King Jesus will be redeemed and bow before him. We, his subjects, are called to be salt and light in our communities, in hospitals, schools, factories, law courts and any other sphere in which we work so that our communities will be leavened by grace and truth, righteousness and mercy.

Chapter 5
Back to basics

Please read Deuteronomy 4:44 - 5:33

In 2003 an Australian newspaper contained an article entitled 'America's most controversial bishop advocates dumping the Ten Commandments'. The article continued, 'John Shelby Spong advocates a twenty-first-century Christianity that doesn't require people to check in their brains when they enter the church door. In practice... this means abandoning outmoded concepts such as ... the ten commandments as the basis of ethics.' We would be naïve to think that negative attitudes towards the Ten Commandments are found only amongst liberal theologians and radical church leaders like Bishop Spong. Several years ago a survey among ministers in a large mainline denomination in the British Isles found that three in every ten parish ministers could not even name the Ten Commandments which God gave to Moses at Sinai. Yet they remain the foundation stone of biblical ethics, not only for Jews, but for Christians as well.

Sadly, even when church members know about the Ten Commandments and accept that they set a worthy standard, many are not very enthusiastic about being taught the Commandments. Some will complain that they are too negative. Others allege that teaching the Commandments fosters a legalistic spirit. Others will point out that they were first pronounced in an age which was very different from the one in which we live today, and insist that we need a more contemporary set of rules to guide our lives. Still others suspect that any set of rules for Christian living has been made redundant by the gospel of Jesus Christ and the working of the Holy Spirit. Surely, they say, our guide is the unwritten principle of love rather than written laws and commandments.

These claims are simply not grounded in the teaching of Jesus. He did not come to abolish the law, but to fulfil it (see Matt. 5:17). When the rich young ruler asked Jesus what he must do to inherit eternal life, Jesus replied, 'If you want to enter life, obey the commandments.' When asked for an explanation, Jesus made it clear that the commandments to which he referred were the Ten Commandments (see Matt. 19:16-19). When Jesus said, 'Love the Lord your God with all your heart and with all your soul and with all your mind...' (Matt. 22:37-40), he was summarising the Ten Commandments so that his hearers might understand them and apply them in their lives. He did not seek to replace the Ten Commandments with something new, but continued in the Mosaic tradition of restating and reapplying the moral law of God to each new generation. This is what Moses sought to do as he expounded the law in Deuteronomy.

The Preface (4:44-49)

'This is the law Moses set before the Israelites. These are the stipulations, decrees and laws Moses gave them when they came out of Egypt and were in the valley near Beth Peor east of the Jordan' (4:44-46a). With these words, which echo his introduction to the first Deuteronomic sermon in 1:1, Moses opened his second sermon. This sermon, which continues through to 26:19, was preached by the same preacher (Moses) and in the same location (Beth Peor, in the plains of Moab).

Back to basics

The preacher's purpose remains the same. These opening verses are a summary of the history set out in the first sermon. Israel's history thus far has been a record of God's goodness in giving them a beautiful land.

> *They took possession of his land and the land of Og king of Bashan, the two Amorite kings east of the Jordan. This land extended from Aroer on the rim of the Arnon Gorge to Mount Siyon (that is, Hermon), and included all the Arabah east of the Jordan, as far as the Sea of the Arabah, below the slopes of Pisgah.* (4:47-49)

The wonderful panorama set before us in these verses was intended to help the Israelites realise what God had already done for them. Not only had he brought them out of Egypt, he had brought them to the brink of the promised land. From the slopes of Pisgah Moses would look into the land (34:1-4); but, he hoped, the Israelites would enter in if they held fast to their covenant with Jehovah.

The focus of the second sermon shifts from history to law; from God's gifts to God's commands. This was because of Moses' concern lest the Israelites copy the idolatry and immorality of the pagans who surrounded them and so forfeit God's blessing. The Ten Commandments and their many applications are the theme of this second Mosaic sermon.

The introduction (5:1-6)

'Hear O Israel, the decrees and laws I declare in your hearing today. Learn them and be sure to follow them' (5:1b). Moses' sermon is an expository sermon, in that it aims to explain the laws of God. Although the text of his sermon is the law, God is the theme of the sermon. Every word from God points to its author and so must every sermon that faithfully expounds God's word. Moses

took his hearers back forty years to the day when God met with the nation of Israel at Mount Sinai and described two things which God did on that day.

First of all, *he made a covenant with the Israelites* (5:2-3). 'The LORD our God made a covenant with us at Horeb.' It was in this setting that God had given his law to Israel and it is very important to remember that Israel's law was covenant law. It flowed from Israel's special privileges as a redeemed people and brought with it special responsibilities. A covenant is a solemn agreement that creates privileges and responsibilities. A covenant with God is always initiated by God as an act of grace. Because God's love for Israel was everlasting, his covenant with Israel was an everlasting covenant. The implications of that covenant outlived the first generation of covenanters.

Jehovah remained the same covenant Lord even after forty years had elapsed since he had made a covenant with Israel at Horeb. The Israelites, however, had changed. A whole generation had died in the wilderness (see Deut. 1:35; Num. 14:32; 32:13). Thankfully, God's covenant with Israel did not die with that rebellious generation. Moses states this in emphatic terms in 5:3. 'It was not with our fathers that the LORD made this covenant, but with us, with all of us who are alive here today.' We might add the qualification that it was 'not *only*' with the people who stood at Horeb that this covenant was made. Their children and grandchildren who stood on the plains of Moab were also parties to God's covenant, heirs of his promises and subject to his commands (see 4:23).

Secondly, *he spoke face to face with the Israelites* (5:4-6). The events of that momentous day are described in detail in Exodus 19:16-20:19. It must have been an overwhelming experience for the Israelites to have the Lord of heaven come so near to them. 'The LORD spoke to you face to face out of the fire on the mountain.' The phrase 'face to face' is literally 'person to person'. God's dealings with Israel were very personal. The experience terrified them, for the Lord spoke 'out of the fire on the mountain' and they realised that they were sinners in the presence of a holy God. Later, in 5:23-27, we will see the fear which this created amongst the Israelites; in anticipation of this Moses describes how he stood as a mediator between Jehovah and Israel. *'I stood between the LORD and you to declare to you the word of the LORD.'* This enabled the people to hear God's words and enjoy a relationship with him. Otherwise their sins and their fears would have created a double barrier driving God from them and them from him.

Thankfully, God had not drawn near to the Israelites to condemn and destroy them, but to deliver them from destruction and draw them to himself. That is what God declared when he spoke to them on the mountain, and in 5:6 Moses records the very words that God had spoken to them. *'I am the LORD your God, who brought you out of Egypt, out of the land of slavery.'* In the verses which follow, God had much more to say; but in these opening words of his address to Israel God reminded them that he was their Saviour. This truth figured prominently in Moses' thinking, right from the time of the exodus.

> Your right hand, O LORD,
> was majestic in power.
> Your right hand, O LORD,
> shattered the enemy.
> In the greatness of your majesty
> you threw down those who opposed you...
> In your unfailing love you will lead
> the *people you have redeemed.*
> (Exod. 15:6-7, 13)

So, when God gave the Commandments to Israel, he gave them after the great works of salvation had been accomplished, in order to help the Israelites to live as redeemed people ought to live. God did not give his Commandments as a way of earning favour, but as a way of reflecting his holiness among the nations.

The *Westminster Shorter Catechism* explains the significance of 5:6 (which it calls the preface to the Ten Commandments) for Christians today: 'The preface to the ten commandments teacheth us, That because God is the Lord, and our God, and Redeemer, therefore we are bound to keep all his commandments' (answer 44). Our salvation in Christ is never accomplished by obeying God's laws, but our salvation always leads to obedience. That is God's design, according to the apostle Paul in Ephesians 2:10: 'For we are God's workmanship, created in Christ Jesus to do good works, which God prepared in advance for us to do.' There is no greater reason for keeping God's commands than the knowledge that God has delivered us from eternal destruction by giving his only Son to be our Redeemer.   NO FOOT IN BOTH CAMPS

> For the grace of God that brings salvation has appeared to all men. It teaches us to say "No" to ungodliness and worldly passions, and to live self-controlled, upright and godly lives in this present age, while we wait for the blessed hope – the glorious appearing of ... Jesus Christ, who gave himself for us to redeem us from all wickedness and to purify for himself a people that are his very own (Titus 2:11-14).

The Ten Commandments (5:7-21)

Before considering each of the Ten Commandments in turn it is good to make some preliminary observations.

The number
They are described in Exodus 34:28 and Deuteronomy 4:13 literally as 'the ten words'. From this we get the English word,

DO I HAVE TO BE A JEW!
WHAT THEY OBSERVING

Back to basics

Decalogue. Ten is a round number, and the Ten Commandments are intended to be a succinct and memorable summary of God's law.

The division
The division of the commandments adopted below is the one traditionally followed by Protestant churches. Jewish commentators have sometimes taken the preface (5:6) as a separate commandment. Roman Catholics and some Lutherans have combined the prohibition of other gods and making idols into a single commandment, while dividing the prohibition of coveting into two commands.

The commandments are often divided into two sections (or tables); one describing man's duty to God (commands 1-4), and the other man's duty to his fellow men (commands 5-10). These two sections are very closely related to each other. Our social obligations are grounded in our devotion to God. It has been suggested that the commandments are listed in order of importance. At best this provides us with only a very rough indication of the relative importance of the commandments. It may well be that God places a greater emphasis on life and family than on property, but it is certainly true that our duty to God comes above all other obligations. This is where God's priorities differ from those of human law-makers. God's honour and worship must take the first place in our lives.

The importance of contemporary application
In Deuteronomy 5 Moses restates the summary of the law which God had given in Exodus 20:1-17. Repetition is a frequently used teaching tool, and Moses used it in his preaching on the plains of Moab when he called on the Israelites to renew their covenant with the Lord. At other times of spiritual renewal in Israel the reading of the law served as a wake-up call for the people (see 2 Kings 23:1-3; Neh. 8:1-3). The prophets of Israel made use of the Commandments in their preaching, to expose the nation's

wickedness (see Jer. 7:9-10; Hosea 4:1-2); and in the New Testament we see our Lord and the writer of James employing the Commandments to convict complacent sinners of their radical sinfulness (see Matt. 5:21-37; James 2:10-11). Those who preach God's word today ought to be diligent students of God's moral law so that they might apply its unchanging precepts to a constantly changing culture.

The first commandment (5:7) GWD FIRST

'You shall have no other gods before me.' This command sets forth Jehovah's demand for total loyalty. He is not content that his people merely acknowledge his existence, for he insists that they must serve him and him alone. Not only must he come first in their affections, but there must be no rivals for their affections. This command reminded the Israelites that they lived every day in God's presence. They were to have no other gods 'in my presence' (or literally 'in my face'). This is the significance of the words *'before me'.* When the Israelites worshipped other gods in their homes or temples, they did so in the very presence of the one true God, because he is everywhere present. That worship was deeply offensive to God. That was strikingly illustrated when the Philistines captured the ark (a symbol of God's presence) and took it into the temple of their god, Dagon, in order to humiliate Israel's God (see 1 Sam. 5:1-5). It was Dagon who was humiliated, for he simply could not stand before God.

The second commandment (5:8-10)

'You shall not make for yourself an idol ... You shall not bow down to them...' The second commandment is closely linked to the first because it regulates the way in which God's people worship him; and this in turn reflects their view of God. Depicting God by means of an idol necessarily gives a defective and demeaning idea of who God is. The commandment prohibits the manufacture of anything which is the product of human artistry – presumably with the understanding that it will be used to depict or worship God. Isaiah, for example, describes

a craftsman who cut down a tree and carved its wood to make an idol (see Isa. 44:13-17). We may think that this command has very little relevance for us. However, in the world of the twenty-first century, we are increasingly exposed to non-Christian cultures and their customs and this brings us into contact with a new pantheon of idols. It is becoming more common nowadays to see images of Buddha or Hindu gods in private homes and in public places. It would be naïve to think that these are merely cultural curiosities. They are, in fact, the instruments of spiritual bondage. We are commanded to 'flee from idolatry' (1 Cor. 10:14) and 'keep [ourselves] from idols' (see 1 John 5:21).

The third commandment (5:11)
'You shall not misuse the name of the LORD your God, for the LORD will not hold anyone guiltless who misuses his name.' Properly speaking, the God of Israel had only one name: Jehovah. By this name his character as the uncreated and unchanging covenant God of Israel was made known and he was distinguished from all other gods. Yet Jehovah was known by many other titles – God Most High, God Almighty and the Lord of Hosts, to name but a few. In the fullness of time his only-begotten Son was given the name Jesus, and the title Christ. The Spirit of God is known as the Holy Spirit, the Counsellor, and the Spirit of truth. All of these names and titles (and many others as well) are used by God's people when they speak about God and when they draw near to God in prayer and worship. This commandment forbids the careless use of God's names and titles. Literally it reads, 'You shall not lift up the name of the LORD your God as a vain thing'. God's name is not to be used in a careless or frivolous way, such as when people worship God with their lips but not with their hearts. God's name is most certainly not to be used in a blasphemous way, as when evil actions, thoughts or motives are ascribed to God. The seriousness of this sin is indicated by the warning that God 'will not hold anyone guiltless who misuses his name'.

God's treasured possession

The fourth commandment (5:12-15)
'*Observe the Sabbath day by keeping it holy, as the LORD your God has commanded you.*' The wording of the commandment differs significantly (but not substantially) from Exodus 20:8-11. The Israelites were not merely to 'remember' the Sabbath day, but to 'observe' it. As well as storing the commandment in their memories, they were to cherish the Sabbath in their hearts and incorporate its underlying principles into their lives. They were to make the day 'holy' by ceasing from all work. The whole family and wider community were also to enjoy a day of rest. '*On it you shall not do any work, neither you, nor your son or daughter, nor your manservant or maidservant, nor your ox, your donkey or any of your animals, nor the alien within your gates.*' The rest which one Israelite enjoyed was not to be bought at the cost of others, who might be forced to work extra hours and forego their day of rest.

The Israelites were to remember their own experience of slavery in Egypt. '*Remember that you were slaves in Egypt and that the LORD your God brought you out of there with a mighty hand and an outstretched arm. Therefore the LORD your God has commanded you to observe the Sabbath day.*' Forced, hard labour had been one aspect of that pitiable condition from which God had redeemed the Israelites when he brought them out of Egypt. When they entered the land of Canaan, many of the Israelites would employ servants to work their farms, and they were to have pity on those who worked for them, just as God had pitied them. In Exodus 20:11 the fourth commandment was grounded on God's rest in Genesis 2:1-2, which followed his work of creation. This continues as the basis on which the Sabbath principle applies to Christians today (Heb. 4:9-10). The additional motive of concern for the welfare of one's fellow Israelite is a characteristic feature of Moses' exposition of the law in Deuteronomy and a reminder that Moses was not content merely to restate the law of God. He sought to apply the spirit of the law to the hearts of his hearers.

The fifth commandment (5:16)
'*Honour your father and your mother...*' The values underlying this commandment stand in contrast to modern western values which glamorise youth and undervalue the wisdom and experience of age. In Biblical times traditional authority was highly regarded. The honour which parents were to receive was derived from their 'weight' or 'gravity' as older people. (When the word 'honour' is used of God, it is sometimes translated 'glory'.) Parents are to be honoured because God has appointed them to lead their families. It is important to remember that this commandment was not addressed exclusively (or even mainly) to young children, but to the nation as a whole. Young children must, indeed, obey their parents for, according to the apostle Paul, that is the right thing to do (Eph. 6:1). Adults, too, must honour their parents in the way they speak about them, listen to them, and care for their needs; although there may be times when they judge it best not to follow all their wishes.

The fifth commandment is the first one to come with a promise attached (Eph. 6:2), and the promise is typical of Moses' preaching in Deuteronomy: '*... so that you may live long and that it may go will with you in the land the LORD your God is giving you*.' The land of Canaan, and the prospect of entering it, is the constant background to Moses' exposition of the law in Deuteronomy. The hope was that generations of Israelites would succeed each other over the centuries to live in the land as parents passed on their inheritance (material and spiritual) to their children. Strong family units were essential to the well-being of the nation as a whole, and at the heart of these family units were parents who ruled their households and children who honoured their parents' authority.

The sixth commandment (5:17)
'*You shall not murder*' is a preferable translation to the more familiar 'You shall not kill'. The Hebrew verb, *ratsach*, refers specifically to unlawful, illegitimate or unsanctioned killing.

Specifically, it refers to the taking of human life. In Scripture, human life is distinguished from that of other animals, for God has drawn a line between mankind and the rest of creation (see Gen. 1:28). God does not condone cruelty, nor does he encourage needless killing of birds or animals (see Deut. 22:6); but he draws a clear distinction between taking the life of an animal and taking the life of a human being. The latter is murder and this command forbids it. The sixth commandment forbids taking human life for purely personal (and therefore illegitimate) reasons. Examples of illegitimate killing include revenge (as when the avenger of blood pursues someone who has killed without malicious intent, Deut. 19:6); jealousy (such as Cain's killing of Abel in Gen. 4:8); lust (as when David ordered the killing of Uriah in 2 Sam. 11:14-15); or personal gain (as when Jezebel had Naboth put to death, 1 Kings 21:7-14). The rationale for this command is that God created mankind in his own image and human life is God's to give or take away.

The seventh commandment (5:18)

'You shall not commit adultery.' The seventh commandment forbids the violation of marriage vows. Adultery is a sin committed by married people who have sex with a person other than their spouse, or by those who have sex with a married person. The law of Moses viewed this as a very serious sin – in fact, one which merited the death penalty. Although the sin of fornication (sex outside of marriage between those who are unmarried) was roundly condemned in the laws of Moses, it was not punished so severely. This was not intended to condone premarital sex, but to highlight the seriousness of adultery. Adultery is a sin which violates solemn vows and a special relationship. Israel's prophets often placed marital unfaithfulness on a par with Israel's idolatry and unfaithfulness to Jehovah (see Hosea 1:2).

The church has been right to see the seventh commandment not simply as a prohibition of adultery, but also an encouragement to sexual purity in all its aspects. 'Marriage should be honoured by all' according to Hebrews 13:4. Our Lord applies this commandment to the hearts and eyes of Christians. 'I tell you that anyone who looks at a woman lustfully has already committed adultery with in his heart' (Matt. 5:28). In the light of our Lord's words, who can claim to be guiltless? Yet by the grace of God there is cleansing for those who repent and turn from sexual sin (see 1 Cor. 6:9-11).

The eighth commandment (5:19)

'You shall not steal.' This commandment forbids the dishonest acquisition of property. Some modern studies of the commandments suggest that the scope of the eighth commandment is very narrow, referring primarily to man-stealing or kidnapping. The same verb is used in Deuteronomy 24:7, which prohibits kidnapping. An example of this is the enslavement of Joseph by his brothers (see Gen. 37:27-28). However, it is unlikely that a commandment as succinct as the eighth commandment was intended to refer to only one form of stealing. It is a summary statement forbidding all forms of dishonestly taking away what belongs to another person. As well as forbidding one Israelite to take away the liberty of another, the commandment forbade him from taking away his neighbour's material possessions, his time, his livelihood, his financial security, his peace of mind and his good reputation. Stealing takes many forms, because property has many forms.

The ninth commandment (5:20)

'You shall not give false testimony against your neighbour.' The ninth commandment uses the language of the courtroom to forbid perjury or dishonest testimony in court. A literal translation would read 'You shall not answer against your neighbour with worthless testimony.' The wording here differs slightly from that of Exodus 20:16. The ninth commandment in Exodus prohibits 'injurious falsehood', while in Deuteronomy its scope is wider and it prohibits 'vain words'. These words may be technically

true, but because of their vagueness and ambivalence they aim
to conceal and deceive. This kind of dishonesty is forbidden by
this commandment. When the people of God speak to others,
their words ought to be transparently honest and edifying
(see Matt. 5:37; Eph. 5:25, 29; Col. 4:6). We should not think
that dishonest speech is a trivial sin which is hardly worth
comparing with really serious sins such as idolatry, murder or
adultery, for the ninth commandment rests upon some of the
most important truths in the Bible. Jehovah is a God of truth
and desires to implant truth and truthfulness into the hearts
and lives of his people.

The tenth commandment (5:21)

*'You shall not covet your neighbour's wife. You shall not set your desire
on your neighbour's house or land, his manservant or maidservant,
his ox or donkey, or anything that belongs to your neighbour.'* This
commandment differs from the nine which come before it, in
that it deals with desires of the heart rather than accomplished
actions. Many systems of law distinguish between offences
that are still incomplete (such as conspiracy and attempt) and
offences that have actually taken place (such as the murder of
a particular person or theft of a specific item). Both are crimes
and carry heavy sentences. In God's eyes, coveting is just as
much a sin as theft or adultery. Indeed, coveting is the sin that
leads to every other sin. Two different Hebrew verbs describe
covetous desire in this verse. *Hamad* (used once in 5:21 and
twice in Exodus 20:17) describes desire which leads to action.
Here in 5:21 it is supplemented with another verb, *awah*, which
describes strong desire. This turns legitimate desires (such as
the desire for a wife and a home) into sinful cravings, such as
the craving of the Israelites for food in the desert (see Num.11:4,
34). This commandment exposes the hidden deceitfulness of
our hearts by challenging us to ask ourselves why we want the
things we desire. All too often it is possible to desire things,
which are otherwise lawful, for all the wrong reasons. When
we examine our hearts we may find that we are motivated by

envy, greed and malice. It was this very commandment which convicted Saul, the proud and self-righteous Pharisee, of his heart corruption before God (see Rom. 7:7).

What happened next? (5:22-31)

After recounting the giving of the Ten Commandments at Sinai, Moses reminded the people of two events which took place before the assembly.

God engraved the law on stone (5:22)

'These are the commandments the LORD proclaimed in a loud voice... Then he wrote them on two stone tablets.' After God spoke, he preserved his words in written form. The spoken word is easily forgotten, and a written record was needed so that the law might be preserved and passed on to future generations. Hence God 'wrote them on two stone tablets' with his own finger (see Exod. 31:18; Deut. 9:10). The form which God used to preserve the Ten Commandments emphasises their unique and permanent significance.

This was a supernatural act which distinguished the Ten Commandments from the other laws which God gave Israel. Although other laws, covering ceremonial, judicial and political matters, were written down in Scripture, their sphere of application was limited to the nation of Israel in the days before the coming of Christ. By contrast, the Ten Commandments are of universal and timeless application. They were foundational and God *'added nothing more'* to them. God did not need to add anything to this summary of the law because its emphasis and balance was just right. It captured perfectly the spirit and ethos of how God expected, and still expects, people to live.

God spoke through Moses (5:23-31)

The Ten Commandments were a perfect, but not exhaustive,

summary of God's law. More instruction was needed if the Israelites were to be made ready for the challenge of obeying the Ten Commandments when they entered the land of Canaan. The people of Israel and their leaders anticipated that God would have more to say to them after he had given them the Ten Commandments.

> *When you heard the voice out of the darkness, while the mountain was ablaze with fire, all the leading men of your tribes and your elders came to me. And you said... 'Go near and listen to all that the LORD our God says. Then tell us whatever the LORD our God tells you. We will listen and obey.' (5:23-27)*

Before they presented their request, they registered their amazement at what had happened that day on the mountain. *'The LORD our God has shown us his glory and his majesty, and we have heard his voice from the fire. Today we have seen that a man can live even if God speaks with him'* (5:24). This was not something that they could take for granted. It is an awesome thing for sinners to enter the presence of the holy God of heaven, as Isaiah saw in his vision of the Lord seated on the throne of heaven. He cried out 'Woe to me! ... I am ruined!' (see Isaiah 6:1-5). At Sinai, Moses had learned that no-one can see God and live (see Exod. 33:20); and the Israelites were as terrified of the sound of God's voice as they had been of the sight of his face. *'But now, why should we die? This great fire will consume us, and we will die if we hear the voice of the LORD our God any longer. For what mortal man has ever heard the voice of the living God speaking out of fire, as we have, and survived?'* (5:25-26).

Yet they strive never to loosen their hold on the truth that sinners *can* hear God's voice and live. This takes us back to the garden of Eden where Adam and Eve, naked and trembling, hid from the *sound* of the Lord God as he walked in the garden (see Gen. 3:8-10). Their fear was understandable, because Adam was under a sentence of death (see Gen. 2:17). What did God have to say to him, except to pronounce his doom? Yet when God did speak to Adam it was to reason with him so that he might lead him to repentance, and set forth the promise of a Saviour. God's voice was amazingly gracious in the circumstances.

Although God is merciful, the Israelites approached him with caution. They knew that they enjoyed a unique privilege, for God had condescended to speak to them through Moses. Moses was a unique man (see Num. 12:7-8) for he was able to speak to God face to face and not die. That is why the Israelites presented their request in 5:27, 'Go near and listen to all that the LORD our God says. Then tell us whatever the LORD our God tells you. We will listen and obey.' They asked Moses to be their mediator and they asked God to speak to them through this mediator. Through that same mediator they pledged obedience to God. This is the only way sinful people can relate to a holy God.

In the New Testament, Moses is described as a mediator. Paul tells us in Galatians 3:19b that 'the law was put into effect through angels by a mediator'. Moses was the mediator through whom God put the law into effect. He was also the mediator who brought the people's needs to God (see Exod. 32:11-14). He was the man who stood in the gap and pleaded for God's mercy. By these actions he pointed forward to the Lord Jesus, who is the one and only mediator between God and man (see 1 Tim. 2:5).

God agreed to the people's request for a mediator. In fact, he did so with enthusiasm. He told Moses in 5:28-29, '*I have heard what this people said to you. Everything they said was good. Oh, that their hearts would be inclined to fear me and keep all my commands always, so that it might go well with them and their children forever!*' God was pleased with their pledge of obedience in 5:27 and acceded to their request, saying to Moses in 5:30-31, '*Go, tell them to return to their tents. But you stay here with me so that I may give you all the commands, decrees and laws you are to teach them to follow in the land I am giving them to possess.'* These were the laws which Moses would teach to the Israelites throughout the rest of his second sermon, especially chapters 12-26.

While there were many 'decrees and laws' which Moses was to teach, there was only one 'commandment'. The word often translated 'commandments' in 5:31 is in fact singular and the verse can be translated, 'I will teach you the whole commandment.' This is the whole of God's law condensed into a single commanding principle – 'Love the LORD your God with all your heart and with all your soul and with all your strength.' Not only is this the guiding principle of the Decalogue (Matt. 22:34-40), it is also the summary of all the laws in Deuteronomy.

What an important principle this is! We may not remember every rule and regulation, but we dare not forget this command. As we face new situations in the changing scenes of life we are called upon to make fresh applications of God's law to our own age and culture. As we meet each new challenge, the question we ask is, 'What does love for God compel us to do?'

Concluding exhortation (5:32-33)

Moses concludes this section of his sermon with his own call to obedience. *'So be careful to do what the LORD your God has commanded you; do not turn aside to the right or to the left. Walk in all the way that the LORD your God has commanded you, so that you may live and prosper and prolong your days in the land that you will possess.'* This call is a typically Mosaic exhortation. It is a call to *determined obedience*. The Ten Commandments summarise the law and sketch out the scope of God's requirements from his people. They touch on every area of Israel's life. The big principles set forth in the Ten Commandments will be applied in detail in the regulations which follow. The really important question for the people was whether they were willing to obey? There was the real danger that they would be distracted and diverted from God's laws. Walking in God's ways is never easy, but when God's people make a conscious and deliberate commitment to serve God they will find that his strength enables them to walk an otherwise impossible path.

Moses' exhortation is also a call to *delight in God's blessing*. Those who walk in God's ways will prosper in the land which God will give them. Moses never intended that obeying God should become a mere drudgery; and obeying God ought never to be a drudgery for his people today. 'This is love for God: to obey his commands. And his commands are not burdensome' (1 John 5:3). 'The man who looks intently into the perfect law that gives freedom, and continues to do this, not forgetting what he has heard, but doing it – he will be blessed in what he does' (James 1:25).

Chapter 6
Teaching God's commands

Please read Deuteronomy 6: 1-25

After giving the definitive summary of the law in the Ten Commandments, Moses impressed upon his hearers the importance of teaching and obeying the law. Many people who know the law, nevertheless fail to obey it themselves or pass it on to their children. This was a danger which the Israelites needed to guard against.

The struggle is a timeless one. Many times we will look back on our actions and ask, 'Why did I ever do that?' Even those who have loved and served God will ask why they still fall into sin year after year. The apostle Paul asked the same question. We find him acknowledging: 'I do not understand what I do. For what I want to do I do not do, but what I hate I do... For what I do is not the good I want to do; no the evil I do not want to do – this I keep on doing... What a wretched man I am! Who will rescue me from this body of death?' (Rom. 7:15, 19, 24).

Paul's struggle starts with the question, 'why don't I do what God wants me to do?' – but it becomes 'How can I do what God wants me to do?' Despair can, by God's grace, lead to a desire for new obedience. That is a very healthy development.

The same concern lay behind Moses' preaching in Deuteronomy. His concern was not simply to teach the law of God to the Israelites. As their spiritual under-shepherd he sought to help them to shake loose from the grip of their besetting sins as they prepared themselves for a new life in the promised land of Canaan. They had not found it easy to obey God during their forty years of wandering through the desert. It wouldn't get any easier when they moved into a land inhabited by idol-worshipping pagans.

Many years earlier, Jehovah had rescued them from slavery in Egypt and called them to live as a nation bound to him in a covenant relationship. At Sinai God had given them his law to show them how to live as his holy nation. This law was summarised in the Ten Commandments, which were supplemented, and explained in detail, by a myriad of rules for the nation of Israel. The Ten Commandments were repeated in Deuteronomy 5 and the detailed regulations expounded in chapters 12 to 26. As they listened to Moses' sermon, some of the Israelites might have said, 'Yes, we know all these commands, but will we be able to obey them?' So in Deuteronomy 6 Moses teaches the Israelites how they and their children are to face the challenge of living a godly and obedient life.

Know God's commands better (6:1-9)

In 6:1 Moses reminded the people of Israel that God's *'commands, decrees and laws'* (which set out both general principles of godliness and detailed application to specific circumstances) were not just words carved on stone. They were to be written all over the lives of God's people. *'These... the LORD your God directed me to teach you to observe in the land that you are crossing the Jordan to possess.'* With this goal in view, Moses sought to engrave the law of God on the hearts and minds of his hearers. Jeremiah reminded the people of Judah that this had always been God's intention and that it would be a high priority when God made a new covenant with Israel. "'This is the covenant I will make with the house of Israel after that time," declares the LORD. "I will put my law in their minds and write it on their hearts. I will be their God and they will be my people'" (Jer. 31:33).

God's goal in giving the law to the Israelites is benevolent. He desires to bless them. God directed Moses to teach his statutes to Israel *so that you, your children and their children after them may fear the LORD your God as long as you live by keeping all his decrees and commands that I give you, and so that you may enjoy long life'* (6:2). Long life is one of the central blessings of the covenant. It is life in the land of blessing, enjoyed by generation after generation of God's people, living in fellowship with their Redeemer. The spiritual dimension of this life in covenant with God is very real. So, too, is the material dimension. *'Hear, O Israel, and be careful to obey so that it may go well with you and that you may increase greatly in a land flowing with milk and honey, just as the LORD, the God of your fathers, promised you'* (6:3). Here, the good life to which God called them is described in terms which must have been very appealing to people who had lived for two generations in a dry and barren desert. The metaphor brings to mind food and drink, but we should remember that these blessings come from the hand of a loving God who provided for all the needs of his people.

And so Moses set about the task of teaching the Israelites how to live as God commanded. *'Hear, O Israel: The LORD our God, the LORD is one'* (6:4). Moses did not start by describing the behaviour which God required, but by describing God himself. The law was simply an extended description of God's character and how the character of a holy God is to be reflected in the conduct and attributes of his people. The doctrine of God may seem to be abstract and mysterious, but it was to leave a very clear and obvious mark on the character of the nation of Israel. 'The LORD our God' is 'Jehovah our God'. 'Jehovah' is not merely the title of the God of Israel, but his name. 'I am the LORD; that is my name!' he exclaims in Isaiah 42:8. In our English versions the fact that God's name 'Jehovah' (or 'Yahweh', as it is sometimes rendered into English) is found in the Hebrew text is commonly indicated by 'LORD' in upper-case letters.

Jehovah is the God who reveals himself to his people. When Jehovah appeared to Moses at the burning bush to send him back to Egypt and lead the Israelite slaves to freedom, Moses asked God to explain what he might say to Pharaoh and the people. When people ask 'Who sent you?' what shall I say? God replied, 'Say to the Israelites, "The LORD, the God of your fathers – the God of Abraham, the God of Isaac and the God of Jacob - has sent me to you." This is my name forever, the name by which I am to be remembered from generation to generation' (Exod. 3:13-15). Jehovah was not an unknown quantity but a person whom they had known and with whom they would have a personal relationship. Moses told the people of Israel that they could describe Jehovah as 'our God'. No other nation dared to expect such dealings with their deities, for they were spirits who dwelt on distant mountain-tops or in the skies and the winds. By contrast, Jehovah is the God who seeks out men and women and makes his covenant with them. He walked and talked with Adam in the Garden of Eden; but most wonderfully, he took human form and dwelt amongst men (John 1:14). Like Paul, we can call Jesus Christ, 'our Lord' (Rom. 1:4; 1 Cor. 1:2).

Jehovah is also described as 'one'. At first sight this is a simple and obvious description for the one living and true God. However, its significance in this setting has puzzled commentators. The following are some of the explanations that have been offered.

Jehovah is unique
The people of Israel lived in a world where it was common to believe in many gods, all of whom had their limited sphere

of influence. Some were gods of war or fertility; or gods who controlled the hills or the plains; or they might display certain traits of character such as strength or generosity. Even if these gods had been capable of existing as the pagans believed they did, Jehovah would not have been like any of them. His holiness and glory differentiate him from all these gods (Exod. 15:11). So, too, did his universal power. In his confrontation with the gods of Egypt God made that abundantly clear. (Exod. 8:10; 9:14) Most especially, his grace and willingness to forgive sin set him apart from the cruel and capricious gods of the heathen (Micah 7:18).

Jehovah is the only God
Monotheism is one of the great truths that the Old Testament taught about God. 'For who is God besides the LORD? And who is the rock except our God?' (Ps. 18:31). 'I am the Lord, and there is no other; apart from me there is no God' (Isa. 45:5). Moses states this truth elsewhere in Deuteronomy (see 4:35, 39; 32:39). We find the same message in the New Testament. 'For there is one God and one mediator between God and men, the man Christ Jesus' (1 Tim. 2:5). 'We know that an idol is nothing at all in the world and that there is no God but one' (1 Cor.8:4). Other so-called gods existed only as figments of the imagination of deluded people, and these words in 6:4 became one of Israel's most distinctive creedal statements. Having said this, they are a statement about the character of God, not an explicit denial of the existence of other gods. Yet when this verse is quoted elsewhere in the Bible, the necessary implication that other gods do not exist comes to the fore. When the prophet Zechariah looked forward to the victorious day of the Lord, he quoted from Deuteronomy 6:4: 'The LORD will be king over the whole earth. On that day there will be one LORD, and his name will be the only name' (Zech. 14:9). When Jesus quoted Deuteronomy 6:4-5 to answer a question about the law, the teacher of the law replied, 'Well said... You are right in saying that God is one and there is no other but him' (Mark 12:28-32).

God's treasured possession

Jehovah is consistent in his behaviour as God
This reflects an inner unity of purpose in the person of God, which theologians describe as the simplicity of God. His actions are not driven by warring impulses which push him hither and thither like the impulses that often drive our actions. Because of this God does not change like a weather-vane (James 1:17); nor is he two-faced, or self-contradictory. As a result, 'God is not a man that he should lie, nor a son of man, that he should change his mind' (Num. 23:19).

A very different view of God was held by the nations surrounding Israel. Paganism (ancient and modern) believes in a god that is essentially unknowable, a mysterious and impersonal force in the world around us. He, she or it dwells in the planets, in the hills and rivers, in the animals and in men and women. All creation is divine and is to be honoured as god. Thus there are many contradictory faces of god and all of them are to be worshipped and appeased. That is why paganism believes in the existence of many gods, some of whom are feminine goddesses of fertility while others are very masculine gods of war. This diversity expresses the multi-faceted mystery of God. Paganism is the most thoroughgoing attack on the truth that Jehovah has revealed about himself. It undermines his uniqueness, his goodness and his consistency. In this creedal statement Moses laid the axe to paganism by emphasising that Jehovah is one person who acts with an inner unity of character and purpose and who rules over all his creation; so when Jehovah revealed himself to Israel, there was no need to seek after other gods. There is no other God. There is no other revelation about God. There is no other name to be acknowledged.

So because of who Jehovah is he is to be loved whole-heartedly. *'Love the LORD your God with all your heart and with all your soul and with all your strength'* (6:5). In the Old Testament, the Hebrew word for 'heart' describes the part of our being in which we process information and make decisions. The 'soul' is our inner being, the seat of our deepest emotions and desires. The word 'strength' does not, as many have assumed, describe our physical might. Nor does it describe our material possessions. It is a word which describes the willingness of God's people to go beyond the bare call of duty; it describes anything which is done to excess. 'Strength' is the overflowing exuberance of God's people when they devote all they have to serving the Lord who rules over the whole universe.

So in 6:4-5 Moses taught both doctrine and ethics. According to the *Westminster Shorter Catechism* (answer 3), this is how we are to summarise the teaching of the whole Bible: 'The Scriptures principally teach what man is to believe concerning God, and what duty God requires of man'. Doctrine and duty are linked, for when we know God as he reveals himself to us we will love him with our whole being; and when we love him we will obey him. Knowing the greatness of God is where the energy comes from. Well, how does it work out in practice? Moses gave four specific instructions.

1. Digest God's commandments (6:6)

'These commandments that I give you today are to be upon your hearts.' When people today speak of the heart they think of it as the seat of their emotions. On Valentine's Day couples send each other flowers and chocolates and cards with big red hearts on them as an expression of romantic love. Our hearts are supposed to be the place where we entertain such emotions. However, in the ancient world the Hebrews used a different imagery to describe their inner beings. Their bowels or intestines were reckoned to be the seat of their feelings and emotions, while the heart represented their ability to think and make decisions (something which people today associate with their brains).

So when Moses encouraged the Israelites to impress God's law on their 'hearts', he was encouraging them to analyse and digest what God had commanded in his laws and to resolve to obey them. He was encouraging them to meditate upon God's word. 'Blessed is the man who does not walk in the counsel of the wicked... but his delight is in the law of the LORD, and on his law he meditates day and night' (Ps. 1:1-2). The knowledge of God's law must not, however, be coldly cerebral. The Psalmist studied God's law because he loved God and he loved his word. 'Oh, how I love your law! I meditate on it all day long' (Ps. 119:97). As a result of his study, he is able to apply God's word to his daily life. 'I have hidden your word in my heart that I might not sin against you' (Ps. 119:11).

2. Teach God's commands to our children (6:7a)
'Impress them on your children...' In practical terms this involved a lot of memory work, as books were rare in the ancient world and people committed such books as did exist to their memories. It was the task of parents to teach their children to memorise the whole of the Scriptures. Even though we have an abundance of books and other ways of storing and presenting information available to us today, the value of God's word stored in our own minds and in the minds of our children is incalculable.

Memorisation of God's law, however, was not the primary focus of Moses' instruction to parents in 6:7a. The Hebrew verb which he used has the root meaning of sharpening a knife. The word of God which we teach to our children is a sharp sword (Heb. 4:12). When we impress it on our children, we seek to teach it incisively so that it penetrates the conscience and makes a lasting impression upon them. Parents are required to impress upon their children the seriousness and spirituality of God's commands. God requires a loving heart as well as a conformed life. God will call each one who has been instructed in the law of God to give an account of his or her actions to him. He knows our lives and he will not let disobedience go unpunished.

3. Talk about what God commands us to do (6:7b)
'Talk about them when you sit at home and when you walk along the road, when you lie down and when you get up.' Talk can sometimes be an alternative to obedience, but it need not be. Talking about God's laws, as Moses describes it here, is intended to be an encouragement to obedience. Christians are commanded to spur one another on toward love and good deeds, and that is why they meet together (see Heb. 10:24-25). In these verses, Moses describes the settings in which Old Testament believers would spur one another on by talking about God's law – the home, sitting around the meal table, travelling on a journey or going to work in the fields, preparing to rest at night and getting up the next morning. Modern equivalents are obvious. Yet many families do not talk much around the meal table because of their hectic schedules or the television in the background. As a result many valuable opportunities for showing the application of the Christian faith to daily life are lost. We need to be both creative and disciplined in making times – whether around the meal table, driving in the car, walking to school, at the beginning of the day, or just before bedtime – to talk about God. Our children will supply us with enough questions to keep us busy.

4. Apply God's commands (6:8-9)
God's commands need to be integrated into our patterns of daily life. Moses used figurative language to describe how we do this. *'Tie them as symbols on your hands and bind them on your foreheads. Write them on the doorframes of your houses and on your gates.'* By the first century AD, many Jews had given these words a very literal application. The Pharisees tied small wooden boxes (called phylacteries), containing scraps of parchment upon which verses from the law were written, to their wrists and foreheads (See Matt. 23:5). Others attached boxes containing a small scroll with words from God's law (a mezusa) to their doors. These cultural traditions completely missed the point of Moses' teaching. God's law was to dwell, not merely in wooden boxes, but in their hearts. When God's law dwelt in their hearts and

minds, the effect would be obvious in their personal conduct and family life. We find a similar concern in the teaching of Paul. 'So whether you eat or drink or whatever you do, do it all for the glory of God' (1 Cor. 10:31).

The ethos of our homes and family life is also to be governed by God's law. God's law is, spiritually speaking, to be on our doorframes and gates. God's law is to stand as a watchman over the influences that we allow to enter into our homes. Christian parents today will make household rules that regulate the kind of television programmes which their children are allowed to keep and the company which their children are allowed to keep. Christian parents will also need to watch over their own lifestyles lest their lifestyles and values become a snare to their children rather than a positive example of godliness.

Fear God and heed his warnings (6:10-19)

The tone of Moses' teaching changes in these verses. His high expectations of the people give way to dire warnings. He anticipated some of the temptations which the Israelites would face when they entered into the land of Canaan and warned that the consequences of falling into sin were dire indeed. *'The LORD your God, who is among you, is a jealous God and his anger will burn against you, and he will destroy you from the face of the land'* (6:15). 'The wages of sin' would indeed be death' (Rom. 6:23). In this section, Moses probes the hearts of the Israelites by describing the situations in which they would be tempted to abandon the Lord their God.

When life is going well (6:10-12)
Moses described the good things that the Israelites would enjoy in the Canaan, *'a land with large flourishing cities you did not build, houses filled with all kinds of good things you did not provide, wells you did not dig, and vineyards and olive groves you*

did not plant. When people have worked hard to achieve their goals, they are often tempted to forget God and take the credit for themselves, as did the rich fool in our Lord's parable in Luke 12:19. Yet when people have everything handed to them on a plate there is also the danger that they will despise their inheritance and take it for granted. This was the temptation which the Israelites would face in Canaan and it would rapidly quench any feeling of gratitude towards Jehovah. *'When the LORD your God brings you into the land he swore to your fathers... be careful that you do not forget the LORD who brought you out of Egypt, out of the land of slavery.'*

The same danger faces people today who live in an affluent community. Many western Christians have been abundantly supplied with homes to live in and food to eat and it is easy to imagine that we are entitled to expect a comfortable standard of living. As a result, possessing and enjoying the good things of this world takes up more and more of our time and energy. How easy it becomes to forget God!

When others do not love God (6:13-14)
'Fear the LORD your God, serve him only, and take your oaths in his name. Do not follow other gods, the gods of the peoples around you.' The Canaanites worshipped other gods. When they concluded their business deals in the market-place, they swore by their gods, for their paganism had thoroughly permeated their culture. At first their pagan customs would be strange and unfamiliar to the Israelites, but in time that would change. They might not realise it as it was happening; but in time they would adapt to their surroundings and adopt the ways of the Canaanites. The same pressure is on us as we live in an increasingly pagan culture. That is why it is so important that we digest and apply God's commands. If it is not God's commands which govern our lives, the standards of the world will shape the way in which we live.

When life brings disappointments (6:16)
'Do not test the Lord your God as you did at Massah.' At Massah, the people of Israel were thirsty and angry (see Exod. 17:1-7) and so they quarrelled with Moses. They believed that God had let them down. Their cynical questions were an insult to God. 'They spoke against God, saying, "Can God spread a table in the desert... can he also give us food? Can he supply meat for his people?"' (Ps. 78:18-22). In response, Moses insisted that God was able to supply all the needs of his people and he urged the Israelites to believe his promises and trust on him. *'Do what is right and good in the LORD's sight, so that it may go well with you and you may go in and take over the good land that the LORD promised on oath to your forefathers, thrusting out all your enemies before you, as the LORD said'* (6:18-19). God was about to expel the Canaanites because they had forgotten Jehovah and refused to serve him. Moses appealed to the Israelites not to make the same mistake.

Moses' teaching in these verses is summarised in the phrase *'Fear the LORD your God'* in 6:13. The fear of Jehovah is a special kind of fear, for it grows out of love. It is a passionate desire to please him in every way possible. The pagans feared their gods because they were unpredictable and cruel, while the Israelites feared Jehovah because he is good and great. This reverent fear is well described in the conversation between Mr and Mrs Beaver and the children in C.S. Lewis' story *The Lion, the Witch and the Wardrobe*. Mr Beaver told Lucy that Aslan, the true king of Narnia, was a lion who would overthrow the powers of evil.

> 'Is he - quite safe? I shall feel rather nervous about meeting a lion.'
> 'That you will, dearie, and no mistake,' said Mrs Beaver...
> 'Then he isn't safe?' said Lucy.
> 'Safe?' said Mr Beaver. '... Who said anything about safe? 'Course he isn't safe. But he's good. He's the King, I tell you.'

Jehovah is the king. He has promised every blessing to his people; and when he gave the Israelites the promised land of Canaan, he gave them more than they could expect or deserve. Yet Jehovah was also a majestic and awesome God, who conquered his enemies and ruled his own people. When the people of Israel had stood at Mount Sinai, Moses had told them that 'the fear of God will be with you to keep you from sinning' (Exod. 20:20). That same fear is to dwell in the hearts of God's people today; and it is this fear which makes us want to keep his commandments.

The fear of God is a sadly neglected, and even unpopular, aspect of Christian piety in the church of today. It seems that, in many circles, God is a buddy who is to be addressed with patronising familiarity. This spirit has affected the worship of many congregations and the devotional lives of many Christians. The consequence is that many professing believers do not love God's law, but resent it and dismiss every challenge to obey it as outdated legalism. Hence many Christians are unwilling have their consciences pricked by the goads of God's law. We need to learn some very basic lessons from the Psalmist. 'Come, my children, listen to me; I will teach you the fear of the LORD' (Ps. 34:11).

Understand the significance of God's commands (6:20-25)

Moses continues to look into the future and anticipate what will happen when the Israelites will enter the promised land. Yes, the Israelites will face temptation, but they will overcome those temptations and a new generation will arise to look back upon God's goodness. *'In the future, when your son asks you...'* (6:20). The setting is the kind of family instruction envisaged in 6:7-9, and this is a sign of spiritual health amongst the people of Israel.

God's treasured possession

When God's people live distinctively holy lives, they will provoke the curiosity of their neighbours. Some may even ask, 'Why do you live the way you do? Why do you not do some of the things that everyone else does?' When Peter wrote, 'Always be prepared to give an answer to everyone who asks you to give the reason for the hope that you have' (1 Peter 3:15), he presumed that Christians would be asked about the way we lived. In this way ethics leads to evangelism.

Moses told the Israelites that their children would also ask them questions. *'What is the meaning of the stipulations, decrees and laws the LORD our God has commanded you?'* (6:20). Are we to imagine that future generations of Israelites would not know the meaning of the commands not to take God's name in vain or to steal or to covet? It is most unlikely that these children would be so ignorant of God's commands that they would ask merely for a technical definition of God's words. We must anticipate that they knew what it meant to take God's name in vain or to steal or covet. What they wanted to know was the significance of these commands. 'Why ought we to keep these commands? Where do they fit into the bigger picture of God's plan?' These are the questions that succeeding generations will ask, and Moses seeks to help parents answer their children's questions.

In 6:21-24 Moses directed the parents of Israel to the story of their salvation. He recounts this story as one who had been there. He described their miserable condition: *'We were slaves of Pharaoh in Egypt'* (6:20). He described God's mighty power: *'The LORD brought us out of Egypt with a mighty hand. Before our eyes the LORD sent miraculous signs and wonders – great and terrible – upon Egypt and Pharaoh and his whole household'* (6:21-22). He described the promised blessings: *'But he brought us out from there to bring us in and give us the land he promised on oath to our forefathers'* (6:23). These blessings depended upon an obedient response to God's word.

Teaching God's commands

The LORD commanded us to obey all these decrees and to fear the LORD our God, so that we might always prosper and be kept alive as is the case today. And if we are careful to obey all this law before the LORD our God, as he has commanded us, that will be our righteousness. (6:24-25)

Three blessings in particular are promised to those who obey – God's goodness (prosperity), life and righteousness. These were the blessings which Israel would enjoy in the land of Canaan. There they would enjoy the bounty of that beautiful land. There they would raise their children and pass their inheritance to a new generation which would love and serve Jehovah. There, too, they would be noted as a people that lived and walked in God's ways. Their visible righteousness would declare to the world that they were the people whom God had chosen and redeemed. It was in this sense that both Abraham and Rahab were considered to be righteous because of their works (see James 2:20-26). This righteousness is a right response to God's mercy. It pleases and glorifies God. That is why the Lord Jesus taught his followers: 'let your light shine before men, that they may see your good deeds and praise your Father in heaven' (Matt. 5:16).

This righteousness does not, however, earn God's mercy. It is built upon and flows out of the saving mercy of God. Over the years many have tried to secure a place amongst God's people by obeying God's law, but they have failed. 'Israel, who pursued a law of righteousness, has not attained it. Why not? Because they pursued it not by faith but as if it were by works' (Rom. 9:31-32). If, as you read this, you are keeping God's commands because you hope that your obedience will earn God's favour and give you a place in heaven, you are very mistaken. You will fail and your efforts will leave you frustrated and miserable. The challenge of the gospel is to acknowledge that we cannot earn God's mercy by keeping his commands. However, we can – and must – receive the righteousness which earns God's favour as a free gift (see Rom. 1:17; 3:21-22). When sinners ask for and receive this gift of righteousness, they discover the most powerful motivation for keeping God's commands - gratitude.

How can we train ourselves to obey God's law? The best training we can receive is that which we receive in the school-room of God's free grace. These verses proclaim the gospel according to Moses, who describes what God had done for the people of Israel. He had saved them from a miserable fate and called them to live holy lives in the land of promise. In the same way, God redeems sinners today 'from all wickedness' in order 'to purify for himself a people that are his very own, eager to do what is good' (Titus 2:14). Hence, our response to God's mercy is to love God and keep his commands.

Chapter 7
God's love for Israel

Please read Deuteronomy 7: 1-26

The message of Deuteronomy is a message of God's grace. It describes the character of God, his love for undeserving sinners, and how he led them into his blessing. It presents the sovereign God who stands at the heart of the gospel. However, many readers of Deuteronomy find it very difficult to see the gospel in Deuteronomy, especially in this chapter which records Moses' instructions to the Israelites to drive out the inhabitants of the land of Canaan before them. When we pause to consider what this task involved, its horror and violence must surely appal us.

In modern times the horror of warfare has become better known to non-combatants than ever before. Whole generations of civilians were caught up in the trauma of the First and Second World Wars. Many people are still stunned when they think about the destructive power of the two atomic bombs that were dropped on the Japanese cities of Hiroshima and Nagasaki in August 1945. More recently, with the advent of television and digital photography, wars have been documented and broadcast into our homes. We have seen the pictorial evidence of ethnic cleansing in the former Yugoslavia and the destruction of Saddam Hussein's regime in Iraq. Our revulsion is entirely appropriate. How can we reconcile the destruction of the Canaanites with the grace of God, or with the teaching of Jesus in the New Testament?

Deuteronomy 7 presents us with this challenge. The message of Moses to the Israelites was clear - the Canaanites must be destroyed.

> *When the LORD your God brings you into the land you are entering to possess and drives out before you many nations... then you must destroy them totally... You must destroy all the peoples the LORD your God gives over to you. Do not look on them with pity and do not serve their gods, for that will be a snare to you (7:1-2, 16).*

Yet this is also one of the most evangelistic chapters in the Old Testament. It is overflowing in its description of God's love. Amazingly, Moses displays not a hint of embarrassment or discomfort at the contrast between these two aspects of God's character. He did not try to soften the sharpness of the contrast. The God who commanded the destruction of the Canaanites also loved Israel with an everlasting love. That love is the key to unlocking the book of Deuteronomy and understanding its message.

1. God's command (7:1-5)

Until this point in Deuteronomy, Moses has been pointing the people of Israel back to what God had done for them in the past. Now Moses points forward and anticipates what will happen when God gives Israel the promised land. *'When the LORD your God brings you into the promised land you are entering to possess and drives out before you many nations...'* (7:1). God is the main actor in these verses. He will give the land to his people, and it will be the place where they enjoy his blessing and dedicate themselves to him without compromise.

The influence of the heathen nations – which often led to compromise and apostasy – was a constant snare to the people of Israel. They are named in 7:1b, '... *the Hittites, Girgashites, Amorites, Canaanites, Perizzites, Hivites, and Jebusites'.* This list of *'seven nations'* is unusual in the Old Testament. (See, however, the reference in Acts 13:19.) Most lists mention only six or fewer nations. Only in Joshua 3:10 and 24:11 are the same seven nations mentioned. In Genesis 15:19-21 a longer list of ten nations is given. The seven nations in the promised land were a strong and formidable foe. They were *'larger and stronger'* than Israel, secure and confident in their walled fortresses. Their strength contrasted with the weakness of the Israelites (see 7:7). They had caused Israel to tremble once before (1:27-28; 7:17). Only a miracle of divine intervention could dislodge them from the land of Canaan so that the Israelites might possess it; but that was exactly what God had promised!

Moses spoke about the seven nations of the Canaanites in past tenses as though these nations were already defeated, for that is how God viewed them. He exhorted the Israelites to advance against them confident of victory. Although God was giving them the promised land, the Israelites must go forward and take possession of it. *'When the LORD your God has delivered them over to you and you have defeated them, then you must destroy them totally'* (7:2).

The verb that Moses used (*haram*) was often used in the accounts of the conquest to describe the destruction of the Canaanites and their possessions. It describes the total elimination of that which has been corrupted by sin. This vindicates the lordship of Jehovah, for those nations which had cast off authority could not escape the reach of his justice. They would not serve him willingly, but they will honour him even in their destruction. As for the Israelites, they must learn an important lesson from the destruction of these nations, namely, that they must have no dealings with evil.

God's treasured possession

It is significant that God did not vindicate his honour by a miraculous intervention, but by the actions of his servants. The Israelites were to share in God's revulsion at the evil of these nations. They must learn to repudiate evil and separate themselves from sin. That is the note on which the chapter begins and ends (see 7:25-26). God did not put his redeemed people into a spiritually sanitised environment; instead, he put them into the real world and commanded them to do battle with the evil that was all around them. Their goal was to purge the land of its sin.

Moses highlighted two fronts on which they would fight this war. The first front was *in their family lives* (7:2b-4). *'Make no treaty with them.'* The word for treaty is the important Old Testament word *berith* or covenant. It describes the covenant between the Lord and his people. It describes an exclusive relationship of love and loyalty. It is impossible to have a treaty with Jehovah and with the heathen. Trying to keep one foot in the Lord's camp and another foot in the camp of the Canaanites would be a recipe for disaster.

The kind of treaty that Moses had in mind was a treaty of friendship secured by marriage. *'Do not intermarry with them...'* Even today we recognise that marriage unites two families as well as two people. In the past this was regarded as one of the most significant aspects of marriage. The marriage of Ferdinand of Aragon and Isabella of Castile in 1469 brought together two small kingdoms to create a united Spain, which became one of the strongest nations in Europe. Intermarriage between the Israelites and the Canaanites would lead to God's enemies becoming Israel's friends.

Not only were the Israelites not to seek marriages with the Canaanites, they were to reject every proposal of marriage from the Canaanites, because the consequences would spell disaster for Israel. *'They will turn your sons away from following after me to serve other gods and the LORD's anger will burn against you and will quickly destroy you.'* Marriage was not to be thought of as an evangelistic tool for the conversion of the heathen, but as the union of compatible people who would become 'one flesh' (see Gen. 2:20b-24). Amongst the people of God, then and now, marriage partners are to be spiritually compatible or equally yoked (see 2 Cor. 6:14). When this principle is ignored, the danger of compromise with the world increases dramatically. This was tragically demonstrated in the history of Israel.

The second front on which the Israelites would wage war against God's enemies was *in the sanctuary of worship* (7:5). *'Break down their altars, smash their sacred stones, cut down their Asherah poles and burn their idols in the fire.'* Intermarriage with the heathen almost inevitably led to the adoption of idolatrous worship, and this is the problem which Moses addressed. Israel was to have no other God apart from Jehovah, nor was Israel to have any idols. These were the first two commands of the Decalogue, and they summarised the essence of Israel's covenant-treaty with Jehovah. Israel was to be devoted to Jehovah and him alone, so the symbols of loyalty to other gods had no place in the land which Israel would receive from her Lord.

This is also a hallmark of biblical holiness. God's people in every age are to consecrate themselves to God by cutting themselves off from idols (see 1 Thess. 1:9; 1 John 5:21). By God's grace, believers in Christ become a new Israel, a spotless bride, purified from idols. The relationship between Christ and his people is like the relationship between a husband and wife (see Eph. 5:31-32). When a man and a woman commit themselves to each other in marriage, they leave their natural families and cleave to each other. Sometimes in their marriage vows they will promise to 'forsake all others'. Their relationship is an exclusive relationship. There is no place for love-letters or friendship rings from old friends.

In the Christian life, there is no room for other gods. Even legitimate material wealth must be put in its rightful place. Jesus said to the rich young ruler, 'Go, sell your possessions and give to the poor, and you will have treasure in heaven. Then come, follow me' (Matt. 19:21). The sinful habits of the past will certainly have no place in the life of grace. 'Have nothing to do with the fruitless works of darkness' (Eph. 5:11). Like soldiers on the battlefield, 'let us throw off everything that hinders and the sin that so easily entangles' (Heb. 12:1).

2. God's love (7: 6-11)

Moses explained why God had commanded the Israelites to purge the paganism of the Canaanites from the promised land. They were a *holy* people, a *chosen* people and a *precious* people. *'For you are a people holy to the LORD your God. The LORD your God has chosen you out of all the peoples on the face of the earth to be his people, his treasured possession.'* Moses based his exhortation on God's words in Exodus 19:5-6, spoken after he had gathered the people of Israel at Sinai and constituted them as His nation. 'Now, if you obey me fully and keep my covenant, then out of all nations you will be my treasured possession. Although the whole earth is mine, *you will be for me a kingdom of priests and a holy nation.'* Here in Deuteronomy, Moses focuses on the divine love which established them in that blessed position.

God's love is not deserved (7:7)
Moses describes two aspects of God's love that cannot be separated. Firstly, *God's affection.* God *'... set his affection on you...'* This was a deep emotional attachment. God's love is the kind of love that just never lets go. Then secondly, Moses described *God's election.* God '**chose you...**' This was a free choice, for God was not constrained to love the people of Israel by anything outside of himself, least of all by anything in the Israelites themselves. Specifically, Moses told them they were not chosen

'because you were more numerous than other people, for you were the fewest of all peoples'. They were, in fact, small and helpless.

In 9:4-6 Moses will tell the Israelites that God did not love them because of their *righteousness*. There was no virtue in them that merited God's blessing. Here he tells them that God did not love them because of their *usefulness*. Conventional wisdom regards large populations as a great bonus. During the nineteenth century, the Russian empire was economically backward, but militarily powerful because it could muster large armies for battle. With its large population, China has been able to accomplish great feats of engineering, such as building the Great Wall. Large populations stimulate economic activity and make their rulers wealthy. However, God did not need a large army to fight his battles; nor did he need a large labour force to subdue the promised land; nor did he need a large population to make him wealthy. God's love for Israel is inexplicable in human terms. It is explicable only in God's terms. God loved Israel because he chose them and set his affection on them. That is why he gave them the promised land. That is the only explanation for God's mercy.

For this reason, too, God gave the gift of his only-begotten Son. 'For God so loved the world that he gave his one and only Son, that whoever believes in him shall not perish but have eternal life' (John 3:16), Yet we sometimes ask, why doesn't everyone believe this wonderful news and receive the salvation that is freely offered to all? The simple answer is that God chooses some, to renew their hearts so that they will believe and be saved. Why, then, does God choose some and not others? The answer to that question is to be found in the 'high mystery of predestination', that 'God, before the foundation of the world was laid, according to his eternal and immutable purpose, and the secret counsel and good pleasure of his will, hath chosen (his elect), in Christ unto everlasting glory, *out of his mere free grace and love,* without any foresight of faith or good works, or perseverance in either of them, or any other thing in the creature, as conditions, or causes moving him thereunto; and all to the praise of his glorious grace" (*Westminster Confession of Faith*, chapter 3.5). It is humbling, yet wonderfully heartwarming, for believers to remember that their privileges in Christ do not rest on their usefulness to God. God has not chosen us because he needs our strength to accomplish his plans. God has chosen the foolish, the weak and the despised, for his own glory (see 1 Cor. 1:26-31).

What is true of believers individually is also true of the church collectively. She is the redeemed community of God's people that has grown out of the nation of Israel, and God loves the church just as he loved Israel (see Eph. 1:22-23; 5:28-29). God's love for his church does not depend on its numbers. Many people today judge the importance of the church as a whole, or an individual congregation, by its numerical strength. Joseph Stalin is said to have asked contemptuously, 'How many divisions has the Pope?' Even Christians will assess the value of their congregation on the basis of its membership list. Size matters only because God wants to see more people reached with the gospel and brought to a saving faith in the Lord Jesus Christ. Size is of no significance when it comes to explaining Christ's love for his church. Christ loves his bride because he loves her, not because she is large and growing.

God's love expresses itself in acts of salvation (7:8)
God did two things to express his eternal, unconditional love. First of all, *he swore an oath.* Moses refers to the covenant that God made with Abraham, and then confirmed to Isaac and Jacob. He had promised to give their descendants the land of Canaan as their inheritance. It was to be the place where they would enjoy blessing and fellowship with God. Then secondly, *God kept that covenant. 'But it was because the LORD loved you and kept the oath he swore to your forefathers that he brought you out with a mighty hand and redeemed you from the land of slavery,*

from the power of Pharaoh king of Egypt' (7:8). He had reached out to the Israelites when they were slaves in Egypt. He had redeemed them from the power of Pharaoh and had delivered them from the land of slavery. He did so by paying a price that made the Israelites his *'treasured possession'* or 'personal treasure' (see 7:6; also 14:2; 26:18). Now he was bringing them home to rejoice over them.

During a lifetime spent serving with the British Royal Air Force in places such as Cyprus, Aden and Singapore, my great-aunt and uncle gathered many interesting artefacts. When they returned to the United Kingdom, they brought these with them and decorated their home with ornaments and furniture from the east. They were special and had many memories associated with them. In a similar way Israel was God's special treasure for he had bought her and brought her home. The same can be said of God's redeemed people today (see Luke 15:6; 1 Peter 2:9; Titus 2:14). In 1 Peter 2:9, Peter echoes the 'personal treasure' analogy of Exodus 19:5-6 and Deuteronomy 7:6 to describe the church as 'a treasure deposited for safe-keeping'. When God redeems us, he takes us under his protection for safe-keeping. He keeps us safe because we are precious to him; and we are precious to him because he has redeemed us 'not with perishable things such as silver or gold... but with the precious blood of Christ, a lamb without blemish or defect' (1 Peter 1:18-19).

God's love is unfailing (7:9-10)
'Know therefore that the LORD your God is God; he is the faithful God, keeping his covenant of love to a thousand generations of those who love him and keep his commands.' Here we see the unique quality of divine love: it never grows weary and it never falters. God's love for Israel will last to a thousand generations. This is quite simply a Hebrew way of saying 'for ever and ever'. In spite of many disappointments and provocations, Jehovah continued to love Israel over the centuries (see Jer. 31:3; Mal. 1:2). Even when they sinned against him and suffered terrible consequences,

God delivered them from their plight because of his covenant of love (see Ps. 106:44-45; Isa. 54:10; 55:3). This was the promise which Solomon claimed in his prayer at the dedication of the temple (see 1 Kings 8:23), and upon which faithful men relied during the dark days of the Babylonian exile (see Neh. 1:5; 9:17-23; Dan. 9:4). Through the centuries God remained faithful to his covenant of love. The apostle Paul rejoiced in that thread running through Israel's history (see Rom. 11:28) and applied the same privileges to believers who are now members of the new Israel and heirs of the new covenant (see Col. 3:12; also 1 John 3:1; 4:10).

Having said all this, Moses adds the qualification in 7:10, *'But those who hate him he will repay to their face by destruction; he will not be slow to repay to their face those who hate him.'* These words are sometimes regarded as an embarrassing intrusion into an otherwise idyllic description of God's love. They are, however, the very core of this chapter, for they also describe God's covenant faithfulness. God is faithful in following through his warnings of judgment as well as in keeping his promises of mercy. It is important that we remember that God's first and greatest love is for his own glory. He is passionately devoted to the victory of his truth and his righteousness. He is passionately opposed to unrighteousness. In his holy zeal he must purge from this world everything that sets itself up against him. Jehovah will demonstrate his holiness and justice by bringing his judgment upon those who break his commands (see Exod. 20:5). The wrath that is about to fall upon the Canaanites for their wickedness will also fall upon the Israelites if they follow in their sinful ways. This will not be a denial of Jehovah's covenant faithfulness, but an expression of it.

God's love demands a response (7:11)
Because God keeps his covenant of love to 'those who love him and keep his commands', Moses adds a word of application here. *'Therefore, take care to follow the commands, decrees and*

laws I give you today.' This is the response God sought from the people of Israel. The same covenant Lord calls for the same response from his people today – trust and obey! When the gospel is preached today, God expects a response. We obey the gospel call by turning from our sins and trusting the Lord Jesus for salvation. We also demonstrate our gratitude to God by living obedient lives. That is why we call people to count the cost of commitment to Christ. 'Take care', said Moses, because a life of disciplined godliness is what God requires from his redeemed people. 'If you love me,' Jesus said, 'you will obey what I command' (John 14:15).

3. God's blessing (7:12-16)

God's specific command for the Israelites at this time was a sombre one. *'You must destroy all the peoples the LORD your God gives over to you. Do not look on them with pity and do not serve their gods, for that will be a snare to you'* (7:16). Yet Moses reminded the people that God had promised to bless them if they obeyed his command. *'If you pay attention to these laws and are careful to follow them, then the Lord your God will keep his covenant of love with you, as he swore to your forefathers'* (7:12).

In the light of what Moses has taught in 7:7-8, it is impossible to believe that God's love might be earned by Israel's obedience, because God's love for Israel was freely bestowed upon undeserving sinners. In 7:13-15 Moses described how God demonstrated his love for Israel.

> *He will love you and bless you and increase your numbers. He will bless the fruit of your womb, the crops of your land— your grain, new wine and oil—the calves of your herds and the lambs of your flocks in the land that he swore to your forefathers to give you. You will be blessed more than any other people; none of your men or women will be childless,*

nor any of your livestock without young. The LORD will keep you free from every disease. He will not inflict on you the horrible diseases you knew in Egypt, but he will inflict them on all who hate you.

Ironically, these were the very blessings which the false gods of the Canaanites purported to offer their devotees. Grain, new wine and oil were the three most important agricultural commodities produced in Canaan and they were commonly attributed to the generosity of Baal (see Hosea 2:5-8). Moses insists that these were the gifts of Jehovah, as were children, livestock and good health (7:14-15). All these were Jehovah's gifts to those who served him. This promise is not a foundation for a gospel of health, wealth and happiness that is popular in some evangelical circles today, but a polemic against the pagan theology of the Canaanites. Closely allied to God's promise to Israel is a warning to those who worship false gods. While he will keep Israel free from *'every disease'*, he will *'inflict them on all who hate you'*, that is, those who hate God and his people and do not obey his commands.

These promises remind us that God's love for Israel was not abstract or theoretical. God expressed his love in his works of providence, and he still does so today. This does not mean that Christians will enjoy constant health and happiness here on earth, and sometimes God's providence is mysterious. There are times when ungodly people receive blessing and God's people do not (see Ps. 73:2-3). This is a mystery that is not easily resolved, but God would have us take note of the earthly blessings that we do enjoy. We are to enjoy our families and our health and our food and our work while we can; and as we do so, give thanks to God for his faithfulness. We must also remember that God also takes away the earthly blessings which he has given when we become worldly and disobedient and make false gods out of his good gifts.

4. God's warning (7:17-26)

Moses returns to the challenge of 7:1-5 and concludes the chapter on the same note as it started – the destruction of the Canaanites. *'The LORD your God will deliver them over to you, throwing them into great confusion until they are destroyed. He will give their kings into your hand and you will wipe out their names from under heaven.'* This was both God's promise and his command.

Moses recognised that obeying God's command in these verses would not be easy. It is not unusual for God's people to find it hard to do what God commands them, but this command was especially daunting. The people of Israel had faced this challenge before, and backed away from it (see Deut. 1:26-33). The stature of the Canaanites and the strength of their cities had terrified the Israelites so that they refused to enter the land of Canaan. Forty years later, with the Israelites gathered on the plains of Moab, Moses anticipated the same objection. *'You may say to yourselves, "These nations are stronger than we are. How can we drive them out?"'* In response to their fears, Moses sought to draw out some lessons from Israel's history.

First of all, Moses reminded them that the Lord had humbled the mighty Egyptians (7:18-21). *'Remember well what the LORD your God did to Pharaoh and to all Egypt...'* A good memory is a great blessing, especially when we can remember what God has done to save and defend his people. The history of redemption is a heritage that we ought to commit to memory, for it shows us what a great God we serve today.

Moses applied that message to the Israelites in his own time. *'The LORD your God will do the same to all the peoples you now fear. Moreover, the LORD your God will send the hornet among them until even the survivors who hide from you have perished.'* There were several types of stinging insects in Canaan that were known as hornets. Some were able to deliver a fatal sting; and it may well have been that the Canaanites were so debilitated by these stings that they were unable to resist the Israelites. It is also possible that the hornet is used figuratively to describe some other assault upon the Canaanites such as disease (the Hebrew word comes from the same root as the word for leprosy) or the armies of Egypt. In Exodus 23:27-28 Moses associates the hornet with confusion and terror. Joshua 24:12 records how the Lord did indeed sent the hornet to drive out the Canaanites. Yet because of Israel's disobedience in failing to pursue the Canaanites from the land, many did remain to cause trouble for the Israelites over the centuries that followed (see Josh. 13:13; 15:63; 16:10; Judges 2:20-22; 3:1).

Secondly, Moses assured the Israelites that the Lord would most certainly drive out the Canaanites before them. The process would be gradual, as Moses described in 7:22-24: *'The LORD your God will drive out those nations before you, little by little.'* There was much common sense in God's strategy. *'You will not be allowed to eliminate them all at once, or the wild animals will multiply around you.'* An important spiritual principle is being taught here. God establishes his kingdom gradually, just as leaven makes a loaf rise in an oven or as a seed germinates underground (see Matt. 13:33; Mark 4:26-29). God's elect are brought to faith one by one and like living stones they are cemented together to build the church. Believers grow in holiness by a process of gradual sanctification which takes rough stones and polishes them to make them beautiful in God's sight. Through the preaching of the gospel over the centuries, the kingdom of Satan is cast down and the kingdom of Jesus Christ is established on earth. As the spiritual battlefront moves back and forward we may fear that a terrible stalemate prevails or, worse still, that God is losing the battle. God would have us be patient and take the long perspective, for he will conquer every enemy gradually, but most assuredly. One by one God's enemies are overthrown so that Christ's kingdom might be established. 'But each in his own turn: Christ, the firstfruits; then, when he comes, those who belong to him. Then the end will come, when he hands over the kingdom to God the Father after he has destroyed all dominion, authority and power. For he must reign until he has put all his enemies under his feet' (1 Cor. 15:23-25).

Thirdly, Moses insists that love for God means hatred of evil (7:25-26). His language is deliberately confrontational, because there can be no neutrality in the spiritual battle between Jehovah and the idols. The people of Israel must be whole-hearted in their dedication to Jehovah or they would be absorbed into the wickedness of the Canaanites. *'The images of their gods you are to burn in the fire. Do not covet the silver and gold on them... Do not bring a detestable thing into your house... Utterly abhor and detest it, for it is set apart for destruction.'* The same Hebrew word for coveting is also used in the Tenth Commandment, which is a general prohibition of coveting, (see Exod. 20:17; Deut. 5:21). Idolatry has nothing to offer the people of God – not even scrap metals.

Moses was able to see the spiritual danger that was hidden even in the trappings of Canaanite religion. The danger lay not in recycling the silver and gold, but in the ideas and lifestyles they represented. Today we are seeing ancient religious ideas being recycled and put to modern uses by the new age movement or the new spirituality. As Christians, we need to be on our guard against old paganism in new guises. We cannot be neutral about anything that diminishes God's honour. 'You adulterous people, don't you know that friendship with the world is hatred toward God? Anyone who chooses to be a friend of the world becomes an enemy of God' (James 4:4). By the same token, love for God leads to a holy hatred of false religion.

Chapter 8
Lessons from poverty and riches

Please read Deuteronomy 8: 1-20

The psalmist resolved, 'I will extol the LORD at all times; his praise will always be on my lips' (Ps. 34:1). This is an amazing statement and one which runs counter to our natural instincts. There are many times when we find it hard to praise God. Do we, for instance, find it easy to praise God as we walk home in the rain? Do we extol God's greatness when we are tired and disappointed? Do we rejoice in God's mercies when we lie in a hospital bed? We know that it is right and proper to praise God at these times, but often we find it hard to count these experiences as blessings.

The thrust of Moses' preaching in the early chapters of Deuteronomy was to urge the Israelites to love and obey God. Typically he did this by looking back over what God had done in the past and by looking forward to what God would do in the future. This double look showed the Israelites many signs of God's blessing which served to confirm his covenant of grace with them. These tokens of God's grace were intended to motivate the Israelites to love, obey and praise God.

In Deuteronomy 8 Moses took the Israelites back to their journey through the desert and pointed them forward to the blessings which they would enjoy in the promised land. These two locations were as different as chalk and cheese. In the *desert* the Israelites endured hunger and thirst; while in the *land* the Israelites would enjoy food and drink. Yet both were important training grounds for the covenant people. *'Know then in your heart that as a man disciplines his son, so the LORD your God disciplines you'* (8:5). When God disciplines his people, he does so with fatherly love, training them to become mature in holiness. In the desert God used the rod to train them, while in the land God used a gentler approach. However by means of carrot and stick God taught them to love, obey and praise him. When the apostle Paul faced this double challenge he was able to say, 'I know what it is to be in need and I know what it is to have plenty. I have learned the secret of being content in any and every situation, whether well fed or hungry, whether living in plenty or in want' (Phil. 4:12).

Returning to Moses' words to the Israelites in Deuteronomy 8, we will find a reminder, an encouragement and a warning.

Moses reminded the Israelites of their hardship in the desert (8:1-6)

This section opens and closes with the recurring exhortation to the Israelites obey God's commands in order that they might enjoy God's blessings in the promised land. *'Be careful to follow every command I am giving you today, so that you may live and increase and may enter and possess the land that the LORD promised on oath to your forefathers... Observe the commands of the LORD your God, walking in his ways and revering him.'* Moses followed his exhortations with explanation and motivation.

'Remember how the LORD your God led you all the way in the desert these forty years' (8:2). The desert is described later in 8:15 as 'the vast and dreadful desert, that thirsty and waterless land, with its venomous snakes'. It was a place where those who lost their way

often died of thirst and starvation. The first European explorers to visit the hot, dry interior of Australia faced similar conditions and their stories are tales of extraordinary courage and suffering. Even today visitors to remote areas of the Australian outback are warned of the dangers that await the unprepared traveller in this unrelenting environment. Moses cast the minds of the Israelites back to the forty years they spent in a very similar environment and explains God's purpose in 8:2-5. There were some important lessons for them to learn in the desert.

i. Lessons about their hearts (8:2)
'God led you all the way in the desert these forty years to humble you and to test you in order to know what was in your heart whether or not you would keep his commands.' We should not think that God did not know their thoughts or was conducting a spiritual experiment with them. God knows all things and God knew what was in their hearts. God wanted them to know what was in their hearts, and he wanted them to know that he knew what was in their hearts.

The hearts of fallen mankind always veer towards that which is sinful. In the days of Noah, 'the LORD saw how great man's wickedness on the earth had become, and that every inclination of the thoughts of his heart was only evil all the time' (Gen. 6:5). The prophet Jeremiah observed this in his own day: 'The heart is deceitful above all things and beyond cure. Who can understand it?' (Jer. 17:9). Our Lord identified the heart as the source of every sinful action. 'For from within, out of men's hearts, come evil thoughts, sexual immorality, theft, murder, adultery, greed, malice, deceit, lewdness, envy slander, arrogance and folly' (Mark 7:21-22).

The sinful heart of man inclines to disobedience just as water is inclined to flow downstream. As a result of this sinful inclination, fallen mankind instinctively reacts against God's commands. He does not want to do what God commands.

He wants to do what God forbids. That instinct became very evident during Israel's time of testing in the desert. When they were hungry and thirsty they instinctively blamed God for their predicament rather than seeking his help. They even reinterpreted the exodus as an act of collective punishment rather than an act of deliverance (see Exod. 14:11-12; 16:2-3; 17:3).

ii. Lessons about God's provision (8:3-4)
'He humbled you, causing you to hunger and then feeding you with manna, which neither you nor your fathers had known...' God humbled the Israelites by bringing them into a place where they might well have starved to death. This was a terrifying experience for them, but God provided for their needs in the most amazing ways. Both their hunger and God's provision were humbling and instructive experiences for them, for they emphasised Israel's total dependence on Jehovah's miraculous provision.

God fed the Israelites with manna. They had never seen anything like it. It appeared mysteriously every morning, as described in Exodus 16:13-15.

> That evening quail came and covered the camp, and in the morning there was a layer of dew around the camp. When the dew was gone, thin flakes like frost on the ground appeared on the desert floor. When the Israelites saw it, they said to each other, 'What is it?' For they did not know what it was. Moses said to them, 'It is the bread the LORD has given you to eat.'

The mysterious, even supernatural, nature of God's provision is made even clearer by the double provision on the sixth day so that the people did not have to gather food on the Sabbath (see Exod. 16:22-26). On the Sabbath, the people rested from all their labours and worshipped the God who provided for all their needs. This bread could have could come from only one source, Jehovah, the God of Israel.

Moses explained the significance of this supernatural provision in 8:3b: '...to teach you that man does not live on bread alone but on every word that comes from the mouth of the LORD'. We might also translate the last words of this verse as follows: 'man does not live by bread alone but by everything that comes from the mouth of God'. Moses had in mind the totality of God's provision for Israel. He did not seek to downplay Israel's need of bread to feed their bodies. In 8:9 he rejoiced over God's provision of bread and called the Israelites to do the same. Nor did Moses seek to imply that spiritual food was more important than bodily food. Both are important (see James 2:15-16). Rather, Moses sought to emphasise that life is possible only when God gives the gift of life (see Gen. 2:7) and sustains it.

The key word in this familiar phrase is the verb 'live'. The Hebrew text uses this word twice in 8:3b: 'man will not live on bread alone but on everything that goes out from the mouth of God man shall live'. The life that Moses describes is more than physical existence. In the Sermon on the Mount, which contains many echoes of Moses' preaching in Deuteronomy, our Lord also taught that life consists of more than food and clothing (see Matt. 6:25). The life which God gives to his covenant people in both Old and New Testament times is life lived in fellowship with him. This fellowship means that we depend upon God for everything, including food, water and clothing. The Israelites enjoyed this miraculous provision in the desert, and Moses reminded them of that in 8:4. 'Your clothes did not wear out and your feet did not swell during these forty years.'

Life in fellowship with God also involves listening to God and learning to obey him. From God's mouth come teaching, instruction and law as well as food and clothing. That is why this section opens and closes with Moses appealing to the Israelites to obey God's commands (see 8:1, 6). All too often the Israelites forgot this. They eagerly sought the material provision, but were less enthusiastic about God's law. It is common for people today to pray for material blessing, yet overlook the need for holiness in their prayers. This ought not to be so, for the good life which God offered to the Israelites had two parts. One part was to enjoy God's provision. The other part was to listen to God and obey his commands. Both proceeded from God's mouth.

The Lord Jesus had clearly learned this lesson from this passage when he quoted from it in response to the devil's temptation in the wilderness. In preparation for his ministry as 'the true Israel' our Lord spent forty days in the wilderness, which are often thought to correspond to the forty years which the Israelites spent in the wilderness. Just as they were tested before they went to claim the promised land, so Jesus was tested before he went to fulfil his Messianic mission. The first temptation recorded in Matthew 4:3-4 questioned both his status as the Son of God and the totality of his reliance upon his Father's provision. 'If you are the Son of God, tell these stones to become bread.' Our Lord's response from Deuteronomy 8:3 reaffirmed his determination to obey his Father's commission, however difficult that might be. In essence, he said that his first priority was to do his Father's will. 'My food ... is to do the will of him who sent me and to finish his work' (John 4:34).

Sometimes faithful obedience will bring earthly hardship. Our Lord is the perfect example of this. The Israelites were imperfect examples, but examples nonetheless, of those who face hardship in the path of obedience. Their path to the promised land went through the terrible desert and along the way they may well have been tempted to ask whether serving the Lord was worth the trouble it brought. These verses show that even in the desert God provides for the needs of his people and that faithfulness brings its reward.

Moses encouraged the Israelites to enjoy the land (8:7-11)

In these verses Moses turned from the forty years in the wilderness and looked forward to the promised land. *'For the LORD your God is bringing you into a good land.'* In contrast to the desert, it is a land with water: *'A land with streams and pools of water, with springs flowing in the valleys and hills'.* That is what made the land of Canaan such a desirable place to live. In contrast with the desert regions around it, it was well watered and able to sustain agriculture.

In 8:8-9a Moses describes the rich produce of the land of Canaan. It was *'a land with wheat and barley, vines and fig trees, pomegranates, olive oil and honey'.* It was capable of producing enough food to feed all its inhabitants: *'... bread will not be scarce and you will lack nothing'.* The God of Israel provided for all the needs of all his people. In Deuteronomy 15:4 Moses states the goal that there ought to be no poor people amongst the Israelites. This was a reasonable and realistic goal, as God had provided the resources necessary to make the ideal a reality. Sadly, the hardness of the people's hearts meant that some amassed great fortunes while others went hungry and so the ideal was never realised (see Deut. 15:11). Since then many centuries of warfare, deforestation and intensive settlement have degraded the land of Canaan. Nevertheless, the land is still fertile and prosperous in contrast to the lands around it.

An added bonus for the Israelites was the mineral resources of the land. It was *'a land where the rocks are iron and you can dig copper out of the hills'* (8:9b). Today, we cannot be sure where these minerals were found or when they were mined. They have been mined to extinction and the land of Israel does not contain iron or copper ores today. The existence of sophisticated cultures in Canaan during the bronze and iron ages bears testimony to the availability of resources to forge these metals. Moses' aim, however, was not simply to describe the rich blessings which the people would enjoy when they entered the promised land. It was to teach the people how to respond to God's blessing.

i. Eat and be satisfied (8:10a)
'When you have eaten and are satisfied, praise the LORD your God for the good land he has given you.' God did not lead the Israelites into the land only to tell them, 'Don't look, don't touch, don't taste.' He encouraged them to eat and enjoy what the land produced. In the Garden of Eden God had told Adam that he was 'free to eat from any tree in the garden' (Gen. 2:16). There was only one exception to God's generous provision, yet that tree – the tree of the knowledge of good and evil – is often the focus of our attention when we read that passage. We overlook the generosity of God in giving every other tree to Adam to enjoy. With similar generosity, God gave the good land of Canaan to the Israelites to satisfy their needs and thereby to confirm his covenant with them. This was a display of God's grace and showed how he sought the happiness of his people.

ii. Praise the Lord your God (8:10b-11)
God also desires the holiness of his people and Moses taught them how to enjoy the land of Canaan in a godly way. When they had enjoyed God's blessings they were to bless God: *'... praise the LORD your God for the good land he has given you'.* The word translated 'praise' in 8:10b is the Hebrew word *barak* or 'bless'. It surprises some to think of the Israelites blessing God for, according to Hebrews 7:7, it is the greater person who normally blesses the lesser. How, then, can mortal men bless God? In this case, Israel blessed God by praising him and thanking him for his blessings to them. When they worshipped God they put their gratitude towards God into words. This is an essential ingredient in a godly life.

Moses reinforced his appeal with a warning in 8:11. *'Be careful that you do not forget the LORD your God, failing to observe his*

commands, his laws and his decrees that I am giving you this day.'
It is unlikely that the Israelites would forget that the Lord
existed or that he had brought them out of Egypt or that he
had given them his laws at Sinai. It was, however, possible that
they would forget to obey God. Even when future generations
remembered those facts of history they often forgot to obey
God's commands. Jeroboam I, for example, remembered the
events of the exodus when he set up golden calves for Israel
to worship. He even gave these gods which he had set up
the credit for the exodus (see I Kings 12:28). However, by his
disobedience, he demonstrated that he forgotten the covenant
Lord of Israel.

When the people of Israel worshipped idols, or broke any of
God's laws, it was as though God had vanished from their minds.
They did not deny his existence. They simply lived as though
God did not exist, and so they became fools (as described in
Psalm 14:1). The same is often true of people today. We know
that God is real, that he has spoken, that he hates sin and that
he loves obedience, but still we become careless and forgetful
and fall into sin. This is the forgetfulness Moses warns the
Israelites against.

What Moses said to the Israelites in 8:10-11 is especially relevant
to those who live in affluent western nations today. Many enjoy
material blessings that would have been beyond the dreams of
previous generations and are still beyond the hopes of many
who live in third world countries. Yet when the latest economic
figures record falling unemployment and rising incomes, do
they remember God and praise him? When did you last hear
a finance minister call his nation to praise God after releasing
the latest economic data? Not only is God not being praised,
his laws are forgotten. Moses made it clear that God will not
allow those who enjoy his goodness to forget him.

Moses warned the Israelites against forgetfulness (8:12-20)

'Otherwise, when you eat and are satisfied, when you build fine houses and settle down, and when your herds and flocks grow large and your silver and gold increase and all you have is multiplied, then your heart will become proud and you will forget the LORD your God' (8:12-14). Moses describes in these verses the consequences of the forgetfulness against which he had warned in 8:11. This has been called 'the dilemma of Deuteronomy' - the fear that the enjoyment of God's promised blessings would erode rather than confirm Israel's faith in God. This last section of the chapter describes would happen if Israel forget her Lord. A fateful scenario unfolds in 8:12-20. Note its five elements.

i. You will enjoy herds and houses (8:12-13)
The blessings described in these verses will accumulate over time. *'Fine houses'* are the product of much careful planning and hard work. It may take many years to build up a quality herd of cattle or flock of sheep. It may take generations to accumulate significant quantities of *'silver and gold'.* As Israel's material prosperity increased her relationship with God deteriorated, but the spiritual consequences of Israel's affluence were not always easy to observe and acknowledge. This is certainly the case in affluent western countries where the church was once a vibrant witness to the gospel, but now has become weak and worldly.

ii. You will forget what God has done (8:14-16)
Moses lists some of God's actions which the Israelites might easily forget. The Lord *'brought you out of Egypt, out of the land of slavery. He led you through the vast and dreadful desert... He brought you water out of hard rock. He gave you manna to eat in the desert.'* The Lord did all these things to humble the Israelites, but they will become proud when they forget those lessons learned in the wilderness.

iii. You will take the credit for yourselves (8:17-18)

When they prosper in the promised land, they will grow into the proverbial 'self-made men who worship their maker'. '*You may say to yourself, "My power and the strength of my hands have produced this wealth for me."*' This is to forget the basic rule of biblical economics – everything belongs to God, and we are stewards who manage his resources. '*Remember the LORD your God, for it is he who gives you the ability to produce wealth and so confirms his covenant which he swore to your forefathers, as it is today.*' God does this by creating the resources which we use, by giving us the strength to use them, by watering the earth and making the sun continue to shine, and by providentially guiding human affairs so that we have the right conditions in which to work productively. When Jesus said that 'the ground of a certain rich man produced a good crop' (Luke 12:16), he meant us to understand that God made the ground fruitful. However, the rich farmer attributed his prosperity to his own skill and foresight. For that reason he was called a 'fool' (Luke 12:20) who had robbed God of his glory.

iv. You will give the credit to false gods (8:19a)

"*If you ever forget the LORD your God and follow other gods and worship and bow down to them...*' In the ancient world the gods were credited with giving rain and prosperity, and Moses warned against giving those false gods any credit for what only the Lord could give. Giving thanks to any god (even a false one) may seem to contradict the self-reliant attitude of 8:17-18. It was, however, perversely appropriate for self-made men to worship man-made gods. These gods were a projection of their own egos and the creation of their own imaginations. Men who live for the things of this world have a deep emptiness within and create gods to satisfy their spiritual hunger. That is why, in our own age, materialism is receding before resurgent paganism. Rather than give the true God the credit for his unseen provision, sinful men would rather give thanks to the gods of their own creation.

v. You will be destroyed (8:19b-20)

This is the climax of Moses' warning. His words are a solemn testimony, recorded for future generations so that no-one can plead ignorance. *'I testify against you today that you will surely be destroyed. Like the nations the LORD destroyed before you, so you will be destroyed for not obeying the LORD your God.'* Destruction was the fate that was about to fall upon the wicked Canaanites; and it would fall even upon the Israelites if they were unfaithful to God. Moses words are emphatic. Destruction would be sure and certain if the Israelites turned from the Lord and followed other gods. Their special status would not protect them if they did not heed God's word.

This solemn warning came to a tragic fulfilment many centuries later when the people of Israel were expelled from the land at the time of the exile. Their prosperity would give way to poverty. This would be a sadly recurring pattern in the lives of many. Pride goes before a fall. Years of plenty are followed by years of hunger. Boom is followed by bust. In this way God disciplined his people. That discipline may come to us in the form of illness or unemployment, drought or disappointment. These are learning experiences under the hand of a sovereign, yet loving God. May we learn to think and talk about these experiences in terms of God's fatherly discipline. May we learn to praise God even as he leads us through difficult times.

Perhaps a harder lesson to learn is to praise God when be blesses us with plenty. Today we may not accumulate flocks and herds or silver and gold. Our wealth may well be stored electronically. In any case, God is the source of every good gift, both in this life and in the life to come. Jehovah was not simply one provider among the many gods of the ancient world, for he has a monopoly on nature's gifts. May we learn to give God the credit for our homes, for our employment, for favourable economic conditions, for political freedoms and for the health and strength which we need to do our work. And when we turn to God to seek his blessing, may we learn to rejoice in everything that proceeds from his mouth.

Throughout the first decade of the twenty-first century, Australia suffered its worst drought on record. Many farmers feared for their livelihood; and even those who lived in the major cities bore with restrictions on their use of water. Many prayed urgently for drought-breaking rains. That was an appropriate thing to do. Yet few prayed with the same urgency for repentance amongst our people. Both rain and repentance proceed from God. We know the importance of rain, yet we need to learn the urgency of repentance out of reverence for God. That is a lesson which God teaches his followers in the wilderness of his discipline.

Chapter 9
Living with a sinful record

Please read Deuteronomy 9: 1-29

In Deuteronomy 9 and 10 Moses addressed the people of Israel about some painful incidents in their past. They were about to receive the promised land of Canaan as God's gift to an undeserving nation. They were, of course, the nation God had delivered from slavery in Egypt, but they were a people who deserved death in the wilderness. Moses reminded them of their sin at Sinai, where they had worshipped a golden calf even as he had been speaking with God and receiving the law on their behalf. In Deuteronomy 10 Moses will remind the Israelites how God rehabilitated them after this incident and led them on towards their promised inheritance in the land of Canaan. There they will be called to serve God with reverend fear and gratitude. Before coming to that point, Moses describes, in Deuteronomy 9, Israel's sin and his own response. Why, we may be tempted to ask, did Moses remind the Israelites of this sinful and embarrassing episode?

Sometimes the actions of our past come back to haunt us and distress us. That is one of the themes of Victor Hugo's novel, *Les Miserables*. The central character, Jean Valjean, stole bread when he was an impoverished young man and was sentenced to many years of hard labour in a prison camp. The memory of those years haunted him for the rest of his life. He escaped from prison and would have been recaptured but for the help of a bishop who gave him the opportunity to start his life over again. He did, and became a wealthy businessman and respected citizen. However he was recognised by one of his former guards, Javert, now an inspector of police. Once again on the run, he hid away in a convent in Paris and took on another new identity. Still Javert caught up with him. 'I know who you are, Valjean. You are still a criminal to me,' said Javert.

Sometimes our conscience may be a Javert crying for justice. It can be hard to live with the record of a sinful past, especially when we come to see how seriously God regards sin. Moses addressed that concern in Deuteronomy 9, when he spoke to the Israelites about their sinful past and their shameful record of rebellion against God. The redeemed people of God need to know that they do not stand on their own merits (that is a perch from which we can easily be toppled), but upon God's mercies. If that were not so, our old sins would easily come back to terrify us.

An important principle (9:1-6)

The Israelites were standing on the plains of Moab, by the River Jordan, about to enter the promised land of Canaan. God was about to do something quite amazing. His people were about to receive their promised inheritance. The fortified cities of the Canaanites would fall into their hands and their mighty warriors would fall before them in battle (see 9:1-2). *'Hear, O Israel. You are now about to cross the Jordan to go in and dispossess nations greater and stronger than you, with large cities that have walls up to the sky.'* These were the very enemies that had so frightened them thirty-eight years earlier. *'The people are strong and tall—Anakites! You know about them and have heard it said: "Who can stand up against the Anakites?"'* At that time the people grumbled against God and refused to enter the promised land when they were encamped at Kadesh Barnea (see 1:26-28). The Anakites and their fortifications, however, would prove to be no match for the people of Israel.

At this point, before they entered the land of Canaan, Moses introduced a word of caution. Remember *who* will give Israel the victory. It will be *'the Lord your God'*. He *'is the one who goes across ahead of you like a devouring fire. He will destroy them; he will subdue them before you'* (9:3). The Israelites were not to pat themselves on the back or take the credit for themselves. *'After the LORD your God has driven them out before you, do not say to yourself, "The LORD has brought me here to take possession of this land because of my righteousness"'* (9:4). Instead, they were to remind themselves that it was because of the wickedness of the Canaanites that the Lord took the land of Canaan from them. *'No, it is on account of the wickedness of these nations that the LORD is going to drive them out before you'* (9:4b). Their hideous idols, their sacrifices of their own children to their gods (specifically forbidden in Lev. 18:21), and their fertility cults had provoked God to anger. This explains why the Canaanites were driven out of the land, but it did not explain why God should want to give it to Israel.

Moses repeats his main point in 9:5 in order to lead up to God's reason for giving the land to Israel. *'It is not because of your righteousness or your integrity that you are going in to take possession of their land; but on account of the wickedness of these nations, the LORD your God will drive them out before you, to accomplish what he swore to your fathers, to Abraham, Isaac and Jacob.'* It was because of his promise to Abraham, Isaac and Jacob that God gave the land to the Israelites. God had made a covenant with Abraham and his family because, in his mercy, he had chosen them to be his people. He had selected them so that they might become a blessing to the whole world. He would give them the land of Canaan so that they might transform it into a land where God was honoured and where his people would be blessed. God keeps his promises; and that was about to be demonstrated in a spectacular fashion.

Just in case the Israelites missed the implications of what he was saying about them, he states emphatically that it was *not* because of Israel's righteousness that they were to be given the land or that God would overthrow the Canaanites on their behalf. *'Understand, then, that it is not because of your righteousness that the LORD is giving you this good land to possess, for you are a stiff-necked people'* (see 9:6). This was the principle that Moses really wanted to drive home. It is a principle of abiding relevance and one that we see demonstrated in God's dealings with mankind from eternity and throughout history.

The apostle Paul described the application of this principle in God's choice of Jacob over Esau in Romans 9:11-13. 'Before the twins were born or had done anything good or bad – in order that God's purpose in election might stand: not by works but by him who calls – she (Rebekah, the boys' mother) was told, "The older will serve the younger." Just as it is written: "Jacob I loved, but Esau I hated."' Jacob was, of course, the father of the nation of Israel; and just as God chose him without reference to any righteousness actions that he might possibly do, so God also chose the nation of Israel 'not because of their righteousness or integrity'. The same principle appears in Titus 3:4-5, where Paul explains why God should offer salvation in Christ to those who follow in Israel's footsteps. 'But when the kindness and love of God our Saviour appeared, he saved us, not because of righteous things we had done, but because of his mercy.' That is why salvation is by faith and not by works. 'And if by grace, then it is no longer by works; if it were, grace would no longer be by grace' (Rom. 11:6). 'For it is by grace that you have been saved, through faith – and this not from yourselves, it is the gift of God – not by works, so that no-one can boast' (Eph. 2:8-9). That is why there is no room for the people of God to boast in their righteousness. 'Where, then, is boasting? It is excluded.

On what principle? On that of observing the law? No, but on that of faith' (Rom. 3:27).

Boasting is what the Israelites would be tempted to do when they captured the cities and the land of Canaan. Boasting is what the self-righteous Pharisee in our Lord's parable did, even in his prayers. 'God, I thank you that I am not like other men – robbers, evildoers, adulterers – or even like this tax-collector. I fast twice a week and give a tenth of all I get' (Luke 18:11-12). Boasting is something that we may be tempted to do when we have become well established in the Christian faith and have established godly habits of life. Perhaps we may quietly boast about all we do for God in the life of our local congregation; or when we lead others to the Lord and see success in our ministries. Yet all such boasting is possible only when we forget what Moses said to the Israelites in these verses. We need to remind ourselves constantly that all these good things are gifts from God and that God does not give us anything because our righteousness merits it. Whatever God gives to his people – whether it was the promised land or the gift of eternal life – is a free gift. God bestows his blessings because of his covenant mercies.

A series of illustrations (9:7-24)

Moses drove home his message about the free mercy of God by reminding the Israelites of their record of rebellion. *'Remember this and never forget how you provoked the LORD your God to anger in the desert'* (9:7a). If the matter were not so serious, the suggestion that the Lord had given the Israelites the promised land because of their righteousness would have been laughable. The people of Israel had a long record of rebellion and disloyalty. *'From the day you left Egypt until you arrived here, you have been rebellious against the LORD'* (9:7b). The idea that God was rewarding them for their record of obedience was like suggesting that Pol Pot, the Cambodian dictator responsible for the tragic deaths of millions, might be a worthy candidate for a Nobel peace prize.

Time did not permit Moses to record every example of Israel's unfaithfulness, but in these verses he lists five. Four of them he mentions very briefly in 9:22-24.

> *You also made the LORD angry at Taberah, at Massah and at Kibroth Hattaavah. And when the LORD sent you out from Kadesh Barnea, he said, 'Go up and take possession of the land I have given you.' But you rebelled against the command of the LORD your God. You did not trust him or obey him.*

At Taberah, the people complained about their hardships and fire from the Lord burned amongst them (Num. 11:1-3). At Massah, the people quarrelled with God because they were thirsty and accused him of bringing them into the wilderness to kill them (Exod. 17:1-7). At Kibroth Hattaavah (which means *graves of lust*), the people complained because they had only manna to eat and no meat (Num. 11:4-34). At Kadesh Barnea, the people listened to the negative report of the spies and refused to enter the promised land (see Deut. 1:26-28).

First of all, and at greater length, Moses reminded the Israelites of their sin at Horeb (or Sinai). *'At Horeb you aroused the LORD's wrath so that he was angry enough to destroy you'* (9:8). There, God had given the Israelites the Ten Commandments; but immediately after they had heard God speak, and while Moses was on the mountain-top to receive the law on tablets of stone, they had made a golden calf and worshipped it. This was a blatant violation of the covenant which God had just made with Israel. That covenant was like a marriage bond and the stone tablets were like the marriage certificate. The Israelites committed spiritual adultery even as their marriage certificate was being filled out. It was as shocking as a husband or wife who flirts with another person at their own wedding reception. It was serious disloyalty and it provoked God to anger.

The Israelites might well have been utterly destroyed at this point, had it not been for the intercession of Moses while he was before God's face on the mountain (see Exod. 32:11-13). His main purpose for being on the mountain-top was to receive the tablets of stone bearing the Ten Commandments, and he stayed for forty days until that task was accomplished (9:9-11). *'When I went up on the mountain to receive the tablets of stone, the tablets of the covenant that the LORD had made with you, I stayed on the mountain forty days and forty nights.'* During that time he must have relied upon God's special provision for he *'ate no food and drank no water'.* He points us forward to the mediator of a better covenant, who spent forty days and nights in the wilderness, relying on every word that proceeds from the mouth of God (Matt. 4:2-4).

At the end of those forty days on the mountain-top God sent Moses back down to the people with words of judgment ringing in his ears (see 9:12-14). *'Then the LORD told me, "Go down from here at once, because your people whom you brought out of Egypt have become corrupt. They have turned away quickly from what I commanded them and have made a cast idol for themselves."'* Not only were they corrupt and disobedient, but destruction hung over them (9:14). *'Let me alone, so that I may destroy them and blot out their name from under heaven. And I will make you into a nation stronger and more numerous than they.'* The history of Israel might have been very different had God acted out this warning and built a new nation out of the family of Moses. We cannot know whether Moses was, even for a moment, tempted to rejoice in the prospect of securing a place among the patriarchs of Israel. Such an unworthy thought might well have appealed to a lesser man, but it does not seem to have entered Moses' mind, as we can see from his actions in 9:15-21.

God's treasured possession

First of all, *Moses made the people aware of the seriousness of their sin* (9:15-17).

> *So I turned and went down from the mountain while it was ablaze with fire. And the two tablets of the covenant were in my hands. When I looked, I saw that you had sinned against the LORD your God; you had made for yourselves an idol cast in the shape of a calf... I took the two tablets and threw them out of my hands, breaking them to pieces before your eyes.*

Some people vent their anger and frustration by smashing things. This kind of vandalism is not to be condoned, but Moses smashing of the stone tablets of the law was not wanton vandalism. It was a symbolic action, a public declaration of the consequences of Israel's sin. Just as the stones lay shattered before them, so too was their covenant with God. They had repudiated it by worshipping an idol.

Secondly, *Moses prayed for the Israelites* (9:18). *'Then once again I fell prostrate before the LORD for forty days and forty nights; I ate no bread and drank no water, because of all the sin you had committed, doing what was evil in the LORD's sight and so provoking him to anger.'* This forty-day period of prayer seems to have taken place after Moses left the mountain-top. He was overwhelmed by the seriousness of what had happened and physically prostrated himself before God. Emotionally he was gripped by fear. *'I feared the anger and wrath of the LORD, for he was angry enough with you to destroy you'* (9:19). Only when we take the wrath of God seriously will we see the need to wrestle in prayer for the lost and to warn them to flee from the wrath that is to come.

Moses was particularly aware of the role played by his own brother, Aaron, in the whole affair (9:20). *'And the LORD was angry enough with Aaron to destroy him, but at that time I prayed for Aaron too.'* When Moses came down the mountain he became aware of Aaron's role in the whole affair. The consequences of Aaron's sin were especially serious as he was the one designated to be Israel's High Priest. If he were swept away by the wrath of God, who would intercede before God for the people? Every sin amongst God's people does damage, but those committed by the leaders of God's people do even greater damage. How important it is to pray for those who lead God's church today! By his prayer in 9:20 Moses stood in the gap left by his brother as a result of his sin and prayed for him. Yet Moses himself had feet of clay and was an imperfect intercessor. Only in the Lord Jesus do we find a perfect intercessor, one who is better than Aaron and Moses (Heb. 3:3; 7:25-27).

Thirdly, *Moses removed the idol from their midst* (9:21). *'Also I took that sinful thing of yours, the calf you had made, and burned it in the fire. Then I crushed it and ground it to powder as fine as dust, and threw the dust into a stream that flowed down the mountain.'* This was only the first step in a series of events which demonstrated God's displeasure at Israel's sin and sought to root out idolatry from their midst. The full story is told in Exodus 32:25-29. The slaughter of three thousand Israelites may sound like a serious over-reaction to Israel's sin, but it averted an even more drastic act of God. Moreover, our Lord urges us to take decisive action to root out sin and the causes of sin from our lives.

> If your right eye causes you to sin, gouge it out and throw it away. It is better for you to lose one part of your body than for your whole body to be thrown into hell. And if your right hand causes you to sin, cut it off and throw it away. It is better for you to lose one part of your body than for your whole body to go into hell (Matt. 5:29-30).

This incident at Horeb helps us to see the nature of Israel's covenant with Jehovah. In particular, it shows us how sinful people can be saved from the wrath of God and restored to fellowship with God. This can happen only through the work of an intercessor who takes seriously the offensiveness of sin. Because Moses shared God's indignation at Israel's idolatry, he refused to sweep Israel's sin under the carpet. Not only was he angry enough to smash the tablets of stone on the ground, he was willing to take up the sword and slay thousands of his own people. Not only did he punish them at the time, but forty years later he reminded them of their sin and its consequences. To many modern readers of the Old Testament, the events of Exodus 32 are a moral outrage, and Moses' willingness to revisit them in Deuteronomy is morose, at best. How can we explain Moses' words here?

Moses was keenly aware that the controlling power of sin, even amongst the redeemed people of God, was a present and persistent reality; see 9:7b, 24. 'From the day you left Egypt until you arrived here, you have been rebellious against the LORD... You have been rebellious against the LORD ever since I have known you.' To cover over this serious problem with a quick fix solution or a superficial gospel is both unconvincing and ineffective. A university student once went to the university chaplain for spiritual counsel because he was troubled about his sins. The chaplain was liberal in his theology and saw his role as a social worker rather than an evangelist. He invited the young man to join him for a drink at a nearby pub, and assured him that the drink would soon relieve his concern. In essence, his advice was to forget about his sins. Many sinners would gladly forget about their sins, if only they could. But they cannot, and they yearn for atonement and forgiveness. They need to be taken to the cross where God has punished the sins of the world, and then to the throne-room in heaven where Christ intercedes for sinners before a holy God whose wrath has been appeased by his death on the cross. As the sinner comes to the cross and the throne-room, he is brought to his knees in heart-felt repentance.

Moses lived many years before the death of Jesus Christ at Calvary; but he knew well the holiness and justice of God which were revealed on the cross when God punished his Son in the place of his people. He also knew well the mercy of God, which gladly yields to the prayers of an intercessor on behalf of his people. Because God is merciful, Moses took the sinful record of his people and laid it before him with repeated prayers for mercy. So may we as we intercede for ourselves and others.

A call to prayer (9:25-29)

Intercessory prayer for the Israelites was an important part of Moses' ministry. After he smashed the tablets of the law before the Israelites he prayed, fasted and destroyed the sinful idol (see 9:18-21). In 9:25-29 Moses takes us back to those forty days of prayer. *'I lay prostrate before the LORD those forty days and forty nights because the LORD had said he would destroy you'* (9:25). Prostration, or lying flat on one's face, was a widely recognised form of body language in prayer in the ancient world. It said that the one who prayed was in desperate need and urgently sought God's help. In 9:26-29 Moses records the substance of his prayer. He came very quickly to the point. *'O Sovereign LORD, do not destroy your people, your own inheritance that you redeemed by your great power and brought out of Egypt with a mighty hand.'* In the verses that follow Moses recorded how he gave God two reasons why he ought to spare the nation of Israel.

First, Moses pleaded Jehovah's covenant faithfulness (9:27). *'Remember your servants Abraham, Isaac and Jacob. Overlook the stubbornness of this people, their wickedness and their sin.'* This is an abbreviated way of reminding God of the promises that he had made to Abraham, Isaac and Jacob. God had promised that he would multiply their descendants and make them into a great nation and give them the land of Canaan as their inheritance. God had made these promises to the patriarchs even though they and their children were sinful people. Clearly implicit in these promises was a promise of grace to the undeserving, and Moses draws on that thread, which runs through God's dealings with Israel.

Secondly, Moses urged Jehovah not to do anything that would jeopardise his reputation among the surrounding nations (9:28). *'Otherwise, the country from which you brought us will say, "Because the LORD was not able to take them into the land he had promised them, and because he hated them, he brought them out to put them to death in the desert."'* Jehovah was known among the nations as a mighty God and a merciful Saviour for his people. He was the God who had smitten the Egyptians with terrible plagues and had parted the Red Sea so that the Israelites might pass through. Moses recoiled from the thought that anyone should think that God had run out of strength and could no longer lead his people. The God of Israel never grows tired, not does he ever need to sleep (Ps. 121:3-4). He also recoiled from thought that God's love could grow cold and turn into hate. Later prophets would speak of an everlasting and unquenchable love (Jer. 31:3; Hosea 11:1-4; Mal. 1:2), and Moses knew the covenant promises that undergirded those statements. For God to deny his love for Israel would have been to deny himself and reduce himself to the level of the petty deities of the nations, who were mere weather-vanes reacting unpredictably to events around them.

One of the pioneer missionaries of the early nineteenth century was Henry Martyn, who served amongst Muslims in India and Persia. On one occasion he heard a Muslim theologian describe Jesus Christ as a lesser prophet than Mohammed, and he recorded how it grieved him to the point of tears that his Saviour was spoken of in such terms. He could not bear to think of Christ Jesus being robbed of his divine honour. Moses, too, was grieved that the nations should think that Jehovah was weak and vindictive like all the false gods of the nations. This passion for the honour of the true God and for the honour of his Son is what creates the impetus for Christian missions. Today, we not only want the nations to know that God is powerful and willing to save his people, but also that they, too, can become his people by faith in Christ and enjoy the blessings of God's covenant.

Moses concluded his appeal by gathering his thoughts in a single, emotionally charged, appeal (9:29). *'But they are your people, your inheritance that you brought out by your great power and your outstretched arm.'* It is important to remember that Moses was deeply exercised about the consequences of Israel's sinful behaviour at Sinai. Moses was himself a sinner who needed to confess his own sin and seek God's mercy; but that was not the burden on Moses' mind when he prayed. Moses had been on the mountain when Aaron set up the golden calf and he was specifically exempted from the judgment which God threatened to bring upon the Israelites (9:14b). Moses was able to stand aside from the people and their predicament, but he used this special position to seek their salvation rather than secure an honoured place in Israel's history. He served as their intercessor or mediator.

In so doing, Moses points us to the Lord Jesus, the only mediator who is totally without sin (see 1 Tim. 2:5). Through his own Son, God did raise up a new Israel, even in the midst of the widespread national apostasy and rejection of God's purposes which our Lord encountered when he came as a man to live amongst men (John 1:10-11). Just as intercessory prayer played a very important role in Moses' ministry, so it was central to the earthly ministry of our Lord (Heb. 5:7). When he warned Simon Peter and his other disciples that they would face temptations which would overwhelm them, he assured them that his prayers would sustain them. 'I have prayed for you, Simon, that your faith may not fail' (Luke 22:32). Our Lord's ministry of intercessory prayer continues today. 'Therefore he is able to save completely those who come to God through him, because he always lives to intercede for them' (Heb. 7:25). Christ Jesus is the believer's Moses, praying for those who trust him. Just as God listened to his servant Moses, he listens today to the prayers of his beloved Son.

This is what draws us to God when we come to see that we are sinners who have rebelled against God over many years. Yes, God is a just and holy God who must punish sin. But he is also a merciful God who hears the prayers of those who fall on their faces and seek his mercy. We are to pray honestly and realistically about our sins, confessing them to God. Even when we are ashamed and embarrassed and unsure whether God would ever have mercy upon sinners like us, we are to come to God in prayer. We are to pray boldly and persistently. And when we have found God's mercy for ourselves, we will pray with a passion for God's glory, asking that God would demonstrate his righteousness in the salvation of sinners.

Chapter 10
Another chance

Please read Deuteronomy 10: 1-22

In Deuteronomy 9 Moses outlined the important principle that God would give the promised land of Canaan to the people, not because of their righteousness, but because of his faithfulness (9:4-6). The incident at Sinai, where the Israelites had made and worshipped a golden calf, demonstrated that the Israelites were, in themselves, no more righteous than the pagan nations around them. Jehovah, by contrast, was very different from the false gods of those nations. Moses showed how this was so as his sermon unfolded and continued into Deuteronomy 10. Because of Moses' intercession, Jehovah saved the Israelites from total destruction and offered them another opportunity to serve him as his covenant people.

As we shall see, it is a source of great encouragement for us today to know that God does not administer a 'one strike and you're out' policy with his people. If he did, very few of us would last long in his family, for we sin against him daily. Sometimes we sin badly. Yet, when they return to him, God restores those who fall and this prompts God's people to praise him.

God's mercies (10:1-11)

Moses described the events which followed Israel's sin and God's wrath at Sinai. Three events in particular told the Israelites that God had spared them the destruction they deserved and that he was willing to give them another chance to serve him.

God gave them another copy of the law on tablets of stone (10:1-5)
'At that time the LORD said to me, "Chisel out two stone tablets like the first ones and come up to me on the mountain. Also make a wooden chest. I will write on the tablets the words that were on the first tablets which you broke. Then you are to put them in the chest'* (10:1-2). These stone tablets recorded the Ten Commandments (or the Ten Words summarising God's law) which God had given to Moses on Mount Sinai. They were written copies of the covenant between God and Israel. A set of stone tablets had been given to Moses when he ascended the mountain for the first time (see 5:22). Moses had smashed those when he came down the mountain to confront the Israelites over the evil they had done in making the golden calves (see 9:17). As we have seen, this was not an act of mindless frustration, but an indication that the Israelites had violated their covenant with Jehovah. Their relationship with God as well as the stone tablets lay shattered and in ruins. Had this been God's last word to Israel, they would have been in dire straits indeed.

Thankfully, God did not leave his people in such a predicament. He took steps to restore the relationship that had been shattered and demonstrated his intention by giving the people of Israel, through Moses, a new set of stone tablets. Note that these were *exactly* the same as before. God instructed Moses that the tablets were to be *'like the first ones'* (10:1); and then he would write on these tablets *'the words that were on the first tablets'*. Moses reported that *'The LORD wrote on these tablets what he had written before, the Ten Commandments he had proclaimed to you on the mountain, out of the fire'* (10:4). Israel's covenant with

Jehovah was the same covenant, renewed and restored. This time the tablets of stone were placed in a box for safe-keeping, so that the people might realise that their covenant with God was an everlasting covenant which they were to remember and rely upon over the centuries. *'Also make a wooden chest. I will write on the tablets the words that were on the first tablets, which you broke. Then you are to put them in the chest'* (10:1b-2).

This was no ordinary chest, but the ark of the covenant.

> *So I made the ark out of acacia wood and chiselled out two stone tablets like the first ones, and I went up on the mountain with the two tablets in my hands... Then I came back down the mountain and put the tablets in the ark I had made, as the LORD commanded me, and they are there now.* (10:3-5)

The Ark, together with its contents, was to be placed in the central sanctuary or most holy place in the tabernacle and later the temple in Jerusalem. Although the ark does not play a major role in the book of Deuteronomy, it was an important symbol of God's presence amongst his people, as we will see in 10:8. On important occasions it was carried before the Israelites as a reminder that the Lord went before them (see Josh. 3:6-17; 6:6-14; 1 Sam. 4:4-6). It was stored in the Holy of Holies where God's glory dwelt amongst his people (see 1 Kings 8:6-11).

The only other references to the ark in Deuteronomy are found in 31:9, 24-26, where the written copies of Moses' exposition of the law at Moab were presented to the priests and Levites who carried the Ark. The references of the ark in Deuteronomy 10 and 31 straddle Moses' exposition of the law of God in chapters 12-26. The law that Moses expounded was nothing other than the Ten Commandments which came from God's mouth at Sinai. Both the words of God and the preaching of Moses were to be written down and preserved for succeeding generations of the people of Israel. Both were important because they were the terms of God's covenant with Israel, the covenant which had been violated by Israel's idolatry and which was now being restored at God's initiative. God's anger had been appeased by the outpouring of his wrath and the intercession of his servant. If the Israelites are to walk as the people of God, they must learn to love and honour God's law. Moses reminded them that the Ten Words of the law had been miraculously written on stone by the finger of God and placed in the ark so that they might dwell in their midst. However, it was of little value to have stone tablets stored in the ark, if the teaching of God's law was not also impressed on their hearts.

God spared the Israelites and Aaron (10:6-7)
The details of the Israelites' onward journey from Horeb seem like an historical footnote, strangely out of place in Moses' sermon at this point. *'The Israelites traveled from the wells of the Jaakanites to Moserah. There Aaron died and was buried, and Eleazar his son succeeded him as priest. From there they traveled to Gudgodah and on to Jotbathah, a land with streams of water.'* The places mentioned in these verses are found in the longer list of stopping places in Israel's journey found in Numbers 33:31-33. We may not be able to pinpoint the exact location of these places on a map, but their very mention reminded those Israelites who stood on the plains of Moab that their sinful forebears had been spared to travel on from Sinai. They had lived to see another day and were not wiped out as Moses had feared.

Neither did Aaron die at Sinai, but at Moserah. *'There Aaron died and was buried, and Eleazar his son succeeded him as priest'* (10:6). Moserah is another name for the area known as Mount Hor which, according to Numbers 20:22-29; 33:37-39, was the site of Aaron's burial. Today, the traditional site of Aaron's burial is marked by a monument known as Aaron's Tomb which can be reached after a six-hour climb from the ruins of the ancient city of Petra. Mount Hor is part of the mountain range which lies to the south-east of the Dead Sea and overlooks the south of

Canaan. It is worthy of note that, like Moses, Aaron died just as the people of Israel were approaching the promised land. Even though his sins prevented him from entering the promised land, God was merciful to Aaron and gave him another chance to serve him. Not only did God spare Aaron's life, he allowed his son Eleazar to succeed him as priest. The significance of this is enormous for, without a priestly intercessor to pray for them, the Israelites would have been unable to approach the Lord or to seek his mercies.

God set the Levites apart for a special ministry (10:8-9)
The stone tablets bearing the Ten Commandments played an important role in the life of the nation, and Moses was told to make a wooden chest in which to store them. This chest, the ark of the Covenant, was the symbol of God's work of atonement (see Lev. 16:2, 14) and the reconciliation which flowed from it. As an indication of the importance of the Ark, Moses appointed the Levites to look after it. *'At that time the LORD set apart the tribe of Levi to carry the ark of the covenant of the LORD, to stand before the LORD to minister and to pronounce blessings in his name, as they still do today'* (10:8). The Levites were appointed to their special ministry when Moses came down from Mount Sinai to rebuke the Israelites because they had sinned by worshipping the golden calf. Only the Levites stood with him at that time when he was God's instrument to visit wrath upon the people's sin (see Exod. 32:27-29). That was, of course, a terrible day for the nation as a whole, but for the Levites it was their finest hour. They rallied to the cause of truth and demonstrated that they loved God more than their own kinsmen and fellow Israelites. This is the kind of loyalty that Jesus sought in his disciples (see Luke 14:26). It marked out the Levites for their special ministry as God's servants amongst the Israelites. 'You have been set apart to the LORD today, for you were against your own sons and brothers, and he has blessed you this day' (Exod. 32:29; see also Num. 3:5-13).

God's treasured possession

In 10:8 Moses described the threefold work of the Levites.

i. They carried the ark of the covenant. The ark was rich in old covenant symbolism. Its lid was the mercy-seat, sprinkled with blood on the Day of Atonement. Over it the cherubim spread their wings, indicating that the God of heaven had drawn near to his people in mercy. Inside were the tablets of stone which the redeemed people sought to obey with new hearts in order to express their love for their Saviour God. When the ark was carried before the people, these great doctrines of atonement, reconciliation and renewal were symbolically proclaimed. It was the task of the Levites to carry this great symbol of God's grace before the people; and as their role developed, they ceased to be mere carriers of the ark and worked alongside the priests as teachers of the law which the ark contained (see 1 Chr. 23:26; 2 Chr. 17:7-9; 19:8-11).

ii. They stood before the Lord to minister. The Levites served the Lord at the altar where the priests offered sacrifices to the Lord. Their work differed from that of the priests in that they stood ready to assist the priests and were not to usurp the work and dignity of the Aaronic priesthood (see Num. 16:8-10). The Levites also stood ready to assist the people as they brought their sacrifices to the priests at the altar. They assisted the people and the priests by slaughtering and skinning the animals. Much of their work was unpleasant and menial and for that reason the ordinary Levites were often despised by the priests and the other Israelites. Any act of service, however menial it appears to be, is made precious by the fact that it is done for the Lord (see Matt. 25:40). This ought to be an encouragement to those who do seemingly menial tasks in the church today, such as sweeping floors, setting out chars and cutting grass (see Ps. 84:10), as well as to those who preach the Word of God and lead the praise of God's people.

iii. They pronounced blessings in God's name. Pronouncing God's blessing or benediction was an important part of Old Testament worship. In Psalm 134:3 the psalmist recorded the words of blessing pronounced by the temple servants upon those who praised the Lord there. 'May the LORD, the maker of heaven and earth, bless you from Zion.' The best known Old Testament blessing was that pronounced by Aaron and his sons in Numbers 6:23-27 (see also Lev. 9:22; Deut. 21:5). These blessings flowed from the sacrifices of atonement which they offered at the altar. The Levites also pronounced blessings in the name of the Lord, and these were an extension of their ministry of God's law. God's blessing rests upon those who hear and obey God's word (see 28:1-13; Rev. 1:3). The apostle Paul pronounced God's blessing upon the believers in Corinth after they had heard and heeded his stern rebukes (2 Cor. 13:14); and it is appropriate that ministers of the word today assure their congregations of God's blessing after they have taken heed to the preaching of that word.

This special ministry of the Levites placed them in a position where they would depend upon the generosity of their fellow Israelites for their livelihood. In 10:9 Moses drew attention to this fact. *'That is why the Levites have no share or inheritance among their brothers; the LORD is their inheritance, as the LORD your God told them.'* Moses will return to this many times in his exposition of Israel's laws in Deuteronomy. The Levites were scattered throughout the tribal territories of the Israelites so that they might minister to all the people of Israel. Originally this was a punishment for the sins of their ancestor, Levi (see Gen. 49:7). Yet what started as a punishment was turned into a blessing. The people of Israel were blessed to have communities of Levites living amongst them in their towns and villages to teach them the law of God. In times of apostasy the true faith and true piety were preserved by those small groups of Levites. We will see how God placed a responsibility upon those who benefited from their ministry to provide for their material needs (14:28-29; 18:1-2), a principle which has implications for the church today (see Rom. 15:27; 1 Cor. 9:11).

Moses reminded his hearers that these three blessings (the new tablets of stone, the fact that they had been spared to continue their journey and the ministry of the Levites) were God's answer to the prayers which he had offered on the mountain-top. *'Now I had stayed on the mountain forty days and nights, as I did the first time, and the LORD listened to me at this time also. It was not his will to destroy you'* (10:10). This was the third forty-day period of prayer during which Moses had interceded for Israel (see 9:11-20), the second period of prayer on Mount Sinai. We can see the great value in persistent prayer. We very easily become discouraged and give up; but there was no weariness on Moses' part, for he had come to realise that persistent prayer leads to the outpouring of God's blessing. This time, however, Moses was able to draw a line under the whole terrible incident at Sinai, for God told him to lead the people onwards towards their promised inheritance. *'"Go," the LORD said to me, "and lead the people on their way, so that they may enter and possess the land that I swore to their fathers to give them"'* (10:11).

What a blessing prayer is! Moses cried out to the Lord not to destroy the Israelites, and the Lord listened to him. There are times when we pray about life and death issues and we can be assured that God hears those prayers. Let us never think that our guilt is too great or that God is too angry to save. The Scriptures assure us that 'the prayer of a righteous man is powerful and effective' (James 5:16b). God sent Moses on his way with the promise that his presence would be with him as he led the Israelites towards the promised land (see Exod. 33:14-17).

Israel's response (10:12-22)

Moses shifts the focus of his sermon from what God had done for his people to what they must do in response. The Israelites had been given a second chance. What would they do with that opportunity? That was as pressing a challenge for the Israelites who stood ready to enter the promised land as it had been for their fathers who sinned at Sinai. Moses posed a question in 10:12a: *'And now, O Israel, what does the LORD your God ask of you...'* This was an important question. The answer to it was made abundantly clear over the centuries (see Micah 6:8). Moses will set out what God expects of his people in his exposition of the law in chapters 12-26, but before he comes to the details of the law he presses home his challenge to the hearts of his hearers. In 10:12 – 11:32 we find many repeated and recurring exhortations to love and serve God. We will hear Moses introduce new ethical emphases which will be taken up later in the exposition of the law (such as a concern for the fatherless, the widow and the stranger); but first Moses draws a link between the character of Jehovah and the response which he seeks from his covenant people.

In 10:12-22 Moses called for three responses to God's mercies.

i. Serve the Lord your God (10:12-13)

> *And now, O Israel, what does the LORD your God ask of you but to fear the LORD your God, to walk in all his ways, to love him, to serve the LORD your God with all your heart and with all your soul, and to observe the LORD's commands and decrees that I am giving you today for your own good?*

The response which God sought from his people is summarized in five words, which summarise the essence of godly living – fear, walk, love, serve and observe. The last four of these activities describe how the people were to live. They were to observe and to obey God's law. They were to serve the Lord. They were to demonstrate their love for God by their actions. They were to conduct themselves in a godly way in all their daily activities. This is total commitment of heart, soul and strength

(6:5) and was possible only when the people feared or revered God with their hearts. That is why the fear of God is given such prominence in the Old Testament (see Ps. 111:10; Prov. 1:7). Not only is it the first principle of wisdom, it is the foundation upon which a godly life is built. If we today are to honour God by the conduct of our lives and our sharing of the gospel of Christ, we must know more and more of his greatness and revere him. Moses opens our eyes to the greatness of God in the verses which follow.

ii. Circumcise your hearts (10:14-20)
It is sometimes said that the religion of the Old Testament was a matter of outward rituals and mere moralism which did little to transform the heart. Nothing could be further from the truth. Jehovah did not set out merely to reform the religious practices or the ethical conduct of his redeemed people while leaving their hearts unchanged. In fact, it would be impossible to reform their religion and morality without also transforming their hearts; and Moses was keenly aware of this as he preached in Deuteronomy. He is also aware that only God can change the hearts of his people and that he does that by drawing near to them to meet with them. In 10:16 Moses will bring one of the central challenges of his preaching to the people of Israel, but first he prepared the way by describing God's character in 10:14-15.

In 10:14 Moses described a God who is entitled to all honour and service, because everything belongs to him. '*To the LORD your God belong the heavens, even the highest heavens, the earth and everything in it.*' Then in 10:15 Moses described a God whom his people would want to serve because he chose them and loved them. '*Yet the LORD set his affection on your forefathers and loved them, and he chose you, their descendants, above all the nations, as it is today.*' There is no tension, in Moses' mind, between the majesty and mercy of Jehovah. The Lord who holds the whole universe in his hands is not too busy or preoccupied to show his love for his people.

Another chance

After reminding the Israelites that it is this majestic Lord who has saved them, he calls for a response in language drawn from God's covenant with Abraham. *'Circumcise your hearts, therefore, and do not be stiff-necked any longer'* (10:16). When God chose Abraham to be the father of his family on earth, he made a covenant with him and gave circumcision to be the sign of that covenant (see Genesis 17:7, 10-14). In Deuteronomy Moses explains the response of the covenant people in terms of love and reverence for God and calls for a circumcision of the heart. Just as the ritual of circumcision involved the cutting away of the flesh of the foreskin, so circumcision of the heart involved the cutting away and removal of evil in the heart. Those whose hearts were circumcised offered whole-hearted obedience and affection to the Lord who had loved them. The bond between Jehovah and Israel was to be a knitting together of their hearts so that electing love led to loving obedience.

The practical implications of this high ideal were set out in Moses' exposition of the law in chapters 12-26, where we will find repeated descriptions of how a circumcised heart will think and act. In particular, Moses will describe the motives that God wants to see in his people's hearts. These high ideals were only imperfectly realised in Israel for, although God loved Israel, Israel failed in her calling to love God. She was a nation circumcised only in the flesh (see Jer. 9:25). Jeremiah called upon the people of Judah in his day to circumcise themselves to the Lord, to circumcise their hearts (see Jer. 4:4). Yet, try as they might, the people of Israel could not circumcise their hearts, just as Nicodemus would find that he could not enter his mother's womb a second time to be born again (see John 3:4). The climax of Moses' preaching in Deuteronomy will come in 30:6 with the promise that what Israel could never do, God would do for them. The heart of God's covenant promise is the total restoration of a fallen and rebellious people. God will circumcise their hearts and call them effectually to himself. This command finds its ultimate fulfilment in the ministry of the

Holy Spirit 'convincing us of our sin and misery, enlightening our minds in the knowledge of Christ, and renewing our wills', with the result that 'he doth persuade and enable us to embrace Jesus Christ, freely offered to us in the gospel' (*Westminster Shorter Catechism*, answer 31).

Just as 10:14-15 paved the way for the great command of 10:16, so Moses followed the command with further reasons why God's people ought to devote their hearts to his law. In 10:17-18 Moses describes the fairness and justice of God. *'For the LORD your God is God of gods and Lord of lords, the great God, mighty and awesome, who shows no partiality and accepts no bribes.'* In what seems to be an aside, Moses challenged the Israelites to meditate on these aspects of God's character and to reflect them in their behaviour towards one another (10:18-19). *'He defends the cause of the fatherless and the widow, and loves the alien, giving him food and clothing. And you are to love those who are aliens, for you yourselves were aliens in Egypt.'* Then in 10:20 Moses appealed to them to behave with integrity, taking seriously the promises they made. *'Hold fast to him and take your oaths in his name.'*

These exhortations in 10:18-20 were no mere aside, for they introduce an emphasis to which Moses will return repeatedly in his exposition of Israel's laws in chapters 12-26 (see 14:29; 16:14, 19; 24:14, 17-22; 26:12-13). Moses made it clear to the Israelites that God is displeased with his people when they declare their love for him, but ignore the needs of the poor and vulnerable in the community. A circumcised heart is also a compassionate heart. In fact, the attitude of our hearts towards the needy around us is often an indicator of whether or not our hearts have been truly circumcised – whether we have been born again!

iii. Praise God (10:21-22)
'He is your praise; he is your God, who performed for you those great and awesome wonders you saw with your own eyes.' This description of Jehovah could mean either that he would make Israel an object of admiration amongst the nations or that

Jehovah was the object of Israel's praise. Both interpretations are possible; but the latter is preferable, because the passage as a whole describes Israel's response to the renewal of God's mercies towards them. Moses called upon the Israelites to praise God because of the 'great and awesome wonders' which he had done for them. In so doing he recalled their deliverance from Egypt (4:34; 7:18-19) and even the blessing they experienced as slaves in Egypt. *'Your forefathers who went down into Egypt were seventy in all, and now the LORD your God has made you as numerous as the stars in the sky.'* It was a relatively small clan which Jacob led down into Egypt (see Gen. 46:27; Exod. 1:5; in Acts 7:14 Stephen counts the number of Jacob's descendants as seventy-five, a figure taken from the Septuagint text of Gen. 46:27 and Exod. 1:5, which incorporates additional information about Joseph's family); but there in the land of slavery at least one of God's promises to Abraham came to fulfilment (see Gen. 15:5; 22:17).

Worship is the proper response of God's people to his mighty acts on their behalf. 'Praise him for his acts of power; praise him for his surpassing greatness' (Ps. 150:2). He is the only God who can act in this way (3:24), and he alone is the one to be worshipped. No other god is willing or able to persevere with unruly and undeserving sinners. No other god can restore those who fall and preserve them from destruction. No other god can demand such total loyalty and uncompromising obedience. No other god can draw from his people such admiration and affection.

A promise for God's people today

We can think of others who have been given a second chance by God. King David committed adultery and then murder (2 Sam. 11); but after he confessed his sin (Ps. 51:1-2) he was told, 'the LORD has taken away your sin. You are not going to die' (2 Sam. 12:13b). Jonah ran away from God's call to preach to the people of Nineveh, but God sent a storm and a great fish to bring him back. In this way God gave Jonah another chance. 'Then the word of the Lord came to Jonah a second time' (Jonah 3:1). Simon Peter deserted the Lord Jesus and denied him three times, but after his resurrection the Lord Jesus specifically sent for Peter (Mark 16:7) and reinstated him as an apostle (John 20:15-19). John Mark deserted Paul and Barnabas on their first missionary journey (Acts 13:13). While Paul would not have him on the team, Barnabas drew near to this immature young man and gave him a second chance (Acts 15:37-39). More importantly, God blessed the restorative ministry of Barnabas and, many years later, Paul would later ask for Mark to be sent to him so that he might help him in his ministry (see 2 Tim. 4:11).

We, too, can thank God for second chances. What would have become of us if God struck us down every time we sinned? What would have become of us if God did not give us another chance when we fell into sin? We can only shudder to think. There are many times when we have failed God and have regretted it. We are not to make light of those failures, but neither ought we to make more of them than God does. They do not necessarily spell the end of our walk with God or the usefulness of our ministries, for God is a merciful God who restores those who fall. Praise him for his mercies!

When God restores us, we are to learn lessons even from our lives of sin. It has been said of John Newton (the slave-trader turned preacher of the gospel) that he was such a great preacher of the gospel because he knew the depths from which he had been saved. Even though his mother had taught him about Jesus Christ and continued to pray for him, he turned his back on God and plunged into every wickedness imaginable. 'Two things I know,' he said. 'I am a great sinner, but I have a great Saviour.' After his conversion he was able to show, with great persuasiveness, the folly of sin. He knew the power of the wickedness from which he had been delivered. He also knew the power of the grace which had saved him. Our lives may not be as dramatic as his, but we, too, would face destruction before the holy wrath of God, were it not for God's patience and the mediatorial work of Jesus Christ. Let us praise God for his patience with us.

Chapter 11
Discipling a new generation

Please read Deuteronomy 11: 1-32

In Deuteronomy 11 Moses continues his urgent appeal to the Israelites to love and serve their covenant Lord with all their heart, soul and strength. *'Love the LORD your God and keep his requirements, his decrees, his laws and his commands always.'* This was Israel's proper response to the mercies of God, but Moses feared that they would forget how the Lord had redeemed them and slip back into idolatry. He had in his mind the terrible events at Sinai where the Israelites had worshipped a golden calf (9:7-21). Had it not been for his prayers, and God's mercies, they would have been destroyed as a nation. Because of his great mercy God spared his people and allowed them to continue on their journey towards the promised land of Canaan. In 10:12-13 Moses records the exhortation he had given them at that time. 'And now O Israel, what does the LORD your God ask of you but to fear the LORD your God, to walk in all his ways, to love him, to serve the LORD your God with all your heart and with all your soul, and to observe the LORD's commands and decrees.' After pausing to set out some very important truths about God's character (10:14-22), which were intended to impress upon the Israelites the importance of loyal obedience, Moses turned again to this theme in 11:1.

Moses knew that the Israelites had short memories. They would very quickly forget the painful lessons they had learned at Sinai and would succumb to the temptation to turn to other gods and worship their idols. So, in the rest of Deuteronomy 11, Moses addressed the problem of Israel's forgetfulness. On the one hand he taught the parents to teach their children (11:2-21); and on the other hand he instructed the children to gather at Shechem to remember what their parents had taught them (11:22-31).

A challenge to the parents (11:2-21)

i. Remember the lessons of the past (11:2-7)
Moses moved swiftly from the general principle in 11:1 to a very specific application in 11:2. *'Remember today that your children were not the ones who saw and experienced the discipline of the LORD your God...'* Here he addressed the remnants of that generation which had been born in Egypt and which had lived through the Exodus and the early years of Israel's wanderings in the wilderness. They had seen

> *the signs he performed and the things he [Jehovah] did in the heart of Egypt, both to Pharaoh king of Egypt and to his whole country; what he did to the Egyptian army, to its horses and chariots, how he overwhelmed them with the waters of the Red Sea as they were pursuing you, and how the LORD brought lasting ruin on them.*

The phrase 'lasting ruin' describes the abiding significance of God's actions at the time of the exodus. A literal reading of the Hebrew text is 'and the Lord destroyed them unto this day'. God had promised that never again would those Egyptians trouble the Israelites (Exod. 14:13), and forty years later the Israelites were still able to go about their lives free from the oppression of their former overlords. God's mighty acts in the past were still shaping the present experiences of God's people.

The generation to whom Moses was speaking in these verses was also that generation which remembered what God *'did to Dathan and Abiram, sons of Eliab the Reubenite, when the earth opened its mouth right in the middle of all Israel and swallowed them up with their households, their tents and every living thing that belonged to them'* (11:5-6). Their rebellion (as well as that of another key conspirator, Korah) is described more fully in Numbers 16. There is no reason to doubt that Moses knew about Korah's involvement in the terrible events of that day. We can be sure that this was etched on his memory, but he mentioned only the actions of Dathan and Abiram from the tribe of Reuben, most probably because they represented the whole Israelite community and put into words their complaint against God (see Num. 16:3). By contrast, Korah seems to have expressed the grievances of the lesser Levites against Aaron and the priests (see Num. 16:4-11). The complaint which most offended Moses at the time was that of Dathan and Abiram, that Moses had brought them out of Egypt, 'a land flowing with milk and honey, to kill us in the desert' (see Num. 16:13-14). They had forgotten that Egypt was the land of slavery and that Canaan, towards which Moses was leading them, was the promised land flowing with milk and honey (see 6:3; 11:9; 26:9, 15; 27:3).

The fact which Moses sought to impress on that generation – which had experienced the exodus and the wilderness years – was that their children had not witnessed these events. Having stated this rather obvious fact in 11:2, he returned to it again in verses 5 and 7 for emphasis. *'It was not your children who saw what he did for you in the desert until you arrived at this place... but it was your own eyes that saw all these great things the LORD has done.'* They were the generation which (like Moses himself) would not enter into the land of Canaan.

When these people had reached Kadesh Barnea they had refused to trust God's promises. Because of their fears, they refused to enter the land to possess it. When the Lord heard what they said, he was angry and swore that 'not a man of this evil generation shall see the good land I swore to give your forefathers, except Caleb' and Joshua (see Deut. 1:35-36). This ban applied only to the adult members of the community and not to those who had been little children at that time. As they gathered with their aged parents on the plains of Moab, they would have had little or no memory of what had happened in Egypt and in the wilderness. They had not 'experienced the discipline of the Lord'; and because of this they would easily forget the lessons their parents had learned through these painful experiences.

Discipline is one of the ways in which God's people learn how to love and serve him. Although the events which Moses described in verses 2-7 were painful, God's primary purpose was not to cause pain but to teach the Israelites moral and spiritual lessons. It is not without significance that the word which Moses used in 11:2 to describe the Lord's 'discipline' is used often in Proverbs to describe the instruction which parents give to their children (see Prov. 1:8; 4:1, 13; 5:12; 6:23; 13:1; 19:27). 'He who ignores discipline despises himself, but whoever heeds correction gains understanding' (Prov.15:32).

Moses encouraged those parents who had learned from the Lord's discipline to pass on what they learned – while they were able – to their children. He will explain how to do this in 11:18-21, but first they must remember what they have discovered. They had discovered *the mighty power of God*, who alone is able to save his people from slavery and death. The God who overthrew the Egyptians would also overthrow the Canaanites, and he has overcome the last great enemy, death, through the death of his Son on the cross (1 Cor. 15:25). They had also discovered *the destructive power of sin*. Israel's own rebellion against God had caused them as much pain and death as the cruelty of the Egyptians. Some parents today have learned the hard way that God's ways are best. They have rebelled against God and suffered the consequences of their sin. Their lives were a mess until God graciously saved them from the pit of their own making. They wonder whether their children will repeat their mistakes before they come to repentance and faith. That is why parents are to pass on the benefits of their experience to their children by warning them about the consequences of sin and encouraging them to walk in God's ways.

ii. Make ready for new challenges (11:8-17)
In 11:8-9 Moses returns to the underlying theme of chapters 6-11, that Israel is to love the Lord their God because he has redeemed them. Love and obedience are to be an expression of thanks. Love and obedience are also the conditions upon which God has promised future blessing – in particular, their enjoyment of the promised land. This is what Moses meant by the phrase 'so that' in verses 8-9.

> *Observe therefore all the commands I am giving you today, so that you may have the strength to go in and take over the land that you are crossing the Jordan to possess, and so that you may live long in the land that the LORD swore to your forefathers to give to them and their descendants, a land flowing with milk and honey.*

The freeness of God's grace never gave his people a green light to continue in sin, nor did it remove the incentive to devote their lives to serving God. The same love and service is expected of those who are saved by the free grace of God in Christ Jesus (see Rom. 6:1-2; Eph. 2:8-10).

When the Israelites entered the land of Canaan, they were to serve God by conquering and subduing the land. In that new land they would face challenges that previous generations of Israelites had not faced when they laboured as slaves in Egypt.

God's treasured possession

In 11:10-12 Moses continued to speak to the remnants of that generation which remembered life in Egypt. He told them to prepare their children for a very different way of life in Canaan. *'The land you are entering to take over is not like the land of Egypt, from which you have come, where you planted your seed and irrigated it by foot as in a vegetable garden.'* The contrast between the two lands is like that faced by the early European settlers when they arrived in Australia. Many of them came in search of land. They did indeed find vast plains in this new land, but it was very different from the land they had left behind. The hot, dry climate of Australia was very different from that of the British Isles and they had to rethink their approach to farming.

The Israelites would face a similar contrast, except that they were moving from a dry land to a comparatively moist land when they settled in the land of Canaan. Farming in Egypt was hard work, because the land could be cultivated only with water from the mighty River Nile. When the Nile flooded, it watered the land and made it fruitful; but beyond the narrow strip of land along the river valley and the delta of the Nile it was necessary to irrigate. Archaeologists are not completely sure how the irrigation systems of ancient Egypt operated, but the most likely explanation is that water was fed into channels by a water wheel rotated by a foot pedal or by a bucket suspended from a finely balanced pole. This latter device, a shaduf, is still in use in Egypt today. If Moses had a device like this in mind, he envisages the Israelite slaves using their feet to open or close gaps in the mud walls of the irrigation channels. This was an intensive method of agriculture, suited to a vegetable plot. Only the backbreaking toil of an army of slaves made it possible to farm a whole land in this way.

By contrast, the land of Canaan was watered by rainfall from above. In 11:11-12 Moses draws out theological lessons from this fact of geography. *'But the land you are crossing the Jordan to take possession of is a land of mountains and valleys that drinks rain from heaven. It is a land the LORD your God cares for; the eyes of the LORD your God are continually on it from the beginning of the year to its end.'* The topography of Canaan was mountainous and its rainfall came from the moist air brought in from the sea and forced to rise over the hills. Therefore the rain fell where it was needed and did not have to be moved about in irrigation channels. Typically, the rain fell in autumn (just before planting) and late spring (before harvest) and it made the ground fruitful. As a result, the Israelites would have a deep sense of God's blessing. Rain was not an accident of geography and climate, but a gift from God and an indication that he was pleased to pour his blessings directly upon them (see Job 36:27-29; Ps. 65:9-11).

The rain that watered the land of Canaan was not always reliable. When the rains failed, the result was famine. This forced the inhabitants of the land to look beyond themselves and the created order around them for help. The Canaanites worshipped fertility gods, such as Baal and Ashteroth, whose speciality was sending rain to make the ground fruitful. The Israelites would be tempted to adopt their ways. This was a temptation which the Israelites were to resist, because only Jehovah can give rain. This brought Moses back to his main theme – to exhort the people to serve Jehovah and him alone (11:13-15).

> *So if you faithfully obey the commands I am giving you today – to love the LORD your God and to serve him with all your heart and with all your soul – then I will send rain on your land in its season, both autumn and spring rains, so that you may gather in your grain, new wine and oil. I will provide grass in the fields for your cattle, and you will eat and be satisfied.*

The constant danger which the Israelites would face in the land of Canaan was that they would eat the good things produced by the land of Canaan and forget the Lord who had given them the land in the first place and who continued to make it fruitful (see 8:12-14). We face the same danger today. Our lives are much easier than those of our grandparents, in that many of us can earn a living without backbreaking physical toil. We enjoy the benefits of modern technology and medical care and many other things beside. We are tempted to give technological explanations for our present blessings and overlook the hand of God in our lives. We forget that 'every good and perfect gift is from above, coming down from the Father of the heavenly lights' (James 1:17). We can be like the rich farmer described by our Lord in Luke 12:16-21, who stored up many things for himself, but was not rich toward God.

Worse still, we can give others the thanks which we owe to God. In recent times there has been a renewed interest in the powers of 'mother earth', and nature itself is sometimes worshipped as an impersonal deity. This is a temptation as old as the hills; but God will not stand by while his glory is given to others. Moses warned the Israelites of the consequences of idolatry in 11:16-17.

> Be careful, or you will be enticed to turn away and worship other gods and bow down to them. Then the LORD's anger will burn against you, and he will shut the heavens so that it will not rain and the ground will yield no produce, and you will soon perish from the good land the LORD is giving you.

The rain which seemed so abundant and reliable in the mountainous land of Canaan would be taken away and they would perish. This actually happened to Israel. That should be a warning to those who confidently assume that abundant natural resources, combined with sophisticated technology and economic management skills, will guarantee our prosperous lifestyles. One blow from God can bring the whole edifice crashing down.

Discipling a new generation

iii. Teach God's word at home (11:18-21)
The temptation to worship other gods was one which would persist over the centuries, and in 11:18-21 Moses outlines three steps which, if followed, would protect not just one generation, but many succeeding generations from idolatry and its disastrous consequences. This is what the Israelites were to do.

a. Fix these words in their minds and hearts (11:18). *'Fix these words of mine in your hearts and minds; tie them as symbols on your hands and bind them on your foreheads.'* Moses returned to the figure of speech which he had used in 6:8, where outward actions indicated an inward appropriation of God's word. It was not by attaching scraps of parchment to the wrist and forehead that the Israelites were to fix God's words in their minds, but by meditating on them, memorizing them and talking about them with like-minded believers. The first two commandments in the Decalogue forbade any expression of loyalty to other gods; and if the Israelites had memorized and meditated on these commands, they would have had a finely tuned internal warning system to protect them against idolatry. Likewise, when we keep God's word in our hearts and on our minds, we will recognize apostasy when it subtly begins to tempt us.

b. Teach these words to their children (11:19). *'Teach them to your children, talking about them when you sit at home and when you walk along the road, when you lie down and when you get up.'* The generation which had not seen God's mighty acts could still hear God's powerful words. God's words were preserved in written form so that the future generations might know his power and experience his grace. In particular, his word calls them from spiritual slavery and points them to the living God. Parents have a particular responsibility to make sure their children hear God's word, not only in formal, congregational gatherings, but also in the informal, routine activities of family life. In today's context, parents might well speak to their children about the things of

God when they mow the lawn, supervise their homework, or go for a picnic, and when they lead family devotions.

c. *Make God's laws visible to all who entered their homes* (11:20). *'Write them on the door-frames of your houses and on your gates ...'* In all probability, Moses intended that this phrase be understood figuratively. Over the years many Jews have applied this instruction literally by placing a box containing a fragment of the Old Testament law on their doorpost. Moses' goal was that when servants and visitors entered an Israelite home they would know immediately that this was a home where the Lord was honoured. That was Joshua's resolve: 'But as for me and my household, we will serve the LORD' (Josh. 24:15b). By contrast, Isaiah describes the corrupting influence of pagan symbols attached to Israel's doors and doorposts (see Isa. 57:8). Some Christians adorn their walls and doors with Christian emblems and Bible verses in order to make the statement that they want their home life to honour God. This is a worthy goal, but one that demands more than emblems and fragments of Scripture. A godly home is one where God is loved, obeyed and worshipped, and this love will overflow in hospitality and service to others.

Moses' instructions in 11:18-21 are very similar to those in 6:7-9. The difference, which is not obvious to the English reader, is that in 6:7-9 Moses addressed the Israelites as a collective singular while in 11:18-21 he addresses the Israelites as a community. This is reflected in the KJV, where 6:7 reads, 'And thou shalt teach them diligently unto thy children', while 11:18 reads, 'Therefore shall ye lay up these my words in your heart'. The movement between singular and plural forms of address in Moses' sermons is an important feature of Deuteronomy and has provoked much comment. Some claim that it indicates a plurality of sources with their distinctive styles, gathered together by a later editor. There is, however, every reason to believe that the alternation of different forms of address was a deliberate feature in Moses' preaching, emphasizing the importance of both individual and collective action on the part of God's people. In Deuteronomy 6:7-9 Moses encouraged individuals to impress God's word on their hearts and teach it to their families, while in 11:18-21 he addressed the community as a whole and encouraged it to take hold of God's law so that it was impressed on its collective psyche. The people of Israel were to be a 'people of the book'. So when they entered the land of Canaan they were to gather to hear God's word and renew their covenant with Jehovah(see 11:29; 27:2-8).

A challenge to the children (11:22-31)

In the final section of the chapter, Moses turned his attention to the children of the exodus generation who were about to enter the promised land. In principle, his message for them was the same as his message for their parents (11:22). *'If you carefully observe all these commands I am giving you to follow – to love the LORD your God, to walk in all his ways and to hold fast to him ...'* They, too, were to love God and walk in his ways. If they were faithful, they would inherit the promises which God had made to their forefathers. In keeping with the everlasting character of God's covenant with Israel, his promises are for parents and their children (see Gen. 17:8). The phrases which Moses used in 11:22 echo 10:12, 20, where Moses set forth Israel's response to God's gracious deliverance at Horeb. Love and obedience are also the essential conditions for future blessing, which Moses describes in terms of the military conquest of Canaan (11:23-25). *'Then the LORD will drive out all these nations before you, and you will dispossess nations larger and stronger than you. Every place where you set your foot will be yours: Your territory will extend from the desert to Lebanon, and from the Euphrates River to the western sea.'*

It is good for us to pause and consider the wonder of the promise which God made to this generation of his people in these verses.

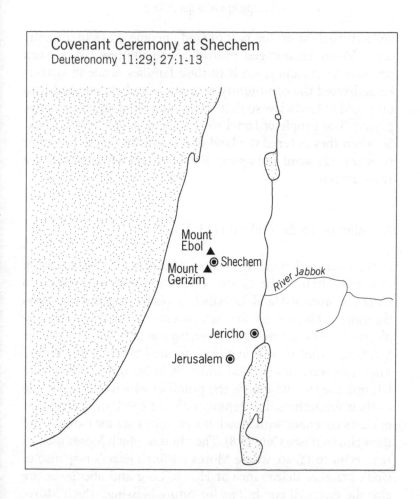

Covenant Ceremony at Shechem
Deuteronomy 11:29; 27:1-13

Mount Ebol
Mount Gerizim
Shechem
River Jabbok
Jericho
Jerusalem

The *extent of the territory* which would be theirs is staggering. It encompassed much more than the land of Canaan, and pointed to the universal nature of Jehovah's dominions (see Ps. 72:8-11). It took many years, and the advent of the monarchy under David and Solomon, before the Israelites would rule territory from the River Euphrates, through the eastern desert, to the Mediterranean Sea (see 1 Kings 4:21). Moreover, the *decisiveness of their* victory would be more than they had expected (11:25). *'No man will be able to stand against you. The LORD your God, as he promised you, will put the terror and fear of you on the whole land, wherever you go.'* Daunting as the Canaanites had once appeared to the Israelites (Num. 13:31-33; Deut. 1:28), they would not be able to stand before the victorious armies of Israel (7:17-19; 9:1-3). The fear of Israel may well be the hornet described in 7:20, for the two spies who went into Jericho discovered that the Canaanites had lost the will to fight because of their fear of the Israelites (Josh. 2:9).

With a similar military metaphor, the Lord Jesus promised his disciples that the well-defended gates of Hades will not be able to withstand the church's witness when she advances in the power of the Holy Spirit to preach the gospel. 'And I tell you that you are Peter, and on this rock I will build my church, and the gates of Hades will not overcome it' (Matt. 16:18). Just as the seemingly impregnable gates of the Canaanite cities collapsed before Israel's armies, so will today's citadels of opposition to the gospel fall before the church. We may find this hard to believe, but we need to remember that victory belongs to our God and his people. 'But thanks be to God! He gives us the victory through our Lord Jesus Christ' (1 Cor. 15:57). 'This is the victory that has overcome the world, even our faith. Who is it that overcomes the world? Only he who believes that Jesus is the son of God' (1 John 5:4b-5). This is what God has promised to his people. This is what will happen as we rest upon his promises.

God's treasured possession

God's promise of victory to this new generation (which we
might call the conquest generation) was conditional upon their
love for God and their obedience to his law. They had some
important choices to make in the coming years and in 11:26-32
Moses emphasised the importance of making the right choices.

i. He set before them two contrasting outcomes (11:26-28)

> *See, I am setting before you today a blessing and a curse -
> the blessing if you obey the commands of the LORD your
> God that I am giving you today; the curse if you disobey the
> commands of the LORD your God and turn from the way
> that I command you today by following other gods, which
> you have not known.*

Both blessing and cursing are acts of God and flow from his
covenant with Israel. Blessing is God's free gift to his people
when they love and serve him, but cursing is God's punishment
falling upon those who turn away from him. Moses will return to
these blessings and curses in his third sermon in Deuteronomy
28-30. He will explain in some detail what each involves in
chapters 28-29, and appeal to the Israelites to seek the blessings
by choosing life in 30:15-20. All their choices would lead back
to one important question – whom will they serve, Jehovah or
the false gods of the nations around them? When they chose to
serve Jehovah as their God, they chose to submit to his Lordship
and enjoy his blessings. Whey they chose to seek other gods,
they chose a path that led to death. That was the choice which
faced generations of Israelites (see Josh. 24:15; 1 Kings 18:21).

The same choice faces us today. The Lord Jesus appeals to us to
enter his kingdom through the narrow gate (see Matt. 7:13-14).
This is something we need to choose to do because, by our birth
as sinners, we have already entered into the 'wide gate' and we
are already walking on the 'broad road' that leads to destruction.
All mankind is walking along one or other of these two paths,

and our everyday choices confirm us in the path we are taking. Sinners choose to stay on the path that leads to destruction; but to enjoy God's blessing we must choose to leave the path of death and seek life in God. How important are the choices we make when we hear the word of God! The gospel places us at a crossroads: one path takes us to eternal life, while the other takes us to eternal death (see Rom. 6:23). To choose Christ is to choose life, while to go in the way of sin is to embrace death. No other choice we make has more contrasting outcomes.

ii. He called them to gather at Shechem (11:29-32)
'When the LORD your God has brought you into the land you are entering to possess, you are to proclaim on Mount Gerizim the blessings, and on Mount Ebal the curses.' Between these two mountains lay the town of Shechem. It was to this place that the Israelites were to gather to renew their covenant with Jehovah once they had entered the promised land. The ceremony itself did not take place until after the conquest, and is described in Joshua 8:30-35; but in 27:1-26 Moses prescribed in more detail what was to take place in that covenant-renewal ceremony. Six tribes standing on Mount Gerizim were to bless the people (27:12) and six tribes standing on Mount Ebal were to pronounce curses (27:13), while the Levites were to recite curses to which all the people were to respond, 'Amen'. In these ways the people would acknowledge the consequences of the choices they would make.

In 11:30 Moses explained God's choice of Shechem as the location of the place where the Israelites were to gather. '*As you know, these mountains are across the Jordan, west of the road, toward the setting sun, near the great trees of Moreh, in the territory of those Canaanites living in the Arabah in the vicinity of Gilgal.*' Shechem was a central location, easily accessible from all parts of Canaan. Its strategic location meant that it was inhabited from very early times. When Abraham arrived in the land of

Canaan, he met with the Lord there and built an altar (see Gen. 12:6-7). It was appropriate that when God, in keeping with his promise, gave Abraham's descendants the land of Canaan, they should gather at Shechem to acknowledge God's faithfulness.

Shechem was also a centre for pagan activity in the land of Canaan. Moses told the Israelites that Mounts Gerazim and Ebal were 'near the great trees of Moreh, in the territory of the Canaanites living in the Arabah in the vicinity of Gilgal'. Genesis 12:6 mentions a tree at Moreh, and here Moses mentions a grove of trees. The sacred sites of the pagans were often marked out by such groves. The place name itself, Moreh, indicates its significance. The word means 'teacher' or 'oracle', and may have been a place where pagan priests were consulted for guidance. Judges 9:37 describes a 'soothsayers' tree' in the vicinity of Shechem. The Gilgal mentioned in 11:30 was not the Gilgal east of Jericho (which Joshua used as his base of operations after crossing into the promised land, Josh. 4:19), but a lesser-known site much closer to Shechem. The name means 'the stone oracle', and it may well have had a function very similar to that of Stonehenge in England, where pre-Christian religious gatherings were held. Clearly the site was well known for its pagan associations.

Yet right here, in the centre of Canaanite paganism, the Israelites were to dedicate themselves to Jehovah. The symbolism of this daring act was enormous. Just as Gideon would set up the altar of the Lord where the altar of Baal had once stood (see Judg. 6:25-28), so the Israelites were to worship the Lord where the false gods of Canaan had once been honoured. The significance of Israel's conquest of Canaan was spiritual and theological as well as military and political. In this way they staked Jehovah's claim over the whole of Canaan. They declared war on the false gods who had once held its inhabitants in bondage. Jehovah will challenge his rivals and cast them down (see 1 Sam. 5:1-4).

Many years later, the Christians of Pergamum would bear witness to the universal lordship of Jesus Christ in a city 'where Satan has his throne' (Rev. 2.13). (Pergamum was renowned as a centre of the cult of emperor worship.) Saint Patrick challenged the power of paganism in pre-Christian Ireland by lighting a fire in defiance of the high king of Ireland on an evening held sacred to the druids. It was a bold move, but full of gospel symbolism as Jesus Christ brought light to a land plunged in spiritual darkness. The gospel advances as its enemies are cast down. According to the *Westminster Shorter Catechism*, this is what we seek when we pray the second petition of the Lord's Prayer, 'Thy kingdom come': 'We pray, That Satan's kingdom may be destroyed; and that the kingdom of grace may be advanced, ourselves and others brought into it, and kept in it...' (answer 102).

Conclusion

The Israelites had been redeemed by God to live as his holy people in the land of Canaan. In Deuteronomy 5-11 Moses has sketched out, in general terms, what this would mean. They were to love God and keep his commandments (11:31-32). *'You are about to cross the Jordan to enter and take possession of the land the LORD your God is giving you. When you have taken it over and are living there, be sure that you obey all the decrees and laws I am setting before you today.'* With these words Moses concluded the general introduction to his second Deuteronomic sermon. He made clear that true religion is heart religion. His people must love him with all their hearts and they must love each other.

Moses does not rest content with a general statement of purpose, for in chapters 12-26 he will give a more detailed exposition of the law which the Israelites are to obey. He will wrestle with some of the temptations they will face and explain why God's commands are for their good. This body of teaching is what the Israelites were to fix in their minds and teach to their children. Just as the exodus generation was to teach the conquest generation about God's mighty works, so each succeeding generation was to train the next generation to love and serve the Lord of Israel.

It is equally important for the church today to train new generations of believers. Paul exhorted Timothy to continue in what he had learned and become convinced of (2 Tim. 3:14-15) and then exhorted him to pass those things on to others. 'You then, my son, be strong in the grace that is in Christ Jesus. And the things you have heard me say in the presence of many witnesses entrust to reliable men who will also be qualified to teach others' (2 Tim. 2:1-2). Parents especially have a unique opportunity and responsibility to train their children in the ways of the Lord. 'Fathers, do not exasperate your children; instead bring them up in the training and instruction of the Lord' (Eph. 6:4).

Chapter 12
God's chosen place

Please read Deuteronomy 12: 1-32

Deuteronomy 12 introduces us to one of the central themes in Deuteronomy – the place which God has appointed as the place for sacrifice and worship. At this place the tribes of Israel would meet to worship God. This was the formal expression of their covenant love and loyalty to Jehovah. This was an acknowledgment that they belonged to him and that he ruled over them. Jehovah declared his sovereignty over his people by determining how, when and where they were to worship. Moses explained the significance of this in his second covenant-renewal sermon, particularly in chapters 12 to 16.

These chapters are a practical and detailed exposition of the first and second commandments, for in them Moses told the people whom they were to worship (Jehovah alone) and how they were to worship him (as he has commanded them in his word). The underlying principle is summarized in 12:32: *'See that you do all I command you; do not add to it or take away from it.'* The purity of Israel's corporate worship was important because it stood at the heart of the covenant relationship between God and Israel and because it declared God's holiness to the nations. This principle is sometimes called the regulative principle of worship and it is just as relevant to the life of the New Testament church as it was to the redeemed community in the Old Testament (see

John 4:24; Col. 2:20-23; Mark 7:6-8). Our worship is an act of obedience in response to God's grace, and not (as is commonly assumed today) an act of self-expression serving our personal happiness.

The regulations of Deuteronomy 12 are built upon the pre-existing 'altar law' of Exodus 20:24-6. 'Make an altar of earth for me and sacrifice on it your burnt offerings and fellowship offerings, your sheep and goats and your cattle. Wherever I cause my name to be honoured, I will come to you and bless you.' The location of this altar was not specified beyond the fact that it would be 'wherever I cause my name to be honoured ...' As the Israelites were nomads at that time, their sanctuary and their altar would move from place to place. However it was very important to regulate their mode of worship as, even in the desert, there were many temptations to adopt the idolatrous practices of their neighbours.

In Leviticus 17:1-7, Moses specifically addressed the challenges of the wilderness. 'Any Israelite who sacrifices an ox, a lamb or a goat in the camp or outside of it instead of bringing it to the entrance to the Tent of Meeting to present it as an offering to the LORD ... – that man shall be considered guilty of bloodshed; he ... must be cut off from his people.' This regulation was designed to prevent offerings being made to the 'goat idols' worshipped by the nomadic tribes who lived in the desert. Moreover, no animal was ever to be slaughtered away from the tabernacle – not even those they would eat for food. This 'lasting ordinance' was both applied and relaxed by Moses in Deuteronomy 12. The core principle that only Jehovah is to be worshipped and that sacrifices are to be offered to him only at the place he would choose is restated (see 12:5). Yet the requirement that animals can be slaughtered for food only at the altar was relaxed (see 12:15).

The relationship between Deuteronomy 12 and other Old Testament passages has generated many theories about the origins of Deuteronomy and the five books of Moses. Higher critical scholars have argued that the altar law of Deuteronomy 12 evolved many years after the time of Moses, in response to the growing disillusionment with Israel's local sanctuaries and the nation's repeated lapses into idolatry and the growing belief that the only way to avoid a total collapse into the worship of Baal was the establishment of one central sanctuary in Jerusalem. Some have argued that this ideal was nurtured under the preaching of the eighth-century prophets or in the late seventh century, leading to the reforms of King Josiah. These theories abound with historical and theological problems; not least their outright denial of Deuteronomy's claim that it was the work of Moses and is the record of his preaching on the plains of Moab just before the Israelites entered the land of Canaan. Those who accept Deuteronomy as the inspired and infallible word of God receive it as God's message delivered through his servant Moses. Let us hear what he has to say about the Sovereign Lord of Israel and the worship of his people.

God's worship must be kept pure (12:1-14)

The opening words of this chapter introduce us to a very significant portion of Deuteronomy. Chapters 12-26 are often called the law code of Deuteronomy. In these chapters Moses gave an exposition of some of the civil and ceremonial regulations which God had given to Israel at Mount Sinai. After four decades to reflect upon the significance of these laws, Moses expounded them at a great covenant-renewal ceremony on the plains of Moab, just before the Israelites moved to take possession of the land of Canaan. He examined the spirit as well as the letter of the law and applied the commandments to heart and life. He stressed the fact that God's good gifts to them call forth willing obedience from his people. In words reminiscent of 6:1-2, Moses introduces this detailed exposition of the law with a reminder of God's promise. *These are the decrees and laws*

*you must be careful to follow in the land that the LORD, the God
of your fathers has given you to possess – as long as you live in the
land.'* The gift of the land is still in the future, but it is described
in a past tense (a prophetic perfect) because the land is as good
as theirs. They are to rejoice in God's goodness and to follow
his commands carefully.

Moses moved from the general principle to its application.
In a sinful world God's people will be tempted to introduce
into their worship practices which are 'culturally relevant' but
offensive to a holy God. Moses made three applications of this
principle in 12:1-14.

i. He applied the principle negatively (12:2-3)

> *Destroy completely all the places on the high mountains and
> on the hills and under every spreading tree where the nations
> you are dispossessing worship their gods. Break down their
> altars, smash their sacred stones and burn their Asherah
> poles in the fire; cut down the idols of their gods and wipe
> out their names from those places.*

In these verses, Moses had his sights set firmly on Canaanite
worship and on the paraphernalia of paganism which the
Israelites would find in the land of Canaan. Typically, the
Canaanites worshipped their gods on hilltop shrines because
they believed that these places offered better access to their
gods. Luxuriant trees, with their fresh green foliage, were
symbols of fertility, and the shady places under their branches
were thought to be appropriate locations to worship the
fertility gods (see 2 Kings 17:10; Jer. 2:20; 3:6). At these places
the Canaanites built altars for sacrifice and set up stones to
indicate their sacred significance. Asherah was the goddess of
fortune or blessing and sacred trees were often dedicated to
her honour. At these groves her devotees called upon her name
and the name of her consort, Baal.

God's chosen place

Not only were the Israelites to avoid these pagan rituals, they were to remove every trace of them from the land where they would live. They were to be ruthless in their purge of the land. Note again what they were to do, 'Destroy... break down... smash... burn... cut down... and wipe out their names.' They were to do these things because they were taking possession of the land and subduing it to the Lord. They themselves were to be God's precious inheritance, a people holy to the Lord (see 7:5-6). Not only were these Canaanite rituals a denial of God's holiness, they were also a constant danger to his people.

For these same reasons, Christians today are to keep their homes and their church buildings free from idols (see 1 Cor. 10:14; 1 John 5:21). Whether they are so-called images of our Lord or images of the false gods of other religions, they can only present a demeaning and deceptive picture of the true and living God, and we ought not to participate in the religious rituals of false religions. The Apostle Paul warned the Christians in Corinth, newly converted from paganism, 'you cannot drink the cup of the Lord and the cup of demons too; you cannot have a part in both the Lord's table and the table of demons' (1 Cor. 10:21). As never before, Christians are exposed to the rituals of false religion – Islam, Buddhism and corrupted versions of Christianity. We are encouraged to engage in multi-faith worship as a path towards mutual understanding and world peace; but this chapter reminds us that our first priority is to give God his place of honour above all. It is an insult to the Lord God to call upon him as merely one of a pantheon of deities, for he is the only God and the only Saviour; and only his Son can bring peace to the world when the nations submit to him. False religions simply expose their devotees to the power of Satan, who uses their rituals to lure men and women away from the only true God and Saviour of our souls.

ii. He applied the principle positively (12:4-7)
In these verses Moses described how the Israelites ought to worship. *'You must not worship the LORD your God in their way.'* Having rejected the shrines and the rituals of the Canaanites, they were to do three things.

a. They were to *seek* the place that God had appointed (12:5). *'But you are to seek the place the LORD your God will choose from among all your tribes to put his Name there for his dwelling. To that place you must go.'* The location of this chosen place, and how the Israelites were to seek it, are questions which have puzzled students of Deuteronomy over the years. The most natural understanding of 12:5 is that there was to be one central sanctuary in Israel and that God would make its location clear eventually. More recent commentators have suggested that Moses intended to leave open the possibility that God might choose many places as a dwelling for his name, perhaps one in each tribal territory, or perhaps one that shifted from place to place. In the centuries which followed the conquest of Canaan, the Israelites gathered in many different places to worship God.

When the Israelites entered the land of Canaan, the first place at which they established an altar was Shechem. This is the town which lay between Mount Ebal and Mount Gerizim, and Moses had directed the Israelites to gather at this spot to give thanks to God for his covenant mercies (see 11:29-30; also 27:4-8; Josh. 8:30-35). At Shechem the ark of the covenant was placed in the valley between the two mountains, in the midst of the people, as a symbol of God's name dwelling amongst them (Josh. 8:33). Although Shechem remained a gathering place for the people of Israel (see Josh. 24:1; 1 Kings 12:1), the ark did not remain there, and it did not become established as the place God had chosen as the dwelling for his name. Later, the ark was based at Bethel and the Israelites went there to seek the Lord (see Judges 20:26-28). Then, towards the end of the period of the judges, the ark was at Shiloh (see 1 Sam. 1:3) and the Israelites gathered there for their major festivals (see 1 Sam. 1:3; also Josh. 18:1). It is difficult to know how widely (or officially) these and other locations were accepted as centres for the true worship of Jehovah.

From Shiloh the ark was taken into battle against the Philistines (see 1 Sam. 4:4), where it was captured and taken to the Philistine cities of Ashdod and Ekron. When the Philistines returned the ark to Israel, it was looked after by the men of Kiriath Jearim (1 Sam. 7:1-2) until David brought it up to his newly captured capital city of Jerusalem (2 Sam. 6:2-15) and kept it in a tent (2 Sam. 6:17). David felt very embarrassed that he should live in a beautiful palace while the ark of the covenant was still kept in a tent (2 Sam. 7:1-2); but this was the situation which prevailed until Solomon built the temple (see 2 Chr. 3:1). At the dedication of the temple in 2 Chronicles 6:3-6, Solomon described the events of that day as the fulfilment of God's promise in Deuteronomy 12:5. 'Since the day I brought my people Israel out of Egypt, I have not chosen a city in any tribe of Israel to have a temple built for my Name to be there... But now I have chosen Jerusalem for my Name to be there.'

With the erection of Solomon's temple, the period of seeking and making do with mobile and temporary sanctuaries was over; but the point to notice is that the prerogative of choosing the location belonged to God (see 2 Chr. 7:11-12; Ps. 132:13-14). He is Lord over every detail of his people's worship. He will choose the places which will be associated with his name and his presence, because the conduct of his people at these places will affect how he is regarded amongst the nations. The pagan nations surrounding Israel could not see Jehovah himself, but they did see Israel and her worship. When the Israelites entered into God's presence and called upon his name they enjoyed a great privilege, but they also carried an awesome responsibility. Sadly, they often presented a poor reflection of God's excellence to the world. For that reason, God regulated very carefully their corporate rituals of worship.

b. They were to *bring* their offerings to the place that God had appointed (12:6). *'There bring your burnt offerings and sacrifices, your tithes and special gifts, what you have vowed to give and your freewill offerings, and the firstborn of your herds and flocks.'* The central sanctuary was the place appointed by God for sacrificial worship. The Israelites were free to pray and praise God in their homes and villages throughout the promised land, but they were to present their sacrifices and offerings at one specified place. Moses lists the kinds of offerings which they were to bring to God's appointed place. 'Burnt offerings' were wholly consumed in the fire on the altar (Lev. 1:3-9), and indicated the worshipper's total consecration to God. The 'sacrifices' were a symbolic meal at which the flesh of the animal was eaten by the worshipper, while the fat and blood were burnt on the altar. As the smoke from the altar ascended to God it symbolized the fellowship which existed between God and the worshipper. The 'tithes' were the tenth of a person's income which belonged to God and indicated God's lordship over all his substance. The 'special gifts', 'what you have vowed' and the 'freewill offerings' were voluntary offerings which were offered as a spontaneous response to God's many blessings upon them. After they had gathered the harvest or looked back on some act of deliverance from danger, their hearts were filled with gratitude and they freely expressed that gratitude by bringing offerings to the Lord. These were public ways of expressing private thankfulness.

The *'firstborn of your flocks and herds'* were also to be were killed and eaten each year at the chosen place (see 15:19-23). These were not voluntary offerings, but they were reminders of how God had saved them. Since the night of the exodus every firstborn child in an Israelite family or from their livestock was consecrated to Jehovah (see Exodus 13:2, 12). This was because their firstborn had been spared while the angel of death went into all the homes of the Egyptians. By a simple act of consecration the Israelites were reminded that they owed their very lives to the covenant Lord. The firstborn of their children were to be redeemed by the consecration of the Levites and by the payment of a sum of money (see Exod.13:13; Num. 3:40-48), but the firstborn of their livestock were to be killed and eaten at the chosen place.

The important thing to note about this chosen place is that it was a place of sacrifice. God's name dwelt at an altar where atonement was made for the sins of his people. There the Israelites were to go in order that they might enter God's presence and meet with him. Today we have no such altar, but we meet with God at Calvary, where the sins of God's people in every age were taken away by Jesus Christ, the Lamb of God.

c. They were to *rejoice* at the place which God had appointed (12:7). Far from being gloomy rituals, Israel's gatherings at the chosen place were to take on the character of a family festival. *'There, in the presence of the LORD your God, you and your families shall eat and shall rejoice in everything you have put your hand to, because the LORD your God has blessed you.'* Moses told the Israelites that they would rejoice because God had blessed the work of their hands. Subduing the promised land would be hard work. The Hebrew phrase which Moses used to describe their labour ('the sending forth of your hand') implies strenuous exertion. Without God's blessing, all our labour will be fruitless (Ps. 127:1); but those who serve him do not labour in vain (Ps. 90:17, 1 Cor. 15:58).

The greatest blessing enjoyed by the Israelites was, however, the enjoyment of God's presence. The gift of the land and the material blessings which flowed from it were earthly tokens of the eternal covenant and its spiritual blessings, chief of which was fellowship with the living God. At the chosen place, the Israelites would enjoy a special measure of God's presence, for God promises to draw near to those who make use of his appointed means of grace. Today there are no 'holy places' for God's people. However, God has appointed means of grace such as prayer, the ministry of the word and the sacraments. Christians who neglect these ordinances are also neglecting the presence of God and will lose much blessing. Only in the presence of God will we have fullness of joy. By the use of God's appointed means, David was able to say,

> You have made known to me the path of life;
> you will fill me with joy in your presence,
> with eternal pleasures at your right hand.
> (Ps. 16:11)

iii. He applied the principle to the current practices of the Israelites (12:8-14)

In these verses Moses restated the principle stated in 12:5-7, this time in anticipation of the day when the Israelites would enter the promised land. *'You are not to do as we do here today, everyone as he sees fit, since you have not yet reached the resting place and the inheritance the LORD your God is giving you.'* Moses would not live to see that day, for he would die in the land of Moab and Joshua would lead the Israelites into the land. Addressing the Israelites, he said, *'But you will cross the Jordan and settle in the land the LORD your God is giving you as an inheritance, and he will give you rest from all your enemies around you so that you will live in safety.'* The rest which Moses set before the Israelites was an end to their wearisome journey through the wilderness and the security of a homeland of their own. During their years of wandering in the wilderness they were always vulnerable to the attacks of their enemies; but that would soon come to an end when Joshua led them into Canaan (see Josh 21:44; 22:4; 23:1). When they entered that rest, they were to seek God's chosen place and there offer their sacrifices to the Lord (see 12:11); and when they came they were to rejoice in the presence of the Lord (see 12:12). The beauty and bounty of the land would give them every reason to rejoice in the goodness of the Lord to them.

God's chosen place

With this foretaste of future blessing, in 12:8-9 Moses gave notice that the current worship practices of the Israelites would no longer be tolerated. During their years in the wilderness, the Israelites set up altars wherever they saw fit in or around the places where they camped. No doubt their nomadic existence meant that they had built many altars in many different locations over the years. God had accepted this as a necessary consequence of their wilderness lifestyle. However, it exposed the Israelites to the temptation to make use of the cultic sites and religious traditions of the desert tribes around them, which inevitably led them into superstition and idolatry. Once they settled in the land of Canaan there would be no reason to relax the altar law and every reason to enforce it. This is what Moses made clear in 12:13-14. *'Be careful not to sacrifice your burnt offerings anywhere you please. Offer them only at the place the LORD will choose in one of your tribes, and there observe everything I command you.'*

Here we see two sides to Jehovah's dealings with his people. On the one hand, we see his gentleness with his erring people. God has no desire to make his commands burdensome for his people. He understands the challenges they face and accommodates his expectations accordingly. In Acts 17:30 Paul describes how God was willing to overlook the sins of heathen nations because they were committed in ignorance. There will, however, come a day when everyone will have to give an account for their actions, and those who persist in their sinful actions will be punished. The other lesson we learn about God is that he is deeply committed to the holiness of his people and their worship. When he has made provision for the spiritual needs of his people – as he did for Israel at the central sanctuary – he expects them to take it. To us God has given prayer and the preaching of his word as means of grace so that we might be strengthened in the faith. Let us take hold of them so that we may serve and obey him.

God's treasured possession

God's laws are not an arbitrary burden (12:15-28)

The regulations expounded in this section may, when we first read them, seem strange and even repulsive. If you do not like the sight of blood, take care, for these verses contain 'slaughterhouse regulations'. They describe where, when and how the Israelites might kill animals for food.

In 12:15 Moses made an important concession to the law forbidding the slaughter of animals away from the altar. *'Nevertheless, you may slaughter your animals in any of your towns and eat as much of the meat as you want, as if it were gazelle or deer, according to the blessing the LORD your God gives you.'* To appreciate the significance of this law we need to remember two things. The first is that during the wilderness years, domestic animals like cattle and sheep could only be killed at the tabernacle (see Lev. 17:3-4). This was intended to prevent the Israelites from offering sacrifices to goat idols at desert shrines (see Lev. 17:7a). The Hebrew verb *zabah* in Leviticus 17:3 and Deuteronomy 12:15 described both the slaughter of an animal for sacrifice and the slaughter of an animal for food, and so animals slaughtered for food were also slaughtered at the tabernacle. The second thing we need to remember is that at that time the Israelites lived in a single camp and in close proximity to the tabernacle. That would no longer be the case when the Israelites settled in the land of Canaan.

After relaxing the law regulating slaughter in 12:15, Moses explained the underlying reasons in 12:20-25. *'When the LORD your God has enlarged your territory as he promised you, and you crave meat and say, "I would like some meat," then you may eat as much of it as you want.'* God planned to give the whole land of Canaan to his people so that they might enjoy his abundant provision for all their needs. He wanted them to enjoy the produce of their flocks and herds, even though they might live many miles from the appointed sanctuary (12:21). *'If the place*

God's chosen place

where the LORD your God chooses to put his Name is too far away from you, you may slaughter animals from the herds and flocks the LORD has given you, as I have commanded you, and in your own towns you may eat as much of them as you want.' They were allowed to kill their cattle and sheep for food, just as they had been permitted to hunt wild birds and animals in the desert. *'Eat them as you would gazelle or deer'* (12:22; see also Lev. 17:13).

These regulations are a further illustration of the principle that God knows and understands the realities of our lives and frames his laws in the best interests of his people. Israel's laws were an expression of God's holiness, but they were also an expression of God's generosity and in them God sought what was best for his people. It is important to realise that God's laws are not arbitrary. They do not arise out of a mean spirit, nor do they burden us with the petty rules which Paul described in Colossians 2:21: 'Do not handle! Do not taste! Do not touch!' God does not delight in withholding good things from his people, but in bestowing them. When Satan tempted Eve in Genesis 3:1-5, he wanted her to think that God's command not to eat from the tree of the knowledge of good and evil was a burdensome restriction on her freedom. God's commands, however, are not burdensome (see 1 John 5:3). They seek our holiness and our eternal joy.

Moses summarized the regulations of this chapter in 12:26-27, and set out their goal in 12:28. *'Be careful to obey all these regulations I am giving you, so that it may always go well with you and your children after you, because you will be doing what is good and right in the eyes of the LORD your God.'* Holiness and happiness are inextricably linked together in God's plan for his people. Our holiness brings God honour and pleasure. It also brings joy and blessing to us. Holiness places us on the path that leads on to even more of God's blessing.

God's treasured possession

Having emphasized that God's laws were not intended to be a burden upon Israel, Moses drew their attention to two areas where God did not relax the regulations concerning slaughter and sacrifice. Even here God's laws brought blessing to his people.

i. The Israelites were not to eat the blood of the animals which they killed in their towns (12:16)
'But you must not eat the blood; pour it out on the ground like water.' This prohibition is explained in verses 23-25 with reference to the law of Leviticus 17:11. *'But be sure you do not eat the blood, because the blood is the life, and you must not eat the life with the meat. You must not eat the blood; pour it out on the ground like water.'* Meat was God's provision for the physical needs of mankind (see Gen. 9:3). The blood, however, represented the life of the animal, and this belonged to God. God has given the gift of life to every living creature, and his ownership of every creature is recognised in the ritual of pouring out its blood. This ritual taught the Israelites that God gives life to all his creatures and their lives are precious to him (see Matt. 10:29).

The pouring of the blood upon the ground prevented it from being used for religious purposes in the local pagan sanctuaries. Blood was sometimes eaten at these shrines as part of a sacred meal; or it might have been offered on an altar to appease the wrath of the false gods. In God's plan of salvation, the shedding of blood represented the laying down of the life of a substitute so that a condemned sinner might live. The only sacrifice that could successfully take away the guilt of sinners was one offered according to God's gracious design. It must be offered God's way and at God's chosen place. The Israelites needed to be reminded of this truth often so as to keep their eyes focused on God's promise to provide, in his time and his place, a perfect sacrifice who would satisfy his perfect justice.

ii. The Israelites were not to eat their tithes and other offerings in their towns (12:17-19)
The prohibition is stated in 12:17 and then in 12:18 Moses states God's purpose underlying the law.

> *Instead, you are to eat them in the presence of the LORD your God at the place the LORD your God will choose—you, your sons and daughters, your menservants and maidservants, and the Levites from your towns—and you are to rejoice before the LORD your God in everything you put your hand to.*

Moses will have more to say about this in 14:22-29 and 26:1-15 when he describes the occasions when Israelite families would gather to celebrate before the Lord. As well as being a means of grace for all God's people, these feasts made regular material provision for the Levites, who were guaranteed a seat at the feast (see 12:12). The Levites received no allocation of land in Canaan, but were to be supported by the generosity of the other tribes when they brought their tithes and freewill offerings to God at the central sanctuary. Because of their neediness, Moses had a particular concern for the Levites, and repeatedly reminded the Israelites to take care of them. *'Be careful not to neglect the Levites as long as you live in your land'* (12:19). If the Israelites feasted on their tithe offerings at home, the Levites who ministered at the sanctuary or in their own settlements might well miss out and go hungry.

The implications of these verses stretch far beyond the challenge to give a tithe of our personal income to the Lord's work. They challenge us to develop and maintain a charitable disposition towards the needy and vulnerable people in our communities. In particular, we are to be alert to the needs of our fellow Christians (see Gal. 6:10). The challenge here is a corporate, as well as an individual, one. The church is to be a channel of practical goodness to those in need. This ministry of mercy is not left to the initiative of individuals, for the Lord Jesus has appointed elders and deacons to receive the tithes and offerings of God's people and disburse them to those in need (see Acts 6:1-6; 5:2; 11:30).

God's rivals will not be tolerated (12:29-32)

This chapter concludes as it commenced with strong words to describe God's revulsion at the idolatry of the Canaanites. Their rituals were *'detestable things the LORD hates"* In 12:29 Moses describes what the Lord will do. *'The LORD your God will cut off before you the nations you are about to invade and dispossess.'* Then in 12:20 he describes what Israel must do. *'And after they have been destroyed before you, be careful not to be ensnared by inquiring about their gods, saying, "How do these nations serve their gods? We will do the same."'*

In some situations curiosity is a good thing. It leads to enquiry, exploration and discovery. There are, however, other situations in which curiosity can be positively dangerous. It is said that 'curiosity killed the cat'. When the Israelites entered the land of Canaan, curiosity about the religion of the Canaanites would prove to be the first step towards imitation. This was because the Israelites had no experience of living a settled agricultural life. For two generations they had been nomadic shepherds; but now they would have to learn how to cultivate the hills and valleys of Canaan. Who better to learn from than the Canaanites? If it were simply a matter of learning how to sow grain or tend grapevines, that would have not have been a problem. The problem was that the false religion of the Canaanites had an enormous influence on the way they farmed the land. Their gods, Baal and Ashtoreth, were fertility gods. They prayed to them to make the land fruitful; and when they gathered the harvest they gave them the credit. The temptation for the Israelites was to imagine that, if these rituals 'worked' for the previous inhabitants of the land, they might 'work' for them. Especially when drought or famine threatened, and it seemed that Jehovah had forgotten them, they would desperately turn back to the old religion for help.

This warning against curiosity about the false religions of Canaan does not mean that Christians today ought never to study false teaching or false religion in the world around us. There may well be times when we are required to do this in order to provide a reasoned apologetic for the gospel. In fact, it is often necessary for missionaries to understand the culture and religion of the people amongst whom they work. When Don Richardson went to work amongst the Sawi people of New Guinea, he found that they instinctively admired Judas' cunning rather than the righteousness of Jesus. This proved to be a real obstacle to reaching them with the gospel, until he discovered their concept of a 'peace child' given by one warring family to another to bring about reconciliation. In this case, false religion was studied with the goal of finding an entrance for the gospel rather than adopting or imitating it, and the latter was what Moses warned against.

The curiosity of 12:30 was a fascination with false religion that nurtured admiration for its claims or teachings. This kind of fascination leads many people today, especially in the secular western world, to explore eastern religions because they seem to offer an inner peace or an alternative to the materialism of the modern age. If only such people could see the true nature of these false faiths, resting as they do on gods that do not exist. In 12:31 Moses solemnly warned the Israelites against turning to the religious alternatives of their day. *'You must not worship the LORD your God in their way, because in worshiping their gods, they do all kinds of detestable things the LORD hates.'* 'Detestable' is a recurring word in Moses' preaching. It expresses a strong visceral revulsion and describes God's attitude towards idols (7:25), those who lead a city astray (13:14), offering defective animals (17:1), witchcraft (18:12), and remarrying a divorced wife (24:4). Here it describes the fertility rituals of the Canaanites.

Why was Moses so 'narrow-minded' when it came to pagan religion? One reason is that Canaanite religion was a particularly gross form of idolatry. Moses spoke as though God's revulsion really needed no explanation or justification. *They even burn their sons and daughters to their gods'* (see also 18:9-10a). Nothing could be more unnatural to any parent. If we as human parents recoil at the thought, how much more must our heavenly Father have grieved at the suffering of these little ones.

However, even if the paganism of the Canaanites had been more sophisticated and shorn of its primitive brutality, it would have been no less offensive to Jehovah, because he is a jealous God who will tolerate no rivals. All the laws of this chapter are really an application of the first commandment: 'You shall have no other gods before me'. God demands total and exclusive loyalty and his people are to love him with all their heart, soul and strength (6:5). Pure worship will always be the first priority and greatest pleasure of those redeemed by grace. However, it is not any kind of worship that will suffice, for we will want to give the God who has redeemed us, through the death of his own Son, the worship that he has commanded in his word. *'See that you do all I command you; do not add to it or take away from it.'*

Chapter 13
The danger within

Please read Deuteronomy 13: 1-18

Moses was keenly aware of the threat which Canaanite worship posed to the spiritual health of the people of Israel. Jehovah tolerates no rivals, so in chapter 12 Moses instructed the Israelites to have nothing to do with the sacred sites or religious rituals of Canaan. To keep them free of these he also told them to seek out the site which Jehovah would choose as the dwelling-place for his name. There they would worship their covenant Lord, just as he had commanded them. 'See that you do all I command you; do not add to it or take away from it.'

In the Hebrew Bible these words are the first verse of chapter 13 (rather than the last verse of chapter 12) and they lead on to a fresh warning about the dangers posed by the Canaanite idolatry all around them. When the Israelites entered the land of Canaan, they would find themselves in a spiritual battlezone and they would need to have their wits about them. Moses did not urge them to back off from the challenge; but he prepared them to face it. The temptation to worship false gods, as well as coming from the nations which dwelt in Canaan, would also, sadly, come from within their own ranks. In this chapter Moses gives three examples of how Canaanite religion might infiltrate the Old Testament church and taught his hearers how to respond to these dangers.

These are challenges which we face today. We are called to live in the world, yet we are to remain distinct from the world. In his great high priestly prayer in John 17, our Lord very deliberately did not pray that his disciples would be taken out of the world, but he did pray that they would be protected from the evil one (see John 17:11, 15). He called his followers to be salt and light in the world (Matt. 5:13-14) so that they might make disciples of the nations (Matt. 28:19). Paul exhorted the Romans not to conform to the pattern of this world, but to be transformed by the renewing of their minds (Rom. 12:2).

This positive involvement in a fallen world presents us with many challenges. We must live alongside fallen people and will, like Lot, often find ourselves grieved and offended by their sin (2 Peter 2:7). We must try to understand the thinking of fallen people so that we can win them for Christ (2 Cor. 10:3-5). John Stott has described this as 'double listening'. On the one hand, 'We listen to the world with critical alertness, anxious to understand it... and resolved ... to discover how the gospel relates to it.' On the other hand, 'We listen to the Word with humble reverence, anxious to understand it, and resolved to believe and obey what we come to understand' (*The Contemporary Christian*, Leicester: IVP, 1992, p.28). The result is 'a vigorous nonconformity' which clearly distinguishes the church from the world and empowers her for witness.

In Chapter 13 Moses describes how the Israelites were to be vigorous nonconformists when they entered the land of Canaan. The word of God was to be their guide and they were to show reverence for every command that God had given them through his servant Moses. That was what Moses taught in 12:32. In Revelation 22:18-19 John echoed those words in the closing verses of the New Testament.

I warn everyone who hears the words of the prophecy of this book: If anyone adds anything to them, God will add to him the plagues described in this book. And if anyone takes words away from this book of prophecy, God will take away from him his share in the tree of life and in the holy city, which are described in this book.

One of the recurring themes of Deuteronomy is the curse that God will bring upon those who add to or take away from God's commands. Here in Revelation it falls upon those who tamper with God's Word.

Israel's vigorous nonconformity would also lead them to reject false teaching even when it came from within the community of God's people. They would need to develop the discernment which enabled them to recognise temptation even when it came from an unexpected angle. Moses describes three examples of how idolatry might infiltrate the people of Israel in unexpected and alarming ways.

A false prophet (13:1-5)

Prophets had an important ministry in Israel, as we will see in 18:14-22, where they are described as God's spokesmen to his people. Sometimes they received their message by means of a dream (Num. 12:6), though Jeremiah described some prophets whose dreams are only lies (Jer. 23:25-32). Sometimes prophets would reinforce their message with miraculous signs (see Exod. 4:1-9; 7:10-23; 1 Kings 17:22-24). False prophets were to be identified by their inability to perform wonders or foretell events (see 18:21-22). Because of this it might have been assumed that anyone who was able to foretell events or perform miracles was a true prophet of the Lord and ought to be heeded, but that was not the case (see Exod. 7:11-12a; 2 Thess. 2:9).

God did allow prophets like this to arise amongst his own people (see 13:1-2), but the Israelites were warned not to heed their message. *'You must not listen to the words of that prophet or dreamer.'* Moses described God's purpose in allowing such a prophet to preach in 13:3b. *'The LORD your God is testing you to find out whether you love him with all your heart and with all your soul.'* We are taught to pray that God would not lead us into temptation, but there are times when God permits us to be tempted, just as Jesus was tempted. At such times we know that God provides us with the strength to overcome temptation and a way of escape from the temptation (1 Cor. 10:13). We also know that God has a good and loving purpose in his dealings with us, just as he had in this instance when he allowed the Israelites to be tested by false prophets. God wanted to know whether they had the kind of devotion which Moses described in 6:4-5. This was the Israelites' confession of faith, but it was possible to say these wonderful words without really loving God whole-heartedly. Only testing in fires of temptation would show the purity of Israel's love for God. Martin Luther recognized that prayer and temptation forged the character of a minister of the gospel, because temptation drives us back to God in repentance, resolving to rely upon his strength.

Israel's testing would drive her back to her covenant Lord so that she might serve him faithfully. This is what Moses highlighted in 13:4. *'It is the LORD your God you must follow, and him you must revere. Keep his commands and obey him; serve him and hold fast to him.'* (See also 10:12-13.) Each of these five commands focuses on Jehovah, the object and centre of Israel's faith. He was Israel's life-giver and Redeemer, and it was the task of the prophets to point the people to him. The Israelites were to be instructed in the law of God (6:6-9; 11:18-20) so that they might become 'a wise and understanding people' (4:6), a people who held fast to him. That is why it was so important that the prophets were trustworthy men who preached the truth about God and who called the Israelites to serve him. The prophets described in these verses were men who *'preached rebellion against the LORD your God who brought you out of Egypt and redeemed you from the land of slavery'* (13:5). Not only did this dishonour Israel's Redeemer; it exposed the Israelites to danger. Our Lord warned that those who follow 'blind guides' will, like them, 'fall into a pit' (Matt. 15:14).

This grave danger explains why a false prophet was to be put to death when he was found to be preaching rebellion against the Lord. *'That prophet or dreamer must be put to death... he has tried to turn you from the way the LORD your God commanded you to follow. You must purge the evil from among you.'* That is what Jehoshaphat did when he purged the Asherah poles from Judah (2 Chr. 19:3). The action is an intense and urgent one because idolatry is a dangerous evil which bears bitter fruit.

The great need of the church today is still God-centred preaching of God's word. While the church today does not have the power to put to death those who preach false doctrine there is still a pressing need to cultivate discernment and to 'test the spirits to see whether they are from God, because many false prophets have gone out into the world' (1 John 4:1). We are to test the sermons we hear, the books we read, the websites we visit and the churches we attend against the standard of God's word. This often means looking beyond how things appear on the surface. All too often preaching and preachers are tested by superficial criteria such as presentational skills and the size of the congregations they gather. In their promotional material, popular preachers will be described as 'gifted communicators' or 'inspirational speakers'. In reality, we ought to be seeking men who are faithful interpreters of Scripture and who are able to speak to the conscience about the sins of our age as well as the ever-relevant message of God's mercies. We are to discern sound preaching and teaching by the content of the message preached (Acts 17:11; 1 Cor. 12:3). The prophet Isaiah warned, 'To the law and the testimony! If they do not speak according to this word, they have no light of dawn' (Isa. 8:20).

Not only must the church test and approve those who are permitted to preach in her pulpits, but the church itself is being tested as it makes these decisions. Just as God tested the Israelites by permitting false prophets to arise in their midst, so he tests the church by allowing false teachers to arise today. Will anyone notice? Will anyone be concerned enough for the integrity of the truth to act? God has no delight in self-righteous, self-appointed, hypercritical heresy hunters; but he does want his people to speak the truth in love so that the church will not be 'blown here and there by every wind of teaching' (Eph. 4:14-15).

A family member (13: 6-11)

This is an especially shocking passage because it describes the effects of apostasy in the family and amongst close friends. Moses described what might happen if one family member secretly enticed another to join with them in idolatry (13:6-7). *'If your very own brother, or your son or daughter, or the wife you love, or your closest friend secretly entices you, saying, "Let us go and worship other gods"...'* Only family members would know that this has taken place, because it took place in the family home. We know that this kind of thing really happened because in Joshua 24:14-15 Joshua urged the Israelites to get rid of the idols that remained amongst them from their days in Egypt as well as the new gods of the Amorites. He declared that he and his family would set an example of undivided loyalty to the Lord. Could it be that Joshua had found it necessary to take firm action against sin in his own household?

The implications of this kind of secret temptation within an Israelite family were serious indeed. The faith of Israel was passed from one generation to the next within families. The bonds of affection and companionship within the family created the trust which enabled the children to accept whole-heartedly what their parents taught them. The family circle might also be widened to admit trusted companions ('your closest friend'; literally 'the neighbour who is as your very soul') who, although not kinsmen, were able to influence the household. When such a friend embraces destructive heresy, the potential for disaster is obvious. Instead of passing on the truth and pointing others to Jehovah, this family member experiments with false religion and entices others to worship unknown gods.

Moses described them in 13:6b-7 as *'gods that neither you nor your fathers have known, gods of the peoples around you, whether near or far, from one end of the land to the other'.* The novelty of these false gods is what made them suspect. The force of this argument is hard for many people today to appreciate as we instinctively assume that anything old must be primitive and in need of replacing, while anything new must be better. Moses argued that Jehovah was to be trusted because he had shown his trustworthiness over many years, while these new gods were untested and therefore untrustworthy. Only Jehovah could be called 'the eternal God' (33:26-27).

The proper response to a family member who incites another to join him in the worship of false gods is described in 13:8-10. *'Do not yield to him or listen to him...'* Obviously the Israelites were not to join in his idolatry, or even to listen to him, but Moses' words here urge an even more resolute response. *'Show him no pity. Do not spare him or shield him.'* This family member was not to be protected from the due process of law.

Even in ancient times there was a legal system in Israel (see 1:9-18; also Exod. 18:17-26), and Moses did not leave the application and enforcement of the first and second commandments to individuals to act as they saw fit. Anyone accused of 'doing evil in the eyes of the Lord' was to have the charge against him properly investigated and established by the testimony of two or three witnesses (17:2-6). In order to deter frivolous testimony, these witnesses were required to be among the first to stone the offender to death (17:7). That law explains the requirement of 13:9. *You must certainly put him to death. Your hand must be the first in putting him to death, and then the hands of all the people.'* In 13:10-11 Moses explained why the penalty was so serious. *'Stone him to death, because he tried to turn you away from the LORD your God, who brought you out of Egypt, out of the land of slavery. Then all Israel will hear and be afraid, and no-one among you will do such an evil thing again.'* To turn an Israelite from serving the living God to serving idols was to turn him away from life to death. It was like leading him back into slavery in Egypt, undoing God's work of redemption. The severity of the penalty was a warning that sin offers nothing but eternal separation from God, which is death. Those who lead sinners to God do a great work (Prov. 11:30; James 5:20); but those who cause others to stumble are guilty of a most heinous sin.

The New Testament equivalent of this procedure is church discipline, which may lead to excommunication (Matt. 18:15-18; 1 Cor. 5:4-5). The goal of church discipline is to bring a sinner to see the gravity of his sin and to repent. Sadly, this ministry is often frustrated by well-meaning friends and relatives of the offender who criticise church leaders when they administer discipline and shield the sinner from rebuke. It is important it is for church members to learn that they, like the members of an Israelite family, also have an important role to play in the administration of church discipline (2 Thess. 3:14; 1 Cor. 5:11).

A rebel town (13:12-16)

The sin of apostasy, if left unchecked, spreads its influence. In these verses Moses described how those who turned from the living God to worship idols would lead not just individuals and families, but whole towns astray (13:12-13a). *'If you hear it said about one of the towns the LORD your God is giving you to live in that wicked men have arisen among you and have led the people of their town astray...'* The phrase 'wicked men' (literally 'sons of Belial' or 'sons of wickedness') was used in the Old Testament to describe particularly nasty individuals who exercised a malign influence over the community. In Judges 19:22 they were violent sexual predators who raped the Levite's concubine as he lodged in the city of Gibeah. In 1 Samuel 10:27, they were the discontents who refused to honour Saul when he was appointed as king over Israel. In 1 Kings 21:10, they were the false witnesses who, at Jezebel's instigation, connived at the execution of Naboth. Here in Deuteronomy 13:12-13 they lead a whole town into idolatry. *"Let us go and worship other gods" (gods you have not known).'*

Because of the seriousness of this sin, and because of the penalty which it attracted, Moses commanded that a thorough investigation into the matter must be launched (13:14-15). *You must inquire, probe and investigate it thoroughly. And if it is true and it has been proved that this detestable thing has been done among you, you must certainly put to the sword all who live in that town.'* Yet again, we see the justice of God displayed in the actions of his people. Only after a proper investigation establishes that the charge is true can a whole city be put to the sword. The law of Moses gave no encouragement for lynch-mob justice or a witch hunt amongst the Israelites. Due process must be followed, and then an appropriate punishment must be administered.

The punishment stipulated in 13:15-16 was certainly severe. *'You must certainly put to the sword all who live in that town.'* Several comments are necessary by way of explanation. First of all, the penalty was severe because the offence was especially serious both in its nature and its impact on the community. The act of leading a whole city astray is described in 13:14 as a *'detestable thing'.* We have already found this word in 7:25 and 12:31, where it described idolatrous worship, the rituals of which are repulsive in themselves, and which is offensive to God because it is a repudiation of his covenant with Israel. The loss of a whole city in Israel was grievous in God's eyes (see Ezek. 33:11). If we are to appreciate just how much this would have grieved God, we should keep in mind how the Lord Jesus wept over the unbelief of Jerusalem in his own day (Luke 13:34).

A second point to observe is the manner of the city's destruction prescribed in verses 15b-16. *'Destroy it completely, both its people and its livestock. Gather all the plunder of the town into the middle of the public square and completely burn the town and all its plunder as a whole burnt offering to the LORD your God. It is to remain a ruin forever, never to be rebuilt.'* To destroy the city meant 'to devote to God by means of destruction'. The verb that Moses used was *herem,* which was often used to describe the destruction of the Canaanites who had lived in the land (see 2:34; 3:6; 7:2; also Josh. 2:10; 6:17; 7:1; 11:1-2) so that Canaan might be made holy to the Lord. The practice has been described as 'a kind of sacrifice to Jehovah', for even the livestock was to be killed. Thus what had been defiled by idolatry might be cleansed by sacrifice.

To highlight this point, Moses instructed the Israelites to gather all the possessions of the people of the apostate city into the main square so that it might be burnt as 'a whole burnt offering to the LORD your God'. The city was 'to remain a ruin, never to be rebuilt'. This is the same curse as Joshua pronounced over the ruins of Jericho in Joshua 6:24-26. The parallels between the destruction of the Canaanites and the punishment of an apostate city in Israel show how seriously God took the sins of his people. They also show that God's desire was not simply to punish the wicked, but to reclaim the city for himself. His aim was to reassert his lordship over his people and over the land of Israel. Even though a wicked generation might perish under his judgment, those who saw the ruin were warned to turn from their sin and serve the God who delivers those who serve him from sin and death.

Some common features

The three examples of apostasy which Moses describes in these verses may seem very far removed from the temptations which we face. It is, after all, most unlikely that we will be invited to go along to a Canaanite shrine and offer a sacrifice to Baal. We will, however, be tempted to make gods of other things and rob the living God of the honour that is due to him. There are several features of the temptations which faced Israel from which we can learn important lessons about the temptations which we face today.

i. The unexpectedness of the temptation
Temptation may well come from the most surprising of sources. This is what makes it so dangerous. Who would expect such a temptation to come from a respected religious leader, or from a family member in a Christian home? Who would expect a whole community of God's people – a congregation or denomination – to abandon God's word and worship a false god? Sadly, such things can happen. This note of warning is sounded in chapter 25.5 of the *Westminster Confession of Faith* in its statement about the church. 'The purest churches under heaven are subject both to mixture and error; and some have so degenerated as to become no churches of Christ, but synagogues of Satan.' Satan's attacks on the church are bold indeed, and he attacks God's people in unexpected ways. We need to be aware of his schemes (2 Cor. 2:11; 1 Peter 5:8).

ii. The nature of the temptation
The temptations described in these verses play upon the human appetite for something new. The men of Athens in Paul's day 'spent their time doing nothing but talking about and listening to the latest ideas' (Acts 17:21). The people of Israel were enticed to follow other gods and to worship them in violation of the first and second commandments. The particular quality of these gods was that they were 'gods you have not known' (see

13:2, 6, 13; also 11:28; 28:64; 29:26; 32:17). As we have seen, they were untested and therefore unreliable gods, in contrast to the unchanging and trustworthy covenant Lord of Israel. Yet it was their unfamiliarity that made them fascinating to the Israelites when they grew bored with the Lord and with the blessings which he so richly poured upon them. Like the younger brother in Luke 15:12, who grew tired of his father's provision and set off in search of a better life in a faraway country, the Israelites would seek the new and exciting gods of Canaan. This is the fascination which the world holds for Christians even today, especially young people who have grown up in godly homes and who have not yet tasted the bitterness of a life without God. Moses' warnings challenge us to remain with the God whom our fathers have known and loved and to listen to those whose testimony is reliable. 'But as for you, continue in what you have learned and have become convinced of, because you know those from whom you learned it, and how from infancy you have known the holy Scriptures, which are able to make you wise for salvation through faith in Christ Jesus' (2 Tim. 3:14-15).

iii. The response to the temptation
The Israelites were to put to death those who enticed others to idolatry (see 13:5, 9, 15). The stoning of false prophets and execution of whole communities are drastic steps to take, and this makes Deuteronomy 13 one of the most shocking chapters in the Old Testament. By this drastic step the Israelites sought to purge idolatry from their midst and to deter others from falling into this serious sin. They recognised the scale of the danger which they faced. If they forsook the Lord, they would face all the curses of the covenant which have been hinted at in 4:26; 6:14-15; 8:19-20, and which will be set out in detail in 28:15-68. We know that every sin is serious (Rom. 6:23), yet some sins are especially serious because they draw men and women away from a life-giving relationship with God. The *Westminster Shorter Catechism* (answer 83) recognizes this distinction as follows: 'Some sins in themselves, and by reason of several

aggravations, are more heinous in the sight of God than others.'
The Lord Jesus recognised that few sins are more heinous than
those which turn people away from God when he warned those
who cause 'these little ones who believe in me to sin' that 'it
would be better for him to have a large millstone hung around
his neck and to be drowned in the depths of the sea' (Matt. 18:6).

A faithful people (13:17-18)

Moses described a fourth scenario in this sad chapter, but it is a
much happier one than the three which have gone before it. In
these verses he described what would happen when the people
of Israel kept themselves from idols and worshipped God
according to his commands. *'None of those condemned things
shall be found in your hands'* (13:17) refers, in the first instance, to
the plunder devoted to God by means of its destruction (13:16).
It also refers more generally to the evil which God told Israel
to purge from its midst by the stringent measures of 13:14b-16.
As well as commanding the Israelites to forsake idolatry, Moses
commanded them to commit themselves whole-heartedly to
the Lord (13:4); and the rest of 13:17-18 is as much a promise as
a command:

> *...so that the LORD will turn from his fierce anger; he will
> show you mercy, have compassion on you, and increase your
> numbers, as he promised on oath to your forefathers, because
> you obey the LORD your God, keeping all his commands that
> I am giving you today and doing what is right in his eyes.*

God's response to Israel's faithfulness will be twofold. First, he
'will turn from his fierce anger'. This was what Moses sought
in his prayer of Exodus 32:12 when God's anger burned against
the Israelites for worshipping the golden calf. At first, God sent
Moses away from his presence so that he might wipe out the
people, but Moses asked, 'Why should your anger burn against

your people, whom you brought out of Egypt with great power and a mighty hand?' God listened to Moses' prayer and relented.

God's second response is to describe what he will do (13:17b-18). 'He will show you mercy, have compassion on you, and increase your numbers, as he promised on oath to your forefathers, because you obey the LORD your God.' The first word in the Hebrew text of 13:18 is the same as in 13:1, 6 and 13. There it was translated 'if', but here it is translated 'because' (NIV, NKJV) or 'when' (KJV). Just as Moses' warnings in 13:1-16 describe things that could and did happen, so verses 17b-18 hold out a very real prospect of God's blessing upon those who love him and serve him. The warnings are real and the consequences of ignoring them are disastrous; yet God's promises are equally real, and it is these which motivate faithful obedience. These promises are the climax of Moses' preaching in chapters 12-13, where he calls Israel to serve Jehovah alone and to worship him as he had commanded in his word.

It is never possible to tolerate little doses of paganism amongst God's people. Many years later Paul warned, 'Don't you know that a little yeast works through the whole batch of dough? Get rid of the old yeast that you may be a new batch without yeast – as you really are. For Christ our Passover lamb has been slaughtered' (1 Cor. 5:6-7). Christians are those who, like the Thessalonian believers, have 'turned to God from idols to serve the living and true God, and to wait for his Son from heaven, whom he raised from the dead – Jesus, who rescues us from the coming wrath' (1 Thess. 1:9-10). The seriousness with which Moses took the actions of those who turned others from the living God back to idols in Deuteronomy 13 underlines the seriousness of the threat posed by paganism. It also demonstrates the reality of the coming wrath from which we need to be saved (Rom. 1:18-23).

The danger within

Many modern readers find Deuteronomy 13 hard to read with profit. Some even find it offensive and question its place in the Christian Bible. They find it intolerable that God could order such violence. Yet we must read this chapter in the light of the New Testament, where we are taught that different weapons have been given to the church to use in her battle against false doctrine and false gods (2 Cor. 10:4-6). One thing that New Testament Christians must learn from Moses and share with him is his passion for the purity of the people of God. Paul was zealous for the purity of the church in Corinth (see 2 Cor. 11:2). We must never lose sight of the fact that God is passionate about his own glory. He is worthy of total obedience and commitment and idolatry is a denial of that. His just indignation will fall upon individuals, families and nations which will not serve him, but his mercy and blessing will overflow to those who do.

Chapter 14
Eating and drinking to God's glory

Please read Deuteronomy 14: 1-29

In this chapter Moses shows what it meant for the Israelites to be a holy people. The chapter opens with an emphatic affirmation of Israel's status as God's adopted nation. 'Sons you are of the LORD your God' is the arresting word order of the Hebrew text of 14:1. The chapter closes with God's promise that he will bless them in all the work of their hands (see 14:29). Covenantal privileges are combined with covenantal obligations; and into this covenantal context Moses introduces teaching about an assortment of ceremonial laws, most of which have to do with eating. These regulations may seem very far removed from the great truths of the gospel, but here Moses presents them as a visible demonstration of Israel's adoption and sonship.

Sonship is one of the great blessings enjoyed by believers. In the New Testament, the apostle Paul expands upon this theme. He wrote to the Galatians, 'you are all sons of God through faith in Christ Jesus' (Gal. 3:26). To the church in Ephesus he wrote, 'In love he predestined us to be adopted as his sons through Jesus Christ' (Eph. 1:4-5). To the church in Rome he wrote, 'You received the Spirit of sonship. And by Him we cry, "Abba, Father"' (Rom. 8:15). The writer to the Hebrews exhorted them, 'Endure hardship as discipline; God is treating you as sons' (Heb. 12:7). Discipline takes many forms. It can take the form of painful rebuke or patient instruction; but in all its forms it is one of the marks of sonship. These New Testament passages build upon the principles and experiences of the people of Israel many centuries earlier.

Israel's sonship (14:1-2)

The special relationship between God and Israel grew out of God's covenant with Abraham (see Gen 17:7); but the first description of Israel as God's son is found in Exodus 4:22, where God gave Moses the following message for Pharaoh: 'This is what the LORD says: Israel is my firstborn son'. The painful experiences of slavery in Egypt and the deliverance from that slavery were, according to the prophet Hosea, Israel's rites of adoption (Hosea 11:1b). Although the language of God's fatherhood and Israel's sonship is used elsewhere in Deuteronomy (see 1:31; 8:5; 32:5-6), only here in 14:1 are the Israelites called 'the children of the LORD'. This significant phrase sets the tone for Moses' exposition of the law. He is God's spokesman passing on fatherly instruction to his beloved children.

Moses draws out the ethical implications of Israel's sonship in 14:2. 'For you are a people holy to the LORD your God.' Holiness of life is the family trait which God expects to see in his children – just as we might look for certain physical characteristics or behavioural traits in human families. Sadly, God did not always see those traits in his family (Isa. 1:2-3). In response to his covenant love, God looked for covenant loyalty, love and obedience. As well as declaring their loyalty to God formally in great national gatherings for worship, the Israelites were to express their loyalty to God informally in the mundane events of daily life. This is why the food laws were so significant in the Old Testament. They were a reminder that God was the Lord of every part of their lives. Jehovah was the Lord over the kitchen and, as Christopher Wright comments, 'A God who governs the kitchen should be not easily forgotten in the rest of life.'

One of the interesting features of Moses' exposition of these laws in this chapter is that he applies to the people as a whole laws which in Leviticus 21:5 (prohibiting mourners from shaving their heads) and Leviticus 22:8 (eating the meat of fallen animals) are applied to the priests. Holiness is not the peculiar characteristic of the priests or one tribe alone, but of the nation as a whole. The whole community of Israel is to be a model of the holiness of God before the nations. This principle is later applied to the church (see 1 Cor. 1:2; 1 Peter 2:5). 'You also, like living stones, are being built into a spiritual house to be a holy priesthood.' Here Peter follows in the footsteps of Moses in applying the priestly regulations to the people of God as a whole.

Moses linked Israel's special status and calling to her election by God (14:2). '*Out of all the peoples on the face of the earth, the LORD has chosen you to be his treasured possession.*' This was the foundation upon which Israel's privileges rested (see 4:37; 7:6; 10:15). God chose Israel because he loved her freely and sought to bless her (see 7:7). Although there was nothing in her that was loveable, she was precious to God and Moses describes her as '*his treasured possession*'. This phrase is also used in Deuteronomy 7:6 and 26:18 as well as in Exodus 19:5, Psalm 135:4 and Malachi 3:17. Israel was like a sparkling diamond or a nugget of gold.

When a prospector searching for gold sees the glint of gold among the stones in his pan he rejoices, for he has found his treasure. In a similar way, the Lord rejoiced when he saw the holiness of his people standing in marked contrast to the nations around them. The idea underlying Biblical holiness is that of being different or distinct from the world. In the New Testament, our Lord used salt and light to describe the distinctiveness of his people (Matt. 5:13-16; Mark 9:50). In

Philippians 2:15 Paul exhorted Christians to shine like stars in a dark and sinful world. This will expose us to the scrutiny and sometimes ridicule of others, and that can be a daunting prospect. Yet it is only when God's people are visibly different and Christlike that they bring glory to God.

In Deuteronomy 14 Moses describes three ways in which Israel was to demonstrate her holiness to the Lord.

Repudiating pagan rituals (14:1b, 21b)

From time to time Moses makes reference to pagan practices. Some of these the Israelites may well have encountered in their journeys thus far. They would most certainly encounter them in the land of Canaan. Moses told them in no uncertain terms to have nothing to do with them.

i. Rituals of mourning (14:1b)

Every culture has formal ways of expressing grief and seeking consolation in the face of death. Bereavement is a brush with eternity which brings out the religious instincts of even the most secular people. The people of Canaan were very religious, and they gave expression to their pagan mindset in the way they grieved for their dead. Two of their rituals are expressly mentioned and both are forbidden. 'Do not cut yourselves or shave the front of your heads for the dead.'

Lacerating the body was a ritual practiced by pagans for several different reasons. Perhaps the best known example of this practice is the frenzied attempts of the prophets of Baal to elicit a response from their gods in 1 Kings 18:28. They imagined that, as blood flowed from the self-inflicted wounds on their bodies, their gods would take notice and send fire from heaven. A more pertinent example is found in Jeremiah 47:5, where laceration was used by the Philistines to gain the attention of their gods at a time of grief. Sadly, too, we find that the practice was current amongst the northern Israelites when Gedaliah was assassinated (see Jer. 41:5); and that it had become the norm in Judah, so that failure to perform this rite (see Jer. 16:6) was a mark of disrespect.

The purpose of this ritual was to harness the power which, according to pagan belief, resided in the creation. The essence of paganism is its belief that the earth has hidden powers and that these can be used in religious rituals and ceremonies to manipulate the gods. Blood, in particular, was believed to have a life-giving power. Shedding blood in a ritual way was believed to bring fertility to the land and guarantee eternal life to the dead as they passed through the various stages of the after-life.

Shaving the front of the head (between the eyes) was a recognized ritual of mourning, though it is hard to know with certainty how and why the practice originated. It is mentioned, along with wearing sackcloth, in Isaiah 22:12 at a time of national disaster and mourning.

> The Lord, the LORD Almighty,
> called you on that day
> to weep and wail,
> to tear out your hair and put on sackcloth.

Surprisingly, in this instance the ritual seems to have enjoyed God's approval. One possible explanation is that, over the centuries, it had lost its pagan connections. Or perhaps disconsolate expressions of grief, which were appropriate at a time when the nation was abandoned by God on account of its sin, were not an appropriate response to the death of a loved one because God's people had the hope of eternal life in covenant with Jehovah. That was and still is a very real source of comfort in affliction.

The mourning rituals of the pagans were offensive to Jehovah and his people because they expressed an ungodly view of life and death. We can identify at least three areas in which the mourning rituals of the pagans led them into false doctrine.

a. A pagan view of death led to contempt for the body. That is why they mutilated their bodies in their grief. They had no idea that their bodies had been made in God's image and they had no hope of the resurrection of their bodies. They believed that when they died their bodies would dissolve back into the earth from which they came, never to be restored. By contrast, Christians believe that their bodies are temples of the Holy Spirit (1 Cor. 6:19) and that even in death their bodies are still united to Christ. As a result, they are to be treated with respect in life and in death.

b. A pagan view of God leads to vain and desperate attempts to gain his attention. These forbidden rituals were part of the pagan's attempt to gain God's attention and harness his power. When it became obvious to the prophets of Baal that their deities were not listening, they became even more desperate in their efforts to make themselves heard. They assumed that the more blood they shed the greater the likelihood of Baal seeing and acting. Yet the Bible assures us that God knows the needs of his people even before they cry out to him (Isa. 65:24). He hears even the unspoken prayers of our hearts (Rom. 8:26-27) as well as our loud cries of anguish, but he is not impressed with the 'many words' of the pagans or the hypocrites who make a public display of their prayers (Matt 6:5-8).

c. A pagan approach to religion gives no comfort in death. The pagans had no confidence that their gods cared about them. These gods might be cajoled into giving them earthly blessings such as rain and harvests, but there was no possibility of a relationship between them and the mortals whose lives they controlled. The after-life was a cold and friendless place where the pagans could hardly dare to hope for any fellowship with the gods they had served on earth. Hence their rituals of mourning for the dead were desperate and hopeless.

By contrast, the Israelites were able to grieve for their dead in a godly way. This was recognized in Ecclesiastes 7:2-4.

> It is better to go to a house of mourning
> than to go to a house of feasting,
> for death is the destiny of every man;
> the living should take this to heart.
> Sorrow is better than laughter,
> because a sad face is good for the heart.
> The heart of the wise is in the house of mourning,
> but the heart of fools is in the house of pleasure.

We see examples of godly grief in David when he mourned for Saul and Jonathan (2 Sam. 1:17-27) and the infant son of Bathsheba (2 Sam. 12:23). We are told that 'Jesus wept' at the grave of his friend Lazarus (John 11:35). The apostle Paul taught the believers in Thessalonica to grieve in a godly way. 'Brothers, we do not want you to be ignorant about those who fall asleep, or to grieve like the rest of men, who have no hope' (1 Thess. 4:13).

ii. Fertility rituals (14:21)
'Do not cook a young goat in its mother's milk.' This unusual command is also found in Exodus 23:19b and 34:26b. The only other references to this practice are found in secular poetry (written in Ugaritic), which appears to commend the practice. We are not told why anyone might want to cook a young goat in its mother's milk, but in all probability it was a magical ritual to harness the life-giving power of the mother's milk. When the offspring was boiled in its mother's milk, the milk might be drunk as an aphrodisiac or sprinkled on the land as a fertilizer. The practice seems to have been bound up with pagan ideas of

the hidden powers that resided in the creation, and the Israelites were to have nothing to do with it.

God's people are to avoid every appearance of evil and every practice associated with false religion. For this reason, Puritans in the Church of England protested that clergy should not wear ceremonial vestments because (although there was nothing inherently sinful about these pieces of clothing) they were closely associated, in the eyes of many people at that time, with the Roman doctrine of the Mass. Today's equivalents – which Christians ought to avoid - might well include things associated with the rituals of the new spirituality (such as crystals, incense and horoscopes).

Distinguishing between clean and unclean foods (14:3-21a)

Israel's distinct identity as the people of Jehovah was reinforced by her food laws. These were vigorously enforced until God released the Israelites from these regulations in the New Testament (see Mark 7:19; Acts 10:9-16). While they were in force, they served a very important purpose. Even today, though we are not bound by them, they continue to teach us some very important lessons about what it means to live as the people of God.

The general principle is stated in 14:3. *'Do not eat any detestable thing.'* The word *detestable* is a strong one and was intended to provoke a visceral revulsion. In Deuteronomy it is used to describe the practices of the Canaanites which included 'all kinds of detestable things the LORD hates' (see 12:31; 13:14). The Israelites were to recoil in horror from practices such as child sacrifice and sacred prostitution. Likewise, they were to turn away from eating unclean foods.

Eating and drinking to God's glory

Having stated the general prohibition in 14:3, Moses told the Israelites what they were allowed to eat in 14:4-21. His teaching is both positive and permissive.

These are the animals you may eat: the ox, the sheep, the goat, the deer, the gazelle, the roe deer, the wild goat, the ibex, the antelope and the mountain sheep... Of all the creatures living in the water you may eat any that has fins and scales... You may eat any clean bird... any winged creature that is clean you may eat.

In the Garden of Eden God had given Adam considerable freedom to eat what he had provided. Moses emphasizes this divine generosity in these verses. Yes, the holiness of God required the Israelites to refrain from eating any detestable thing, but we are not to overlook the expansiveness of God's provision. God created everything to be received and enjoyed with thanksgiving (see 1 Tim. 4:4-5); but for a time in the history of Israel, for good spiritual and pastoral reasons, God placed some restrictions on their freedom by distinguishing between clean and unclean. In this section Moses divided all living creatures into four groups – animals, fish, birds and insects. Within these four groups Moses described the distinction between clean and unclean.

a. Animals (14:4-8). The clean animals are listed in 14:4-5 and their characteristics are described in 14:6. *'You may eat any animal that has a split hoof divided in two and that chews the cud.'* These were the characteristics which were commonly found in the domesticated farm animals, with which the Israelites had close daily contact. Unclean animals were defined as unclean because they did not have these characteristics. Three animals are listed as unclean because they fall short of the rule, having only one of the two commonly recognized characteristics of a clean animal (14:7-8).

However, of those that chew the cud or that have a split hoof completely divided you may not eat the camel, the rabbit or the coney. Although they chew the cud, they do not have a split hoof; they are ceremonially unclean for you. The pig is also unclean; although it has a split hoof, it does not chew the cud. You are not to eat their meat or touch their carcasses.

b. *Fish* (14:9-10). Moses distinguished between clean and unclean fish. *'Of all the creatures living in the water, you may eat any that has fins and scales. But anything that does not have fins and scales you may not eat; for you it is unclean.'* Free-swimming fish have fins and scales to enable them to live, move and breathe in their aquatic environment. This is what we might expect of fish, and such creatures were considered clean to eat. Other water creatures might burrow in the mud, crawl along the seabed or cling to rocks, so they did not have fins and scales. These creatures were considered abnormal and so were not to be eaten.

c. *Birds* (14:11-18). Moses distinguished between clean and unclean birds simply by listing those which were unclean. The Israelites were permitted to eat any clean bird (14:11), but he did not provide any examples. It may be that a clean bird is any bird not listed among the unclean birds and which does not share their characteristics. The unclean species of birds are listed in 14:12-18. *'But these you may not eat...'* It is not always easy to identify, from the Hebrew words and phrases in these verses, specific species of bird. It is important to remember that Moses used the language of his day, not the terminology which we would find in a modern ornithological textbook. Many of the bird types are named only here and in Leviticus 11:13-19. Some of the phrases are quite broad in their scope and may refer to a type of bird rather than a single species: for instance, 'any *kind* of falcon, any *kind* of raven, ... any *kind* of hawk, ... any *kind* of heron'. The expression used here is similar to that in

Genesis 1:21b: 'So God created ... every winged bird according to its *kind*'. Yet each kind had its own characteristics.

Nor is it easy to identify the characteristics which made these species offensive and therefore unclean. Some birds in this list have unpleasant characteristics. The screech owl (other translations include nighthawk and male ostrich) in 14:15, for instance, was thought to be cruel. This propensity to violence is reflected in its Hebrew name. Likewise the great owl in 14:16 had a strident call. However the stork in 14:18 was respected for its selflessness and kindness to its offspring. Its Hebrew name derives from the verb 'to be good or kind'. Many of these unclean birds were birds of prey, including the eagle of 14:12. This eagle was in fact was a kind of vulture which ate the rotting flesh of dead animals. Others are mentioned elsewhere in the Old Testament as birds which inhabit ruins and deserts. Into this category come the little owl (14.16; see also Ps. 102:6), the great owl and the desert owl ((14:16-17; see also Isa. 34:11). The solitary habits of these birds set them apart from domesticated birds which may be eaten.

d. *Insects* (14:19-20). Moses distinguished between clean and unclean insects. *'All flying insects that swarm are unclean to you; do not eat them. But any winged creature that is clean you may eat.'* In contrast to the first three categories of living creatures,' he opens this section on insects with a prohibition. Eating unclean insects was forbidden. Unclean insects were those which swarmed, presumably over dead bodies. As well as being repulsive in themselves, these insects were carriers of disease. Winged insects, by contrast, were regarded as clean and could be eaten. There is no explanation of why winged insects were to be regarded as clean, but a fuller description and some examples are given in Leviticus 11:21-22. Locusts and grasshoppers were to be regarded as clean. This may have been because they were grass- rather than flesh-eating insects.

Over the centuries, many theories have been put forward to explain why some creatures were to be regarded as clean and others as unclean. The distinction did not originate with Moses, as it influenced how many animals of each species Noah was to take into the ark (see Gen. 7:2, 8) and which animals he sacrificed to the Lord. (Gen 8:20). The three most common explanations of the distinction between clean and unclean are those based on hygiene, religious practice and ethical purity. Yet all three raise as many questions as answers.

a. Hygiene. Some animals are notorious for their disgusting habits or as carriers of disease. It has often been suggested that the food laws sought to eliminate these from Israel's diet. The pig is a forager and, if its meat is not processed properly, those who eat it can ingest harmful parasites. Animals, birds and insects which eat the flesh of fallen beasts also fall into this category. Yet even the meat of some of the clean animals presents similar dangers, while some of the forbidden animals (camel and rabbit, for instance) have been safely eaten since ancient times. As a general principle the sixth commandment teaches us to take care of the health and well-being of ourselves and others by serving up wholesome and healthy food, but this does not seem to be the principle which underlies the food laws of Israel.

b. Religious significance. Some of these detestable animals were associated with idolatrous rituals. The pig was commonly offered on pagan altars and its flesh was mentioned with holy revulsion in Isaiah 65:4 and 66:17. However, the recognised symbol of Baal in Canaanite religion was a bull and cattle were often sacrificed to him by his devotees, yet this did not render cattle unclean in the sight of Jehovah or his people.

c. Ethical symbolism. Over the years, both Jewish and Christian commentators have observed the habits of the animals mentioned in the Old Testament food laws and drawn moral lessons from them. These have then been offered as the rationale for distinguishing clean and unclean animals. For instance, the dirty habits of the pig are said to represent filthy thoughts and actions which we ought to avoid in our conduct, whereas the sheep was to be considered clean because it loyally followed its shepherd, as God's people ought to do. Ingenious though these moral explanations may be, they are too subjective to be convincing.

More modern commentators have stressed that holiness in the laws of the Old Testament is closely connected with ideas of wholeness, completeness and conformity to what is normal. Clean animals are said to conform to the pattern of what we might expect of them. For instance, there are certain qualities and features which we might expect of creatures which live and move on the land, while different qualities might be expected of creatures which live in water. Clean animals will conform to the former, while clean fish will conform to the latter. Those creatures which do not conform are to be considered unclean. This leaves the question, what is normal and who makes that judgment? God, who created all creatures after their kind (Gen 1:21-22, 24-25), defines what is normal and in his sovereign wisdom distinguishes clean and unclean. In the Garden of Eden, God distinguished one tree from all the rest and told Adam not to eat from it, thereby testing Adam's loyalty to him. In the food laws, God tested and displayed the loyalty of his covenant people. He reminded them that they were holy to the Lord. They were not to follow the example of the nations around them, but to be different from them as they obeyed God's commands. Although the details of these dietary laws are not binding on Christians today, we live in a similar theological framework as people who have been set apart from the world to reflect the holiness of God in everything we do.

Fallen animals (14:21a)

Moses gave one final dietary prohibition to the people of Israel. *'Do not eat anything you find already dead...'* Even if the animal might otherwise have been regarded as a clean animal, it was not to be eaten if it had been attacked and killed by a wild animal or if it had died of natural causes. The explanation, no doubt, is that its blood had not been drained from the carcass and that blood was not to be eaten (see 12:16, 23; Lev. 17:10-14).

This prohibition did not apply to non-Israelites (see 14:21a). In fact, Israelites were expressly permitted to sell the flesh of such an animal to non-resident foreigners and even to give it free of charge to a resident foreigner who had settled in their midst. *'You may give it to an alien living in any of your towns, and he may eat it, or you may sell it to a foreigner.'* Resident foreigners were often very needy people, and Moses encouraged the Israelites not to waste the food (clearly this permission assumes that the food was fit to eat) but to help the person in need. This modified the law in Leviticus 17:15, which required that 'anyone, whether native-born or alien, who eats anything found dead or torn by wild animals must wash his clothes and bathe with water, and he will be ceremonially unclean till evening; then he will be clean', and anticipated the emphasis which our Lord placed upon compassion to those in need even when that seemed to conflict with the rules of ceremonial purity (see Matt. 12:11-12; Luke 10:30-37). However, the underlying principle remains intact – there is a clear distinction between the redeemed people of Israel and all other nations. Moses reinforced that distinction in 14:21. *'You are a people holy to the LORD your God.'*

Bringing tithes and offerings (14:22-29)

The principle of tithing was deeply embedded in Israel's laws. Leviticus 27:30-33 required the Israelites to give the Lord a tenth of all their grain and their livestock. Numbers 18:21-24 explained that the tithe was to be given to the Levites. This was their inheritance in the land of Canaan and provided for their material needs so that they might devote themselves to their special calling. Moses restated this general principle in 14:22. *'Be sure to set aside a tenth of all that your fields produce each year.'* Although only the produce of their 'fields' is mentioned in this verse, we should not take this to mean that Moses intended to exclude from their obligation a tithe of their livestock. The reference is general and extended to all the produce of their farms.

In 14:23, however, Moses describes something else which the Israelites were to do with their tithe and other offerings. *'Eat the tithe of your grain, new wine and oil, and the firstborn of your herds and flocks in the presence of the LORD your God at the place he will choose as a dwelling for his Name, so that you may learn to revere the LORD your God always.'* This chosen place will come to occupy a position of great importance in the religious life of the Israelites. We have seen that it was *the* place where they were to offer sacrifices when they entered the land of Canaan (12:5-7). We will see that it was where they would gather on joyful pilgrimages (16:5-6, 11, 15, 16). This chosen place was also where they would gather to eat some of the produce which they had given to the Lord as their tithe. The religious significance of these tithe festivals is further explained in 26:1-15, where Moses gave the Israelites declarations to recite every time they brought their tithe. They were to remember their history and give thanks to God for his goodness. In 14:23 Moses explained that they were to 'learn to revere the LORD your God always'. The Israelites revered God by acknowledging that he was the owner of all they possessed and the giver of all they enjoyed. In the verses which follow, Moses describes two tithe festivals which were held in Israel.

i. The annual tithe feast (14:22-26)
This was to be held every year *'in the presence of the LORD your God at the place he will choose as a dwelling for his name'*. Moses anticipated that it might be very difficult for some Israelites to bring their tithe from the more remote areas of Canaan to the place which God would choose for his sanctuary, so he made provision for this in 14:24-26.

> But if that place is too distant and you have been blessed by the LORD your God and cannot carry your tithe (because the place where the LORD will choose to put his Name is so far away), then exchange your tithe for silver, and take the silver with you and go to the place the LORD your God will choose. Use the silver to buy whatever you like: cattle, sheep, wine or other fermented drink, or anything you wish. Then you and your household shall eat there in the presence of the LORD your God and rejoice.

The people were permitted to bring cash rather than produce, but the end result was the same. They would feast together in celebration of God's bountiful provision.

This commonsense approach to the tithe festival demonstrates Moses' desire in Deuteronomy to apply God's law faithfully and sensitively to the new circumstances which would prevail when the Israelites took possession of the land of Canaan. God's laws are not and were never intended to be burdensome (1 John 5:3); but over the centuries the teachers of the law reinterpreted and reapplied the laws so as to make them burdensome. Jesus chided them for this in Matthew 23:4. 'They tie up heavy loads and put them on men's shoulders, but they themselves are not willing to lift a finger to move them.' The tithe law is a case in point, as its demands were multiplied (see Matt. 23:23) and the opportunity it offered to rejoice in God's bounty was lost. It is hard to imagine a happier way of tithing than that which Moses prescribed in these verses, where he called the Israelites to 'eat the tithe... in the presence of the LORD ... and rejoice'. Having acknowledged the importance of rejoicing in God's bounty, the question remains, 'Why did Moses encourage the ordinary Israelites to eat the very tithe which was intended to support the Levites and maintain God's sanctuary?

The reminder in 14:27 shows that the annual tithe feast and God's concern for the Levites were connected. *'And do not neglect the Levites living in your towns, for they have no allotment or inheritance of their own.'* We should not imagine that the Israelites ate all (or even most) of the produce which they brought to the annual tithe feast. That would have been impossible for all but the most gluttonous. In 2 Chronicles 31:4-5 there is an account of the tithe festival during days of revival in the reign of King Hezekiah.

> He ordered the people living in Jerusalem to give the portion due to the priests and Levites so that they could devote themselves to the Law of the LORD. As soon as the order went out, the Israelites generously gave the firstfruits of their grain, new wine, oil and honey and all that the fields produced. They brought a great amount, a tithe of everything.

Then Azariah, the chief priest, was able to report to the king that 'since the people began to bring their contributions to the temple of the LORD, we have had enough to eat and plenty to spare, because the LORD has blessed his people, and this great amount is left over' (2 Chr. 31:10). By bringing the tithe to the central place, provision was made for the Levites who ministered there. The central tithe feast was both an incentive and a mechanism by which the produce of the land was brought to the Levites whose ministry centred on the central place of sacrifice.

By means of this feast Moses established a time, a place and an occasion at which the people brought their tithes to the Lord. As the people gathered to eat the tithe feast they were able to exhort and encourage each other in this good work. We can also see how the apostle Paul made use of the regular gatherings of the early church on the first day of each week to encourage those early believers to gather their collection for the needy in the Jerusalem church (1 Cor.16:1-3). Both Moses and Paul encouraged cheerful giving amongst God's people (see 2 Cor. 9:7, 15). It is therefore quite appropriate to make our contributions to the work of the gospel as part of a congregational worship service. Whatever the setting, however, the spirit of thanksgiving is vital. 'Each man should give what he has decided in his heart to give, not reluctantly or under compulsion, for God loves a cheerful giver' (2 Cor. 9:7).

ii. The special tithe year (14:27-29)
The central sanctuary was where many of the Levites served God, and the yearly tithe feast provided for them and their families. There were, however, many other Levites who lived amongst the Israelites in their towns and communities and Moses had a special concern for them (14:27). *'Do not neglect the Levites living in your towns...'* Like the rest of the Levites, they received no allocation of tribal land in Canaan (see 10:9; 12:12; 18:1; Josh. 14:4; 18:7). These rural Levites laboured under another disadvantage, as they were not in a position to eat the tithe which the Israelites would bring to the central place which God would choose as his dwelling-place. Moses was aware of the predicament of these rural Levites and sought to alleviate it in his retelling and refining of Israel's laws. See 18:6-8 for another example of this.

In these verses Moses instituted a series of localised tithe feasts every third year (14:28). *'At the end of every three years, bring all the tithes of that year's produce and store it in your towns, so that the Levites... and the aliens, the fatherless and the widows who live in your towns may come and eat and be satisfied...'* Rather than that year's tithe being taken to the central sanctuary, it was to be stored locally so that the Levites and other needy people in the area might be fed.

These special arrangements encourage us to be sensitive to the needs of those we tend to overlook, and to make special provision for them. We might think of pastors in small and struggling congregations who, like the rural Levites, tend to be overlooked by those in more prosperous situations. We might think of the homeless and disadvantaged in our own country and the needy in the third world. Do we make special provision for them in our personal and congregational budgets? God's material blessings are to overflow from us 'in many expressions of thanks to God', just as they did in the life of the Corinthian church (2 Cor. 9:12).

Not only were the Levites and other disadvantaged groups to eat from this triennial tithe, they were to 'eat and be satisfied'. No-one was to have any reason to come like young Oliver Twist and ask for more. This feast was to be a demonstration that God's provision is never stingy but always overflowing. A laden table is a recurring motif in Scripture, picturing God's abundant grace to those he saves (see Ps. 23:5-6; Isa. 25:6; 55:1-2; Matt. 8:11; 22:4; Rev. 19:9).

Unfortunately, those who enjoy an abundance of God's material provision are sometimes exposed to the danger of thinking that they can do very well without God. In Deuteronomy 6:11, 31:20 and Hosea 13:6, to be 'satisfied' is to be in spiritual danger. Moses warned the Israelites lest they 'forget the Lord' when they were 'satisfied' and 'turn to other gods'. In 8:10 he exhorted the Israelites to 'praise the LORD your God' when they had eaten and were satisfied. Tithing plays an important role in this struggle with temptation, because it reminds us that everything we have comes from God. It also reminds us of the needs of others and involves us in caring for them. This is of great spiritual value for Christians living in situations where wealth can easily become a snare (see Mark 4:19, 1 Tim. 6:10, 17-19).

The chapter choses with a typically Mosaic explanation of why the Israelites ought to practise tithing (14:29b): *'so that the LORD your God may bless you in all the work of your hands.'* The prophet Malachi may well have had this chapter in mind when he exhorted the people of his day to bring the whole tithe into God's house (Mal. 3:10). Just as Moses had done, Malachi reminds the people of Judah that they were God's treasured possession (compare 14:2 with Mal. 3:17) and that God distinguished between the righteous and the wicked (Mal. 3:18). Yet in Malachi's day God's generosity was openly doubted (Mal 3:14). That is why Malachi exhorted the people to discover God's goodness for themselves. '"Test me in this," says the LORD Almighty, "and see if I will not throw open the floodgates of heaven and pour out so much blessing that you will not have room enough for it"' (Mal. 3:10). This was the kind of blessing which Moses sought for Israel

Chapter 15
Rest for the burdened

Please read Deuteronomy 15: 1-23

In this chapter Moses expounds three laws which apply the Sabbath principle to the lives of the Israelites. This is the principle which is summarised in the fourth commandment, and we find the distinctive wording of the fourth commandment in Deuteronomy 5:15 echoed in 15:15. What is particularly surprising and challenging is the fact that the application of the Sabbath principle was much wider than sanctifying the Sabbath day.

The Sabbath principle takes us back to creation and reminds us that everything and every person belongs to God. God owns our lives, our land, our time and everything else we possess. Even when God allows mankind to exercise stewardship over the earth, its creatures and other people, all these still belong to God. Moses taught the Israelites to recognise Jehovah's lordship by relinquishing control over a portion of their possessions and returning them to him. For instance, God's lordship was recognised by resting or ceasing from normal activities on the seventh day. God himself had rested on the seventh day and instructed mankind to follow his example (see Gen. 2:1-3). Not only did the Israelites rest from their routine labours on the Sabbath day, they rested their land and remitted debts in the seventh year, they released their slaves and certain animals were not put to work. By placing these restrictions on their normal, and otherwise legitimate, economic activity, God's people learned that labour and wealth creation were not their highest goals. They lived to glorify and enjoy the Lord who had made them.

Another valuable lesson which the people of Israel were to learn from the application of the Sabbath principle was God's compassion for the oppressed and vulnerable in their midst. By placing a check upon their freedom to exploit to the maximum their land, servants and animals, God protected those who tend to get crushed under the steam-roller of economic progress. Moses was especially mindful that the Israelites had once been oppressed in Egypt (see 15:15), and he wanted them to care for those who laboured for them.

The humanitarianism of these verses points to the ultimate expression of God's compassion in his Son, the Lord Jesus Christ. It was our Lord who called the 'weary and burdened' to himself and offered them 'rest'. By contrast with the demands of the worldly master, his yoke is easy and his burden is light (Matt. 11:28-30). He recognised in the prophecy of Isaiah a description of his own mission 'to proclaim freedom for the prisoners... to release the oppressed, to proclaim the year of the Lord's favour' (Luke 4:18-20). When he had completed his work of redemption he entered his rest (Heb 1:3), and provides an everlasting Sabbath rest for the people of God (Heb. 4:9). This is what Christians celebrate each Lord's Day, which is the weekly Christian Sabbath given to us by God for physical rest and spiritual nourishment. For this reason, our Lord said that the Sabbath was made for man (Mark 2:27). When we sanctify that day by resting and renewing our souls with the bread of life we recognise that 'the Son of man is Lord even of the Sabbath' as well as being Lord of all.

These themes of God's lordship, cessation from normal activities and compassion for the needy are expressed in Moses' exposition of the three laws before us in this chapter: the remission of debts (15:1-11); the release of slaves (15:12-18); and the dedication of firstborn animals (15:19-23).

The remission of debts (15:1-11)

Here Moses gave a fresh application of an existing law. The closest parallels in the earlier Mosaic legislation were the laws in Exodus 23:10-11 and Leviticus 25:1-7 requiring the Israelites to leave their land unploughed and unused every seventh year. This allowed the poor and the wild animals to gather what the land produced naturally. However, it may well have created hardship for those who relied for their living on cultivating that land, especially if they had to borrow money or grain to feed their families. Moses addressed the concerns of those in this position.

a. The law itself (15:1-3)
The law itself is stated succinctly in 15:1. *'At the end of every seven years you must cancel debts.'* The very simplicity of the law demands some further explanation, and this is provided in 15:2-3.

> *This is how it is to be done: Every creditor shall cancel the loan he has made to his fellow Israelite. He shall not require payment from his fellow Israelite or brother, because the LORD's time for cancelling debts has been proclaimed. You may require payment from a foreigner, but you must cancel any debt your brother owes you.*

Even this explanation leaves us asking several questions.

i. *When did the seventh year come around?* There was a fixed cycle in the rhythm of life in Israel and every seventh year was regarded as special. In that Sabbath year, everyone would cease planting and sowing, and allow their land to rest. When the Feast of Tabernacles came around in that seventh year, the people were to gather before the Lord to hear the reading of the law (see 31:10-11). These Sabbath years were largely ignored during Israel's later history. That was one of the reasons why God punished them with the exile (see 2 Chr. 36:21). In Nehemiah 10:31 the people of Jerusalem covenanted to rest their land every seventh year and cancel all debts. Clearly they linked the practice of cancelling debts with the Sabbath year. Here in 15:2 this special year is greeted as '*the LORD's time for cancelling debts...*' It was a time of God's appointment for the purpose of displaying his mercy. So, irrespective of when the loan was made in the seven-year cycle, the debt was to be released when the seventh year came around.

ii. *What kind of loan was to be cancelled?* Most people today (at least in the developed world) carry some level of debt. It may be a mortgage on their house, a loan to buy a car or to pay for their education, a credit card debt, or even a commercial loan to set up a business. Yet it is most unlikely that when Moses commanded the Israelites to remit debt every seventh year that he had these kinds of commercial loans in view. A law such as we find in 15:1 would invite cynical exploitation in modern financial markets! We need to keep in mind that loans in ancient Israel were generally for charitable purposes. They were taken out only in times of special hardship by people who were at their wits' end. Nehemiah 5:3-4 describes how the impoverished people of Judah took out loans to buy food for their families and to pay their taxes. There was nowhere else to turn. In Psalm 112:5 giving and lending are described as acts of charity performed by a good man. Here in 15:2 the loans are characterised as acts of brotherly love made to '*a fellow Israelite*' (literally 'a neighbour and brother'). Hence payment must not be exacted from him during the seventh year.

Foreigners are specially excluded from the benefits of this law (15:3). *'You may require payment from a foreigner...'* The foreigners referred to here were travelling merchants who temporarily resided amongst the Israelites in order to trade with them. They are to be distinguished from the resident aliens who had taken up permanent residence amongst the Israelites, and whose interests were often protected in Deuteronomy. Loans made to the travelling merchants would clearly have been commercial loans. Those who took them out did so for the purpose of making a profit and would have known the risks involved. By contrast, the brother in need is at the mercy of the markets and is accorded the protection of God's law, *'...but you must cancel any debt your brother owes you.'*

iii. *How was the loan to be cancelled?* Older interpreters (both Christian and Jewish) assumed that the law required a total cancellation of the remaining debt in the seventh year. The rabbis sought to find a way around this interpretation of the law because it discouraged lenders from lending, as Moses recognised in 15:9. More recent commentators have questioned whether Moses ever intended a total cancellation of the debt in the seventh year and have emphasised the parallel with the law requiring the land to be released from cultivation during the seventh year. From this practice they argue that only the repayment due during that seventh year was to be suspended. The similarity between these two laws is a significant one but, on balance, the traditional interpretation of the law is the most probable one. It is unlikely that a suspension of repayments would have provoked the response anticipated in 15:9.

b. The underlying ideal (15:4-6)
Moses explained why it was right and proper to expand the application of the Sabbath principle to require the remission of debts on the seventh year in 15:4. *'However, there should be no poor among you, for in the land the LORD your God is giving you to possess as your inheritance, he will richly bless you.'* This may

seem like a utopian dream. Thankfully, there is a place for godly idealism amongst God's people. Throughout history there have been those who have sought to free those who are slaves and to lift the poor out of poverty because these are worthy goals. Today many are seeking to 'make poverty history' and their goal, if not always their methods, is biblical. Christians ought to work and pray for a just and fair society (see Isa. 58:10; Acts 4:34-35). In Deuteronomy Moses taught the Israelites how to build such an ideal community on earth (see also 24:14-15, 19-22)

This high ideal can only come about by following God's ways and with the enjoyment of God's blessing (see 15:5). The Israelites would enjoy great prosperity in the promised land and see an end to poverty in their midst *'if only you fully obey the LORD your God and are careful to follow all these commands I am giving you today'.* If the Israelites had obeyed this law, and other laws which protected the interests of the needy in their midst, they would have been delivered from poverty. Yet, because the rich and powerful in the community ignored and evaded these laws, the rich got richer and the poor got poorer. The failure of the Israelites to obey these laws (as recorded in the histories of Israel and especially in the denunciations of the prophets (see Amos 2:7; 5:11; Hab. 2:6-7) should not blind us to the very real prospect which God set before his covenant people. A society without poverty was not to be thought of as an impossible dream, but as a realisable prospect if only God's people would walk in his ways. In 28:1-14 Moses will return to this theme when he describes the blessings which an obedient people would enjoy. 'The Lord will open the heavens, the storehouse of his bounty, to send rain on your land in season and to bless all the work of your hands.' This blessing would come upon rich and poor alike when the nation faithfully obeyed God's commands.

As a result of God's covenant blessing the nation of Israel will achieve a place of strength and pre-eminence among the nations (15:6). *'For the LORD your God will bless you as he has promised, and you will lend to many nations but will borrow from none. You will rule over many nations but none will rule over you'* (see also 28:12b). Moses anticipated Israel's role as a commercial power and the centre of a great empire. This vision was realised during the reign of King Solomon, when Israelite merchants traded with many other nations (1 Kings 9:26-28; 2 Chr. 1:15-17) and many peoples were subject to Israel's king. However, the ultimate fulfilment of this promises is to be found in the time of the messianic king whose reign will bring prosperity and righteousness (Ps. 72:3) in such abundance that the righteous will flourish and the poor will be delivered from their affliction (Ps. 72:7, 12-14).

c. The sad reality (15:7-11)

Moses moved from the lofty ideal of a nation submitting to God's righteous rule to the present reality of the people who stood before him. There were many poor people amongst the Israelites. Moses acknowledged this indirectly in 15:7. *'If there is a poor man among your brothers in any of the towns of the land that the LORD your God is giving you, do not be hard-hearted or tight-fisted towards your poor brother.'* Moses also acknowledges that this was inevitable in a sinful world (15:11). *'There will always be poor people in the land.'* Our Lord quoted these words to rebuke his disciples when they criticised a woman who had anointed him with expensive perfume (see Matt. 26:11; Mark 14:7). When Jesus said 'the poor you will always have with you', he was not encouraging indifference to their needs, but reminding his disciples that they had an ongoing obligation to the needy around them which required regular acts of generosity. Moreover, by quoting from this passage, Jesus reminded his disciples that Moses had challenged mean-heartedness in all its forms.

As well as recognising that there would always be poor people among the Israelites, Moses acknowledged that there would also be mean people in their midst (15:7, 9). *'Be careful not to harbour this wicked thought: "The seventh year, the year for cancelling debts, is near," so that you do not show ill will toward your needy brother and give him nothing.'* His response was both positive and negative. Negatively, he told the Israelites what they were not to think or say in their hearts. The 'wicked thought' in 15:9 is literally, a 'word of Belial'. (Belial is not a person, but an abstraction for evil, so in 13:13 'sons of Belial' are 'wicked men'. In that verse they brought destruction upon a city, while here 'wicked thoughts' bring God's censure upon those who think them.)

Moses specifically had in view those who were unwilling to lend to needy neighbours for fear that they would be unable to repay the debt before the seventh year and so their investment would be lost. The fact that this law would have been well-nigh impossible to police suggests that its goal was to search the spiritual condition of the heart. We sometimes make jokes about mean people (or ethnic groups with a reputation for tight-fistedness), but in reality this is a serious matter. It is sobering to remember that our ungenerous thoughts and actions are examined by God (see Heb. 4:12). How often have we turned away those in need because we fear the cost of compassion? Yet generosity to the needy is as important a command as godliness.

Positively, Moses commanded the Israelites to be generous (15:8, 10, 11b). *'Rather be open-handed and freely lend him whatever he needs... Give generously to him ... Therefore I command you to be open-handed towards your brothers and towards the poor and needy in your land.'* Generosity is one way of demonstrating the righteousness of God in the lives of his people. The righteous person will lend to the poor because they are in need, and not because they seek a return on their investment. 'They are always generous and lend freely' (Ps. 37:26). 'Good will come to him who is generous and lends freely, who conducts his affairs with justice... He has scattered abroad his gifts to the poor, his righteousness endures forever; his horn will be lifted high in honour' (Ps. 112:5, 9).

The release of slaves (15:12-18)

God's compassion was also reflected in the labour laws of his people. Hebrew slaves were to be set free after six years of service (15:12). *'If a fellow Hebrew, a man or woman, sells himself to you and serves you six years, in the seventh year you must let him go free.'* This passage is an elaboration of the law found in Exodus 21:2-6 and aims to shows that the Israelites are bound to each other by bonds of brotherly affection. Moses described the enslaved Israelite as 'a fellow Hebrew' or 'your brother, a Hebrew'. This is the only time the designation 'Hebrew' is used in Deuteronomy. It calls to mind the social origins of Abraham's family.

God had called Abraham from Ur of the Chaldees and so he became a wandering nomad. In Genesis 14:13 he is described as 'Abram the Hebrew'. He was called this because he was a nomad. When his descendants settled in Egypt they, too, were known as Hebrews (see Exod. 1:15-19; 2:6-7, 11-13, etc.). This adjective 'Hebrew' describes them as 'those from beyond'. It may well refer to their origins beyond the River Euphrates. In the Old Testament it is mostly used by non-Israelites to describe Israelites. In Egypt, the Hebrews were a rootless underclass of aliens who stood out in contrast to the native Egyptians. Even when God liberated them from slavery and settled them in a land of their own, there were those who fell upon hard times. Their only option would be to sell themselves into servitude. Yet even these Hebrews were not to be regarded as slaves, but hired labourers (see Lev. 25:39-40), for God has set his people free from slavery.

Those who share in the enjoyment of this freedom are to love each other with brotherly affection. This is what made Israel's laws unique. They were not burdensome requirements, but the natural expression of kindness in those who have experienced God's grace. Brotherly affection shows itself in several ways in Moses' exposition of this law.

a. Men and women slaves were equally protected
In 15:12 Moses stated that the fellow Hebrew might be *'a man or woman'* (literally a 'Hebrewess'); while in 15:17 he says, *'Do the same for your maidservant.'* This was probably implicit in the law of Exodus 27:2-6, but according to Exodus 21:7-11 women who had been sold as concubines were not to go free as menservants did. If they were dismissed by their master they were not free to remarry, but were to be supported for the rest of their lives (see 2 Sam. 20:3). However, when Moses revisits this law and expounds it in the light of the law of brotherly love, women who had been sold as household servants or field labourers benefit from this law just like their male colleagues.

b. The released slave was not to be sent away empty-handed
When a servant was taken into the household of his master, he was provided with shelter, food and clothing. So when he left his master's service there was a real danger that he might starve. Freedom from servitude might not be as attractive as it first appeared, unless the cycle of poverty and debt which had led the unfortunate individual to sell himself into servitude was broken. Hence Moses instructed the master to give the departing slave a substantial golden handshake (15:13-14) so that he might establish himself as a free man and feed his family. *'And when you release him, do not send him away empty-handed. Supply him liberally from your flock, your threshing floor and your winepress. Give to him as the LORD has blessed you.'*

c. Moses' exhortation was grounded upon God's deliverance of the Israelites in Egypt
'Remember that you were slaves in Egypt and the LORD your God redeemed you. That is why I give you this command today'

(15:15). Moses attached a similar exhortation to the fourth commandment in 5:15, where the Sabbath principle required that everyone be allowed one day of rest per week. That same principle also required that slaves be given rest from their labours in the seventh year of their service. The promise of rest is one of the great blessings which God holds out to his people (see Matt. 11:29; Rev. 14:13). God is concerned about those who are being worn out by excessive toil, but he is also concerned about the whole person, body and soul. He knows that when his people enjoy physical rest they will be better able to appreciate the eternal rest which awaits them in heaven.

d. Moses envisaged that a servant who loved his master might want to stay in his household
There were several reasons why a slave might want to stay with his master when the time came for his release. Exodus 21:4 explains that the slave and his family might belong to the same master and the family would not be free to leave with him in the seventh year. A slave might reluctantly stay with his master in order to retain his family. Moses, however, does not envisage a slave staying with his master merely for these reasons. He describes a slave who will stay with his master for reasons of brotherly affection. *'But if your servant says to you, "I do not want to leave you," because he loves you and your family and is well off with you then take an awl and push it through his ear lobe into the door, and he will become your servant for life'* (15:16-17).

The paradox of willing servitude is a reminder that the law of brotherly love placed demands on workers as well as their masters. They were to love their masters and serve them loyally. The apostle Paul applied this principle to slaves in his day, some of whom were believing slaves working for believing masters (see Eph. 6:5-8; Col. 4:22-25; Titus 2:9-10). Willing servitude is also a pointer to our relationship with the Lord Jesus, who has set us free from slavery to sin in order that we might dedicate ourselves to him as slaves to righteousness (see Rom. 6:18,22; 1

Cor. 7:22; Eph. 6:6). Our Lord made himself a slave to his Father's will in order that he might secure our salvation (see Ps. 40:6-8; Heb. 10:5-7). Psalm 40:6 alludes to the ear-piercing ceremony of 15:17 by which a slave renounced his right to go free in the seventh year. 'Sacrifice and offering you did not desire, but my ears you have pierced...' How much more ought we to dedicate ourselves publicly and willingly to a lifetime of service to the Master who has loved us and blessed us so richly.

e. Moses probed the hearts of those who were obliged to free their slaves
'Do not consider it a hardship to set your servant free, because his service to you these six years has been worth twice as much as that of a hired hand' (15:18). Not only were masters to comply with the law requiring the release of their slaves, but they were to do so willingly and joyfully. Moses warned them not to be like Pharaoh, who complied with God's demands very unwillingly. In fact, he only allowed the Israelites to go free after his country had been devastated by ten plagues. God is just as eager to see a right attitude in the hearts of his people as he is to see right actions in their lives. Moses nurtured such an attitude by pointing out to masters that they had benefited from six years of hard labour and by promising God's blessing on those who keep his commands (15:18b). *'And the LORD your God will bless you in everything you do.'*

Later generations forfeited God's blessing because they failed to obey this law, or did so very reluctantly. At a time of crisis in Judah, King Zedekiah and his subjects made a solemn covenant with each other to release their slaves when they became aware that they had been neglecting the law of Deuteronomy 15:12-18 (see Jer. 34:8-10). They did so only when the Babylonian armies were pounding at the gates of Jerusalem. Yet when the threat of God's judgment receded, the people took their slaves back into slavery and so incurred even more of God's wrath. How very like Pharaoh! This was a violation, not only of their covenant with each other in Jeremiah 34:8, but also of God's covenant with Israel (see Jer. 34:12-16). As a result of this infidelity, their freedom of movement would be severely curtailed (see Jer. 34:17). 'Therefore, this is what the LORD says: You have not obeyed me; you have not proclaimed freedom for your fellow countrymen. So I now proclaim 'freedom' for you, declares the LORD – 'freedom' to fall by the sword, plague and famine. I will make you abhorrent to all the kingdoms of the earth.'

Human masters may often be greedy and oppressive. It is only to be expected that fallen men will exact everything due to them (and more if possible). However, the mediator of God's new covenant is a master who brings liberty to those who are enslaved. The ideals which Moses proclaimed in 15:12-18 may never find perfect fulfilment in a fallen world, but they will be fulfilled in the one who came 'to proclaim freedom for the prisoners... to release the oppressed, to proclaim the year of the Lord's favour' (Luke 4:18-19).

The dedication of firstborn animals (15:19-23)

Firstborn sons are very special people. As a firstborn son himself, the author of this commentary must admit some bias. However, in all seriousness, we cannot but note the special position accorded to a firstborn son in Israel. Jacob said of his firstborn son, 'Reuben, you are my firstborn, my might, the first sign of my strength, excelling in honour, excelling in power' (Gen. 49:3). It was quite normal for the firstborn to receive his father's blessing and the family inheritance. The Mosaic law even gave special status to the firstborn males of the sheep and cattle (see Exod. 13:2, 11-16; 22:29b-30; Num. 18:15-19). Even a cursory reading of these texts shows that the principle applied to sons applied to calves and lambs as well. In 15:19 Moses turned Israel's attention to this law. *'Set apart for the LORD your God every firstborn male of your herds and flocks'* (15:19a).

In 15:19b-23 Moses explained how the Israelites were to set apart their firstborn lambs and calves to the Lord. In keeping with the Sabbath principle he commanded, *'Do not put the firstborn of your oxen to work, and do not shear the firstborn of your sheep.'* They were set apart for religious use and as they waited for the day when they were taken to the sanctuary they were not to be put to ordinary uses. The consequence of this was that their economic potential was not to be tapped.

These firstborn animals were to be dedicated to the Lord. Every Israelite family was to gather in the presence of the Lord at one of the three pilgrim festivals described in Deuteronomy 16 (see 16:16-17). When they went up to worship the Lord they were to take with them their firstborn animals. *'Each year you and your family are to eat them in the presence of the LORD your God at the place he will choose.'* As we saw in 12:11-14 and 14:22-27, eating these offerings in the presence of the Lord was a mechanism for bringing the produce of the land to the central place where they became available for the support of the Levites and priests. The firstborn animals were dedicated to the Lord during those times of sacrifice and feasting, repentance and rejoicing.

The only time when a firstborn animal was not to be eaten in the presence of the Lord was if it had any physical defects (15:21). *'If an animal has a defect, is lame or blind, or has any serious flaw, you must not sacrifice it to the LORD your God.'* Only perfect animals were to be offered to the Lord or eaten in his presence. The same rule applied to those animals which were offered as sacrifices to the Lord (see Lev. 22:17-22 for more examples of what made an animal defective). The Israelites were often tempted to offer second-best to the Lord. The prophet Malachi rebuked them for offering sacrifices to the Lord which would have been unacceptable to their earthly governor (see Mal. 1:6-8). However, even a defective firstborn animal was to be dedicated to God and eaten by his people in their home towns, so long as they observed the laws governing animal slaughter in

12:15-25. *'You are to eat it in your own towns. Both the ceremonially unclean and the clean may eat it, as if it were gazelle or deer. But you must not eat the blood; pour it out on the ground like water.'*

The purpose of this law was to remind the Israelites that every animal born to them was a gift from God and belonged to God. The firstborn animal was an appropriate reminder of this fact because it 'opened its mother's womb', as the Hebrew idioms expressed it. The firstborn was the sign of his father's strength and his mother's ability to bear offspring, and in due time more offspring might well be expected.

The special place given to the firstborn was also used to illustrate Israel's special privileges as a people dedicated to God. In Exodus 4:22 God claimed the people of Israel as his firstborn son. He told Pharaoh that they were not to be put to work for him. 'Israel is my firstborn son ... Let my son go, so that he may worship me.' Yet again we see that Israel's special status was marked out by resting from ordinary tasks.

This law also anticipates the provision of a Saviour of God's people. The law required that a firstborn son in an Israelite family should be redeemed by the payment of five shekels of silver (see Num. 18:16; Exod. 13:13). By contrast, the firstborn of the flock or herd was not to be redeemed, but sacrificed on the altar (see Num. 18:17). When God's firstborn Son, the Lord Jesus (see Col. 1:18; Heb. 1:6), came into the world, he was dedicated to the Lord and the sacrifice required by Moses was made on his behalf (see Luke 2:22-24). In spite of this sacrifice, he was not spared from the death which awaited him. His heavenly Father gave up his eternally firstborn son in order to redeem many sons and daughters on earth – a new Israel who would look to him for salvation. He himself did not claim the exemption which any human firstborn could have claimed. He made himself like a firstborn from the flock. When we set our Lord's ministry against the background of Israel's laws, we see how much he was willing to humble himself for our salvation. He did not evade death by redeeming his own life; he offered himself as the sacrificial lamb so that others might eat and rejoice.

Conclusion

The nation of Israel became God's firstborn son because God redeemed them from slavery in Egypt and adopted them as his own. They were doubly devoted to the Lord. They belonged to Jehovah both by creation and redemption. Every Israelite belonged to the Lord. So did every animal and every inch of the promised land. There was no such thing as private property, for everything was held in trust for God. The Sabbath principle recognised this fact by releasing debts in the seventh year, releasing slaves after six years' service, and dedicating firstborn animals to God.

Redemption in Christ makes believers a people doubly devoted to God. 'You were bought with a price. Therefore honour God with your body... do not become slaves of men' (1 Cor. 6:20; 7:23). We recognise God's Lordship when we return our tithe to him, offer worship on the Sabbath day, and show compassion to our brothers in need. They, like us, belong to God. 'I tell you the truth, whatever you did for one of the least of these brothers of mine, you did for me' (Matt. 25:40).

Chapter 16
The pilgrim festivals

Please read Deuteronomy 16: 1-17

Deuteronomy roots the spiritual life of the Israelites in their history. Over and over again, Moses appealed to the Israelites to remember their history so that they might have God's power and faithfulness impressed on their minds (see 4:10; 5:15; 7:18; 8:2; 9:7; 11:2; 15:15). This would strengthen their faith and encourage greater obedience. The call to remember was often coupled with warnings not to forget (see 4:9, 23; 6:12; 8:11, 14, 19; 25:19). The importance of both the call to remember and the warning against forgetfulness was noted in the Psalms (see Ps. 78:42; 106:7, 13, 21). Yet all too often, and sometimes very quickly, the Israelites forgot their history and forsook the Lord their God.

God knew that even his own redeemed people had faulty memories; so he provided regular reminders of his goodness and mercy towards them. Three times a year the people of Israel were to make a pilgrimage to the place God had chosen in order to remember God's mercies and to acknowledge their covenant with Jehovah. These three pilgrim festivals were the Feast of Passover and Unleavened Bread, the Feast of Weeks and the Feast of Tabernacles. These became an established feature of Israel's national calendar (see Exod. 23:14; 2 Chr. 8:13). As well as setting out the liturgy of these festivals, Moses explained their purpose and encouraged whole-hearted participation. In these verses Moses called the people of God to gather for worship.

The Feast of Passover and Unleavened Bread (16:1-8)

The Feast of Passover and Unleavened Bread was a double celebration. It lasted for a week and included three elements. First of all, the people sacrificed the Passover animal on the anniversary of the night they left Egypt (16:1). Then for six more days they would eat unleavened bread (16:3-4). Finally, they held a sacred assembly on the last day of that Passover week (16:8b). The purpose of this festival was to help the Israelites remember how the Lord had led them out of slavery in Egypt. Note three significant features of this week-long celebration.

1. The Passover meal (16:1-4)
The Feast of Passover was celebrated on one of the most important dates in the Israelite calendar, the fourteenth day of the first month. *'Observe the month of Abib and celebrate the Passover of the LORD your God, because in the month of Abib he brought you out of Egypt by night.'* The month of Abib (later called Nisan) was designated the first month of the year for the Israelites, to honour the significance of the exodus. The Israelites were to observe the whole month as a special month, because in the middle of this month they gathered to celebrate the feast of Passover and Unleavened Bread. Moses restated God's purpose in 16:3b: *'so that all the days of your life you may remember the time of your departure from Egypt'.* In 16:6 the very time of the feast is specified. *'You must sacrifice the Passover in the evening, when the sun goes down, on the anniversary of your departure from Egypt.'* The feast was rooted in the history of Israel's salvation from slavery in Egypt.

i. *The main dish* (16:2). *'Sacrifice as the Passover to the LORD your God an animal from your flock or herd...'* We often associate

Passover with the sacrifice of a lamb. Certainly a lamb was slain on the first Passover night, when the Israelites daubed its blood on their doorposts (see Exod. 12:3). In New Testament times the custom of killing and eating a lamb was well established (see Mark 14:12; Luke 22:7). This imagery of a sacrificial lamb was used by the New Testament writers to describe the Lord Jesus (see 1 Cor. 5:7; 1 Peter 1:19). However, in Deuteronomy Moses did not specify a lamb. His command in 16:2 allowed for the sacrifice of a lamb from the flock or a calf from the herd. See also Numbers 28:19 and 2 Chronicles 35:9. Perhaps this allowance was made because at this stage in their journey cattle were more readily available for some of the Israelite tribes. The tribes which had been allocated land east of the Jordan had many cattle (see 3:19).

It may well be that that the lack of detail in the Passover law in Deuteronomy points to the principle of substitution rather than the details of the ritual. The point to note is that God had made special provision for the deliverance of the Israelites through the sacrifice of a substitute. The sacrifice which they offered reminded the Israelites of the last and worst of the ten plagues which devastated Egypt. Yet when the angel of death went through the land to slay the firstborn in every family, they were spared. What a terrible night for the Egyptians! Yet what a great deliverance for Israel, because they were covered by the blood of the slain sacrifice. That night the Israelites roasted and ate the meat of the animal whose blood had saved their lives. They were to eat every last piece of meat (16:4b). '*Do not let any of the meat you sacrifice on the evening of the first day remain until morning.*' That must have been a very sobering thought.

ii. *The side dish* (16:3-4). The Passover animal was to be eaten along with bitter herbs and bread made without yeast (see Exod. 12:8). Here Moses mentioned only the bread without yeast. '*Do not eat it* (that is the Passover sacrifice) *with bread made from yeast, but for seven days eat unleavened bread, the bread of affliction, because you left Egypt in haste – so that all the days of your life you may remember the time of your departure.'* The unleavened bread is called 'bread of affliction' because it reminded them of their time as slaves in Egypt. It may well have been that a simple unleavened flat loaf was all they had the time or means to prepare when they were slaves. On the night they left Egypt they ate unleavened bread because they left in haste, and did not have time to wait for the yeast to rise. They were eager to leave the place where they had suffered so much. That was a fact which they later forgot. Some of the Israelites even looked back with longing on the days when they had eaten meat and fish and vegetables in Egypt (see Exod. 16:3; Num. 11:5). It is amazing how we can forget what God has done for us, yet remember with pleasure what the world has to offer us! Another reason why the Israelites left in haste was that the window of opportunity was a small one. In the agony of his grief Pharaoh gave the command that the Israelites should leave Egypt, but he would soon change his mind (Exod. 14:5). The Israelites must seize the opportunity of salvation when it presented itself, just as people today must seek the Lord while his mercy is offered to them (see 2 Cor. 6:2).

An alternative translation of the phrase 'in haste' (16:3) would be 'in fear and trepidation'. The Israelites did not march out of Egypt like a victorious army with trumpets sounding and banners flying. They left Egypt fearfully, looking over their shoulders and wondering where they would go next. They had a slave mentality and were unsure what freedom would feel like. Their deliverance was a mighty and miraculous work of God. They had played little or no part in planning or accomplishing it. They were simply swept up in God's work of liberation.

As well as being slaves, the Israelites were also sinners in the presence of a holy God. Because of this, the unleavened bread took on a new and spiritual significance. Not only were they to eat unleavened bread during the Passover week, but every trace of leaven was to be removed from their midst (16:4). *'Let no yeast be found in your possession in all your land for seven days.'* Perhaps because yeast caused a process of fermentation and disintegration, it was associated with moral corruption (see New Testament examples in the teaching of our Lord; Matt. 16:6; Mark 8:15). At Passover time in the Old Testament, the removal of yeast symbolised an active campaign to purge sin from their lives and to walk in the ways of the Lord. The Lord who had saved them from slavery also sought to deliver them from the idols and immorality of Egypt. That was what they were to remember as they purged the yeast from their midst and ate unleavened bread.

2. The location of the celebration (16:5-7a)
The first Passover was celebrated by the Israelites as a family feast in their own homes in the land of Goshen. During their years in the wilderness the Israelites continued to celebrate the Passover in their homes (see Exod. 12:46), which were gathered around the tabernacle. When the people entered the promised land that togetherness would be lost as they settled down in their tribal lands throughout Canaan. Yet when it came to the first month of each year, the Israelites were to gather at one central place to celebrate the Passover. This is the distinctive feature of the Passover law in Deuteronomy. Moses has already made reference to this in 16:2, and in 16:5-7a he spells out the implications. *'You must not sacrifice the Passover in any town the LORD your God gives you except in the place he will choose as a dwelling for his Name. There you must sacrifice the Passover... Roast it and eat it at the place the LORD your God will choose.'*

The significance of this chosen place has been explained in Deuteronomy 12. This was a place which God would reveal once the Israelites entered the promised land. The Israelites were to seek it out so that they might bring their sacrifices there to offer them to the Lord and rejoice in his mercies. They were to make sacrifices at this one central location rather than at the many shrines which were to be found on almost every hilltop in

Canaan. Those were the places where the pagans worshipped their false gods. Not only were the Israelites to destroy these sacred sites, they were to have nothing to do with them and the rituals associated with them. In order to avoid the danger of being tainted by pagan worship at these shrines, the Israelites were to offer sacrifices – and that included the Passover sacrifice –at the place which God had chosen for himself. Later we find that Hezekiah and Josiah were commended for gathering the people together at the temple in Jerusalem to celebrate the Passover (see 2 Chr. 30:1-11; 35:1-6).

From this practice we can learn that it is good for God's people to gather together to worship him and remember his mercies (see Ps. 122:1-2; 133:1). This plays an important role in preserving the integrity and identity of the church. Today we gather together to hear God's word and receive the sacraments. These are means of grace given to the church collectively, and not to individual believers or families. The gathering of the Israelites teaches us to value the collective life of the church.

We also learn the importance of remaining distinct from the world in which we live. God has chosen and called his people to be different from the sinful world in which they live. For the Israelites, that meant not offering sacrifices at the shrines of Canaan. For the church today, it means knowing the culture in which we live and rejecting those aspects which clash with the holiness of God. By the way in which we worship, by the values we hold to, by the lives we live we are called to be a people who stand out from the culture around us. This kind of counter-cultural holiness requires courage and insight, yet it is essential to the survival of the church. Our Lord taught this when he described citizens of the kingdom of heaven as 'the salt of the earth' (Matt. 5:13).

3. The closing assembly (16:7b-8)
A whole night was given over to eating the Passover meal and

remembering how the Lord had delivered his people from slavery in Egypt. Clearly the meal was a substantial one (the whole of the sacrificial animal was to be consumed in one evening, 16:4b) and it was eaten with thoughtful remembrance. Afterwards the Israelites were to go back to their tents (16:7b). *'Then in the morning return to your tents.'* When Moses gave this instruction, the Israelites were still nomads encamped east of the Jordan, preparing to enter the promised land. At that time they lived in tents. Later, when they settled in the promised land, they would travel up to Jerusalem every year to keep the Passover. There they would slaughter their Passover animal and eat the feast within Jerusalem before returning to their tents outside and all around the city. They would live in tents for six days, eating bread without yeast, and then on the seventh they would hold a special assembly (see 16:8b). *'For six days eat unleavened bread and on the seventh day hold an assembly to the LORD your God and do no work.'*

This final assembly was the climax of the Passover season. During the Passover week the people rested from the unrelenting physical labour that characterised their lives. No doubt the children would play together while their parents talked and relaxed. The week-long celebration gave them an opportunity to reflect on the spiritual significance of the Passover sacrifice and the unleavened bread. At the time of King Hezekiah's great Passover feast, 'the Israelites who were present in Jerusalem celebrated the Feast of Unleavened Bread for seven days with great rejoicing, while the Levites and priests sang to the LORD every day, accompanied by the LORD's instruments of praise' (2 Chr. 30:21). On that occasion the Israelites so enjoyed this time of celebration that they continued for seven more days (2 Chr. 30:23). The more normal pattern was to end the week by holding an assembly that compressed the remembering and rejoicing of the previous seven days into one service of worship. We do not know what kind of liturgy was followed during the assembly, but we might well assume that sacrifices were offered, praise was sung and prayers of thanks were said.

Today, Christian believers are given an even clearer view of their privileges in Christ through the preaching of God's word and the administration of the sacraments. When we come to the Lord's Table, we remember the completed work of the Lord Jesus, our Passover lamb (see 1 Cor.5:7). Yet do we appreciate how great these privileges are? Do we rejoice as we gather with God's people? Do we sense Christ's presence as we come to the Lord's Table? Do we wish we could continue and enjoy more, or do we look anxiously at our watches, longing to get away? May we know more of the joy of the Lord in our personal devotions and public gatherings.

The Feast of Weeks (16:9-12)

Gratitude is the outstanding characteristic of the second pilgrim festival described in this chapter, the Feast of Weeks. It was celebrated seven weeks after the Passover (16:9). *'Count off seven weeks from the time you begin to put the sickle to the standing corn.'* Passover took place at the beginning of the harvest (typically just before the barley was harvested), while the Feast of Weeks took place shortly after the completion of the harvest (typically just after the wheat was gathered in). Later, the feast came to be known as Pentecost, a name taken from the phrase 'fifty days' in the Septuagint translation of Leviticus 23:16.

Detailed descriptions what happened at the Feast of Weeks are found in Leviticus 23:15-22 and Numbers 28:26-31. The nation was to 'hold a sacred assembly and do no regular work' (Num. 28:26). The required sacrifices were to be offered as the firstfruits of the grain harvest were presented to God.

In Deuteronomy Moses does not repeat the ceremonial details. Instead, he distils their spiritual significance. The Feast of Weeks was an expression of gratitude. The blessings of the harvest were to be an annual reminder of God's goodness and a prompt to the Israelites to express their thankfulness to God. Parents often find that they have to prompt their children to say 'thank you', or write a letter of thanks, when they receive a gift. In the excitement of the moment they easily forget. Our Lord observed that forgetfulness amongst a group of ten lepers whom he healed of their leprosy. Only one returned to give thanks (see Luke 17:15-18). The Feast of Weeks taught the Israelites to pause in the midst of one of the busiest seasons of their year to acknowledge what God had done for them. It taught them two lessons about gratitude to God.

i. A freewill offering (16:10)
'*Then celebrate the Feast of Weeks to the LORD your God by giving a freewill offering in proportion to the blessings the LORD your God has given you.*' This freewill offering consisted of produce from the land (including grain, wine and meat) and was given in addition to the tithe. No specific amount was prescribed. The giver was encouraged to give whatever he thought appropriate. Moses simply urged the Israelites to give 'in proportion to the blessings the LORD your God has given you'. The apostle Paul applied this principle when writing to the church in Corinth on the subject of giving to support needy Christians. 'Each man should give what he has decided in his heart to give, not reluctantly or under compulsion, for God loves a cheerful giver' (2 Cor. 9:7). A cheerful giver is one who has seen the goodness of God and responds with gladness.

As we read this passage today we do well to remind ourselves that we have even more reason to be grateful to God than the Israelites had when they celebrated the Feast of Weeks. We have received the greatest of all God's gifts, the gift of God's beloved Son and the salvation which he offers (2 Cor. 9:15). God has blessed us with the riches of salvation. 'So then, just as you received Christ Jesus as Lord, continue to live in him, rooted and built up in him, strengthened in the faith as you were taught, and overflowing with thankfulness' (Col. 2:6-7). We show our thankfulness by bringing our offerings to support the work of the church. We also show our gratitude by offering our time and talents to the Lord's service, by offering our hearts in love and our lips in the singing of God's praise, and by offering our lives in total surrender to his Lordship. 'Therefore, 1 urge you, brothers, in view of God's mercy, to offer your bodies as living sacrifices, holy and pleasing to God – this is your spiritual act of worship' (Rom. 12:1).

ii. Communal rejoicing (16:11)
'And rejoice before the LORD your God at the place he will choose as a dwelling for his Name – you, your sons and daughters, your menservants and maidservants, the Levites in your towns, and the aliens, the fatherless and the widows living among you.' As this celebration was a feast, we may assume that the rejoicing took place around a meal table. The food was supplied by those who gave generously from the produce of their land. The guest list was long and inclusive. Moses included people who might not normally have been invited. As well as close relatives and household members (which included servants) the Israelites were to invite needy and vulnerable members of the community. This is a recurring feature of Moses' teaching in Deuteronomy (see 12:12, 18-19; 14:27-29).

Three needy groups are mentioned here: the Levites who lived at a distance from the central sanctuary, the aliens who did not own land, and the fatherless and widow who had no family head to protect them. The Levites were included in this list because they had no tribal land from which to derive a living. They were allocated towns within the territory of the other tribes, and they depended on the generosity of their fellow countrymen. Also included in this list were landless aliens and the fatherless and widows, who would not have been able to access the benefits of their family's inheritance. They depended on the generosity of others in their family and the wider community. Moses encouraged the Israelites to be mindful of the needs of these groups because the whole nation had once been destitute in Egypt.

In 16:12 Moses places Israel's gratitude in its historical and theological context. *'Remember that you were slaves in Egypt, and follow carefully these decrees.'* At that time they were landless slaves, labouring in the fields of their Egyptian masters. Everything they gathered went to others. Yet God led them out of slavery, and they were now a redeemed people. In gratitude they were to obey all the laws which God had given to Moses at Sinai, including these laws which regulated the pilgrim feasts. By the second century BC the Feast of Weeks came to be associated with the giving of the Law at Sinai, because it was reckoned that it had taken the Israelites seven weeks to travel from Egypt to Sinai. The gratitude expressed at this festival was channelled into loving and generous obedience by the laws given to Moses.

Christian readers now associate Pentecost with the outpouring of the Holy Spirit upon the disciples in Acts 2. Although Luke does not labour the symbolism of the Old Testament festival in his account of the Spirit's outpouring, it is significant that God chose this as the day when he would pour out his Spirit upon his renewed Israel, the church. Just as the Feast of Weeks followed the exodus, so the Christian Pentecost followed the redemptive exodus which Jesus accomplished at Calvary. The three thousand who were added to the church on that day (Acts 2:41) were the firstfruits of an even greater harvest gathered through the preaching of the gospel.

There is a link, too, between the theological significance of the Jewish Pentecost and that of the Christian Pentecost. Just as the giving of the law at Sinai channelled the gratitude of a redeemed people, so did the giving of the Spirit in Jerusalem. His mighty indwelling prompted them to live winsomely as citizens of God's heavenly kingdom on earth. They gladly shared their material blessings with each other (Acts 2:45; 4:32). They also shared their spiritual blessings with the needy nations of the world (Rom. 15:27). This group of Spirit-filled Israelites then started to look beyond themselves to the Gentiles who were still aliens to the grace of God (Eph. 2:12).

The Feast of Tabernacles (16:13-15)

Some Old Testament ceremonies sound very unattractive by modern standards. They involved the slaughter of animals, the sprinkling of blood and the burning of flesh. These may seem quite repulsive to many people today. However, the Feast of Tabernacles is one Old Testament ceremony which we might have enjoyed attending. Its outstanding characteristic was joy in the Lord. Moses exhorted the Israelites to keep this yearly festival in 16:13-15.

Let's try to observe what it would have looked like through the eyes of a child. If you had grown up in a small village in Israel, the routine of life would have been fairly humdrum. Yet one night, as you go to bed, your father tells you to get a good night's sleep tonight because tomorrow the whole family will set off on a long journey. 'Where are we going?' you ask. 'Jerusalem,' is the reply. Looking ahead to the journey you ask your father, 'Where will we stay and what shall we eat?' Your father tells you, 'We will camp out in the open, underneath the stars, and you will eat all your favourite food.' Bewildered, you ask, 'How will we be able to afford all this?' Your father replies that God has been very good to his people and provided an abundant harvest so that there will be enough food to feed all the families in your village through the winter months. And so the whole community goes up to Jerusalem to give thanks to the Lord.

The Feast of Tabernacles had a prominent place in the affections of God's people. While other Old Testament festivals were solemn reminders of the sin and misery from which God had delivered his people, this feast was an emphatically joyful celebration. It impressed upon the Israelites a deep sense of God's goodness towards them. Elsewhere in the Bible it is simply called 'the feast' (see 1 Kings 8:2; 12:32; Psalm 81:3; John 7:8). At the conclusion of the Feast of Tabernacles our Lord made his great declaration about the work of the Holy Spirit in the heart of the believer. 'If anyone is thirsty, let him come to me and drink. Whoever believes in me, as the Scripture has said, streams of living water will flow from within him' (John 7:37-38). Let's look at what Moses had to say about this feast.

i. When the festival took place (16:13)
'Celebrate the Feast of Tabernacles for seven days after you have gathered the produce of your threshing-floor and your winepress.'
The Passover and Feast of Weeks were celebrated in spring and early summer, either side of the grain harvest. Only after the grapes and olives had been gathered in, in the autumn when the harvest was complete, did the Israelites celebrate the Feast of Tabernacles. Leviticus 23:33 specified the date of this feast - the fifteenth day of the seventh month. The backbreaking work of gathering the harvest was over. The barns were full. There would be enough food to feed the people through the winter.

Many people today may not find it easy to appreciate the significance of a harvest festival like the Feast of Tabernacles. Few of us have experienced the hard physical work of harvesting grain with a hand-held sickle, or the pressure of gathering the harvest before the weather breaks. Most of us buy our food at supermarkets and it is always there when we need it. Yet we have busy seasons in our lives. Teachers have exams to mark and reports to write at the end of the school year. Accountants have their busy season at the end of the financial year. Shopkeepers are very busy in the weeks leading up to Christmas. Fire-fighters are in great demand during dry, hot summers. After these busy seasons we are glad to rest and give thanks for God's provision and protection.

ii. How the festival was celebrated (16:14-15a)
Moses spelled out three important features of this feast. They were to celebrate this feast joyfully, unitedly (the whole community joining together) and centrally (at the place which God would choose).

Moses does not mention the *shelters* (or tabernacles) which gave this feast its name. The law of Leviticus 23:40 would have been well known. It describes the materials from which temporary shelters were constructed. They were similar to the shelters which villagers built when they encamped in their vineyards during the grape harvest. Yet their purpose was to remind the Israelites of the forty years their ancestors had spent in the wilderness before entering the promised land. By dwelling in tents for one week every year they were reminded that, even though they now had a homeland of their own and even though their barns were full, they were still pilgrims with their eyes set on a better land (Heb. 11:13, 39). Their joy was thus centred upon God himself.

The Israelites celebrated the Feast of Tabernacles *joyfully* because their focus was upon the Lord who had blessed them. '*Be joyful at your Feast...*' Nehemiah 8:13-17 describes an occasion when this command was taken very seriously. It may seem strange that Moses should teach such a command. After all, joy is not something that we can turn on. Or is it? Paul issues a similar command in Philippians 4:4. 'Rejoice in the Lord always, I will say it again: Rejoice!' We can subject our emotions to our wills, and above all to the gospel. Godly joy is not an erratic and uncontrollable feeling, but a fruit of the Spirit's work inside us (Gal. 5:22). It is found in the Lord and focuses on him.

The Israelites celebrated the Feast of Tabernacles *inclusively* because everyone was invited (16:14). *'Be joyful at your Feast—you, your sons and daughters, your menservants and maidservants, and the Levites, the aliens, the fatherless and the widows who live in your towns.'* The guest list for the feast is the same as that in 16:11. It is noteworthy that 'aliens' were invited to join the feast, as they did not live in tents during the feast like native-born Israelites (Lev. 23:42). Presumably this is because the aliens were not members of the redeemed community. Yet they were to enjoy the generosity of those who had been redeemed. This generosity was a testimony to the grace of Israel's God and held out the hope that they too might one day come to enjoy Israel's privileges.

The Israelites celebrated the Feast of Tabernacles *centrally* because they went to a designated place (16:15a). *'For seven days celebrate the feast to the LORD your God at the place the LORD will choose.'* This requirement is characteristic of Moses' teaching in Deuteronomy (see 12:5), as it sought to keep Israel's celebrations free from the influence of the worship which took place at pagan shrines. Even though the Feast was a happy occasion, it was also a holy occasion. Every seventh year the Feast of Tabernacles provided the occasion for a communal reading of the law (see Deut. 31:9-13). It was by no means inconsistent with the joy of the occasion that the Israelites should 'listen and learn to fear the Lord' (Deut. 31:12). It is important that God's people learn to celebrate God's mercies according to God's commands.

iii. Why the Israelites celebrated this festival (16:15b)
It was typical of Moses to explain why the Israelites ought to do as God had commanded. In 16:15b he included a reason which went beyond what they might have expected. *'For the LORD your God will bless you in all your harvest and in all the work of your hands, and your joy will be complete.'* They might have expected Moses to refer back to the harvest which they had just gathered. Instead, he pointed forward towards promised

blessings. This is understandable as the Israelites had not, at that time, entered into the land of Canaan. There was an air of expectancy amongst them as they looked forward to God's provision in the land of promise. Only then would their joy be 'complete' or 'unspoiled'. A literal translation of the last phrase of 16:15 reads, 'it will be only joy'.

There were, no doubt, many times when Israelites read these words with incredulity. Times when their lives were touched by tragedy and sadness, rather than joy. Even in the promised land there were times when they sowed in tears and reaped no harvest. They would bring such distress upon themselves by their own sinful conduct. At such times there was little to celebrate when the autumn came. What were they to do? In such times they were taught to look forward to a better harvest. Psalm 126:5-6 describes those whom God has redeemed out of exile.

> Those who sow in tears
> will reap with songs of joy.
> He who goes out weeping,
> carrying seed to sow,
> will return with songs of joy,
> carrying sheaves with him.

Psalm 67:6-7 looks for a harvest from the ends of the earth when Jehovah is acknowledged by all nations.

> Then the land will yield its harvest,
> and God, our God, will bless us.
> God will bless us,
> and all the ends of the earth will fear him.

Our Lord anticipated such a harvest even among the Samaritans in John 4:35. 'I tell you, open your eyes and look at the fields! They are ripe for harvest.' He saw people who would hear the gospel and enter the kingdom of heaven. In Matthew 9:37-38 he urged his disciples to pray for such a harvest. 'The harvest is plentiful but the workers are few. Ask the Lord of the harvest, therefore, to send out workers into his harvest field.' Paul longed for such a harvest amongst those to whom he ministered (see Rom. 1:13; 2 Cor. 9:10). The final harvest is still to come (see Matt. 13:37-39). For those who reject the gospel it will be a time of misery. But for those who have accepted the Saviour it will be a time of perfect joy. Will that joy be yours? (1 John 1:4).

Conclusion (16:16-18)

In this summary Moses listed the three festivals and their common features. *'Three times a year all your men must appear before the lord your God at the place he will choose...'* The invitation was universal. All Israel was to gather for the nation as a whole had been redeemed by God and richly blessed by him. The mention of 'all your men' did not exclude women or children. Often whole families came to worship together. An example of this is the family of Elkanah and his two wives in 1 Samuel 1:3-8. The men who appeared before God came as representatives of their families and when they came they brought their families with them. By their presence they were saying what Joshua said in Joshua 24:15: 'But as for me and my household, we will serve the LORD'.

As the men of Israel and their families gathered for the festivals, they brought an offering. *'No man should appear before the LORD empty-handed. Each of you must bring a gift in proportion to the way the LORD your God has blessed you.'* As they gathered in God's presence they were to acknowledge God's blessing in their lives. Everything they possessed had been given to them by God himself. Sadly, it is all too easy to go through life getting and spending and enjoying the good things that God had given us, but forgetting God himself. The purpose of these three annual festivals was to create in the hearts and minds of the Israelites a consciousness of God that permeated their lives throughout the rest of the year. As a result of that God-consciousness they gathered at God's appointed place to present their offerings. The evidence of their love and gratitude towards God was that they did not come empty-handed.

When we come to God as sinners seeking his pardon and acceptance, we come empty-handed. 'Nothing in my hand I bring. Simply to thy cross I cling.' Yet when our sins have been forgiven and we have been adopted into God's family, we appreciate how richly God has blessed us. Everything we possess takes on a new significance. Every day that we live is an opportunity to serve God. Every meal that we eat has been provided by the God who loves us and strengthens us for his service. Thus we do not want to come to God empty-handed. We bring him our thank offerings. 'Ascribe to the LORD, O families of nations, ascribe to the LORD glory and strength. Ascribe to the LORD the glory due to his name; bring an offering and come into his courts' (Ps. 96:7-8). We want to sing his praises (Heb. 13:15) and offer our whole being in his service (Rom. 12:1).

Chapter 17
Judges and kings

Please read Deuteronomy 16:18 - 17:20

Every community, however strong its moral foundations, needs to be governed by rulers. It needs laws which are recognised by all and it needs officers who will enforce them. Moses recognised this in his exposition of the laws which God had given him at Sinai. In 16:18 –17:20 he explains the laws which regulated Israel's civil rulers. Many of the laws in this section concern matters which many people today might think of as secular. Yet in Moses' eyes, nothing was secular, for every area of Israel's life was subject to the rule and regulation of Jehovah, Israel's covenant Lord.

Moses ministered God's word at a time when Israel was a theocracy. Jehovah was not only Israel's Redeemer, but her king, and he was explicitly recognized as such. Rulers were appointed and sustained in office by his authority. Civil rulers were, therefore, not regarded as a necessary evil but as instruments of God. They were to 'rule over men in righteousness' and 'in the fear of God' (see 2 Samuel 23:3; Psalm 2:10-12; 72:2).

No modern nation stands in exactly the same position as Israel in Old Testament times. It was both a religious and political entity. Its public institutions had the character of both church and state. One of the challenges which face the Christian reader of the Old Testament is the application of these regulations today. Do they apply to civil rulers or to church authorities or to both? Most Christians will acknowledge that the civil laws of Israel apply principles of righteousness which find their perfect expression in the Lord Jesus, the king and head of the church. Thus these principles guide ministers and elders who rule the church (1 Tim. 5:17; Heb. 13:7, 17).

Some Christians, because of their high regard for the authority of God's law, take the view that these and other judicial laws apply automatically to rulers today. Others note the obvious differences between ancient and modern society and the accomplishment of redemption in Christ, and argue that the civil laws given to Israel have served their purpose and were never intended to apply to every nation in every age. The Westminster divines bridged these two positions by noting that 'to them (the people of Israel) also, as a body politic, he gave sundry judicial laws, which expired together with the state of that people, not obliging any other now, further than the general equity thereof may require' (*Westminster Confession of Faith*, chapter 19.4). It is those principles of equity that we will seek to identify as we study these laws, so that we may apply them in our modern setting.

The New Testament church is a multi-ethnic and international community which cannot be confined within the boundaries of any single nation. It is found in countries which have for many centuries been influenced by the gospel as well as in countries where Christians are a tiny minority and the culture is profoundly antichristian. Yet in both settings the church bears testimony to its rulers and calls upon them to rule righteously. Church and state are distinct entities, yet both are equally subject to the Lord Jesus Christ, who has been give all authority in heaven and earth and who rules over all things for the sake of the gospel (see Matt. 28:18; Eph. 1:22-23).

Paul taught church leaders how to rule justly (see 1 Tim. 3:15; 5:17-20; Titus 1:5). He also recognised that civil rulers have an important function within the overall framework of God's kingdom. They are ordained by God to suppress evil and encourage those who do what is right (see Rom.13:1-5). Their task is to create the conditions in which the church can carry out its task of proclaiming the gospel. In both cases Paul applied general principles to specific challenges.

That is what Moses did when he expounded Israel's laws about rulers to the Israelites of his day. He did so because the people themselves were to appoint suitable rulers from their midst, and because Israel's rulers needed to know how to rule well as servants of the Lord. The underlying principle was that God was Israel's Father and he ruled his people as a father rules his household. For this reason many commentators regard Deuteronomy 17 and 18 as an extended meditation upon the fifth commandment. This command placed checks on the way rulers ruled and explained why the people ought to respect their rulers.

Judges and their role (16:18 – 17:7)

The need for a judge to adjudicate in disputes between Israelites became obvious to Moses soon after the exodus (see Exod. 18:13-26). He gladly took the advice of Jethro, his father-in-law, to 'select capable men from all the people – men who fear God, trustworthy men who hate dishonest gain – and appoint them as officials over thousands, hundreds, fifties and tens. Have them serve as judges for the people at all times' (Exod. 18:21-22). In 1:9-16 Moses reminded the people of this incident. As the nation increased in size the need for leaders grew, so in 16:18-20 Moses laid out a framework for Israel's system of justice. *'Appoint judges and officials for each of your tribes in every town the LORD your God is giving you and they shall judge the people fairly.'* Judges were to adjudicate between parties to a dispute, hopefully by giving a decision which would resolve the dispute. Officials assisted the judges by implementing the decisions which the judges handed down. There are four features of Israel's system of justice which are worthy of comment.

i. It was to be accessible

The judges and their courts were to be within easy reach of every Israelite. That is the significance of the provision in 16:18a: 'Appoint judges in every town the LORD your God is giving you...' Justice is a noble goal, but realistic steps need to be taken to accomplish it. These included the appointment of suitably qualified judges, and their placement in communities where the people lived. In the wilderness, the Israelites went to the tabernacle to seek justice. When they entered the land of Canaan, they would not be able to do that as they were spread throughout the whole land of their inheritance. It was necessary that the infrastructure of justice be expanded to allow for the peaceful resolution of disputes. Local courts were to be set up 'in every town', literally 'in all your gates'. Traditionally, the local elders who adjudicated disputes sat in the area near the city gate. When opportunities for the peaceful resolution of grievances were not available they would build up and create social tension (see 2 Sam. 15:3-4). This was at odds with the ideal of covenant brotherhood in Israel.

ii. It was to be reliable

Moses described the quality of the justice which the judges were to administer in 16:18b-19. *'... and they shall judge the people fairly. Do not pervert justice or show partiality. Do not accept a bribe, for a bribe blinds the eyes of the wise and twists the words of the righteous.'* These are basic rules of natural justice which have been adopted as the ideal in many legal systems. In Israel judges were to make their decisions on the basis of God's law rather than on the basis of their self-interest. God's law is righteous, whereas human motives are often mixed. Moreover

God's law is transparent and unchanging, whereas human self-interest fluctuates. Hence judges were not to be influenced by the self-interest of those who were rich enough to offer bribes, or powerful enough to threaten the judges. We can see the value of these ideals today in countries where corruption is common. Everyone suffers from the resulting uncertainty. Often entrepreneurs are reluctant to invest in a country where their investment could be lost because of an erratic decision of a corrupt official. Reliable justice is a blessing which flows from God's common grace and reflects God's faithfulness (see Prov. 29:4).

iii. It was covenantal
The ideals of 16:19 have been adopted in almost every human community, but the rationale given in 16:20 is peculiar to the redeemed people of Jehovah. *'Follow justice and justice alone, so that you may live and possess the land the LORD your God is giving you.'* Moses was more than a law-giver. He was a preacher of the word of God and as such he constantly reminded the Israelites of the grace which Jehovah had lavished upon them and the covenant which he had made with them. He exhorted the people with passion and emphasis. 'Justice, justice you will pursue' is a literal reading of 16:20. If they obeyed Jehovah in this matter, he would keep his covenant promises and they would live for a long time in the land. Security in the land of promise is the recurring promise of Deuteronomy. The emphasis is not on the length of an individual's life, but on the quality of life enjoyed by the redeemed community. It is life protected, sweetened and enriched by the righteousness of God. The social legislation of Deuteronomy sought to foster social cohesion and harmony. For this a fair system of justice was essential.

iv. It was sacred
Everything in Israel was sacred, including many aspects of life which people today think of as secular. We have seen that agriculture had a religious underpinning. The same was true

of the administration of justice. God's name was to be invoked every time God's law was applied (see 1:17). In the ancient world this would have been considered quite normal. It was taken for granted that judges would seek divine guidance and perform religious rituals when they administered justice. The all-important question which faced Israel's judges when they entered the land of Canaan was which god would guide them? For Moses, there was only one answer – Jehovah! From this he drew two implications.

a. Israel's judges must not seek guidance from false gods, nor must their religious rituals be those of the pagans around them (16:21–17:1).

> Do not set up any wooden Asherah pole beside the altar you build to the LORD your God, and do not erect a sacred stone, for these the LORD your God hates. Do not sacrifice to the LORD your God an ox or a sheep that has any defect or flaw in it, for that would be detestable to him.

This is a repetition of similar prohibitions found elsewhere (see 7:5; 12:3; also Exod. 34:13; Lev. 26:1). Asherah poles were fertility symbols erected by the Canaanites, often beside standing stones and sacrificial altars. In ancient literature Asherah was sometimes referred to as the 'goddess of oracles'. At these sacred sites ancient judges sought a message from their gods, especially when it was hard to decide between the competing claims of two parties. Asherah would guide them through the impasse, or so they hoped.

Moses returned to his prohibition of Asherah poles and pagan rituals in order to make it very clear that there was no need for such help. He taught the Israelites that they were not to administer justice on the basis of oracles from false gods, for righteous judgment can only be given on the basis of the word of God. Many years later, in the reign of King Jehoshaphat, we find a godly king purging the land of Asherah poles (2 Chr. 19:3). This reform was then followed by the appointment of judges who would 'judge for the Lord' when they gave their decisions (2 Chr. 19:4-7). By purging away pagan superstition, Jehoshaphat paved the way for true justice based on the sound principles of God's law.

b. *Israel's judges must be pro-active in purging evil from the Lord* (17:2-7). *'If a man or woman living among you in one of the towns the LORD gives you is found doing evil in the eyes of the LORD your God in violation of his covenant, and contrary to my command has worshipped other gods, bowing down to them or to the sun or the moon or the stars of the sky... take the man or woman who has done this evil deed to your city gate and stone that person to death.'* Any violation of God's covenant with Israel was 'evil' in God's sight. He hated evil (see 12:31) with the same intensity as he loved his people. Because corrupt worship brought the curses of the covenant upon the whole nation, judges were to purge such practices from their midst.

Idolatry was the definitive act of covenant disloyalty (see 4:15-27). Its various forms are listed in these verses – worshipping false gods such as Baal or Ashteroth and bowing down to the heavenly bodies. These were serious matters and the people were encouraged to report any such behaviour to the judges (17:4): *'and (if) this has been brought to your attention...'* The judges were then to investigate these reports (17:4b): *'then you must investigate it thoroughly'*. They had a pro-active role, rather like that of the prosecutor-judge in the civil law systems of continental Europe.

The judges' investigation was to be a thorough one. No allegation was to be given any credence without evidence. Moses knew the deceitfulness of the human heart and ordered safeguards against a miscarriage of justice resulting from hasty action based upon a malicious accusation. First of all, the accusation must be supported by at least two witnesses whose testimony agreed with each other (17:6). *'On the testimony of two or three witnesses a man shall be put to death, but no-one shall be put to death on the testimony of only one witness.'* This is an important rule and was applied more generally (see 19:15). It was especially important that the witnesses agreed in cases where a death sentence was possible (see Num. 35:30). This rule of evidence reflects God's concern for justice and truth. Israel's legal system was to reflect these attributes of her covenant Lord. This requirement was violated by the Jewish authorities when the Lord Jesus was condemned to death on the testimony of witnesses whose story was evidently a mass of contradictions (see Mark 14:59). The church, like Israel, is to reflect God's concern for fairness in her dealings with those who are accused of serious sin for no accusation is to he heard against an elder unless it is brought by two or three witnesses (see 1 Tim. 5:19; Matt. 16:18).

Another safeguard is found in 17:7. Those who gave evidence of idolatry to the judges were to consider the potential outcome of their testimony. *'The hands of the witnesses must be the first in putting him to death, and then the hands of all the people.'* Those who were willing to give testimony in court were to follow their words with actions. This was surely calculated to discourage frivolous or vexatious accusations. Our Lord's words in John 8:7 had a similar effect on those who claimed to have caught a woman in adultery and asked Jesus to condemn her. 'If any one of you is without sin, let him be the first to throw a stone at her... At this, those who heard began to go away one at a time...' This requirement reminded the witness that a charge of idolatry was a serious matter indeed and that he would give an account to God for his words. It is important for us to remember that we too will give an account to God for every word that we have spoken (Matt. 12:36) and that our words have the power to kill and destroy (Prov. 18:21a; James 3:5-8).

The goal of Israel's system of justice was to preserve purity of the covenant people (17:7b). *'You must purge the evil from among you.'* Idolatry was a 'detestable thing' and 'evil in the eyes of the Lord'. The penalty was a severe one and had the effect of removing evil-doers from the community (17:5). *'Take the man or woman who has done this evil deed to your city gate and stone that person to death.'* The people as a whole had a part to play in the process of purging evil from their midst. *'The hands of all the people'* were to take up stones against the idolater. This may seem barbaric by modern standards, but it was the way in which the whole community indicated its endorsement of God's holy law and its repudiation of idolatry.

The New Testament equivalent of this judicial process is the exercise of church discipline. As well being an act of pastoral oversight exercised by the elders of the church, it is a judicial process to be administered fairly. Although ministers and elders do not have the authority to impose fines or imprisonment, and certainly not a death sentence (these powers rightly belong to the civil authorities, see Rom. 13:4), they have been given the keys of the kingdom (see Matt. 16:19; 18:18) and they may exclude offenders from the privileges of membership within the visible church (1 Cor. 5:5).

The purpose of church discipline is to preserve the purity of the church community and preserve the honour of the church's head, very much like the purpose of Israel's judicial system. It is well summarised in chapter 30.3 of the *Westminster Confession of Faith*: 'Church censures are necessary for the reclaiming and gaining of offending brethren; for deterring of others from the like offences; for purging out of that leaven which might infect the whole lump; for vindicating the honour of Christ, and the holy profession of the gospel; and for preventing the wrath of God, which might justly fall upon the church, if they should suffer his covenant, and the seals thereof, to be profaned by notorious and obstinate offenders.'

The court of reference (17:8-13)

The central court described in these verses was a court of reference rather than a court of appeal (17:8). *'If cases come before your courts that are too difficult for you to judge ... take them to the place the LORD your God will choose.'* The right to refer the matter to the central court belonged to a local court rather than an aggrieved party who did not like the decision given by a local judge. The matter taken to the central court was one which the local judges realised was too difficult for them, so they sought a ruling from the more experienced judges of the central court.

These difficult cases are described by an unusual Hebrew expression in 17:8. They were 'too wonderful' for the local judges to adjudicate. The same Hebrew expression is used, in other contexts, to describe God's miraculous acts in Egypt (Exod. 3:20), the intricacy of the human body (Ps. 139:14), the stone in which the builders rejected but which became the capstone of the temple (Ps 118:22-23). In Deuteronomy 30:11 Moses told the Israelites that the message of God's covenant mercies was not 'too difficult for you'. In other words, they were able to understand that message and act upon it. However, here in 17:8 it describes issues and problems which required wisdom and insight that the local judges did not have. This kind of wisdom was not to be gained merely through the experiences of daily life. These cases required an evident measure of wisdom from God.

Moses provides several examples of these difficult cases in 17:8: *'bloodshed, lawsuits or assaults'*. 'Bloodshed' refers to the distinction between wilful murder and involuntary homicide. This is an important distinction in most criminal codes; and amongst modern common law jurists merely defining the distinction between murder and manslaughter has been a point of contention. Assessing the facts of a particular case can be even more difficult. In modern courts, that decision is often left to a jury. 'Lawsuits' refers to civil disputes over property, straying animals and inheritance claims. 'Assaults' refers to the injuries done to a person and the appropriate level of compensation to be given by the person who caused the injury. It is never easy to assess the monetary value of an eye or a leg. These are hard questions to answer satisfactorily, and local courts were able to hand them on to a panel of experts. There, wisdom might be sought in a multitude of counsellors (Prov. 11:14).

By acknowledging the necessity for this court of reference, Moses recognised the fallibility of the local judges. Judges can and do make mistakes. Their mistakes can sometimes rob innocent people of their life and livelihood. That is a terrible evil, and one which every system of justice ought to seek to avoid. Most legal systems draw on the wisdom of experienced judges. Israel's legal system went further and drew on the wisdom of God. King Solomon recognised this when he asked God to give him the wisdom he needed to rule. 'So give your servant a discerning heart to govern your people and to distinguish between right and wrong' (1 Kings 3:8). God granted Solomon's request and enabled him to make wise adjudications (1 Kings 3:28).

True wisdom for every difficult decision we face continues to come from God. 'For the LORD gives wisdom, and from his mouth come knowledge and understanding' (Prov. 2:6). This encourages us to search God's word, as the psalmist did in Psalm 119:97-100.

Oh, how I love your law!
I meditate on it all day long.
Your commands make me wiser than my enemies,
for they are ever with me.
I have more insight than all my teachers,
for I meditate on your statutes.
I have more understanding than the elders,
for I obey your precepts.

Praise God that he is able to fill up the deficiencies in our wisdom when we acknowledge our need. 'If any of you lacks wisdom, he should ask God, who gives generously to all without finding fault, and it will be given to him' (James 1:5).

The central court was located near the central sanctuary, where sacrifices were to be offered to Jehovah. Thus the local judges were to refer cases to *'the place the LORD your God will choose'* (17:8). Moses exhorted the people in 17:9, *'Go to the priests, who are Levites, and to the judge who is in office at that time. Inquire of them and they will give you the verdict.'* The judges of the central court were priests and Levites, and they were meant to be the custodians of God's law (see 31:9). They were also charged with the task of presenting the king with the Book of the Law (see 17:18). They were to teach the people what God's law required of them. 'For the lips of a priest ought to preserve knowledge and from his mouth men should seek instruction – because he is the messenger of the LORD Almighty' (Mal. 2:7). An extension of this role was helping the local courts to apply God's law to difficult cases.

The president of the court is referred to simply as 'the judge'. He did not sit alone when he gave judgment, but sat as the leading officer of the court. Very possibly he was the court's spokesman. Some commentators suggest that he was an experienced and gifted local judge seconded to the central court, but most probably he was also a priest or Levite. In 2 Chronicles 19:8-11 we find that a number of laymen served alongside the priests in a similar court in Jerusalem at the time of King Jehoshaphat. He appointed the high priest to preside over a bench consisting of other priests and Levites to adjudicate on any matter concerning the Lord; while the leader of the tribe of Judah presided over the same bench when it considered 'any matter concerning the king' (17:11). In both spheres God's wisdom was needed to administer justice. Jehoshaphat prayed, 'may the LORD be with those who do well.'

Moses exhorted the Israelites to recognise the authority of this new central institution and to abide by its decisions in 17:10-13.

You must act according to the decisions they give you at the place the LORD will choose. Be careful to do everything they direct you to do. Act according to the law they teach you and the decisions they give you. Do not turn aside from what they tell you, to the right or to the left.

The location of the court, the participation of priests and the application of God's law in this central court gave it great authority. The judges who served on its bench were servants of Jehovah and to show contempt for their decisions was equivalent to showing contempt for Jehovah. In 17:12-13 Moses prescribed the penalty for such contempt. *'The man who shows contempt for the judge or for the priest who stands ministering there to the LORD your God must be put to death. You must purge the evil from Israel. All the people will hear and be afraid, and will not be contemptuous again.'* The penalty was severe and was intended to deter those who would challenge the authority of the fledgling central institutions of the Israelite nation as it established itself in the lawless land of Canaan. It was also intended to deter those who would challenge the authority of Jehovah to rule as Lord over his own redeemed people.

Modern judges do not hold exactly the same position as did judges in Israel's theocracy, but they are still 'ministers of God'. In that sense their work is not totally secular. They have been ordained by God and must give an account to him for the way in which they rule. We must respect them and submit to them even when we do not agree with their decisions. Peter tells us, 'Submit yourselves for the Lord's sake to every authority instituted among men' (1 Peter 2:13). The same principle was stated by the apostle Paul in Romans 13:4-5:

For he is God's servant to do you good. But if you do wrong, be afraid, for he does not bear the sword for nothing. He is God's servant, an agent of wrath to bring punishment on the wrong-doer. Therefore, it is necessary to submit to the authorities, not only because of possible punishment but also because of conscience.

Elders who rule the church also find themselves having to address increasingly complex pastoral issues. Giving pastoral counsel to God's people often requires us to balance several biblical principles and think our way around new challenges. Every case of church discipline is overwhelming in its implications. Yet we must not run away from this important ministry in the life of the church. Not only is faithful discipline one of the marks of a true church, it is a means of blessing. Those who administer it need wisdom. It is a great blessing to know that we are able to pray to the head of the church for guidance and to seek his wisdom in Scripture. He provides resources of help and wisdom through the wider church community. We find an example of this in Acts 15, where the fledgling church in Antioch sought help from the mother church in Jerusalem after certain men had come from Judea teaching what sounded like a dangerous deviation from the apostolic gospel (see Acts 15:1-4). The decree from this gathering of the apostles and elders of the wider church served to strengthen the local congregations (Acts 15:30-32).

The law of the king (17:14-20)

In these verses Moses describes an institution which did not exist during his own lifetime – the monarchy. In fact, it did not come into existence in Israel until many years after his death. Yet Moses looked forward to the day when Israel would have a human king and set out the legal and spiritual framework within which he would rule. *'When you enter the land the LORD your God is giving you and have taken possession of it and settled in it...'*

Although Moses performed many of the functions of a king, he was never considered to be Israel's king. Jehovah was Israel's king and Moses taught the Israelites to acknowledge him as such in 33:5. Following the deaths of Moses and Joshua, Israel was ruled by a series of judges. They were not thought to be kings either. In Judges 8:23 Gideon refused to be Israel's king or to allow his sons to be made king. The judges were raised up by God to lead the Israelites against a specific threat (see Judg. 8:1; 12:1). Yet Moses could foresee the day when the Israelites would want a king to gather the tribes and lead them in battle (17:14b): *'... and you say, "Let us set a king over us like all the nations around us"'.* Moses had seen the institution of monarchy in Egypt and the nations around them. Its benefits as well as its drawbacks were known to Moses and the Israelites even at this stage in their history.

Moses was surprisingly positive about the possibility of the people asking for a king. Although he did not encourage the request, he did not discourage it either. He simply told the people to acknowledge the higher authority of Jehovah in the process of selecting a king. *'Be sure to appoint over you the king the LORD your God chooses.'* This is in marked contrast to Samuel's response to the people's request for a king towards the end of his life (see 1 Sam. 8:3-5). Samuel interpreted this as a vote of no confidence in him (see 1 Sam. 8:6). The Lord told Samuel not be so concerned about his own honour, for it was the honour of Israel's heavenly king which had been slighted (see 1 Sam. 8:7-8). Their request was 'an evil thing... in the eyes of the Lord' (1 Sam. 12:12, 17, 19), but the Lord was still willing to grant their request and give them a king to rule over them.

Israel's request for a king may have come from impure motives, but it was something that Jehovah himself had already anticipated. Although Samuel did not refer to Deuteronomy 17, his response to Israel's request indicates a familiarity with the concerns which Moses had expressed and the framework which he had laid down several centuries earlier. Compare 1 Samuel 8:11-17 with Deuteronomy 17: 16.

Moses set out a series of checks and balances which would prevent the abuse of kingship in Israel. History has shown that 'power corrupts and absolute power corrupts absolutely'. Only Jehovah can be trusted to exercise absolute power righteously, because he is a holy and incorruptible God. Human kings who ruled as his vassals needed to be reminded of their limitations from the very moment of their enthronement. In fact, the very method of their appointment reminded them that they were subject both to God and his people. They were chosen by God and appointed by the people. *'Be sure to appoint over you the king the LORD your God chooses.'* God revealed his choice (see 1 Sam. 10:1, 24; 16:12-13; 1 Kings 8:16b; Psalm 89:3-4) to the people. Thus they became God's instruments in placing the king on the throne (1 Sam. 10:24; 2 Sam. 2:4; 5:3). The king could never claim a divine right to tyrannise the people who had appointed him. He remained one of the people whom Jehovah had redeemed and over whom Jehovah ruled.

The king was to be a member of the covenant community (17:15b-17). *'He must be from among your own brothers. Do not place a foreigner over you, one who is not a brother Israelite.'* He must be a true Israelite. In a time of crisis the people might be tempted to ask a powerful neighbour to rule over them. Submitting to the rule of a foreign king might be a smart move, when strategic considerations are taken into account. Yet this would inevitably lead the people away from their exclusive commitment to Jehovah. This happened when King Ahab took Jezebel, a heathen princess, as his queen (1 Kings 16:31-33). It was vitally important that the titular head of the covenant people was subject to Jehovah and his laws.

Other limitations were placed on Israel's king. These limitations were intended to make Israel's king very different from the kings of other nations (17:16-7).

The king, moreover, must not acquire great numbers of horses for himself or make the people return to Egypt to get more of them, for the LORD has told you, "You are not to go back that way again." He must not take many wives, or his heart will be led astray. He must not accumulate large amounts of silver and gold.

In order to survive, ancient kings were required to flaunt their wealth and power. They kept a large stable of horses, not merely for personal pleasure, but in order to put an army into the field. They married many wives in order to establish political alliances and win allies. Gold was able to buy anything and anyone. So horses, wives and gold were emblems of worldly power and worldly kings zealously hoarded them.

By contrast, Israel's kings were to rely upon the Lord's strength. 'Now I know that the LORD saves his anointed; he answers him from his holy heaven with the saving power of his right hand. Some trust in chariots and some in horses, but we trust in the name of the LORD our God' (Ps. 20:6-7). Sadly King Solomon did not follow the counsel of Moses and the psalmist in this matter. Not only did he marry many heathen princesses who led his heart astray (1 Kings 11:1-6), but he accumulated great wealth (1 Kings 10:14-17, 27) and imported horses from Egypt (1 Kings 10:28-29). Moses specifically warned kings of Israel against sending their people back to Egypt (17: 16b). This may have been a simple prohibition on horse trading with the nation that had so recently oppressed the Israelites. Or it may have referred to the terrible practice of kings who sold their subjects as slaves or mercenaries in order to obtain luxury items such as horses. Solomon's lavish spending on his buildings, horses, and wives placed a terrible burden on his people. These burdens led to growing resentment and the break-up of his magnificent kingdom. If only he had heeded Moses' warning!

There was one final reminder that the king's power was limited by God (17:18-20). *'When he takes the throne of his kingdom, he is to write for himself on a scroll a copy of this law, taken from that of the priests, who are Levites.'* The Levites were custodians of the law. They preserved the scrolls and taught their contents to the people. They were to serve as teachers to the king himself. At a time when books were rare, because they had to be copied by hand, the king was required to make a copy of the law for himself. The scroll described in this verse contained the summary of the law which Moses expounded on the plains of Moab. This has come down to us as the book of Deuteronomy. At first it was preserved by the Levites who served at the central sanctuary (31:9). Then it was associated with the other books written by Moses and became an integral part of the Hebrew Scriptures. This summary of the law was not a second law or an addition to the law that was given at Sinai. That is what some understand the name Deuteronomy ('second law') to mean. Instead, Deuteronomy is a summary and reapplication of the law. Its name comes from the Septuagint translation of the phrase 'copy of this law' in 17:18.

The ritual of receiving and copying the book of the law at the king's enthronement was to be followed by a lifetime of reading and meditating upon God's law (17:19).

> *It is to be with him, and he is to read it all the days of his life so that he may learn to revere the LORD his God and follow carefully all the words of this law and these decrees and not consider himself better than his brothers and turn from the law to the right or to the left.*

A Bible gathering dust is of little value. It is like medicine in the cabinet or food that is never eaten. God's word cries out to be read and digested inwardly. This applied to kings just as much as it applied to their subjects. When kings lose sight of the fact that they are servants of God and of the people they rule, they become a menace. They have many opportunities to abuse their position.

It was the custom when a victorious Roman general was being feted on his triumphal procession through Rome, that a servant beside him would whisper in his ear, 'Sir, remember that you are mortal'. The book of the law was a constant whisper in the ears of Israel's kings that they were mere men, answerable to Israel's divine king. Many people today imagine that they are kings of a different kind. They imagine that they are autonomous kings over their private lives, free from all moral restraints. The word of God whispers in the consciences of each one of us to remind us that we are subject to the authority of the King of kings.

Moses concludes this section with a promise to the king who read God's law and obeyed it (17:20b). *'Then he and his descendants will reign a long time over his kingdom in Israel.'* The same promise was made to David in 2 Samuel 7. When God declined David's offer to build him a temple in Jerusalem, he promised that David's son Solomon would build that temple and that Solomon's offspring would reign forever on the throne of Israel. 'When your days are over and you rest with your fathers, I will raise up your offspring to succeed you, who will come from your own body, and I will establish his kingdom... Your house and your kingdom will endure forever before me; your throne will be established forever' (2 Sam. 7:12, 16).

This promise was fulfilled in David's greatest son, King Jesus, whose kingdom is an everlasting kingdom. He has been given all authority in heaven and earth (Matt. 28:18). Yet before he was exalted and enthroned, he lived as a model citizen on earth. He was subject to his earthly parents (Luke 2:51) and he paid his due to the tax collectors (Matt. 17:24-27). He meditated on God's law and was able to quote it aptly (Luke 4:1-12, 17-21). He became a brother to those whom he would save and rule (Heb. 2:11-12, 17). In all these ways he followed the ideal set out by Moses for Israel's kings.

In the kingdom of Jesus there is none of the arrogance of earthly rulers. Jesus contrasted his authority with that of the secular rulers of his day.

> Jesus called [his disciples] together and said, 'You know that the rulers of the Gentiles lord it over them, and their high officials exercise authority over them. Not so with you. Instead, whoever wants to become great among you must be your servant, and whoever wants to be first must be your slave - just as the Son of Man did not come to be served, but to serve, and to give his life as a ransom for many' (Matt. 20:25-28).

Those who exercise authority within the church are to follow his example of servant leadership (1 Peter 5:1-3). Likewise, those who exercise authority in the political sphere have no better model to follow, for they too rule as men under authority (Luke 7:8). Citizens of such a king will, like him, renounce worldly ways and worldly attitudes 'for the world and its desires pass away, but the man who does the will of God lives for ever' (1 John 2:17).

Chapter 18
Spiritual leaders

Please read Deuteronomy 18: 1-22

It is a great privilege to lead God's people. With that privilege come responsibility and scrutiny. Moses laid down rules and guidelines for those who ruled the people of Israel. His goal was to prepare the people of Israel to live as a well-ordered and godly community in the land of Canaan. For this to happen they would need central institutions and leaders to administer them. In chapter 17 we read what he had to say about judges and kings. In chapter 18 we move from civil rulers to spiritual leaders.

Moses taught the Israelites about the privileges and responsibilities of their spiritual leaders – the Levites and the prophet. He also explained their obligations to their pastors. Those leaders were entitled to the support and respect of the people. Some commentators regard this whole section (16:18 – 18:22) as an application of the fifth commandment, with civil and religious leaders exercising a father-like authority from God, who is the source of all authority. Whether or not Moses based his teaching in this chapter on the fifth commandment, he did teach about the mutual obligations of the people and their spiritual leaders. First he considered the priests and Levites (18:1-8), and then the prophets (18:9-22).

The priests and Levites (18:1-8)

The tribe of Levi offered continuity and stability to the religious life of the people of Israel. In contrast to the prophets, who were raised up by God as the need arose, the Levites and priests ministered constantly amongst the people, albeit with varying degrees of faithfulness. Two groups are mentioned in 18:1. *'The priests, who are Levites—indeed the whole tribe of Levi...'* The tensions between the two groups named here – 'the priests' and 'the whole tribe of Levi' – provide the background for Moses' teaching in the verses which follow.

The priests were those Levites descended from Aaron (Exod. 28:1). Elsewhere in the Old Testament, they are described as 'the sons of Aaron' (Lev. 1:5; 22:2). They alone were allowed to offer sacrifices at the altar, and from this ministry some of them derived a comfortable living. Others were not satisfied with what God had provided for them and abused their ministry to enrich themselves, as we can see when we read about the activities of Hophni and Phinehas in 1 Samuel 2:12-17. They were often contemptuous of the other clans from the tribe of Levi and the important work which they did.

Some of these other clans from 'the whole tribe of Levi' were singers, some were gatekeepers, some helped with the work of slaughtering and skinning the sacrificial animals, some lived in the towns and villages of Israel, where they gathered the tithe and taught the people. All of these ministries were important, because they supported the ministry of sacrifice at the altar. The whole tribe of Levi was characterised as a priestly tribe, even though not every Levite was a priest. Moses therefore warned against any haughtiness on the part of the priests, who might think that, because they served at the altar, they could look down on the Levites who served in other spheres. The underlying goal of his teaching was to protect the interests of 'the whole tribe of Levi'. He described the common inheritance of the whole tribe of Levi in 18:1-2; the entitlements of the priests in 18:3-5; and the free movement of all Levites in 18: 6-8.

i. The common inheritance (18:1-2)

Moses described the provision which God made for the whole tribe of Levi. This was quite different from the provision which God made for the other tribes in Israel, for the Levites 'are to have no allotment or inheritance with Israel'. The other tribes were to receive an allocation of land when they entered Canaan (see Josh. 15-19). They were to divide this land amongst their families so that they might grow crops and raise their animals and support their families. The Levites, however, received no such allocation. They lived here and there in the midst of the other tribal territories. In these territories certain towns were set apart for the Levites (see Josh. 21; Num. 35:1-5); but they had no contiguous area which they could call their own. Moses regularly brought this fact to the attention of the other Israelites (see 10:9; 12:12; 14:27, 29) in order to remind them of their responsibility to provide for the Levites.

The Lord appointed the Levites to minister to the spiritual needs of the other Israelites (10:8-9). 'The LORD set apart the tribe of Levi to carry the ark of the covenant of the LORD, to stand before the LORD to minister and to pronounce blessings in his name, as they still do today. That is why the Levites have no share or inheritance among their brothers.' When Moses blessed the tribes of Israel, he said of Levi that 'He teaches your [Jehovah's] precepts to Jacob and your law to Israel. He offers incense before you and whole burnt offerings on your altar' (Deut. 33:10). As they performed their ministry at the altar, the Levites were to receive their inheritance, for 'they shall live on the offerings made to the LORD by fire, for that is their inheritance' (18:1b). As we see in 18:3-5, the priests and Levites were to receive a portion of the offerings brought by the people as a remuneration for their work and as a means of supporting them and their families. They were to look upon their special status as an inheritance from the Lord. Their ministry was to be handed down from one generation to the next within the tribe of Levi as a sacred commission. The Levites were not to think that they had drawn the short straw in God's allocation of resources to the tribes, for theirs was a special inheritance. There is no greater privilege on earth than serving the Lord and caring for the spiritual needs of his people.

Moses described the special privileges enjoyed by the Levites in spiritual terms in 18:2. 'They shall have no inheritance among their brothers; the LORD is their inheritance, as he promised them.' Not only were they able to serve the spiritual needs of the Israelites, they were to enjoy a special relationship with Jehovah. The Lord had made this promise to Aaron and the rest of the Levites in Numbers 18:20. 'You will have no inheritance in their land, nor will you have any share among them; I am your share and your inheritance among the Israelites.' This promise is stated in language very similar to Deuteronomy 4:20; 9:29; 32:9, where Israel is described as the Lord's inheritance. (See also Ex. 34:9; 1 Sam. 26:19; 2 Sam. 20:19; Ps. 28:9; 33:12; Joel 3:2.) Israel was described in this way because the Lord took a special delight in her, choosing her to be his peculiar treasure and entering into a covenant with her. The Lord took upon himself an unbreakable obligation to bless the nation of Israel because it was his inheritance. The language of inheritance is the language of covenant love and loyalty.

When Moses spoke of the Levites having the Lord as their inheritance, he was describing a privilege that even the other Israelites did not enjoy. The Lord had made a special covenant with Levi and his tribe (see Mal. 2:4-6). Like the other Israelites, the Levites rejoiced in the knowledge that the Lord was their Redeemer and knew that they could rely upon the Lord to provide for all their material and spiritual needs. But they enjoyed more. They enjoyed the privilege of ministering at the altar and teaching God's law to God's people. This brought them into an especially close connection with Jehovah himself. As they taught God's law, they had opportunity to meditate on it and so walk with the Lord. As they offered sacrifices, they were able to enter the glory of God's presence. When the New Testament apostles sought to describe the privileges which believers enjoy under the new covenant, they did so in terms very similar to those of the Levites and priests. These gospel privileges are not limited to one tribe or group within the New Testament Israel. All believers may enter God's presence clothed in the righteousness of Christ. 'Therefore, since we have been justified through faith, we have peace with God through our Lord Jesus Christ, through whom we have gained access by faith into this grace in which we now stand' (Rom. 5:1-2). All believers are also called to special service. 'Therefore, I urge you, brothers, in view of God's mercies, to offer your bodies as living sacrifices, holy and pleasing to God – this is your spiritual service.' (Rom. 12:1, based on the NIV with modifications)

The greatest privilege of the Levites in Old Testament times was not their special status in the community, but their special relationship with the Lord. It was not their ministry, but the Lord himself whom they served. Some of the priests forgot this and greedily guarded their status and the privileges which went with it. This is a perennial temptation for those who serve God in full-time ministry. One of the dangers which faces those in Christian ministry today is that of becoming absorbed in the work of the church to the detriment of our relationship with the Lord. Some may enjoy the status which the work brings or the success which results from their labours. Some are gifted speakers, while others really enjoy getting alongside people. It is important that Christian ministers love the work of ministry; but first and foremost they must be lovers of God. He must be our greatest delight and treasure.

ii. The priests' provision (18:3-5)
The Levites enjoyed many spiritual blessings in Israel, but

these alone did not provide for their material needs. These verses summarise the ways in which Jehovah provided for the material needs of the Levites, who had no tribal lands of their own. In 18:2 Moses stated that 'They shall live on the offerings made to the LORD by fire'. These were the offerings of flesh and grain sacrificed on the altar. In the Hebrew text they are simply called 'fire offerings', because they were offered to Jehovah in the fires of the altar. This phrase occurs many times in Leviticus 1 – 7, where it describes the burnt offering, the grain offering, the fellowship offering, the sin offering and the guilt offering. Some of these offerings were completely consumed on the altar, while others were only partly burnt. What was left provided food for the priests and Levites and their families (see Lev. 2:10; 6:26; 7:28-36). Other offerings were not burnt at all, but were given in their entirely to the priests (see Lev. 7:12-14).

In 18:3 Moses describes what portion of those offerings was to be given to the priests, that is, the family of Aaron, which was one clan within the tribe of Levi. *'This is the share due to the priests from the people who sacrifice a bull or a sheep: the shoulder, the jowls and the inner parts.'* The priests were to receive a just and fair portion of the sacrifice as food to eat. Moses gave a rule of thumb assessment of what a fair share might be, mentioning three parts of the animal. In Leviticus 7:34 he had commanded that a more generous share be given to the priests from the fellowship offering. 'From the fellowship offerings of the Israelites, I have taken the breast that is waved and the thigh that is presented and have given them to Aaron the priest and his sons as their regular share from the Israelites.' It is not surprising that a more generous portion might be given from the fellowship offering as it involved sharing God's bounty amongst God's people as an expression of gratitude to God. In Deuteronomy Moses states the rules which applied more widely. It established a minimum legal standard which applied to all animal sacrifices so that the priests did not miss out on the provision which was rightfully theirs.

Spiritual leaders

In years to come another problem arose. Some priests used their monopoly on the altar to enrich themselves. In 1 Samuel 2:12-16 we read of the two sons of Eli, Hophni and Phinehas, greedily demanding the best cuts of meat and using the threat of violence to get what they wanted. Not only did the people suffer from this despicable behaviour, but we can only assume that the other Levites who served God away from the place of sacrifice lost out in the distribution of food. Laws such as Moses' rule of thumb guide in 18:3 were designed to ensure that there was equity in the distribution of the inheritance amongst priests and Levites.

Another source of income for the priests was from the tithes and firstfruits which the people offered to Jehovah (18:4). *'You are to give them the firstfruits of your grain, new wine and oil, and the first wool from the shearing of your sheep.'* These were the first portion of the produce of the land from the yearly harvest. In Exodus 23:19 and Numbers 18:12-13 Moses commanded the Israelites to bring this produce to the Lord so that it might be shared amongst the sons of Aaron. How much of the crop was to be offered as the firstfruits of the harvest is not stated in these passages. However, in Deuteronomy 14:22 Moses told the people to set aside a tenth of all their produce each year for the Lord. This was to be eaten in the presence of the Lord at the place which God had chosen as a dwelling for his name. The people were not to eat all of this produce themselves, for they were commanded to invite the needy, including the Levites, along to the feast. This feast was a way of thanking God for his goodness to them and distributing a portion of the harvest to the central altar, where it might be distributed amongst the priests and Levites for their support.

An example of how this system worked is found in 2 Chronicles 31:2-5. Here King Hezekiah ordered the people living in Jerusalem to bring in 'the portion due to the priests and Levites so that they could devote themselves to the Law of the Lord'.

This was part of Hezekiah's wider reform programme to restore true worship in Judah. In order for his goal to be realised, there needed to be a body of spiritual leaders who would teach God's word and lead the people in worship. These leaders depended upon the people they served for support and encouragement. A biblically-oriented church will always have a high regard for its leaders whose task it is to teach God's word and lead God's people in worship. That regard manifests itself not only in deep affection but also in practical, material support. The apostle Paul applied this Old Testament practice to the New Testament church in 1 Corinthians 9:13-14. 'Don't you know that those who work in the temple get their food from the temple, and those who serve at the altar share in what is offered on the altar? In the same way, the Lord has commanded that those who preach the gospel should receive their living from the gospel.' He makes an even broader application in Galatians 6:6: 'Anyone who receives instruction in the word must share all good things with his instructor'.

In 18:5 Moses repeated, as if for emphasis, the rationale underlying God's provision for the Levites and priests: '... for the LORD your God has chosen them and their descendants out of all your tribes to stand and minister in the LORD's name always'. In 18:3-4 Moses concerned himself with the portion due to the priests, but the scope of his concern in 18:5 broadens to embrace the ministry of the whole of the tribe of Levi, for the whole tribe had been chosen by God for a special ministry. Those who benefited from their ministry were under a legal obligation to provide for them. Moses' intention is not so much to teach the Levites their rights, as to teach the Israelites their obligations. When the situation was right the apostle Paul was willing to sacrifice such rights for the same of the gospel (see 1 Cor. 9:12). Yet the people of God must know and abide by their obligations to their spiritual leaders.

iii. The free movement of Levites (18:6-8)
Moses addressed the issue of workers' entitlements in a way which resembles modern labour laws (18:6). *'If a Levite moves from one of your towns anywhere in Israel where he is living, and comes in all earnestness to the place the LORD will choose...'* One of the goals of the European Union has been to establish a single market for goods and services which would allow for a more efficient use of resources and encourage economic growth. The theory is that when workers are free to move from one place to another it alleviates unemployment in some places and labour shortages in others. Moses gave a similar law to the people of Israel to guarantee the free movements of Levites. Some Levites would try to restrict the movement of rural Levites from the countryside to the place where the central sanctuary was located by denying them access to the benefits that were provided there for the priestly tribe. Their motives were selfish. They did not want to have to share their inheritance with others, even those from their own tribe.

Rural Levites had an important ministry. They taught God's law to the people who lived in the countryside and small towns of Israel. Often they had an itinerant ministry, travelling amongst the people to teach them and to gather tithes. They did not have a comfortable and settled life. In 18:6 the phrase 'where they are living...' might better be translated, 'Where they are sojourners...' Their travels would sometimes bring them back to the central sanctuary. This law guaranteed to rural Levites the right to minister at the central sanctuary (18:7). *'He may minister in the name of the LORD his God like all his fellow Levites who serve there in the presence of the LORD.'* It also guaranteed them a share in God's provision for the Levites (18: 8). *'He is to share equally in their benefits even though he has received money from the sale of family possessions.'* Commentators have quibbled over what Moses meant by these last words. As Levites did not own land, it probably refers to the sale of personal belongings. This indicates that some Levitical families intended to sell up and move to the city. Their sale of goods provided them with some ready capital to establish themselves in a more promising location, but it made others jealous and gave them an excuse for denying the newcomers a share in the tribal revenues.

Moses had no desire to protect the interests of those whose reasons for moving from the countryside to the central sanctuary were mercenary. The law provided specifically for those who came 'in all earnestness' (18:6), motivated by a desire to serve God and his people. What grieved Moses most was the underlying attitude of greed and the lack of compassion. One of the great themes of Deuteronomy is the brotherhood of God's people. All Israelites are brothers, and they were to care for each other in time of need (see 15:7). This obligation to provide mutual support and encouragement was especially strong amongst the Levites who, as a tribe, relied upon the generosity of their brother Israelites. How could they fail to appreciate the need of those who served God in full-time ministry? Sadly, such gross insensitivity was all too possible. Paul saw it even at the Lord's Table in the church in Corinth (see 1 Cor.11:17-21).

Even today, we see large differences between the salaries of ministers in larger city congregations and those who serve in smaller or struggling rural congregations. This is a disparity which church leaders ought not to resign themselves to as a necessary consequence of economic rationalism. Or we might consider differences in income between believers within the same congregation. We ought never to suggest that those who earn six-figure salaries ought to be ashamed of their earning potential; but Christians must be concerned for their fellow-believers in times of need (see James1:27; Matt. 25:34-40). We need to work hard to create a bond of brotherly love amongst those who labour for God.

The Prophet (18:9-21)

The prophet was God's messenger, raised up to speak to the nation as the times demanded. When kings, priests and the people as a whole became corrupt, the prophet called them to repent and renew their covenant loyalty to Jehovah. He also foretold God's deliverance through the promised Messiah. These ethical and messianic emphases gave Israelite prophecy its unique character. In these verses Moses explains how and why God raised up prophets for his people. Ancient peoples sought explanations of the world in which they lived, but to Israel God gave a revelation of himself.

i. The hunger for prophetic insight (18:9-14)
In ancient times people were constantly confronted by events they could not explain – a thunderstorm, an eclipse of the sun or moon, a sudden death – and they found these mysteries unsettling. After they lost the knowledge of the true and living God, many primitive peoples attributed these phenomena to the spirits who were supposed to inhabit the world of nature. In order to discover what was about to happen to them (and avoid any impending disasters), people turned to these spirits and tried to manipulate them. Certain individuals were believed to have the ability to communicate with these spirits and harness their magical powers. These false prophets had an important role in Canaanite religion. Moses warned the Israelites against turning to them (18:10). *'When you enter the land the LORD your God is giving you, do not learn to imitate the detestable ways of the nations there.'* In 18:10-12 Moses listed nine detestable practices by which the Canaanites sought to discover the mysteries of the universe around them. The Israelites were to avoid them completely.

Four of these detestable practices were ways of predicting future events.

a. Passing a son or a daughter through a fire (18:10) was not merely a sacrifice to a false god, it was a trial or a test in which deductions were made from the child's response to the flames. This cruel practice was particularly offensive to God. Sadly, it became common in Israel and was practised by kings of both Israel and Judah (see 2 Kings 16:3; 17:17; 21:6). Israel was not to use this method to make any kind of enquiry, whether it was addressed to the false gods of Canaan or to Jehovah himself (see Ezek. 20:31).

b. Divination (18:10) was a means of obtaining oracles from a god. Divination was often associated with the practice of passing a child through the fire, and the two practices often took place at the same time. There were other methods of divination: here the more general practice is distinguished from one specific method. The elders of Moab hired Balaam to practice divination against Israel in the hope that they might uncover Israel's hidden weakness and destroy them (see Num. 22:7; 23:23).

c. Sorcery or soothsaying (18:10) is another form of divination. It was practised by the Canaanites (Judg. 9:37) and the Philistines (Isa. 2:6) and by the people of Judah at the time of Manasseh (2 Kings 21:6; 2 Chr. 33:6). In the time of Jeremiah sorcerers and others falsely foretold that the people of Judah would not serve the king of Babylon (Jer. 27:9). The Hebrew term suggests that the sorcerers hummed like an insect (perhaps while in a trance) or interpreted the humming sound made by insects.

d. Interpreting omens (18:10) was also linked with divination. An omen was a natural event, such as an earthquake, an eclipse or the migration of birds, to which a special significance might be attributed. In earlier times the practice might merely involve the application of common sense, acute observation and shrewd insight, as was the case when Laban discovered that he had been blessed by God on account of Jacob (see Gen. 30:27). When he was the ruler of Egypt, Joseph had a cup which he used for this purpose. It has been suggested that the play of sunlight on the liquid in the cup conveyed images which a skilled observer might interpret. The dangers of superstition arising from this practice are obvious and this was surely one of the Egyptian practices which the Israelites were to abandon. As time passed, its pagan overtones became increasingly obvious and Moses outlawed it in Israel.

Two more of these detestable practices were ways of manipulating future events.

e. Witchcraft (18:10) involved the use of special herbs or drugs which were believed to have hidden powers and could be used to achieve outcomes which were unattainable by more conventional means. The magicians of Egypt performed miracles by means of these secret arts (Exod. 7:11). Such practices are not to be tolerated in Israel (Exod. 22:18), for it is God who does mighty wonders by his own power. In Micah 5:12 God foretold the eradication of witchcraft (both the secret rituals and the substances used) from Israel.

f. Casting spells (18:11) involved binding or tying knots. Literally, the phrase describes one who ties another up in knots. It has been suggested that those who practised this secret art tied magic knots which were intended to bind their enemies. In addition to tying knots, those who performed this craft also recited spells or incantations which were designed to bring bad fortune on others (Isa. 47:12) or even to charm a snake (see Ps. 58:4-5).

Then Moses mentions three more detestable practices which involved consulting the dead.

g. A medium (18:11) is someone who consults or seeks help from the spirit of a dead person. The best known example of this practice is found in 1 Samuel 28:7, where Saul, who had by that time completely turned away from Jehovah (1 Chr. 10:13-14), sought a medium through whom he might seek guidance from the spirit of Samuel. In past times Samuel had spoken God's word to Saul; but now Saul had no word from the Lord and was bereft of good counsel. Saul's darkness clearly illustrates the tragic outcome from which Moses sought to deliver the Israelites.

h. A spiritist (18:11) is someone who regularly consults a 'familiar spirit' for guidance in spiritual matters. This spirit becomes familiar by constant recourse, and is one who knows what is going on in the spirit world. Where a medium purported to be able to make contact with many different spirits as the need arose, the spiritist claimed access to one particularly well-informed member of the spirit world. The practice was often associated with the work of a medium (see Lev.19:31; 20:6, 27; 1 Sam. 28:3, 9; Isa. 8:19; 19:3).

i. Necromancy (18:11). Necromancy, or consulting the dead, is a general term to describe what a medium or a spiritist does. It may also include the activities described in Isaiah 65:4, where some sat amongst the graves and performed religious rituals. The purpose of these 'secret vigils' is not clear to us, but they were clearly offensive to God.

These occult practices were attempts by ancient peoples to investigate the mysteries of the world in which they lived. Curiosity is a very positive quality when it leads people to observe God's creation in the light of what he has revealed about himself. However, these ancient peoples had suppressed and then forgotten what God had revealed about himself (see Rom. 1:18-20). They were blinded by 'the god of this age' (2 Cor. 4:4) and their curiosity pushed them into an unholy alliance with Satan to discover 'the secret things' which God had not chosen to reveal. Moses warned the Israelites against all such occult practices (18:12a). *'Anyone who does these things is detestable to the LORD.'* The occult practices of the Canaanites were every bit as offensive to God as their idolatry (18:12b). *'Because of these detestable practices the LORD your God will drive out those nations before you.'* If the Israelites were to enjoy God's blessing in the land, they must *'be blameless before the LORD'* (18:13) and rid the land of their magic (18:14). *'The nations you will dispossess listen to those who practise sorcery or divination. But as for you, the LORD your God has not permitted you to do so.'*

Moses' warning against the occult is as relevant today as it was in his own generation. Modern science is able to explain many natural phenomena. People today turn to meteorologists when they want to know what the weather will bring, and to seismologists when they want to know the likelihood of an earthquake or tsunami occurring in their area. However, there is still much in our world that is mysterious. The details of tomorrow remain a closed book. That is why many people turn to horoscopes and tarot cards. Some will seek to read the future in tea leaves and others will consult mediums and spiritists. With the rise of the new spirituality the occult is becoming increasingly acceptable in popular culture and its pagan underpinnings are overlooked or even lauded. We live in an age of pagan resurgence. Our response to this challenge ought to be that of the prophet Isaiah. 'When men tell you to consult mediums and spiritists, who whisper and mutter, should not a people enquire of their God? Why consult the dead on behalf of the living? To the law and to the testimony! If they do not speak according to this word, they have no light of dawn' (Isa. 8:19-20).

ii. The institution of prophecy (18:15-19)
In contrast to the myriad of detestable Canaanite practices which aimed to unlock divine mysteries, the Israelites were to listen only to God's authorised spokesmen, the prophets. Moses gave the people both a promise and a command in 18:15.

God's treasured possession

'The LORD your God will raise up for you a prophet like me from among your own brothers. You must listen to him.' It is difficult to exaggerate the significance of this promise. A silent god would forever remain a distant and mysterious figure; sovereign perhaps, but not a Saviour. Only when God spoke to his people could they come to know him as their covenant Lord God. The good news of the Bible is that God has spoken (see Heb. 1:1), and that he has spoken to bring salvation to his people.

Moses developed his point by reminding the Israelites of their request at Sinai (see 18:16). *'For this is what you asked of the LORD your God at Horeb on the day of the assembly when you said, "Let us not hear the voice of the LORD our God nor see this great fire any more or we will die."'* A fuller account of this request is given in 5:26-27. When the Israelites saw the cloud of glory and heard the awesome sound of God's voice they realised that they could not stand before such a holy God and listen to his words, so they asked Moses to approach God on their behalf and relate back to them what he had to say. They asked Moses to be their mediator and they pledged themselves to listen to what God said through him. God endorsed their request in 5:28 and his response is recorded here in 18:17-19. *'The LORD said to me: "What they say is good. I will raise up for them a prophet like you from among their brothers..."'* The twofold promise of a prophet (first of all described by Moses in 18:15 and then in God's own words in 18:18) refers to a collective singular or a succession of prophets raised up by God. Over the years there would be many men who succeeded Moses and spoke God's word to the people. These verses set out the distinctive character of Israel's prophets.

a. The prophet's calling. God said *'I will raise up for them a prophet...'* Israel's prophets were called by God and not self-appointed. Before God called them he shaped and trained them for the ministry to which he called them. We can think of the training that Samuel received as a young man in the sanctuary at Shiloh (see 1 Sam. 1:28; 2:18). But it was the voice of God that called Samuel to be a prophet (see 1 Sam. 3:4-13). Likewise, Elisha received invaluable training as he followed his mentor Elijah (see 1 Kings 19:21; 2 Kings 2:9-10). Helpful as this was, his calling came directly from God (see 1 Kings 19:16b, 19; 2 Kings 2:13-15). See also Isaiah 6:8 and Jeremiah 1:4-5.

b. The prophet's identity. The true prophet was to be like Moses, *'...a prophet like you from among their brothers.'* He was to be a member of the covenant community and not like Balaam, a hireling from a pagan race (see Num. 22:4-5). It is worth noting that when the Israelites made use of the occult to uncover mysteries they often had to turn to foreign practitioners of these arts such as the Philistines in Isaiah 2:6. When Israel turned to foreign prophets they invariably turned to false gods.

c. The prophet's inspiration. Moses assured the people that the true prophet of the Lord was totally reliable because, said the Lord, *'I will put my words in his mouth.'* While the people heard the familiar accents of a man, the words were God's. When the Lord called Jeremiah to be a prophet he reached out and touched his mouth and said, 'Now, I have put my words in your mouth' (Jer. 1:9). The true prophet was able to say with confidence, 'Thus says the Lord'. For anyone to make this claim without divine inspiration would be arrogant blasphemy. Yet God has spoken through his servants the prophets and Peter describes the implications for New Testament as well as Old Testament believers in 2 Peter 1: 21. 'For prophecy never had its origin in the will of man, but men spoke from God as they were carried along by the Holy Spirit.' We are to receive the inspired words of God's servants not merely as the words of men, but the very word of God.

d. The prophet's responsibility. Because God has placed his word on the lips of his servant, the prophet must not remain silent. *'He will tell them everything I command him.'* The prophet must speak to the people so that they might hear God's warnings and respond to his offers of mercy. The prophet may not speak selectively, for he must tell the people all that God has chosen to reveal. When young Samuel was afraid to tell Eli what the Lord had told him, the old priest warned him, 'Do not hide it from me. May God deal with you, be it ever so severely, if you hide from me anything he told you' (1 Sam. 3:17). There were times when Jeremiah grew weary under the heavy burden of his ministry, but he knew that he dare not keep silent (Jer. 20:9):

> His word is in my heart like a fire,
> a fire shut up in my bones.
> I am weary of holding it in;
> indeed, I cannot.

'Woe to me if I do not preach the gospel!' Paul exclaimed in 1 Corinthians 9:16. A solemn responsibility was laid upon his shoulders which was akin to the responsibility which rested on the shoulders of an Old Testament prophet.

A heavy responsibility also rested upon those who heard the prophet whom the Lord had raised up. Moses told the Israelites in 18:15b. *'You must listen to him.'* As Moses has explained in chapter 13, this does not remove the responsibility to listen critically to what the prophets say. If a prophet were to lead the people astray he must be rejected, but if he speaks the truth from God he must be heard and obeyed, for he speaks the word of the Lord. Moses recorded God's own warning to anyone who refused to listen to the words of a human prophet in 18:19. *'If anyone does not listen to my words that the prophet speaks in my name, I myself will call him to account.'* There will be no defence for those who have rejected God's word, only condemnation. They have not merely rejected God's servants; they have rejected God himself.

These words of 18:15 were applied by God the Father to the Lord Jesus when he appeared alongside Moses and Elijah on the Mount of Transfiguration in Matthew 17:5. Moses and Elijah were the greatest of the Old Testament prophets, but even their glory paled beside the revelation of the Son of God. When Moses and Elijah disappeared, Peter suggested building three tabernacles to honour Moses, Elijah and Jesus, the three great prophets who had appeared together. The Father's response was emphatic, 'This is my Son, whom I love; with him I am well pleased. Listen to him!' Jesus is the greatest prophet of all. He is more than a prophet, for he is God's own Son. If human prophets were to be heard, so must Jesus.

The New Testament apostles saw Jesus as 'the prophet' of whom Moses spoke in 18:15, the perfect embodiment of a prophetic minister. He is a prophet, but he is greater than all the prophets, for he is not merely God's spokesman, but God's Son. His words reveal the way of salvation. The *Westminster Shorter Catechism* describes this aspect of his work: 'Christ executeth the office of a prophet, in revealing to us, by his word and Spirit, the will of God for our salvation' (answer 24). As he preached in the temple courts shortly after the resurrection of Jesus, Peter described Jesus as the long-awaited prophet and called his hearers to respond to the good news he had proclaimed. Peter   quoted the words of 18:15, 19. ' For Moses said, "The Lord your God will raise up for you a prophet like me from among your own people; you must listen to everything he tells you. Anyone who does not listen to him will be completely cut off from among his people"' (Acts 3:22-23; see also John 1:21; 6:14; 7:40; Acts 7:37). The privilege of hearing God's words brings responsibility. Along with the promise comes the warning. To be cut off from God's people is to be cut off from God himself. What a terrible prospect! Yet God's purpose in sending all the prophets and finally his own Son was not primarily to condemn the world, but to reveal the mystery of salvation so that we might be saved through hearing and believing the gospel.

iii. The danger of false prophecy (18:20-22)
Anything that is valuable will be counterfeited. Moses knew that false prophets would arise in Israel. He addressed that challenge in 13:15; but here he repeated his warning and reminded the Israelites of the penalty in 18:20. *'A prophet who presumes to speak in my name anything I have not commanded him to say, or a prophet who speaks in the name of other gods, must be put to death.'* Note the two forms which false prophecy would take. On the one hand, a false prophet might claim to speak as the representative of Jehovah. What he said might contain elements of truth. He might sound like a true prophet; but the Lord had not sent him and he would bring no benefit to his hearers (see Jer. 23:32). Some false prophets gave false hope to those who heard them (see Jer. 23:16); but their promises of God's blessing were wishful thinking designed to pander to popular sentiment. Even though this prophet speaks in God's name, he is no better than the heathen who practice divination (see Jer. 14:14).

Another, and more blatant, example of false prophecy is the prophet *'who speaks in the name of other gods'.* He leads the Israelites to break the first commandment, for they were to have no other God but Jehovah. In Exodus 23:13 Moses had warned the Israelites, 'Be careful... Do not invoke the names of other gods; do not let them be heard on your lips.' Here he went further, for they were not to listen to false gods or their messengers.

In both instances the false prophet was to be put to death. A true prophet was to be heard with rapt attention, but a false prophet was to be repudiated in the strongest possible terms. *'Do not be afraid of him.'* Because the distinction between true and false prophets had such important consequences, Moses anticipated an obvious question in 18:21. *'You may say to yourselves, "How can we know when a message has not been spoken by the LORD?"'* It was easy to tell when a false prophet claimed to speak in the name of a false god, for his own words would condemn him. It was less easy to tell when a prophet who claimed to speak in the name of Jehovah did so without divine authorisation. Prophets, by the very nature of their ministry, had no official accreditation agency. They registered God's protest against the establishment! Yet true prophets did bear the marks of authenticity, and in 18:22 Moses describes how God's people were to recognise where these marks were lacking. *'If what a prophet proclaims in the name of the LORD does not take place or come true, that is a message the LORD has not spoken.'* This is the test which the courageous Micaiah applied in his show-down with Ahab and his court prophets (see 1 Kings 22:28). Jeremiah also applied this test to those who prophesied peace and security before the destruction of Judah in Jeremiah 28:9.

Important though this test is, it does not tell the whole story and must be subject to obvious modifications. Some true prophets warned of coming judgments which never came because those who heard their message took heed and repented (see Jonah 3:10). Others, who were false prophets, were able to foretell counterfeit signs and wonders and use the credibility gained by this to lead the people into idolatry (see 13:1-2). In spite of these things, the Israelites were not listen to their words. Most importantly however the nature of Messianic prophecy did not lend itself to short-term fulfilment. Many true prophets made predictions which would not be fulfilled until many centuries after their death (see, for example, Isa. 7:14; 53:10-12; Jer. 31:31-34; Micah 5:2; Zech. 9:9). The authenticity of a true prophet is established by the consistency and integrity of his ministry over the long haul, and this would often be recognized only after his death. The authority of the Old Testament prophets has been confirmed by the fulfilment of what they said about the coming of the Messiah (see Luke 24:27; Rom. 3:21; 2 Cor. 1:20; 1 Peter 1:10-11). Although the people of Israel had to wait for many centuries, everything they foretold has come to pass.

Jesus chided the religious leaders of his day for being able to recognise the authenticity of dead prophets, but totally unable to recognise the spirit of prophecy in him. 'Woe to you, teachers of the law and Pharisees, you hypocrites! You build tombs for the prophets and decorate the graves of the righteous. And you say, "If we had lived in the days of our forefathers, we would not have taken part with them in shedding the blood of the prophets..."' (Matt. 23:29-30). 'You diligently study the Scriptures because you think that by them you possess eternal life. These are the Scriptures that testify about me, yet you refuse to come to me to have life' (John 5:39-40). In Jesus we see both the authentication of Old Testament prophecy and the prophet whose words are true.

Conclusion

Moses taught the people of Israel to value their spiritual leaders, the Levites, the priests and the prophets. They were to submit to their teaching and provide for their needs. Spiritual leadership is no less important today. The apostle Paul reminded Timothy that the work of an elder in the New Testament church was 'a noble task' (1 Tim. 3:1). Paul rejoiced in the privilege of preaching 'the unsearchable riches of Christ' (see Eph.3:7-9). The letter to the Hebrews tells believers that they have a responsibility to their spiritual leaders (see Heb. 13:17). 'Obey your leaders and submit to their authority. They keep watch over you as men who must give an account. Obey them so that their work will be a joy, not a burden, for that would be of no advantage to you.' Spiritual leaders stand in such a position because their office is ordained by God and has been established for the spread of the gospel and the strengthening of the church. It is a ministry that needs to be understood both by those who serve as leaders in the church and by those whom they serve. Too often a lack of mutual understanding leads to disappointment and recrimination within the church.

Chapter 19
Places of refuge

Please read Deuteronomy 19: 1-21

Deuteronomy 19 introduces us to a new section in Moses' exposition of the law. Whereas chapters 12 – 18 have focused on the central institutions around which the people of Israel were to unite when they entered the promised land, chapters 19 – 25 focus on the administration of civil and criminal justice in local communities. Most of the references to elders (who administrated Israel's legal system at the grass-roots level) in Deuteronomy are to be found in these chapters. We might also note that Moses shifted his focus from applying the first table of the law (which acknowledges a man's duty to Jehovah) to applying the second table of the law (which governs a man's duty to his neighbour).

One of the questions that have puzzled students of Deuteronomy over the years concerns the structure of the law code in chapters 12 – 26, and how this relates to the Decalogue. It has often been claimed that the laws expounded in these chapters are an application of the Decalogue and follow the order of the commandments. The problem with this claim is that those who make it find it hard to agree which laws expound which commandment. Some laws relate to several commandments, while others are hard to categorise. Some commentators give the impression that they are trying to bludgeon an unwilling text into a framework of their own creation. While the general principle that the laws of Deuteronomy expound and apply the Decalogue is readily admitted and some recurring themes may be noted, it is suggested that Moses exposition of the law code in Deuteronomy 12 – 26 gathers around broad themes rather than specific commandments.

The exposition of Deuteronomy 19 – 25 in the following chapters of this commentary will proceed on the assumption that Moses' primary concern was not to follow a neat literary structure, but to address the pressing pastoral issues of his day. He groups the laws of Israel around topics which were of pressing relevance to the community he was addressing in his covenant-renewal sermons. The first aim of every pastor-teacher is to address the spiritual needs of God's people. Moses concentrated on those laws which the Israelites most needed to hear because they addressed the very issues which they would face when they came into contact with the wickedness of Canaan. On the other hand, some of the commandments are hardly even alluded to, or their teaching is covered in a sketchy kind of way.

The central institutions of Israel were the focus in chapters 12 – 18. In these chapters Moses explained the significance of the first and second commandments, which forbade the worship of other gods and all forms of idolatry. The laws of 14:22 – 15:23, requiring tithing, remission of debt, release of servants and setting apart of firstborn animals, applied the Sabbath principle found in the fourth commandment. When Moses expounded the laws concerning civil and religious leaders in chapters 17 and 18, he explained the wider significance of the fifth commandment, which made submission to parents and other authority figures a mark of submission to the authority of Jehovah. The first five commandments were believed by the Jews to belong to the first table of the law, while the second table of the law was believed to begin with the sixth commandment, 'You shall not kill'. The next three chapters, Deuteronomy 19 –

21, apply this commandment by outlining a series of measures to protect the sanctity of human life.

In a society where life was considered cheap, it should come as no surprise that three whole chapters would be devoted to teaching the sanctity of human life. God alone may determine when it is a time to die. God does this in sovereign and mysterious ways through the outworking of his providence. He also works to uphold the sanctity of life through the public administration of justice. This is what people today call 'the rule of law'. It is a blessing which God bestows on mankind.

Cities of Refuge (19:1-13)

The people of Israel knew that Jehovah was their refuge in times of danger. Linked to the idea that Jehovah was their refuge were descriptions of God as a 'stronghold' (Ps. 9:9), 'an ever-present help in trouble' (Ps. 46:1), holding them in his 'everlasting arms' (Deut. 33:27, as well as their 'rock' and their 'shield' (2 Sam. 22:3). So when an Israelite was in danger from a mortal enemy, he would flee to God's altar for safety. There, in the presence of God, his life would be safe. During Israel's years in the wilderness, the altar in the tabernacle had been that place of refuge (see Exod. 21:13-14). However, Moses could see that when the Israelites moved into the promised land, one central altar would provide little protection for an Israelite in the outlying districts when he was pursued by someone seeking his life.

In Numbers 35:6 Moses had given the instruction that six of the towns to be allocated to the Levites in the land of Canaan were to be designated 'cities of refuge'. Although that phrase is not used in Deuteronomy, Moses refers to them. In 4:41-43 Moses set aside three additional cities, this time on the east of the Jordan (Bezer, Ramoth and Golan) which were places 'to which anyone who had killed a person could flee if he had unintentionally killed his neighbour without malice aforethought'. Here in 19:1-13, Moses anticipated the appointment of three more cities of refuge west of the Jordan and explained how they were to operate. He also explained why they were an important part of the social infrastructure of the covenant people. The focus is on the kind of community which the redeemed community of Israel was to be, not merely on details of jurisprudence. To find out how these ideals were put into practice we can read Joshua 20. But first let's consider some characteristic features of Moses' sermon on the topic.

i. The cities are set in a context of grace (19:1-3)
'When the LORD your God has destroyed the nations whose land he is giving you, and when you have driven them out and settled in their towns and houses then set aside for yourselves three cities centrally located in the land the LORD your God is giving you to possess.' Before any of these cities of refuge could be established, the land must first come into Israel's possession. We are reminded that the land of Canaan was God's gift to his covenant people. That was grace! It was not a matter of 'if' but of 'when' Israel possessed the land, because God has promised it to them. When they enjoyed security in the land, they were to consider the needs of those whose lives were in danger.

The next command, in 19:3 has been variously translated. *'Build roads to them...'* (NIV), thus ensuring that they are easily accessible; or 'you shall measure the distances' (ESV), thus ensuring an even distribution throughout the land. In both cases the goal is the same. These cities are to be made easily accessible to every Israelite in the land. The Israelite whose life is in danger should be able to find sanctuary in the land that God had given them, even after its borders had been greatly extended.

ii. The law restrained sinful actions amongst God's people (19:4-7)
God wanted his people to dwell safely in the land, free from

the fear of arbitrary violence. Even though they were God's redeemed people, they were not perfect people and bad things happened in their midst. They could be careless and at times even malicious in their dealings with each other. God gave laws to keep the consequences of their sinfulness to a minimum. In this section Moses addresses a situation where carelessness on the part of one person can lead to violence on the part of another (19:4). *'This is the rule concerning the man who kills another and flees there to save his life—one who kills his neighbour unintentionally, without malice aforethought.'* The killer may have been careless or even reckless (and if he has, he has brought some degree of guilt upon himself) but if he did not intend to cause injury or death he does not deserve to die, because he is without 'malice aforethought'. It is a testimony to the genius of Israel's laws that this phrase is still used in many modern systems of criminal law to distinguish the crimes of murder and manslaughter.

In 19:5 Moses explained simply and clearly, in words intended for the layman, what manslaughter was. He gave an example from daily life. *'For instance, a man may go into the forest with his neighbour to cut wood, and as he swings his axe to fell a tree, the head may fly off and hit his neighbour and kill him. That man may flee to one of these cities and save his life.'* In our day, we might have taken as an example a death resulting from careless driving, or an accident at work because machinery has been badly maintained. The person who has accidentally caused the death of another was not to be pursued and killed, but was permitted to flee to a city of refuge. The necessity for this provision would have been obvious to everyone in the ancient world, where blood-feuds could last for generations. This is spelled out in 19:6. *'Otherwise, the avenger of blood might pursue him in a rage, overtake him if the distance is too great, and kill him even though he is not deserving of death.'* The 'avenger of blood' was a relative of the deceased who had the responsibility of redeeming the family's honour by extracting retribution according to the *lex talionis* (of which more later). Such a man was not likely to be a fair judge. In the heat of his anger he could not be expected to ask whether the killing was accidental or not, and so might add evil to evil.

The cities of refuge did not, however, allow the killer to escape from justice. What ought to happen when the killer arrived at the gates of a city of refuge is described for us in Joshua 20:4-5, 'When he flees to one of these cities, he is to stand in the entrance of the city gate and state his case before the elders of that city... If the avenger of blood pursues him, they must not surrender the one accused, because he killed his neighbour unintentionally and without malice aforethought.' There at the city gate (where the elders traditionally sat to administer justice) the claims of the fugitive as well as those of the avenger were subjected to cool-headed and impartial scrutiny. Only a fugitive with a valid defence was to be admitted. Once admitted to the city, he was not permitted to leave until the death of the high priest (see Num. 35:28). The city preserved his life from the avenger, but it also proved to be a place of incarceration; and in both ways it served the interests of God's justice. The avenger was restrained from shedding innocent blood, yet the killer was made to reflect on the fact that he had taken a life. The God who is concerned about sparrows holds every human life as precious in his sight (see Matt. 10:29-31). He has placed his law like a hedge around the life of every human being. He commands us to respect the law and those who enforce it (see Rom. 13:3-5). His love for human life is the rationale behind this law. Moses spelled that out in 19:7. *'This is why I command you to set aside for yourselves three cities.'*

iii. Obedience leads to further blessing (19:8-10)

Moses had great hopes for the people of Israel. In 19:1 we observed that Moses opened his exposition of the law concerning cities of refuge by anticipating the conquest and settlement of Israel's promised inheritance in Canaan. He returned to this to this hope in 19:8. *'If the LORD your God enlarges your territory, as he promised on oath to your forefathers, and gives you the whole land he promised them...*' This is an amazing promise. Moses' description of 'the whole land' back in 1:7-8 stretched 'to Lebanon, as far as the great river, the Euphrates'. See 11:24, Genesis 15:18 and Joshua 1:3-4 for other expansive description of Israel's inheritance. There is no evidence that the Israelites ever expanded to possess all these territories, but Moses strove to keep the hope alive, even as he explained the law governing cities of refuge. God's great promises and Moses' great faith shone through amidst the details of Israel's legal system. Ultimately his hopes were not to be realised in the establishment of a greater Israel, but in the greater kingdom of Israel's Messiah. It is the kingdom of Jesus Christ that will extend 'from the River to the ends of the earth' (Ps. 72:8). We might ask ourselves whether our hopes for the kingdom of Jesus Christ match the boldness of Moses' faith.

Yet a new note enters 19:8, a note of pastoral realism. While 19:1 looks forward to the day 'when' Israel will drive the nations from the land of promise, 19:8 admits that God's promises are conditional. *'If the LORD your God enlarges your territory... because you carefully follow all these laws I command you today—to love the LORD your God and to walk always in his ways...'* Moses' high hopes for Israel were conditional upon their obeying God's commands. He summarised the whole body of Israel's law in relational terms, for God wants his people to love him and walk with him. Obedience is not mechanical or impersonal, but an act of grateful and loving discipleship. Israel's discipleship involved the setting apart of three cities of refuge to which an endangered killer might flee (19:9). God told Israel to do this so that the sixth commandment might not be broken (19:10). *'Do this so that innocent blood will not be shed in your land, which the LORD your God is giving you as your inheritance, and so that you will not be guilty of bloodshed.'* When the people of Israel obeyed God's laws, they enjoyed more and more of his blessing.

Even in Old Testament times, Israel's blessedness consisted in much more than possessing material things such as land. The land was the place where the Israelites might dwell with God free from guilt and pollution. The Israelites were to keep the sixth commandment so that they might live in the land free from the guilt of bloodshed. In this sense obedience is its own reward, allowing those who live godly lives to enjoy a clean conscience and blessed access to God. We might compare the anguished prayer of David in Psalm 51:14 with his confidence as he drew near to God in Psalm 26:1-3. In the former he confessed that he had committed murder and prayed, 'Save me from bloodguilt, O God'. In the latter he prayed,

> Vindicate me, O LORD,
> for I have led a blameless life;
> I have trusted in the LORD
> without wavering.
> Test me, O LORD, and try me,
> examine my heart and my mind;
> for your love is ever before me,
> and I walk continually in your truth.

iv. Living with the reality of sin (19:11-13)

Moses' great hopes of Israel were earthed in some biblical realism. He longed for the day when the land of Israel would be free from the shedding of innocent blood, but he recognised that the people had sinful hearts. Hatred and murder were the realities of daily life, and that was not going to change overnight. Yet Moses strove to change the hearts and lives of fallen sinners by preaching God's law. God's moral law shows men that their thoughts and actions are evil. The application of Israel's civil law reinforced the message from the pulpit and sought to restrain the worst consequences of human sin. In 19:11-12 Moses recognised that wilful murders will be committed and prescribed the community's response should the killer try to abuse the system of refuge. *'But if a man hates his neighbour and lies in wait for him, assaults and kills him, and then flees to one of these cities, the elders of his town shall send for him, bring him back from the city, and hand him over to the avenger of blood to die.'* The elders here are the elders of the city where the victim (and possibly the perpetrator) lived. Their role was quite distinct from that of the avenger of blood. They were to pursue justice, not merely vengeance. They were to work through the established channels by extraditing the killer to face the consequences of his actions.

Premeditated murder is a serious crime which calls for the most serious penalty the law can impose. Examples of premeditated murder are given in Numbers 35:16-21a. 'If a man strikes someone with an iron object so that he dies, he is a murderer; the murderer shall be put to death. Or if anyone has a stone in his hand that could kill, and he strikes someone so that he dies, he is a murderer; the murderer shall be put to death.' Judges within the English Common Law tradition have rightly described these crimes as 'murder most foul'. In Israel, the murderer was to be handed over to the avenger of blood, who would then execute the death penalty (19:12b) on behalf of the whole community. His right to seek vengeance was recognised in Numbers 35:21b.

Quite naturally, we recoil from a system which smacks of summary justice. We know that 'lynch-mob justice' hardly deserves to be called justice at all. In our own day we are wary of individual vigilantes who take the law into their own hands, with terrible results. This concern must have been shared by some in Israel as Moses urged the elders not to be reluctant to hand the killer over to the avenger of blood (19:13). *'Show him no pity.'* Literally, 'do not look with pity on him'. Those who might have been reluctant to allow the law to take its course were to remember what the killer had done and consider the consequences of his actions. From the perspective of a holy God, the actions of the killer were abominable. The Israelites must learn to look upon the issues of the day as God saw them.

'You must purge from Israel the guilt of shedding innocent blood, so that it may go well with you.'

The language of 19:13 is reminiscent of 13:8-9, where Moses urged the Israelites to purge idolatry from their midst, showing no pity even to their closest relatives. This was not an easy thing to do, yet such rigorous faithfulness was the condition upon which God promised his blessing. Just as Canaanite idolatry proved to be a snare to many, so unpunished murder created a moral atmosphere within which human life was considered cheap and expendable. Moses' application of the principle of the sanctity of human life contained in the sixth commandment acknowledged that sometimes even a precious life must be sacrificed in order to protect the sanctity of every life. This is the principle which God had stated in Genesis 9:6. 'Whoever sheds the blood of man, by man shall his blood be shed; for in the image of God has God made man.'

Law Courts (19:14-21)

Essential to the effective operation of the cities of refuge was some form of judicial process. City elders served as judges in ancient Israel and their work is described in Deuteronomy 19:12 and Joshua 20:4-6. They assessed the claims of the killer who sought asylum and decided whether he ought to be handed over to the avenger of blood. The competing claims of the killer seeking asylum and the avenger seeking retribution could only be assessed properly when appropriate evidence was brought before the elders. The rest of this chapter describes what kind of evidence ought to be heard.

When the elders of Israel sat as judges to decide cases, they too were a refuge to which people in danger would flee for safety and justice. As well as being a refuge for the accidental killer whose life was being sought by the avenger, they were a refuge for the widow and labourer whose livelihoods were in danger of being swallowed up by the rich and powerful. They were the people to whom the innocent could go to find safety from the malice of the lynch-mob. Israel's courts were places to which people could go to seek justice. Justice is a high priority for a holy God, who delights to protect the lives and livelihoods of his people. However, before expounding the moral and theological basis for the rules of evidence in Israel's law courts, Moses drew his hearers' attention to a law which seems strangely out of context.

i. The Boundary Stone (19:14)

'*Do not move your neighbour's boundary stone set up by your predecessors in the inheritance you receive in the land the LORD your God is giving you to possess.*' Moses anticipated a time when the Israelites will have been in the land of Canaan for a long time. By that time portions of land would have been allotted to each family. Although this fact would be well established in the minds of the people, the precise location of the boundaries between properties would not always have been easy to pinpoint. Even today the same can sometimes be said about some international boundaries. Take, for instance, the border between Northern Ireland and the Republic of Ireland. Although this is an international boundary it is, in some places, marked only by a hedge or a ditch. In other places it runs through farms and fields and even, in one instance, down the middle of a village street. Some farmers have joked that they cross an international border to bring in their cows for milking.

The portions of land allocated to Israelite families were not easy to define. The land of Canaan had few natural, and even fewer man-made, boundaries. In order to mark out a family's inheritance, large stones were set up at key points along the boundary. In ancient Mesopotamia it was customary to set up stones to mark out a king's grant of land to his subjects and a list of curses against anyone who dared to remove them might be written on these stones. This custom may lie behind the inclusion of such a curse in 27:17. It was all too easy for a strong man to cheat on his neighbour by moving the boundary stone, and so 'roll back' his inheritance. References to this practice in Proverbs 22:28; 23:10; Job 24:2; Hosea 5:10 indicate that it was not uncommon in Israel and that the consequences for the most vulnerable people in the community (the widow and the fatherless) were serious. In particular, Hosea pointed the finger at Israel's princes and warned that God's wrath would be poured on them like a flood of water. 'Judah's leaders are like those who move boundary stones. I will pour out my wrath on them like a flood of water' (Hosea 5:10).

The question which puzzles many readers is why Moses introduced this law at this point. It has been suggested that to deprive a person of his livelihood is as serious as taking his life and, as the sixth commandment underlies this section of Moses' discourse, he was concerned about the murderous consequences of economic injustice. It is also possible that Moses was concerned about what might happen should demarcation disputes escalate into violent clashes. Although the parties to such a dispute may not have had 'malice aforethought', it would not be long before a hot-headed response to a provocative move of the boundary stone resulted in someone getting killed. Israel's judges may well have found that such disputes often resulted in killers seeking refuge in one of the designated cities.

A better explanation of why Moses expounded this law at this point in his sermon is to link 19:14 with the laws in 19:15-19 ensuring the reliability of witnesses in court. Both boundary markers and witnesses in court ought to be trustworthy. When testimony presented before judges cannot be trusted, the integrity of the system is undermined and it is the weakest in society who suffer most. When the 'law of the jungle' prevails, the strong can always look after themselves. In Israel, God's law operated to protect the weak, who cannot look after themselves.

God's law insisted upon righteousness and honesty in people's dealings with one another. At this point, we see the influence of the ninth commandment entering the civil law code: 'You shall not give false testimony against your neighbour.' Because all God's commands are part of a package, it should therefore come as no surprise that the conduct which Moses condemns in this chapter breaches several commands at the same time. False testimony takes many forms. Lying in open court and the clandestine movement of a boundary stone are equally offensive to God. We can bear false witness by innuendo and silence, as well as by brazen declarations of untruth. Even though our dishonesty may be hidden from others, it can never be hidden from God. It is particularly offensive to him when the innocent lose their life or the vulnerable their livelihood.

ii. The General Rule (19:15)
The general rule in Israel's law of evidence was that one witness was not enough to convict a man accused of any offence. This was spelled out in the laws which imposed the death penalty for idolatrous worship (17:6) and murder (Num. 35:30). This safeguard was especially important when a person was on trial for his life and an unreliable witness could result in a fatal miscarriage of justice. Here in 19:15 Moses applies the rule to all kinds of cases. *'One witness is not enough to convict a man accused of any crime or offence he may have committed. A matter must be established by the testimony of two or three witnesses.'*

Eye-witness testimony is notoriously unreliable. Even those who were present to see the events in question unfold before their eyes can make many mistakes in recounting and retelling their story. They make assumptions and are swayed by their prejudices. Upon examination a witness may find that his memory is unreliable. It is surely not acceptable to deprive a man of his life, liberty or even his property on the basis of such an uncorroborated accusation. For that reason, 'a matter must be established by the testimony of two or three witnesses'. Yet even when two witnesses who have seen the same event give their testimony, they may give quite different accounts of what they saw. There may be cases where the evidence is so evenly balanced that it is impossible to tell whose testimony is to be believed. Yet their testimony can be weighed, sifted and compared.

This law is quoted in the New Testament as an example of God's justice (Heb.10:28). 'Anyone who rejected the law of Moses died without mercy on the testimony of two or three witnesses.' It is applied as a rule of fairness in the life of the church when discipline is called for (see Matt. 18:15-17; 1 Tim. 5:19). Both Christians in general and elders in particular are protected by the requirement that charges of sinful conduct against them are not to be entertained unless supported by the testimony of two or three witnesses. 'If your brother sins against you, go and show him his fault, just between the two of you. If he listens to you, you have won your brother over. But if he will not listen, take one or two others along, so that "every matter may be established by the testimony of two or three witnesses."' A few verses later our Lord adds the comment that 'if two of you on earth agree about anything you ask for, it will be done for you by my Father in heaven'. The 'two' mentioned here may well be those witnesses whose testimony leads to a blessed purging of the church, rather than, as is commonly assumed, two or three who agree to petition the Lord in prayer.

The apostle Paul drew upon the language of 19:15 (and other Old Testament passages) to explain why he contemplated a third visit to the church in Corinth (see 2 Cor. 13:1). He wanted to teach what he had taught during his two previous visits because 'every matter must be established by two or three witnesses'. This is a rather free application of the principle in Deuteronomy. Here the two or three witnesses were in fact the same person – Paul himself. Yet he sought to pass on basic gospel truths to 'many witnesses', whose collective testimony to the gospel would be compelling (see 1 Tim. 6:12; 2 Tim. 2:2). He wanted its truth to be established 'beyond all reasonable doubt'.

iii. Malicious witnesses (19:16-20)

The consistent testimony of two or more witnesses will generally be quite reliable, unless it has been fabricated by conspirators. Such a conspiracy is described in Kings 21:8-13, where Jezebel sought to dislodge Naboth from his family inheritance. In spite of her despotic ways, Jezebel did not ignore the rule that 'a matter must be established by the testimony of two or three witnesses'. She simply steered around it by procuring multiple false witnesses against Naboth. She instructed the elders of Naboth's city, 'Seat two scoundrels opposite him and have them testify that he has cursed both God and the king. Then take him out and stone him to death.' This incident exposes a weakness in the law of 19:15 – a malicious witness. In 19:16-18 Moses described what Israel's judges were to do should they suspect that a malicious individual (or group of individuals) was bearing false testimony. *'If a malicious witness takes the stand to accuse a man of a crime, the two men involved in the dispute must stand in the presence of the LORD before the priests and the judges who are in office at the time.'*

A *'malicious witness'* is one who intends to cause harm to another person by giving false testimony in court. The Hebrew word for malice often describes physical violence leading to injury and death (see Gen. 6:11; 49:5; Judg. 9:24; 2 Sam. 22:3). Sometimes that violence may be verbal and psychological, but it leads to physical harm, as did Sarah's treatment of Hagar in Genesis 16. The false witnesses of 19:16 attack their opponent by telling lies in court. They are content to leave the physical violence to the executioner; but in God's eyes they are as guilty as the man who takes up a sword to kill his neighbour. They are worthless witnesses who rise up and breathe out violence (Ps. 27:12).

Where two witnesses give conflicting testimony it is not east to conclude which (if either) is a malicious witness. Yet it was the task of the judges to assess the reliability of each (19:17). *'The two men involved in the dispute must stand in the presence of the LORD before the priests and the judges who are in office at the time.'* Deciding who was in fact telling the truth required a superhuman measure of wisdom. During the time of the monarchy, kings were expected to possess such wisdom (2 Sam. 14:20) and Solomon was indeed given it (1 Kings 3:28). Before the Israelites had a king they took difficult cases to the priests and judges who served at the central sanctuary. These men sat 'in the presence of the LORD' and were able to draw on his wisdom. They heard only the most difficult cases, those which were too difficult for the local courts to handle (17:8). As well as deciding whether a killer had acted with malice aforethought, they were called upon to decide whether a witness had spoken with intent to deceive. No doubt they took into account the known character of the witness and his visible demeanour, but they also sought wisdom from God at the place where God had made his name to dwell. Today we do not go to the 'chosen place', for Christ has done away with the sacrificial system and we find in him the wisdom of God (1 Cor. 1:30). Whatever difficult decisions we are called upon to make today, we are to make on our knees before him.

The judges who sought wisdom from God were not exempted from the hard work of examining the witnesses before them (19:18a). *'The judges must make a thorough investigation...'* The judges were not to rely on their 'gut feelings' about the case, but they must follow a proper and rigorous process. They were to find out all the relevant details of the case. They were to ask searching questions and follow up leads to find out who was telling the truth and who was trying to deceive. Through this process of investigation they must come to a just conclusion. These lines of enquiry were not to be dismissed as unspiritual. Nor were they to be neglected in the hope that God would give them his wisdom. God expects his people both to pray and to think as they seek wisdom to address the thorny questions of life.

Once the judges came to a conclusion, they were to take decisive action (19:18b-19): *'and if the witness proves to be a liar, giving false testimony against his brother, then do to him as he intended to do to his brother. You must purge the evil from among you.'* False testimony was regarded as a very serious offence in Israel. 'You shall not give false testimony against your neighbour' (Deut. 5:20). Moses was particularly concerned at the effect which perjury would have on the unity of God's family. The malicious witness had used his testimony as a weapon to destroy his 'brother'. His brother is not just another anonymous person, but one with whom he had the closest bonds of fellowship within God's covenant with Israel. As well as establishing a relationship between God and his people, this covenant had established a whole network of relationships between the Israelites. All this was under attack by the ungodly conduct of a malicious witness, and severe penalties were applied. If he had falsely accused his neighbour of murder, he was to receive the penalty for murder.

In 19:20 Moses explained why a malicious witness was to be penalised so severely. *'The rest of the people will hear of this and be afraid, and never again will such an evil thing be done among you.'* We might have hoped that a redeemed people would obey their Redeemer's laws out of love and loyalty; but that is not always so in a fallen world. The Israelites needed to learn that their sinful actions would have earthly as well as eternal consequences. Fear of those earthly consequences was to be an important teacher for them. The fear described in 19:20 was not simply the fear of judicial punishment, but the fear of Jehovah himself, whose laws were administered by Israel's judges. Even today rulers are described as 'God's servant, an agent of wrath to bring punishment on the wrong-doer' (Rom. 13:4). The fear of earthly judges and their judgments is designed to bring sinful men to their knees before God so that they might flee from the wrath to come. At least one convicted wrong-doer, as he received the due reward for his crimes, sought mercy and was assured entry into Paradise (Luke 23:40-43). That is the goal of the penalties prescribed in these verses.

iv. The Law of Restitution (19:21)
It is often said that one the first principles of justice is that the penalty ought to fit the crime. In 19:19a that principle was applied to the penalty for the crime of perjury. The consequences are followed through in 19:21. *'Show no pity: life for life, eye for eye, tooth for tooth, hand for hand, foot for foot.'* Where a malicious witness had given testimony which would have resulted in the loss of a life, he was to lose his life. Where he had given testimony which would have resulted in the loss of an eye, he was to lose his eye. This law of restitution stated one of the basic principles of the Old Testament legal system. In Exodus 21:23-25 and Leviticus 24:17-21 it was applied in civil actions where one person was asking the judges to impose appropriate penalties upon one who had caused injury or death. This is sometimes called the *lex talionis* or the law of retribution. It is one of the most caricatured and reviled teachings of the Mosaic law. Yet many modern critics misunderstand it.

The law of retribution was a rule of common sense. It aimed to prevent excessive punishment. If a man's words or actions would have resulted in another losing his life, then he deserved to pay with his own life. However, if he has merely knocked out another person's tooth, then a lesser penalty must apply. The law of retribution was the principle on which the provision of places of refuge in 19:1-13 rested. It allowed the avenger of blood to pursue the killer (19:6). Yet it did not allow the person who had no 'malice aforethought' to face the death penalty. The law of Moses did not sanction arbitrary or excessive punishments, but in the name of justice it did demand retribution. This is a basic principle in any legal system. To remove the idea that evil actions call for a just reward (that is retribution or punishment) is to sanction moral apathy; and that is the first step to moral anarchy.

It should be noted that the law of retribution was never intended to be the only (or even the main) rule governing the individual's response to those who had offended against them. It was a principle which shaped Israel's legal system. Moses' great concern in Deuteronomy was to teach how a godly community was to be ordered. An individual may well forgive a person who offends against him or his family, but still pass on information to the authorities or press charges in court. Jesus drew on this distinction in his clarification of the law of retribution in Matthew 5:38-42.

> You have heard that it was said, "Eye for eye, and tooth for tooth." But I tell you, Do not resist an evil person. If someone strikes you on the right cheek, turn to him the other also. And if someone wants to sue you and take your tunic, let him have your cloak as well. If someone forces you to go one mile, go with him two miles. Give to the one who asks you, and do not turn away from the one who wants to borrow from you.

By the time Jesus spoke these words, the law of retribution had become a charter for personal claims. As in our day, people knew their rights and insisted on them right down to the last detail. Jesus criticised this self-seeking spirit. He went further and taught his followers not to resist the claims made upon them by those who dragged them into court. There are times when a Christian may well judge that God's honour is better served by foregoing his or her right to take legal action than pressing that right (see 1 Cor. 6:7). The motive must be one of selfless love to God and our neighbour.

One final point to note is that the law of retribution undergirds God's dealings with mankind. God is a just God and he deals justly with a fallen race. When we violate his laws, God must seek retribution. Our guilt is like that of King David. It is 'bloodguilt' deserving death (see Ps. 51:10). 'The wages of sin is death...' (Rom. 6:23). The God of Israel who taught the principle of retribution has not disappeared. Nor has he been transformed into a different, more acceptable deity by the writers of the New Testament. From before the creation of the world God had planned to satisfy his justice by the sacrifice of his Son on the cross. 'God presented him as a sacrifice of atonement, through faith in his blood. . . He did this to demonstrate *his justice* at the present time, so as to be just and the one who justifies those who have faith in Jesus' (Rom. 3:25-26).

Many passages of Scripture, in both the Old and the New Testaments, teach that God in his mercy has provided a substitute to stand in our place and bear his wrath (see Gen. 22:13-14; Exod. 12:1-11; Isa. 53:4-6; Mark 10:45; John 1:29; 1 Cor. 15:3; Gal. 1:3-4; 1 Peter 2:24; Heb. 9:27-28; Rev. 5:9). These, and many other passages, will only make sense to us when we grasp the divine necessity for retribution. God accepted the sacrifice of his only Son because we had forfeited our lives by our sin. 'Life for life.' His life was laid down for ours.

Conclusion

The law of Moses provided a city of refuge for those who did not deserve to die because they had not hated their neighbour. It also provided protection for those who were unjustly accused of any offence. This was an act of God's mercy. The gospel of Jesus Christ, however, provides a refuge for those who *are* justly accused of many crimes against God and who *do* deserve to die. This is the greatest of all God's mercies! In order that we might enjoy God's mercies and receive his forgiveness, God allowed his Son to find no place of refuge. On the cross he endured desolation, isolation and condemnation. He bore the sins of many, so that our guilt might be taken from us. Let us therefore flee to him to find refuge from the wrath of God. Our only refuge is to be found in the mercy of God. 'The name of the LORD is a strong tower; the righteous run to it and are safe' (Prov. 18:10).

Chapter 20
The rules of war

Please read Deuteronomy 20: 1-20

Alone amongst the books of Moses, Deuteronomy contains laws that regulate the conduct of war. These are mostly found in Deuteronomy 20, but other relevant passages include 21:10-14 (marrying a captive woman), 23:9-14 (uncleanness in the army camp), 24:5 (a newly married solider) and 25:17-19 (conflict with the Amalekites). In these laws Moses shows that war may have a place in Jehovah's plans; but it must be conducted in a godly way. Almost inevitably, war seems to unleash the worst excesses of human cruelty. It was this conduct that the laws in this chapter aimed to curb.

Many people today need to be reminded of the horrors of war. We hear reports of atrocities perpetrated in Afghanistan and Iraq and other conflicts, yet most of us have grown up with no first-hand experience of war. This is a great blessing, yet it can dull our awareness of the horrors of war. The generation which lived through the First World War carried to their graves a keen collective memory of the slaughter in the trenches and yearned never to go to war again. After the Second World War, nations banded together to renounce war as an instrument of policy, resolving to go to war only if absolutely necessary to defend themselves. The words of Isaiah 2:4: 'They shall beat their swords into plowshares, and their spears into pruning hooks; nation shall not lift up sword against nation, neither shall they learn war any more' – were inscribed on the so-called Isaiah Wall opposite the United Nations Headquarters in New York. Every year most western nations hold ceremonies of remembrance for those who died in the two world wars and other conflicts and give thanks for the peace and security which we enjoy as a result.

Many others need no reminder of the horrors of war. In the fifth century AD (a time when wars were all too common), Augustine set out three criteria by which Christians might judge whether a war was just and necessary. Over the years these have become widely recognized bench-marks. The war must be waged for a just purpose (that is, for bringing an end to injustice and restoring peace), it must be waged by a legitimate authority, and it must be conducted in a just and humane way. This last criterion points to the need for rules to govern the conduct of war – and in modern times armies are bound by the rules of the Geneva Convention. Though these rules provide only partial protection for the civilians and combatants who are caught up in conflict, many have reason to be thankful for them. In large measure, Christian teaching about a just war has been derived from the rules of war which God gave to the people of Israel.

Moses' inclusion of the rules of war in his exposition of the law code in Deuteronomy was timely. The Israelites were getting ready for the conquest of Canaan. At God's command they would dispossess the inhabitants of the land. This would involve much loss of life. If we were to use a modern phrase we might call it 'genocide' or 'ethnic cleansing' (see 7:1-6; 9:3b; 12:29; 31:3-6). Both those who were cleansed from the land and those who did the cleansing would be deeply affected by the bloodshed. Even in times of relative peace those were brutal times when human life was short, nasty and often cheap. Yet the sixth commandment (5:17) prohibited murder and sought to instil a regard for the sanctity of cheapened human life. In chapters 19-21 Moses applied the sixth commandment to those areas of community life where its message was most needful, and the conduct of war was one of them.

In ancient times, war came and went with the seasons (2 Sam. 11:1). Yet Israel's war against the Canaanites was not an ordinary war, initiated by a human king for his own political ends. It was a holy war initiated by Jehovah to accomplish his righteous purposes. The sins of the Canaanites could no longer be tolerated (see Gen. 15:16; Deut. 9:4), and Jehovah would use the Israelites as his instruments to purge idolatry from the land (see 20:16-18). However, even though this was Jehovah's war and the slaughter of the Canaanites was an act of righteous judgment, there was a very real danger that the Israelites would conduct themselves in an ungodly way. Armed conflict releases brutal passions which can be hard to control, but the laws of this chapter sought to control them by reminding the Israelites of some basic principles of a just war waged for the sake of Jehovah.

Preparations for War (20:1-9)

War is a dangerous enterprise and nations do not go to war without careful planning (see Prov. 21:31a; Luke 14:31). Most leaders will focus on their tactical and political plans for war, but Moses adds a spiritual dimension to Israel's preparation for war. The Israelites fought for Jehovah and sought his help.

i. The assurance of God's presence (20:1-4)
Moses anticipated that Israel's armies would face much larger and stronger opponents when they went to war. 'When you go to war against your enemies and see horses and chariots and an army greater than yours, do not be afraid of them, because the LORD your God, who brought you up out of Egypt, will be with you.' Israel

345

was one of the smallest of nations (7:7) and she was militarily inferior to her neighbours. While they had horses and chariots, Israel had only foot-soldiers. This was the equivalent of sending infantry to fight tanks. Understandably, the soldiers would be afraid as they waited to go into battle. Often the armies of Israel would go into battle as the underdog (see Josh. 11:4-8; 1 Sam. 13:5-6; 2 Chr. 14:8-11; 20:2-3) yet Moses encouraged them not to be afraid. This was the recurring message of the prophets and kings who followed in Moses' footsteps (see Josh. 11:6; 2 Chr. 20:15; 32:7; Isa. 8:12; Jer. 42:11). Jehovah was their 'ever-present help in trouble' (Ps. 46:1).

This timeless truth needed timely application, and there was no more appropriate time for the Israelites to be reminded that the Lord was their strength than when they were about to go into battle. So when the Israelites were about to go into battle for real, 'the priest' (probably the High Priest, or possibly some other priest specially appointed for the task) would go before the troops to exhort them (20:2-4). 'Hear, O Israel, today you are going into battle against your enemies. Do not be faint-hearted or afraid; do not be terrified or give way to panic before them. For the LORD your God is the one who goes with you to fight for you against your enemies to give you victory.' His opening words, 'Hear, O Israel', echo Moses' exhortation in 6:4, reminding the soldiers that they were the people of Jehovah, called to serve him, even on the battlefield. As they fought Jehovah's battles they were not to be afraid, for he would give them the victory. They knew this in theory, but in the heat of battle or under the pressure of a surprise attack they might easily be overwhelmed by fear. The gist of what the priest said in 20:3 is 'Do not now be terrified... for the Lord your God goes with you'.

There are different degrees of fear. In his exhortation, the priest recognises that the soldiers' level of fear will increase as the battle draws near. 'Faint-heartedness' is a sense of unease at the back of the mind while trouble is still some distance away.

'Fear' is a much stronger sense of apprehension as the danger approaches. It is at this point that brave men face their fears and overcome them. 'Terror' is a state of emotional turmoil in the midst of horrific events. Sometimes terror can lead to 'panic' when a person's resolve breaks down and he flees the field of battle. The priest's exhortation strengthened the soldiers' resolve to stand firm before their fears, so that when they faced the terrors of the battlefield, they would not panic and run. He strengthened them with the knowledge that they did not fight on their own, for Jehovah went with them to fight against their enemies. He is a mighty warrior (Exod. 15:2-4) who fights to deliver his people (1:30).

We should not think that these words from the priest gave the Israelites a green light to start wars and expect God to come to their aid. That is how God's relationship with Israel has sometimes been understood. It makes Jehovah serve the petty ambitions of sinful men. Joshua was forcefully reminded that Jehovah was neither 'for Israel' nor 'for their enemies' (see Josh 5:14). However, the army belongs to the Lord and is to be 'for him'. This doctrine had the effect of limiting Israel's freedom to start wars. Only when God led his people into conflict could they be assured of victory. When the Israelites went to war presumptuously, they were doomed to defeat (see 1:42-44; also 2 Chr. 11:2-4). That is why Israel's leaders sought God's leading before they led their people into battle (see 1 Sam. 30:7-8; 2 Sam. 5:18-19). God gave no unconditional promise of victory to Israel's armies. He fought with them only when they fought his battles in his way. This warns us against too hasty assumptions that God will bless the work of our hands. God is with us only when we submit to his lordship and follow his leading.

Furthermore, this doctrine challenged conventional military thinking. If Jehovah had planned to win his battles with large armies and military might, he would never have made Israel to be his chosen nation (7:7); but he did choose Israel and he warned her kings not to accumulate large armies or mounted cavalry (see 17:16). These were the conventional indicators that a nation was ready for war. Yet in God's battle plans they are not necessary (see 1 Sam. 14:6; Ps. 18:29; 20:7; 33:16-17; Hosea 14:3), and even powerless against the might of Jehovah (2 Chr. 14:12-13; Isa. 37:36). Victory was assured when the Israelites could say, like David, 'with your help I can advance against a troop... In God I trust; I will not be afraid' (Ps 18:29; 56:11). The proclamation of 20:2-4 could only be made when a faithful nation was faithfully following its covenant Lord.

Christians, too, need words of encouragement as they make ready to engage in spiritual warfare. Our enemy is powerful (1 Peter 5:8) and often invisible (Eph. 5:11-12). The devil is like a roaring lion seeking us for his prey. When we face his assaults in our own strength we will easily be overwhelmed. Death, too, is an enemy, the last enemy (1 Cor. 15:26). As with the Israelites, the odds may seem to be stacked against us. Yet we are strengthened by the words of our great High Priest, 'surely I am with you always...' (Matt. 28:20). We are exhorted, 'Finally, be strong in the Lord and in his mighty power. Put on the full armour of God so that you can take your stand against the devil's schemes' (Eph. 6:10-11).

ii. An allowance for human weakness (20:5-8)
The basic principle that the armies of Israel fought Jehovah's battles in Jehovah's strength influenced every aspect of Moses' thinking about war. He encouraged the Israelites to rely on the might of Jehovah rather than their own might. This resulted in some practices that would be considered bizarre in most armies. One example is the set of exemptions from military service set out in these verses. Because Jehovah receives more honour when his victories are won by a small and outnumbered army, the recruiting officers were to remove from the ranks of the army all those who need not be there. '*The officers shall say to the army...*' These were the officials who kept a record of

men who were eligible to fight and (as there was no standing army in Israel before the monarchy) mobilised them for war as the need arose. A different title is used to describe the officers in 20:9 who led the soldiers into battle.

We see how this principle was applied in practice in God's instructions to Gideon as he prepared to fight the Midianites in Judges 7:2-3. After all those who were afraid were sent home, another test was applied (Judg. 7:5-6) to reduce Gideon's army to only 300 men. Clearly, divine logic is being applied here. God wanted to make it abundantly clear that his strength, not human resources, would win the battle. Jehovah's armies were to be composed of willing volunteers who offered themselves to be instruments of his power (Ps. 110:3).

As well as indicating Jehovah's power, the exemption law demonstrates Jehovah's compassion for those experiencing the daily demands of family life or beset by fear. The recruiting officers were to ask the recruits four questions. In these questions Moses listed four exemptions from military service.

a. *'Has anyone built a new house and not dedicated it?'* Anyone who had built a new house but had not yet 'dedicated' it was to go home and live in it (20:5). The same word is used in 1 Kings 8:63 for the dedication of the temple, though a less formal event is envisaged in this verse. The man who built a new house for his family dedicated it by moving into it and enjoying it.

b. *'Has anyone planted a vineyard and not begun to enjoy it?'* Anyone who had planted a vineyard but had not begun to enjoy its fruit was to go home and enjoy the results of his labour (20:6). Because of the law which dedicated the firstfruits of a vineyard to God (Lev. 19:23-25), a man who planted a vineyard might be exempt from being called to fight for up to five years.

c. *'Has anyone become pledged to a woman and not married her?'* Any man who had pledged to marry a woman was to go home and marry her, lest he die in battle and someone else marry her (20:7). If another man had married her and started a family, the name of the deceased warrior would have been lost from the family tree of Israel. That was a highly undesirable outcome for the Israelites (see 25:5-6; Num. 27:1-11; Ruth 4:5, 10). God's promise of a land to Abraham's descendants would only be fulfilled if there were heirs to inherit it, so family life was protected and allowed to flourish. For the same reason this exemption was extended to married men during the first year of their marriage (see 24:5).

Taken together, these first three exemptions show that winning wars did not suspend every other priority in Israel. The goal of Jehovah's war was to bring Israel into possession of his promised mercies. God had promised to bring them into a fertile land where they would enjoy its bounty and train their children to love and honour God. It would be strange if the Israelites had won their war but ruined their community life and decimated their families. That, according to Deborah in Judges 5:6-7, was a very real danger. God's laws of war kept in view the need to preserve as well as destroy, by ensuring that there were homes, families and vineyards for the victorious soldiers to return to. Moses demonstrates that Jehovah is not a bloodthirsty deity who gloried in slaughter, but a covenant Lord who delighted to bless his redeemed people.

d. *'Is any man afraid or faint-hearted?'* One final question sought out those who were simply afraid to fight (20:8). We can imagine how this exemption might be abused if it were applied to modern conscript armies. Naïve as the question may seem, it served a very important function in Jehovah's army. The Israelites were victorious when they fought in reliance upon God's power. As well as being psychologically infectious, fear was spiritually dangerous. If the Israelites did not believe God's promises of deliverance, they were not likely to call upon him in prayer; and if they did not call upon him, they would not be saved. The fear that the officers were to identify and root out of Israel's army was the fear that fills the hearts of God's people when they have lost sight of God and his power.

It is all too possible for Christians today to lose sight of God's power and fall into the grip of fear. We may be afraid when we face temptation, opposition, the onset of illness or the prospect of death. Fear is a natural response to forces which we cannot understand (2 Cor. 7:5). However, there are times when fear gets in the way of doing what God has called us to do, when fear quenches boldness and keeps us silent, when fear keeps us from attempting new things for God. Did fear lie behind John Mark's departure from the apostolic mission team in Acts 13:13? There may be times when we need to step aside from important tasks until we learn to overcome our fears. Thankfully, the Lord Jesus does not ask us to leave his army when we are afraid, but gives us his word to encourage us (Ps. 56:3-4) and his Spirit to strengthen us (Rom. 8:15; 2 Tim. 1:7) when we are afraid.

iii. The appointment of commanders (20:9)

After the recruiting officers had gathered the army, commanders (literally 'princes of the host') were to be appointed over them (20:9). *'When the officers have finished speaking to the army, they shall appoint commanders over it.'* Moses does not say who was to appoint the commanders, nor does he define their role. Elsewhere we read of commanders who led 'thousands', 'hundreds' and 'fifties' (1 Sam. 8:12; 22:7; 2 Kings 1:9; Isa. 3:3). In Deuteronomy 1:15 the same phrase is used to describe tribal officials who governed Israel in civilian affairs at a local level.

Leadership is an important theme in Deuteronomy, for Moses was keen to raise up a new generation of leaders in Israel. As well as appointing leading men from the tribes (1:15), he was preparing Joshua to take over from him and lead the people into the land of Canaan (31:7-8). Gifted and godly leadership at a variety of levels was vital for true religion to prevail in Israel (see 17:18-20; 31:9-13; 32:45-47). Human leaders, however, do not take the place of Jehovah, who is the ultimate commander. He is the one who went before Israel and led her armies into battle. It was he who raised up commanders to serve him, and this law reminded them that they were 'men under authority'. In the same way the church's leaders today are under-shepherds and servants of the Chief Shepherd, the Lord Jesus, the king and head of God's church (1 Peter 5:2-4).

The Conduct of War (20:10-20)

In the second half of chapter 20, Moses set out the rules of war when Israel's armies went beyond the borders of their own land (see 20:10-15, 19-20). Today, wars of aggression and conquest are outlawed under international law, but until very recent times they were accepted as inevitable. In ancient times kings who had the resources went to war each year in the spring (1 Chr. 20:1). Although God's law did not forbid this opportunistic approach to warfare, it did regulate it and restrain some of its worst features by insisting that a besieged city be offered the opportunity to surrender (20:10-15) and that the fruit trees around a besieged city be spared (20:19-20). In the midst of this section (20:16-18) Moses describes what was to happen when the Israelites attacked the cities of the Canaanites which had been promised to them. Moses called for the total destruction of the Canaanites and it seems that no restraints were to be placed upon the conduct of Israel's armies. That was not the case, for whenever the armies of Israel went out to fight, they fought as Jehovah's army. Their goal was the victory of his righteous kingdom and their guide was his law.

i. Cities beyond the borders of the promised land (20:10-15)
These verses assume that Israel would go to war beyond her

boundaries, either to prevent an attack from a hostile neighbour or to extend her influence (20:10a). *'When you march up to attack a city...'* When that happened, Jehovah required a level of discipline and restraint amongst the common soldiers that was very high by the standards of the day. The very first thing that the advancing army was to do as it approached an enemy city was to make it an offer of peace (20:10b). The terms of the offer are stated in 20:11. *'If they accept and open their gates, all the people in it shall be subject to forced labour and shall work for you.'* These were the terms sought by the representatives of Gibeon, who deceitfully pretended to have travelled from a distant land to make a peace treaty with Israel (Josh. 9:6). The Gibeonites were allowed to live, but they were to be 'woodcutters and water-carriers for the entire community' (Josh. 9:21). This was the 'covenant of peace' between the Gibeonites and the Israelites. Similar treaties were made between Israel and other nations (see 2 Sam. 10:19). Even though the city of Rabbah did not surrender to the Israelites, its people were shown some leniency after its capture in 2 Samuel 12:29-31. Its people were put to work, labouring 'with saws and with iron picks and axes', while others made bricks. Although this was a humiliating climb-down for the leaders of the city, it meant that they and their people avoided wholesale slaughter.

There was much wisdom in seeking a negotiated surrender. Winston Churchill once said that 'Jaw, jaw is better than war, war'. Even for the conqueror, a victory at the negotiating table is better than victory on the battlefield. Even the militaristic German Chancellor Otto von Bismarck preferred to achieve his ends by diplomacy rather than conflict, for he knew the costliness of war. Yet the 'offer of peace' was not a cynical ploy dictated by worldly wisdom, for it reflected the character God. The Collect for Peace in the Book of Common Prayer addresses God as 'the author of peace and the lover of concord'. Jesus urged his followers to be lovers of peace as well. 'Blessed are the peacemakers, for they shall be called sons of God' (Matt.

5:9). Christians should work hard to be peacemakers in their families, churches, and communities, and in their contribution to good relations between nations and peoples.

Moses described what could happen to a city if it refused the offer of peace (20:12). *'If they refuse to make peace and they engage you in battle, lay siege to that city.'* He anticipated that the Israelite army, advancing in the power of Jehovah, would be victorious (20:13). *'When the LORD your God delivers it into your hand, put to the sword all the men in it.'* A whole generation of fighting men would perish and it would be a long time before that city would be able to raise a new army. *'As for the women, the children, the livestock and everything else in the city, you may take these as plunder for yourselves. And you may use the plunder the LORD your God gives you from your enemies.'* (20:14) The women, children and livestock were to be 'consumed' or completely absorbed into the Israelite nation. In this way the defeated nations were made to bow before Israel's God.

We may recoil from the violence of Israel's methods and recognise that no-one can be brought into God's kingdom today by violence or the threat of violence (2 Cor. 10:4). Men and women are brought into God's kingdom only as their hearts are renewed by the power of the gospel. However, those who will not submit to Jesus Christ when they hear the gospel preached to them here on earth will submit to him when he comes as the conquering king and judge of all the earth. Then it will be too late to fall upon their knees and accept his offer of peace for he has come 'to proclaim ... the day of vengeance of our God' (Isa. 61:2). Every knee will bow before him and every tongue will confess that he is Lord (Phil. 2:10); but not everyone who falls before him on that day will enjoy his salvation. That is why it is so important that each one of us surrenders to his claims now and submits to him as Saviour and Lord.

ii. Cities within the promised land (20:16-18)
Thus far Moses has been setting out the rules of warfare for

'ordinary' military campaigns, In 20:19-20 he will return to that theme. In the short section from verse 16 to verse 18, Moses sets out the rules which govern 'holy' warfare. They are very different, and in 20:16 Moses prefaces his remarks with 'However'. He told the Israelites what they must do when they conquer the land of Canaan (20:16): '... in the cities of the nations the LORD your God is giving you as an inheritance, do not leave alive anything that breathes'. This was a unique war. In a series of decisive strikes, Jehovah would give his people the inheritance he had promised to Abraham. Even as Moses spoke, the Israelites were assembled on the plains of Moab waiting for the order to move forward. When that order came, they were to fight with all their might. They were to obliterate the Canaanites completely (20:17). 'Completely destroy them—the Hittites, Amorites, Canaanites, Perizzites, Hivites and Jebusites—as the LORD your God has commanded you.' This list of six nations is an abbreviated version of the list in 7:1 and the even longer list in Genesis 15:19-21. That list followed God's promise to Abraham that his descendants would return to the land of Canaan to possess it after 'the sin of the Amorites' had 'reached its full measure' (Gen. 15:16).

Jehovah had been very patient with the Canaanites as their wickedness spiralled out of control for hundreds of years. They were an example of what Paul described in Romans 1:21-25:

> For although they knew God, they neither glorified him as God nor gave thanks to him, but their thinking became futile and their foolish hearts were darkened. Although they claimed to be wise, they became fools and exchanged the glory of the immortal God for images made to look like mortal man and birds and animals and reptiles. Therefore God gave them over in the sinful desires of their hearts to sexual impurity for the degrading of their bodies with one another. They exchanged the truth of God for a lie, and worshipped and served created things rather than the Creator—who is forever praised. Amen.

Theirs was a downward spiral into 'ever-increasing wickedness' (Rom. 6:19), and the time had come to stop it. The Canaanites had refused to listen to the testimony of their consciences or godly men like Abraham who had lived in their midst, and now God must bring the consequences of their sinful actions to bear upon them. He is the judge of every nation and he will do only what is right and just.

Moses described the forthcoming purge of the Canaanites in sacred terms. As he did in 7:2-4, here too in 20:17 he used the theologically verb *herem* in his command to 'destroy' them. This indicates that the land was to be dedicated to Jehovah and restored to his rule by the total destruction of the Canaanites. By means of this 'holy' war the sovereignty of Jehovah over the land and its inhabitants was vindicated. By this means, too, a serious pastoral problem was to be averted (20:18). *'Otherwise, they will teach you to follow all the detestable things they do in worshiping their gods, and you will sin against the LORD your God.'* The nightmare scenario for Moses was that the Israelites would receive the land from Jehovah and then give thanks to the false gods of the nations around them. This was to violate the first and second commandments, and indeed the whole of God's covenant with them. The consequences of such an outcome would be the moral and spiritual destruction of the nation which God had chosen to bring salvation to the world. If they had totally fallen away back then, the prospects for us today would be bleak indeed. It is in this light that we must read these verses and appreciate that Jehovah did not lightly command the slaughter of whole nations.

The methods which the Israelites were to employ do not carry over into the actions of God's people today, but the goal of moral and spiritual purity does. We are to have nothing to do with false gods and false worship that does not honour the triune God. The apostle Paul allowed no room in the life of the church or the lives of individual Christians for the pagan worship of his day. 'The sacrifices of pagans are offered to demons, not to God, and I do not want you to be participants with demons. You cannot drink the cup of the Lord and the cup of demons too; you cannot have a part in both the Lord's table and the table of demons' (1 Cor. 10:20-21). Paul would have had no time for the multi-faith worship gatherings of our day or the new age syncretism that is revolutionising the popular view of God. We need to remember that Jehovah has not changed from the days of Moses and Paul. He is not willing to be worshipped as one god amongst many, nor will he accept 'politically correct' worship, for that is 'detestable to him'.

iii. Cutting down trees (20:19-20)

The destruction caused by war takes many forms. As well as causing loss of life amongst combatants and civilians, war can destroy a nation's economy, environment and social infrastructure. Today we describe this as the 'collateral damage' of war. One of the abiding visual images of the first Gulf War is the burning oil wells of southern Iraq, which continued to burn for many months after the war ended. On top of that we can think of the destruction of bridges, roads, schools and hospitals. Moses was aware of the damage which could be caused to the environment and economy even by the unsophisticated techniques of ancient warfare, and in 20:19-20 he sought to restrain it.

These verses prohibit the destruction of trees (20:19). '*When you lay siege to a city for a long time, fighting against it to capture it, do not destroy its trees by putting an axe to them, because you can eat their fruit.*' Trees might have been cut down to obtain timber for building siege machines or lighting fires to destroy a city's defensive fortifications, or possibly as part of a scorched-earth policy to make the land unproductive and uninhabitable. Fruit trees, and especially olive trees, were a valuable source of nourishment in the hot, dry Mediterranean lands. Even today, the destruction of a family's olive grove can have devastating consequences, and has been used by Israeli forces as a collective punishment against Palestinian communities.

Moses' reasoning in 20:19b may sound strange to modern ears. *'Do not cut them down. Are the trees of the field people, that you should besiege them?'* It seems as though he is more concerned about trees than people. He sanctioned the siege of a whole city, which could result in the loss of many human lives. In fact, he even permitted some trees to be cut down for the construction of siege works (20:20b): *'You may cut down trees that you know are not fruit trees and use them to build siege works until the city at war with you falls.'* He permitted the use of non-fruit-bearing trees for siege works because he recognised that war is sometimes necessary; and if a war must be fought it should be prosecuted with vigour so that it does not drag on interminably. However, he sought to lessen the collateral damage which war might inflict upon the wider community by prohibiting the destruction of food-producing fruit trees.

Moses recognised that wars do not last for ever. Those who wage war must consider the peace which will follow. A victory which leaves a wasteland is a victory for no-one. Moses gave this law to protect trees, but he also gave the law to protect the livelihoods of those who would live to pick up the pieces after the battle. As well as reflecting the humanitarian concerns so prevalent in Deuteronomy, this law reflects God's delight in the world he has made (see Gen. 1:31, 8:21-22). Those who love God will also cherish and protect the world which he made. They will also recognise that God has placed the creation under mankind. The trees exist to provide for the needs of man, not vice versa.

Conclusion

The laws of Deuteronomy 19 – 25 are a sobering reminder that we live in a fallen world in which nasty things happen. God does not ignore the nastiness of life in a fallen world. He has given laws which, if faithfully obeyed and applied, will restrain the evil around us. War and the threat of war (see Matt. 24:6; Mark 13:7; Luke 21:9) is a reminder that our world is still in 'bondage to decay' and 'groaning as in the pains of childbirth' (Rom. 8:21-22). Yet as the kingdom of God spreads, through the influence of the gospel, the worst excesses of warfare will be restrained and eventually war itself will cease (see Ps. 46:9; Isa. 2:4; Micah 4:2). This is because the king of God's kingdom is none other than the 'Prince of Peace' (Isa. 9:6), who makes peace by removing 'the dividing wall of hostility' between man and man (Eph. 2:14). The peace which the Lord Jesus has made between sinners and a holy God (Eph. 2:18) is to have a leavening influence on every area of human activity. In the laws of Deuteronomy we see how the grace of God aims to regulate many forms of sinful conflict, not least when nations go to war with each other. The 'renewal of all things' which God sought to bring about through the laws of Israel will reach its consummation in a universe brought under King Jesus, where nation will no longer make war against nation, where wars will cease to the ends of the earth, and where there will no longer be any of the evil which calls forth the holy anger of Jehovah.

Chapter 21
Sins that pollute the land

Please read Deuteronomy 21: 1-23

Many superstitious ideas are associated with death, especially violent death. It is thought that the spirits of those who have died a violent death haunt the place where violence was done to them and so their ghosts are a reminder of an evil that has not been righted. Back in 1483 the teenage King Edward V of England and his younger brother, Richard, Duke of York, were murdered in the Tower of London. It was widely suspected that they were killed by their uncle, who became King Richard III. We cannot know for sure who killed the boy princes, as no-one was ever brought to justice. This horrific crime continues to baffle those who investigate it. Even today it is claimed that the ghosts of the murdered princes haunt the Tower where they were murdered. The whiff of evil hangs in the air.

The Book of Deuteronomy has no place for primitive superstition, but it does take seriously the consequences of violence. Acts of violence and bloodshed are said to pollute the land which God gave to the Israelites. In chapter 21, Moses continued his exposition of the sixth commandment, which prohibited unlawful killing. In chapters 19 and 20 Moses addressed the two most common causes of violent death in Israel, blood feuds and warfare. Here in chapter 21 he addressed some of the causes of blood feuds and some of the consequences of warfare.

The consequences of an unlawful killing were noted in Genesis 4:10-12, where the Lord called Cain to account for killing his brother, Abel. 'Listen! Your brother's blood cries out to me from the ground. Now you are under a curse and driven from the ground, which opened its mouth to receive your brother's blood from your hand. When you work the ground, it will no longer yield its crops for you.' In Numbers 35:33 Moses commands, 'Do not pollute the land where you are. Bloodshed pollutes the land, and atonement cannot be made for the land on which blood has been shed, except by the blood of the one who shed it.' The problem to which Moses pointed was not the agitated spirits of the dead, but the broken law of God. Even the worst of sinners know that something very evil has taken place when another person has been murdered. There is something in all of us that cries out for justice. How much more does a holy God cry out for atonement when his law has been violated? The theme which unites this chapter is the defilement that flows from the shedding of innocent blood. The chapter begins and ends with laws which protect the land from such defilement (see 21:9; 21:23b).

The other laws which Moses expounded in this chapter deal with a range of different situations arising out of warfare and family conflict. For instance, the victim found lying in a field in 21:1 might well be a victim of a feud between families. If there were no satisfactory way of resolving the tension, someone in the community would make assumptions and set off a new round of blood-letting. So, too, the law regarding the captive woman taken as a wife in 21:10-14 was an extension of the law on warfare in 20:10-15. When family life was so complex, there was a real danger that family tensions might spill over into violence. In his preaching of the Decalogue Moses engaged thoughtfully and realistically with the complexities of life in the community which he served as a spiritual leader. It was not an easy task! Nor is ours today as we seek to apply the same laws in a world where stable family units are increasingly rare and the sanctity of human life is being challenged by new technologies.

An Unsolved Murder (21:1-9)

These verses address the problem of an unsolved murder. Not only was this a puzzle for those whose task it was to enforce the law, it was a challenge to the security of the whole community. When my father was a boy, the rural community in which he lived was shocked by the discovery of a dead body lying by the roadside. The victim, it turned out, was a Turk. This exotic detail made the case a talking-point for miles around. What had brought this stranger all the way from Turkey to the quiet Northern Irish village of Tamlaght O'Crilly? Why had his journey ended in tragedy? Who had killed him? Was it a travelling companion who had quietly disappeared? Or was it some outwardly respectable member of the local community? These and other unanswered questions had chilling implications. Moses knew that an unsolved murder is a worrying problem for the community.

Every murder is evil in the sight of God, and this is the heart of the problem. The problem for the Israelites was made all the more serious by the fact that a murder had taken place in 'the land the LORD your God is giving you to possess' (21:1). This was holy land, given to the Israelites by Jehovah so that they might display his holiness as they lived in brotherhood within its bounds. Murder, like idolatry, had no place in God's land, for it defiled the land. The usual solution to this problem was to find the murderer and punish him with death (see Gen. 9:6; Num. 35:33b). However, in this case 'it is not known who killed him'. The unacknowledged and unpunished evil will not simply go away, but will continue to offend God and to affect the community.

The authorities could not simply close the file on this homicide. First, they must assign responsibility for dealing with the case to some appropriate body (21:2). *'Your elders and judges shall go out and measure the distance from the body to the neighbouring towns.'* These were the elders from all the towns in the locality. They served as local judges (see 16:18; 19:12), and they were to measure the distance from the body to the neighbouring towns and allocate responsibility to the nearest town. The people of that town were not to be held responsible for the killing, nor were they obliged to compensate the victim's family. They were, however, required to administer an atonement ritual (21:3-4). *'The elders of the town nearest the body shall take a heifer that has never been worked and has never worn a yoke and lead her down to a valley that has not been ploughed or planted and where there is a flowing stream. There in the valley they are to break the heifer's neck.'*

The details of the ritual are unusual and their significance is uncertain. At first glance, it may appear that the killing of the animal was a substitutionary sin-offering. This is unlikely, because the animal was killed by having its neck broken. That was not the way sacrificial animals were killed. In Exodus 12:46 we are told that the Passover lamb was to have none of its bones broken. Yet in Exodus 13:13 and 34:20 the law required that if a firstborn donkey was not redeemed by sacrifice it was to be disposed of by having its neck broken. It is significant that the heifer was to be taken to a desolate and uncultivated place, near a fast-flowing mountain stream (not a seasonal or dry river-bed) before its neck was to be broken. This secluded spot was the kind of place a murderer would seek out to commit his crime. It was also the kind of place that an execution would be carried out. The best explanation of this ritual is that the heifer represents the guilty person and its neck is broken in a mock execution. The guilt of the murderer is then symbolically carried away in the fast and ever-flowing waters of the mountain stream. Those who are guiltless in the whole affair are assured that a just and holy God will not punish the innocent for the sins of others.

The priests played an important role in the ritual (21:5). *'The priests, the sons of Levi, shall step forward, for the LORD your God has chosen them to minister and to pronounce blessings in the name of the LORD and to decide all cases of dispute and assault.'* Their participation in the ritual indicated that God was working through this ritual to cleanse the consciences of his people. The priests and Levites played a role in judicial decision-making in Israel (see 17:9); but here there was no case for them to adjudicate, because no-one had been charged with an offence. Their main role was to preside at the altar. Although the killing of the heifer was not a sin-offering, it was presented to the Lord as an atonement (21:8a) so that the whole town might be cleared of any association with the killing.

The elders of the town were to act on behalf of their community (21:6-8a).

> *Then all the elders of the town nearest the body shall wash their hands over the heifer whose neck was broken in the valley, and they shall declare: 'Our hands did not shed this blood, nor did our eyes see it done. Accept this atonement for your people Israel, whom you have redeemed, O LORD, and do not hold your people guilty of the blood of an innocent man.'*

When the elders washed their hands over the heifer, they were saying by that action that they and the people they represented had no involvement in the dead man's murder. When we read of this hand-washing, we may be tempted to think of Pontius Pilate, who washed his hands to indicate that he bore no responsibility for the death of Jesus in Matthew 27:24. This is not a helpful parallel. As the Roman governor who ordered the execution of Jesus, Pilate could not avoid responsibility for his actions. His

365

hand-washing was a smokescreen designed to cover up his guilt. A better parallel is with David in Psalm 26:6. 'I wash my hands in innocence, and go about your altar, O LORD.' The psalmist was able to write these words, not because he was free of all sin, but because he had followed God's instructions and was now purged of his guilt. His conscience was clear.

With words as well as actions the elders declare that their town bears no guilt in the murder of an innocent man. They have done everything they can to investigate the matter and they are not hiding a murderer in their midst. They recognise the fact of corporate guilt and acknowledge the communal implications of one person's sinful action. At times of spiritual renewal, the Israelites were not slow to acknowledge that they had tolerated sin in their midst and that it had serious implications for them all (see Neh. 1:6-7; Isa. 6:5; Dan. 9:5-11.) Where there was guilt to acknowledge, they acknowledged it, and distanced themselves from the sinful actions of their fellow Israelites. However, where there was no guilt they confessed this before God. By this ritual they acknowledged the seriousness of the evil that had taken place, yet declared that they had no part in it. *'And the bloodshed will be atoned for. So (in this way) you will purge from yourselves the guilt of shedding innocent blood, since you have done what is right in the eyes of the LORD'* (21:9). The community could have a clear conscience about the matter when the seriousness of the evil act and its corporate implications were fully recognised, when an honest examination of the situation and full confession of what was known was made before God, and when the prescribed ritual was performed.

The priests had the solemn task of presiding at the ritual execution and hearing the elders' declaration. We are not told exactly how they were to conduct themselves as the ceremony took place. It may well have been that they made a formal acknowledgment of the elders' words and pronounced that

God's requirement had been met. In this way they may have put the people's minds at rest by declaring their community free from all guilt in the matter. What we can say for certainty is that this priestly function is fulfilled under the New Covenant by the Lord Jesus, who has offered himself as an atonement for the sins of the world. The apostle Paul set forth the implications of his death for the community of believers in Romans 8:1. 'Therefore, there is now no condemnation for those who are in Christ Jesus.' The evil of sin has been put to rest and the angry law has been pacified. We can have a clean conscience in the midst of a sinful world.

A Captive Woman (21:10-14)

Moses regulated a practice that was common in the ancient world. After battle, a victorious army would take the wives and daughters of their defeated enemy and enslave them to gratify their desires. Rarely were these women given the security and dignity of being a wife. Often they lived lives of degradation and abuse. By contrast, the law in Israel allowed the men who were victorious in battle to take the women of the city they conquered (see 20:14); but it also required them to take them as their wives (21:10-11). *'When you go to war against your enemies and the LORD your God delivers them into your hands and you take captives, if you notice among the captives a beautiful woman and are attracted to her, you may take her as your wife.'* The ancient practice was tolerated rather than encouraged, and its worst excesses regulated. The legal framework is similar to that which permitted men to divorce their wives in 24:1-4. Jesus explained that this dispensation had been granted because men's hearts were hard (Matt. 19:8, Mark 10:5) and not because divorce was acceptable to God. It was an accommodation to human sinfulness and deeply embedded cultural practices. However, such an accommodation ought not to guide the behaviour of Christians today. We are not to make this law a justification for enforced marriage and bigamy, but we are to dig down to its underlying principles.

One of the problems with taking a captive woman as a wife was that she would almost invariably come from non-Israelite stock. The law of 20:10-15 allowed the armies of Israel to spare the non-combatants amongst these populations when they went to war beyond the boundaries of Canaan. However, these women were pagans, and paganism was to have no place in Israel, so the law requires the woman to put away her old identity when she was taken as a by an Israelite man (21:12-13a) *'Bring her into your home and make her shave her head, trim her nails and put aside the clothes she was wearing when captured.'* Her unbrushed hair, untrimmed nails and unkempt clothes were expressions of her grief following the defeat of her city and the death of her family. This young woman was desolate and without hope. For all she knew, her father and mother were dead; and the only place where she might find a place of safety was in the home of one of her captors. Moses instructed the Israelite man who took her to allow her time to grieve and then to give her such a home (21:13b). *'After she has lived in your house and mourned her father and mother for a full month, then you may go to her and be her husband and she shall be your wife.'*

Whatever her past life, the captive wife was encouraged to lay it behind her and take up a new identity within her new family and within the nation of Israel. Although the circumstances were very different, she was encouraged to do what Ruth did when she embraced the family and nation of her late husband. She pledged to Naomi, 'Your people will be my people and your God my God' (Ruth 1:16). Like Solomon's bride, she is to forget her people and father's house (Ps. 45:10) so that she might find a new home. Hopefully, she too will find shelter under Israel's God.

Her new status protected her from further humiliation. Although she came into her new home as a captive and a

Gentile, she could leave only as a free-born Israelite. Moses gave a pre-nuptial warning to the husband in 21:14: *'If you are not pleased with her, let her go wherever she wishes. You must not sell her or treat her as a slave, since you have dishonoured her.'* As we see in 22:13-19 and 24:1, even married women were often very vulnerable in those days. Malachi rebuked the men of Israel for violating their marriage obligations at will (Mal. 2:14), because such self-indulgent conduct was displeasing to God. God's compassion extended to these Gentile captives who had endured the indignity of a forced marriage. They were not to endure the added humiliation of rejection and divorce. Marriage, after all, is God's way of providing security and protection for those who are weak. That need for security is ultimately met only in covenant with God, through Jesus Christ, in whom there is a deep covenantal equality for in him 'there is neither Jew nor Greek, slave nor free, male nor female, for you are all one in Christ Jesus' (Gal. 3:28).

A Firstborn's Inheritance (21:15-17)

Polygamy is almost unheard of today in the western world, but it was widely practised in ancient times. Its painful consequences are recognised in the Bible (see Gen. 29:16-30:24; 1 Sam. 1:1-8). Not only did wives have to compete for their husband's affection, but their children often found themselves competing for their father's inheritance. It was only natural that a father would favour the children of his favourite wife, even if this conflicted with the natural order of succession.

Even though it was contrary to God's declared purpose in Genesis 2:24, the law of 21:15-17 did not outlaw polygamy. It did, however, limit the freedom of a father to allocate his inheritance when he had more than one wife and family. It was not uncommon for a man to favour one wife and settle his inheritance upon her children. *'If a man has two wives, and he loves one but not the other, and both bear him sons but the firstborn is the son of the wife he does not love...'* Literally, the final phrase reads 'the son of the wife he hated'. This is an instance of 'hate' in Scripture meaning to love one person less than another. In a rather puzzling statement of our Lord in Luke 14:26 he speaks of his disciples hating father and mother, wife and children. That simply meant that they loved Jesus more. Similarly, Elkanah loved Hannah more and Peninnah less in 1 Samuel 1:5: 'But to Hannah he gave a double portion because he loved her'.

As a result of such unequal affection a husband might leave a larger inheritance to the son of his favourite wife, even though he was not his firstborn. The Old Testament records several instances of a younger son receiving the rights of the firstborn. In Genesis 27:25-29, Jacob rather than Esau received the blessing of the firstborn by deceiving his father. Jacob was encouraged to seek the blessing due to the firstborn by his cunning mother, but in Romans 9:11-13, the reversal of the natural order to favour the younger son is presented as a manifestation of God's sovereign will to elect those whom he will bless. Likewise in Genesis 48:12-14, Joseph expected his father to bless his firstborn son Manasseh Israel crossed hands to bestow a greater blessing upon Ephraim and his descendants (see Gen. 48:19).

While such freedom appropriately belongs to God when he bestows his blessings, it is open to blatant abuse when exercised by sinful men. The consequences of open favouritism in families can be deadly (see Gen. 37:3, 19-20), so the law limited the freedom of the father to favour younger sons (21:16). *'When he wills his property to his sons, he must not give the rights of the firstborn to the son of the wife he loves in preference to his actual firstborn, the son of the wife he does not love.'* This did not exclude younger sons from receiving a portion of their father's estate, but a special (or double) portion belonged to the firstborn (21:17). *'He must acknowledge the son of his unloved wife as the firstborn by giving him a double share of all he has. ... The right* (or just portion) *of the firstborn belongs to him.*' The extent of this portion is hard to quantify because land was owned by families in Israel rather than individuals. The extended family as a group would continue to farm the whole area which belonged to them collectively even after the firstborn received his inheritance, so his block of land would not have been visibly bigger than the rest. It may well be that the portion which the firstborn received was figurative, a position of pre-eminence in the family decision-making process. Similar words were used in 2 Kings 2:9 to describe the inheritance of prophetic power and insight which Elisha sought from Elijah. This designated Elisha as Elijah's spiritual heir.

Moses explained why the firstborn son was to receive the double portion of his father's inheritance in 21:17. *'That son is the first sign of his father's strength.'* It was only proper, therefore, that he should inherit a position of leadership and prominence in the decision-making processes of the family. In Psalms 78:51 and 105:36 the firstborn children of Egypt, who were slain by the angel of death, are called 'the firstfruits of (their father's) manhood'. The point of such language is not to encourage a macho attitude in men (after all, the mother has expended far more strength in delivering the child), but to indicate that God has started to raise up a new generation to serve him. Even firstborn animals, because they were the first to emerge from their mother's wombs, were set apart as special in Israel (see 15:19). Sons, in particular, are a blessing from the Lord (Ps. 127:3), because they provide security for parents in their old age and for the family as a whole. In recognition of God's blessing, a father was to bestow special generosity on his firstborn.

This framework shapes our thinking about the Lord Jesus. His birth to a virgin marked a new stage in God's plan of salvation and a new manifestation of his divine power. Very appropriately, he was recognised as God's firstborn (see Rom. 8:29; Col. 1:15, 18; Heb. 1:6), and the people of God are to rejoice in him. Even his brothers are to submit to his pre-eminence in the family of faith. Because he poured out his life as a sacrifice for many, he has received a double portion of his Father's blessing. From this blessing he pours abundant blessing upon his beloved people.

A Rebellious Son (21:18-21)

Family solidarity was a high priority in Israel. The fifth commandment taught both adult and infant children to honour their parents (5:16). Children who attacked or cursed their parents were to be put to death (Exod. 21:15, 17; Lev. 20:9). In 27:16 the Levites call out before the people 'Cursed is the man who dishonours his father or his mother' and the people respond, 'Amen'. The problem which these laws addressed is much more serious than temper tantrums in unruly infants. In 21:18 Moses described the problem of a headstrong young man who has grown into an unruly and socially disruptive adult. *'If a man has a stubborn and rebellious son who does not obey his father and mother and will not listen to them when they discipline him.'* He has gotten himself into bad company and is set on a course of self-destruction.

The actions of this rebellious son affect the well-being of the whole family. Other children may be led astray. The family inheritance may be endangered. The family itself and its name may not 'live long ... in the land the LORD your God is giving you'. The parents are urged to take action before it is too late. Their first step was to counsel their son and restrain his bad behaviour. When every effort to discipline him at home had failed, they were to take him to the local elders (21:19). *'His father and mother shall take hold of him and bring him to the elders at the gate of his town.'* The elders were involved because the problem could not be resolved within the family. The parents needed outside help before the anarchic influence of this young man spread to other families. Painful though it must have been, the parents were to acknowledge the full extent of the problem in their family (21:20). *They shall say to the elders, "This son of ours is stubborn and rebellious. He will not obey us. He is a profligate and a drunkard."* The same vocabulary is found in Proverbs 23:20-21 and 28:7. 'Do not join with those who drink too much wine or gorge themselves on meat, for drunkards and gluttons become poor and drowsiness clothes them in rags... a companion of gluttons disgraces his father.' The folly of the dissolute and the drunkard destroys both the individual and his family, while timely discipline may save a young man from death (see Prov. 19:18).

It is possible that the elders may have exhorted the young man to turn from his evil ways, but if that did not happen Moses prescribed the severest penalty for the unruly son (21:21a). *Then all the men of his town shall stone him to death.* Severe as the penalty was, it could be administered only after the elders gave their permission. Under Roman law, and some other ancient law codes, a father had the power of life and death over members of his family. No Israelite father was given such power. Both father and mother were to act together when they took their son to the elders, for the responsibility to discipline children belonged to them both (see Prov. 1:8). Often a mother's compassionate influence has modified a father's rage. However, even the parents together could not take the law into their own hands. The elders were to establish the truth of their claims; and if the son's rebellion was as serious as the parents had said, they were to sentence him to death. The penalty was severe, but the procedure aimed to prevent the hysteria of the lynch-mob.

The underlying purpose of justice in Israel was spiritual (21:21b). *You must purge the evil from among you. All Israel will hear of it and be afraid.* By means of this law and its application, God was sending a message to the nation as a whole, not only to young men high on testosterone. God was grieved by the actions of a rebellious son; and the nation of Israel was in danger of becoming a rebellious son. Jehovah was a Father who loved his people and had redeemed them from slavery (see 1:31; 32:6; also Exod. 4:22; Hosea 11:1). Yet the Israelites were stubborn and rebellious. '"Woe to the obstinate children," declares the LORD...' (Isa. 30:1)

> All day long I have held out my hands
> to an obstinate people,
> who walk in ways not good,
> pursuing their own imaginations.
> (Isa. 65:2)

> A stubborn and rebellious generation,
> whose hearts were not loyal to God,
> whose spirits were not faithful to him.
> (Ps. 78:8)

Just as the law prescribed death for the rebellious son, so Jehovah, with a heavy heart, brought death and destruction upon unfaithful Israel.

Although Israel was an unfaithful and rebellious son, God was a Father who remained faithful to his covenant promises (see Hosea 11:8; Ps. 103:13-14; Jer. 33:10-11). He yearned to show mercy even to rebellious Israel. His mercy to fallen Israel is depicted in our Lord's parable of the loving father who scans the horizon every day looking for the prodigal's return (Luke 15:20). When the prodigal son did return, the father rejoiced 'for this son of mine was dead and is alive again' (Luke 15:24). The law of 21:21 underlines the seriousness of that word 'dead'. It is not merely a rhetorical way of saying 'separated from me', for this young man had brought himself under the curse of God's broken law (Luke 15:18b). Yet, in Christ, mercy triumphs over judgment, and the loving father was able to receive back the rebellious son. This is possible only because of the sacrificial death of God's sinless son.

Sins that pollute the land

A Criminal's Corpse (21:22-23)

Capital punishment is a controversial topic today. Many modern nations have abolished it, but until the twentieth century it was considered to be an essential instrument in the administration of justice. In order to deter others from committing the same offence, executions often took place in public, and the mutilated body of the felon was held up for all to see. At other times victims were executed for political reasons. According to Josephus, the Romans crucified 3,600 Jews over a period of several months as they laid siege to Jerusalem in AD 70. In one day they crucified 500 people, and eventually 'there was not enough room for the crosses and not enough crosses for the bodies'. While the Old Testament is clear in its support for the death penalty for murder (Gen. 9:6) and other serious offences, there is a warning in these verses against any macabre display of the bodies of those who have been executed. The death of a sinner, even one who has been a notorious criminal, is not something in which God takes pleasure (see Ezek. 33:11), and this is reflected in the law concerning the corpse of an executed criminal.

The most common method of execution in Israel was stoning rather than hanging or beheading. After the execution, a victim's body might sometimes be hung up for all to see. When the Israelites defeated the king of Ai (Josh. 8:29) and the five Amorite kings (Josh. 10:26) their bodies were hung on trees to demonstrate that these men died as a judgment from God. King David ordered that the murderers of Ish-bosheth be executed and their bodies hung up by the pool of Hebron as a demonstration of his horror at what they had done (see 2 Sam. 4:12). The Philistines, after defeating Saul at the battle of Gilboa, had his body and the bodies of his sons hung up on the walls of Beth Shan (see 1 Sam. 31:10, 12). This was an act of pure vindictiveness, and the men of Jabesh Gilead demonstrated their regard for Saul by retrieving the bodies and giving them a decent burial.

God's treasured possession

In this law, Moses acknowledged the legitimacy of the death penalty for certain offences, and the value of demonstrating God's hatred of the evil which he has committed by exposing his corpse to public display (21:22). *'If a man guilty of a capital offence is put to death and his body is hung on a tree...'* However, the law places a restraint upon the practice of exposing the criminal's corpse to public humiliation (21:23). *'You must not leave his body on the tree overnight. Be sure to bury him that same day...'* The administration of God's justice in Israel was designed to purge the land of evil. Moses gives this as the reason for the law in 21:23b: *'...because anyone who is hung on a tree is under God's curse. You must not desecrate the land the LORD your God is giving you as an inheritance.'* An executed criminal was visibly and obviously under God's displeasure, for he had receiving the God-ordained consequences of his actions (see Luke 23:41a). Yet God's displeasure does not last forever once the just penalty has been administered.

This teaches us a very important lesson about God's character. He is just, but he is not vindictive. He has no desire to keep a memorial of the sins of his people always before him.

> He will not always accuse,
> nor will he harbour his anger for ever;
> he does not treat us as our sins deserve
> or repay us according to our iniquities.
> (Ps. 103:9-10)

> Who is a God like you,
> who pardons sin and forgives the transgression
> of the remnant of his inheritance?
> You do not stay angry forever
> but delight to show mercy.
> (Micah 7:18)

Sins that pollute the land

When God punishes sin, he does so in order to save his people. When a murderer or idolater was executed and his corpse buried, the defilement of sin was purged from the land of Israel by the administration of justice.

The death of the Lord Jesus on the cross was also a demonstration of God's justice. Even though Jesus himself had done no wrong, he took upon himself the sins of his people and 'God made him who had no sin to be sin for us' (2 Cor. 5:21). In Galatians 3:13 Paul quotes from this law to demonstrate how completely the Lord Jesus entered into our accursed condition. 'Christ redeemed us from the curse of the law by becoming a curse for us, for it is written: "Cursed is everyone who is hung on a tree."' Peter probably had this law in mind when he said that Jesus' killers put him to death 'by hanging him on a tree' (see Acts 5:30; 10:39). Not only was Jesus executed on the cross, he was humiliated, rejected and accursed. His sufferings and death demonstrated the horrific nature and the terrible consequences of the sins which he bore – our sins. He was despised by men and alienated from his Father. He suffered as the worst of criminals because we have committed the worst of sins.

Yet Jehovah does not cling to his anger forever. Just as the corpse of the cursed criminal was not exposed to shame indefinitely, so the cursedness of our Lord on the cross did not endure forever. When his suffering and death had satisfied divine justice, our Lord Jesus cried out, 'It is finished', breathed his last and committed his spirit to his Father. When he died his body was taken from the cross and buried by those who loved and revered him (see Matt. 27:57-61; Mark 15:42-47; Luke 23:50-56; John 19:38-42; 1 Cor. 15:4a). Although his humiliation continued while he was 'under the power of death' and his body rested in the grave, the time for wrath had passed. When his public humiliation came to an end, the curse resting upon those who are united to him by faith was removed forever.

God's treasured possession

Those who trust in Christ can rejoice that, because of him, our heavenly Father does not stay angry with us forever.

God presented him as a sacrifice of atonement, through faith in his blood. He did this to demonstrate his justice, because in his forbearance he had left the sins committed beforehand unpunished – he did it to demonstrate his justice at the present time, so as to be just and the one who justifies those who have faith in Jesus (Rom. 3:25-26).

Because he bore the curse, that curse and its defilement is removed and 'therefore there is now no condemnation for those who are in Christ Jesus' (Rom. 8:1).

Chapter 22
Brotherly love and fleshly lust

Please read Deuteronomy 22: 1-30

Since mediaeval times it has been common to list lust, gluttony, greed, sloth, wrath, envy and pride as the seven deadly sins. This list has shaped the popular idea of what sin is. It has nurtured the mistaken belief that sins are obvious and blatant evils which most decent people can easily avoid. The Bible shatters this comforting notion. Sin is *any* failure to do or to be what a holy God requires. Sin is omission just as much as it is action. Failing to love our brethren is just as sinful as any deliberate violation of the Ten Commandments.

In Deuteronomy 22 Moses continued his exposition of the Second Table of the Law, which started back in chapter 19. He explained the way of life which God required of his redeemed people. He devoted three chapters (19-21) to explaining the implications of the sixth commandment, but he did not devote the same amount of teaching time to each commandment. He expounded the implications of the seventh commandment ('You shall not commit adultery', 5:18) in just over half a chapter (22:13-30). Before coming to these verses we find in 22:1-12 a miscellany of laws which stands between Moses' exposition of the sixth and seventh commandments. Some of the laws in this section reflect the aim of the sixth commandment to protect the lives and livelihoods of mankind. Some protect the welfare of birds and animals. Others reflect the concern of the seventh commandment to protect the integrity of marriage and the sexual purity of God's people. All of these laws showed the Israelites how they were to live as a holy people in the midst of a fallen world.

A Pause to Reflect (22:1-12)

In this section we find a diverse array of laws which regulate some very mundane activities. Although these verses are sandwiched between the portions which expound the sixth and seventh commandments, other commandments underlie some of the laws in this section. Applications of the eighth and tenth commandments are found in 22:1-4, while the rationale of the fifth commandment is quoted in 22:7. So this section is not simply a bridge allowing our thoughts to move from the sixth to the seventh commandment; it is an opportunity to stop and reflect on the nature and purpose of Israel's laws. We may ask, 'How did these laws help God's people to live the holy life which God seeks?' We ought also to ask, 'What is their message for us today?' Before we start to ponder how and why Moses selected this batch of laws for explanation at this point in his sermon, let's look at the laws themselves. They may be grouped together under five headings.

i. Lost Property (22:1-4)
Many people today complain that we live in an age which has lost its sense of community and duty. When we see people in trouble, we prefer to turn and look the other way. 'Don't get involved' is the advice often given, even to an off-duty doctor passing the scene of an accident. By contrast, the key phrase in this short selection of laws is the command not to ignore what we see (22:1, 4). 'Do not ignore it...' Literally, 'do not hide your eyes' when you see a problem. The problem may be a straying animal (22:1). 'If you see your brother's ox or sheep straying, do not

ignore it but be sure to take it back to him.' Or it may be an item of lost clothing (22:3). *'Do the same if you find your brother's ... cloak or anything he loses.'* Or it may be that one of his animals is in trouble (22:4). *'If you see your brother's donkey or his ox fallen on the road, do not ignore it. Help him to get it to its feet.'* The central concern of this law is not just a neighbour's property, but the neighbour himself and his welfare. A modern equivalent might be a man standing along the roadside with steam hissing from the radiator of his car. Help him!

A similar law is found in Exodus 23:4-5. It required an Israelite to help even his enemy when his animals wandered off or collapsed under their load. This enemy may well be an adversary in a quarrel or a lawsuit. If the law applied even to an enemy, it certainly applied to his 'brother' Israelite. In Deuteronomy Moses regularly reminded his hearers that every Israelite was a brother, whether he was a close neighbour or distant stranger. In 22:2 he recognised that the brother 'may not live near you' or 'you do not know who he is'. Still, he is a brother and is to be helped out of reverence for God. This sense of community obligation is a challenge to us when we are too self-centred or just too busy to stop and help another in need. The good Samaritan who stopped to help the man who had fallen amongst thieves was a true neighbour to that man (Luke 10:36-37). He was a truer Israelite to him than the priest and Levite who passed by.

ii. Dress Codes (22:5, 12)

Two laws in this section deal with the way in which the people of Israel were to dress. One prohibited gender cross-dressing (22:5). *'A woman must not wear men's clothing, nor a man wear women's clothing...'* The other required distinctive tassels on the corners of the heavy outer cloak (22:12). *'Make tassels on the four corners of the cloak you wear.'* Unconnected as these two laws may at first appear, they taught the Israelites that their very clothing ought to distinguish them from the nations around them.

The prohibition against gender cross-dressing applied not only to items of clothing, but to any article typically worn by either a man or a woman. It referred to jewellery, ornaments or weapons. In some Middle Eastern countries, it is still customary for men to wear daggers attached to their belts as a fashion accessory and for women to wear distinctive headgear. The purpose of this law was that women should look like women and men should look like men. God made men and women different but complementary (see Gen. 2:21-25), and neither should blur the distinction. This is an important distinction, for in 22:5 Moses describes God's strong disapproval of cross-dressing, *'for the LORD your God detests anyone who does this.'* The word 'detestable' has already been used in Deuteronomy to describe such activities as child-sacrifice (12:31), instigating idolatry (13: 14), unclean food (14:3), offering flawed sacrifices (17:1), and the occult (18:9, 12). It describes God's attitude towards the practices of the heathen.

In ancient times cross-dressing was incorporated into some pagan rituals, during which men crossed over into the realm of women and women crossed over into the realm of men as they both sought to cross over into the realm of the gods. Immoral and even homosexual behaviour was often associated with these rituals. Underlying them was a pagan theology which holds that there is no distinction between the Creator and the creature. All is one and one is all. Hence all distinctions between gender and species, flesh and spirit are more barriers to be broken down. The goal of the pagan ritual was to break down these barriers in order to achieve a deeper union with the divine spirit which permeates the universe. We can hear an echo of this old paganism in the calls of modern liberal theologians for the church to embrace homosexuality and thereby follow the leading of God's Spirit. Contrary to this false theology is the worldview of the Bible which accepts the distinctions embedded in the natural order as flowing from the will of our Creator. Animals have been created according to their kind.

Men and women, although equal in redemptive privilege (Gal. 3:28), are distinct in their genders and they are to reflect this in the way they dress.

The short law in 22:12, requiring tassels on the four corners of an outer cloak, had a simple and practical purpose. These tassels were made from twisted thread and prevented the outer cloak from lifting and exposing a person's nakedness. The same concern was expressed in a different context in Exodus 20:26. The tassels became (and still are) a distinctively Jewish form of dress. They had the effect of identifying the Israelites as a distinct people and reminding them of their special privileges and responsibilities.

> You will have these tassels to look at and so you will remember all the commands of the LORD, that you may obey them and not prostitute yourselves by going after the lusts of your own hearts and eyes. Then you will remember to obey all my commands and will be consecrated to your God. I am the LORD your God, who brought you out of Egypt to be your God. I am the LORD your God (Num. 15:39-41).

Modesty is an important component in Christian character and conduct today (see 1 Cor. 12:23). Paul's words to women in 1 Timothy 2:9-10 show that modesty affects more than merely the way we dress; but it certainly does make our sense of what is appropriate to wear very different from that of unbelievers. Christians dress modestly so as not to attract sinful looks or stimulate lustful thoughts. Yet even our modesty may well bring the world's hostility upon us. John Bunyan describes how this happened to Christian and Hopeful as they passed through Vanity Fair on their way towards the heavenly city. 'The Pilgrims were clothed with such kind of raiment as was diverse from the raiment of any that traded in that fair. The people, therefore, of the fair made a great gazing upon them: some said they were fools; some that they were bedlam; and some, they were outlandish men.' They were, in fact, clothed in holiness as befits the people of God.

iii. Birds' nests (22:6-7)

Moses demonstrated God's concern for all his creatures, including wild birds, in this law. *'If you come across a bird's nest beside the road, either in a tree or on the ground, and the mother is sitting on the young or on the eggs, do not take the mother with the young. You may take the young, but be sure to let the mother go...'* Many Jewish rabbis who commented on the Old Testament law agreed that this was the least of all the Old Testament laws. No doubt they did not rank little birds high amongst God's priorities. Yet the very fact that Moses taught the Israelites about such a seemingly insignificant topic is in itself significant. Jesus echoed this teaching in Matthew 6:26, 10:29. 'Look at the birds of the air; they do not sow or reap or store away in barns, and yet your heavenly Father feeds them.' 'Are not two sparrows sold for a penny? Yet not one of them will fall to the ground apart from the will of your Father.' God cares for his creatures because he created them for his own glory.

> Each little flower that opens,
> Each little bird that sings,
> He made their glowing colours,
> He made their tiny wings:
>
> He gave us eyes to see them,
> And lips that we might tell
> How great is God Almighty,
> Who has made all things well.'

The significance of this law is indicated by the promise which followed it (22:7b). *'... so that it may go well with you and you may have a long life'.* This is the same promise as that which undergirded the fifth commandment (see 5:16), and it has led some to suggest that this law was designed to honour motherhood. Without mothers there would not be any future generations of sparrows, nor would there be future generations of Israelites to possess the promised land. The primary concern of the law, however, is the preservation of life. Because God is the Creator of all living creatures, their lives are precious to him. While God has given mankind the right to kill birds and animals for food (see Genesis 9:3), we are not to kill God's creatures wantonly. In fact, a concern for their own food supply ought to compel mankind to care for God's creatures. Moses balanced the legitimate human need for food with the importance of preserving the birds and animals which God has made. By taking the mother and her eggs for food, the eater made sure that there would be no more food from that source. This law is similar to that of 20:19 which forbade the destruction of trees during a siege. This law challenges us to consider how short-term greed affects the lives and livelihoods of others and how it impacts on the world around us.

The sixth commandment not only forbade murder, it required 'all lawful endeavours to preserve our own life, and the life of others' (*Westminster Shorter Catechism*, answer 68).

iv. A roof-top safety feature (22:8)
Flat roofs were common in the Bible lands. They provided an extra room for sleeping on hot summer nights and a secure place to store produce after the harvest. Rahab hid the Israelite spies under stalks of flax which were drying on the roof of her house in Jericho (see Josh. 2:6). The Philistines revelled on the roof of their temple in Gaza (see Judg. 16:27). Samuel received guests on the roof of his house (see 1 Sam. 9:25). David relaxed at the end of the day on the roof of his palace (see 2 Sam. 11:2). From ancient times the roof-top was an important centre of household activity. With so much traffic to and from the roof, it was easy to foresee that someone might fall and be injured. That is why Moses required the builder of a new house to *'make*

a parapet around your roof so that you may not bring the guilt of bloodshed on your house if someone falls from the roof'. A death in such circumstances was manslaughter.

The general principle is that people are to be held accountable for their negligence when that negligence results in the death of another. Another application of this principle is found in the law in Exodus 21:29 which makes the owner of a bull responsible for a death caused by the bull 'if... the bull has had the habit of goring and the owner has been warned but has not kept it penned up'. These laws are a reminder that, even when they contain the phrase 'you shall not', God's commands are positive. Every command carries within it a positive requirement. This is particularly true of the sixth commandment which requires 'all lawful endeavours to preserve our own life, and the lives of others' (*Westminster Shorter Catechism*, answer 68).

Because God has placed his law as a hedge around human life, we are to do everything that we reasonably can to protect others from foreseeable dangers. Few of us will have flat roofs on our houses, but in other ways we are to keep our homes and property from becoming death-traps. Those who have a backyard swimming pool ought to have a fence around it. Our electrical wiring ought to be well maintained. If we need to keep drugs or dangerous chemicals in our homes, they ought to be stored away securely, beyond the reach of inquisitive children. We ought to keep our cars in a roadworthy condition before we offer anyone a lift; and when we are on the road we ought to drive carefully. On such matters the sixth commandment has a clear message.

v. Mixtures that shouldn't be mixed (22:9-11)
Three commands in a row forbid the mixing together of things that are different. Taken together, they highlight the distinction between type and species which God, the Creator, has built into the creation.

In 22:9 Moses forbade the planting together of seeds from different plants. 'Do not plant two kinds of seed in your vineyard; if you do, not only the crops you plant but also the fruit of the vineyard will be defiled.' A more general command is found in Leviticus 19:19: 'Do not plant your field with two kinds of seed.' The law in Deuteronomy refers only to seed planted 'in your vineyard'. Israel was described as Jehovah's vineyard (see Isa. 3:14; 5:1-7; Jer. 12:10), and from this vineyard Jehovah sought the good fruit of righteousness. More often than not, God found that the weeds of rebellion had been planted in his vineyard (see Isa. 5:2), so this law was probably intended to be symbolic of the purity which God sought amongst his people. It was also an expression of God's sovereignty over the people of Israel and their land. Both belonged to Jehovah, and when they broke this law they forfeited to him their land and everything which grew in it. 'Defiled' literally means 'sanctified' or returned to the Lord. If this is so, the ultimate application of this law came when God removed the people of Israel from the land at the time of the exile and took this defiled vineyard back to himself.

In 22:10 Moses commanded, *'Do not plough with an ox and a donkey yoked together'.* This practice was common in the ancient Near East, and has been observed in more modern times amongst Palestinian farmers. It was, however, a practice forbidden to the people of Israel. This was a reminder that their way of life was different from that of the nations around them. The law was also symbolic of the fact that the Israelites were set apart from all other nations and were not to enter unequal alliances with their neighbours (see Deut. 7:2-4). This principle is one which applies to Christians today. 'Do not be yoked together with unbelievers. For what do righteousness and wickedness have in common?' (2 Cor. 6:14).

In 22:11 Moses commanded, *'Do not wear clothes of wool and linen woven together'.* This cloth was a mixture of fibres derived from animals and plants (sheep and the flax plant) and was therefore considered unnatural. The word describing the mixture of the fibres was adapted from another language, most probably that of the Egyptians, and indicates that the practice was imported from other nations. Israel's practice in this area was to be visibly and characteristically different. We have already seen that Israel was not to adopt the dress codes of her neighbours, and this is another instance of her distinctiveness.

While there is considerable diversity in the laws of 22:1-12, two themes bind them together and indicate the general purpose of Israel's laws.

'Love the LORD your God with all your heart' (Deut. 6:5; 11:1). Love for God makes God's people stand out as different from the nations surrounding them.

i. *Distinctiveness.* Just as God the Creator has embedded distinctive qualities in his creatures (he distinguished day and night, land and sea, and the different kinds of animals, birds and fish from each other), so God the Redeemer has distinguished his chosen people from all other nations (see Exod. 19:5; Deut. 7:6; 14:2; 26:18-19). God's grace marked the people of Israel for special blessings and called forth a special response. The Israelites were to love the Lord with all their heart and live as his people. This distinctively godly way of life affected the way farmers ran their farms, and builders built houses; how the Israelites treated birds and animals and clothed ourselves. The lifestyle choices which they made in these areas marked them visibly as redeemed people. The same should be true of Christians today. Our Saviour died on the cross 'to redeem us from all wickedness and to purify for himself a people that are his very own, eager to do what is good' (Titus 2:14). True Christianity is 'to keep oneself from being polluted by the world' (James 1:27). Our purity is not now regulated by the ceremonial laws of the Israelites; but it does manifest itself in a visibly different approach to work, family life, material possessions and how we use the time and talents God has given us.

ii. Brotherliness. The Hebrew word *ah* ('brother') occurs six times in the text of 22:1-4 (though the English translation '"brother' appears only four times in the NIV). The Israelites were to look upon each other (even when they lived on the far side of the land) as brothers and sisters in covenant with the Lord. The commands to love one's neighbour flowed naturally from the first and greatest command, which was to love the Lord (6:5). The desire to create a community of brothers has been embraced by many over the years, yet it has rarely been realised. The slogan of the French Revolution was 'liberty, equality, fraternity'. Sadly, these ideals were forgotten when the revolutionaries soon turned their hostility upon each other and plunged the whole of Europe into war. Only when men's lives are reshaped by God's grace and God's law will the ideals of brotherhood be realised. Only God's grace can change our inherently sinful hearts and reshape our selfish habits.

In the New Testament church, bonds of brotherhood in Christ transcend the boundaries of ethnic identity. This brotherhood is built on the doctrine of adoption in Christ. 'You are all sons of God through faith in Christ Jesus. There is neither Jew nor Greek, slave nor free, male nor female, for you are all one in Christ Jesus' (Gal. 3:26-28). 'Therefore, as we have opportunity, let us do good to all people, especially to those who belong to the family of believers' (Gal. 6:10).

The sanctity of marriage (22:13-30)

The Israelite community was a family of families. In order for the community as a whole to enjoy stability and cohesion, so too must its families. The relationship between husband and wife lies at the heart of family life, and their loyalty to each other is guarded by the seventh commandment. 'You shall not commit adultery' (5:18). In these verses, Moses explained some of the implications of this command. He described the kind of conduct which was incompatible with God's plan for marriage and which was to be purged from Israel: infidelity before marriage (22:13-21), adultery within marriage (22:22) and the violation of a woman pledged in marriage (22:23-27). He addressed the consequences of rape (22:28-29) and forbade a man from marrying his stepmother (22:30). It is sobering to think that these kinds of conduct took place amongst a redeemed people. Yet they did! There were matters that were to be addressed firmly, honestly and lovingly by the ministry of God's word.

i. Infidelity before marriage (22:13-21)
The infidelity in question in these verses is that of a woman who has fallen foul of her recently-wed husband (22:13-14). *'If a man takes a wife and, after lying with her, dislikes her and slanders her and gives her a bad name, saying, "I married this woman, but when I approached her, I did not find proof of her virginity."...'*
Evidence of the newly-wed wife's virginity might have been the blood-stained bed-covering from the consummation of the marriage. In some ancient cultures this cloth was preserved by a girl's family, and even paraded through the village, as a sign of the girl's chastity and the family's honour. Another explanation of the husband's charge has been offered, on the assumption that no man would make such an accusation knowing that his charge could be so easily rebutted. It has been suggested that, instead of questioning her chastity, the husband has discovered that the girl has not yet reached puberty. In an age when girls might marry in their early or mid teens, this might indeed have been an issue. In this case the Hebrew word *betulim* would describe the evidence of her monthly period. This interpretation of the charge does, however, seem to be a strained one.

Moses proceeds to describe two outcomes in such cases. In 22:15-19 he describes what would happen *if the charge was rebutted by the girl's parents.* *'Then the girl's father and mother shall bring proof that she was a virgin to the town elders at the gate.'* The father asserted his good faith in giving his daughter in marriage (22:16) and imputed evil motives to the man who brought the accusation (22:17a). The cloth which covered the couple's bed on their wedding night would provide conclusive evidence to rebut the man's charge (22:17b), and he was to be punished by the elders (22:18). The word *'punish'* means to discipline as a father would discipline a son (see 21:18) and as God disciplined Israel (see 8:5, 4:36). It strongly suggests that the punishment would involve a beating with rods. The man's penalty was financial as well as physical (22:19a). *'They shall fine him a hundred shekels of silver and give them to the girl's father, because this man has given an Israelite virgin a bad name.'* The fine was twice the bride price which he had paid for his wife and the money was to be paid to the girl's father because he had impugned the integrity of her whole family.

Not only will the husband who makes a false accusation face public humiliation and be made to redeem the honour of the girl's family, he will be obliged to offer his wife life-long security in his household (22:19b). *'She shall continue to be his wife; he must not divorce her as long as he lives.'* Divorce is an outcome which God hates (Mal. 2:16), yet Moses permitted men to divorce their wives in certain circumstances. Because of the hardness of their hearts Israelite men took advantage of this permission (see Matt. 19:8) to suit their selfish and vindictive desires. The vindictive accusation of the husband in these verses is a perfect illustration of the hardness which Jesus condemned. We might think that a woman would be better off away from the tyranny of such a man. However, in those days, while divorce freed a man of his responsibilities towards his wife, it offered very little to the woman. A divorced or 'desolate woman' would endure social isolation and economic insecurity. Her new freedom might well be the freedom to starve on her own. Many women today would find little consolation in a law prohibiting divorce and so perpetuating marriage to a man who had treated her so shamefully. However, in the setting of the ancient world this law was a significant safeguard for the woman. Having humiliated his newly-wed wife once by forcing her to defend her honour before the city elders, the vindictive husband was not allowed to do the same a second time by divorcing her.

In 22:20-21 Moses described the second possible outcome when a man brought a charge of unfaithfulness against his newly-wed wife. He described what would happen *if the husband's charge was proved to be true*. *'If, however, the charge is true and no proof of the girl's virginity can be found...'* The bloodstained cloth from her first intercourse is not at hand because she was not a virgin when the marriage was consummated. This seems to place an unfair burden on the girl and her family to prove her innocence. There may well have been instances where the girl had not been promiscuous, yet she was unable to produce evidence of her virginity. No doubt the elders would have ruled on the peculiar circumstances of each case as it arose. However, in these verses Moses laid down the general rule. Where an unmarried woman had been sexually promiscuous while living in her parental home she was guilty of a serious offence (22:21b). *'She shall be brought to the door of her father's house and there the men of her town shall stone her to death. She has done a disgraceful thing in Israel by being promiscuous while still in her father's house.'* The phrase 'a disgraceful thing in Israel' describes an act of folly which ought never to have taken place amongst the redeemed people of God. It described the rape of Dinah in Genesis 34:7; the covetousness of Achan in Joshua 7:15; the pack rape of a Levite's concubine in Judges 20:6,10; Amnon's advances upon his sister Tamar in 2 Samuel 13:12; and adultery amongst Judah's leaders in Jeremiah 29:23. The people of Israel were to demonstrate their rejection of all such conduct. *'You must purge the evil from among you.'*

The scene of her execution was *'her father's house'*. Her promiscuity had brought shame upon her family and may well have indicated a failure on the part of her parents. King David failed to rebuke his sons when they started to go astray, and his silence contributed to their waywardness. It is hard to rebuke those we love when we see them drifting into serious sin. It is especially hard to restrain a young person taking their first steps into adulthood when the attractions of sin are very powerful and an overbearing approach can provoke a rebellious response. Yet it is the responsibility of parents to set an example of fidelity in their own marriages and to speak with their children about God's design for sex and moral purity. The penalty which Moses prescribed reminded parents that they were accountable for the actions of their children while they lived under their roof. However, it must be emphasised that even after parents have faithfully taught their children and set an example of godliness for them, young people may still make wrong choices and they will live with the consequences.

The penalty prescribed in 22:21 is also a reminder that sexual sin is a serious matter. In the eyes of many people today, sexual activity between consenting adults is a matter of personal choice – a human right! Yet the Scriptures of both Old and New Testaments insist that sex before marriage is a serious offence in God's eyes. 'Marriage should be honoured by all, and the marriage bed kept pure, for God will judge the adulterer and all the sexually immoral' (Heb. 13:4). On 1st January, 1536, Hugh Latimer, the Bishop of Worcester, presented a New Year's gift to King Henry VIII with the words of this verse inscribed on it. At the time, Henry was pursuing the young Jane Seymour while still married to Anne Boleyn. Latimer's courageous honesty could easily have cost him his life but, as a minister of the gospel, it was his duty to speak God's truth. God's law is no more popular today! Yet the church today still needs to declare what God says about sexual purity. God requires abstinence before marriage, and purity within it.

ii. Unfaithfulness within marriage (22:22)
The second evil to be purged from amongst the people of Israel was unfaithfulness within marriage. This was expressly forbidden in the seventh commandment (5:18). 'You shall not commit adultery.' Here Moses prescribed the penalty for violating that commandment. *'If a man is found sleeping with another man's wife, both the man who slept with her and the woman, must die.'* The underlying concern of this law is to protect God's institution of marriage and reflect his holiness. The holy God of Israel hates unfaithfulness in marriage (and every other area of life), whether that unfaithfulness is committed by a man or a woman. In other ancient law codes, a wife was regarded as the property of her husband. While she was punished severely in the event of her unfaithfulness, the man with whom she was unfaithful was not. By contrast, in Deuteronomy an unfaithful wife is regarded as a free moral agent who, along with her lover, has made a wicked choice. Both are punished on an equal footing.

Both the man and the woman have violated key principles underlyng God's covenant with Israel. The man who has slept with *'another man's wife'* has violated the principle of neighbourliness. In Leviticus 18:20 and 20:10 the innocent husband is described as 'your neighbour'. In Israel it was important that a man be able to trust his neighbour; but who can trust an adulterer? The adulterous wife has violated the principle of faithfulness. This is the quality which Jehovah displayed towards his redeemed people, and he expects to find faithfulness in them. Just as Jehovah had married Israel and stayed with her through thick and thin, so he expected husbands and wives to stay faithful to each other through the ups and downs of their marriage. That is why adultery and idolatry were often mentioned in the same breath in the Old Testament. Idolatry was spiritual adultery (Hosea 4:12; 9:1; Jer. 13:25-27), and adultery was tantamount to a rejection of Jehovah. The Israelite who violated his or her marriage vows could easily violate the covenant with God.

For this reason adultery was one of the sins expressly forbidden in the Decalogue and its prescribed penalty was death. Generally the sentence was administered by stoning (see verses 21, 24; also Ezek.16:40). This expressed the whole community's repudiation of the evil-doer and his or her evil. '*You must purge the evil from your midst.*'

iii. Violation of a marriage pledge (22:23-27)

This third evil to be purged from the midst of the people was very decidedly the act of a predatory male who induces a young woman to have sex with him (22:23). '*If a man happens to meet in a town a virgin pledged to be married and he sleeps with her ...*' In the ancient world, betrothal was a much more serious commitment than is engagement today in the Western world. It was a binding promise which could be enforced in the courts. When a 'bride price' had been paid to the girl's family she took on a new status, even though she continued to live in her father's home until her wedding day. The man who violated her had effectively '*violated another man's wife*' (22:24). The consequences for the man were serious, for he had committed an offence worthy of death. However, the outcome for the girl who was seduced would depend on her complicity in what happened.

Two scenarios are described in these verses. The consequences for the girl would be very different. The first scenario is described in 22:23-24 where the intercourse between a man and the betrothed girl was consensual and both must be put to death. '*You shall take both of them to the gate of that town and stone them to death—the girl because she was in a town and did not scream for help...*' Her consent is inferred from the fact that help was at hand, but she chose not to seek it. This may seem like a naïve and unfair reading of her situation, for it is sadly possible to imagine situations in which a rape victim is too afraid or to traumatised to shout out for help. However, we should not miss the point, which is that Moses was giving a rule of thumb guide to help the elders in Israel to distinguish consensual intercourse from rape. It is also a reminder that when God provides 'a way out' from temptation and sin (see 1 Cor.10:13) we must take it, lest by our silence we become as guilty as the one who tempts us.

In the second scenario (see 22:25-27), intercourse is to be regarded as not consensual. *'But if out in the country a man happens to meet a girl pledged to be married and rapes her, only the man who has done this shall die.'* Even if the girl had cried out for help in that remote place, there would have been no-one to rescue her. Literally, 'there was no saviour (*moshiah*) for her'. In spite of the shame which she may feel as a victim of a terrible crime, she has done nothing wrong. *'Do nothing to the girl; she has committed no sin deserving death. This case is like that of someone who attacks and murders his neighbour, for the man found the girl out in the country, and though the betrothed girl screamed, there was no-one to rescue her.'* No stigma attaches to her. The guilt of this crime rests on the man's shoulders. With some emphasis, Moses insisted that the man, and *only* the man, was to die.

Underlying this law is a principle which has important implications for Christians today. We must say no to sin! Clearly, the women placed in these scenarios were not in control of their situation, but they did have choices to make as they responded to the advances of a sinful man. We too may find ourselves forced to endure things that are repugnant to us, but we should never become willing partners to sin. Just as Joseph resisted the advances of Potiphar's wife in Genesis 39:8-12, we should flee from sexual immorality (1 Cor. 6:18) and from 'the evil desires of youth' (2 Tim. 2:22). We are not to remain in situations where we will be easy prey to the tempter, nor ought we to 'walk in the counsel of the wicked or stand in the way of sinners or sit in the seat of mockers' (Ps. 1:1). Rather, when we are tempted, we ought to cry out to the Lord Jesus for help 'because he ... is able to help those who are being tempted'

(Heb. 2:18). When we cry to him for help, we shall find that he is a deliverer near at hand, able and willing to rescue us.

Two further laws bring this section to a conclusion.

i. The rape of a girl not pledged in marriage (22:28-29)
As Moses applied God's law to those who violated a woman pledged in marriage, another terrible scenario came to mind – the violation of a virgin who had not been pledged in marriage. While this was not adultery, it violated all the norms of behaviour which the seventh commandment commended. As well as forbidding the violation of marriage, it requires 'the preservation of our own and our neighbour's chastity, in heart, speech, and behaviour' (*Westminster Shorter Catechism*, answer 71). Hence it forbids 'all unchaste thoughts, words and actions' (*Westminster Shorter Catechism*, answer 72).

Moses describes the man's sinful action in 22:28. '*If a man happens to meet a virgin who is not pledged to be married and rapes her and they are discovered...*' Although the verb used to describe the man's violation of the girl does not imply violent assault, as in 22:25, his crime is properly called rape. The girl had not consented to intercourse and she is not censured in any way. The man is censured and his punishment set out in 22:29a. '*He shall pay the girl's father fifty shekels of silver...*' This sum of money was the customary 'bride price' which a prospective husband would have paid to the girl's father when she was pledged in marriage (see Exod. 22:16). The man's action has seriously reduced the girl's ability to find a suitable husband, so he must marry her himself. '*He must marry the girl, for he has violated her. He can never divorce her as long as he lives.*' The fact that he can and must offer the girl he has violated a secure home probably saved the man's life, as the death penalty was the most common punishment for violations of the seventh commandment.

God's treasured possession

The requirement of 22:29b may seem more like a punishment for the young woman than a protection. After all, what woman would want to marry the man who has raped her? That is why the law allowed the father the right to refuse to give his daughter to the man (Exod. 22:17). Presumably he would not want to give her to a man who would treat her badly. The purpose of the law was to force the man to take care of the woman whom he had wronged. There would now be few men who were willing to marry her. The requirement of marriage was an expression of God's concern for the vulnerable, analogous to the law protecting women taken as captives in war (21:14), and the law protecting women falsely accused of promiscuity before marriage (22:19b). Women who were unable to marry found themselves in a terrible predicament. Ruth and her mother-in-law Naomi were fortunate to find security in the home of a man who loved her (see Ruth 4:13-14). The law of Moses sought to instil within the Israelite community a God-given concern for those who, through no fault of their own, found themselves in a similar position.

We should note that the man's obligation to marry the girl he had raped did not arise from the possible arrival of a baby, but from the fact that he had had sexual relations with her. These alone did not create the marriage. Establishing that compact required a further step, but it was one which the man's actions demanded. In God's plan for mankind, sexual intimacy is reserved for a husband and a wife and implies a commitment to a life-long companionship (see Gen. 2:24). Sexual coercion and even consensual sexual promiscuity inevitably lead to confusion and misery as people say one thing with their bodies while thinking quite the opposite in their minds. The availability of contraception allows many people today to seek casual intercourse merely for personal pleasure, while avoiding long-term commitment or responsibility. This is not what God planned when he blessed mankind with the pleasure of physical intimacy. That is why many who seek happiness in casual sex find that their pleasures leave them with bitter frustration and deep emptiness.

ii. Marriage to a stepmother prohibited (22:30)
Although this verse is found at the end of chapter 22 in our English translations, it is the first verse of chapter 23 in the Hebrew Bible. This would place it in the context of regulations governing ceremonial purity. It is, however, best understood in the context of the seventh commandment, for it required a man to honour the marital relationship between his father and stepmother. *'A man is not to marry his father's wife; he must not dishonour his father's bed.'*

Although the text simply refers to 'his father's wife', it is unlikely that it would have referred to his mother. Incestuous relations between a man and his mother were prohibited in Leviticus 18:7. However, in an age when men took multiple wives, it was not uncommon for a man to have several stepmothers. It was believed that a man's position as head of the family and heir to his father's estate would be secured by marrying his father's wives and concubines after his death. By this practice Absalom sought to establish his authority after overthrowing his father, King David (2 Sam. 16:22); and Adonijah sought to stake his claim to the throne after the death of King David (1 Kings 2:17, 22). Perhaps because of these motives, the practice was considered repugnant (Gen. 35:22; 49:4) and worthy of God's curse (27:20).

The phrase used in 22:30b to describe the practice is noteworthy. 'He must not dishonour his father's bed' literally reads, 'he must not uncover the corner' of his father's robe. When the corner of a man's robe was lifted, his nakedness was exposed and he was exposed to shame. The phrase is used here as a figure of speech, for 'a man's robe' was symbolic of the love and protection which he offered his wife (see Ruth 3:9; Ezek. 16:8). When a son married his deceased father's wife or concubine, it was because he had refused to offer her a home and provision within his household. In that way he exposed the inability of the deceased man to care for his wife. That dishonoured his memory. Hence the fifth commandment as well as the seventh was violated by the man's actions.

Conclusion

Some of these verses make unpleasant reading. Adultery, rape and incest are some of the ugliest sins committed by mankind. They have caused unspeakable distress to many people throughout the ages and are still wounding people who live near us, perhaps even people we know. It is important to remember that every sin is ugly in God's sight and that their consequences are earthly and eternal, for 'the wages of sin is death'. It is not only the seven deadly sins that lead to death. Behind these sins lie the sins of selfishness, anger, covetousness and lack of brotherly love. As he expounded God's law, Moses has shown us that neglecting our duty to love our neighbour can cause him damage (22:1-4) and even death (22:8). He has shown us that inappropriate clothing can expose an unchaste heart which is just as ugly as that of the adulterer or rapist.

Yet even the ugliest sin can be cleansed by the outpouring of God's mercy. The apostle Paul found every kind of immorality in the city of Corinth during the first century. He confronted sinners with the consequences of their sin; but he assured them that even the ugliest of sins can be pardoned and its guilt washed away by the blood of Christ Jesus.

> Do you not know that the wicked will not inherit the kingdom of God? Do not be deceived: Neither the sexually immoral nor idolaters nor adulterers nor male prostitutes nor homosexual offenders nor thieves nor the greedy nor drunkards nor slanderers nor swindlers will inherit the kingdom of God. And that is what some of

you were. But you were washed, you were sanctified, you were justified in the name of the Lord Jesus Christ and by the Spirit of our God (1 Cor. 6:9-11).

Chapter 23
The Lord's assembly

Please read Deuteronomy 23: 1-25

Many people today view religion as a personal and purely private matter. Whatever they choose to believe about God, how they practise their faith and whether they participate in the activities of any community of faith are considered to be matters left to the discretion of the individual. Many of those who do identify themselves with a particular group of believers do so because it aids their personal journey of faith. This individualistic and non-institutional approach to popular religion stands in marked contrast to the religion of the Bible, which emphasises the collective identity and activity of God's people.

In the New Testament, the followers of Jesus Christ are described as 'the body ...the church' (Col. 1:18); 'God's household' (1 Tim. 3:15); and 'God's flock' (1 Peter 5:2). They are those whom God has called out of the world to be 'his very own, eager to do what is good' (Titus 2:14). Here Paul uses the language of the Old Testament to describe the church. The Old Testament describes how God called Abraham and his descendants to be a special nation. An important day in their history was the day when the Lord God came down on Mount Sinai and gave them his law (Deut 4:10). He made a covenant with them and they became his nation – the Lord's assembly. Deuteronomy describes that day at Sinai as 'the day of the assembly' (9:10; 10:4; 18:16). This was the first of many times when the people of Israel would be called together in the name of Jehovah. These were special occasions because the Lord's people were holy (Exod. 19:5-6, 10-11; Num. 16:3). Both their conduct and their membership were to be regulated by God's law. Thus far in his exposition of the law Moses has shown how God's law regulated the conduct of the Israelites. In this chapter we will hear what God had to say about who might be regarded as members of the Lord's assembly. Moses explains the implications of holiness for the nation of Israel.

The boundaries of the Lord's assembly (23:1-8)

These verses (as well as the following section, 23:9-14) are often regarded as a further application of the seventh commandment. They tell us who may or may not enter the Lord's assembly. The seventh commandment was relevant to this question because sexually immoral behaviour is offensive to God and those whose guilt remains unresolved have no place in the kingdom of heaven (1 Cor. 6:9-10). Sexual immorality not only alienates those who commit it from God, it leaves a bitter legacy for future generations. Moses describes a number of groups who were excluded from the Lord's assembly because of their own actions or the actions of others. Three categories of people were specifically excluded from the Lord's assembly:

i. Eunuchs (23:1)
'*No-one who has been emasculated by crushing or cutting may enter the assembly of the LORD.*' These were men who had been rendered incapable of having children by a deliberate human action such as 'crushing or cutting' rather than a congenital defect. Our Lord recognised this distinction in Matthew 19:12. 'For some are eunuchs because they were born that way; others were made that way by men.' It is the latter kind of eunuch to

whom Moses referred, that is, those who became eunuchs by mutilation. Mutilation of any kind was forbidden by Moses (14:1); but the mutilation of a man to make him into a eunuch was considered particularly offensive because the ritual was associated with an act of dedication to a heathen god. By contrast, Jehovah did not take any pleasure in infertility. He was glorified when his people had children (Gen. 1:28) and trained them in the ways of the Lord (6:7).

In the ancient world, men were made into eunuchs in order that they might serve in the harems of oriental despots. They worked amongst the wives and concubines who served the lust and pride of a megalomaniac king. Kings in Israel were to be very different from these ostentatious despots who ruled over other nations (17:16-17). The law of 23:1 is a repudiation of the customs associated with worldly monarchy. In spite of this the biblical record tells us that eunuchs served as royal officials in Israel. See 1 Kings 22:9; 2 Kings 8:6; 9:32; Jer. 34:19; 38:7. In each of these verses the word *saris*, meaning 'eunuch', is used, though in all but one instance the NIV translates it as 'official'.

As the story of salvation unfolded, we find that the grace of God was extended to eunuchs so that they were able to find a place amongst God's people. Although their condition was offensive to God, his mercy was able to restore them to a right relationship with him. These were men who had been abused and exploited in a sinful world, but God would show them mercy. Although they were denied the opportunity to have physical descendants (a very important blessing in Israel), they could have an everlasting place in God's family (see Isa. 56:3-7). In fulfilment of this promise, we find that one of the earliest converts to Christianity in the book of Acts was both a eunuch and a foreigner who had come to pray in Jerusalem (Acts 8:27). By the grace of God, he was washed from his sin and went home rejoicing (Acts 8:36-39).

ii. Children born of a forbidden marriage (23:2)
Another category of people excluded from the Lord's Assembly
is described in 23:2. *'No-one born of a forbidden marriage nor
any of his descendants may enter the assembly of the LORD...'*
In some Bible versions (for example the KJV and RSV) the
offspring referred to in 23:2a are described as illegitimate.
This is a misleading translation of a difficult Hebrew word. In
Zechariah 9:6 it describes the legitimate offspring of Israelites
who had married foreigners contrary to God's command.
Nehemiah describes some of these marriages, their detrimental
consequences and his vigorous response (Neh. 13:23-27). It is
possible that this law may also have applied to children born as
a result of incest or to one of the shrine prostitutes mentioned
in 23:17-18.

The exclusion of a person born in such circumstances may seem
harsh and unloving; even out of keeping with God's character.
We know that the Lord does show his mercies to outcasts; but
the purpose of the law was to explain why there were outcasts
in the first place. Not only does God's law define sin, it also
shows us the consequences of sin. Sin alienates us from God
and God from us. Some sins are particularly serious. Their tragic
consequences will affect the lives of many generations. The
descendants of the excluded person were also excluded from
the Assembly *'even down to the tenth generation.'* This may be a
colloquial way of saying that the exclusion would last for as long
as anyone could imagine, that is, virtually for ever. However, it
does show that the exclusion was not indefinite. The alienation
which sin creates lasts until a Redeemer can reconcile outcasts
to a new fellowship with God through the gospel. Mercy will
triumph over the bitter legacy of sin – eventually.

iii. Ammonites and Moabites (23:3-6)
These two peoples were also excluded from entering the
Lord's assembly, 23:3. *'No Ammonite or Moabite or any of his
descendants may enter the assembly of the LORD, even down to*

the tenth generation.' They were descended from Lot, whose two daughters bore sons to him as a result of incest after the destruction of Sodom (Gen. 19:30-38). This sorry history may have led Moses to link the Ammonites and Moabites with those born of a forbidden relationship in 23:2. However in 23:4 Moses gave another explanation for their exclusion. *'They did not come to meet you with bread and water on your way when you came out of Egypt.'* In fact, they actively opposed the progress of the Israelites: *'... and they hired Balaam son of Beor from Pethor in Aram Naharaim to pronounce a curse on you.'* In Numbers 22-24 Moses recorded an account of how the Moabites incited Balaam to use divination (Josh. 13:22) against the Israelites. Nehemiah used the same argument in Nehemiah 13:1-3 (quoting Moses' words verbatim) when he urged the people of Judah to purge the temple of the merchandise stored there by Tobiah the Ammonite. There is no record in the Pentateuch of the Ammonites behaving maliciously against the Israelites as they travelled towards the land of Canaan, as did the Moabites. Yet they, too, incurred God's displeasure because they did not come to help the Israelites. This was a failure to help strangers in need. Hospitality was considered a sacred duty amongst the desert peoples.

More important than the breach of social custom was the contempt which was shown to the people of God. This was an offence to Jehovah, the One who dwelt in the midst of his people. Moses retold the story of Balaam and the Moabites because it provided him with an opportunity to remind the people of Israel just how much God loved them. In spite of the hostility which they faced from the nations around them, they were protected by the Lord who loved them (23:5). *'However, the LORD your God would not listen to Balaam but turned the curse into a blessing for you because the LORD your God loves you.'* Clearly Moses revelled in this truth! See 4:37; 7:8; 10:15; 33:3. There is in 23:5 an echo of God's promise to Abram in Genesis 12:3. 'I will bless those who bless you, and whoever curses you I will curse.' The victory of the Israelites over the Moabites and Ammonites was an example of God blessing Israel as she faced the attacks of her enemies. It was also an example of how God turned the curses of her enemies back upon them. As a result of their hostility towards Israel, the Moabites brought the hostility of Jehovah upon themselves and they were (with a few exceptions, such as Ruth) cut off from the living God and from the assembly of his people (23:6). *'Do not seek a treaty of friendship with them as long as you live.'*

This teaches us that it is a serious thing to show, by our words and actions, contempt for the people of God. They are the apple of his eye and beloved by God. Even today there are many who hold God's people in contempt. Sometimes they show that contempt by refusing to heed their witness, just as Noah's contemporaries refused to heed his warnings of the flood. At other times they are active in ridiculing and persecuting the people of God. Their attitudes and actions demonstrate that they have no place amongst those who will inherit the kingdom of heaven.

Notwithstanding the three exclusions from the Lord's assembly in 23:1-6, two groups are singled out for special kindness (23:7). *'Do not abhor an Edomite, for he is your brother. Do not abhor an Egyptian, because you lived as an alien in his country.'* The Edomites were descended from Jacob's brother, Esau (Gen. 25:24-26, 30) and were to be looked upon as distant cousins. More surprising is the special mention of the Egyptians in 23:7. Although the Egyptians had enslaved the Israelites for many years (Exod. 1:8-14; 3:7), there was another side to the complex relationship between Israel and Egypt. Moses highlights it in the explanation attached to this regulation: *'...you lived as an alien in his country'*. When famine threatened to destroy Jacob's family in Canaan, Egypt offered them a place of security (Gen. 46). They became aliens under the protection of a foreign power.

We can see God's wonderful providence in this turn of events, because God had sent Joseph to Egypt ahead of the rest of his family and raised him up to be the ruler of the land. Egypt was God's instrument to preserve his people when they were threatened with starvation. Later, at the time of the exodus, when the Israelites were slaves rather than welcomes guests in Egypt, there were many in Egypt who were favourably disposed towards the Israelites and helped them as they went (Exod. 12:36). This memory of the welcome which Jacob had received and the help which the departing Israelites had received ought to teach the Israelites to show kindness to those strangers who settled in their midst. Although Edomites and Egyptians were, like all others from the heathen nations around them, to be excluded from the Lord's assembly when they first came to settle in Israel, their exclusion lasted only for three generations (rather than the ten prescribed in 23:2, 3). *'The third generation of children born to them may enter the assembly of the LORD'* (23:8). The passage of time removed the offence of their past.

Here is an Old Testament example of the principle of inclusion. Those who came to dwell in the midst of God's people were able to become God's people. They are not to be abhorred as were the heathen and their rituals. The verb used in the commands of 23:7 is closely related to the detestable things of 12:31. The assumption underlying this command is that the Edomites and the Egyptians who came to live amongst the Israelites would renounce their idolatry (Isa. 19:23-25) and embrace the God of Israel. The great example of this was Ruth, who came to take refuge under the wings of the God of Israel (Ruth 2:12). When she resolved to stay with Naomi her mother-in-law, she renounced not just her nationality but her old religion in order to join the people of God's covenant. 'Your people will be my people and your God my God' (Ruth 1:16). The Lord's assembly, therefore, was not to be defined by purely ethnic criteria. God had chosen Israel to be his people, but he could also choose others as well. God chose to include Rahab the prostitute, Ruth the Moabitess,

Cornelius the centurion and the Ethiopian eunuch. He has chosen sinners from every nation to be his people, and he calls them through the gospel. Truly every nation on earth is blessed in Abraham's blessed Seed (Gen. 12:3). Yet it is not the passage of time which removes the offence of our past sins and allows us to be included amongst God's people. It is the sovereign grace of God which adopts us into God's family (Eph. 1:5), and it is the blood of Jesus Christ which cleanses us from all defilement (1 John 1:7).

The purity of the Lord's assembly (23:9-14)

From time to time, the people of Israel would assemble to go to war against their enemies. War can be a very messy business; but even in their encampment they were to conduct themselves with godly purity as becomes 'the armies of the living God' (1 Sam. 17:26). Two laws in this section apply this general principle, which is stated in 23:9. *'When you are encamped against your enemies, keep away from everything impure.'* The focus broadens to include personal cleanliness as well as moral purity.

i. Nocturnal emission (23:10-11)
'If one of your men is unclean because of a nocturnal emission...' Literally, the phrase is 'an accident by night'. One plausible explanation of the ambiguous phrase 'accident by night' is that he had urinated where he lay because the latrine was too far away or the night air was too cold for him to go out. Not only was this unpleasant for the man concerned, it was unhygienic and posed a threat to the health of his fellow soldiers. Because of the proximity of this law to other laws drawing out the implications of the seventh commandment, another explanation of the phrase is that it was a euphemism to describe an emission of semen. The law of Leviticus 15:16-17 specifically describes such an occurrence, which may well result from impure thoughts and actions, and prescribes a very similar response.

Moses describes what the man is to do in 23:10b-11: *'he is to go outside the camp and stay there. But as evening approaches he is to wash himself, and at sunset he may return to the camp'.* Here, Moses required the man to remove himself from the camp, wash his whole body and return at sunset. It is significant that, while the physical washing could have been completed in a few minutes, the process was to take a whole day. The law required both outward cleanliness and inward purity. The outward and physical washing of the man's body represented an inward examination of his heart and a pursuit of moral purity. The *Westminster Shorter Catechism* reminds us that the goal of the seventh commandment was to purge 'all unchaste thoughts, words, and actions' (answer 72). Often it is not enough merely to try purge evil thoughts; we must replace them with pure ones (Phil 4:8-9).

ii. Bodily waste (23:12-14)

This law concerned the important matter of how soldiers were to dispose of bodily waste while living in a makeshift military camp. Until modern times, dysentery often killed more soldiers in the field than the sword. It was therefore important for those who laid out the encampment to consider how and where waste was to be disposed (23:12). *'Designate a place* (literally, a *hand* or a *pointer) outside the camp where you can go to relieve yourself.'* Not only were they to appoint a place some distance away from where the soldiers ate and slept, they were also to erect a sign pointing to it. With earthy realism, Moses gave the men detailed instructions about what they were to do when they went to relieve themselves (23:13). *'As part of your equipment have something to dig with, and when you relieve yourself, dig a hole and cover up your excrement.'* These instructions aimed to prevent the spread of disease.

There was, however, a theological purpose underlying this law. Moses spelled it out in 23:14: *'For the Lord your God moves about in your camp...'* Although invisible to the eye, God's presence in the camp of Israel's armies was visibly represented by the ark of the covenant (see Num. 10:33; Josh. 3:3-6; 6:6-7; 1 Sam. 4:3). The Lord God came amongst his people for their *good*. He came *'to protect you and to deliver your enemies to you'*. It is a great encouragement to God's people to know that 'God is our refuge and strength, an ever-present help in trouble' (Ps. 46:1). The promise of God's presence was given to his people at times when they faced a difficult task and needed the assurance that God was with them. Just as Jehovah promised that he went with the armies of Israel as they fought the Lord's battles, so the Lord Jesus promised that he would be with his disciples as they went to make disciples of the nations. 'And surely I am with you always, to the very end of the age' (Matt 28:20b). The young Scottish martyr, Margaret Wilson, put it like this: 'the Lord sends none a-warring on their own charges'. He is surely with his own people when they are encamped for battle.

However, as well as extending protection to his people, God's presence exposed them to his scrutiny. God sees everything that happens in the midst of his people (Ps. 139:1; Heb. 4:13). This placed a duty upon the Israelite soldiers to conduct themselves in a godly way within the camp. *'Your camp must be holy, so that he* (Jehovah) *will not see among you anything indecent* (literally, the 'nakedness of a thing') *and turn away from you.'* In particular, Moses was concerned lest the Israelites expose their private parts in a public place. This concern for modesty distinguished the Hebrew people from many of the nations around them, and it can be traced back to the fall. When God made Adam and Eve they were naked, yet they knew neither sin nor shame (Gen. 2:25). The entry of sin into the world through Adam's sin made him feel ashamed before God (Gen. 3:8, 10) and it filled his mind with sinful thoughts, so God covered his nakedness with 'garments of skin' (Gen. 3:21). In recognition of our condition it is still appropriate that we cover our bodies before God and others. In 1 Corinthians 12:22-23 Paul commends the practice of treating the less honourable parts of our body with special honour. This is for the honour of God who sees everything.

God is a holy God who hates all impurity. When the people of God tolerated impurity in their midst, the Lord their God turned away from them and withdrew his blessing. The defeat of the Israelites at the hands of the Philistines and the capture of the ark in 1 Samuel 4 was a demonstration of what could happen should God withdraw his presence. The ark itself provided no guarantee of victory when the hearts and lives of the people of Israel were filled with impurity (1 Sam. 4:10-11). When King David committed the serious sins of adultery with Bathsheba and plotting the murder of Uriah, he suffered something worse than defeat on the battlefield. He lost the joy of salvation and sensed that God had taken away the Holy Spirit from him. The restoration of these is what he pleaded for in Psalm 51:11-12. If we are to stand firm in the Lord and resist the attacks of the evil one, we must make holiness a priority. We will want to give God's Spirit no reason to turn away from us.

The characteristics of the Lord's community (23:15-25)

A new section of the law code begins at 23:15 and continues through to 24:5. Like 22:1-12 it is a transitional section. The laws explained by Moses in these verses deal with a diverse array of issues. Some concern the sanctity of marriage (24:1-5) and moral purity (23:17-18). In others a new emphasis emerges – honesty in the people's dealings with God (23:21-23) and each other (23:19-20, 24-25). The later prepare the way for 24:6-22, where the implications of the eighth commandment ('You shall not steal') are addressed more fully. As in 22:1-12, these diverse laws highlight two key principles of the law of Moses – Israel is to be visibly different from the nations around her, and Israel is a brotherhood of redeemed people.

i. The Refugee Slave (23:15-16)
Runaway slaves seem to have been a perennial problem in ancient times. Their plight often provoked a very unsympathetic response. When David asked Nabal for help, he was taken for just another unruly servant. 'Many servants are breaking away from their masters these days. Why should I take my bread... and give it to men coming from who knows where?' (1 Sam. 25:10-11) The people of Israel ought to have a more sympathetic approach, as they were themselves a nation of runaway slaves. Moses set out the Israelite response in 23:15-16. *'If a slave has taken refuge with you, do not hand him over to his master. Let him live among you wherever he likes and in whatever town he chooses. Do not oppress him.'*

Other nations set very harsh penalties for a runaway slave and anyone who offered him sanctuary. Both faced the sentence of death. Their laws required the return of a runaway slave to his master, even if the master lived in another jurisdiction. This posed a problem for the Israelites, who were forbidden to make any treaty or alliance with their neighbours (23:6). Any agreement to send back runaway slaves would have required negotiation and agreement with the heathen nations. So, in marked contrast with the customary practices of the day, the Israelites allowed a runaway slave who came from another nation the opportunity start a new life as a free man. The runaway was not to be sent back to his master and he was protected by the laws protecting aliens from ill-treatment (Exod. 22:21).

The goal of this law was to make the nation of Israel a beacon of righteousness in the midst of a fallen and groaning world. Just as the Statue of Liberty in New York beckoned the huddled masses of nineteenth-century Europe who longed to be free, so the nation of Israel was a place of refuge for those who groaned under the yoke of slavery. This role was taken over by the Messiah, who became the true fulfilment of Israel's destiny. He himself would be 'a light for the Gentiles, to open eyes that are blind, to free captives from prison, and to release from the dungeon those who sit in darkness' (Isa. 42:6-7). The Messiah's message is one of freedom and hope for those in bondage (Isa. 61:1; Luke 4:17-20). Until the time when he would come to grant that everlasting freedom, the stranger was to be given refuge in Israel as a foretaste of the true and lasting liberty which can be enjoyed only in union with Christ and in fellowship with the living God (see 2 Cor. 3:17; Gal. 5:1).

ii. Shrine Prostitutes (23:17-18)

One of the most bizarre and offensive aspects of Canaanite religion was the practice of sacred prostitution. We may find it hard to understand the thinking behind the practice, but the men and women who offered themselves for sex at the Canaanite shrines were considered to be holy because they were dedicated to the service of a particular heathen god. Those who worshipped at the shrines of gods such as Baal or Ashteroth would have sex with these prostitutes, believing that this sacred intercourse brought them closer to their gods. As a result, they were able to pray more effectively for the things they desired. Moreover, it was believed that Baal and Ashteroth were fertility gods and that the sight of humans having intercourse with their servants would encourage them to procreate with nature so that the harvests would be more abundant and the flocks and herds more fruitful. So prevalent was this practice amongst the ancient Canaanites that Judah's daughter-in-law, Tamar, posed as a shrine prostitute to get his attention in Genesis 38:21-26.

Decisive action was needed to prevent this Canaanite practice from gaining acceptance amongst the Israelites, so in 23:17 Moses gave a clear command. *'No Israelite man or woman is to become a shrine-prostitute.'* In spite of this law, the practice of sacred prostitution became common in Israel and Judah (1 Kings 14:24). Reforming kings such as Asa, Jehoshaphat and Josiah had to purge the shrine prostitutes (as well as many other pagan practices) from the kingdom (1 Kings 15:12; 22:46;

2 Kings 23:7). There was even the danger that the practice of sacred prostitution might infect the worship of Jehovah. To show the extent of God's abhorrence, Moses continued in 23:18, 'You must not bring the earnings of a female prostitute or of a male prostitute into the house of the LORD your God to pay any vow, because the LORD your God detests them both'. Moses did not mince his words. He describes the earnings of these female and male prostitutes respectively as the 'pay of a harlot' and the 'wages of a dog'. The sexual practices in which they engaged were abhorrent to God and even the money they earned from them was unacceptable to him. The Lord does not want 'dirty money'. He wants holiness in the hearts and lives of his people.

This law may well have lain behind the response of Simon the Pharisee (Luke 7:37-39) when he saw 'a sinful woman' pour a jar of expensive perfume on the Lord Jesus. He was outraged and could not understand how Jesus would allow her to make this offering to him. Her expensive perfume was no doubt bought with the profits of prostitution, and may well have been one of the tools of her former trade. God certainly repudiates the sin of immorality and will judge those sinners who refuse to repent. However, he extends mercy to sinners who repent and turn their allegiance from idols to the true and living God. Even the prostitute can become holy to the Lord. Jesus shocked the Pharisees of his day by telling them that the tax collectors and the prostitutes were entering the kingdom of heaven ahead of them (Matt. 21:31).

iii. Charging Interest (23:19-20)

The law against charging interest was one of the most distinctive features of Old Testament economics. It rested on the belief that the people of God ought to help each other during times of need. One way of helping those in utter distress was to lend them food or the money they needed to buy food. The purpose of such loans was to relieve distress, not to make a profit. In Exodus 22:25 and Leviticus 25:35-37 Moses explained that the law against charging interest was a measure to help the needy and linked it to the law against charging inflated prices when food was short. In 23:19 Moses extended the scope of the law beyond loans of food or money. *'Do not charge your brother interest, whether on money or food or anything else that may earn interest.'* The positive teaching which lay behind this law was that the Israelites were to lend freely to each other in times of need (see 15:8; also Ps. 37:26; 112:5; Prov. 19:17).

Like the law which required the cancellation of debts in 15:1-3, this law applied only to Israelites (23:20a). *'You may charge a foreigner interest, but not a brother Israelite...'* The foreigner referred to here was not a stranger who had sought refuge and lived as a permanent resident amongst the people of God. Instead he was a merchant who had come to trade with them. Although not nearly as common as they are today, commercial loans were not unknown in the ancient world. They offered entrepreneurs the opportunity to expand their enterprise and increase their profits. It was thus entirely appropriate that the entrepreneur who borrowed the money should share some of those profits with the person from whom he had borrowed it. Interest rates in the ancient world were often exorbitant. Ancient records indicate that rates of between 20% and 50% were not uncommon. While an entrepreneur might be able to pay interest at those levels, a person whose crops had failed and whose family faced starvation could not.

Moses prompted a generous response to those in need with the promise of God's blessing (23:20b): *'... so that the LORD your God may bless you in everything you put your hand to in the land you are entering to possess'*. This echoes a similar promise in 14:29 and 15:10. It is the promise which underlies the covenantal wisdom of Proverbs 19:17: 'He who is kind to the poor lends to the LORD, and he will reward him for what he has done'. Not only will the Lord pay the interest on what had been lent to the needy, but he will abundantly repay the lump sum with both earthly and heavenly blessing (see Matt. 6:19-21). God loves a cheerful giver, one who gives of his material possessions to supply the needs of others as well as to support the work of the church (2 Cor. 9:7; also Luke 6:34-36). God's people will never suffer loss as a result of such generosity, for God is no man's debtor.

iv. Vows to God (23:21-23)

A vow is a solemn promise made to God. It may indicate gratitude for past blessings, or it may a desire for yet more blessing. Jacob (Gen. 28:20), Jephthah (Judg. 11:30), Hannah (1 Sam. 1:11) and probably the apostle Paul (Acts 18:18) all made vows to God. Typically, the person who vowed promised to do some act of service to God if he would bestow a particular blessing. In Old Testament times it was the custom to offer a sacrifice at the altar (12:6) in thanksgiving for God's blessing. These vows were entirely voluntary. They were *'freely'* made (23:23b); and in 23:22 Moses stated that *'if you refrain from making a vow, you will not be guilty'*. See also Ecclesiastes 5:4-6. However, once a vow had been made, a binding obligation rested upon the person who made it (23:21, 23). *'If you make a vow to the LORD your God, do not be slow to pay it, for the LORD your God will certainly demand it of you and you will be guilty of sin... Whatever your lips utter you must be sure to do...'*

The principle which underlies this law is the faithfulness of God. God keeps his promises; and he expects his people to keep theirs. He is the Lord who entered into a covenant with his people. 'He is the faithful God, keeping his covenant of love to a thousand generations of those who love him and keep his commands' (7:9). Not only were the Israelites to fulfil their vows, they were to do so quickly. *'Do not be slow to pay it.'* Slowness was almost as blameworthy as total neglect of the vow. In business there is a saying 'slow pay is no pay'. People who do not pay their bills on time can cause serious cash flow problems for small (and not so small) businesses. Jehovah did not depend upon the offerings which his people brought to him, but the man who was slow to pay what he had promised to God showed that his love for God had grown cold and his spiritual zeal had turned to lethargy. He was robbing God of the honour due to him. By contrast, those who know the power and grace of God will be 'a willing people' in the day of his power.

Another lesson which we learn from this law is that our words are important. The words that we say, even when uttered rashly, are not to be swept aside. 'Do not protest to the temple messenger, "My vow was a mistake." Why should God be angry at what you say and destroy the work of your hands?' (Eccles. 5:6). That is why we ought to think before we speak. When we do make promises, we are obliged to follow them with action. The godly man is identified in Psalm 15:4 as one who keeps his oath 'even when it hurts'. Jesus applied this principle not only to the vows we make to God, but also to the words we say to our fellow men. 'Simply let your "Yes" be "Yes" and your "No", "No"; anything beyond this comes from the evil one' (Matt. 5:37). He reminds us that on the day of judgment we will give an account for every careless word we have spoken (Matt. 12:36).

However, it is legitimate to make promises to God Even today, Christians may bind themselves with lawful oaths. These do not earn God's favour or extract blessing from him. God is, in fact, more willing to bless his people than we can ever know. However vows can and do express our devotion to God. The *Westminster Confession of Faith* (chapter 22.1) describes the practice of making vows before God as follows: 'A lawful oath is a part of religious worship, wherein, upon just occasion, the person swearing solemnly calleth God to witness what he asserteth or promiseth; and to judge him according to the truth or falsehood of what he sweareth.' In this law Moses warns us to examine our hearts before we make any such vow. We are to ask ourselves whether we appreciate the significance of what we promise to do, whether we love God deeply and whether we have the will to persevere in what we have promised. When we are able to make such vows and fulfil them, our lives will reflect God's faithfulness.

v. Gathering crops (23:24-25)
God cared for the poor and needy among his people. His compassion can be seen in the significant number of laws in Deuteronomy which protect their interests. In this law Moses encouraged the Israelites to make allowance for the needs of the very poorest of the people, who could only find food by gathering it from the property of others. They had nowhere else to turn. So they were allowed to enter their neighbour's property and take what they needed. Yet the poor were not to take advantage of the generosity of others. This short section contains two very similar laws which taught the same lesson. The law of 23:24 is set in the vineyard. *'If you enter your neighbour's vineyard, you may eat all the grapes you want, but do not put any in your basket.'* The law of 23:25 is set in the grain field. *'If you enter your neighbour's cornfield, you may pick the ears with your hands, but you must not put a sickle to his standing corn.'* Repetition is a common Old Testament teaching tool. It tells us to take note of what has just been said because it is important. Pharaoh had two very similar dreams to warn him of the famine which was about to strike Egypt (Gen. 41:32).

These laws recognised that a passer-by had a right to enter the property of another to gather produce in a moment of need. However, they did not allow the person who went in to gather produce and take it away so that he might give or sell it to others. *'Do not put any in your basket... you must not put a sickle to his standing corn.'* These laws were designed to relieve occasional and unexpected need, the kind that might occur when a person is on a journey and far from family and friends. Even an Israelite who lived in another town or belonged to another tribe was still a neighbour. These laws were not meant to impoverish those who owned land, nor were they designed to relieve the larger issue of poverty in Israel. Other laws addressed that challenge, such as the laws requiring the release of slaves and the remission of debt (see 15:1-18). The law of gleaning in Deuteronomy 24:19-22 made seasonal provision for the poorest in the community to share regularly in the produce of the land. This law, by contrast, provided for the occasional and unexpected need. Our Lord's disciples made use of it when they were hungry and walking through a cornfield (see Matt 12:1).

Even today there are many people in our communities who have fallen on hard times. The causes of their distress are many. Unemployment, family breakdown, mental illness, substance abuse and sheer folly result in some of the most vulnerable people in our community going hungry and becoming homeless. As Christians we need to learn to see them and respond in a godly way. We should not make their folly an excuse for lack of generosity on our part. In keeping with the spirit of these laws, we should be willing to sacrifice a little of what the Lord has given to us to meet their basic needs of food and shelter.

Chapter 24
A bulwark for the needy

Please read Deuteronomy 24: 1-22

It has been said that law is about power. Those who make the laws do so to protect their own wealth, power and prestige. There may be some truth to this claim when it is applied to fallen human beings, but God's law is built on very different foundations. God has chosen the poor to enjoy his riches (Jas 2:5); he hears their cry (Ps 34:6); he rescues them from those who oppress them (Ps 35:10); he raises them from the dust (Ps 113:7); and he does no special favours for the rich at the expense of the poor (Job 34:19) for all men are the work of his hands. These aspects of God's character are reflected in his law and in Deuteronomy 24-25 Moses gathered together a series of instructions which demonstrate God's concern for the poor and the powerless.

Each of these laws is an application of one or more of the Ten Commandments. In 22:13 – 23:14 Moses collated a series of laws about sexual and moral purity which flow from the seventh commandment. This is followed by a 'transitional section' in 23:15 – 24:5 which contains a diverse array of laws. From 24:6 onwards, Moses moves to a new theme. He expounds and applies the eighth, ninth and tenth commandments. At this point in Moses' sermon it becomes very difficult to divide the laws into orderly sections systematically and consecutively applying these three commandments. It is fair to say that several commentators have laboured hard to produce such a division, often by highlighting basic principles of conduct which underlie the commandments, such as fairness or honesty. The problem remains that these divisions seem to be forced upon the text rather than arising out of it.

The underlying theme through most of chapter 24 is God's desire to protect the weak. The eighth commandment forbids dishonest actions. The ninth commandment forbids dishonest words – particularly when uttered under oath in a court. The tenth commandment forbids the covetous thoughts which often motivate dishonest words and actions. These commands have had a powerful influence for good. They protect the weak against the strong. In particular, Moses aimed to regulate social institutions – marriage, the legal system and the ownership of land – to prevent them becoming oppressive to the most vulnerable members of the Israelite community.

Marriage (24:1-5)

Family life, both in the ancient world and today, provides us with examples of the best and the worst in human behaviour. We can see families which love and care for their members. We can also see abuse and cruelty. The prevailing social customs in the ancient world provided little legal protection for women and children when those who ought to have protected them sought to harm them. Husbands sometimes married in the hope of gaining land or money and were quick to dispense with surplus wives. The laws in this section aimed to prevent husbands from playing fast and loose with their marriage commitments and to encourage husbands to be faithful to their wives.

i. The law against remarriage (24:1-4)
This law deals with a very specific and unusual situation – the

remarriage of a couple who have divorced, after the wife has been through a second marriage. However, it sheds light on marriage and divorce in Israel. This is the only passage in the Old Testament where we find clear and direct teaching on the conduct of divorce. Malachi 2:16 tells us that God hates divorce. However this law indicates that divorce was tolerated in Israel. Jesus explained that this was a temporary measure to accommodate the hardness of men's hearts (see Matt. 19:8). God did not give men the freedom to divorce as they pleased, for the law imposed two restrictions.

a) There must be proper grounds for divorce (24:1a). A man could divorce his wife only when she did something *'displeasing to him'*. This might include almost anything which was offensive to him, but was less serious than adultery. That would have required death by stoning, not divorce (see 22:22). The same phrase is used in 23:14 to describe conduct that is unseemly or immodest in the sight of God. For this reason the rabbis who followed the teaching of Shammai argued that divorce could be granted only for an unseemly act, whereas the rival school of Hillel argued that even a trivial act (such as burning a meal on the stove) or a woman's appearance could justify divorce. Clearly, Jesus regarded both of these schools as unduly lax. Only 'marital unfaithfulness' (Matt. 19:9) can justify the dissolution of a marriage. To this the apostle Paul adds desertion by an unbelieving spouse (1 Cor. 7:15) as a ground for divorce.

b) The proper procedure for divorce must be followed (24:1b). The husband who divorced his wife must place in her hand a *'certificate of divorce'* and *'send her from his house'*. The certificate protected the woman against slander and innuendo and made it possible for her to remarry and find the security of a new home (24:2). The husband's action in sending his wife away was a public statement that the marriage was ended.

The finality of this action was reinforced by the law of 24:4. *'Then her first husband, who divorced her, is not allowed to marry her again after she has been defiled. That would be detestable in the eyes of the LORD.'* It is very possible that this law was a response to a recurring problem in Israel. In order to understand this law and its significance, we ought to try to think ourselves into the life-setting of the wife in question here. After being divorced by one husband, a second husband 'dislikes her' and has divorced her. We are not told what the grounds of the divorce were, simply the motive. The woman is presented as the victim of a man who has abandoned her. Yet again she is sent from her home. In desperation, she contemplates returning to her first husband. This is firmly forbidden by Moses, on the grounds that this is 'detestable in the eyes of the Lord' because she would be 'defiled'. On a superficial reading, it seems that the law stigmatised the woman unfairly. The Hebrew word translated 'defiled' was often used to describe the guilt associated with adultery, and the Hebrew text makes it clear that it was she who would be defiled. However, Moses does not level an accusation against the woman, but against the man who has forced her into this predicament. Remarriage to her first husband is simply not an option, because this would make her second marriage look like an adulterous affair. However, no restriction is placed on the divorced woman's freedom to enter a third marriage with another man. The first husband, however, must live with the consequences of his own sinful actions.

The goal of this law was to discourage men from frivolous or hasty divorce. Men sometimes used marriage to gain a woman's inheritance. When it was spent, they would dismiss her for a wealthier bride. Some may have reasoned that they could always go back to their first love at some later date. Such behaviour exploited women and offended God. This law insisted that divorce, like marriage, has lifelong consequences. It was only ever to be contemplated as a last resort and for good biblical reasons. Jesus applied the spirit of this law when he insisted that any man who divorced his wife for any reason other than marital unfaithfulness, and married another woman, committed adultery (Matt. 19:9). 'Therefore what God has joined together, let man not separate.'

Biblical teaching on the sanctity of marriage and God's abhorrence of divorce is very necessary today. Because men and women stand on a much more equal footing in the modern world than in the time of Moses, divorce is no longer the special privilege of men. Although divorce is no longer used as a means of oppressing women, it causes much grief to families and to God. It dishonours God when many professing Christians are almost as willing to seek the option of divorce as those who make no profession of faith. Many resent being told that God places a higher priority on our faithfulness than our personal happiness. Nevertheless, the principles underlying this law must have a place in the pulpit and the counselling room.

ii. Exemption from public duty (24:5)
As well as discouraging divorce, the law of Moses encouraged a positive attitude towards marriage. *'If a man has recently married, he must not be sent to war or have any other duty laid on him. For one year he is to be free to stay at home and bring happiness to the wife he has married.'* This law protected a young couple from obligations which might have distracted them from the important task of establishing a loving relationship with each other. Then, as now, building a strong marriage is hard work. If the marriage had been arranged by their families, the newly-weds might not have known each other very well and would have little in the way or romance to draw them towards each other. During their first year of marriage both of them would have had a lot to learn about each other and about the demands of married life.

The law of Deuteronomy 24:5 builds on the law of 20:7, which allowed a recently married husband to go home to his wife lest he die in battle. It would have been considered a disaster for the man's family if he had died with no heir to carry on his name and inherit his property. This exemption extended to *'any other duty'* or any form of public service.

During that first year of marriage *'he is to be free to stay at home and bring happiness to the wife he has married'.* In Proverbs 5:18 Solomon encouraged husbands 'to rejoice in (or with) the wife of your youth', but this law goes further. The husband is to 'bring happiness' to his wife. This meant taking a special interest in her welfare and seeking her happiness; providing for her needs materially, emotionally and spiritually. In particular, he was to join with her in starting a family. We see what those words 'bring happiness' mean when we read Ruth 4:13-16 and observe the joy in the home of Ruth and Boaz when their son Obed was born. The psalmist describes this as a blessing from the Lord.

> He settles the barren woman in her home
> as a happy mother of children.
> Praise the LORD.
> (Ps. 113:9)

This law provides wise guidance for young Christian couples today. In the early days of their courtship and marriage they should not cut themselves off from their still-single friends. Those friends will be greatly helped and encouraged to see the formation of a healthy and loving Christian marriage. However, a young couple needs to make sure that they are not so absorbed in social activities and even church ministries that they have little time for each other as they seek to establish the patterns of a healthy marriage.

The Legal System (24:6-18)

Western civilization owes a great deal to the principles which undergird these and similar verses in the Old Testament. The rule of law is a thoroughly biblical concept and it protects many of our daily actions and transactions. It is reassuring to know that banks and other powerful institutions are subject to regulations which prevent them from abusing their power. The same is true of insurance companies, government departments, the police and even the courts themselves. One of England's greatest judges, Lord Denning, would often quote the dictum, 'Be you never so high, the law is above you'. Implicit in this phrase is the claim that there is one who stands over the whole human race as the Supreme Law-giver. Moses taught that Jehovah is that Law-giver. He called the rich and powerful to bow before him. These laws prevented Israel's legal system from being used by the strong to oppress the weak. The justice and mercy of Jehovah gave Israel's laws of contract, slavery, public health and criminal sentencing their distinctive flavour.

i. Security for a loan (24:6, 10-13, 17b)
The loans described in Deuteronomy were, for the most part, loans to the very poor in times of utter desperation. The poor borrowed money to feed their families when their crops had failed and their barns were empty. This is why the law prevented the lender from charging interest (see 23:19). At such times the lender, too, might find himself in financial difficulty, so a delicate balance had to be struck. A lender was allowed to ask the borrower to pledge some item of his property as security for the loan. A pledge was simply a guarantee that the borrower would repay the money he had borrowed. Three laws in this section regulate what may be pledged and how the lender may claim that to which he is entitled.

a) He is not to rob the debtor of daily bread (24:6). *'Do not take a pair of millstones – not even the upper one – as security for a debt, because that would be taking a man's livelihood as security.'* The significance of a household hand-mill for grinding grain can be illustrated by the story of a Japanese nobleman who was building a mighty fortress for himself and his retainers. He was greatly hindered in this work by the shortage of stone for building, so he appealed to the people who lived in the vicinity for any stone they could spare. Stone walls and even stone coffins were offered as building blocks; but one poor widow had nothing to offer but her stone hand-mill. It was only about twenty inches in diameter, but the nobleman was so impressed by the gesture that he spread the story far and wide to encourage others to give. To this day, visitors to the castle are still told the story and shown the round stone in the fortress wall.

Although this story has echoes of the story of the poor widow in Mark 12:41-44, it makes another very important point. The hand-mill was a prized possession in every household because it was used every day to grind grain and provide the flour from which bread was made. To take away even one of the stones would have made the device useless and robbed the family of their daily bread. Just as it was an act of amazing generosity to give the millstone, it would have been an act of cruel injustice to take it from a poor man – even one who has pledged it as security for a loan. It would have left him and his family to starve.

b) He is not to rob the debtor of his dignity (24:10-11). *'When you make a loan of any kind to your neighbour, do not go into his house to get what he is offering as a pledge. Stay outside and let the man to whom you are making the loan bring the pledge out to you.'* The creditor was to allow the debtor to choose which of his belongings would be given as security for the loan. He was also to respect the privacy of the debtor's personal space. What often upsets those who have been the victims of a burglary is the thought that a stranger has invaded their privacy and gone through their personal belongings. This is an affront to their personal dignity and security. This is what this law protects.

The Rev J. B. Armour was one of the leading political radicals in Ulster during the late nineteenth and early twentieth centuries.

A bulwark for the needy

He was one of the few Presbyterian ministers to support Irish Home Rule. His outlook on life was shaped during the Irish land wars of the mid-nineteenth century. As a young boy, he remembered the horrific scenes of the landlord's bailiffs coming to evict tenants who could not pay their rents. Not only would the family be left homeless; but their tables and chairs, pots and pans, and even children's toys would be taken and sold to pay the family's debts. Such callous indignity grieves the heart of a merciful God.

c) He is not to rob the debtor of warm clothing (24:12-13, 17b). *'If the man is poor, do not go to sleep with his pledge in your possession. Return his cloak to him by sunset so that he may sleep in it...'* When a man was so poor that his most valuable possession was his cloak – or overcoat – he was in dire straits indeed. This was the only thing that he could offer as a pledge when he borrowed money. Should the lender want to take possession of his security, he was not allowed to keep it overnight. The nights could get very chilly in Israel and the cloak was a very necessary covering. The inconvenience of returning the cloak every evening and reclaiming it every morning would surely discourage the lender from claiming such a pledge. If the borrower was a poor widow, the lender was not allowed to take her cloak at any time of the day as a pledge (24:17b). *'Do not ... take the cloak of the widow as a pledge.'* The old were especially vulnerable and an even greater level of protection was extended to them.

The goal of this law is not simply to discourage selfish and oppressive conduct, but also to encourage thoughtful and generous behaviour. It was an Old Testament application of the 'Golden Rule' which figured so prominently in our Lord's teaching in the Sermon on the Mount (see Matt. 7:12). Every act of kindness prompted a response. Two responses are described in 24:13b. First, there is the response of the debtor who has been treated kindly by his creditor: *'Then he will thank you...'* He will be more eager to repay the debt. This is an important responsibility and a demonstration of brotherly love to the lender, as Paul taught in Romans 13:8. Secondly, there is God's response to the kindness of the creditor: '...and it will be regarded as a righteous act in the sight of the LORD your God'. God, who sees everything, will see the generosity and forbearance of the creditor and regard it as a righteous act of obedience (see 6:25). Each act of kindness sets off a chain of responses which leavens the communal and spiritual life of the people of God.

ii. Enslavement (24:7)

Slavery was an inescapable reality in the ancient world, even amongst the redeemed people of Israel. Sometimes an Israelite might sell himself into slavery in order to pay his debts (see 15:12). The law of Moses did not abolish the practice of slavery, but it certainly did not give it the seal of divine approval. It regulated the practice so that its most obnoxious aspects might be moderated. One of the most offensive forms of slavery was involuntary slavery, or man-stealing, and this is roundly condemned in 24:7. 'If a man is caught kidnapping one of his brother Israelites and treats him as a slave or sells him, the kidnapper must die. You must purge the evil from among you.'

Throughout the first half of the nineteenth century, a great debate raged in the United States of America over African slavery. Some Christians sought to justify the practice of slavery from the way it was accommodated in the Old Testament and from the fact that it was nowhere condemned in the New Testament. The opponents of slavery responded to these arguments that American slavery was illegal and immoral because the African slaves had been stolen. The African slave trade was simply a violation of the eighth commandment and this law in 24:7. The words 'kidnapping' and 'kidnapper' in this verse translate the same Hebrew verb as was used in the commandment, 'you shall not steal' (see Deut. 5:19; Exod. 20:15). To enslave a man is to rob him of his freedom, dignity, family and the fruits of his labour.

A bulwark for the needy

In this law Moses associates harsh treatment of the slave as an inevitable consequence of his enslavement. The phrase 'treat him as a slave' translates a verb which means 'to deal tyrannically with' another person. It is also used in 21:14. This was possible only when the slave had been sold to foreigners who were not bound by the laws of Moses, which would have given him some protection. At the very least, an Israelite slave in Israel would have had the hope of release in the seventh year (see 15:12). However, this slave languishes in the hands of idolaters, excluded from the privileges of citizenship in Israel and without hope in the world (see Eph. 2:12). The spiritual implications are even more tragic than the implications for his physical well-being. For these reasons the crime of man-stealing was punishable with death. It was the only application of the eighth commandment to attract the death penalty. This was because it robbed a man not only of his property, but also of his place amongst the covenant people of God.

iii. Quarantining infectious diseases (24:8-9)

This law called for public-spirited honesty during an outbreak of infectious diseases. '*In cases of leprous diseases be very careful to do exactly as the priests, who are Levites, instruct you. You must follow carefully what I have commanded them.*' Moses referred to the laws in Leviticus 13-14 which described what the people ought to do if they suspected that they had an infectious skin disease or if they noticed mildew in their clothing or houses. They were to go immediately to the priest, who would examine the affected area, and either pronounce it clean or, if he was unsure, place the person under quarantine. If it became clear that the person had an infectious disease, he would sent him away from the community to lie in isolation. The skin diseases described in Leviticus 13 and Deuteronomy 24:8 cover a wide range of ailments, many of which were less serious than the dreaded illness known as leprosy or Hansen's disease. However, even the less serious infections could have very unpleasant consequences, and their spread was feared just as have been the plague in the Middle Ages and AIDS in more recent times.

A concern for the welfare of others ought to have been sufficient reason to abide by this law. However, experience shows us that human beings often take the path of least inconvenience to themselves, even though that endangers the health and lives of others. Recent epidemics of SARS and swine flu have been spread by the carelessness of some who failed to take adequate precautions or failed to seek medical help. That was why Moses reinforced the law with an exhortation in 24:9. *'Remember what the LORD your God did to Miriam along the way after you came out of Egypt.'* She was stricken with leprosy because she refused to accept that the Lord had made Moses his spokesman and given him a status which surpassed that of her and Aaron (see Num. 12:1-15). The Levites were God's servants appointed for the good of the people. By following their instructions, an infectious outbreak could be contained; but despising their instructions would cause the disease to spread all the more.

iv. Prompt payment of wages (24:14-15)
Casual labourers were another vulnerable group in Israel. For a variety of reasons they had no land of their own from which to earn a living. This may have been because they were foreigners who had come to live in Israel and had received no tribal allocation. It may have been because they were Israelites who had left their tribal allotment to find work in the towns. Some of them would have worked as casual labourers, often being hired for one day at a time. This law urged the Israelites to treat them fairly (24:14). *'Do not take advantage of a hired man who is poor and needy, whether he is a brother Israelite or an alien living in one of your towns.'* This general principle was given a specific application in 24:15. *'Pay him his wages each evening before sunset, because he is poor and counting on it'* (see also Lev. 19:13).

A bulwark for the needy

This law harks back to a time when women went to the market every morning to buy food for their families. They could only do this if the breadwinner had brought home enough money the previous evening. The labourer depended on his daily wage because his family was looking to him for their daily bread. There were many times when the labourer needed his wages a lot more than the employer needed his labour. This allowed employers to exploit the vulnerability of their workers by delaying or even denying them their wages. God's command was clear and simple – pay your workers promptly.

The Israelites had a special reason for paying their labourers fairly and promptly. The wording of 24:15b is a deliberate reminder of Israel's plight when they were slaves in Egypt, *'Otherwise he may cry to the LORD against you, and you will be guilty of sin.'* When the Israelites were oppressed in Egypt, they cried out to the Lord for mercy and he heard them (Exod. 3:9). Some Israelite employers were following in the footsteps of Pharaoh. God would come to the aid of their labourers and visit his wrath upon them. They would stand 'guilty of sin' before God because God is the guarantor of every contract in the work-place and in the market-place. Just as surely as God would punish the adulterer and idolater, so he would call the dishonest employer to give an account of his actions.

Unscrupulous employers are found in every age. In the first century AD, James addressed this challenge to them: 'Look! The wages you failed to pay the workmen who mowed your fields are crying out against you. The cries of the harvesters have reached the ears of the Lord Almighty' (James 5:4). Even today we hear news reports of factory workers who have not been paid their wages for three months. It is disturbingly common for large manufacturing firms to delay paying what they owe to smaller firms which supply them with materials, sometimes with the intention of driving these small firms out of business. Economic progress has certainly not eliminated injustice.

v. Personal responsibility for criminal activity (24:16)
God demanded that his standards of fairness apply in criminal trials, particularly when it came to fixing a penalty. The guilty, and only the guilty, were to be punished. *'Fathers shall not be put to death for their children, nor children put to death for their fathers; each is to die for his own sin.'* This principle presented a radical challenge in the ancient world where the principles of 'guilt by association' and 'collective punishment' were widely accepted, even in the law courts. For instance, in one ancient Mesopotamian law code it was stipulated that if a builder's shoddy workmanship had caused the death of another man's son, the builder's son was to be put to death. Even in Israel, it was not uncommon for those in power to put to death the children of their rivals and opponents lest they become a focus for discontent. This law expressly forbade such a policy. It is quoted in 2 Kings 14:5-6, where King Amaziah is commended for executing only the officials who had murdered his father and sparing the lives of their sons.

The principle underlying this law is restated in Ezekiel 18 as a riposte to the public mood of cynicism about God's dealings with Israel. This was expressed in the proverb, 'The fathers eat sour grapes, and the children's teeth are set on edge' (Ezek. 18:2). The people had failed to realise that sin has radical consequences. Its consequences spill over into the lives of others and cascade down the generations, leading many away from God. The sins of the fathers bring grief and punishment even to the third and fourth generation of those who hate God (see 5:9-10). Yet while the accumulated sins of many generations resulted in the nation of Israel being taken into exile, each generation would have to bear the responsibility for its own sins. When they stood before the heavenly judge, they would not be held guilty of their fathers' sins, only those which they had committed. 'The soul who sins is the one who will die' (Ezek. 18:4, 13, 18). Ezekiel drew on this and other laws from Deuteronomy to press home his point that each person is accountable to God for his own actions. In so doing, Ezekiel vindicated the justice of God, who deals with each one according to their actions

vi. Summary (24:17-18)
A general command not to '*deprive the alien or the fatherless of justice*' in 24:17 summarises the thrust of this whole section. The nation of Israel was to care for its poor through the justice administered by its courts. The courts were to be a refuge for the poor where they could gain a fair hearing, rather than an ally of powerful interests biased against them. As if to reinforce this goal, Moses linked the general principle to one of the examples of injustice which concerned him, the recurring theme of the poor who were forced into debt. In 24:17b he supplemented the law of 24:12-13, warning the creditor not to take a widow's cloak as a pledge. Moses moved with alacrity from general principles to specific applications. He was a preacher who left his hearers in no doubt what God's word required of them.

Moses grounded this section, and indeed the whole of the Deuteronomic law, on Israel's redemption (24:18). '*Remember that you were slaves in Egypt and the LORD our God redeemed you from there. That is why I command you to do this.*' Moses will return to this same exhortation in 24:22 after he has explained the responsibilities of land-owners to the poor. The deliverance of the Israelites from slavery in Egypt had many implications for the way they behaved towards each other and, in the midst of his explanation of Israel's laws, Moses regularly pointed his hearers to the bigger picture. He placed the detailed regulations of the Deuteronomic law in the theological context of God's mercies to Israel. He asked and answered three questions which the Israelites might well have asked. First of all he explained the principle which God wanted them to apply. Then he explained how God wanted them to apply basic principles. Finally he explained to the Israelites why they should behave as God had commanded them. This took them back to first principles. The Israelites were to treat the poor and needy in their midst with justice and compassion because God is a merciful God who hates injustice, and that was how he had treated them. There is no greater motivation to godly living in all its dimensions than the knowledge that God has delivered us from sin and misery and forgiven all our sins.

The Ownership of Land (24:19-22)

The land of Canaan was God's gift to his redeemed people. It had been promised to Abraham many years earlier. When the Israelites took possession of it they were reminded that God is a faithful God who keeps his promises. As the story of the Bible unfolds, we see that the land was the first instalment of even greater blessing in a redeemed world. Although the land of Israel was replete with spiritual symbolism, we should not overlook the fact that it was a material gift. Its earthiness is significant. From this promised land the people of Israel were to obtain their food and clothing; yet this did not always happen. For a variety of reasons there would always be some who missed out on the benefits of land-owning. As a result they went hungry.

Israel's system of landholding contributed to this unhappy outcome. When the Israelites entered the land, portions were allocated to each tribe, clan and family. These portions were passed from father to son. It was assumed that each clan would look after the widows and orphans of a relative who died. Yet that was not always the case. On occasions, fathers were more concerned to protect the inheritance of their own sons than the interests of distant relatives. Then there were the foreigners who were part of no tribe and had no allocation of land. Ruth and Naomi provide us with examples of needy people who had neither land nor employment (see Ruth 1:3-5, 19-21). The God of Israel had made provision for them, and Moses explained that provision in 24:19-22.

A bulwark for the needy

These verses contain three parallel laws which restricted the liberty of a land-owner to gather every last grain from the produce of his land. The owner of a grain field was not permitted to return for a sheaf of grain which he had overlooked (24:19). *'When you are harvesting in your field and you overlook a sheaf, do not go back to get it.'* The owner of an olive grove was not allowed to beat the branches (the traditional method of removing ripe olives from the tree) of his trees for a second time (24:20). *'When you beat the olives from your trees, do not go over the branches a second time.'* The owner of a vineyard was not to search the vines for any cluster of grapes which had been overlooked (24:21). *'When you harvest the grapes in your vineyard, do not go over the vines again.'* These overlooked crops were to be left for the stranger, the orphan and the widow. When we add to this the requirement in Leviticus 19:9-10 and 23:22 that a land-owner was not to reap to the very edges of his field, we see that a generous amount was to be left for the needy. This challenges our modern preoccupation with efficiency and productivity. The profit motive is not to be our only guiding principle. It has been observed that God's word inculcates a positive work ethic in those who embrace a biblical worldview. Here Moses teaches us that at least as important as industry and efficiency is loving God and caring for the needy amongst our neighbours.

There are two further lessons which we learn from the method which God employed to provide for the needy in Israel.

i. God gave them a stake in the economy. The left-over produce was not given to the poor as an act of charity, but as an obligation. It became the property of the alien, the orphan and the widow. When they went onto the land-owner's property, they did not come for a hand-out but to take what God had allocated to them. In this way their dignity was respected. Neither was the land-owner able to boast about his generosity.

ii. God's provision gave them the dignity of work. The stranger, the orphan and the widow did not beg for a gift, but worked to gather their food. Ruth worked 'steadily' in the fields of Boaz and had a substantial amount of grain to show for her labours (see Ruth 2:7, 17-18). Work is a blessing from God. The ability, and the desire, to work reflects the image of God the Creator in mankind. It would have done the landless poor no favours to create for them a welfare-dependent lifestyle which neither offered them the opportunity nor encouraged them to work with their hands. The churches of the New Testament demonstrated God's concern for the needy, but the apostle Paul laid down the stipulation that 'if a man will not work, he shall not eat' (2 Thess. 3:10).

Moses encouraged land-owners to provide for the needy with a promise of compensation from God (24:19b, 20b, 21b). *'Leave it for the alien, the fatherless and the widow, so that the LORD your God may bless you in all the work of your hands.'* He also reminded them of their past (24:22). *'Remember that you were slaves in Egypt. That is why I command you to do this.'* When their forefathers had cried out to God because of their poverty and misery, God had listened to their cry, redeemed them and led them into a land of blessing. It was now incumbent upon them to care for the poor and needy in their midst. Sadly, as Christopher Wrights observes, 'when Israel forgot its history, it forgot its poor'. God did not want them to forget either. Moses constantly reminded them of the exodus, their journey through the wilderness and the conquest of Canaan so that they might rejoice in the grace of God and renew their commitment to obey all his commands, including these laws which protected the poor.

The story of salvation which we tell and retell today takes us beyond the land of Canaan to the cross at Calvary. The proclamation of the gospel reminds us of our history as slaves to sin, condemned to everlasting misery, cut off from God. It reminds us that we have been delivered from death and led into the kingdom of light. Those who profess to know God as their Saviour are to demonstrate the love of God in acts of kindness towards their needy neighbours. William Wilberforce was so concerned about the plight of African slaves that he worked for their freedom because he was so keenly aware that he had been a slave to sin until God delivered him. His evangelical faith instilled within him a social conscience.

Paul reminded the Corinthian Christians of the poverty which the Lord Jesus endured on their behalf. 'For you know the grace of our Lord Jesus Christ, that though he was rich, yet for your sakes he became poor, so that you through his poverty might become rich' (2 Cor. 8:9). The poverty which Jesus endured on earth was for their salvation. As a result 'rich generosity' welled up within them towards their needy brothers and sisters in the Lord (2 Cor. 8:2-3). This is the kind of generosity which Moses sought to encourage amongst the Israelites as he reminded them of their blessings under the Old Covenant.

Chapter 25
God's justice practically applied

Please read Deuteronomy 25: 1-19

When we read through this chapter it can be very hard to identify a common theme. 'What is the big idea?', we ask. The diverse array of laws in this portion of God's word takes us from the courtroom to the farmyard, the family home, a street brawl, the market-place and finally an encounter with a group of foreigners. In all probability these laws were a response to recurring problems which faced the Israelite community, the details of which are unknown to us today. However, from Moses' response to those problems we see that God's law gave clear instructions about every sphere of life, and we must be willing to search God's law to find what it has to say to us. Those who study God's law will discover what God hates and what God loves; and they will be able to work out the implications of God's goodness, holiness, justice and compassion.

The very diversity of the laws in this chapter is significant. This is a reminder that Jehovah was a sovereign Lord, who ruled every area of the lives of his people. This truth was articulated dramatically by Abraham Kuyper. 'In the total expanse of human life there is not a single square inch of which the Christ, who alone is sovereign, does not declare, "That is mine!"' There was a time when the judges who crafted the English common law acknowledged that God's moral law was the basis for the judgments they made. Sadly, that consensus has been lost as Western nations have become increasingly secular. We pray that a fresh outpouring of God's grace will restore a Biblical moral consensus. However, as we study the detail of Deuteronomy's laws, we are challenged to consider what a godly community might look like in our day – and to pray for it.

In Deuteronomy 25 we see how God's laws applied in six very different scenarios arising amongst the people of Israel.

A convicted criminal (25:1-3)

The proper administration of justice has been a recurring concern of Moses in his exposition of Israel's laws (see 1:15-18; 16:18-20; 17:8-13; 19:15-21; 24:16-17). He returns to it again in this section. Those who go to court must be able to do so in the expectation that they will get a fair hearing and an unbiased decision. *'When men have a dispute, they are to take it to court and the judges will decide the case, acquitting the innocent and condemning the guilty.'* They should also be able to expect that an appropriate penalty would be handed down from the judges. In some instances the law prescribed a specific penalty for a particular offence (see 22:24; 22:29; 25:12, where death, the payment of fifty shekels of silver and the cutting off of a hand are the prescribed penalties). Mostly, however, the penalty was left to the discretion of the judge who heard the case. Judges might order that an offender be beaten as a punishment for his crime or as a deterrent to others. Should that happen Moses gave instructions which governed how the beating was to be administered (25:2-3):

> *If the guilty man deserves to be beaten, the judge shall make*
> *him lie down and have him flogged in his presence with the*
> *number of lashes his crime deserves, but he must not give him*

more than forty lashes. If he is flogged more than that, your
brother will be degraded in your eyes.

Not only were judges to act fairly in determining whether a
person had done anything wrong, they must administer any
penalty humanely.

The law in Exodus 21:20 mentioned the possibility of death
resulting from a severe beating. 'If a man beats his male or
female slave with a rod and the slave dies as a direct result, he
must be punished...' This kind of cruelty was not acceptable in
any circumstances and most certainly not from those whose
task it was to administer justice in God's name. When corporal
punishment was administered, a limit was set to protect the
life of the man receiving the punishment. Later Judaism took
this restriction so seriously that it reduced the number of lashes
permitted to thirty-nine, lest the limit be exceeded by accident
(see 2 Cor. 11:24). The judge who imposed the sentence was to
be present to supervise its application so that he might make
sure that only the proper number of lashes was given and that
they were not applied with unnecessary cruelty.

The underlying concern of this law is set out in 25:3b. '*If he is
flogged more than that, your brother will be degraded in your eyes.*'
Even though he was a law-breaker, he was still a member of
the covenant community and a 'brother'. His reputation and
honour was protected by law and by the whole community.
To degrade a person robbed him of the 'weight' or 'worth' that
was rightfully his as a person created in the image of God. This
law applied the biblical doctrine of creation even to criminals,
whose lives and persons were often held cheap by others. Yet
it is how a community treats the wretched and despised in its
midst that demonstrates its regard for God – or lack of it.

Biblical teaching on the nature of man underpinned the penal
reforms in nineteenth-century England which were initiated

by people like Elizabeth Fry. After hearing the preaching of an American Quaker called William Savery, Fry took an interest in the poor, the sick and those in prison. She visited those incarcerated in Newgate prison in London and was appalled by what she saw. Especially in the women's section of the prison she saw the prisoners and their children cooking, washing and sleeping in tiny, overcrowded cells. She saw that the prisons of her day fell far short of the humanitarian ideals which Moses sought to apply in Deuteronomy.

A Working Animal (25:4)

Although animals were not created in God's image, nor were they brought into a covenant of redemption, they were still God's creatures and precious to him. The redeemed people of Israel were to treat them as such, with compassion and respect. This was an expression of their righteousness before God, according to Proverbs 12:10, for 'a righteous man cares for the needs of his animal'. This principle is given application in 5:14, 22:4, 6-8 and here in 25:4. *'Do not muzzle an ox while it is treading out the grain.'*

The ox described in this law was a domesticated animal which worked for its owner. One of its tasks was to remove the grains of wheat or barley from the stalks by walking over them as they were spread out over the threshing-floor, perhaps also pulling a large flat piece of wood with stones embedded in it, called a threshing sledge. Naturally, the ox would be tempted to eat some of the grain at its feet, just as a fruit-picker working in an orchard or berry farm might be tempted to eat some of the fresh fruit he had just picked. In Israel, the poor were not prevented from entering a neighbour's vineyard or cornfield to gather food to eat (23:24-25). They were allowed to glean after the harvest (24:19-22). Even the ox was allowed to eat what it needed. It was not to be prevented by a muzzle, which a mean-spirited owner might affix to the animal's mouth to prevent it from getting its just desserts.

This law was quoted by the apostle Paul in two of his letters. On both occasions Paul applied the principle underlying this law to the conduct of the Christian church. 'The elders who direct the affairs of the church well are worthy of double honour... For the Scripture says, "Do not muzzle the ox while it is treading out the grain" and "The worker deserves his wages"' (1 Tim. 5:18).

> Who tends a flock and does not drink of the milk? Do I say this merely from a human point of view? Doesn't the Law say the same thing? For it is written in the Law of Moses, "Do not muzzle an ox while it is treading out the grain." Is it about oxen that God is concerned? Surely he says this for us, doesn't he? (1 Cor. 9:9).

Paul does not arrive at this principle by spiritualising or allegorising the text. He acknowledged the primary meaning and application of the law. God is concerned about the welfare of animals, and so should we be. However, there is a bigger principle to apply, one derived from the compassionate character of God. God is concerned about people as well, particularly those in need. Paul's argument followed the logic of the Lord Jesus in Matthew 6:26, where he said, 'Look at the birds of the air; they do not sow or reap or store away in barns, and yet your heavenly Father feeds them. Are you not much more valuable than they?' Since God has made provision for the birds, will he not also make provision for those who serve him by preaching the gospel? Yes, and he makes that provision through those who hear the gospel and are saved by it (1 Cor. 9:11). 'If we have sown spiritual seed amongst you, is it too much if we reap a material harvest from you?'

A deceased brother's widow (25:5-10)

In Israel, it was the responsibility of the extended family to provide for those in need. Widows were often amongst the neediest in the community. One of the ways in which the extended family provided for a widow in their midst was the practice of levirate marriage. This practice involved the brother of the deceased husband marrying his sister-in-law so that she might have children who would inherit his brother's property and continue his name. Moses made this a requirement in Israel (see 25:5-6).

This custom was very common in the ancient world and still exists in parts of Africa, Asia and the Middle East. Even before Moses gave this law we read the sad story of Tamar, Judah's daughter-in-law, in Genesis 38. When her first husband, Er, died, Judah asked Er's brother Onan to do his duty as a brother-in-law and lie with Tamar. However, Onan avoided providing offspring for his brother, and the Lord put him to death. After that, Judah was reluctant to offer Tamar his youngest son, so Tamar went to extreme lengths to become pregnant, much to the embarrassment of her father-in-law.

Another, more indirect, testimony to the thinking which lay behind this custom is found in the story of Ruth. Naomi rued the fact that she was too old to have more sons to offer to Orpah and Ruth after their husbands Mahlon and Kilion died (see Ruth 1:12-13). Eventually Ruth found an Israelite husband in Boaz, who was not a brother, but a close relative and her kinsman redeemer. The custom which prevailed in Ruth's case was similar, but not identical to what is described in 25:5-6. The practice is mentioned again in Matthew 22:23-27, where a hypothetical situation was put to Jesus by the Sadducees in order to make the doctrine of the resurrection appear in a ridiculous light. Even though the practice of levirate marriage was not common amongst Jews in the time of Jesus, it was known to them through this law in 25:5-6. These verses describe the custom and its purpose in the covenant community of Israel.

i. It provided for the living woman (25:5). Moses described a family setting where *'brothers are living together'.* In Israel several generations of a large extended family would live together in the same encampment or around a common courtyard. Adult brothers would raise their own families under the watchful eye of the family patriarch. Each family would have its own space, but everyone would have eaten together around a common table. In this setting the needs of the weaker members of the family were seen and provision was made. When the system worked, the outcome was idyllic. See Psalm 133:1: 'How good and pleasant it is when brothers live together in unity.' However, the realities of family life were not always so pleasant.

When her husband died, a widow might be excluded from the family inheritance or even exploited sexually. The law required the widow to stay within her late husband's family (25:5a). *'If brothers are living together and one of them dies without a son, his widow must not marry outside the family.'* Literally, 'she must not become the wife of an outsider'. She is to stay within the family support mechanism and not become a wandering vagrant or lapse into a life of prostitution. Nor was she to be exploited by the men of her husband's family. They were to protect and provide for her and if one of them wanted to claim conjugal rights with her (literally, 'to go in to her'), he must take her as his wife (25:5b). *'Her husband's brother shall take her and marry her and fulfil the duty of a brother-in-law to her.'* The Hebrew language formed its own special word to describe his responsibility 'to do what any decent brother-in-law ought to do'. He would provide a home for his sister-in-law and raise up children for her and his deceased brother.

ii. It perpetuated the name of the deceased brother (25:6). *'The first son she bears shall carry on the name of the dead brother, so that his name will not be blotted out from Israel.'* This law expressed a deeply-held concern in Israel. The blessings of God's covenant with Israel were enjoyed within families and passed on to succeeding generations. God's goodness was not an abstract concept, but took many tangible forms, one of which was the family inheritance. The family portion was passed from father to son as a visible token of God's everlasting faithfulness. The new generation which arose to take the place of those who had gone before them was a sign that God's blessing continued to rest upon those who had died. Hence 'a righteous man will be remembered forever' (Ps 112:6), and 'the memory of the righteous will be a blessing' (Prov. 10:7a). By contrast, the wicked will be forgotten and their name will be blotted out because they will have no descendants (Ps. 9:6; 109:13; Prov. 10:7b). Thus it was a terrible outcome when a man died without an heir to inherit his portion of land and perpetuate his name (Judg. 21:3, 6-7). Moses addressed this problem in 25:6. This law made the biologically impossible legally possible by declaring that the first son of the levirate marriage would carry on the name of the deceased husband.

The responsibility of the deceased man's brother was taken very seriously indeed. Even though there were no criminal penalties should he refuse to do his duty as a brother-in-law, he would face sustained community pressure (25:7-11). *'However, if a man does not want to marry his brother's wife, she shall go to the elders at the town gate and say, "My husband's brother refuses to carry on his brother's name in Israel. He will not fulfil the duty of a brother-in-law to me."'* If the stigma of being reported to the authorities did not persuade him, he would face a serious lecture from the elders (25:8a). *'Then the elders of his town shall summon him and talk to him.'* If he still refused to do what was expected of him he must renounce his rights to marry the woman and, by implication, receive any property that went with her. Moreover, he will become an object of humiliation (25:8b-9). *'If he persists in saying, "I do not want to marry her," his brother's widow shall go*

up to him in the presence of the elders, take off one of his sandals,
spit in his face and say, "This is what is done to the man who will
not build up his brother's family line."' We see a version of this
ritual in Ruth 4:6-8, where Boaz stepped in to marry Ruth
when a closer relative refused to do so lest he endanger his own
immediate family's inheritance. Of course, Ruth was delighted
that the other man stepped aside and allowed Boaz to marry
her, because she had come to love Boaz. That may explain why
Ruth did not spit in the other man's face or humiliate him
publicly; or it may simply have been that the customs had been
modified over the years. However, the full rigour of the law as
Moses stated it required that the selfish and indifferent brother
should be shamed publicly. The contempt expressed in this
public ritual was akin to the gift of a white feather to men who
refused to fight for their country in times of war.

The humiliation of the unsandalled man was passed on to his
descendants (25:10). *'That man's line shall be known in Israel as*
The Family of the Unsandalled.' This was a fitting punishment for
a man who refused to raise up an heir for his deceased brother
and so preserve his name in Israel. Because of his refusal, his
own name would be blighted for ever. In this unexpected way
the memory of the deceased brother would live on through the
shame of the brother who lived.

Shame is a very powerful, but dangerous motivation. Moral
indignation can easily degenerate into manipulation. Yet Paul
urged the Thessalonians to take note of those who neglected
their responsibility to work and support their families and to
keep away from them (2 Thess. 3:6, 14). 'Do not associate with
him in order that he may feel ashamed.' Someone who does not
provide for his family 'has denied the faith and is worse than an
unbeliever' (1 Tim 5:8). That Paul was willing to give this counsel
shows how the early church viewed the sin of neglecting the
needy within one's family. This was a lesson which they had
learned from Moses.

A vulnerable assailant (25:11-12)

When Moses gave permission for a disappointed widow to humiliate her neglectful brother-in-law, he may have had some misgivings. What if this gets out of hand? What message is being sent to others who prefer violent action to peaceful dispute resolution? The wife mentioned in 25:11-12 needed no encouragement to take direct and violent action against her enemies and those of her family. Moses described a violent scenario. *'If two men are fighting and the wife of one of them comes to rescue her husband from his assailant, and she reaches out and seizes him by his private parts...'* The response of the woman was to take direct action against the man (literally, 'a brother') who was attacking her husband. We might have some sympathy for the woman, as she acted out of loyalty to her husband in order to protect him. However, she went well beyond the bounds of acceptable behaviour. She seized the assailant by his private parts, literally 'that of which he is ashamed'. At least three considerations explain why her actions are inexcusable.

i. The private parts of a man bore the covenant sign of circumcision. Her action treated both the man and the sign of God's covenant mercies to Israel with unacceptable disrespect.

ii. An assault on the man's genitals could cause lasting damage, the result of which might be that the man would be unable to father children. He would then face the same fate as the brother who died without issue in 25:5. This was a serious matter.

iii. Her actions exposed human nakedness in a shameful and sinful way. It was for a very good reason that God had covered the naked bodies of Adam and Eve with animal-skin clothes in Genesis 3:21. Even in the daily matters of personal hygiene the Israelites were to take care not to expose their nakedness accidentally (see 23:14). When a man's nakedness was exposed as a result of a deliberate assault, this was certainly not to be condoned.

The penalty prescribed in 25:12 shows how seriously the woman's action was viewed. *'You shall cut off her hand. Show her no pity.'* This is the only instance in the laws of Moses where mutilation was specifically required. The *lex talionis* of 19:21 permitted a hand or foot to be cut off if that was the damage which an assailant had caused his victim. Some commentators have suggested that cutting off her hand in 25:12 is a euphemism for some form of female circumcision. Although the practice of female circumcision was widely practised in the ancient world, there is no clear evidence of its practice in Israel and the law of 14:1 demonstrates an abhorrence of cruel and unusual bodily mutilation. However, even the amputation of a hand is a terrible punishment, and it was to be administered without pity as in 7:16, 13:8 and 19:13.

This severe law applies the principle that the end never justifies the means. It is never right to take the law into our own hands or respond to wrong-doing with wrong-doing. Those who have been duly appointed to administer justice are God's servants to punish evil (see Rom. 13:4). We are not to usurp their role by setting ourselves up as judges and executioners. Moreover, Jesus encourages Christians to respond to violence with meekness (see Matt. 5:39) and Paul lists 'brawling' among the sins of which Christians are to rid themselves (see Eph. 4:31). It is particularly inappropriate for women to conduct themselves in a violent and indecent way. God has given fathers and husbands the responsibility of protecting their womenfolk. It is not for a wife to go into a fight to protect her husband, for she is 'the weaker partner' (1 Peter 3:7). Not only are godly women to dress modestly, they are to conduct themselves with modesty, purity and reverence (1 Peter 3:1-4).

A Dishonest Merchant (25:13-16)

The need for standard weights and measures was recognised at an early stage in Israel's history. Precious metals were measured by a recognised unit, the 'sanctuary shekel' (see Exod. 30:13, 24; 38:24-26). Later, the standard measure was set by order of the king (see 2 Sam. 14:26). However, the dishonest merchant carried around two sets of measures in his bag of tricks. It contained two sets of stones to be used to measure weight. Or it might contain two containers (literally, an *ephah*) to measure capacity. An *ephah* was the standard unit for measuring out dry goods such as grain or flour. It amounted to 6 gallons or 22 litres. The trickster had a lighter stone or a smaller container to use when he was selling. This meant that he gave his customers less than they paid for. He also had a heavier stone or a larger container when he was buying. This meant that he got more for his shekel than he was entitled to. With sleight of hand he would produce whichever set of weights and measures best served his advantage.

This common practice was forbidden in Israel (25:13-14). *'Do not have two differing weights in your bag—one heavy, one light. Do not have two differing measures in your house—one large, one small.'* See also Leviticus 19:35-36. The book of Proverbs describes God's abhorrence of dishonest weights and measures (see Prov 11:1; 16:11; 20:10, 23), as did the prophets (see Hosea 12:7, Amos 8:5 and Micah 6:11). To encourage the Israelites to act honestly, and perhaps contrary to their sinful habits, Moses added two explanations to the basic law.

i) The promise of God's blessing upon those who kept his commands (25:15)
'You must have accurate and honest (literally 'complete and righteous') *weights and measures, so that you may live long in the land the LORD your God is giving you.'* We have seen that the Israelites laid great stress on the transfer of the promised

inheritance from one generation to the generations which followed them. In this way the Israelites would live long in the land that God had given them. However, only those who obeyed God's law would 'live long in the land'. God's covenant people were to be characterised by honesty, because nothing tarnishes his reputation like dishonesty amongst his people.

Even today many unbelievers are hardened against the gospel by the dishonest reputation of some professedly Christian businessmen. In church they recite the Ten Commandments, yet on a Monday morning in their places of business they violate them. The story is told of an encounter between W. P. Nicholson, a fiery Irish evangelist, and a tailor who lived in a town where Nicholson was leading an evangelistic campaign. The tailor was a sceptic and protested that he would never attend any of the services, so Nicholson called to issue a personal invitation. When he did so, the tailor proceeded to show Nicholson his ledger, which recorded many long-unpaid accounts. Some of the debtors were Christians in the town, who clearly had no intention of paying the tailor for the work he had done. Their hypocrisy was a stumbling block to this man.

ii) The warning of God's hostility upon those who break God's commands (25:16)
'For the LORD your God detests anyone who does these things, anyone who deals dishonestly.' 'Detests' is a word that occurs often in Deuteronomy. It describes God's attitude towards idolatry and gross immorality. In Proverbs 11:1; 20:10, 23 it describes how the Lord views the tools of a dishonest merchant. Moses told the Israelites that God detests the dishonest merchant himself. God's holy wrath is not abstract and impersonal. It is provoked by the violation of his covenant with Israel and it is passionate (Ps. 7:11). Some sins may seem petty and insignificant to us, but every violation of God's commands is a personal offence against him. God is not swayed by the argument that 'everyone does it nowadays'. God calls upon his people to live holy lives so that

they might transform the wicked world around them (Phil. 2:14-16). His wrath will fall upon the petty cheat just as surely as it will fall upon the cold-blooded murderer or the flagrant adulterer. It is the conviction of this awesome truth that drives respectable sinners out of their complacency to repent and seek mercy from God.

Remember the Amalekites (25:17-19)

In these final verses of chapter 25, Moses looked beyond the boundaries of the covenant community to those nations which were Israel's enemies and showed how God's justice applied to them as well. We have already heard the sentence which God pronounced on the Canaanites in Deuteronomy 7:1-5 and 12:1-3. Here is a specific pronouncement concerning the Amalekites, who did not live in the land of Canaan but in the territories south of the Dead Sea. As the Israelites had journeyed through the wilderness, the Amalekites had attacked them. Moses commanded the Israelites to remember their hostility (25:17-18). *'Remember what the Amalekites did to you along the way when you came out of Egypt. When you were weary and worn out, they met you on your journey and cut off all who were lagging behind; they had no fear of God... Do not forget!'*

The Amalekites were a desert people descended from Amalek, a grandson of Esau (Gen. 36:12). Thus they were distant cousins of the Israelites. Israel's journey from Egypt towards the land of Canaan took them through the areas where the Amalekites lived (Num. 13:29). Even before the Israelites reached Sinai, the Amalekites attacked them at Rephidim (Exod. 17:8-16). With the support of Moses' prayers, Joshua overcame the Amalekites in battle. Afterwards the Lord told Moses, 'Write this on a scroll as something to be remembered and make sure that Joshua hears it, because I will completely blot out the memory of Amalek from under heaven' (Exod. 17:14). The attacks to which Moses

God's justice practically applied

refers in 25:17-18 may have taken place after that battle as well as sporadically over the next forty years of tramping through the wilderness. They targeted the stragglers at the tail-end of the procession, literally, 'those who were shattered'.

By the ethical code of desert nomads, this was a despicable thing to do. They attacked the women and children, those who could not defend themselves. Moses explained that they acted in this way because there was no fear of God in their hearts (see 25:18b). Even though the Amalekites did not know Jehovah as their covenant Lord, they ought to have known him as their Creator, the One who made the heavens and the earth. God had written his law on their hearts. When Abraham went down to Gerar, he concluded that there was no fear of God in that place (Gen. 20:11) and pretended that Sarah was not his wife. Yet even there, Abimelech respected the sanctity of God's holy institution of marriage and returned Sarah to Abraham. This was an example of how the fear of God the Creator can influence the conduct even of those who do not know God as Saviour.

The vast and awesome desert was an especially appropriate setting in which to learn the fear of God. T. E. Lawrence (better known as Lawrence of Arabia) described the fear which fell upon him and his fellow soldiers as they entered Wadi Rum, a canyon south of the Dead Sea in an area which may have been known to both the Israelites and the Amalekites.

> The hills drew together until only two miles divided them: and then, towering gradually till their parallel parapets must have been a thousand feet above us, ran forward in an avenue for miles... Our little caravan grew self-conscious, and felt quite dead, afraid and ashamed to flaunt its smallness in the presence of the stupendous hills.

In spite of the awesome splendour of the desert, the Amalekites clearly had no sense of the holiness of the One who made those hills, for they were not ashamed to violate the code of conduct which he had written on their hearts. We might say the same of many today who admire the beauty of the world around them, yet never worship its Creator. Not only do they not worship him, they throw off all restraint and rebel against his commands. Their ears are deaf to God's word.

God, however, listens to the cries of his people. He saw the plight of the Israelites and heard their prayers for help. He pronounced his sentence upon those who afflicted them. Because of their hostility towards God's people, the Amalekites would be removed from the face of the earth (see Exod. 17:14). In 25:19 Moses combined God's promise of salvation to the Israelites with his warning of destruction for the Amalekites. *'When the LORD your God gives you rest from all the enemies around you in the land he is giving you to possess as an inheritance, you shall blot out the memory of Amalek from under heaven. Do not forget!'* The Israelites will become the instruments of divine justice. This is a solemn reminder that those who stand in the way of God's redemptive plans and oppose them will bring destruction upon themselves. Sadly, what brings salvation to one, results in condemnation for others.

The fact remains that no-one who stands against God and his people will succeed, whether it is a desert tribe, a mighty empire or a totalitarian dictator. It may appear for a time that those who cruelly oppress the church have gained the upper hand; but they will fall before the King of kings. Later kings of Israel, Saul and David, humbled the Amalekites. By the time of King Hezekiah they had been all but eliminated (1 Chr. 4:45). The mighty Babylonian empire rose up and oppressed God's people but, when it had served God's purpose, it collapsed and fell. In its time the Roman Empire persecuted the early church, but it too was conquered by the sign of the cross. Many alive today can remember when the Soviet Union and militant communism seemed to threaten the churches of Eastern Europe with extinction. How rapidly it has passed into history! So, too, will every power that despises God and hurts his people.

Although we should not overlook the human tragedy that was necessarily involved in the elimination of the Amalekites, we should see it as a part of the bigger struggle between God and Satan. Ultimately, God will win and all his enemies will be defeated. Not only will they be defeated, but their memory will be removed and the trouble they cause God's people will be no more. Isaiah looked forward to the day when God would create a new world order and banish fear from the minds of his people. 'Behold, I will create new heavens and a new earth. The former things will not be remembered, nor will they come to mind' (Isa. 65:17). In that new Jerusalem 'there will be no more death or mourning or crying or pain, for the old order of things has passed away' (Rev. 21:4), while outside the holy city will be the wicked who have opposed God's people (Rev. 22:15).

Yet we live in a live in a sinful world, and so long as that is the case we cannot ignore the reality of evil. Moses instructed his hearers to remember the Amalekites and what they had done. 'Do not forget!' The Israelites were to remember because God remembers every word and action and will bring everything into judgment (Eccles. 12:14). Let us remember that God is holy and just. Let us examine our hearts and lives and be sure that we are amongst the covenant people whose names will live forever.

Chapter 26
Three declarations

Please read Deuteronomy 26: 1-19

Nothing warms the heart of a preacher more than signs that his hearers are responding to the message. Some congregations are very responsive and indicate their agreement with loud exclamations. Others are less responsive and a look, a smile or a comment afterwards at the church door indicates their appreciation of the sermon. The most important response to the preaching of God's word is not words of approval, but submission and obedience to the Lord who speaks through his word. In this chapter Moses' second Deuteronomic sermon is drawing to a close and he sets out the response which he seeks. He appeals to the Israelites to declare their allegiance to Jehovah. In chapters 5 – 25 Moses summarises the laws which God gave to Israel and urges them to obey those laws. Finally, in chapter 26, Moses sets out a liturgical response to the preaching of God's law.

Moses has already shown the Israelites that God expected from them a response to the preaching of his word. 'Hear now, O Israel, the decrees and laws I am about to teach you. Follow them so that you may live and may go in and take possession of the land that the LORD, the God of your fathers is giving you' (4:1). 'Acknowledge and take to heart this day that the LORD is God in heaven above and on the earth below. There is no other'

(4:39). 'Hear, O Israel: The LORD our God, the LORD is one. Love the LORD your God with all your heart and with all your soul and with all your strength' (6:4-5).

> And now, O Israel, what does the LORD your God ask of you but to fear the LORD your God, to walk in all his ways, to love him, to serve the LORD your God with all your heart and with all your soul, and to observe the LORD's commands and decrees that I am giving you today for your own good? (10:12-13).

These appeals come to a climax in 30:19, where Moses calls upon the Israelites to grasp the offer of life with God. 'Now choose life, so that you and your children may live and that you may love the LORD your God, listen to his voice, and hold fast to him.'

In this chapter Moses records three declarations which indicate Israel's willingness to serve and obey God. They were to be recited on important occasions in the life of the community as reminders that the Israelites were a nation which belonged to Jehovah, which had been blessed by him and which was under obligation to serve him. By placing these declarations in the context of God's covenant with Israel, Moses shows that they were reminders of God's grace. Because they speak of the grace of God, these covenant rituals speak to us as well and show us the abiding significance of Israel's law code. They give the grateful response of a redeemed people. Redeemed people will be people who serve and worship God daily.

The first of the firstfruits (26:1-11)

The first declaration which Moses described in this chapter took place at harvest time (26:1-3).

Three declarations

When you have entered the land that the LORD your God is giving you as an inheritance and have taken possession of it and settled in it, take some of the firstfruits of all that you produce from the soil of the land that the LORD your God is giving you and put them in a basket.

Although the offering of the firstfruits from the soil was a yearly event (see 18:4 and Num. 18:12-13), which took place in association with the pilgrim festivals, this formula is mentioned nowhere else in the Old Testament. This has led some commentators to suggest that it was to be used only once, when the Israelites celebrated their first harvest in the promised land. This is an unlikely suggestion, as 26:3 indicates that the ceremony was intended to become a regular feature in Israel's life. *'Then go to the place that the LORD your God will choose as a dwelling for his Name and say to the priest in office at the time...'*

Although many priests held office over the years, this ordinance was sadly neglected. When the people gave thanks for the harvest, all too often they gave thanks to Baal (Hosea 2:8). It is significant that the declaration was to be made at the central sanctuary dedicated to the worship of Jehovah. By appointing this central sanctuary, God intended to direct the people away from the hill-top shrines where Baal was acknowledged as 'the god of the harvest'. The point of this declaration was to reaffirm the fact that Jehovah, not Baal, had given the harvest.

There were actually two declarations which the grateful Israelites were to make before the Lord. The first declaration acknowledged *present happiness* (26:3). *'I declare today to the LORD your God that I have come to the land the LORD swore to our forefathers to give us.'* They traced their present blessedness back to the promise which God had made to Abraham. In fulfilment of that promise God had given them the land of Canaan. In that land they enjoyed earthly security, for God provided them with grain and wine, flocks and herds. There, too, God dwelt with them and blessed them with the fellowship of an everlasting covenant. They were always to remember that God keeps his promises. Today we, too, can enjoy eternal security because God has kept his promises and given to his people every spiritual blessing in Christ Jesus. Those who are united to Christ in saving faith declare in their worship that God is faithful and has bestowed eternal life on his people.

The second declaration acknowledged *past deliverance* (26:5-10). The worshipper linked his present happiness in the land of promise to the history of his people. He described three stages in his nation's history. First came the *distress of his ancestors* (26:5-6). *'My father was a wandering Aramean, and he went down into Egypt with a few people and lived there and became a great nation, powerful and numerous.'* The wandering Aramean was Jacob. He was so called because his ancestors came from the land of Aram in Mesopotamia. In Genesis 24:10, the region of Abraham's birthplace is described as Aram Naharaim (literally, 'Aram of the two rivers'); and in Genesis 25:20, 28:5; 31:20, 24 Abraham's kinsmen are called Arameans. Jacob went there to escape the fury of his brother Esau and married. Although he prospered in that land, he was often cheated by his father-in-law, and returned to Canaan. There a severe famine threatened the lives of his family, so he sought refuge in Egypt. This explains why Jacob is called 'a wandering Aramean'. 'Wandering' can also mean 'perishing', and on many occasions his life was in peril. Mercifully, God raised up a deliverer for Jacob and his family, in the person of Joseph. Yet, many years later, when Joseph had been forgotten *'the Egyptians ill-treated us and made us suffer, putting us to hard labour'*. Jacob's family had jumped out of the frying-pan of famine into the fire of slavery.

The second stage in this brief historical survey was the *deliverance wrought by God* (26:7-8). *'Then we cried out to the LORD, the God of our fathers, and the LORD heard our voice and saw our misery, toil and oppression. So the LORD brought us out of Egypt…'* The Israelite's declaration recalls God's assurance in Exodus 3:7-9 that he had heard the cries and seen the suffering of his people and would deliver them from slavery; it also recalls God's promise in Exodus 6:6-7 that he would bring them out from slavery. 'I am the LORD, and I will bring you out from under the yoke of the Egyptians. I will free you from being slaves to them, and I will redeem you with an outstretched arm and with mighty acts of judgment.' No human power can frustrate the plans of an Almighty God when he sets out to deliver his people.

The third stage of Israel's history is *delight in the blessings bestowed by God* (26:9-10). The outcome of God's mighty actions was that the Israelites were able to enjoy the fruit of the promised land, as God had promised many years earlier. 'So I have come down to rescue them from the hand of the Egyptians and to bring them up out of that land into a good and spacious land, a land flowing with milk and honey' (Exod. 3:8). In 26:9 the Israelite worshipper acknowledged the fulfilment of that promise. *'He brought us to this place and gave us this land, a land flowing with milk and honey.'* This familiar description of Canaan was first used in God's promise to the Israelites (Exod. 3:8, 17) and later repeated by Moses in Deuteronomy 6:3 and 11:9. It brings to mind images of sweetness and plenty and reinforced the fact that the Israelites were a truly blessed people to live in a land blessed by God with many natural resources. The firstfruits of these blessings were now to be brought as a thank-offering to God (26:10a). *'And now I bring the firstfruits of the soil that you, O Lord, have given me.'*

The point to note is that the giver returned to God what God has first given to him. In fact, everything we have has been received from God. When we come to understand and accept this simple but profound fact, we are able to take a holy delight in all of God's good gifts. The psalmist was able to sing with great joy about God's provision of rain to refresh and enrich the soil and the flocks which graze in the meadows. 'You care for the land and water it; you enrich it abundantly. The streams of God are filled with water to provide the people with grain, for so you have ordained it. You drench its furrows and level its ridges; you soften it with showers and bless its crops. You crown the year with your bounty, and your carts overflow with abundance. The grasslands of the desert overflow; the hills are clothed with gladness. The meadows are covered with flocks and the valleys are mantled with grain; they shout for joy and sing' (Ps. 65:9-13). That is why the apostle Paul was suspicious of those who taught others to abstain from God's good gifts (1 Tim. 4:3). They forgot that 'everything God created is good, and nothing is to be rejected if it is received with thanksgiving' (1 Tim. 4:4-5).

We give thanks to God both by our words and our actions. As well as reciting words of thanks, the Israelite brought his offering to the sanctuary (26:10b). *'Place the basket before the LORD your God and bow down before him.'* This act of giving was a reminder that God's generosity demands a response. Much will be expected from those to whom much has been given. One of the consequences of this offering was that needy people in Israel would be able to feed on the firstfruits (26:11). *'And you and the Levites and the aliens among you shall rejoice in all the good things the LORD your God has given to you and your household.'* The offerings made to the Lord were not hidden away in barns or used to enrich the priests, but to feed those who owned no land of their own. This has been a recurring theme of Moses in Deuteronomy. The point which Moses sought to make was very simple and practical – those who love God must show love for their neighbour. Those who love their neighbour will themselves be blessed. Our Lord (in a saying recorded by Paul in Acts 20:35) taught the same lesson, for 'it is more blessed to give than to receive'.

Three declarations

The tithe of the third year (26:12-15)

The firstfruits were a token offering. They pointed forward towards something that was not fully known. Only after the harvest had been safely gathered in would the full extent of God's provision be known. By contrast, the tithe was a more precise offering. The Israelites were to give to the Lord one tenth of all that the land produced. When the Israelites had the harvest in their barns, they could work out how much to set aside for the Lord. Then they would bring their tithe to the central sanctuary (14:22-27), where it was eaten in a thanksgiving feast before the Lord. Every third year there was to be a departure from this pattern, which Moses described in 14:28-29. Instead of taking the tithe to the central sanctuary, the people would store it in their towns and villages to make provision for the needy in their midst (26:12). 'When you have finished setting aside a tenth of all your produce in the third year, the year of the tithe, you shall give it to the Levite, the alien, the fatherless and the widow, so that they may eat in your towns and be satisfied.'

The principle underlying this triennial tithe was a noble one but, like anything good, it was liable to abuse. As the produce was to be eaten in the local community rather than at the central sanctuary, there was a heightened danger that the Israelites would use the tithe of the third year in ways that the Lord had not intended. Some of the tithe might even be taken to the local sanctuaries and eaten as part of rituals associated with the worship of Baal. Moses countered this danger by requiring people to make a pledge or declaration before the Lord (26:13-15). Some have suggested that the declaration was made by each Israelite family which went to celebrate the Feast of Tabernacles at the central sanctuary. This is nowhere stated in Deuteronomy, and it is more likely that the declaration was made in the towns of Israel as the triennial tithe was placed in the local tithe barns for the benefit of others. The Levites could not police the actions of the Israelites in their home towns, but

God sees everything (Ps. 7:9; Rev. 2:23; Heb. 4:13). Note three features of this declaration.

First of all, it contained *a declaration of obedience* (26:13-14). *'I have removed from my house the sacred portion and have given it to the Levite, the alien, the fatherless and the widow, according to all you commanded... I have obeyed the LORD my God; I have done everything you commanded me.'* Although the declaration refers to the whole of God's law, its focus is quite specific. The Israelite declared that he had kept the tithe law in particular. The 'sacred portion' was his tithe to the Lord. He has ring-fenced that portion of the harvest which he owed to the Lord so that it did not get diverted to other uses. Now he places it at God's disposal. He has 'purged' it from his property. Here he uses a word which was often used to describe how evil was to be removed from Israel (see 22:21, 22, 24). Although it is used here in a very different context, the choice of words indicates that the Israelites were to be intentional and scrupulous about tithing. God must not be robbed of anything that rightfully belongs to him (see Mal. 3:8-10a).

Later Judaism took this scrupulosity to extremes. Jesus rebuked the Pharisees who tithed even their spices – mint, dill and cummin – but neglected 'the more important matters of the law – justice, mercy and faithfulness' (Matt. 23:23). Jesus did not rebuke them for their desire to measure out what belonged to the Lord. He did rebuke them for their motive. They were moved by a desire to be seen to do the right thing rather than by love for God. The first of God's commands is to love him with all our hearts; and out of love the Israelite worshipper declared his determination to hold nothing back from God. We too must love God with all our hearts and with all our possessions. That is why many Christians have found tithing to be an important part of their stewardship of what God has given them. When they receive their pay packet (whether that comes to them in a literal or electronic form), they set aside a portion to give to the work of God's kingdom just as they set aside money to buy food or pay bills. It is all too easy for our tithe to get lost in the midst of many financial commitments, unless we calculate it and mark it off as the Lord's.

Secondly, it contained *a denial of uncleanness* (26:13b-14). *'I have not turned aside from your commands nor have I forgotten any of them.'* After this general denial, the Israelite made three specific denials. These refer to pagan practices for which some might well have used the produce of their land. *'I have not eaten any of the sacred portion while I was in mourning.'* Being present in a home where a family member has died would have brought the Israelite into close proximity with a dead body and made him ritually unclean under Israelite law. However, a more serious matter would have been any participation in specifically pagan rites of mourning. That this is what the declaration describes may well be indicated by the fact that the only other use of the Hebrew word used here for mourning is found in Hosea 9:4 where unacceptable sacrifices are likened to the 'bread of mourners'. Both were tarnished with paganism.

Two further denials most probably refer to rituals of death and mourning. *'Nor have I removed any of it while I was unclean'* is a denial that the Israelite has touched the tithe offering after having contact with a dead body. *'Nor have I offered any of it to the dead'* is a denial that he has used the tithe in a ritual designed to make provision for the dead in the after-life. It was common in the ancient world to offer food to the gods, both to appease their anger against the person who had died and to provide for the material needs of the departed. The offensiveness of these overtly pagan practices should have been obvious to Moses' hearers, and it may simply be that the Israelite is declaring that he had not used the tithe for the funeral feast of a family member. Even if that were the case, it was not the purpose for which the triennial tithe was set apart. It was to be used to make provision for 'the Levite, the alien, the fatherless and the widow, according to all [God] commanded'.

Thirdly, it contained *a prayer for continued blessing* (26:15). *'Look down from heaven, your holy dwelling-place, and bless your people Israel and the land you have given us as you promised on oath to our forefathers, a land flowing with milk and honey.'* God's blessing comes from above. 'Every good and perfect gift is from above, coming down from the Father of the heavenly lights, who does not change like shifting shadows' (James 1:17). This is not to deny that God works powerfully in every place or to confine him to one section of the universe. The point of the Israelite's declaration is that the God of Israel is highly exalted. He stands high above us and is greater than any of his creatures.

> As the heavens are higher than the earth,
> so are my ways higher than your ways
> and my thoughts than your thoughts.
> (Isa. 55:9)

Not only is he higher than us, Jehovah is greater than all other so-called gods.

Jehovah has, however, reached down to take an active interest in the lives and welfare of fallen mankind on earth. He has bound himself to the nation of Israel by making a covenant with them. He made promises and he keeps them. He led them into 'a land flowing with milk and honey'. God's mercies were manifested in obvious and earthly ways. In his prayer, the Israelite acknowledged those mercies and sought even greater blessing in days to come. Can we see the signs of God's mercies around us? Nothing gives us greater encouragement to pray and to worship God than the promises which he makes and keeps. They teach us to acknowledge existing blessing as we give thanks and to anticipate future blessing in our petitions. They teach us to look around us with gratitude. They also teach us to look up to God with wonder and joy.

The covenant declaration (26:16-19)

Moses concluded his second covenant-renewal sermon (chapters 5-26) in much the same manner as he started it. He appealed to the Israelites to love and obey the Lord who had saved them (26:16). *'The LORD your God commands you this day to follow these decrees and laws; carefully observe them with all your heart and with all your soul.'* He had made similar exhortations in 5:1, 6:1 and 12:1. No doubt he hoped that the Israelites had a better understanding of these laws and decrees after having listened to Moses' sermon. Yet the goal of preaching is not merely to inform the mind. The recurring danger of nurturing a congregation of sedentary sermon-tasters is one which concerned James, the New Testament letter writer. 'Do not merely listen to the word, and so deceive yourselves. Do what it says' (James 1:22).

Yet the response of God's people to what they hear preached ought never to be routine or mechanical, like that of a platoon of soldiers on the parade ground responding to the commands of their drill sergeant. That response ought to be an overflow of gratitude from a heart renewed by grace. In 26:17-19 Moses records two declarations which both cultivate and express the covenant fellowship between Jehovah and Israel. It is possible that these declarations were drafted for use at the covenant-renewal ceremony over which Moses presided on the plains of Moab. They echoed the promises made at Sinai (Exod. 24:1-8). Here is the substance of the covenant.

i. Israel's declaration (26:17)

Moses described the substance of Israel's response to Jehovah's mercies. *'You have declared this day that the LORD is your God and that you will walk in his ways, that you will keep his decrees, commands and laws, and that you will obey him.'* Because Jehovah had chosen Israel to be his people, Israel responded by acknowledging Jehovah as her God. The very words which covenant people were to say were, 'You are my God' (Jer. 30:22; Hosea 2:23). In the New Testament we hear a similar declaration of faith from Thomas, the doubting disciple, when he repented of his scepticism and acknowledged the risen Jesus. 'My Lord and my God', he declared in John 20:28. Because Jehovah is Israel's God, the people promised that they would keep his commandments and obey him. There was little point professing that Jehovah was God, if they were not willing to submit to his claims over their lives. This simple profession, 'We will obey him,' would have enormous implications for the covenant people. It made them different from all the nations around them.

The same profession transforms the lives of Christian believers today. When we profess faith in the Lord Jesus, we pledge ourselves to live godly lives which bring honour and pleasure to God. Some do this at their baptism, while others do so when they make a profession of faith and join the church. There may be times later on in our Christian life when we are convicted of specific sins and humbled by the grace of God and in response we pledge ourselves to reform our ways according to God's word. This is what Peter calls 'the pledge of a good conscience towards God' (1 Peter 3:21). It is important to remind ourselves of the promises which we have made to God. They strengthen our resolve to do what love requires.

ii. Jehovah's declaration (26:18-19)

It may seem strange that this declaration follows that of the people in 26:17. After all, doesn't God's declaration that Israel is his chosen nation precede Israel's declaration that they will serve him? Logically, that is the order of events in Israel's salvation. Yet God's willingness to reach out to Israel set up a dialogue between himself and his people which assured them of their blessed condition. In his great mercy God responded to their responses. *'And the LORD has declared this day that you are his people, his treasured possession as he promised, and that you are to keep all his commands.'*

The description of the Israelites as 'his treasured possession' takes us back to Sinai, where the descendants of Jacob were declared to be the nation of Israel (Exod. 19:5). God promised that if the Israelites kept his law fully they would continue to enjoy a special relationship with the Lord who held the whole earth in his hands. God kept his promise; and several times in Deuteronomy Moses reminded the Israelites that they really were God's treasured possession (see 7:6; 14:2). They were precious in God's eyes because he had made them and chosen them, and not because of anything they had done. This is grace. The grace of God takes unworthy sinners and changes them into something beautiful. Grace finds a worthless pebble on the beach and transforms it into a precious gem. Grace saves sinners and makes them precious to God.

If ever the Israelites stopped and asked 'Why did God choose an unworthy group of people like us to be his treasured possession?' Jehovah's declaration in 26:19 gave the answer. *'He has declared that he will set you in praise, fame and honour high above all the nations he has made and that you will be a people holy to the LORD your God, as he promised.'* They will be praised and famous and honoured amongst the nations so that God might also be praised and famous and honoured through them. When, after many centuries, the band of redeemed slaves became a great empire under King Solomon, all their splendour served one purpose only - the glory of God. This was what the Queen of Sheba saw in 1 Kings 10:9 when she described Solomon and his kingdom. 'Praise be to the LORD your God, who has delighted in you and placed you on the throne of Israel. Because of the LORD's eternal love for Israel, he has made you king, to maintain justice and righteousness.' Yet the Israelites often forgot why God had blessed them.

Many centuries later, the prophet Jeremiah quoted from 26:19 to describe God's purposes for Israel. The people of Israel had become proud, so Jeremiah enacted a parable by hiding a new linen belt in a crevice in the rocks. As we might expect, it was ruined after many months of exposure to the elements. The point of the parable was to demonstrate that in this way the pride of Israel would come to ruin. The Israelites had to see that their pride was folly. Only when they served the Lord would they be able to stand tall among the nations. Jeremiah made that belt a picture to describe Israel's restoration. "'For as a belt is bound around a man's waist, so I bound the whole house of Israel and the whole house of Judah to me," declares the Lord, "to be my people for *my* renown and praise and honour"' (Jer. 13:11). 'I will cleanse them from all the sin they have committed... Then this city will bring *me* renown, joy, praise and honour before all nations on earth that hear of all the good things I do for it; and they will be in awe and will tremble at the abundant prosperity and peace I provide for it' (Jer. 33:8-9). Jeremiah explicitly claimed the honour for the Lord who would save Israel.

So as we enjoy the riches of God's grace, we are to consider how we can turn them over to God's honour. Do we acknowledge that our material possessions and spiritual privileges come from God? Do we acknowledge that if God treated us as we deserved he ought to sweep us away in judgment? Do we praise God that he has loved us while we were repulsive to him and that while we were still sinners Christ died for us? Do we acknowledge that our hope of eternal life is grounded in the work of Jesus Christ? Do we acknowledge that anything that is good and holy in our lives is the fruit of the Spirit's work within us? 'Who has ever given to God, that God should repay him?

Three declarations

For from him and through him and to him are all things. To him be the glory forever! Amen' (Rom. 11:35-36).

Chapter 27
Covenant renewal

Please read Deuteronomy 27: 1-26

In ancient Greece, Damocles was a courtier of Dionysius, the ruler of Syracuse. Once, in his naïveté, he commented to his master that rulers must live very happy lives because they possessed great wealth and power. Dionysius responded by inviting Damocles to a banquet, which he thoroughly enjoyed, until Dionysius told him to look towards the ceiling. High above his head was a sword suspended by a single horsehair. This was meant to illustrate the vulnerability of those who think themselves most fortunate. Their wealth and power can be quickly taken away.

The people of Israel were about to receive many blessings when they entered the land of Canaan. Over the following centuries they would grow prosperous. The surrounding nations would come to admire and envy them. Yet in Deuteronomy 27 and the following chapters, Moses reminded this privileged nation that its blessings could be taken away. The riches of Canaan could be lost, not as the result of an arbitrary turn of fate, as the ancient Greeks believed, but by the righteous judgment of Jehovah. Moses warned that serious consequences would follow if the Israelites did not keep their covenant with Jehovah and obey his commands. This chapter turns the reader's attention to the commands and the curses of God's covenant.

Moses knew that he would not enter the land of Canaan. As his earthly life drew to an end, he led the Israelites in a covenant-renewal ceremony on the plains of Moab. On that day Moses recited and expounded the law which God had given to him for the Israelites. 'Keep all these commands that I give you today.' This was the day on which the Israelites declared their allegiance to Jehovah (26:17), and it is referred to in 28:1; 29:10; 30:11-19 as 'today'. In fact, the whole book of Deuteronomy was written as a memorial of that covenant renewal which strengthened the resolve of the people to face the challenges which lay before them.

Moses knew that the people needed effective leadership in the challenging years that lay ahead. God had appointed Joshua to take his place. He would need the support of the elders and priests who had worked alongside Moses. In the remaining chapters of Deuteronomy Moses prepared for a smooth transition to a new generation of leaders. He does not stand alone as the preacher of God's law, but shares the platform with the elders and the priests. The opening exhortation to keep God's commands in 27:1 came from 'Moses and the elders of Israel'. Then in 27:9 'Moses and the priests, who are Levites,' call the people to be silent before God. Training the next generation of leaders is an important element in the forward planning of any organisation, and especially so amongst the people of God. Not only did Moses train Joshua and the elders who served alongside him, but Elijah called Elisha to follow him and gathered a group of disciples around him (1 Kings 19:19, 2 Kings 2:3, 15). In the New Testament, Jesus devoted much time away from the crowds to training the twelve to continue the work which he had started. Paul trained Timothy and instructed him to train others (2 Tim. 2:2). As well as preaching the word and evangelising the lost, it is important that our churches train and equip God's people for service.

In this chapter Moses told the Israelites and their leaders how they were to teach succeeding generations about their covenant with the Lord. Covenant renewal was not something that happened only once. It was a way of refreshing a living relationship with God and passing on the faith of Israel to a new generation. At Moab, the Israelites renewed the covenant which they had made at Horeb. Even that covenant was a confirmation of the covenant which God had made with Abraham many centuries earlier. Here, Moses takes up the command which he had given in 11:29-32. When the Israelites took possession of Canaan they were to gather at Shechem to thank God for the gift of the land and to renew their covenant with him. Chapter 27 anticipates that covenant renewal by describing what the Israelites were to do.

Set up stones and write God's law on them (27:1-4, 8)

Every Monday I write out a list of things I aim to accomplish that week. I know that unless I do that the urgent demands of daily life will crowd out those things that are really important. Some people write a note and leave it on their desk or attach it to the fridge door to remind them of an urgent project to be tackled. We do these things because our memories often fail us. We hope that seeing will lead to remembering.

Moses commanded the people to write a message on stone to remind them of God's laws. They were to do this after they entered the land of Canaan and reached the place near Mount Ebal where they were to renew their covenant with the Lord (27:2-3a). *'When you have crossed the Jordan into the land the LORD your God is giving you, set up some large stones and coat them with plaster. Write on them all the words of this law...'* These stones were to be painted with a white plaster so that the words (painted in black) would stand out clearly against this background. This was an Egyptian custom, in contrast to the Mesopotamian custom of carving letters into stone. God had carved his laws onto tablets of stone with his own finger (Exod. 31:18, Deut. 9:10); but the Israelites used paint. This is a reminder that the techniques of men are always inferior to the mighty power of God. Nevertheless, these painted stones taught some important lessons.

i. The permanence of God's laws
God's law was written on stone because stone stands the test of time. In Ireland it is possible to visit stone circles and monuments which were built 3000 years before Christ. We know very little about the people who built them, but their stones remain as monuments to a long-lost civilisation. God's law was written on stone because it abides from one generation to the next. It does not merely reflect the values or preferences of one generation. It communicates the unchanging righteousness and everlasting instructions of our Creator. Many today question the relevance of a law code given to desert nomads in the second millennium BC, because they have forgotten that God is their maker and that he reveals himself in his law. In it he shows every generation how he would have them to live.

ii. The importance of communicating God's word clearly
Moses told the Israelites how they were to write the law of God on the stones (see the comments on 27:2-4 above) for a purpose. The contrast between the white plaster background and the black lettering made it easy for the reader to see and read the words. God's law was there before him in black and white. Moses repeated that point in 27:8. *'And you shall write very clearly all the words of this law on these stones you have set up.'* Throughout Deuteronomy Moses' aim has been 'to expound this law' (1:5). Not only did Moses seek to make the Israelites aware of what God said in his laws and commands, he wanted them to understand what these laws meant. He preached the law of God so that the Israelites might understand it, because

if they did not understand it they were unlikely to obey it with all their hearts. When we understand why a command has been given, and that it has been given for our own good, we are more likely to want to follow it. Clear and compelling communication was a high priority for Moses.

Preachers and teachers of God's word have a similar goal today. Sometimes sermons are muddled and unclear because preachers have not invested time and energy into the study of the Scriptures. Other preachers aim to impress listeners with their learning, yet their displays of erudition only serve to distract hearers from the message. Some preachers speak in theological generalities or religious clichés, but never tell people what God wants them to do. We must give clear and specific direction. Yet we must always remind people that they cannot keep God's commands apart from the inward, renewing work of God. Deuteronomy is a beautiful example of preaching that does justice to both God's law and God's grace. The stones were to be a monument to the absolute demands of God's holy law. As we shall see, they are also a pointer to God's grace.

iii. The reason why Israel ought to obey God's law
Moses specified when ('*When you have crossed the Jordan...*') and where ('*on Mount Ebal*') these stones were to be set up (27:4). This was very significant information. Just as the Ten Commandments were only given to the Israelites after God had delivered them from slavery (Exod. 20:2), so these stones were set up as a memorial to God's law only after the people entered their promised inheritance. There is no thought of the Israelites obeying God's commands in order to earn their redemption or the blessings of the covenant. These were freely given by God, and the Israelites were to respond with humble and heart-felt obedience. The land of Canaan was one of the central blessings promised by God to Abraham and Mount Ebal lay deep inside the promised land. It overlooked the town of Shechem, which is 40 kilometres north-west of Jericho. By the time they reached

Shechem, they would have taken possession of a significant portion of the promised land.

Moreover, Shechem was the place where God had promised Abraham that his descendants would possess the land in which he wandered as an alien. 'Abram travelled through the land as far as the site of the great tree of Moreh at Shechem...The LORD appeared to Abram and said, "To your offspring I will give this land." So he built an altar there to the LORD' (Gen. 12:6-7). When Jacob returned to the land of his birth from his exile in Paddan Aram, he went to Shechem and set up an altar where he worshipped the mighty God of his fathers (Gen. 33:18-20). Jacob worshipped at that altar because Jehovah had remembered the promise to Abraham and had brought him back home. When the Israelites went to Shechem to worship God, they were to remember Jehovah's promise to Abraham and rejoice in its fulfilment. In 27:3 Moses followed his instructions with a reminder that the land they were about to receive was 'a land flowing with milk and honey, just as the LORD, the God of your fathers, promised you'. When they started to enjoy the blessings of this land, they were to remember the One who had given it to them and recommit themselves to him in humble and heart-felt obedience.

Build an altar and offer sacrifices (27:5-7)

Moses knew that the Israelites were stubborn people, who often refused to live as God instructed them. In spite of their status as the people of the covenant, their sins would provoke God to be angry with them. How could such people live in fellowship with a holy God? That is why Moses told the people to build an altar and offer sacrifices on it. 'Build there an altar to the LORD your God, an altar of stones.' A covenant has been defined as 'a bond sealed in blood', and sacrifice was an important element in any covenant-renewal ceremony.

Covenant renewal

The altar was to be constructed very simply. It was to be built *'with stones from the field'* (27:6). These were simply shapeless pieces of rock that farmers cleared from their land as they ploughed it. *'Do not use any iron tool upon them'* (27:5b). Artistic ingenuity would not make the altar any more pleasing to God. In fact, it might well import pagan symbols and ideas into the worship of Jehovah. Moses feared that the Israelites would use their tools to do more than merely knock the rough edges off the stones, but might well decorate the stones with religious motifs. This was an anathema to Moses. Even today, people think that they can devise their own ideas of who God is and use them to adorn their worship. Human art and ingenuity can sometimes obscure the truth that God has revealed and corrupt the simplicity of worship. That is why the second commandment 'forbiddeth the worshipping of God by images, or any other way not appointed in his word' (*Westminster Shorter Catechism*, answer 51).

The altar was built for sacrifice (27:6b-7). *'Offer burnt offerings on it to the LORD your God. Sacrifice fellowship offerings there, eating them and rejoicing in the presence of the LORD your God.'* Two types of sacrifice are mentioned. The burnt offerings were the sheep or bullocks burnt in their entirety, indicating that the worshipper was totally dedicated to God. The fellowship offerings were partly burnt on the altar and partly eaten by the worshippers. This was symbolic of a meal table around which God and his people enjoyed fellowship. As a result of the atoning sacrifice, sins were forgiven and a new relationship was created which allowed the sinner to dwell in harmony with God. This was a time of 'rejoicing in the presence of the LORD your God'.

We all enjoy being invited to a friend's house for a meal. What makes those times special is not just the food we eat, but the fact that others care about us and want to spend time with us. God redeems a people for himself in order that he might have fellowship with them. This is an amazing thing. It is not a simple matter for God to invite sinners into his presence. Sin and rebellion drive us from God and God from us, but God deals with sin by means of sacrifice. In Psalm 50:5 God issued his gracious invitation, 'Gather to me my consecrated ones, who made a covenant with me by sacrifice'. God's covenant with Israel was a bond of love sealed with a sacrifice. The altar on Mount Ebal was a timely reminder that the people of Israel were sinners drawing near to a holy God. Their only way into a restored relationship with God was the altar where atoning sacrifices were made. As the writer to the Hebrews put it, 'without the shedding of blood there is no forgiveness' (Heb. 9:22). Yet through the shedding of blood, the Israelites were invited to God's banquet. The same invitation is extended to us, except that it is through the death of Jesus that we are invited to 'dwell in the house of the LORD for ever' (Ps. 23:5-6).

Consider the implications of God's covenant (27:9-13)

In the United Kingdom, some of those who have served the community in an outstanding way are given honours by the queen. They may be invited to a special ceremony in Buckingham Palace to receive their award. For them, this is a once-in-a-lifetime occasion, something they will never forget. Yet members of the royal family might visit Buckingham Palace and have dinner with the queen so often that these visits become quite routine and even a little tedious. There was a danger that the Israelites would come to look upon their access to Jehovah in a similar light. Moses warned them against adopting a careless attitude toward their spiritual privileges and took steps to guard them from that danger.

First, Moses, together with the priests, called for a period of silence and reflection (27:9-10). *'Be silent, O Israel, and listen!'* The Israelites were to observe this time of silence before the Lord on the plains of Moab as part of the covenant-renewal ceremony over which Moses presided shortly before his death. At this ceremony they would confess their faith aloud and verbally declare their allegiance to Jehovah. But first there was to be a time of silent reflection on what those words mean. There is 'a time to be silent and a time to speak' (Eccles. 3:7). There is a time to be still before the Lord and consider his mighty works. 'Be still, and know that I am God; I will be exalted among the nations, I will be exalted in the earth' (Ps. 46:10). 'But the LORD is in his holy temple; let all the earth be silent before him' (Hab. 2:20).

> Be silent before the Sovereign LORD,
> for the day of the LORD is near.
> The LORD has prepared a sacrifice;
> he has consecrated those he has invited.
> (Zeph. 1:7)

Might it be that Zephaniah was inviting the people of Judah to renew their relationship with God by following the pattern that Moses set here – first silence, then sacrifice?

Some of the great events of church history have included times of silence. During periods of revival intense silences have often preceded or followed the preaching of the word. Such was the effect of the preaching that those who listened were riveted to their seats, unable to talk or leave a place where God's presence was so mightily manifested. These must have been precious times of reflection on the might and mercy of God. When the National Covenant of Scotland was signed in Greyfriars' churchyard in Edinburgh on 28th February 1638, the covenant document was read to a large assembly. The terms of the covenant were then explained to the people, defended, and read again. Then there followed a period of silence before the Covenanters came forward to sign their names on the parchment. Some signed with their own blood, such was the depth of their commitment to the cause of Jesus Christ. In the silence they had searched their hearts and consecrated themselves to God. Likewise, in

Moab, the Israelites were encouraged to search their hearts as they made a solemn commitment to the Lord.

Moses explained the significance of this ceremony. *'You have now become the people of the LORD your God.'* We are not to understand this to mean that the Israelites had not previously been the people of God. God promised Abraham that he would have many descendants and 'I will be their God' (Gen. 17:8). In consequence of this, they would be his people. When the Israelites were slaves in Egypt, God referred to them as 'my people': 'I have indeed seen the misery of my people... I am sending you to Pharaoh to bring my people the Israelites out of Egypt' (Exod. 3:7, 10). Their status as the people of God was confirmed at Sinai when God made a covenant with them (see 29:1b). God promised, 'Now if you obey me fully and keep my covenant, then out of all nations you will be my treasured possession... a kingdom of priests and a holy nation' (Exod. 19:5-6). At Moab Moses yet again confirmed their status as the people of God.

In the silence and solemnity of the occasion they were to reflect on that fact and its significance. It may have seemed hard to believe that a nation of slaves might be the special treasure of the God who had created the whole earth and every other nation. Why hadn't God taken one of the larger and more powerful nations? Might not the Lord abandon them? Would he keep his promises to them? Covenant renewal was a way of answering these, and many other, questions. It was a way of confirming Israel's special status. As the Israelites reflected on all that God had said to them through Moses, they heard the words of reassurance: 'Yes, hard as it may be to take in, you really are the people of the living God'. In the same vein of wonderment John reminded the early Christians, 'How great is the love that the Father has lavished on us, that we should be called children of God! And that is what we are!' (1 John 3:1).

In the silence they also heard the challenge to be what they already were. In other words they were to live out the reality of what they had become. They were to live godly lives (27:10). *'Obey the LORD your God and follow his commands and decrees that I give you today.'* If this seems like a strange thing to ask, all we need to do is to look at our own lives. Many professing Christians will see ungodly actions and attitudes in themselves when they look into the mirror of God's word. Do these things mean that we are no longer the people of God? No, but they do challenge us to become what God has saved us to be. This is the same challenge as Paul put to the Corinthians. 'Get rid of the old yeast that you may be a new batch without yeast – as you really are' (1 Cor. 5:7). The call to live a new life is based on God's gift of a new status.

The second step which Moses told the people to take in order to avoid the danger of taking their spiritual privileges for granted would have to wait until they took possession of the promised land (see 27:11-26). In 27:12-13 Moses prescribed a communal recitation of the curses and blessings of the covenant by all the tribes of Israel. *'When you have crossed the Jordan, these tribes shall stand on Mount Gerizim to bless the people: Simeon, Levi, Judah, Issachar, Joseph and Benjamin. And these tribes shall stand on Mount Ebal to pronounce curses: Reuben, Gad, Asher, Zebulun, Dan and Naphtali.'* The ceremony itself is described in Joshua 8:30-35, which tells us that the priests brought the ark of the covenant and placed it in the midst of the people.

The setting for this gathering was calculated to reinforce some very important messages. It will help us if we can picture the scene. The people of Israel gathered at Shechem in the valley between two mountains. To the south lay the gentle slopes of Mount Gerizim. Here six tribes stood *'to bless the people'.* To the north was the rugged and broken outcrop of Mount Ebal. Here the six other tribes stood *'to pronounce curses'.*

It has been suggested that the tribes were a silent, symbolic witness to the covenant and that their respective histories recalled both blessing and cursing. The six tribes who stood on Mount Gerizim were descended from the sons of Jacob's two wives, Leah and Rachael. They included Simeon (the second son of Israel), Levi (the priestly tribe), Judah (the tribe from which the Messiah would come), Joseph (the father of Ephraim and Manasseh, and the one who received the double portion due to the firstborn; see 33:13-17) and Benjamin. The six tribes who stood on Mount Ebal were descended from the sons of Jacob's servants, Bilhah and Zilpah. They included Reuben (the firstborn who lost his privileges because of his sin; see Gen. 35:22, 49:4), Gad, Asher, Zebulun, Dan and Naphthali.

Others suggest that the tribes recited aloud the blessings and curses of the covenant similar to those found in Deuteronomy 27-28. No words are prescribed here, so we cannot be sure what the tribes actually said. The curses which follow in 27:14-26 were to be spoken by one tribe only, the Levites. As we read on into the chapters which follow we will come to the substance of the curses and the blessings, but the point that Moses sought to make is that there must be a means whereby the people of God speak to each other about the promises of blessing and the warnings of judgment. Whether by their words, by their actions, or by their mere presence, the tribes of Israel exhorted each other to heed God's warnings and claim his promises. They encouraged each other to be faithful to God and live as his people.

This is what the New Testament calls fellowship or 'speaking the truth in love' (Eph. 4:15). The Scriptures teach us that we cannot live godly lives in isolation from the people of God. We need the strength that comes from being part of God's community. We need to be grafted into the vine, gathered within the sheepfold and connected to the body. Within the community of God's people, we have a responsibility to exhort one another.

See to it, brothers, that none of you has a sinful, unbelieving heart that turns away from the living God. But encourage one another daily, as long as it is called Today, so that none of you may be hardened by sin's deceitfulness... And let us consider how we may spur one another on toward love and good deeds. Let us not give up meeting together, as some are in the habit of doing, but let us encourage one another – and all the more as you see the Day approaching (Heb. 3:12-13; 10:24-25).

By our presence at worship; by our prayers at the prayer meeting; by a letter, a phone call or a quiet word we can encourage others. We too need that encouragement from others.

Hear the curses recited by the Levites (27:14-26)

After all the tribes had proclaimed blessings and curses, the tribe of Levi had a special task (27:14). *'The Levites shall recite to all the people of Israel in a loud voice...'* There then follows a series of twelve curses in 27:15-26, which the Levites were to shout out to the people. An explanation of the consequences of Israel's disobedience will be found at greater length in 28:15-68. But in this communal recitation and response the curses of the covenant are summarised and acknowledged. This list of twelve curses (sometimes called the dodecalogue) is a negative counterpart of the Ten Commandments. It gathered together specific examples of the kind of behaviour with which God was displeased. It might also be thought of as a summary of Moses' preaching in chapters 12-26, highlighting his main pastoral concerns and addressing the pressing moral challenges facing the community.

i. *Idolatry* was a perennial temptation for the Israelites. Perhaps for that reason the first curse in this list (27:15) was upon *'the man who carves an image or casts an idol.* This was a clear violation of the second commandment (5:8-10).

ii. *Family solidarity* was important because the family was the sphere within which spiritual blessings were transmitted from one generation to the next. This is why the fifth commandment required children to honour their parents (5:16). Here in 27:16 the Levites pronounce, *'Cursed is the man who dishonours his father or his mother.'*

iii. One of the recurring concerns in Deuteronomy has been Moses' desire *to protect the needy* in the community from exploitation at the hands of those who were rich and powerful. This is reflected in three of the curses: *'Cursed is the man who moves his neighbour's boundary stone'* (27:17); *'Cursed is the man who leads the blind astray on the road'* (27:18); *'Cursed is the man who withholds justice from the alien, the fatherless or the widow'* (27:19).

iv. *Sexual purity* was an urgent pastoral issue in Israel. The Israelites were under constant pressure to adopt the offensive behaviour of the nations around them. In 27:20-23 four curses warn against actions that violated the seventh commandment (5:18). *'Cursed is the man who sleeps with his father's wife, for he dishonours his father's bed'* (27:20). *'Cursed is the man who has sexual relations with any animal'* (27:21). *'Cursed is the man who sleeps with his sister, the daughter of his father or the daughter of his mother'* (27:22). *'Cursed is the man who sleeps with his mother-in-law'* (27:23).

v. Regard for *the sanctity of human life* was another distinctive feature of Israel's laws which stood out in contrast to the conduct of those who had no fear of God. The sixth commandment (5:17) forbade all forms of unlawful killing. God's attitude towards unlawful killing is reflected in the two curses in 27:24-25. *'Cursed is the man who kills his neighbour secretly'* (27:24). *'Cursed is the man who accepts a bribe to kill an innocent person'* (27:25).

vi. The final curse reminded the Israelites that every one of God's commands was binding on them (27:26). *'Cursed is the man who does not uphold the words of this law by carrying them out.'* If they violated even one command they were law-breakers and, as such, they were subject to God's curse. This is a basic biblical precept (James 2:10). In the New Testament, sin is defined as 'lawlessness' (1 John 3:4). Sin is not an abstract and ill-defined concept. God has shown us the kind of conduct he requires of us (Micah 6:8) and sin is failure to do what God requires. It is, according to the *Westminster Shorter Catechism*, 'any want of conformity unto, or transgression of, the law of God' (answer 14). Sin is not a subjective concept, dependent upon an individual's response to a particular situation. It is objectively defined by God. The person who steps beyond the line which God has drawn is a sinner under the wrath and curse of God.

One of the features of Moses' teaching in Deuteronomy is his application of God's law to the whole of life. As well as governing what a person does in public, the laws of Israel governed his hidden thoughts, motives and actions. These secret sins are rarely, if ever, brought before any earthly judge. The curses which the Levites recited were designed to bring them before the court of human conscience. Two secret sins are specifically mentioned in 27:15 and 27:24. In verses 17, 20-23 and 25, curses are pronounced on activities that tend to be done furtively, such as moving a boundary stone or sexual sin or accepting a bribe. As these curses were read publicly, those who had violated God's commands secretly were reminded that they would face the consequences of their actions before the judge of all the earth.

After each of these curses had been read aloud, the people were to respond with the word 'Amen'. These declarations were not pious platitudes but acknowledgments of personal responsibility before God. By saying 'Amen' the people were praying, 'If I do any of these things, may God's curse fall upon me, just as God has warned.' Yet this is not how we generally pray. In fact, it would be fair to say that these verses (and similar passages in the chapters that follow) are probably amongst the least-loved passages in the Bible. When you go into many Christian bookshops you will find posters, key rings and mugs with encouraging texts printed on them. Yet have you ever bought a key ring to remind you that 'Cursed is the man who does not uphold the words of this law by carrying them out'? We do not readily say 'Amen' to these words.

Yet this is where the gospel begins. Each one of us needs to say 'Amen' to the fact that we are sinners who have rebelled against God and are worthy of eternal death. In Old Testament times even believers were to acknowledge that their sins could have serious consequences. Many Israelites would perish because of their wicked ways (see Ps. 95:10-11; 1 Cor. 10:5; Heb. 3:16-18). The writer of Hebrews applies the same lesson to professing Christians under the New Testament. 'See to it, brothers, that none of you has a sinful, unbelieving heart that turns away from the living God' (Heb. 3:12). We are not to be complacent about disobedience, for the consequences of our sins are serious. Those who stray from God will perish.

On a positive note, we also need to remember that the curses pronounced by the six tribes in 27:13 came from Mount Ebal. That is where the altar for offering sacrifices during the covenant renewal at Shechem was to be located. This is significant. The covenant curse cuts sinners off from God, but God has opened up a way back into his favour. The wages of sin is death, but God has already provided a way of life. That is what Abraham discovered when he went, at God's command, to sacrifice his son Isaac on Mount Moriah. Unknown to Abraham, a ram caught by its horns was waiting there. This animal was to be sacrificed in place of Isaac (Gen. 22:13). In Shechem the Israelites found that on the mountain of cursing God had provided an altar on which sacrifices of atonement were to be offered. By these the covenant curse was to be removed.

The New Testament has an even more amazing story to tell. In Galatians 3:10 Paul quotes from 27:26 to teach us that God cannot simply forget about the sins which we have committed and the curse which he has pronounced on those who broke his law. 'All who rely on observing the law are under a curse, for it is written: "Cursed is everyone who does not continue to do everything written in the Book of the Law."' We cannot be saved from the wrath and curse of God by keeping the law, because we cannot and do not keep the whole law perfectly. When fallen human beings imagine that they will go to heaven because they have lived a good life, they invite God to examine their lives. Just how good have those lives been? God requires absolute perfection; and by his standards we fall far below that which is acceptable in God's sight. Hence, Paul's conclusion in Galatians 3:11: 'Clearly no-one is justified before God by (keeping) the law'.

However, God has opened a way for law-breakers to live. In Galatians 3:13 Paul quotes again from Deuteronomy, this time from 21:23. Here again he refers to the curse. 'Christ redeemed us from the curse of the law by becoming a curse for us, for it is written: "Cursed is everyone who is hung on a tree."' The greatest act of God's mercy was not to ignore the curse of the broken law, but to transfer it from his people to his Son. As he poured out his wrath on Jesus at Calvary, he removed the curse from us.

How then can we escape the curse of God? Only by asking God for mercy and trusting in the One who has already been cursed in our place. God will certainly punish those who rebel against his law, but he will not punish the same sin twice.

God's treasured possession

Payment God cannot twice demand,
First, at the bleeding Surety's hand,
And then again at mine.

Have you said 'Amen' to this promise?

Chapter 28
Blessings and curses

Please read Deuteronomy 28: 1 - 29: 1

Most of us prefer good news to bad news. That is understandable, for good news lifts our spirits while bad news depresses us. This is why many of us prefer to hear the promises of God rather than his warnings. In the past it was the practice of some Christians to dip into a 'promise box' when they needed a spiritual pick-me-up. This contained a selection of Bible verses with precious promises just waiting to be 'claimed'. No doubt those who dipped into the Scriptures in this way had excellent intentions, but their practice cultivated bad habits in handling the Scriptures. Verses were taken out of context and the practice did little to foster an appreciation of the whole message of the Bible. Few people ever gathered a collection of curses and warnings and dipped into these for their spiritual edification! However, in the Bible blessings and curses stand together.

The book of Deuteronomy proclaims a message of good news for the nation of Israel – and for those of us who read it today. The good news for the people of Israel was that God loved them and had chosen them to be his special people. His love was free and undeserved and confirmed in the promises which he had made to their forefathers. In faithfulness to those promises God had delivered them from slavery in Egypt, led them through the wilderness and brought them to the point where they were about to enter the wonderful land of Canaan. God had made a covenant with them and reaffirmed that covenant at Sinai. There God had shown them how they were to walk in a path that led to righteousness and blessing.

This was good news, but there was also bad news. Lots of bad news! The balance between good news and bad news, promise and warning, blessing and cursing is struck in Deuteronomy 28. The good news comes first and is found in the blessings of 28:1-14. However, the bulk of this chapter is devoted to the warnings and curses of 28:15-68. This litany of disasters is almost overwhelming. It makes this one of the most difficult chapters in the Old Testament for the modern reader to read with profit. It would not, however, have taken ancient readers by surprise.

In the ancient world, covenants or treaties between a king and his subjects were quite common and had their own peculiar style. This chapter shares some of those features. When a powerful king was on the rise and establishing his authority over newly-conquered peoples, he made sure that everyone knew where they stood by setting out what was expected of them in the form of a covenant or treaty. That treaty described what would happen if the people obeyed their king and what would happen if they rebelled. Typically, a short summary of the promised benefits would be followed by a lengthy summary of the threatened disasters. The aim was to leave no room for doubt in the minds of those who read the treaty (or more probably heard the treaty being read) that they were now subjects of a very powerful king and that it was in their interests to submit to his rule. The treaty used words to create 'shock and awe' among the population.

In some respects the book of Deuteronomy follows the literary form of these ancient treaties, but it has its own very distinct purpose and message. It was a message about Jehovah – a great king who ruled his people with grace. Moses' aim in

Deuteronomy 28 was to sum up the implications of the law which he expounded in chapters 12 – 26. Some have suggested that the blessings and curses recorded in this chapter were given for the covenant renewal that Moses had commanded the Israelites to observe at Shechem (between Mount Ebal and Mount Gerizim) after they entered Canaan (see 27:2-8, 11-26; also Josh. 8:30-35). They may well have been used for that purpose; but they are recorded in this chapter in connection with the covenant renewal at Moab. There the Israelites renewed their commitment to Jehovah. There they claimed afresh God's promises and committed themselves to obey his law. They rejoiced in God's blessings and trembled before his curses.

God's blessings (28:1-14)

Here is the good news. God has already blessed his people richly and he will continue to bestow his blessing upon them. The following verses summarise the extent and the details of the blessings which God has promised to his people Israel.

i. The promise of God's blessing, (28:1-2)
'The LORD your God will set you high above all the nations on earth.' Moses highlights the generosity of Jehovah towards Israel. He is a God who gives. He has given them his law and he will give (the verb translated 'set' by the NIV is the verb 'to give') them a place of prominence among the nations. This vivid phrase personifies God's blessing and depicts it as seeking, pursuing and overtaking the people of Israel. They did not seek God, but he sought them and overwhelmed them with his mercies. They will have more than they ever expected. In a similar vein, Paul describes the sheer unexpectedness of God's blessing in Ephesians 3:20. We too are encouraged to expect great things from God, for he has promised abundant blessing to his people.

There is, however, a condition to God's promise. *'If you fully obey the LORD your God and carefully follow all his commands that I give you today... All these blessings will come upon you and accompany you if you obey the LORD your God.'* Three things were expected of the Israelites. First, they were to *hear* the preaching of God's law, for through it God spoke to them. The same verb, in a very emphatic form, was also used in the famous appeal of 6:4: 'Hear, O Israel, The LORD our God, the LORD is one.' Before anyone can enter a right relationship with God, they must hear his words, because faith comes through hearing the word (see Rom. 10:14-17). Secondly, they were to *keep* God's law. They were to preserve God's word and pass it on to their children. They were to hold it in reverent awe and resolve to obey it. They were to cultivate right attitudes and regular habits of reading and meditating on God's law. Then, thirdly, they were to *do* what God commanded in his law. The Israelites were not to be passive listeners or theoretical followers only. They were to be activists in the best sense of the word. They were to be men and women whose lives reflected what they had heard.

We should not imagine that Israel's obedience earned the blessings which are set out and promised in the verses which follow. We will see in 30:6 that the ability to obey God proceeds from a 'circumcised heart'; and this is a gift from God. Every blessing which God bestows proceeds from his grace, and his grace redirects the lives of his people into paths of righteousness. God's grace or his undeserved love continues to be the most powerful influence in the lives of God's people today. Grace checks us when we are tempted. Grace warns us when we go astray. Grace also rewards us when we are faithful.

ii. The extent of God's blessing (28:3-6)
From time to time Christians need to be encouraged to count their blessings. In these verses Moses gave the Israelites a brief and memorable summary of the blessings which God had promised to them. Six rhythmical sentences, each beginning

with the word 'blessed', made these lines easy to memorise and repeat. They may have been taught to children and used in family worship; or they may have been recited at larger gatherings of the Israelites, such as the covenant renewal at Moab or Shechem (see 27:12). The Israelites must never allow themselves to forget God's promises.

The promises of 28:3-6 show how God's blessing touched every aspect of the daily lives of the people. *'You will be blessed in the city and blessed in the country... You will be blessed when you come in and blessed when you go out.'* From a modern perspective, the Israelites lived simple lives, dominated by the need to provide food for themselves and their families. They cultivated the ground, they tended their flocks and herds, and they ground grain and baked bread every day. Many people today imagine that this simple rural lifestyle must have been a blissfully happy one. Often it was the reverse. It was one of grindingly hard work, and often fraught with insecurity. When the rains failed, the crops also failed and the livestock perished. There would be no bread on the table and their children would starve. God's promise in 28:4-5 addressed these basic concerns. *'The fruit of your womb will be blessed, and the crops of your land and the young of your livestock – the calves of your herds and the lambs of your flocks. Your basket* (used to gather produce) *and your kneading trough will be blessed.'*

Today, our food supply is much more secure and we tend to take these things for granted. Therefore we need to be encouraged to look upon the simple things of daily life – our children, our work, our meals – as blessings from God. Do we rejoice in God's goodness as we cook an evening meal or go for a walk with our children? The psalmist knew that only a God who is higher than the heavens and who never sleeps could promise such blessing. 'The LORD watches over you – the LORD is your shade at your right hand; the sun will not harm you by day, nor the moon by night. The LORD will keep you from all harm – he will watch over your life; the LORD will watch over your coming and going both now and for evermore' (Ps. 121:5-8).

iii. The details of God's blessing (28:7-13)
After the poetic summary of Israel's blessings in 28:3-6, Moses describes these and other blessings in greater detail.

The passage begins and ends with promises of *military and political blessings* (28:7, 13).

> *The LORD will grant that the enemies who rise up against you will be defeated before you. They will come at you from one direction but flee from you in seven... The LORD will make you the head, not the tail. If you pay attention to the commands of the LORD your God that I give you this day and carefully follow them, you will always be at the top, never at the bottom.*

This was a timely promise, as the Israelites were just about to enter the land of Canaan, where they would meet strong enemies. In the strength that God supplied, the Israelites would overpower these enemies and enjoy supremacy in their region. They would possess the promised land and dwell securely in it. God's promise addressed the needs of the moment.

The next set of promises held out *economic and agricultural blessings* (28:8, 11-12).

> *The LORD will send a blessing on your barns and on everything you put your hand to. The LORD your God will bless you in the land he is giving you... The LORD will open the heavens, the storehouse of his bounty, to send rain on your land in season and to bless all the work of your hands.*

The land which God gave to the Israelites was fertile and would give a rich return for their labours. As a result of these natural blessings, the people of Israel would prosper and find themselves in a position where they could lend to the nations. *'You will lend to many nations but will borrow from none.'* Interest rates in the ancient world were often exorbitant, and debt was a crippling burden. Because of her prosperity, Israel would be able to avoid this snare and enjoy a significant measure of independence and prestige amongst the nations.

At the heart of this passage is the greatest promise of all, the promise of *spiritual blessing* (28:9-10). *'The LORD will establish you as his holy people, as he promised you on oath...'* Israel's spiritual blessings will mark her out as unique amongst the nations. The people of Israel were holy because the Lord had chosen them to be his own and set them apart from other nations. His solemn declaration confirmed their unique status (see 7:6; 14:2, 21). Holiness is promised to them as a blessing from God (see 26:19). The Israelites would need to learn that holiness is a way of living, not a mere title given to the covenant people. They would also need to learn that holiness is not a burdensome duty, but the greatest of God's blessings. This is a lesson we struggle to comprehend today. Yet Robert Murray McCheyne was able to say that what promoted holiness in his life also promoted true happiness. This is an attitude which God gives us when the Spirit of holiness dwells within.

> Blessed is the man
> who does not walk in the counsel of the wicked...
> but his delight is in the law of the Lord
> and on his law he meditates day and night.
> (Psalm1:1-2)

When God blesses his people, he makes a powerful statement to the surrounding nations (28:10). *'Then all the peoples on earth will see that you are called by the name of the LORD, and they will fear you.'* When God's people are established as holy, they are placed like lamps on a lampstand so that others might see their light. Moses has described Israel's example to the nations in 4:6-8. When the Israelites obey God's commands, the nations will look on in amazement and comment on it. Not only will they be amazed, they will fear. True holiness can be unnerving and intimidating to sinful people, because it exposes their sinfulness and the emptiness of man-made religion. Simon Peter fell on his knees before Jesus and pleaded, 'Go away from me, Lord; I am a sinful man!' (Luke 5:8). When the holiness of the living God dwells in the lives of redeemed people, it has a similar effect on others. When Jesus came among the Gadarenes and healed the demon-possessed man, the pagans of the region were terrified at what had taken place asked Jesus to leave them (Mark 5:17).

Israel's holiness was simply a reflection of the holiness of Jehovah. Yet that made them God's witnesses to a fallen world (see Isa. 43:10). That is the church's calling today (see Acts 1:8). Ours is the privilege of speaking about Jesus Christ and proclaiming his gospel. Underlying that verbal proclamation must also be the visual proclamation of holy lives.

God's Warnings (28:15-68)

And now for the bad news – God's warnings to his own redeemed people. After recounting the blessings which God had promised to those who followed God's commands, Moses described what would happen if the Israelites did not obey the Lord their God. *'However, if you do not obey the LORD your God and do not carefully follow all his commands and decrees I am giving you today, all these curses will come upon you and overtake you...'* In 28:16-19 Moses reversed the language of 28:3-6.

> *You will be cursed in the city and cursed in the country.*
> *Your basket and your kneading trough will be cursed.*
> *The fruit of your womb will be cursed, and the crops of your land, and the calves of your herds and the lambs of your flocks.*

Blessings and curses

*You will be cursed when you come in and cursed when you
go out.*

Just as God intended to make his promises memorable, so he
intended to make his warnings memorable as a check upon
the sinful tendencies of his people. Every sphere of their lives
would be blighted if they were disobedient and turned away
from Jehovah.

Moses highlights the fact that there will be no escape from God's
rebuke in 28:15, where he says that the curses of these verses
will pursue and overtake the Israelites. The same verb is used in
28:2 to describe the blessings which overtake Israel, and again
in 28:45 to describe the curses which pursue her. It is a vivid
expression. In Genesis 31:25 it describes Laban pursuing Jacob
and in Exodus 14:9 it describes the Egyptian chariots as they
bore down on the terrified Israelites. God's warnings are not
idle threats. His justice is dynamic, as the prophet Zechariah
saw in his vision of a flying scroll thirty feet long and fifteen feet
wide. 'This is the curse that is going out over the whole land;
for according to what it says on one side, every thief will be
banished, and according to what it says on the other, everyone
who swears falsely will be banished' (Zech. 5:3). This flying scroll
will be sent by God to 'visit' the wrong-doer. There is no escape
from divine justice. We are warned that our sin will find us out.

This awesome and soul-searching message was explained at
some length by Moses in 28:20-68 as he applied it prophetically
to the nation of Israel. His whole discourse is permeated by an
intense desire to prevent the nation of Israel from falling into
unbelief. There is much detail, and even repetition, in these
verses, but one point is clear – the Israelites will not prosper
if they forsake Jehovah. Each new section describes how the
Israelites will be reduced to a new level of distress, until they
reach a tragic climax in 28:68. This was a difficult message for
Moses to preach, because he loved the people whom he had led

for forty years and longed for their salvation even when they fell into serious sin (see Exod.32:11-14). Yet Moses did not flinch from preaching a hard truth. Just as Robert Murray McCheyne preached about hell with tears in his eyes, so Moses preached about the curses which would fall upon the Israelites and warned them to flee from the wrath to come.

Let's note five stages in Moses' warnings in 28:20-68.

i. Distress (28:20-26)
'The LORD will send on you curses, confusion and rebuke in everything you put your hand to, until you are destroyed and come to sudden ruin because of the evil you have done in forsaking him.' In particular, Moses introduces three tragic scenarios, to which he will return again and again throughout the chapter – disease drought and defeat. In 28:21-22 he lists a string of extremely unpleasant diseases, some of which are hard to identify with medical precision today.

> *The LORD will plague you with diseases until he has destroyed you from the land you are entering to possess. The LORD will strike you with wasting disease, with fever and inflammation, with scorching heat and drought, with blight and mildew, which will plague you until you perish.*

Their combined effect was to cause the Israelites to perish. In 28:23-24 he describes the cruel impact of drought when the sun would burn ferociously in the sky and the soil would become as hard as clay fired in a kiln. *'The sky over your head will be bronze, the ground beneath you iron.'* Here, too, the result is that the Israelites will be destroyed. *'The LORD will turn the rain of your country into dust and powder; it will come down from the skies until you are destroyed.'* In 28:25 he holds out the prospect of total and ignominious defeat at the hand of their enemies. *'You will come at them from one direction but, flee from them in seven.'*

Compare this with the days when Jehovah gave them decisive victories over their enemies (see 28:7).

These tragic reversals of Israel's fortune indicate the removal of God's blessing because Israel has violated the covenant. Note that the Lord himself would send the plagues and strike the land and cause them to be defeated in battle. The Lord will abide by the terms of the covenant had made with Abraham. In 28:26 Moses recalls the covenant ratification ceremony of Genesis 15:9-11, where Abraham brought a heifer, a goat and a ram as well as a dove and a young pigeon to the Lord, cut their carcasses in two and arranged them opposite each other. This was a way of saying, 'May such terrible things happen to me and my descendants if we are unfaithful to God'. He hoped it would only be a symbol and a warning, so he drove away the birds of prey lest they consume the carcasses completely. Yet this destruction would indeed fall upon the people of Israel. '*Your carcasses will be food for all the birds of the air and the beasts of the earth, and there will be no-one to frighten them away.*' There will be no-one to make intercession for the Israelites at that time when God's wrath is about to fall upon them. Their distress will be self-inflicted and tragically predictable.

God warns us that 'the wages of sin is death' (Rom. 6:23). God will deal with those who disobey him just as he has said. God's justice ought not to take us by surprise. Yet it will take many by surprise because they suppress these unpopular truths which trouble their consciences.

ii. Despair (28:27-37)
In this section Moses returns to the disasters which he has described in the previous verses. In 28:27 and 35, Moses describes the painful illnesses which will afflict them. '*The LORD will afflict you with the boils of Egypt and with tumours, festering sores and the itch, from which you cannot be cured... The LORD will afflict your knees and legs with painful boils that cannot be cured, spreading*

from the soles of your feet to the top of your head.' In 28:36a he holds out the prospect of military defeat and expulsion from the land. *'The LORD will drive you and the king you set over you to a nation unknown to you or your fathers.'* The root cause of their problem is idolatry. Yet the worship of foreign gods in a foreign land will become their punishment. *'There you will worship other gods, gods of wood and stone.'*

A new dimension to their distress appears in 28:30-33 – the so called 'futility curses'. *'You will be pledged to be married to a woman, but another will take her and ravish her. You will build a house, but you will not live in it. You will plant a vineyard, but you will not even begin to enjoy it.'* These are unnatural and unexpected outcomes which, if Israel had loved and obeyed Jehovah, should never have happened. The laws of Deuteronomy 20:5-7, 22:23-24, 28-29 sought to prevent these outcomes in a well-ordered covenant community.

However, when Israel violates her covenant with Jehovah nothing works as it should.

> *Your ox will be slaughtered before your eyes, but you will eat none of it. Your donkey will be forcibly taken from you and will not be returned. Your sheep will be given to your enemies, and no-one will rescue them. Your sons and daughters will be given to another nation, and you will wear out your eyes watching for them day after day, powerless to lift a hand. A people that you do not know will eat what your land and labour produce, and you will have nothing but cruel oppression all your days.*

This is what the Bible calls vanity or futility (see Ecc. 1:2; Rom. 8:20; Eph. 4:17). God has made everything to serve his good purposes, but human sin turns those purposes on their head and forfeits the blessing that could be enjoyed. Yet so long as we live in the midst of God's creation, the good things which God offers to us, and which we desire, remain tantalizingly close, but beyond our grasp.

I can think of a friend who was expelled from his home in the north of Cyprus following the Turkish invasion in 1974. His family home was less than a mile from the boundary which divided the island, and clearly visible from the Greek Cypriot side. It was so close, yet totally inaccessible. In 28:34 Moses describes the effects of Israel's frustration. *'The sights you see will drive you mad.'*

The characteristic theme of this section is the psychological effect of Israel's physical distress (28:28). *'The Lord will afflict you with madness, blindness and confusion of mind.'* In Zechariah 12:4 these words describe the panic which will come upon Israel's enemies. Here they describe Israel's fate. Israel will become like a blind man groping about in the middle of the day because he cannot see where he is going. This blindness is worse than physical blindness. It is an inability to see where God's purposes are leading and an unwillingness to look to God for guidance. For such there is no hope, no light on the horizon. They can see no saviour coming to help them.

The tragedy of this state of mind is that it is self-inflicted. It is the result of a steadfast refusal to see the light of God's truth and grace. Jesus described the condition of those who refused to enter his kingdom or acknowledge him, when he came as the Saviour of the world. 'Light has come into the world, but men loved darkness instead of light because their deeds were evil' (John 3:19). 'The eye is the lamp of the body. If your eyes are good, your whole body will be full of light. But if your eyes are bad, your whole body will be full of darkness. If then the light within you is darkness, how great is that darkness!' (Matt. 6:22-23). Sin pollutes everything, including the way our minds and emotions work. That is why fallen sinners need not only to be saved from guilt and death but also transformed by the renewing of their minds (Rom. 12:2).

iii. Disaster (28:38-48)

Here Moses describes what will happen to Israel's agriculturally-based economy should God withdraw his blessing. A string of natural disasters would devastate the land.

> *You will sow much seed in the field but you will harvest little, because locusts will devour it. You will plant vineyards and cultivate them but you will not drink the wine or gather the grapes, because worms will eat them. You will have olive trees throughout your country but you will not use the oil, because the olives will drop off.*

As a result of these disasters Israel will become weakened and lose status in the eyes of their neighbours (28:43-44). *'The alien who lives among you will rise above you higher and higher, but you will sink lower and lower. He will lend to you, but you will not lend to him. He will be the head, but you will be the tail.'* The aliens described here are the remnants of the Canaanites whom the Israelites ought to have purged from the land. Instead, they will prosper at Israel's expense and their prosperity will be Israel's disgrace. This is the opposite of the blessing promised in 28:12-13.

In 28:45-48 Moses summarises his message thus far. *'All these curses will come upon you... because you did not serve the LORD your God joyfully and gladly in the time of prosperity...'* God wanted willing obedience from his people. After all, he had loved them, delivered them from slavery and promised them the earth. Was it asking too much that they should devote themselves to him? God wanted the Israelites to serve him with a smile on their faces, yet too quickly their religion became a mechanical affair whereby they did the right thing in order to get the desired result. At times they even did the wrong thing if they thought that another god would offer them a better deal. The painful curses which would fall upon Israel 'will be a sign and a wonder to you and your descendants for ever'. They would be a reminder that Israel was not free to shop around in the religious supermarket in order to find a better god. Israel belonged to Jehovah; and if she ever forgot that fact, hunger and thirst, nakedness and poverty were the rods that Jehovah would use to drive her back to him. *'Therefore ... you will serve the enemies the LORD sends against you. He will put an iron yoke on your neck until he has destroyed you.'*

What a contrast between the happy service of 28:47 and the iron yoke of 28:48! Who would reject the former and choose the latter? Yet that is what many Israelites did. It is also what many people do today. Like Saul of Tarsus in his pre-conversion days, they kick against the goads of gospel truth (Acts 26:14) and reject the salvation that is freely offered to them. The natural disasters which we see on our news bulletins remind us that God will not allow mankind to reject him and shop around for a better option. Everlasting destruction will be the fate of those who persist in this path.

iv. Disintegration (28:49-57)

From 28:49 onwards the instruments of Israel's humiliation will no longer be the Canaanites in their midst, but *'a nation ... from far away, from the ends of the earth, like an eagle swooping down, a nation whose language you will not understand'.* When this *'fierce-looking nation'* invades it will *'devour the young of your livestock and the crops of your land until you are destroyed. They will leave you no grain, new wine or oil, nor any calves of herds or lambs of your flocks until you are ruined'* (28:51). In other words, they will destroy the basic fabric of life, depriving Israel of her daily food. They will also destroy Israel's military defences (28:52). *'They will lay siege to all the cities throughout your land until the high fortified walls in which you trust fall down. They will besiege all the cities throughout the land the LORD your God is giving you.'* Sadly, the Israelites would come to rely on these blessings rather than on the Lord who gave them. They no longer looked upon the Lord as their tower of refuge (see Ps. 18:2, Prov. 18:10).

Even more alarming than the disintegration of Israel's national infrastructure would be the disintegration of her moral and social cohesion. In 28:53-57 Moses describes some of the atrocities which would take place when their cities were besieged. His account makes our flesh creep. *'Because of the suffering that your enemy will inflict on you during the siege, you will eat the fruit of the womb, the flesh of the sons and daughters the LORD your God has given you.'* No-one will escape the degrading and brutalising effects of Israel's tragedy. *'Even the most gentle and sensitive man among you will have no compassion on his own brother... The most gentle and sensitive woman among you – so sensitive and gentle that she would not venture to touch the ground with the sole of her foot...'* Ancient streets were squalid dumping-grounds for household refuse, but the well-to-do could avoid the squalor by riding in a carriage or being carried on a palanquin. Yet when their very survival demanded it, even the wealthy were willing to get their feet and hands dirty in order to provide food for their stomachs. She will *'begrudge the husband she loves and her own son or daughter the afterbirth from her womb and the children she bears.'* What a repulsive meal! It is hard to tell what was more offensive in these actions: the cannibalism, or the selfish disregard for family members. A community that sinks to this has plumbed new depths of moral depravity and social disintegration. These things actually happened in the unfolding tragedy of Israel's departure from Jehovah (see 2 Kings 6:28; Lam. 2:20; 4:10).

v. Destruction (28:58-68)
The Israelites must have been startled when they heard Moses speak these words. He foretells in graphic details the horrors of the removal of the covenant people from the promised land.

Blessings and curses

This happened many centuries later and was the undoing of everything Moses longed for in Deuteronomy. As well as bringing upon the people all the illnesses mentioned in previous verses (see 28:59), the Lord *'will bring upon you all the diseases of Egypt that you dreaded'.* They will take the place of the Egyptians in the drama of the exodus and they will be fatally weakened by this series of plagues. They will enter a new captivity (28:61). *'The LORD will also bring on you every kind of sickness and disaster not recorded in this Book of the Law, until you are destroyed.'* They will be reduced to a numerically insignificant remnant (28:62), for it will please the Lord to *'ruin and destroy'* them (28:63). Then in 28:63 the Israelites heard words that would have shocked them as they stood expectantly on the plains of Moab. *'You will be uprooted from the land you are entering to possess.'*

Could that really happen? How could God take any pleasure in the destruction of his chosen people? Many centuries later the prophet Ezekiel would reassure the exiles of Judah that the Lord takes no pleasure even in the death of the wicked! See Ezekiel 33:11. We should never think of the Lord as one who is malicious or gleeful in the administration of his judgments. Nothing could be further from the truth. However, he will not recoil from doing what is right and just – even though that involves visiting his people with judgment. If he did not spare his own Son, but delivered him up for us all when he bore the sins of mankind (see Rom. 8:32) he will not spare Israel – or the church – when the time for judgment comes. In fact, God's righteous judgment begins with the church (see 1 Peter 4:17).

In 28:64-68 Moses describes prophetically what God's judgment on Israel would look and feel like. *'Then the LORD will scatter you among all nations, from one end of the earth to the other. There you will worship other gods – gods of wood and stone, which neither you nor your fathers have known.'* The exile would be a deeply traumatic experience for the people of Israel. The physical trials of defeat and dislocation would give way to centuries of anxiety and soul searching. *'There the LORD will give you an anxious mind, eyes weary with longing, and a despairing heart.'* Many would be tempted to think that God had turned his back on his people for ever (see Amos 8:11-12).

From our historical vantage-point we know that the exiles of Israel went to Assyria and Babylon. Only a few went to Egypt. Yet Egypt loomed large in Moses' mind when warned the Israelites, *'The LORD will send you back in ships to Egypt on a journey I said you should never make again'.* This is what we would expect from someone living in Moses' day, when the humiliations of Egypt were still fresh in the collective memory of the Israelites. They had no desire to return to their unredeemed state in the land of slavery. Yet even worse humiliations awaited them should they forsake the Lord their God. *'There you will offer yourselves for sale to your enemies as male and female slaves, but no-one will buy you.'* At least Pharaoh had needed and wanted the services of his Israelite slaves (see Exod. 14:5). In the day of their desolation they will be without work, identity or dignity. At this point only Jehovah would love them or desire them. There would be no other god who was willing to pay anything for such worthless slaves.

The point that Moses wanted the Israelites of his day to understand was that Jehovah had already redeemed them from slavery and that they were precious to him. So precious, in fact, that he had made them his precious possession and he wanted them to love and serve him all their days. From the vantage-point of the cross we know that God loved Israel, and his New Testament Israel, so much that he was willing to pay the ultimate price to redeem them from the consequences of their sin and rebellion. That price was the life of the Lamb of God, his own precious Son (see 1 Peter 1:18-19; John 3:16).

In an amazing turn of events, this point was brought home to a servant girl in the home of Lady Huntingdon, a friend of the great preacher George Whitefield. Lady Huntingdon had invited Whitefield to preach to a group of her aristocratic friends. They were shocked by a throwaway comment of Whitefield, when he said that Jesus was willing to take 'even the devil's castaways'. Yet a poor servant girl who happened to be listening to the sermon was arrested by the phrase. She reasoned that if Jesus would take 'even the devil's castaways', he would take her, miserable sinner that she was. Before we can appreciate the redeeming power of that love we must come to see and acknowledge our miserable condition as sinners who have turned away from God and are suffering the consequences.

Conclusion

The combination of curses and blessings which we find in this chapter continues into the New Testament. In the gospel of Matthew we find both blessings (or beatitudes, as they are often called, in Matt. 5:3-12) and curses (the series of woes which our Lord pronounced on those who rejected him as Messiah in Matthew 23). In the big picture of God's plan of salvation, mercy triumphs over judgment because the Lord Jesus came to undo the curse and restore the fallen people of Israel. Deuteronomy 28 provides us with the background information which we need to understand what he did and why he suffered on the cross. The devastation which hung over disobedient Israel explains the desolation which came upon Jesus at Calvary. There he became a 'thing of horror and an object of scorn and ridicule to all the nations' (28:37). There he cried out in pain and shame, 'My God, my God, why have you forsaken me?' (Matt. 27:46). His atoning work creates a new world, from which the curse of sin will be removed forever (see Rev. 21:4; 22:3).

Chapter 29
Looking back and looking forward

Please read Deuteronomy 29: 1-29

Some preachers are granted the opportunity of knowing that a particular sermon may well be their last. As his health was failing, a veteran preacher decided to preach one final sermon. He chose 2 Corinthians 13:14 as his text: 'May the grace of the Lord Jesus Christ, and the love of God, and the fellowship of the Holy Spirit be with you all.' He had pronounced this apostolic blessing at the close of over three thousand worship services which he had led during his years in ministry. It was fitting that he concluded his preaching ministry expounding this portion of Scripture.

When the apostle Paul addressed the elders of the Ephesian church in Acts 20:17-38, he believed that he might never see them again (see verses 25, 38). This was going to be his final opportunity to speak to them. Although Paul may have been mistaken in this belief, it energised him to speak with great urgency about the central emphases of his ministry. 'I consider my life worth nothing to me, if only I may finish the race and complete the task the Lord Jesus has given me – the task of testifying to the gospel of God's grace... I have not hesitated to proclaim to you the whole will of God... so be on your guard! Remember that for three years I never stopped warning each of you night and day with tears' (Acts 20:24, 27, 31). The forthrightness which characterised Paul's address to the Ephesian elders is also evident in Moses' final sermon in Deuteronomy 29 and 30.

This is the final sermon in a series of three covenant-renewal addresses preached by Moses shortly before his death in the land of Moab. The first of these sermons (chapters 1 – 4) was predominantly historical. The second sermon (chapters 5 – 26, 28) was predominantly an exposition of the law and its significance. The third sermon (chapters 29 – 30) recaps all that has gone before and is evangelistic in its tone. The warnings of chapter 29 and the urgent appeals of chapter 30 are the climax of the whole book of Deuteronomy. The renewal of Israel's covenant with Jehovah was not merely a national event with priests and elders as the main participants. Each and every Israelite was called to choose Jehovah as their Lord and serve him with all their being.

Moses addressed the Israelites on the plains of Moab (29:1). *'These are the terms of the covenant the LORD commanded Moses to make with the Israelites in Moab, in addition to the covenant he had made with them at Horeb.'* The significance of this verse has long been a matter of debate. In the Hebrew Bible this is numbered as 28:69, suggesting that it is a summary and conclusion of that chapter, and indeed the whole of Moses' second sermon, which expounded the laws of Israel and their significance. There is, however, a marked similarity between this verse and 1:1 and 4:44-45, which introduce Moses' first and second sermons. This suggests that 29:1 actually opens Moses' third and final sermon, which is a brief and final exposition of God's covenant with Israel. This seems to be confirmed by the reference to 'the terms of this covenant' in 29:9 – picking up the reference in 29:1. The focus of this final sermon is not the details of Israel's laws, which were given at Sinai and restated in Moses' second sermon in Deuteronomy. Instead, it summarises all that God had graciously done for Israel and the whole-hearted response which God sought from his covenant people.

Looking back and looking forward

The preamble to the covenant (29:2-8)

Moses loved to tell the old, old story of Israel and her Lord. It is a story which the Israelites knew and loved, but it was worth telling again. At the beginning of the story, Israel is in bondage in Egypt; but by the story's end the Israelites are on the verge of entering the promised land.

This story tells *God's mighty acts* at the time of the exodus (29:2-3). *'With your own eyes you saw those great trials, those miraculous signs and great wonders.'* The miraculous plagues which fell upon Egypt, culminating in the death of the firstborn and followed by Israel's passage through the Red Sea, demonstrated God's great power and how he broke Egypt's iron grip upon the Israelites. Only a powerful God could deliver his people from such a predicament. In the New Testament, Jesus Christ is similarly shown to be God's Son and the Saviour of mankind by 'miracles, wonders and signs' (see Acts 2:22; Heb. 2:4). We are to pay careful attention to these mighty acts, for they are part of *our* story of salvation.

In Pharaoh's case, these mighty miracles were also *'trials'* which tested the character of his heart (see also 4:34; 7:19). They showed just how stubborn he was in resisting God. He preferred to destroy his country and even himself, rather than submit to God's word. Before we point the finger at Pharaoh, it is right and proper for us to recognise that God's mighty deeds also test us. When they are set before us they are meant to evoke a response of reverence, adoration and trust. Do they? Or have they become just another ancient fable?

This story also tells of *God's miraculous provision* in the wilderness (29:5-6). *'During the forty years that I led you through the desert, your clothes did not wear out, nor did the sandals on your feet. You ate no bread and drank no wine or other fermented drink.'* The Israelites did, of course, eat manna during their years in the wilderness. Moses' point was that they did not eat bread prepared by human hands. They drank water from the rock (8:15); but they did not drink wine or any other drink that they themselves had prepared. To highlight the fact that God himself provided all these basic necessities, Moses records the very words that Jehovah had spoken to the Israelites. *'I did this so that you might know that I am the LORD your God.'* Only Jehovah could have made such an abundant provision in the wilderness (see Ps. 78:23-25).

This story also recounts *God's military conquest* of the Amorite kingdoms east of the Jordan (29:7-8). *'When you reached this place, Sihon king of Heshbon and Og king of Bashan came out to fight against us, but we defeated them. We took their land and gave it as an inheritance to the Reubenites, the Gadites and the half-tribe of Manasseh.'* Needless to say, the Israelites did not conquer these kingdoms in their own strength. God handed these kingdoms over to them as a foretaste of the blessings yet to be enjoyed west of the Jordan, in Canaan itself.

This story of God's goodness to Israel, in all its many aspects, set the scene for Moses' appeal to the Israelites and sought to motivate their response. God's mercies had been freely given and lavishly bestowed on his chosen people. Obedience was to be Israel's response. In spite of everything that had happened, the Israelites so often failed to recognise that it was Jehovah who had blessed them. Moses introduces this sobering thought in the very heart of his story (29:4). *'But to this day the LORD has not given you a mind that understands or eyes that see or ears that hear.'* This explains why they murmured against Moses and against the Lord so often during their wilderness journey. It also explains why they had set up golden calves and given them the credit for their deliverance from Egypt (Exod. 32:8). In years to come, the Israelites would turn to many other gods because their eyes failed to see how much Jehovah had done for them (see Isa. 6:9-10).

Moses explained that Israel's spiritual blindness and foolishness was a consequence of *God* not giving them a mind that could understand or eyes that could see. This was not an attempt to blame God for Israel's actions. After all, Moses had warned the Israelites that God would hold them accountable for the choices which they freely made and that God most certainly did not force them to serve idols. The point that Moses sought to make in this verse was that spiritual insight is a gift from God and that until God gives this gift, all people will walk in spiritual darkness.

Paul saw the same spiritual blindness in the Israelites of his own day. 'Their minds were made dull, for to this day the same veil remains when the old covenant is read. It has not been removed, because only in Christ is it taken away' (2 Cor. 3:14). Elsewhere, Paul wrote to tell the Corinthians that Jesus Christ is the source of spiritual wisdom (1 Cor. 1:30). Only when he sends forth his Spirit can we see our fallen condition and God's wonderful provision. Without that work, the Israelites could not learn the lessons that God was teaching them in the wilderness. Nor could they recognise the promised Messiah when he came to them (see John 1:11; 5:39-40). Nor can we appreciate or appropriate the grace of God offered in the gospel of Jesus Christ without that work of the Holy Spirit. 'The god of this world has blinded the minds of unbelievers, so that they cannot see the light of the gospel...' (2 Cor. 4:4). We can see in the stubbornness and rebellion of the Israelites just how deep that darkness is. Yet we can praise God that Jesus Christ is the light of the world, whose light shines even into that darkness (see John 1:4, 9; 8:12).

The parties to the covenant (29:9-15)

After tracing the story of their salvation thus far, Moses addressed the people who were standing before him on that day in Moab when the Israelites renewed their walk with God. He told them what God expected of them (29:9). *'Carefully follow the terms of this covenant, so that you may prosper in everything you do.'* Moses' purpose in chapters 29 and 30 is to summarise 'the terms of the covenant' so that Israel might live and proper as the people of God. The law was a means to an end. The end was that the Israelites would love Jehovah with all their hearts. The prosperity promised here is spiritual and moral as well as material, for the verb which Moses uses is commonly used to describe the wisdom which God gives to those who fear him. It is found in David's final charge to Solomon just as he was about to become king (see 1 Kings 2:3). Solomon, of course, was known for his wisdom; and that wisdom was a gift from God.

In the verses which follow Moses describes the two parties to the covenant and some of their outstanding qualities.

i. Israel's diversity
Moses addressed the whole nation of Israel, listing in 29:10-11 the different types of people who were part of the covenant community. Here we see Israel's diversity.

> *All of you are standing today in the presence of the LORD your God – your leaders and chief men, your elders and officials, and all the other men of Israel, together with your children and your wives, and the aliens living in your camps who chop your wood and carry your water.*

It is significant that Moses includes in this list the people who were often overlooked as unimportant as well as the leaders, tribal chiefs and public servants. Women and children are mentioned as well as the men; foreigners like the Gibeonites, who performed menial tasks (see Josh 9:21, 23, 27) are mentioned alongside the established families in Israel.

Moses' list reminds us that a similar diversity is found within the New Testament church. This, too, is an extended family united in covenant with God. The metaphor of the human body with its many parts, each possessing different levels of honour, is used to describe the church. 'We have different gifts according to the grace given us...' (see Rom. 12:6-8). In our congregations some will preach and administer the sacraments, others will serve as elders or deacons or members of the property committee, while others will make tea, stack chairs, sweep the floor, greet visitors or drive the minibus. There are many modern-day equivalents of wood-choppers and water-carriers. Yet everyone in God's house stands in the presence of the covenant Lord. What a privilege! He values our service, but more importantly, he seeks our fellowship.

ii. God's faithfulness
The faithfulness of the covenant Lord is affirmed in 29:12-13.

> *You are standing here in order to enter into a covenant with the LORD your God, a covenant the LORD is making with you this day and sealing with an oath, to confirm you this day as his people, that he may be your God as he promised you and as he swore to your fathers, Abraham, Isaac and Jacob.*

The Israelites were standing in the presence of their Lord, just as soldiers stand to attention when they are on parade before their commanding officer. That is the significance of the word 'standing' here and in 29:10. What an awesome privilege is theirs! They stand in God's presence so that they might 'enter into' a covenant with him. The same verb has also been used to describe the Israelites as they crossed the River Jordan and entered into the promised land. Their covenant relationship with Jehovah was just as real as the pastures and vineyards and olive groves of Canaan. This covenant had been made with their ancestors 'Abraham, Isaac and Jacob'; and now it was being confirmed with them. Jehovah assured them that they would be 'his people' and he would be their God.

Jehovah was the other party to the covenant. Indeed without his gracious initiative there would have been no covenant. Because of his faithfulness Israel can stand before him with hope and confidence. At Sinai, when the Israelites 'heard the voice out of the darkness' they feared lest they would be consumed by the holiness of God (see 5:23-26); but now, through Moses the mediator of the old covenant, they are able to stand in God's presence and live. Today, we have a better mediator than Moses. Jesus Christ is the mediator of a new covenant (see Heb. 9:15; 12:24). Through him we gain blessed access to our heavenly Father (see Rom. 5:2; Heb.10:19-22). For the Christian believer, God is no longer a distant, terrifying deity. He has sought us out and drawn us to himself. He is our covenant partner. When we are assured of this fact there ought to be a wonderful freshness in our walk with God.

God's faithfulness extended not only to that generation which stood before him in Moab, but to the generations which followed them (29:14-15). *'I am making this covenant, with its oath, not only with you who are standing here with us today in the presence of the LORD our God but also with those who are not here today.'* Children still unborn would live in the land of promise and enjoy the blessings of fellowship with the living God because Jehovah is faithful to his promises. Those who enjoy his mercies are also bound by his covenant; so those children would also be bound by 'the terms of this covenant'. They would be called to give an account of how they responded to God's word and obeyed God's law. When Jehovah gave his law to Israel he commanded fathers to teach his laws to their children 'so that the next generation would know them, even the children yet to be born, and they in turn would tell their children. Then they would put their trust in God and would not forget his deeds but would keep his commands' (Ps. 78:5-7).

Many centuries later, in the New Testament, we find that God's faithfulness continues undiminished. We read of believers like

Timothy who were children of the covenant (2 Tim. 1:5; 3:14-15) and the Galatians who were 'children of promise' (Gal. 4:28). Upon them came the fullness of God's promises in Christ and they in turn were to pass on what they had received to others (see 2 Tim 2:2). It is a great joy to see saving faith in the hearts of our spiritual children, but our first responsibility is to teach God's word to our physical children, our own 'flesh and blood'. These 'children of the covenant' enjoy real blessing and carry a heightened responsibility to seek the Lord so that they might serve him.

The problems which threatened the covenant (29:16-21)

The covenant between God and Israel required total commitment from both parties. There was never any question about God's love for Israel, but there were very real questions hanging over Israel's commitment to serve the Lord and him alone. Idolatry was Israel's perennial Achilles' heel. Moses had warned against it in 4:15-19 and 13:1-18 and he returned to Israel's track record in 29:16. *'You yourselves know how we lived in Egypt and how we passed through the countries on the way here. You saw among them their detestable images and idols of wood and stone, of silver and gold.'*

Clearly, this was not a new temptation. When the Israelites left Egypt they had taken with them some of the religious practices of that land. Even after the severe rebuke which they received after the incident at Sinai when they worshipped a golden calf (see Exod. 32:1-33:6), they clung to their idols and even carried them into the land of Canaan. There Joshua, towards the end of his life, challenged them to throw away those gods of Egypt (Josh 24:14). As they journeyed through the wilderness they picked up new 'gods' from the desert tribes and the nations east of the Dead Sea (29:17). *'You saw among them their detestable* (the same word is used in Daniel 11:31; 12:11 to describe 'the abomination which causes desolation' that would be set up in the temple) *images and idols of wood and stone, of silver and gold.*' An unusual Hebrew word is used to describe these idols. They are depicted as shapeless and lifeless blocks of wood. Isaiah would later employ sarcasm to describe the futility of such wooden idols in Isaiah 44:9-20. Here in 29:17 Moses emphasises the offensiveness of such idols.

The temptations which faced Israel in Egypt and in the wilderness were not going to disappear any time soon. So in 29:18 Moses addressed the challenge of 'today'. *'Make sure there is no man or woman, clan or tribe among you today whose heart turns away from the LORD our God to go and worship the gods of those nations...*' Idolatry was a sin which continued to tempt the covenant people at every level. Individuals were tempted to turn away from the living God. Families were tempted to set up idols shrines in their homes, at which children would see their parents praying to false gods. At times of national crisis whole tribes, and even the Israelite nation as a whole, might well turn to false gods for help and transfer their allegiance to them.

Most dangerous of all was the person who set up an idol secretly (27:15) and enticed others to join him in worshipping it (13:6). This is described in 29:18b as a *'root among you that produces such bitter poison.'* The idolatry of the Egyptians and the Canaanites also produced bitter fruit (32:32), but it was done openly so that everyone could recognise it for what it was. Secret idolatry amongst the Israelites spread unseen like a long underground root whose shoots spring up where one least expects them. From hidden idolatry there would spring an array of other sins as diverse as they were ugly – sexual immorality, violence, dishonesty and unbelief.

Even though few people today are going to be tempted to set up idols of Molech or Baal, the same bitter root spreads its influence today. The writer to the Hebrews warns, 'See to it that no-one misses the grace of God and that no bitter root grows up to cause trouble and defile many. See to it that no-one is sexually immoral or is godless like Esau, who for a single meal sold his inheritance rights as the oldest son' (Heb. 12:15-16).

Linked to the insidious danger of secret idolatry is the almost limitless capacity for self-deception which lies in the human heart. Moses gave an example of this in 28:19. *'When such a person hears the words of this oath, he invokes a blessing on himself and therefore thinks, "I will be safe, even though I persist in going my own way."'* Here the idolater pronounces a blessing on himself, and congratulates himself that no evil will befall him. He imagines that he will be safe (literally, 'peace will be upon me') even though he persists in going his own way. His smugness is both amazing and offensive. The words which follow in 29:19b are not easy to translate. Two alternative interpretations have been offered. One takes them as the words of the idolater, stating his cynical determination to persist in idolatry. Although his actions may bring disaster to the land, he himself will be spared, and so he persists in his idolatry. The other, more common, interpretation (see NIV) takes these words as Moses' description of the consequences of his idolatry. *'This will bring disaster on the watered land as well as the dry.'* God's wrath will fall on the whole land as a result of the idolater's actions.

The idolater may live in a dream world of denial, but everyone else will face the reality of God's judgment. The idolater may justify his actions within his own unreliable conscience (see Romans 2:15); but he cannot evade 'this oath' (29:19) in which God has sworn to punish the unrighteous.

The LORD will never be willing to forgive him; his wrath and zeal will burn [literally, 'smoulder' or 'bring forth smoke'] *against that man. All the curses written in this book will fall upon him, and the LORD will blot out his name from under heaven. The LORD will single him out from all the tribes of*

God's treasured possession

*Israel for disaster, according to all the curses of the covenant
written in this Book of the Law' (29:20-21).*

These verses describe the sober reality of judgment and the
shocking intensity of God's wrath. They challenge our smug
and cosy ideas about God's character. His hatred of evil is the
passionate expression of his love for truth and righteousness.
'God is a righteous judge, a God who expresses his wrath every
day' (Ps. 7:11). Paul described this link between God's wrath
and his righteousness in Romans 1:18-19. 'The wrath of God
is being revealed from heaven against all the godlessness and
wickedness of men who suppress the truth by their wickedness,
since what may be known about God is plain to them, because
God has made it plain to them.' This wrath came upon his fellow
Israelites because they rejected and killed the Lord Jesus and
persecuted the church (see 1 Thess. 2:14-16). 'The wrath of God
has come upon them at last.' Here is the culmination of *all the
curses of the covenant written in this Book of the Law'*.

It is important to note that this terrible fate will fall only on those
who reject God's warnings. Paul explained in 2 Thessalonians
2:10b-12 that those who perish under the wrath of God do so
only because 'they refused to love the truth and so be saved'. This
is the setting in which we must understand God's unwillingness
(29:20) to forgive the man who boasts that he can get away with
idolatry (29:19). The word used in 29:20 for Jehovah's forgiveness
describes his ability to obliterate every trace of Israel's sin (other
Hebrew words focus on other aspects of God's forgiveness, such
as his ability to cover sin over and turn away wrath). It is at the
core of God's promise in 2 Chronicles 7:14: 'If my people who
are called by my name, will humble themselves and pray and
seek my face and turn from their wicked ways, then will I hear
from heaven and will forgive their sin and will heal their land'.
God has no desire to see even the idolater perish, but before
the idolater can be forgiven he must repent. If he will not ask
God to wipe out his sin, then his name will be blotted out from
under heaven. Moses speaks of the terrible consequences of

persisting in sin so that the Israelites would take heed and not set out along that path in the first place. Prevention is always better than having to seek a cure.

The prospect of covenant termination (29:22-28)

In this section Moses turned the attention of his hearers from the temptations of the present to the consequences of Israel's sins over the centuries to come; from the sins of individuals to the judgment which would fall upon the nation as a whole. Moses anticipated a time when the sins of individual Israelites had festered and infected whole families, towns and tribes. Indeed, the whole community has been affected and it seems that the covenant itself lies in ruins.

Moses described two groups of people who would see the consequences of Israel's idolatry and rebellion – their own descendants and the people of other nations (29:22). *'Your children who follow you in later generations and foreigners who come from distant lands will see the calamities that have fallen on the land and the diseases with which the LORD has afflicted it.'* The *'children'* were future generations of Israelites. Even though they had not yet been born, they were also parties to God's covenant with Israel. From God's viewpoint on the proceedings, they were present with their fathers on that day that Israel renewed its covenant with Jehovah. They would see and experience what their parents did not see and refused to acknowledge – the painful consequences of sin. The *'foreigners'* were non-Israelites, to whom Israel was meant to have been a beacon of hope. In better circumstances they might have seen the wisdom of God's laws (4:6-8) and the wonder of God's grace. Instead, they saw the fury of God's wrath.

The next few verses describe how their curiosity would be aroused by terrible scenes of devastation before them. 'The whole land will be a burning waste of salt and sulphur –

nothing planted, nothing sprouting, no vegetation growing on it. It will be like the destruction of Sodom and Gomorrah, Admah and Zeboiim, which the Lord overthrew in fierce anger.' The destruction of Sodom and Gomorrah is described in Genesis 19:1-29; while Hosea 11:8 refers to the destruction of the nearby cities of Admah and Zeboiim. To this day the precise location of these cities remains a mystery, though we know the general area, and it remains a desolate salt plain south of the Dead Sea. In the Old Testament these cities came to symbolise the vilest of sin and the judgment of God upon it (see Amos 4:11; Isa. 1:9; 13:19; Jer. 23:14; Zeph. 2:9). Perhaps the eerie photographs of the smoking ruins of Hiroshima and Nagasaki after they were destroyed by atomic bombs in August 1945 can capture something of the horror described in these verses.

What was particularly shocking to Moses' hearers was that Israel would lie in smoking ruins and that foreigners would see her and be appalled. Moses captures their horror in 29:24. *'Why has the Lord done this to this land? Why this fierce, burning anger?'* This question would be on everybody's lips, including those of Moses' hearers as they contemplated this distant prospect. After all, Israel was no ordinary land. It was the home of God's chosen people. How could Jehovah deal with his land and his people in this way? Questions like this were a standard feature of secular treaties at that time and we find them elsewhere in the Old Testament (see 1 Kings 9:8-9; 2 Chr. 7:21-22; Jer. 22:8-9). Not only did they verbalise the fears which troubled many Israelites, they also drew attention to the severity of God's judgment upon the sins of his people. They heighten the dramatic tension of the passage by pointing forward to, yet delaying, the answer which God will give through his prophets.

Moses' answer to the wide-eyed question of 29: 24 is given in 29:25-28. 'And the answer will be: "It is because this people abandoned the covenant of the LORD, the God of their fathers, the covenant he made with them when he brought them out of Egypt.'" They broke the covenant by turning away from the God of their fathers and turning to other gods who were unknown and untested (29:26). *'They went off and worshipped other gods and bowed down to them, gods they did not know, gods he had not given them.'* In 29:27-28 Moses foretells the exile as the consequence of Israel's idolatry. *'Therefore the LORD's anger burned against this land, so that he brought on it all the curses written in this book. In furious anger and in great wrath the LORD uprooted them from their land and thrust them into another land, as it is now.'* The Israelites would arrive back at square one! Once again they would end up as wandering nomads. Just as they stood on the edge of the land of Canaan, trying to catch a glimpse of the riches it contained, they would weep in a foreign land, trying to remember the glories they had lost.

This awful prospect brought Moses and his hearers back to the awful message of 28:64-68. Those verses were the climax and conclusion of Moses' second Deuteronomic sermon. Yet Moses is still only halfway through his third and final sermon. What will become of Israel? Does God have even greater disaster in store for them? Will he seek their final destruction or will he bring forth an amazing deliverance? That question must have intrigued and perplexed Moses' hearers. What would become of their children?

A pause for reflection

It is at this point, in the middle of his sermon, that Moses paused to caution against idle curiosity about future events (29:29a). *'The secret things belong to the LORD our God...'* The secret things were those future events which are known to God but which God has chosen not to reveal to us. God may choose to reveal his plans by speaking through his servants, the prophets. He has often done so (see, Isa. 7:14, Micah 5:2). However, when God does not choose to reveal his plans, we must not fill in the gaps with our speculations. When God keeps silent, so must his messengers and his people.

The reverse is also true. When God has spoken, we must take note and act. Moses made this clear in 29:29b: '... *but the things revealed belong to us and to our children for ever, that we may follow all the words of this law'*. To follow the laws of God is not merely to study and explain them, but to do what they say. God's commands are given to direct our lives towards him. God's promises and warnings are given to motivate us to live holy and obedient lives, and to teach God's ways to our children (see 6:5-6).

As parents watch their children grow up, they sometimes ask themselves what they will grow into. What career will they pursue? What talents will emerge? How will their character develop? Most importantly of all, for believing parents, is the question of their children's salvation. Will they accept or reject Jesus Christ and his offer of salvation? These are questions which will be answered only in the fullness of God's time. In the meantime we must devote ourselves to doing what God has commanded us to do – to love, serve and obey him.

Chapter 30
God's promise

Please read Deuteronomy 30: 1-20

One of the saddest stories I have ever heard was that of a man who had come to the conclusion that there was no hope of salvation for him. He had grown up in the church and had heard the gospel many times. He had become a church member and sat regularly at the Lord's Table. Yet he feared that his heart had never been renewed by the grace of God and that he had never truly embraced Jesus Christ as his Saviour. On top of all this, he was convinced that God had for ever passed him by. He had tasted the good things of God's word, but he had not swallowed them, and now he had no appetite for the things of God. He feared that his heart was hardened beyond recovery. Is there any hope for such a man?

In Deuteronomy 30 Moses brought words of promise to a nation which had heard God himself speak to them at Sinai. Over the following forty years they had often sat under the ministry of Moses. Yet many of them had hardened their hearts. In the coming centuries many more would repeatedly ignore what they heard. When the wrath of God eventually fell upon them in the form of invasion and exile, they would despair of any hope of salvation. Yet in this chapter Moses stored up a word of hope for those future generations. He also challenged those who stood before him to renew their faith and hope in Jehovah.

God's treasured possession

This chapter concludes Moses' final covenant-renewal sermon. In the first part of his sermon Moses reminded the Israelites of how God had dealt with them in the past (29:1-15) and warned them of the terrible consequences which would follow if they turned away from God (29:16-28). As his hearers paused to reflect on the secret purposes of God (see 29:29) they must have trembled at what Moses would say next. Yet Moses concluded his sermon, not with a message of final destruction, but with a promise of salvation. In 30:1-10 Moses set out God's promise for the future, and in 30:11-20 he called upon his hearers to turn to the Lord in repentance and faith that very day. This chapter is the evangelical climax of Deuteronomy.

There is also a message of hope for the modern reader in this chapter. As long as we can hear the preaching of God's word, there is hope for us. Salvation is freely and openly held out to each one of us. The ancient Romans had a saying, 'While I breathe, I hope'. As long as we can breathe, we can call upon the name of the Lord. When we call upon his name he will hear and bestow his salvation. Only those who will not come to him are without hope, for they cut themselves off from 'the grace that could be theirs' (Jonah 2:8).

God's promise to a future generation (30:1-10)

In the first half of the chapter Moses looked into the future and saw the fulfilment of all God's promises and warnings. '*When all these blessings and curses I have set before you come upon you...*' In this brief phrase, Moses surveyed Israel's future. They would enter the promised land of Canaan and enjoy its bounty, but they would lose it all because of their unfaithfulness. God's blessing would be swallowed up by God's curse. Israel would find herself scattered among the nations, in slavery and in exile. Yet even there it would not be too late to turn to the Lord and seek his mercy. He will deliver them from their misery if only they will turn to him. That is God's promise. This is the message which Moses develops in the verses which follow.

In these verses Moses proclaims the call of grace to which the people of Israel must respond. This is the message which will be preached by the prophets over the centuries and it will call for a certain type of response. God will not be satisfied with a token response; nor with a cold and half-hearted response. What God seeks from his people is that they turn from their rebellion and turn back to him with all their heart and soul. Three times in 30:1-10 the phrase 'with all your heart and with all your soul' describes how Israel must turn to the Lord. In 30:2 it anticipates what would happen if the Israelites return to the Lord. In 30:6 it describes God's desire, for God wants them to return to him. And 30:10 describes what will happen when they return to the Lord. From these verses we can lean three important lessons about going back to God.

i. The necessity of a whole-hearted return to the Lord (30:1-5)
As the people of Israel languish in exile, a change will take place within them. Moses describes that change in 30:1: '*When all these blessings and curses I have set before you come upon you and you take them to heart* (or cause your heart to turn) *wherever the LORD your God disperses you among the nations...*' A distant and hazy memory of the blessings promised by Moses, and the curses with which he warned them, will come back to their minds. Words that had been suppressed and ignored for generations will come back to haunt the memories of this prodigal nation. We might think of the turning-point in the fortunes of the prodigal son in our Lord's parable. 'When he came to his senses, he said, "How many of my father's hired men have food to spare, and here I am starving to death"' (Luke 15:17). When he remembered his father's generosity all those years earlier, he came to his senses. He longed to be back in his father's house and he took the first step back to his father.

Remembering God's promises and warnings is the first step towards true repentance. That is why it is such a blessing to have God's Word planted in our minds. A sinner may wander far from God; but if he has been taught God's word, he can never excise that totally from his memory. Parents may not be able to stop their children wandering from God, but they can plant his truth in their minds so that there will be something there to recall in later years. If it is not in their minds, it cannot awaken their consciences and call them to repentance. Yet when God's word has been stored in the sinner's heart, it can be God's way of turning him back to himself even after many years of spiritual apathy.

The conversion of William McKay, a famous surgeon in nineteenth-century Edinburgh is a case in point. When he went to medical school, his mother gave him a Bible and urged him to read it. Sadly, he became so engrossed in his studies that he never read his Bible. In fact, he fell in with bad company, became a heavy drinker, and sold his Bible to feed his habit. In time he became a successful and famous surgeon, who seemed to be able to work wonders. One day a man who had been badly injured in a factory accident was brought to him. He could do nothing to save the man's life, so Dr McKay made the poor man comfortable and left him in the care of a nurse. During those last hours of his life the poor man wanted only one thing, his book. After the man died, Dr McKay asked if the man had received his book. The nurse replied that he had and pointed to it under the pillow on which the man had laid his head. When Dr McKay lifted the pillow, he saw that the book was a Bible. In fact, it was the very Bible that his mother had given him many years earlier and which he had disposed of so contemptuously. He remembered his mother and her concern for his soul and, with tears streaming down his face, went to his room to read that Bible. This strange providence had turned his heart back to the promises and warnings of God.

God's promise

Moses promised that when the Israelites remembered his words and returned to the Lord he would restore her fortunes (30:3). *'Then the LORD your God will restore your fortunes...'* Some translations read, 'return your captivity'. A literal translation of the original is that the Lord will 'turn your turnings'. This is God's desire to restore the nation of Israel to a state of covenant blessedness. One specific outworking of God's promise would be their restoration from exile (30:3b). *'Then the LORD your God will... have compassion on you and gather you again from all the nations where he scattered you.'* However far away she has wandered, God would bring her back (30:4). *'Even if you have been banished to the most distant land under the heavens, from there the LORD your God will gather you and bring you back.'* When he brings them back, he will restore everything that they have lost and he will bless them with even greater blessing (30:5). *'He will bring you to the land that belonged to your fathers, and you will take possession of it. He will make you more prosperous and numerous than your fathers.'*

The contrast between Israel's predicament and God's promise is striking. However deep her predicament, however distant she is from God, however difficult the task of restoration may be, God will restore her. God will even cross the desert to build a road through the desolate wastes so that he might bring her home again (see Isa. 35:8-10). Again, we might think of the prodigal son in the far country, in the mire of his own making. There, too, we see that no sin is too offensive and that no sinner has gone too far to be restored to God's favour. However, no sinner will ever be restored unless he turns to the Lord. Moses emphasised the condition attached to the promise in 30:2 (and also 30:10). *'When you and your children return to the LORD your God and obey him with all your heart and with all your soul according to everything that I command you today, then the LORD your God will restore your fortunes and have compassion on you.'* This is what Israel had to do. This is what we too must do, for only those who 'repent and believe the good news' will enter the kingdom of God (Mark 1:15).

ii. The genesis of a whole-hearted return to the Lord (30:6)
Moses' promise prompts some important questions. Why won't the Israelites turn to Jehovah and seek his blessing? Why will they wait so long and endure so much misery? Why would Israel have to go into exile before she would seek the Lord? Could it have been that the Israelites did not know what God wanted them to do? Moses had told them what God required of them. 'Love the LORD your God with all your heart and with all your soul and with all your strength' (6:5). And when they fell short of this high ideal they were told, 'Circumcise your hearts, therefore, and do not be stiff-necked any longer' (10:16). Just as physical circumcision removed a piece of flesh from the foreskin, so heart circumcision removed the evil thoughts, attitudes and desires of the heart. When they loved the Lord in their hearts, their words and actions would follow.

In his exposition of the law in Deuteronomy 12-26, Moses explained what it would mean for Israel to love the Lord their God with all their heart, soul and strength. By doing this, he explained what a circumcised heart is like. One of the outstanding characteristics of Moses' retelling of the law in these chapters is his emphasis on the heart. There could be no room in their hearts for other gods, because they were to love Jehovah with all their heart. They were also to love their neighbour. They were not to have a mean-spirited attitude when a poor man asked for a loan (15:10); they were to send away a freed slave with a parting gift (15:13); they were to return a neighbour's animal when it strayed (22:1); and they were not to take advantage of a hired labourer (24:14). These laws did more than merely regulate outward conduct, for they shaped the attitudes of the heart.

God's promise

It soon became obvious that these commands required more of the Israelites than they were able to give. They overwhelmed the Israelites, not because the conduct they required was difficult in itself, but because the hearts of the people were disinclined to do them. It is not hard to give thanks to the God who has given us everything we have or to show kindness to the hungry. Yet people with sinful hearts are inherently selfish and always want to put themselves first. Israel's failure to obey God's laws would highlight this sad phenomenon.

Yet Israel's failure to keep God's commands was an example of how man's extremity can be God's opportunity. Moses promised that God would make it possible for the Israelites to do what they found impossible (30:6). *'The LORD your God will circumcise your hearts and the hearts of your descendants so that you may love him with all your heart and with all your soul, and live.'* God would make it possible for them to turn from their sins and return to the Lord their God. God would make it possible for them to seek his mercy and find salvation. When they turn to the Lord they will find that he is a merciful God who delivers sinners from the wages of their sin.

This promise was taken up by the prophet Jeremiah in his promise of a new covenant (see Jer. 31 and 32). There the Lord of the everlasting covenant promised that he would reach out to his exiled people and restore their fortunes. 'I will never stop doing good to them, and I will inspire them to fear me, so that they will never turn away from me' (32:40). God would bring this about by writing his law on their hearts.

> 'This is the covenant that I will make with the house of Israel after that time,' declares the LORD. 'I will put my law in their minds and write it on their hearts. I will be their God and they will be my people. No longer will a man teach his neighbour, or a man his brother, saying, "Know the LORD," because they will all know me, from

the least of them to the greatest,' declares the LORD. 'For I will forgive their wickedness and will remember their sins no more' (Jer. 31:33-34).

Repentance will flow from the new heart which God can and will give to his people and then forgiveness will follow repentance.

This is the pattern which God follows today to bring about the salvation of his chosen people. It shows how totally dependent we are upon the grace of God. We love God only because he loved us first. We seek him because he first sought us. We turn to him in our need because, first of all, he restored our fortunes. We are to give him all the glory for our salvation, for he has made our repentance and saving faith possible. When we pray for someone who has shown unrelenting hostility to the gospel, we are to remember that God can change even the hardest of hearts. If anyone is ever tempted to give up hope that he or she might find God's salvation, remember that what God has done for others he can do for you. Ask him!

iii. The consequences of a whole-hearted return to the Lord (30:7-10)
When his people come seeking him, God will not ignore them. He will respond to their cry. In these verses Moses anticipates three aspects of God's response.

a. God will remove the curse (30:7). 'The LORD your God will put all these curses on your enemies who hate and persecute you.' He will remove from Israel the sad and painful consequences of their sin and visit them upon their enemies. God will punish the nations justly for their cruelty towards Israel.

b. God will restore their blessing (30:8-9a). 'You will again obey the LORD and follow all his commands I am giving you today. Then the LORD your God will make you most prosperous in all the work of your hands and in the fruit of your womb, the young of *your livestock and the crops of your land.'* Moses anticipates the blessings which he pronounced in 28:4. He describes a land free from God's judgment, flourishing under God's blessing. Once again it will be a land flowing with milk and honey. This will be a visible sign that God loves his people. In these promises of earthly blessings God points to a greater, everlasting and heavenly blessedness.

c. God will rejoice in heaven (30:9b-10). *'The LORD will again delight in you, and make you prosperous, just as he delighted in your fathers...'* God's mercy will triumph over his judgment (James 2:13). In 28:63 Moses had warned rebellious Israel that it would 'please' God to destroy them. He uses the same Hebrew verb, meaning to rejoice or exult, in 30:9b. God delighted over Israel's punishment because he is a God who loves justice, but he delights even more in their repentance and restoration because he is a God who loves to show mercy (Micah 7:18). The prophet Zephaniah anticipated the fulfilment of this promise (Zeph. 3:14-17) when he predicted that Jehovah would rejoice over the people of Judah with singing when he restored them after the exile. In the New Testament we are told that there will be rejoicing among the angels in heaven when even one sinner is saved (Luke 15:7, 10). In the parable of the lost son, there is rejoicing when he returns (Luke 15:23-24). When the older brother questioned the soundness of his father's judgment, the loving father insisted, 'But we had to celebrate and be glad, because this brother of yours was dead and is alive again; he was lost and is found' (Luke 15:32).

These verses give hope to anyone today who has wandered far from God. They also contain a message to those who once professed faith in Christ, but have in more recent times slidden away from God. When they hear God's call to return and seek him, they are daunted by the prospect. They may come Hlike the tax-collector in Luke 18:13, who was unable even to lift up his eyes as he entered the temple. 'How will God receive me?'

they may ask. 'Will he look at me with a scowl and cast me out of his presence?' No, for the Saviour receives repentant sinners with rejoicing. This is the Saviour God who promised to restore the fortunes of Israel even when they were far away in exile. He will give them a heart to seek him. When they seek him, he will rejoice that his mercy has borne fruit.

Moses' plea to his hearers (30:11-20)

Once I was asked to speak to a group of primary school children about the work of a minister. One of the children was not really satisfied with my explanation and asked the disconcerting question, 'What do you actually do?' Her question was a good one and it made me ask myself what, in the midst of much activity, God had called his ministers to do. The standard answer is that ministers preach God's word. But what does preaching involve? At the very least it involves passing on information from the Bible. However, simply passing on information about the Bible is not preaching. Something more takes place when a servant of God preaches the living word of God. True preaching seeks the salvation of sinners, the sanctification of believers, the perfection of the saints, and the edification of the church. It labours for a response.

Moses' message in his final sermon has been clear and simple: God will restore his people when they turn to him. This is the promise which Moses wants the Israelites to remember and take to heart. In times of apostasy, when the Israelites had wandered far from the Lord and were suffering the consequences of their sins, the Lord would restore their fortunes when they returned to him. This was the gospel which Moses preached to his own generation.

In 30:11-20 the focus of Moses preaching moved from the restoration of Israel in the future to the response of Israel in the present. *'See, I set before you today life and prosperity... Now choose life, so that you and your children may live...'* (30:15, 19). Soon Moses would leave them and they would never hear his voice again. A great sense of urgency came over him. He knew these people well. For forty years he had led them through the wilderness. He knew how hard and sinful their hearts could be. On many occasions they had heard God's word and rejected it; so he returned to his summary of the law in 30:11. *'Now what I am commanding you* (literally, 'now this command') *today is not too difficult for you or beyond your reach.'* Moses knew that the Israelites needed to hear God's word over and over again so that they might repent and return to the Lord. Moses knew that it was not enough simply to teach them God's commands. He needed to plead with them and to set God's word before them as attractively and as compellingly as he could.

A good chef works hard to make the food which he prepares presentable and appetising. Not only is the food nourishing, but your mouth will water when you see it. By contrast, I can remember some very unattractive school dinners which consisted of soggy vegetables and tough meat. It looked as though the cook did not really care whether we ate the food or left it, and the inevitable consequence was that much of it was thrown in the bin uneaten. Sadly, that is the response of many to the word of God because some sermons are sound and nourishing, but unappealing. Moses does not adopt a 'take it or leave it' attitude to his preaching. He passionately wanted the Israelites to hear God's commands and obey them, because this was the way of salvation. It was said of John Wesley that each one of his hearers knew that he cared for their souls and longed for them to believe and be saved. That is one of the hallmarks of true preaching. It was the outstanding feature of Moses' final sermon. In 30:11-20 Moses gave three reasons why the Israelites ought to heed God's word and seek the life which God offers.

God's treasured possession

i. The accessibility of God's word (30:11-14)

God's law played a vital role in Israel's salvation. It was the life-giving message which awakened in the Israelites an awareness of their sin and a desire to return to Jehovah for mercy. Its message was one which the Israelites needed to hear over and over again, and which any Israelite could understand and obey. First, Moses stated this fact negatively. *'Now what I am commanding you today is not too difficult for you or beyond your reach.'* In other words, it did not place impossible or unrealistic demands upon those who heard it. The same phrase is found in Psalm 131:1, where the Psalmist says that he does not delve into obscure ideas that were beyond his understanding. It is also found in Genesis 18:14, where God asked Abraham *'Is anything too hard for the Lord?'* The simplicity and reasonableness of God's command is explained further in 30:12-13. *'It is not up in heaven, so that you have to ask, "Who will ascend into heaven to get it and proclaim it to us so we may obey it?" Nor is it beyond the sea, so that you have to ask, "Who will cross the sea to get it and proclaim it to us so we may obey it?"'* God did not call upon his people to go to the ends of the earth to discover some hidden mystery or perform some Herculean feat of bravery in order that they might be saved.

In the ancient world many tales were told of men travelling to the ends of the earth in order to find the secret of eternal life and happiness. According to eastern legend, Buddha set out to find enlightenment and, after many years of wandering and searching, found it while meditating under a lotus tree. In more modern times the Beatles went to India to explore eastern religion and claimed to find an inner peace which they had not found in the west. These are examples of people who went to great lengths to find a word from heaven. Moses told the Israelites that they did not need to set foot outside their camp in order to find such enlightenment. If we want to find eternal life and peace with God today, we need only open the Bible and follow God's directions.

God's promise

Moses was not suggesting that the Israelites would be saved simply by obeying the Commandments. There is no suggestion in these verses that God's favour can be earned by works of obedience. Rather, Moses was saying that if the sinful Israelites were to be saved, they must hear God's law, for the law brought them to their knees. It was the sign that pointed a lost traveller back into the right path. It was like a crowbar which a workman uses to prize loose a rock that is stuck fast. It was like a prod which a herdsman uses to push a recalcitrant animal in the right direction. God's law fulfils a similar function in the lives of believers today, as we see in the case of the rich young ruler. When he asked Jesus how to inherit eternal life, Jesus pointed him to the commandments (Mark 10:17-19). He would never inherit eternal life by obeying these, but by recognising his failure to keep them he would be pointed more clearly to God's way of salvation in Christ.

That is why Paul quoted from Deuteronomy 30:12-13 in Romans 10:6-9, where he describes the righteousness that comes by faith and not by works.

> But the righteousness that is by faith says: 'Do not say in your heart, "Who will ascend into heaven?"' (that is, to bring Christ down) 'or "Who will descend into the deep?"' (that is, to bring Christ up from the dead). But what does it say? 'The word is near you; it is in your mouth and in your heart,' that is, the word of truth which we are proclaiming: That if you confess with your mouth, 'Jesus is Lord,' and believe in your heart that God raised him from the dead, you will be saved.

This is evangelical obedience. It is the believer's response to God's command. Both Paul and Moses highlight the essential simplicity of the gospel. All that we need to know and do in order to be saved can be stated very simply and succinctly. It has been stated for us in the Scriptures. God calls us to trust him and the provision he has made for sinners.

Moses repeated this claim positively in 30:14. *'No, the word is very near you; it is in your mouth and in your heart so that you may obey it.'* Moses guards against the danger of mysticism. He was not referring to an inner light, supposedly lodged within the heart of every man. Moses was speaking to a nation that had received God's law at Sinai and which had heard that law preached often. Moses focused their thoughts on that word. It was in their hands. For them, turning to God and doing as he said was simple. The simplicity of God's command is demonstrated in the story of Naaman, the Syrian general who came to Israel seeking a cure from his leprosy. Elisha the prophet told him to go and wash seven times in the River Jordan. The very simplicity of the remedy was offensive to Naaman (2 Kings 5:11-14). For Peter, the simplicity of God's provision meant having his feet washed by Jesus (John 13:8). For Peter's hearers on the day of Pentecost, it meant repenting of their unbelief and being baptized in the name of Jesus Christ for the forgiveness of sins (Acts 2:37-38).

God's words may be simple and uncomplicated, but that does not mean that following them is easy. The words of Jesus to the rich young ruler were simple. 'Go, sell everything you have and give to the poor, and you will have treasure in heaven. Then come, follow me' (Mark 10: 21). Yet how hard it was for this young man to do! It may be just as hard for some of us to yield our lives to God. It may be too humiliating to admit that we are naked, blind and poor sinners who need to ask for forgiveness from God. Or we may be willing to ask God for help now and then, but are very reluctant to submit to the sovereign lordship of Jesus Christ over every part of our lives.

Many of us stand in the same position as those Israelites. We live in reputedly Christian nations. We have attended churches where the word of God has been faithfully preached for years. We have heard God's word in sermons, we have read it in pamphlets and we have seen it on posters and billboards. This is a blessing for which we ought to be very thankful. Yet what are we to do with that knowledge? May we delight in God's word by reading and meditating upon it and above all by obeying it. After all, God gave his law to Israel so that they might obey it.

ii. The alternatives to God's mercy (30:15-18)
Moses' heart-felt desire was that the Israelites would seek God's mercy and enjoy the life which he can give. In 30:19 he called upon them to 'choose life'; but first he set before them two alternatives. *'See, I set before you today life and prosperity, death and destruction.'* This helped them to grasp the importance of the decision which they all had to make.

The starkness of the choice which Moses presented to the Israelites is obvious. 'Life' and 'death' are clear opposites. They are the outcomes of two very different ways of life. In Matthew 7:13-14 Jesus told his hearers that those who refused to enter his kingdom were on a broad path that led to death, while those who followed him along the narrow path were on the road that leads to life. 'Prosperity' and 'destruction' (literally, 'good' and 'evil') is the other set of opposites which Moses describes. They, too, are the outcomes of the choices which the Israelites will make. Good choices result in God's goodness or prosperity being bestowed on them; while evil choices result in the unravelling of God's goodness or destruction for them. How very different these outcomes are! The Israelites would not need to think long or hard before choosing which they preferred. It was, to use the colloquial expression, a 'no-brainer'. No-one in his right mind would choose death or destruction. No person aware of the issues would deliberately reject life or prosperity. Yet that is what many Israelites did. The choices they made in their daily lives had consequences which they had not anticipated.

So in 30:16-18 Moses restated the choice which faced the Israelites in terms of obedience and disobedience. *'For I command you today to love the LORD your God, to walk in his ways, and to keep his commands, decrees and laws; then you will live and increase, and the LORD your God will bless you in the land you are entering to possess.'* When they loved God and walked in his ways they would enjoy God's blessing. The alternative and its consequences are described in 30:17-18.

> *But if your heart turns away and you are not obedient, and if you are drawn away to bow down to other gods and worship them, I declare to you this day that you will certainly be destroyed. You will not live long in the land you are crossing the Jordan to enter and possess.*

This was the choice which faced the Israelites every day, in many simple but unexpected ways. Often they did not realise that they were making ultimate choices, but they were. When they planted their crops, they would seek heavenly blessing to make their land fruitful. To whom would they turn, Jehovah or Baal? When they gathered in the harvest, to whom would they return thanks? To whom would they give their tithe? When they took a wife; when they entered a business deal or signed a contract; and in a host of other areas they had to choose whether they would follow God's ways, or the ways of the Canaanites and their deities. These choices were outward indicators of the ultimate choice which faced the Israelites – to serve Jehovah or the idols.

The same choice faces us. Will we serve the one true and living God who reveals himself in Scripture and in the person of Jesus Christ? Or will we serve a multitude of false gods fashioned out of our own ideas and dreams? This is a very real choice, and it is one which we face every day. We may not always be aware that we are making a choice that has such enormous, even eternal, consequences. I remember speaking with one young man who had grown up in a Christian home but had chosen to follow the world rather than Christ. When I pointed out the consequences of his choices, he retreated into denial. 'I haven't turned away from God,' he protested, 'I'm just taking time out'.

His decision to put God on to the periphery of his life was in reality a choice to reject God and his offer of life.

We need to face the fact that earthly and ethical choices have eternal consequences. You may have heard the saying (often attributed to Ralph Waldo Emerson): 'Sow a thought, and you reap an act; sow an act, and you reap a habit; sow a habit, and you reap a character; sow a character, and you reap a destiny'. Let us honour and obey God in all the choices we make in our daily lives, for by the choices we make, we select our ultimate destiny, either life or death!

iii. The accountability of God's people (30:19-20)
It is a great privilege to hear God's words. However, with privilege comes responsibility and accountability. Accountability simply means that we are called upon to give an account of what we have received. In the parable of the talents, each of the servants was asked to explain what he had done with the talents given to him (see Matthew 25:19). Likewise, when we hear God's word, God checks up upon our response. We are not allowed to hear the gospel and just walk away as though nothing of significance has happened. Moses emphasised Israel's accountability by calling upon heaven and earth to take note that they had heard his words. *This day I call heaven and earth as witnesses against you that I have set before you life and death, blessings and curses.'*

The calling of witnesses was a common feature of secular covenants. Often, heathen gods were cited as witnesses to the vows of loyalty and submission taken by a conquered people. Moses knew that Jehovah is the only true God and ultimately Israel would give account to him. He reminded them that the whole creation around them could see and hear what the Creator had said and done. The prophets of the Old Testament often used this device in their preaching. It demonstrated that there was no excuse for Israel's sin.

> Hear, O heavens! Listen, O earth!
> For the LORD has spoken:
> I reared children and brought them up,
> but they have rebelled against me.
> (Isaiah 1:2)

Listen to what the LORD says:

> 'Stand up, plead your case before the mountains;
> let the hills hear what you have to say.
> Hear, O mountains, the LORD's accusation;
> listen, you everlasting foundations of the earth,
> for the LORD has a case against his people;
> he is lodging a charge against Israel.'
> (Micah 6:1-2).

Moses appealed to the heavens and the earth to witness the fact that he had spoken God's word to Israel (see 4:26; 31:28; 32:1). Why did he do this? The heavens and the earth can neither hear nor speak. Are we to understand this as nothing more than a rhetorical device? The significance of Moses' appeal to heaven and earth is that God created them, and in them the might and glory of Israel's Creator was visible for all to see. Just as the psalmist lifted his eyes to the hills as he set off on his journey, knowing that the Creator of the hills was his helper (see Ps. 121:1-2), so Moses knew that the Creator of heaven and earth had heard his words and would call Israel to account. This makes his appeal in 30:15 all the more urgent. So he renews his appeal to Israel in 30:19b-20. *'Now choose life, so that you and your children may live and that you may love the LORD your God, listen to his voice, and hold fast to him. For the LORD is your life, and he will give you many years in the land he swore to give to your fathers, Abraham, Isaac and Jacob.*

In similar vein, the apostle Paul warned his readers in Romans 1:18-20 that no human being has any excuse for rejecting the gospel which he preached because 'God's invisible qualities – his eternal power and divine nature – have been clearly seen, being understood from what has been made, so that men are without excuse'. The inanimate creation bears silent, yet constant, testimony to its mighty Creator, who sees and hears everything. Even the self-professed atheist has heard this testimony in his conscience. So when we speak the gospel to unbelievers, the very creation around us corroborates our message.

Just a few weeks before he died a martyr's death in 1680, Richard Cameron preached on the text 'And ye will not come to me that ye might have life' (John 5:40) at Crawfordjohn in the rugged southern uplands of Scotland. His appeal to his hearers echoed Moses' message in these verses.

> Look over to Shawhead and these hills, and take a look at them; for they are all witnesses now and when you are dying they shall all come before your face. We take every one of you as witness against another; and will that not aggravate your sorrow when they come into your mind and conscience saying, 'We heard you invited ... to take Christ, and we were witnesses, and yet ye would not.'

A second Moses stands before us and calls upon us to choose Him for he is 'the way and the truth and the life' (John 14:6).

Chapter 31
The promise of God's presence

Please read Deuteronomy 31: 1-30

As he set out for his first day at kindergarten, my son took a firm grip of my hand and said, 'Daddy, will you go with me?' I assured him that I would, knowing that the prospect of entering a new and unfamiliar situation makes us all feel uncomfortable. Especially so if we go on our own. At times like these we can draw great comfort from the promise of our heavenly Father that he will be with us always.

In Deuteronomy 31 Moses encouraged Joshua and the Israelites with this promise. He was preparing them for the challenge of entering the land of Canaan. He would no longer be their leader, but Jehovah would go before them. This was Moses' message in the opening chapters (1 – 3) of Deuteronomy. He would not enter the promised land with them, but his task was to 'commission Joshua, and encourage and strengthen him, for he will lead this people across and will cause them to inherit the land that you will see' (3:28). Now, as the book draws to a close, Moses returns to this theme. The closing chapters of Deuteronomy (31 – 34) describe the transition from the leadership of Moses (who had brought them from Egypt to Moab) to the leadership of Joshua (who would lead them from Moab into Canaan itself).

Moses knew that change is unsettling; and the Israelites were facing many changes in the coming years. Not only would they have a new leader: they would leave behind their nomadic lifestyle and settle into a new, agricultural, way of life. In the midst of these many changes there would be one rock-solid certainty. Jehovah never changes. The Lord of the covenant will remain with his people.

The encouragement of God's promise (31:1-8)

Moses' long life was drawing to an end (31:1-2). *'Then Moses went out and spoke these words to all Israel: "I am now a hundred and twenty years old and I am no longer able to lead you..."'* Even though he was one hundred and twenty years old, Moses was still a remarkable man. 'Moses was a hundred and twenty years old when he died, yet his eyes were not weak nor his strength gone' (34:7). He was not forced to retire because of physical frailty or by an arbitrary age limit, but by God's decree. Moses had lost his temper with the people when he struck the rock in the wilderness, and in so doing he had dishonoured God. As a result, God decreed that Moses would not enter the promised land (see 1:37; 3:23-27; 4:21; 32:50-51; also Num. 20:12). Moses quotes God's decree: *'The Lord said to me, "You shall not cross the Jordan."'* This must have been a crushing disappointment for Moses, but he did not dwell on the personal disappointment. Instead he accepted God's decision and moved on to describe God's promise.

Moses assured the people of Israel that they would not face the challenges that lay before them without a leader (31:3a). *'The LORD your God will cross over ahead of you. He will destroy these nations before you, and you will take possession of their land.'* Jehovah would accomplish this mighty feat through his chosen servant, Joshua (31:3b). *'Joshua also will cross over ahead of you, as the Lord has said.'* Over the years the Lord had been grooming

Joshua to take over from Moses. With God's help, Joshua would be a vigorous and successful leader, but without God's help he would be powerless. It is amazing yet wonderful that the Lord should choose people like Joshua (and us) to accomplish his grand designs.

Jehovah's plan for the conquest of Canaan and the removal of the Canaanites from the land is set out more fully in 31:4-5. *'And the LORD will do to them what he did to Sihon and Og, the kings of the Amorites, whom he destroyed along with their land. The LORD will deliver them to you, and you must do to them all that I have commanded you.'* The Lord himself will do all this. Joshua's task was to follow everything that the Lord had commanded him to do. It was as though he was simply to hold out his hand to receive blessing from Jehovah.

With this reassurance in mind Moses issued two challenges. First of all, he spoke to *the people as a whole* in 31:6. *'Be strong and courageous. Do not be afraid or terrified because of them* (the Canaanites), *for the LORD your God goes with you; he will never leave you or forsake you.'* The second challenge was addressed *to Joshua personally* (see 31:7-9). *'Be strong and courageous, for you must go with this people into the land that the LORD swore to their forefathers to give them, and you must divide it among them as their inheritance.'* These words of exhortation are very similar to those spoken to the people, except that they describe Joshua's peculiar calling. He was to go with the people as their leader in the battles to come and to divide the land of Canaan amongst the tribes of Israel.

This would be a daunting task. Moses reminded Joshua that he did not face the challenge alone (31:8). *'The LORD himself goes before you and will be with you; he will never leave you nor forsake you.'* Moses describes God's presence in two ways. First he describes it *positively,* by telling what the Lord will do. He will 'walk with you'. The verb is a present participle indicating continuous ongoing activity. The presence of Jehovah amongst his covenant people is dynamic and active, not an abstract concept. 'The LORD watches over you - the LORD is your shade at your right hand... The LORD will keep you from all harm – he will watch over your life; the LORD will watch over your coming and going both now and for evermore' (Ps. 121:5, 7-8).

Moses also describes God's presence *negatively*, by telling what the Lord will not do. *'He will never leave you or forsake you.'* This is a very emphatic negative. Jehovah will not forsake Joshua and the Israelites as they enter the promised land. In fact, he will never abandon those he has redeemed at such great cost – ever! Many years later, and after much provocation, he asks in Hosea 11:8, how he could ever abandon the people he has chosen and loved. Jehovah has entered into a covenant with his people and it is an everlasting covenant. Because of that promise he will never abandon his people.

The promise of God's presence with his redeemed people is a gospel promise. It is central to the Bible's story of salvation. It is all about restoring that blessedness which Adam lost as a result of the fall. Before Adam sinned, God had walked and talked with him in the Garden of Eden. Those had been happy times, but they were soured by Adam's sin so that Adam and Eve hid when they heard the sound of the Lord in the garden (Gen. 3:8). In his mercy God reached out to Adam and his fallen descendants. We read that 'Enoch walked with God' (Gen. 5:22). When Jacob set out from Bethel God told him, 'I am with you and will watch over you wherever you go' (Gen. 28:15). When God called Moses to lead the Israelites out of slavery he promised, 'I will be with you...' (Exod. 3:12). After the people sinned and went through a time of testing in the wilderness God assured Moses, 'My presence will go with you, and I will give you rest' (Exod. 33:14).

We can cite examples of how God drew near to the Israelites so that they might enjoy his presence, but they are all overshadowed by the promise in Isaiah 7:14 of a Saviour who will be called Immanuel. 'The virgin will be with child and will give birth to a son, and will call him Immanuel.' In Matthew 1:23 the angel who appeared to Joseph explained the significance of that promise. 'Immanuel – which means, "God with us."' And so 'the Word became flesh and made his dwelling among us' (John 1:14). Jesus is the promised presence of God.

This explains the devastation felt by the disciples when Jesus spoke about his departure from them. They grieved at the prospect of losing their beloved teacher. Yet their grief went deeper, for they feared that the hope of Israel was about to disappear from them. They had longed for the day when God would dwell in their midst to deliver them from the curse of sin and the scourge of their enemies. Having just arrived, is he to remove himself to his Father's presence again? At that moment of grief, Jesus spoke to his disciples of another comforter, the Holy Spirit 'to be with you forever... He lives with you' (John 14:16-17). This third person of the Godhead is also God with us.

The practical and pastoral significance of this promise is described in 31:8b. *'Do not be afraid; do not be discouraged.'* Discouragement dogs the steps of all who serve as leaders of God's people. The work is demanding and sometimes bears little fruit. Preachers labour hard to preach the gospel and may see few conversions. Elders faithfully watch over the flock, but find that their work is unappreciated and their counsel ignored. Those who work with youth are sometimes heartbroken to see a promising young Christian reach his teenage years and drift with the world. Satan is especially active in his attacks upon those who lead God's people. Sharp and hurtful criticism can come even from within the church. Were it not for the fact that God is with us and gives us strength many of us might well have fallen by the wayside. That is why Moses reassured Joshua with this promise. It is a promise to which Joshua will need to return on many occasions over the coming years.

The significance of God's law (31:9-13)

God is present with his people in all places and at all times. In 31:1-8 Moses has reaffirmed this promise for the benefit of Joshua and the Israelites. No doubt one of the reasons why Moses felt the need to reassure his fellow Israelites was that they did not always have a clear understanding and hence a keen sense of the reality of God's presence. In ancient communities most people would have believed that spiritual beings were everywhere around them, but they were never sure whether they would help them or hurt them. They could not really claim to know these spiritual beings. Moses insisted that there is only one real and living God, and that his presence pervades the whole universe. He has chosen Israel to be his people. He travels with them and he will bless them if they follow him faithfully. The Israelites had heard this promise many times, but often they did not take it to heart. They were afraid that they might have stepped beyond the reach of Jehovah's power into the orbit of some 'other god'. They knew about God's omnipresence as a propositional idea, but it did not affect the way they lived and thought about him.

The same can be said of many people today. How often have we failed to appreciate the limitlessness of God's power and presence? Sometimes believers sense that God has forsaken them. This may be because they have sinned and a guilty conscience seems to tell them that God is too holy to desire any fellowship with them. Or it may be because they are going through hard times and feel aggrieved that God has not stepped in to stop their suffering. They cry, 'Where was God when I asked for help?' At such times it is important to learn *how* to draw near to God and cultivate a sense of his presence.

Through the rest of this chapter we will see how Moses taught the Israelites to walk with Jehovah so that they might know assuredly that he was with them. This would be a vitally important spiritual discipline during the turbulent times ahead when Moses handed over the baton of leadership to Joshua and when Joshua led the Israelites into the land of Canaan. Some commentators can see a concentric pattern from 31:9 to the end of this chapter. This section begins with Moses writing the law (31:9-13) and ends with him placing the written law beside the ark (31:24-29). Then in 31:14-15 Moses describes the commissioning of Joshua, and returns to that ceremony in 31:23. At the centre of the passage Moses describes a song of witness which the Israelites were to sing. Note how the structure of the passage tells us that this song serves a very important pastoral purpose. The song itself is found in chapter 32, but in 31:19-22 Moses describes how and why the Lord told him to write it down. The Israelites will enjoy God's presence as they hear his word and respond in worship. There is no greater blessing on earth than to join with God's people in the worship of our Creator. It gives a blessed foretaste of heaven.

However, before God's people can enjoy the privilege of worship they must first of all hear God speak. God had spoken to his people on Mount Sinai and Moses had written out his commands (31:9). *'So Moses wrote down this law and gave it to the priests, the sons of Levi, who carried the ark of the covenant of the LORD, and to all the elders of Israel.'* The law given at Sinai was the high-water mark of God's revelation at that stage in the history of redemption. As a result of the exodus, the Israelites were in a blessed situation, and their privileges were confirmed by the covenant which God made with them at Sinai. Their obligations were summarised in the 'ten words' or Ten Commandments (5:1-22). To that summary of the law was added a further series of 'commands, decrees and laws' (5:31) which Moses received on the mountain and which he was to teach to the Israelites. These laws are found in Exodus, Leviticus and Numbers and restated in Deuteronomy, but we are not told how much of this law Moses gave to the Levites at this point.

Some have suggested that 'this law' which Moses gave to the priests was merely a copy of the Ten Commandments, while others suggest that it included the more detailed stipulations in chapters 12 – 26, and others suggest that most of Deuteronomy was written out and handed over. A similar phrase is found in 27:3, where Moses commanded the people to write 'all the words of this law' on whitewashed stones once they had entered the land of Canaan. Those stones were to be set up for all the people to see (27:8). This suggests that Moses wrote out a shorter portion of the law, such as the Ten Commandments or even the law code of chapters 12 – 26. However, when Ezra read 'the Book of the Law of Moses' in the time of Nehemiah, 'he read it aloud from daybreak till noon ... in the presence of the men, women and others who could understand' (Neh. 8:3). Even allowing that some time might have been taken up with interruptions and explanations, this suggests that a much longer section was written out and handed over, possibly the whole of Deuteronomy or even the five books of Moses.

After writing down the law for the benefit of future generations, Moses handed the scroll over to the priests and all the elders of Israel. These were the religious and civil leaders of the Israelites and they represented the whole nation. Moses recognised the important role which they would play in the days to come. He recognised that Joshua would not be able to lead the Israelites into the land of Canaan without their help and support. Succession planning is an important theme running through these final chapters of Deuteronomy as Moses equips Joshua and others to lead the people in God's ways. The priests and elders will have the important task of teaching God's word to the people and encouraging them not to depart from it. Later (31:24-27) we will be told what the Levites were to do with the scroll; but for now their role as guardians of the written law is identified. In the days before printing, when books were copied by hand, there were very few books available. Those that did exist were precious. This book was especially precious as it contained the written record of God's law, telling the Israelites how they were to live and walk with him. The task of Israel's leaders was to preserve and propagate this law.

One of the ways in which they were to do this was by reading the law publicly (31:10-11). *'Then Moses commanded them: "At the end of every seven years, in the year for cancelling debts, during the Feast of Tabernacles, when all Israel comes to appear before the LORD your God at the place he will choose, you shall read this law before them in their hearing."'* Three times a year the tribes of Israel were to gather in God's presence at the place which God had chosen for his name to dwell (16:16). These were annual reminders that Jehovah dwelt with his people. The Feast of Tabernacles reminded the Israelites that he had travelled with them through the wilderness and provided for all their needs in that desolate place. Yet every seventh year there was an added dimension to the Feast of Tabernacles. The reading of the law reminded them that God had come down onto Mount Sinai and spoken to them. Amazingly, they were still able to hear his voice years later, because his words had been recorded in Scripture. The wonder of the written Scriptures is that they are a living word. When they are read God is present, speaking to those who listen.

As time passed the Feast of Tabernacles came to be associated with the ingathering of the harvest and the reading of God's law anticipated a spiritual ingathering of those who would hear God's voice and respond with repentance and faith. The whole nation was to hear the reading of the law (31:12). *'Assemble the people—men, women and children, and the aliens living in your towns—so that they can listen and learn to fear the LORD your God and follow carefully all the words of this law.'* Special mention is made of those who did not know God's law – the aliens who had come to settle amongst the Israelites and the children growing up amongst the Israelites (31:13). *'Their children, who do not know this law, must hear it and learn to fear the LORD your God as long as you live in the land you are crossing the Jordan to possess.'* If this practice had become established as a regular feature of life in Israel (and there is reason to believe that it did not), then every Israelite would have heard the reading of the law in this solemn setting at least once during his or her formative years. If subsequent generation of Israelites had only heeded Moses' instruction one wonders whether the law would have fallen into such a state of neglect as it obviously had by the days of King Josiah (see 2 Kings 22:8).

It is unusual for Christians today to listen to lengthy Scripture readings in church. A paragraph, or a chapter at most, is commonplace. Yet Moses commends the public reading of a lengthy portion. It may have taken hours! In the oral culture of ancient Israel this would not have been unusual. We live in a very different culture and may not think that it is appropriate to incorporate a six-hour Bible reading into one of our church services. However, we do need to remember that the books of the Bible were written to be read aloud, and in their entirety. Paul may have had this in mind when he instructed Timothy to devote himself to the public reading of Scripture (1 Tim. 4:13). Paul's own letters were also written as undivided units and were read as such to gatherings of early Christians (Col. 4:16). Yet we often read bite-sized sections of the Scriptures and mull over isolated devotional thoughts. As a result, we may well fail to see the flow and recurring emphases of the story of salvation. Only as we read larger portions of Scripture will we see the climax and true significance of the story. An antidote to superficial habits of Bible reading is the practice of setting aside several hours to read a large book or several smaller books in one sitting.

The folly of God's people (31:14-30)

In spite of God's promise that he would go with his people, the Israelites often turned away from him and lost any sense of his presence and protection. Eventually the covenant people wandered so far away from God that the covenant between Jehovah and Israel seemed broken beyond repair. Yet the problem had been there all along because of the underlying sinfulness of human nature. Moses describes that sinfulness and the problems it brings in this section. As the folly and rebellion of the Israelites increased, they would need to learn how to acknowledge their sinfulness and seek God's mercies. They would also need special reassurance that Jehovah would continue to be their God and would walk with them as he had with Moses over the past forty years. Hence the setting for this final section is the formal handover from Moses to Joshua. This is described in 31:14-15.

The Lord told Moses to bring Joshua to the tent of meeting (31:14). *'Now the day of your death is near. Call Joshua and present yourselves at the Tent of Meeting, where I will commission him.'* The 'tent of meeting' is the phrase often used in Exodus-Numbers to describe the tabernacle. The tabernacle was the place where God met with his people and their representative leaders (Exod. 25:22; 29:42; 30:36). The atoning sacrifices that were offered at the tabernacle made it possible for the Israelites to approach God and enjoy fellowship with him. There, too, God made his will known to the Israelites. One commentator has said that the phrase might easily be paraphrased as 'the tent of revelation'. This is the only place in Deuteronomy where the tabernacle is mentioned. Significantly, it is the place where God meets with his people to appoint their leaders.

The awesome nature of God's appearance is described in 31:15. *'Then the LORD appeared at the Tent in a pillar of cloud, and the cloud stood over the entrance to the Tent.'* The cloud had been a visible manifestation of God's presence during Israel's years of wandering in the wilderness. A pillar of cloud led the Israelites on their journey (Exod. 13:21-22; Deut. 1:33) and protected the Israelites from the onslaught of Pharaoh's army (Exod. 14:19).

It manifested the glory of Jehovah in the wilderness (Exod. 16:10) and the awesome majesty of Jehovah at Sinai (Exod. 19:9, 16; Deut. 5:22). The symbolism of the cloud demonstrated the impenetrable mystery of God. His presence is palpable, but the essence of his being is hidden from mankind unless and until he chooses to reveal himself. When God speaks, he draws back the veil and reveals himself. For this we can give thanks, for without a true knowledge of God there is no possibility of a right relationship with God.

The reason why God appeared at the tent of meeting and the message which he came to communicate are described in 31:23. *'The LORD gave this command to Joshua son of Nun: "Be strong and courageous, for you will bring the Israelites into the land I promised them on oath, and I myself will be with you."'* It is typical of God's dealings with his people that promise and command go hand in hand and God's message for Joshua contains both. He commanded Joshua to be strong and courageous. This is another way of encouraging Joshua to be strong in his faith, and courageous in his obedience. His task was to lead the Israelites into the land of Canaan and wrest it from the Canaanites. This would be no little task and would demand all the faith and courage he could muster. Jehovah nurtures that faith with the assurance of his presence. He reaffirms the words of promise which Moses had given in 31:7-8. Now Joshua hears them from God himself. He would need all the encouragement he could get. So, too, would future generations of Israelites; for dark and testing times lay before them.

The Lord made this abundantly clear when he spoke to Moses in the tent of meeting (see 31:16-18). These verses describe the downward spiral into apostasy which will take place after his death and the removal of his godly influence. First of all the Israelites will turn to other gods (31:16a). Here the common Old Testament analogy of spiritual adultery is used to describe Israel's actions. *'These people will soon prostitute themselves to the foreign gods of the land they are entering.*' The analogy was sadly appropriate, as the worship of Canaanite gods often involved literal adultery with shrine prostitutes (see Hosea 4:10-14; 5:3-4; 6:10; 9:1). By their immorality and idolatry the Israelites will break their covenant with Jehovah (31:16b). *'They will forsake me and break the covenant I made with them.'*

As a result of their actions, Jehovah will withdraw from the Israelites (31:17). *'On that day I will become angry with them and forsake them; I will hide my face from them, and they will be destroyed.'* This seems to oppose God's recurring promise that he will be with his people. Yet the purpose of these disasters was to awaken the Israelites to the fact that they had driven God from their midst. *'Many disasters and difficulties will come upon them, and on that day they will ask, "Have not these disasters come upon us because our God is not with us?"'* When they start searching their hearts and asking the hard questions, they will have arrived at the turning-point described in 30:1; and when they return to the Lord, he will restore their fortunes. In order to bring this about God will make use of many hardships, but also the ministry of his servants. Moses did three things to encourage the Israelites to repent and return to the Lord – he wrote out a song (31:19-22), placed the law beside the ark (31:24-27) and assembled the people together (31:28-30).

i. *God's song* (31:19-22). This song is not like the songs which we commonly sing in worship. Worship songs have as their primary purpose the praise of God and thanksgiving for his mercies. The song which we will find in 32:1-43 describes God's greatness and the gratitude of those who enjoy his mercies, but its express purpose was to make the Israelites aware of their sinfulness (31:19). *'Now write down for yourselves this song and teach it to the Israelites and make them sing it, so that it may be a witness for me against them.'* We are given a foretaste of what it contains in 31:20-21. It anticipated the beauty of the land which God will give to Israel (31:20a). *'When I have brought them into the land*

God's treasured possession

flowing with milk and honey, the land I promised on oath to their forefathers, and when they eat their fill and thrive...' (see 32:13-14). It was not the land in which the Israelites lived that led them away from God. The land was a good land, 'flowing with milk and honey' (31:20). The root cause of their sinful acts was to be found within their hearts. This is what Jesus taught his disciples in Mark 7:20-23. 'For from within, out of men's hearts, come evil thoughts, sexual immorality, theft, murder, adultery, greed, malice, deceit, lewdness, envy, slander, arrogance and folly. All these come from inside and make a man "unclean".'

The song observed that Israel's prosperity led the people to despise the one who made them prosper (31:20b): *'...they will turn to other gods and worship them, rejecting me and breaking my covenant'* (see 32:15-18). It reinforced the warning that disaster would flow from disobedience (31:21). *'And when many disasters and difficulties come upon them, this song will testify against them, because it will not be forgotten by their descendants. I know what they are disposed to do, even before I bring them into the land I promised them on oath.'*

This cycle of God's blessing leading to prosperity, rebellion and judgment is one which will characterise the history of Israel in the books of Judges and Kings. It will become all too familiar as the centuries pass. Yet even before the Israelites entered the land God knew what would happen, because he knew the inclination of their hearts. God told the people what would happen in their midst even before they entered the land. We should not imagine that the Israelites were prisoners of fate, sleep-walking towards disaster. Rather, we should see this as the path which sinful Israel would freely choose to walk. God knew their hearts and warned them, thus leaving them with no excuse for their actions when they walked into sin. This song was to be sung as a warning to awaken the consciences of Israel and call the people serious self-examination.

ii. God's law (31:24-27). Not only did Moses write out the law (31:9), he gave a copy of the written law to the Levites, who placed it beside the ark of the covenant (31:24-26). *'After Moses finished writing in a book the words of this law from beginning to end, he gave this command to the Levites who carried the ark of the covenant of the LORD: "Take this Book of the Law and place it beside the ark of the covenant of the LORD your God..."'* This may explain why Moses and Joshua were called to the tent of meeting in 31:14. The ark was kept in the innermost room of the tabernacle, often called the Holy of Holies, the room into which the High Priest went once a year on the Day of Atonement. Although the book of the law would have remained invisible to the rest of the Israelites, the fact that it was placed there made an important statement to them (31:26b). *'There it will remain as a witness against you.'* It served the same purpose as the song.

Just as the song reminded the Israelites of God's goodness as well as their ingratitude, rebellion and inevitable destruction, so did the reading of the law. Moses spoke out of his long and bitter experience of Israel's sinfulness (31:27). *'For I know how rebellious and stiff-necked you are. If you have been rebellious against the LORD while I am still alive and with you, how much more will you rebel after I die!'* Even his powerful influence upon the Israelites during his lifetime had not been able to stop them from sinning. He feared worse to come after he died. He was unable to leave the Israelites with the confidence which Paul had in the Christians in Philippi. 'Therefore, my dear friends, as you have always obeyed – not only in my presence, but now much more in my absence – continue to work out your salvation with fear and trembling, for it is God who works in you to will and to act according to his good purpose' (Phil. 2:12-13). Paul's confidence was based upon the work of one greater than Moses, the mediator of the new covenant, whose blood has washed away every sin and at whose command the Holy Spirit is poured into the heart of every believer. There would be many frustrations and failures before that day would come, but the plan of salvation remains constant through the ages. God's purpose is to save for himself a people made holy and preserved from destruction by his indwelling presence. The sanctifying work of God's law points towards this ultimate end.

iii. God's assembly (31:28-30). One of Moses' very last actions as Israel's leader was to convene an assembly of God's people. The purpose of this assembly was to teach the song which he had been told to write out in 31:19. So that this song might reach the whole nation, Moses gathered the people together for a national assembly. First, he assembled the leaders and representatives of all the people (31:28). *'Assemble before me all the elders of your tribes and all your officials, so that I can speak these words in their hearing and call heaven and earth to testify against them.'* By calling heaven and earth to testify against them, Moses anticipated the opening words of the song (see 32:1-2) and reflected the rhetoric of his preaching in 30:19. So in 31:30 Moses set about his task and *'recited the words of this song from beginning to end in the hearing of the whole assembly of Israel'*. It is one of the distinguishing features of God's dealings with mankind that he gathers the people he saves into assemblies to build them up in their faith and obedience. Here, in the assembly of Israel, we have a prototype of the ministry of the church today. It is so important that each one of us gathers regularly in the assembly of God's people to sit under the ministry of his word.

The danger that Israel would turn away from the Lord kept Moses focused on his calling right to the very end of his life. The Lord himself had alerted Moses to this danger and its consequences in 31:16-18; and we can see that Moses took this danger very seriously, for in 31:29 he passed the warning on to others. *'For I know that after my death you are sure to become utterly corrupt and to turn from the way I have commanded you. In days to come, disaster will fall upon you because you will do evil in the sight of the LORD and provoke him to anger by what your hands have made.'* Such was his concern for the Israelites that he was not content merely to record and preserve God's law and God's song, he took steps to ensure that the people would hear God's word and sing the Lord's song. The claims of God must be heard by all and taken to heart. The preacher's passion which we saw in chapter 30 continued even into the succession ceremony in chapter 31, because Moses longed that future generations should continue to love and serve the Lord.

The transfer of leadership from Moses to Joshua was not aimed simply at filling the gap in the life of the nation which would be left by the departure of Moses; but at multiplying appropriate forms of ministry for the people of God. Moses was remarkably innovative in this regard. We have seen how he involved the elders (31:9) and the officials (31:28) in the work of preserving and promoting God's law. We have also seen how Moses established the seven-yearly reading of the law at the Feast of Tabernacles (31:10-11). The song of witness was another method of calling the people to repentance and faith. This song may well have been taken back to the towns, villages and homes of Israel to be sung in a wide range of settings. The methods were diverse, but the aim was one and the same: to pass on Israel's faith so that future generations would serve Jehovah and walk in the light of his presence.

Chapter 32
A song of witness

Please read Deuteronomy 32: 1-52

One of the longest-running radio programmes in the history of broadcasting is *Desert Island Discs*. It was first broadcast by the BBC in 1942. Each week since then a well-known personality has been invited to select favourite pieces of music to take with them to an imaginary desert island. Naturally, their favourite songs and musical items have been those which remind them of positive experiences in their lives or offer comfort for the difficult days ahead. It is interesting to consider what songs we might choose if we were asked to make a similar selection. The familiar words of the twenty-third psalm would, no doubt, be the choice of many Christians. Others love the hymns of Wesley, Toplady or Watts. Still others are drawn to more modern lyrics and their contemplative tunes.

Perhaps we would find it hard to settle on only one song because our moods vary, and as they change we are drawn to different songs. There are times when we want to sing songs that are vibrant and triumphant. At other times we are drawn to songs which are slow and majestic. At times of sadness, a minor key will be more appropriate.

In Deuteronomy 32 we find a song that is commonly called *The Song of Moses*. It is hard to place this song in any of the commonly-accepted categories of worship songs. Much scholarly endeavour has gone into categorising this portion of Scripture. Some call it a covenant lawsuit, others call it a prophetic utterance, while others call it a hymn of praise. It contains adoration for God and warnings for his people, as well as a call to repentance and promises of mercy. Its message is rich and varied.

In 31:19 Moses has already told us what kind of song it is. It is a song of witness. At God's command, Moses was to write down the words of this song and teach them to the Israelites as 'a witness for me against them'. It was not Moses' song at all – it was and is God's song. That is why Moses 'recited the words of this song from beginning to end in the hearing of the whole assembly' (31:30). Unlike other songs in the Old Testament, this song was not primarily a song of praise, nor was it a lament or confession, though hopefully it would lead to those actions. It was a warning, intended to prompt reflection and self-examination. It was like a splash of cold water in the faces of the Israelites. It was intended to help them remember the challenge of Moses' sermons on the plains of Moab. We might describe this song as a set of poetic sermon notes.

God's covenant with Israel (32:1-6)

An appropriate title for this song might be *The Song of the Covenant*. It highlighted many of the most important features of the covenant which God had made with the people of Israel and so recently renewed on the plains of Moab. This covenant would need constant renewal over the generations to come. In this song Moses describes the terms and implications of the covenant, but first in 32:1-6 he describes the parties involved.

First of all, in 32:1-2 Moses describes *the witnesses* who could confirm that he had taught the Israelites faithfully about God

A song of witness

(32:1). *'Listen, O heavens, and I will speak; hear O earth, the words of my mouth.'* Earlier, in 4:26 and 30:19, Moses had called heaven and earth to act as witnesses that the people had heard Jehovah's offer of life to those who followed him and his warning of death to those who forsook him. There were also indirect references to heaven and earth acting as witnesses in 4:36 and 31:28. The prophet Isaiah also called upon heaven and earth to hear the message that he brought to the people of Judah. 'Hear, O heavens! Listen, O earth! For the LORD has spoken...' (Isa. 1:2), Here, too, the heavens and the earth serve as witnesses to God's covenant with his people.

Why were these witnesses considered necessary? We should not think that these witnesses served to add clarity and credibility to God's message. They complemented and added solemnity to the preaching of God's servants – in this case Moses. This is because 'the heavens declare the glory of God' (Ps. 19:1). The glory of the creation was a visible reminder of the glory of the invisible God.

Although God's word is powerful, when we hear its message, we sometimes very quickly forget what we have heard. We imagine that God's warnings do not really apply to us and we are unaffected by what we have heard. The word is like the seed which falls on the path and which the birds of the air take away (Luke 8:5, 12). By contrast Moses' prayer is that his hearers will take in what they hear and be spiritually enriched by it (32:2). *'Let my teaching fall like rain and my words descend like dew, like showers on new grass, like abundant rain on tender plants.'* God assures us that this will indeed happen.

> As the rain and the snow
> come down from heaven,
> and do not return to it
> without watering the earth
> and making it bud and flourish,

so that it yields seed for the sower and bread for the eater,
so is my word that goes out from my mouth:
It will not return to me empty,
but will accomplish what I desire
and achieve the purpose for which I sent it.
(Isa. 55:10-11)

Then in 32:3-5 Moses introduces *the genius who initiated the covenant*, Jehovah himself.

I will proclaim the name of the LORD.
Oh, praise the greatness of our God!
He is the Rock, his works are perfect,
and all his ways are just.
A faithful God who does no wrong,
upright and just is he.

Moses described the character of God in these lines, drawing particular attention to his faithfulness. This is always a reason for praising God. He described God's faithfulness by comparing him to a rock (32:3). This striking metaphor sets the tone for the rest of the song and it is used to describe God in verses 15, 18, 30 and 31. In the desert, a rock was a fixed point by which a traveller might find his bearings and plot his course. By contrast, the shifting sand dunes were treacherous guides and many travellers perished amongst them.

God's people can rejoice that he is their rock. His *righteous standards* do not change from generation to generation or from circumstance to circumstance. 'His works are perfect, and all his ways are just.' His *covenant mercies* do not change with the passing of time. He is 'a faithful God who does no wrong, upright and just is he.' He will never abandon his people, or let them down. He will never close his ears to their cries, but will hear them and answer them when they repent and seek his mercy.

Then in 32:5-6 Moses describes *the people* who were drawn into fellowship with Jehovah through his covenant, the nation of Israel. Sadly, there was a striking contrast between God's faithfulness and Israel's unfaithfulness (32:5). *'They have acted corruptly toward him; ... they are... a warped and crooked generation.'* Moses may have anticipated Israel's future unfaithfulness, as he did in 28:45 and 31:16-18; or he may simply speak out of his long experience of Israel's sinfulness in the wilderness. In either case, he describes their behaviour as totally inappropriate for a people in covenant with Jehovah.

In 32:6 he asks, *'Is this the way you repay the LORD, O foolish and unwise people?'* Simply because of who Jehovah is, he deserved Israel's total loyalty. Anything less ought to have been unthinkable. Yet the Israelites did not really think about who Jehovah is or view their actions in the light of his holiness and greatness. Do we take time to mediate upon the character of God, especially as it is described for us in his great titles? 'Father' and 'Creator' are just two mentioned in 32:6. There are many more besides, and they give us a wonderful insight into who God is and what he expects of us. We are to give him the honour a son gives his father (see Mal. 1:6). We are to acknowledge him as distinct from and greater than all his creatures (see Rom. 1:25). These are important words to mediate upon because, as the Puritan preacher Stephen Charnock put it, 'It is impossible to honour God as we ought, unless we know him as he is'.

The consequences of the people's unfaithfulness are described in the sombre words of 32:5. *'To their shame they are no longer his children, but a warped and crooked generation.'* That chilling prospect was taken up by the prophet Hosea when he named one of his sons Lo-Ammi or 'not my people' (Hosea 1:9). Isaiah described the painful disappointment of the heavenly Father when he saw the rebellious behaviour of his children in Isaiah 1:2-3.

"I reared children and brought them up,
but they have rebelled against me.
The ox knows his master,
the donkey his owner's manger,
but Israel does not know,
my people do not understand."

Although they had the name of being God's people they did not live like his people. Yet Jehovah simply could not cast them away.

How can I give you up, Ephraim?
How can I hand you over, Israel?
How can I treat you like Admah?
How can I make you like Zeboiim?
My heart is changed within me;
all my compassion is aroused.
(Hosea 11:8).

Although they renounced their privileges as children, God never renounced his responsibilities as a Father.

What an example this sets to earthly fathers. There may be many occasions when we are exasperated with our families; but we are called to be patient and loving. We are to remember that we, too, are unworthy children of a patient and loving Father. How comforting it is to know that he will never leave us or cease loving us.

God's goodness to Israel (32:7-18)

Even though Israel's history was often shameful and embarrassing for the Israelites, Moses did not hesitate to remind the Israelites of it, because it was a story of God's great goodness towards them. That is why Moses, in 32:7, urged them to remember it.

> *Remember the days of old;*
> *consider the generations long past.*
> *Ask your father and he will tell you,*
> *your elders, and they will explain to you.*

The most trustworthy people in the community were considered to be the old. Moses urged the Israelites to ask those whom they could trust. It was their responsibility to pass on their history from one generation to the next. This song may have served as an aid for fathers as they taught their families about God and all that he had done for Israel. Children, too, had a responsibility to seek out and remember their father's instruction.

Succeeding generations of Israelites were to remember that *God had chosen them* out of all the nations 932:8-9). Jehovah is the *'the Most High'* who rules over every nation and gives them the lands in which they live.

> *When the Most High gave the nations their inheritance,*
> *when he divided all mankind,*
> *he set up boundaries for the peoples...*

We have already seen how God allocated land to the Moabites and Edomites (2:9, 20-23). In the New Testament, Paul made the same point to show the philosophers of Athens that the God of Israel is the Lord of all the earth (see Acts 17:26). His primary purpose, however, in ruling over the nations was to bless his chosen nation, his channel of salvation for all nations. '*He set up boundaries for the peoples according to the number of the sons of Israel.*' In other words, the blessings which God bestowed upon them were subservient to the blessing which God bestowed upon his most favoured nation (32:9). '*For the LORD's portion is his people, Jacob his allotted inheritance*' (see also 9:26). Just as the land was Israel's covenant blessing, so the people of Israel were Jehovah's covenant blessing. They were his treasured possession (7:6, 14:2, 26:18), chosen to bring him special pleasure by living in loving obedience to his laws.

The people of Israel were also to remember that *God had led them* through the desert (32:10-12). Moses described the setting - Israel's forty years in the desert as they journeyed from Egypt to the promised land (32:10).

> *In a desert land he found him,*
> *in a barren and howling waste.*
> *He shielded him and cared for him;*
> *he guarded him as the apple of his eye.*

There is a strong contrast between the hostile environment in which the people found themselves and the wonderful protection which God provided (32:11).

> *Like an eagle that stirs up its nest*
> *and hovers over its young,*
> *that spreads its wings to catch them*
> *and carries them on its pinions.*

The powerful eagle with its wings outstretched was believed to toss its young into the air and catch them on its wings. This is a wonderful picture of God's protection of his people (see Ps. 91:4). He is like the shepherd going into the wilderness to bring home the lost sheep (32:12a). '*The LORD alone led him; no foreign god was with him.*' See also Psalm 23:1-3; Luke 15:3-7; John 10:1-4. This is a word picture full of encouragement for the believer. Our paths may take us into hard and inhospitable places, but a powerful Saviour leads and protects us. As with the people of Israel, we acknowledge that God is the only one we can turn to for help at such times.

A song of witness

The people of Israel were also to remember that *God had brought them* into the promised land (32:13-14).

> *He made them ride on the heights of the land*
> *and fed them with the fruit of the fields.*
> *He nourished them with honey from the rock*
> *and with oil from the flinty crag,*
> *with curds and milk from the herd and flock...*
> *You drank the foaming blood of the grape.*

These lines were written in anticipation of Israel's entry into Canaan. As they sang this song over the coming years, they reminded themselves that the land of Canaan was indeed a land flowing with milk and honey (11:9; 26:9, 15; 27:3; 31:20). It was filled with many natural blessings. Even where the land appeared unproductive, it yielded a rich reward to those who laboured it.

Because of God's abundant provision for the material needs of his people in the land of Canaan they prospered. In their prosperity they are compared to a fattened animal (32:15). *'Jeshurun grew fat and kicked; filled with food, he became heavy and sleek.'* The irony of Israel's behaviour is indicated by the title Moses gave the Israelites. *'Jeshurun'* means 'the upright one'. It described Israel as the servant of the Lord God (Isa. 44:2; see also 33:5, 26). Israel's behaviour in 32:15-18 was anything but upright. They fell in love with their material possessions and grew fat. It may have been their waistlines which expanded as they enjoyed the rich fare of Canaan, or it may have been their barns which bulged with produce. They prospered in every imaginable way. However, the irony of their material prosperity was that it led to spiritual amnesia (32:15b). Israel *'abandoned the God who made him and rejected the Rock his Saviour'.* They even gave thanks to the false gods worshipped by Canaanites for the blessings which they had received from the hand of Jehovah (32:16). *'They made him jealous with their foreign gods and angered him with their idols.'*

Moses was scathing in his denunciation of these non-existent gods (32:17). They were

> *... demons, which are not God—*
> *gods they had not known,*
> *gods that recently appeared,*
> *gods your fathers did not fear.*

Although they had no objective existence in themselves, they gave the powers of evil (which, tragically, are real) a foothold in their lives. Their baneful influence was all too obvious to Moses – and to Paul during his ministry in Corinth (see 1 Cor. 10:19-21). These ancient gods kept reappearing in new forms, so that Moses described them as *'gods that recently appeared'.* A large part of their appeal was their novelty. And so the Israelites of old, *'deserted the Rock, who fathered'* them and *'forgot the God who gave (them) birth'.* Many people today are fascinated by religions that offer something new. Like the Israelites of old, many people today turn away from the everlasting God, whose gospel is unchanging, seeking a new spirituality and a new faith. Ironically they find the same old gods dressed in the garb of contemporary culture.

Israel's behaviour is a reminder that all mankind is naturally religious. We feel the need to give thanks to someone or something for the blessings we receive. That is why human beings create idols for this very purpose and give thanks to the wrong person for the blessings we have received from God. In 1872, the Conservative government of Benjamin Disraeli extended the vote to the working classes in England. Shortly afterwards it was voted out of office and William Gladstone was elected prime minister. One commentator quipped that those so recently added to the electorate had received the vote from

Mr Disraeli and said 'thank you' to Mr Gladstone. How unfair! Yet how many people today receive blessings from God and say 'thank you' to luck, their hard work, mother earth or the government of the day. This is every bit as offensive to God as the idolatry of the people of Israel.

God's judgment upon Israel (32:19-27)

When the Israelites abandoned the Lord as their God, he rejected them as his people. In the introduction to this song Moses reminded his readers of Jehovah's warning that he would hide his face from them and they would be destroyed (see 31:17). This was the terrible outworking of divine justice and righteousness, and Moses taught the people to reflect on that fact as they sang this song. A time would come when he would not listen to them or answer their prayers. There would be no deliverance from the hand of their enemies, because God was sending these enemies as the agents of his judgment. The time for mercy had passed, for his repeated warnings had fallen on deaf ears. Now God would be deaf to their cries. It is sobering to remember that the same fate awaits those who reject the Lord Jesus and will not embrace the mercies offered to them in the gospel. The righteous judge will say, 'Away from me, you evildoers' (Matt. 7:23). 'They will be punished with everlasting destruction and shut out from the presence of the Lord and from the majesty of his power on the day he comes to be glorified in his holy people' (2 Thess. 1:9-10).

In these verses Moses described three different facets of divine justice. First of all, it was the action of a *grieving father*, 32:19-20. *'The LORD saw this and rejected them because he was angered by his sons and daughters... children who are unfaithful.'* Only a father or mother could grieve this much, and only children could cause this much grief, because there is no relationship more tender than that between parents and children. To be rejected and reviled by a friend is bad, but it is far worse to be reviled by our children. It is unbearably painful, yet God was rejected by his own children, the people of Israel. In such a situation parents may have to face the hard reality and tell their children that such behaviour is not acceptable in the family home. Israel could not worship other gods and continue to rely on God's goodness, but it grieved God to discipline his children.

Then, secondly, it was the action of a *passionate Saviour* (32:21-22).

> *They made me jealous by what is no god...*
> *I will make them envious by those who are not a people;*
> *I will make them angry by a nation that has no understanding.*
> *For a fire has been kindled by my wrath...*

Jealousy is a deadly passion, and God is said to be jealous because he is passionate about his people. He loves them deeply and longs for their salvation. He yearns for their loyalty, and when they sin his anger burns like a fire. Yet God's passionate anger was not the end of the matter, for God wanted his people to be passionate about him. If they were not passionate about God, he promised to work within their hearts to make them passionate. The very nations which administered God's justice would stir them to seek a restoration of their precious relationship with Jehovah.

This truth was taken by the apostle Paul and applied to the nation of Israel in the context of his missionary work amongst the Gentiles (see Rom. 10:19). The gospel blessings enjoyed by the Gentiles were a reminder to the Israelites that they had been rejected by God because of their unbelief (see Rom. 10:16). Yet God would not allow them to continue in unbelief, for the faith of the Gentiles would stir Israel to jealousy and, ultimately, saving faith in Christ. 'Israel has experienced a hardening in part until the full number of the Gentiles has come in. And so all Israel will be saved...' (Rom. 11:25-26). In Romans 10:19 Paul quoted from Deuteronomy 32:21 to show that even God's rejection of Israel arose from his passionate love for them and would result in the salvation of many – both Jews and Gentiles.

Thirdly, God's rejection of Israel was the action of a *faithful judge* (32:23-26). '*I will heap calamities upon them... I will send wasting famine against them, consuming pestilence and deadly plague...*' These were the calamities about which Moses had warned the people in 28:15-68. They were the consequences of covenant-breaking disobedience. The song describes a time when God can warn no longer but must do what he has promised. He does so with a heavy heart, for he is a loving Father. But he acts with a resolute hand because his own justice demands it. Jehovah is like a judge handing down a sentence to a convicted criminal. He has no choice. To allow Israel to continue in its rebellion unchecked would have made God and his covenant an object of contempt. These covenant calamities remind us that the faithfulness of God has two sides. On the one hand it proclaims blessing to those who love God and serve him with all their heart, but on the other hand it assures those who despise God and disobey him that they cannot escape his judgment. The faithfulness of God forces us to ask ourselves 'how shall we escape if we ignore such a great salvation?' (Heb. 2:3).

God's justice is one of his most misunderstood and misrepresented characteristics. It is very common for people today to describe the administration of God's justice as unfair and unloving. We often hear the greatest demonstration of God's justice – the death of his Son on the cross – as an obscene travesty of justice. These slanderous accusations have a long history, and in 32:27 we have an ancient manifestation of the same blindness.

> *I dreaded the taunt of the enemy,*
> *lest the adversary misunderstand*

and say, 'Our hand has triumphed;
the LORD has not done all this.'

In this instance, the accusation levelled against God was that he was powerless to deliver his people from the hostility of his enemies. Those enemies thought that they were in control of history and able to do whatever they liked to the people of Israel. The boasts of the Assyrian commander in 2 Kings 18:33-35 come to mind as an example of this foolishness – 'How then can the LORD deliver Jerusalem from my hand?' He and many others failed to realise that they were able to lift their hands against the people of Israel only because God willed it in the fulfilment of his purposes.

Notwithstanding the fact of his sovereignty over all things, Jehovah was grieved at the foolishness of the claims which would be made by those who oppressed his people. This was because of his zeal for his own glory. He is also very zealous for the honour of his chosen people. He will restore them to their former glory (see Zech. 1:14-16). When he reveals his zeal for his people, his enemies will be put to shame (see Isa.26:11). God's justice is always revolutionary. It knocks the proud off their perch and raises up the humble into God's favour (see Luke 1:51-52). This is a message which our proud world needs to hear today.

God's appeal to the nations (32:28-43)

This section describes God's dealings with the Gentile nations which oppress the people of Israel. They will be God's agents of judgment upon Israel. They will do terrible things to the people of God and they will bring God's judgment upon themselves. However, God has a message of grace, not only for the Israelites, but also for them.

A song of witness

In 32:28-35 God describes the folly of *the nations*.

> *They are a nation without sense,*
> *there is no discernment in them.*
> *If only they were wise and would understand this,*
> *and discern what their end will be.*

They imagined that their own strength had put Israel's armies to flight (32:30). They did not realise that such a thing would have been impossible unless Israel's Lord had allowed it to happen. Israel's calamities were like the sufferings of Job, which God permitted for his own purposes (see Job 1:12; 2:6). Satan's power to hurt Job was restrained by the higher power of God, who rules all things. We can take comfort from that when we feel the hurtful attacks of Satan and evil men, for the Lord has drawn a line beyond which they cannot pass.

The nations which attacked Israel simply did not know Israel's God. They made a serious miscalculation by thinking that Jehovah was just like their own imaginary and powerless gods. But, wrote Moses, *'their rock is not like our Rock... Their vine comes from the vine of Sodom...'* Their gods were quite unable to give them victory over Israel. Only Jehovah could do that. Their gods supplied them with spiritual poison which weakened and destroyed them. Their gods led them deeper and deeper into sin and brought them increasingly under the wrath of God.

> *Have I not kept this in reserve*
> *and sealed it in my vaults? ...*
> *their day of disaster is near*
> *and their doom rushes upon them.*

It was true that God had raised them up to chastise his people, but it was unthinkable that they should ever overthrow his rule on earth. That is as likely to happen as the prospect that a band of impoverished pirates might overthrow the armies of a superpower. Recently, a group of pirates based along the coast of East Africa attacked a Chinese merchant vessel and took several Chinese seamen hostage. The response of the Chinese navy was swift. The sailors were rescued and the pirates were punished. Likewise, God will not let the heathen nations think that they are stronger than him.

Then in 32:36-38 God describes the folly of *Israel*. They had abandoned Jehovah to join the nations in worshipping their discredited gods. Jehovah will ask them,

> *Now where are their gods,*
> *the rock they took refuge in,*
> *the gods who ate the fat of their sacrifices...*
> *Let them rise up to help you!*
> *Let them give you shelter!*

There is a bitter irony here. The nations were powerless to touch Israel because their gods were weak, yet in its hour of need Israel turned to these impotent gods. In so doing they abandoned 'the Rock' and planted their feet in quicksand. They were like many today who seek salvation from any and every source except the God of the Bible. They seek doctrines 'to suit their own desires' but have no time for the Word of God or sound doctrine (see 2 Tim. 4:3).

Yet God's warnings point towards his mercy. He warns those whom he would save and shows mercy towards those who hear his warnings. In 32:39-42 God speaks about himself. These verses describe who God is and what he will do.

> *See now that I myself am He!*
> *There is no god beside me.*
> *I put to death and I bring to life,*
> *I have wounded and I will heal...*

A song of witness

These words would be insufferable arrogance if they came from the lips of anyone other than Jehovah. He alone can combine judgment and mercy. He combines them in the oath he swore (32:40). *'I lift my hand to heaven and declare: As surely as I live forever...'* As the writer to the Hebrews points out, he swore by himself because there is no-one greater than he (see Heb. 6:13-14). His character guarantees the salvation of his chosen people.

Two aspects of God's character come into view in these verses – his justice and his mercy. Both offer hope to the people of Israel. Because he is a just God he will punish those who have dealt so cruelly with Israel (see 32:41-42).

> *When I sharpen my flashing sword*
> *and my hand grasps it in judgment,*
> *I will take vengeance on my adversaries.*

Moses repeated this promise in order to confirm it in 32:43. *'He will avenge the blood of his servants; he will take vengeance on his enemies.'* It may be hard to link these actions with salvation until we remember that the destruction of the Egyptians in the waters of the Red Sea was the defining moment of the exodus (see Exod. 14:30-31). From that day on the Israelites knew that they had been freed from slavery and were free to do whatever the Lord wanted them to do.

Because he is also a merciful God, Jehovah holds out the promise of salvation to those who call out to him. In the final verse of this section he appeals to both Israel and the nations, 32:43.

> *Rejoice, O nations, with his people,*
> *for he will avenge the blood of his servants;*
> *he will take vengeance on his enemies*
> *and make atonement for his land and people.*

This is an amazing verse because the destinies of Israel and the nations are brought together. Both will be subject to God's judgment, but Israel had the hope of better things. Israel at least had the hope that its sins would be atoned for. The atonement described in this verse is the covering over of sin that took place when a sacrificial animal was slain and its blood sprinkled on behalf of the sinner. This is what the High Priest did for the whole community of Israel every year on the Day of Atonement (see Lev. 16:16). This symbolised the greatest of all God's blessings, according to Psalm 32:1: 'Blessed is he who whose transgressions are forgiven, whose sins are covered'. The nations will rejoice along with the people of Israel, for they too will benefit from the atonement which God makes for Israel.

This promise came to a glorious fulfilment when the Lord Jesus became 'a merciful and faithful high priest in service to God' in order that 'he might make atonement for the sins of the people' (Heb. 2:17). The 'people' for whom he made atonement included Gentiles as well as Jews. Paul explained in Romans 15:8-9: 'For I tell you that Christ has become a servant of the Jews on behalf of God's truth, to confirm the promises made to the patriarchs so that the Gentiles may glorify God for his mercy'. To confirm this claim, Paul quotes from Deuteronomy 32:43 and calls the Gentiles to rejoice that salvation is offered to them. These verses point to universal rejoicing because the coming of Jesus to make atonement for sinners is 'good news of great joy that will be for all the people' (Luke 2:10).

Concluding exhortation (32:44-47)

The concluding verses of chapter 32 contain two short sections of historical narrative. The first of these, 32:44-47, tells us that *'Moses came with Joshua son of Nun and spoke all the words of this song in the hearing of the people'.* Moses was faithful in all the tasks which God gave him to do (see Num. 12:7, Heb. 3:5). Moses was accompanied by Joshua, his companion and successor, as he taught the song to the people. This reminds us that the song of witness was part of the succession plan, enabling a smooth transition from one generation of leaders to another. It was important that the next generation, and the generations following it, should teach the same message as Moses had taught. Moses' goal was to ensure a smooth transition and the continuity of biblical ministry.

In 32:45-46 Moses concluded the song with an exhortation of his own, repeating almost word for word what he had said to the Israelites back in 6:6-9. *'When Moses finished reciting all these words to all Israel, he said to them, "Take to heart all the words I have solemnly declared to you this day, so that you may command your children to obey carefully all the words of this law."'* Moses was the messenger, but the message came from God and demanded a response. The Old Testament Israelites were to listen to Moses' words with the same reverent submission as the Christian believers in Thessalonica when they heard the preaching of Paul many centuries later. They heard Paul's message 'not as the word of men, but as it actually is, the word of God, which is at work in you who believe' (1 Thess. 2:13).

Moses explained the abiding significance of his words in 32:47. *'They are not just idle words for you – they are your life. By them you will live long in the land you are crossing the Jordan to possess.'* The purpose of this song was not simply to teach interesting facts about God, but to point them to a right relationship with God. This relationship was one of trust and obedience, walking with the Lord who loved them and led them to freedom. This is life. This is what Moses held out to them with such passion in 30:20: 'For the LORD is your life, and he will give you many years in the land he swore to give to your fathers, Abraham, Isaac and Jacob.' The promise of long life in the land of promise pointed towards what the Lord Jesus would later call 'life to the full' or 'everlasting life' (John 10:10, 6:47). We can live that life and enjoy its pleasures only when we hear God's words and believe them. That is why the psalmist said, 'Your promise preserves my life' (Ps. 119:50). That is why Peter and the other disciples refused to turn away from their Lord when many others abandoned him. 'Lord, to whom shall we go? You have the words of eternal life' (John 6:68).

A personal note (32:48-52)

This is a sad postscript to the song of witness. On the very same day as Moses taught this song to the people, he went to the top of Mount Nebo to survey the promised land (32:48-49) and prepare to die (32:50). *'There on the mountain that you have climbed you will die and be gathered to your people, just as your brother Aaron died on Mount Hor and was gathered to his people.'* Aaron's death is described in Numbers 20:22-29. The reason why he, too, did not live to enter the land is given in Numbers 20:12; 27:12-14. It is perplexing that this sad end to Moses' life is recorded so often in Deuteronomy (see 1:37; 3:26-27; 4:21-22). In these verses the guilt of the people is emphasised. Moses suffered loss as their representative, bearing the consequences of their sin. However, in the present passage the focus is on the guilt of Moses and Aaron rather than that of the people. This is not to deny that the people were rebellious, but to acknowledge that their leaders were also sinners. Moses struck the rock in petulant anger. By striking the rock, when God had told him simply to speak to it, Moses turned the people's attention from God's miraculous provision and focused it on an act of a man. Moses did not honour God as holy before the eyes of the people.

Why does the Achilles' heel of Moses, the heroic preacher of Deuteronomy, receive so much attention? Possibly because the song of witness has sought to point out the danger of unfaithfulness. If a man as faithful as Moses can be barred from the promised land because of this single act of unfaithfulness, then future generations may well be removed from the land because of their many acts of unfaithfulness. This is a warning about the serious consequences of seemingly trivial sins.

Another reason why we are told about Moses' tragic death is that Moses is not the hero of Deuteronomy. God is! God is the Saviour of his people and Moses was an instrument in his hands. Moses was a servant through whom God's people came to hear the gospel and believe. He was a sinful and imperfect preacher. Like all preachers, he did well to remember his shortcomings.

Today, preachers and people alike hear this same warning as they read the list of Old Testament heroes of faith in the book of Hebrews.

> See to it, brothers, that none of you has a sinful, unbelieving heart that turns away from the living God. But encourage one another daily, as long as it is called Today, so that none of you may be hardened by sin's deceitfulness. We have come to share in Christ if we hold firmly till the end of the confidence we had at first. As has just been said: 'Today, if you hear his voice, do not harden your hearts as you did in the rebellion' (Heb. 3:12-15).

Chapter 33
A blessed nation

Please read Deuteronomy 33: 1-29

There is a popular Christian song with the refrain, 'Count your blessings, name them one by one'. The song continues to tell us that, as we do this, we will be surprised to discover how much God has done for us. This is a good habit to cultivate. Yet, human nature being what it is, we are often more inclined to voice our complaints and list our demands than to acknowledge what God has done for us. It is easy for an older generation to lay the blame for this on the mindset of a younger generation and the modern preoccupation with immediate personal gratification. The problem is, in fact, timeless. The people of Israel were quick to forget what God had done for them. Within a few days of their deliverance from death at the hands of the Egyptians at the Red Sea they grumbled because there was no water for them to drink in the desert (Exod. 15:24). It was as though they had forgotten what God had done for them. On many occasions over the next forty years, indeed right up to the moment of his death, Moses reminded them how God had blessed them.

In Deuteronomy 33 we read Moses' last words to the people of Israel – and they were words of blessing. *'This is the blessing that Moses the man of God pronounced on the Israelites before his death'* (33:1). He describes the blessedness of the nation which God has chosen. Some of those blessings were already in their hands, while others would come to them only after they entered the land of Canaan. Each one of these blessings came, not from Moses, but from the hand of God. In 33:6-25 he addressed each tribe specifically; and in 33:26-29 he spoke more generally about Israel's God and Israel's blessedness.

The blessings of this chapter are a fitting conclusion to Deuteronomy. The thrust of Moses' ministry throughout this book has been God's goodness to his people and their response of love and obedience. The most visible example of God's goodness has been his promise of the land of Canaan (see, for example, 1:6-8; 11:24). One commentator very helpfully links this chapter to the theme of the book as a whole, telling us that it 'puts flesh on the theme of covenant blessing'. It describes the promised land in all its beauty and bounty. The language is richly poetic, employing eye-catching imagery and memorable phrases to help the Israelites to see in their mind's eye what life in the land of Canaan would look like. Here we see how literary technique was put to pastoral use to help the Israelites remember what they were often in danger of forgetting.

Moses' strenuous efforts to display God's goodness to his people are an example and encouragement for those whose task it is today to teach the word of God. It is their responsibility to reinforce the message of Psalm 1:1-2 and show how great God's blessings really are.

> Blessed is the man
> who does not walk in the counsel of the wicked
> or stand in the way of sinners
> or sit in the seat of mockers.
> But his delight is in the law of the LORD,
> and on his law he meditates day and night.

It is the privilege and responsibility of all God's people to think often about these blessings.

A blessed nation

The Lord who blesses (33:2-5)

Before describing the specific blessings pronounced upon each of the twelve tribes, Moses pointed the attention of the people to the majesty and glory of Jehovah. On this note the chapter opened and closed.

Moses described the *mountain-top appearance* of God in 33:2.

> *The Lord came from Sinai*
> *and dawned over them from Seir;*
> *he shone from Mount Paran.*

The three mountains named in this verse were places where God had revealed himself to the Israelites during their wilderness travels. Mount Sinai (better known in Deuteronomy as Horeb (see 4:10-14; 5:2-4) was the mountain where God had given the law to Israel. Mount Seir was the mountainous area south and east of the Dead Sea where the Edomites lived (see 2:2-5, 8, 12). Its inhabitants were hostile towards the Israelites as they passed through, yet even here God 'shone forth' on his people's behalf. The location of Mount Paran (see also Hab. 3:3) is uncertain. The wilderness of Paran lay north-east of Mount Sinai, along the western side of the Gulf of Aqaba, and Mount Paran was one of the peaks there. The Israelites would have passed this way as they travelled from Sinai towards Kadesh Barnea and the southern approaches to the land of Canaan.

Mountains were significant landmarks along Israel's journey from Egypt to Canaan. In the ancient world it was commonly believed that God revealed himself to mankind on the tops of mountains. That is why many worship sites were found on mountain-top locations. This was a reminder that God is exalted far above all his creatures, mankind included. There is a great gulf fixed between the king of heaven and his subjects. Only by God's gracious initiative can that gulf be bridged, as

God condescends to come down and bless his people. That is why even the terrifying events at Sinai were to be thought of as an act of mercy.

The presence of angels is a sign that God has come amongst his people. '*He came with myriads of holy ones.*' In 33:1 the 'holy ones' do not refer to God's redeemed people, but to the heavenly spirits who stand in his presence day and night. They were present when he gave the law at Sinai (see Acts 7:53; Gal. 3:19). They heralded the birth of the Son of God (see Matt. 1:20-23; Luke 2:9-14). They will herald the glorious return of the Lord Jesus (see Matt. 13:41; 24:31; 2 Thess.1:7). Their presence is always an indicator that the God of heaven has come into this world.

In 33:3 Moses explained why Jehovah chose to come down and reveal himself. '*Surely it is you who love the people...*' This verse is the only place in the Old Testament where this particular Hebrew verb occurs. It describes the *merciful love* of God. It means to embrace with affection. When God drew near to the Israelites, he hugged them to himself. He took hold of their hands and led them.

Then Moses described the *magisterial instruction* which God gave in 33:3b-5. There at Sinai God gave laws to Moses for the people of Israel to obey. '*At your feet they all bow down, and from you receive instruction.*' Moses had in mind the day when the Israelites and their representative leaders assembled on the slopes of the mountain and God made a covenant with them (33:5b).

> *He was king over Jeshurun*
> *when the leaders of the people assembled,*
> *along with the tribes of Israel.*

Jeshurun is a poetic description of the people of God (see 32:15; 33:26). It means the upright one and describes God's ideal for his people. They were redeemed to be 'upright ones', characterised by holiness. There is an ironic play on words here, for those who *bow down* at his feet and submit to his law (33:3b) will stand *upright* (33:5b). True dignity is not built upon self-aggrandisement, but upon humble repentance before God.

Blessings for the tribes (33:6-25)

It is an indication of Moses' significance in the history of Israel that we find this series of blessings at the end of his life. He is placed on a par with the patriarchs, the founding fathers of the nation of Israel. Just as Jacob blessed his twelve sons on his deathbed (see Gen. 49:1-28), so Moses blessed their descendants when they had grown into tribes. There are important parallels between Jacob's blessing and the blessings pronounced by Moses in this chapter, but there are also some significant differences. Moses listed eleven tribes, omitting the tribe of Simeon and listing Joseph in place to the two tribes of Ephraim and Manasseh. For some of his sons Jacob had sharp words (see Gen.49:4-7, for example); but in this chapter Moses' words contain a more consistent emphasis on blessing.

i. Reuben (33:6). Reuben is mentioned first because he was the firstborn son of Jacob. The marginal reading in the NIV is the preferred translation of this verse: '*Let Reuben live and not die, but let his men be few*'. This tribe settled east of the Jordan (see 3:12, 16-17) and was often exposed to attack from desert nomads (see 1 Chr. 5:18-22). In spite of its vulnerability, the tribe of Reuben survived these ordeals, though its size and influence were small. 'Few' means that its population was easy to count.

ii. Judah (33:7). Although Judah became one of the most important tribes in Israel, the blessing in 33:7 is one of the shortest in this chapter. This is consistent with an early dating of Deuteronomy, as the Messianic significance of the tribe of

Judah was not yet as clearly established in the nation's thinking in the time of Moses as it would be centuries later after the time of David and Solomon. Moses' prayer anticipated the struggles of the conquest when each tribe went out to war against the local Canaanites in order to take possession of its allotted portion of land.

> Hear, O LORD, the cry of Judah;
> bring him to his people.
> With his own hands he defends his cause.
> Oh, be his help against his foes.

Although the tribes fought as tribal regiments, they fought on behalf of the nation as a whole. As the fighting men went into battle the whole tribe would ask for God's protection so that its warriors might return home safely.

iii. Levi (33:8-11). Moses' blessing upon Levi acknowledged its special role in Israel. The Levites were spiritual leaders. Theirs was a challenging task, which Moses was well able to understand, having led the people of Israel for forty years. He described their *tasks* in 33:8, 10. They were teachers who guided the people by using the sacred lot (*'Your Thummim and Urim belong to the man you favoured'*) and by teaching God's word to Israel (*'He teaches your precepts to Jacob and your law to Israel'*). They were also priests who presented the people's sacrifices to God (33:10b).

Moses described the *trials* they faced in their work (33:8). The worst of these was the hostility of the people they served. *'You tested him at Massah; you contended with him at the waters of Meribah.'* A fuller account of these trials can be found in Exodus 17:1-7 and Numbers 20:1-13. Moses and Aaron were from the tribe of Levi and they faced the wrath of the disgruntled Israelites. Interestingly, the 'you' in 33:8 refers to Jehovah, for he was the one who was testing Moses through the grumbling of his people in the wilderness. God tests his people to demonstrate that his power and grace are at work in them. That is why we are encouraged to rejoice in the midst of trials (see 2 Cor. 12:9-10; James 1:2). This is a great encouragement to those who lead God's people, for testing times are certain to come their way.

Moses described the *sacrifices* which they must inevitably make in the course of their ministry (33:9). These arise from the very nature of spiritual leadership, which demands uncompromising loyalty to God.

> *He said of his father and mother,*
> *'I have no regard for them.'*
> *He did not recognise his brothers*
> *or acknowledge his own children,*
> *but he watched over your word*
> *and guarded your covenant.*

This refers to the events of Exodus 32:26-29, when the Levites stood with Moses against their fellow-Israelites after they had worshipped the golden calf at Sinai. A similar commitment is called for from all who would follow the Lord Jesus as subjects in his kingdom (see Matt. 10:37-38; Mark 10:28-30).

Because of their sacrificial service for the Lord, they will be *honoured* (33:11).

> *Bless all his skills, O LORD,*
> *and be pleased with the work of his hands.*
> *Smite the loins of those who rise up against him;*
> *strike his foes till they rise no more.*

Moses and the Levites who followed him must have wondered why God allowed them to face such bitter opposition. For a time God allowed them to be tested, but ultimately he would vindicate them and judge their opponents. God will delight in their work and reward it. Similarly, in the New Testament church, elders are described as doing a 'good work' and as being worthy of 'double honour' (see 1 Tim. 3:1; 5:17).

iv. Benjamin (33:12). The tribe of Benjamin enjoyed a special place in Jehovah's affections, just as Benjamin, the youngest son of Jacob's favourite wife, enjoyed a special place in his father's affections (see Gen.42:4, 38; 44:20-22, 30-34). *'Let the beloved of the LORD rest secure in him, for he shields him all day long.'* This tribe was Jehovah's darling and Moses gave it a special title – 'the beloved of the LORD'. The Hebrew word translated 'beloved' comes from the same root as Jedadiah, the special name given to David's son, Solomon, in 2 Samuel 12:25 (see also Neh. 13:26). It indicated the deep and irrevocable love of God. God's love was the ground of Benjamin's security for it protected him from every danger and disturbance.

The last line of 33:12 describes a very special privilege which Benjamin enjoyed. Here the translation given by the NKJV is to be preferred: *'And he shall dwell between his shoulders'.* 'He' refers to Jehovah, who dwelt in the midst of Benjamin and sheltered him by his presence. This is probably a prophetic reference to the location of the temple between two rocky outcrops (literally shoulders) on Mount Zion. The boundary between Benjamin and Judah ran along the southern slopes of Mount Zion (see Josh. 15:8; 18:16), and the temple site was right on that boundary. After it was built, the temple became a visible symbol of God's presence amongst his people, and a blessing for all the people of Israel. Today, in Christ believers enjoy God's presence and protection. That was Paul's prayer in Ephesians 3:16-17: 'I pray that out of his glorious riches he may strengthen you with power through his Spirit in your inner being, so that Christ may dwell in your hearts through faith'.

v. Joseph (33:13-17). The blessing upon the tribe of Joseph calls for particular notice because it is one of the longest in the chapter. Only the blessing on Levi contains as much substance. The descendants of Joseph formed two tribes, Ephraim and Manasseh. Of these two tribes, Ephraim became the more important and was the leading tribe in the northern kingdom. It rivalled Judah for national pre-eminence. Surprisingly, Moses used royal language to describe the descendants of Joseph; language which we might have expected him to attribute to the tribe of Judah. The language of 33:13-16 is reminiscent of the blessing which Isaac intended for the firstborn in Gen 27:27-29.

May the LORD bless his land
with the precious dew from heaven above
and with the deep waters that lie below;
with the best the sun brings forth
and the finest the moon can yield;
with the choicest gifts of the ancient mountains
and the fruitfulness of the everlasting hills;
with the best gifts of the earth and its fulness
and the favour of him who dwelt in the burning bush.

Moses drew upon his own experience of God's special mercy to describe this special blessing (33:16). *'And the favour of him who dwelt in the burning bush.'* Here Moses refers to the appearance of Jehovah in the flames of a burning bush in the desert. Fire was a characteristic of God's revelation of himself to Moses (see 4:12; 5:22). It spoke of his purity and power to destroy. Yet from the bush God promised Israel's salvation, not its destruction. God's message was one of favour. That favour will rest on Joseph. Why did Moses single out Joseph for such a blessing?

Joseph had been a favourite son of his father (see Gen. 37:3). He concluded from a series of dreams that God had chosen him for a very special task (see Gen. 37:5-11). He was correct. God made Joseph the instrument of deliverance for his whole family and for the land of Egypt as well. God made Joseph the ruler over his brothers so that the lives of many might be saved (see

Gen.50:20). Not only was he a prince among his brothers, he was a prince whose royal power was used to bring salvation. *'Let all these rest on the head of Joseph, on the brow of the prince among his brothers.'*

The might of Joseph's royal power is described in 33:17.

> *In majesty he is like a firstborn bull;*
> *his horns are the horns of a wild ox.*
> *With them he will gore the nations,*
> *even those at the end of the earth.*

The 'wild ox' was an animal of proverbial strength, also mentioned in Psalm 22:21; 92:10; Job 39:9-10. In some older translations it is referred to as 'the unicorn'. It was said to have been as large as an elephant though, since Bible times, it has been hunted to extinction. Joseph was to enjoy the legendary strength of this beast. It is possible that its two horns may represent the division of Joseph into the two tribes of Ephraim and Manasseh (see 33:17b). *'Such are the ten thousands of Ephraim; such are the thousands of Manasseh.'* These tribes were about to take on the Canaanite armies in battle on the battlefield, and Moses' blessing assured them that he would give them the strength they needed to face this onerous task, just as he had helped their ancestor Joseph when the might of Egypt was arrayed against him.

vi. and vii. Zebulun and *Issachar* (33:18-19). These tribes were descended from the fifth and sixth sons of Leah (see Gen.30:17-20), and they are often mentioned together. They were blessed jointly by Moses. Their tribal territories lay side by side in the northern section of the promised land. Zebulun was by the coast (see Gen. 49:13), while Issachar lay inland. Moses called them to rejoice. *'Rejoice, Zebulun, in your going out, and you, Issachar, in your tents.'* This is a poetic way of exhorting these tribes to rejoice in the enjoyment of God's goodness whether they are at home in their tents or out and about their daily work. At all times they were to praise God (see Ps. 34:1). The blessings mentioned in 33:19b may refer to Zebulun's location by the sea. *They will feast on the abundance of the seas, on the treasures hidden in the sand.* Both tribes were able to earn a living from fishing and trade. The coastal strip where they lived was noted for the manufacture of dye from shellfish and glass from the sand.

The prosperity enjoyed by these tribes would encourage them to acknowledge Jehovah as the giver of every blessing and to call others to do the same (33:19a). *They will summon peoples to the mountain and there offer sacrifices of righteousness.* Note that this is true worship, not a syncretistic mix of paganism and the worship of Jehovah. The sacrifices offered are those which God had commanded and they were offered for the glory of God (see Mal. 3:3; John 4:23-24). Their worship was a powerful witness to the true God. The 'peoples' who are summoned to worship Jehovah may be Israelites as well as other nations. This happened after the Israelites returned from exile (see Zech. 8:20-21).

The location of 'the mountain' to which the 'peoples' will be summoned in 33:19 has prompted some discussion. The explanations offered are mostly tentative. John Calvin identifies the mountain as Mount Zion in Jerusalem. Most modern commentators link it with Mount Tabor, where a local shrine may have been located. This subsequently sank into gross paganism (see Hosea 5:1). This scenario sits uneasily beside the hostility which Deuteronomy displayed towards the plethora of local shrines in Canaan. It is therefore wise to agree with Calvin and see it as a pointer to the as yet unidentified location which God has chosen (see 12:5) and to which he will call his people. This is the place where God's people will offer their sacrifices.

viii. Gad (33:20-21). Moses blessing commences in a roundabout manner, by blessing the One who enlarged the territory of this tribe (33:20). *'Blessed is he who enlarges Gad's domain!'* Jehovah himself is the object of Moses' praise, for it was he who made this tribe mighty in battle and who gave it its territory. Yet Gad was active in the pursuit of what God had promised.

> *Gad lives there like a lion...*
> *He chose the best land for himself;*
> *the leader's portion was kept for him.*

Gad's warlike qualities were like those of a lion and he received a 'lion's share' when the land was divided amongst the tribes. The 'best land' was the land east of the Jordan which Gad (as well as Reuben and eastern Manasseh) had sought for themselves as soon as it had been wrested from the Amorites (see 2:24 – 3:20; Num. 32:1-5). This land was especially suitable for livestock, which the Gadites possessed in abundance. 'The leader's portion' may refer to Moses' decision as the leader of the nation to allocate the land to them, or it may refer to the status of Gad as one of the leading tribes. After many years Gad absorbed its neighbouring tribe, the Reubenites, and became the most powerful tribe east of the Jordan.

In 33:21 we see a dynamic combination of tribal ambition and national unity.

> *When the heads of the people assembled,*
> *he carried out the LORD's righteous will,*
> *and his judgments concerning Israel.*

The Gadites fought hard to extend their territory. They must have prayed like Jabez, who asked God to enlarge his boundaries (1 Chr. 4:9-10). Yet they knew that they were not fighting for themselves alone, but for their fellow-Israelites and for their Lord. Moses permitted them to possess their pasturelands east of the Jordan on the condition that they went west into Canaan to fight alongside the other tribes. This was 'the LORD's righteous will, and his judgment'. Not only was it right and proper that the Gadites fight alongside their brothers, this was God's command (see Num. 32:20-25). When God spoke, these mighty warriors could do nothing but submit to him.

ix. Dan (33:22). The shortest of the blessings was that for the tribe of Dan. *'Dan is a lion's cub, springing out of Bashan.'* Dan's original territory was not in Bashan at all, but west of the Jordan in the Aijalon Valley. Bashan lay to the east of the Jordan, running from the river valley to the mountains. It was an ideal natural habitat for lions and one of these fierce animals was used to describe some of Dan's less admirable qualities. Young lions will often shy away from a fight with a more powerful opponent. When Dan found that the Canaanite inhabitants of their allocated territory put up strong resistance, they migrated north and seized the area around Laish (see Judg. 18). Their actions in that chapter were vicious and opportunistic – traits that are characteristic of a young lion, but not indicative of a people trusting in God's promises or submissive to his will.

x. Naphtali (33:23). Another short, but beautiful, blessing is found in 33:23.

> *Naphtali is abounding with the favour of the LORD*
> *and is full of his blessing;*
> *he will inherit southward to the lake.*

Naphtali's territory stretched from the highland plateau north-west of the Sea of Galilee to the lowland areas further south along the upper reaches of the River Jordan and the shores of the Sea of Galilee. These areas were (and still are) noted for their outstanding beauty and rich vegetation. Its greatest blessing, however, was spiritual.

It was *'the favour of the Lord'* which made Naphtali overflow with blessing. God's favour is his undeserved goodness. Because of his favour he dispensed his blessings amongst the tribes of Israel. Moses' distinctive vocabulary of grace is taken up in the New Testament to describe the purpose of our Lord's earthly ministry. 'The Spirit of the Lord is on me, because he has anointed me ... to proclaim the year of the Lord's favour' (Luke 4:18-19). Not every believer will be blessed with earthly goods, but every believer will overflow with God's goodness. 'And God is able to make all grace abound to you, so that in all things at all times, having all that you need, you will abound in every good work' (2 Cor. 9:8; see also Col. 2:7).

xi. Asher (33:24-25). Last, but by no means least, comes Moses' blessing on Asher.

> *Most blessed of sons is Asher;*
> *let him be favoured by his brothers,*
> *and let him bathe his feet in oil.*

The warmth of Moses blessing is indicated by a play on words. Asher's name means blessed or happy (see Gen. 30:13). The blessings which Moses predicted for this tribe flow from its geographical location on the Mediterranean coast between Tyre in the north and the Kishon River in the south. The area was famed for the cultivation of olives, from which oil was produced. Such was the abundance of oil which this region produced that the sons of Asher, figuratively at least, could 'bathe (their) feet in oil'.

The coastline of Asher was one of Israel's frontier areas. Over the centuries, many invading armies marched through its territory. Consequently, it was dotted with fortified towns within which the inhabitants might seek protection. Moses' promise that *'the bolts of your gates will be iron and bronze and your strength will equal your days'* would have been a welcome reassurance. Israel's safety lay in the fact that God watched over them (Psalm 121:5) and gave strength to those who faithfully obeyed his commands (11:8).

Blessings for the whole nation (33:26-29)

After describing the blessings bestowed upon each of the tribes individually, Moses returned to his main point, the blessing bestowed upon all the Israelites as the chosen people of God. Israel's greatest blessing was her covenant with Jehovah. He was the source of every blessing. He was to be the object of their delight. Before listing some of the blessings which they enjoyed in 33:28-29, Moses explains why Jehovah was to the object of their delight. In 33:26 Moses asserts that *'there is no-one like the God of Jeshurun'.* He is the God of the nation that walks uprightly and that makes both him and his people stand out as unique. The uniqueness of Jehovah is an important theme in Deuteronomy (see 4:35; 6:4; 32:12, 39). Many ethical and theological implications are drawn from this truth, not least that only Jehovah can save and only Jehovah is to be worshipped. In 33:26-27 Moses elaborates by describing three reassuring qualities which mark him out as unique.

a. *He is high above* (33:26). He *'rides on the heavens to help you and on the clouds in his majesty'.* In the ancient world those who rode into battle on horses and chariots were feared by ordinary foot soldiers, who walked. Jehovah was greater than any horses or chariots because he 'rides on the heavens'. He harnessed the forces of nature to do his will and made the angels his servants (see Ps. 18:10; 68:32-33; 104:3). Human plans are often frustrated by the unpredictable forces of nature, but God's plans are not (see Isa. 55:9). We walk on the ground, but he rides on the heavens. He commands the wind and the rain and they do his bidding.

God uses his divine power 'to help you'. This distinguished Jehovah from all other gods. The pagans believed that the gods used their powers capriciously and selfishly. They might intervene in the lives of mortals to relieve their boredom or to frustrate the designs of rival deities. Only Jehovah declared his eternal love for his people and sought to help them. God's help is salvation. God helps his people by delivering them from destruction.

b. *He is underneath and all around* (33:27). *'The eternal God is your refuge, and underneath are the everlasting arms.'* The word 'refuge' is similar to that which Moses used in Psalm 90:1, the Psalm of Moses. 'Lord, you have been our dwelling-place throughout all generations.' During their years in the wilderness God was a fortress around them, moved with them, and protected them on their journeys. The fire and the cloud were symbols of his presence and protection. When the Israelites entered the land of Canaan those symbols would not go with them, but Jehovah would continue as their refuge. They would live in cities that had walls and gates, but they would need reminding that their safety was to be found in their Lord and not in their fortifications (see Ps. 125:2).

Moses' words describe the strength and the tenderness of God, as well as his strength. *'Underneath are the everlasting arms.'* He assured the Israelites that God would cradle them as a mother holds her baby. This is a startling description of God and an amazing combination of qualities. Moses has reminded us that God's mighty arm has been stretched out in judgment against Israel's enemies (see 4:34; 5:15; 7:19; 9:29; 11:2; 26:8). Here, those same arms are stretched out to embrace his people. They are 'everlasting' because God's covenant with his people is everlasting. His love and mercy last forever therefore his arms will embrace for ever.

A blessed nation

The same merciful Lord embraces those who trust in the Lord Jesus. When we are physically weak, he remains strong; when we have grown weary from doing good, he delights to do us good; when we have fallen into sin and require chastisement, he restores and embraces us; when we have listened to bad counsel and lost our way, he brings us back into the paths of righteousness; and when we grapple with death, the last enemy, his arms refuse to let go. The Lord Jesus himself has given us this assurance, 'I give them eternal life, and they shall never perish; no-one can snatch them out of my hand' (John 10:28; see also Rom. 8:38-39).

c. *He goes in front* (33:27b). *'He will drive out your enemy before you, saying, "Destroy him!"'* The Israelites were not to fall asleep in God's arms. Moses was preparing them for battle. The promised land was not an empty land. Its Canaanite inhabitants were well armed and ready for battle, but God would drive them out (see 7:20; Josh. 2:9). We can hear Jehovah's war-cry as he goes before his people and urges them on to victory.

This is how the Lord Jesus is described in Hebrews 2:10. 'In bringing many sons to glory, it was fitting that God, for whom and through whom everything exists, should make the author of their salvation perfect through suffering.' He is also called the 'author' of our salvation in Hebrews 12:2. The word which the writer to the Hebrews used describes a scout who went ahead to clear the path for those who would follow. In modern warfare this role has been taken over by special forces who go in to 'take out' key elements of the enemy's infrastructure. The Lord Jesus, by his death and resurrection, has destroyed the capacity of Satan's kingdom to oppose the advance of the gospel. He now sends the church to 'destroy' what remains of Satan's doomed kingdom. He assures us of victory (see Rom. 16:20; 1 Cor. 15:57; Col. 2:15).

God's treasured possession

So in 33:28-29 the focus shifts from the unique glory of Israel's God to the unique blessedness of God's people. Moses asked a rhetorical question, *'Who is like you, a people saved by the Lord?'* The blessings enjoyed by the Israelites are described in military terms because Moses anticipated the invasion, conquest and settlement of the land of Canaan. We can note three aspects of Israel's blessedness in these verses.

a. Secure in isolation (33:28a). *'So Israel will live in safety alone.'* The explanation of their security is to be found in the word 'alone'. Israel was unique because God had chosen her to be 'his treasured possession' (see 7:6). This isolated Israel from other nations. Her isolation was to be spiritual and moral. She was to think and live differently from other nations because she was a nation in covenant with God (see Num. 23:9). Her isolation was also geographical, for when she took possession of the promised land and drove out her enemies she would dwell alone, without neighbours or enemies.

> Shepherd your people with your staff,
> the flock of your inheritance,
> which lives by itself in a forest,
> in fertile pasturelands.
> (Micah 7:14).

Yet God does not expect us to live in splendid isolation from the world around us (see Matt. 28:19; John 17:11, 15, 18). Although God has very deliberately placed us in the world, he intends that we live as people who are not 'of the world'. He has chosen and redeemed us so that we might be 'a people that are his very own, eager to do what is good' (Titus 2:14). God's people will always be distinct from the world around them. This keeps us from falling away from grace and into sin. Matthew Henry makes this telling comment: 'Our specialness as God's people... will be our security. Our singularity will be our safety and satisfaction... The more we dwell alone the more safely we will dwell.' In other words, eternal security belongs to those who walk with God and grow in holiness.

b. *Blessed by earth's riches* (33:28b).

Jacob's spring is secure
in a land of grain and new wine,
where the heavens drop dew.

Jacob is another name for the people of Israel. Here they are compared to a spring of water, constantly bubbling up from the ground. This is a poetic way of describing how new generations of Israelites will arise to enjoy God's blessings in the land and so perpetuate the covenant people. They would live in a land watered by the springs which flowed from the Judean hills. The land which God promised to Israel was not desert or scrub, but a rich land (see 11:10-12; Gen. 27:28). In 33:13 this richness was promised to Joseph, but here in 33:28 it is promised to the whole nation.

The material prosperity represented here by grain and wine is not peculiar to God's redeemed people. Other nations also enjoyed those blessings. Our Lord acknowledged that God 'causes his sun to rise on the evil and the good, and sends rain on the righteous and the unrighteous' (Matt. 5:45). What made Israel's blessings unique was the covenant love of God which accompanied them. Grain, new wine and oil were covenant blessings (see 11:14-15). All that the Israelites saw in the promised land was a reminder of God's great love for them.

We, too, must learn to appreciate our material possessions in a new, God-centred way. God is in total control over the world around us and everything that it contains (see Ps. 24:1). He controls the weather, the economy, the international situation. Sometimes he chooses to bless us and sometimes he chooses to withhold material blessing. In either case God does what is best for us (see Rom. 8:28). If we are to count ourselves blessed even when we are badly treated, how much more ought we to count ourselves blessed when we receive material blessing from God's hand. 'Praise the Lord... forget not all his benefits' (Ps. 103:2).

c. *Victorious in battle* (33:29b). *'He is your shield and helper and your glorious sword.'* Moses reminded the people of Israel that God protected them from the attacks of their enemies and that he struck terror into their enemies. With him in their midst, Israel's advance into the promised land was guaranteed a successful outcome. *'Your enemies will cower before you and you will trample down their high places.'* Israel's enemies would tremble in defeat and disarray. Their trembling is not to be confused with the trembling of those who revere God, as described in Isaiah 66:2 ('This is the one I esteem: he who is humble and contrite in spirit, and trembles at my word.'). This is not the trembling of those who humble themselves before God, but the trembling of those who are terrified by his judgments. The armies of Israel were the instruments of God's judgment.

Today, God subdues the forces of evil with different weapons. 'The weapons we fight with are not the weapons of the world. On the contrary, they have divine power to demolish strongholds' (2 Cor. 10:4). We use words as our weapons (2 Cor.6:7). 'In truthful speech and in the power of God; with weapons of righteousness in the right hand and in the left.' The words we use are none other than the words of the gospel. 'Take up the shield of faith, with which you can extinguish all the flaming arrows of the evil one. Take the helmet of salvation and the sword of the Spirit, which is the word of God' (Eph. 6:16-17). Yet this spiritual battle is just as real as that which the Israelites fought. We are prone to discouragement and battle fatigue just as they were. We are tempted to avoid the battle because the enemy appears strong. Yet we are encouraged by the promise of victory. 'In all these things we are more than conquerors through him who loved us' (Rom. 8:37).

Conclusion

Do we appreciate our blessings? Do we rejoice to belong to the church of Jesus Christ and to be numbered amongst his people?

If not, why not? Could it be that someone reading this chapter has not yet come to enjoy the blessings of salvation which belong to God's people? Could it be that the reader professes to be a Christian, but has never grasped how wide and deep is God's redeeming love? Could it be that you have never taken the time to consider what God has done for the salvation of his own? You may have listed God's blessings; but have you really thought about them? More to the point, have you asked God for them? Ask God to bless you and to fill your heart with a godly contentment that leads on to worship and service.

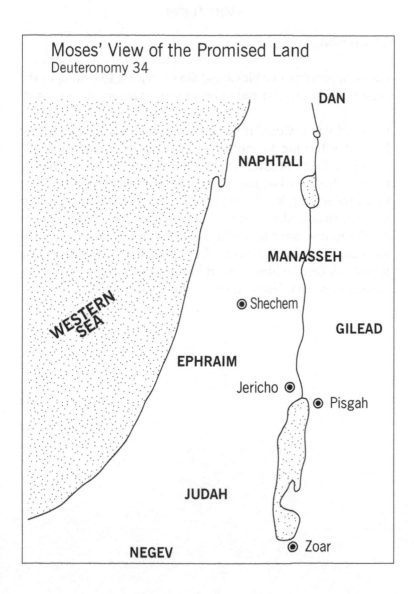

Moses' View of the Promised Land
Deuteronomy 34

DAN

NAPHTALI

MANASSEH

⊙ Shechem

WESTERN SEA

GILEAD

EPHRAIM

Jericho ⊙

⊙ Pisgah

JUDAH

NEGEV

⊙ Zoar

Chapter 34
Dying in hope

Please read Deuteronomy 34: 1-12

One of life's frustrations is an unfinished task. Some of us are very good at making lists of the things which we aim to do, but by the end of the day there are still letters to write, chores to finish, people to see and phone calls to make. We never seem to get to the end of the list, and some tasks seem endless. As I look from my study window, I will sometimes see the gardener in the park opposite my home gathering leaves. Eventually he gathers them into a pile and carts them away. Yet within a few days the park is again strewn with leaves and bark from the constantly shedding gum trees and he starts his work all over again. It is also said that a mother's work is never done, and many are the times when a mother of young children will look wearily at the pile of dirty clothes in the laundry just before dropping into bed. She knows that this ever-growing pile will be there to greet her in the morning.

As Moses drew towards the end of his life and ministry, he knew that he would leave one great task unfinished. He had led the people of Israel out of Egypt and through the wilderness for forty years, but he would not lead them into the promised land of Canaan. He had been a great leader and a great teacher, yet he would not live to see God's people living in God's land under God's law. He would die outside Canaan in the land of Moab.

God's treasured possession

In some old graveyards you may sometimes see a headstone in the form of a broken pillar. Usually it is erected over the grave of a person who had died young or in the prime of life and it symbolises a life that has been cut short and brought to an untimely end. As we read chapter 34 we might think that this has been Moses' fate. Yet, in God's eyes, there is no such thing as an 'untimely' death or a life cut short. For each one of us there is 'a time to die' (Eccles. 3:2) and that time is God's time. The Psalmist was able to say to God, 'my times are in your hands' (Ps. 31:15). To us it may seem strange, and even unfair, that Moses did not live to see the Israelites enter the promised land, but there are important lessons in this. God's plans are always perfect, though we can only see a tiny part of them. Each person plays a small part in the bigger drama and exits the stage before another takes his place. Very few are permitted to see how others will build on their work. That is why many of us will end our lives with a sense that we have accomplished only a fraction of what needs to be done in the work of God's kingdom.

In Deuteronomy 34 Moses left the stage and Joshua took over as Israel's leader. This chapter weaves together two important threads which run through Deuteronomy. The first was *the promise of the land,* which was the most visible of God's promises to Israel (see 1:6-8). The second thread was *the role of Moses.* Moses was the leader who reminded the Israelites of God's promises and taught them God's law. Yet Moses did not enter the land. What lessons can we learn from this unfinished task of Moses?

Much of this chapter was clearly written by an author other than Moses. We are not told who he was, but he is in a position to look back over the life and death of Moses. He assessed the significance of Moses' legacy. Conservative commentators who accept the Mosaic authorship of the rest of the book of Deuteronomy have long held the view that this chapter (and possibly other editorial comments) were penned by an editor who also wrote under the inspiration of the Holy Spirit. John Calvin comments, 'It is not certain who wrote this chapter; unless we admit the probable conjecture of the ancients, that Joshua was its author. But since Eleazar the priest might have performed this office, it will be better to leave a matter of no very great importance undecided.' Whoever the author might have been, he saw that Moses left heap upon heap of unfinished business to those who came after him. Yet he died in hope of one who would lead God's people into their everlasting inheritance.

Moses surveyed the land (34:1-4)

Moses knew that the end of his life was imminent (see 31:2, 14; 33:1). Chapters 31 – 33 describe the public preparations which he made for his departure. The moment of his death, however, was a very private occasion. Its location is described in 34:1a. *'Then Moses climbed Mount Nebo from the plains of Moab to the top of Pisgah, across from Jericho.'* It may be that Nebo and Pisgah were two names for the same peak; or it may be that Nebo was the name of the mountain peak while Pisgah was the name of the range of mountains. It is significant that the location of Moses' death overlooked Israel's point of entry into the promised land. Moses died on its very doorstep.

Very deliberately *'the Lord showed him the whole land'* (34:1b) and Moses surveyed it (34:4). *'I have let you see it with your eyes.'* His eyes moved anti-clockwise around the land from north to south (34:2-3). First of all he looked to the north *'from Gilead to Dan, all of Naphtali'.* Then he looked west to *'the territory of Ephraim and Manasseh, all the land of Judah as far as the western sea'.* Then Moses looked south to *'the Negev'* or the southern desert. Returning to the foreground, Moses saw *'the whole region from the valley of Jericho, the City of Palms, as far as Zoar'.* This fertile area around Jericho lay just below Moses, on the other side of the Jordan valley. Often the view from Nebo is obscured by a heat haze, but on a clear day the view is breathtaking. It must have been a clear day when the Lord showed Moses the view, as he was able to see the Mediterranean Sea, which lay about 100 km to the west. The promised land in all its splendour lay before him.

God described the theological significance of this wonderful sight (34:4a). *'This is the land I promised on oath to Abraham, Isaac and Jacob when I said, "I will give it to your descendants."'* This is the promise which had sustained the faith of Israel over many years. Now Moses could see the land in the distance. He had led Abraham's descendants to the point where they were about to possess their promised inheritance. We are not told what Moses' response to the scene before him was, but it must have been one of wonderment. John Keats described the excitement of discovery in his poem *On First Looking into Chapman's Homer.* He compared his discovery of an ancient text, which had hitherto been closed to him, with that of the first Spanish explorers to set eyes on the Pacific Ocean:

> Or like stout Cortez, when with eagle eyes
> He stared at the Pacific – and all his men
> Looked at each other with a wild surmise –
> Silent, upon a peak in Darien.

Moses' emotions must have been very mixed as he stood on Mount Nebo. He had longed for the day when the Israelites would leave the desert and enter the land 'flowing with milk and honey'. In 33:6-25 he had cast his mind's eye over the land as he blessed the tribes. There he pictured how each tribe would enjoy the inheritance which God had promised to them. Now, at last, Moses could see the land, but he was not permitted to enter into it (34:4b). *'I will let you see it with your eyes, but you will not cross over into it.'*

Dying in hope

In her novel *Wild Swans*, the Chinese writer, Jung Chang, describes the heartache of the Chinese people during the Cultural Revolution. Her mother, a Communist Party official fallen from favour, was sent into exile in the dusty plains of western China and she was allowed to make one brief visit to see her. On the return journey her mother made a last-minute decision to bring her a bowl of soup as a parting gift. On one side she could see her mother walking towards her. On the other she could see the bus coming to collect her. Her mother was unable to reach her before the bus did, and she never drank the soup. She was unable to say farewell, but could only look out of the back window of the bus until her mother disappeared from view. Her frustration was agony.

We know why God did not allow Moses to enter the land, for Moses has told us in 32:48-52. It was because of his sinful response when the people complained that there was no water to drink. God had told him speak to the rock so that water would gush out, but in his frustration Moses struck the rock. Moses did not trust God enough to speak to it as he had been told. His punishment was that he was not permitted to enter the land. Why, then, did God show him the land he was not permitted to enter? Was Jehovah dangling it in front of him, like a toy before a child, only to snatch it away when his interest was fully aroused? Was he teasing Moses? Was this a cruel and unworthy thing for Jehovah to do?

There is a more satisfactory explanation of why God showed Moses the land. In the ancient world, it was customary to view property as part of the process of buying it. Genesis 13:14-16 describes how Abraham viewed the land which God had promised to his descendants.

> The Lord said to Abram ... 'Lift up your eyes from where you are and look north and south, east and west. All the land that you see I will give to you and your offspring

for ever. I will make your offspring like the dust of the
earth, so that if anyone could count the dust, then your
offspring could be counted.'

Although Abraham was a nomad in that land, it was as good
as his because God has covenanted to give it to him. Abraham
surveyed the land as an act of faith and hope. He believed God's
promise and anticipated possession of the land. This was what
it meant to walk in covenant with Jehovah.

By the time of Moses' death, Abraham's descendants had grown
into a large nation and were about to possess the land in which
their ancestor had wandered as a nomad. God had renewed the
covenant which he had made with Abraham and reaffirmed
his promises to them. We have seen that Moses became the
mediator of that covenant. He had stood between Jehovah and
Israel, so that the Israelites might hear God's words and live
(5:27). As mediator, Moses bore the people's guilt. When they
grumbled against God, Moses suffered the consequences (see
1:37; 3:26-27; 4:21-22). As their representative and mediator he
died before they entered the land. In so doing, Moses pointed
forward to a better mediator, whose atoning death secured an
everlasting inheritance.

As the mediator of God's covenant with Israel, Moses also took
possession of the promised land. He was the representative
of the whole nation and he took possession of the land by
viewing it. After viewing the land, Moses died and bequeathed
it to Israelites. Not only was he a mediator, he was a testator.
A testator is someone who makes out a will and leaves an
inheritance for those who come after him. But first the testator
must die before they can benefit from the terms of the will. The
writer to the Hebrews drew upon this analogy in Hebrews 9:15-
17, where he describes Jesus Christ as the Mediator of a new and
better covenant. 'In the case of a will, it is necessary to prove

the death of the one who made it, because a will is in force only when somebody has died.' That is why it was necessary for Jesus Christ to die before his chosen people could receive their heavenly inheritance. On a different mountain, the Mount of Transfiguration, he was permitted to see, along with Moses and Elijahence the , the glory which both he and his people would inherit (see Luke 9:31, where Jesus is compared to Moses, because he will bring about an 'exodus' or 'departure' for those he saves through his death on the cross).

It was fitting that Moses should survey the land before he died. Like Abraham, he lived and died anticipating God's provision of a homeland. So did every other Old Testament believer.

> All these people were still living by faith when they died. They did not receive the things promised; they only saw them and welcomed them from a distance. And they admitted that they were aliens and strangers on earth... Indeed they were longing for a better country – a heavenly one (Heb. 11:13, 16).

This forward look is still an essential part of the faith of Christians. The New Testament teaches us that the promises of God to Abraham and his descendants are fulfilled in Christ. Through his ministry the kingdom of God has been established on earth (see Mark 1:15). However, the kingdom of God on earth is still to come. There is so much that remains to be revealed and enjoyed by believers.

> Christ was sacrificed once to take away the sins of many people; and he will appear a second time, not to bear sin, but to bring salvation to those who are waiting for him... Therefore, since we are receiving a kingdom that cannot be shaken, let us be thankful, and so worship God acceptably with reverence and awe (Heb. 9:28, 12:28).

This forward look is important because it keeps us from becoming complacent with what we already enjoy. This is a real danger, especially in those times when all seems to be going well in our churches and personal lives. At such times the edge goes off our spiritual hunger.

How keenly do we pray, 'Your kingdom come. Your will be done on earth as it is in heaven'? How keenly do we anticipate our heavenly inheritance? Do we think of ourselves as strangers in this world? Or perhaps, might it be true that our earthly possessions really are our greatest joy? How important it is to cultivate a godly discontent with our earthly lives! How important it is to survey, with eyes of faith and eager longing, the better country which God has prepared for his believing people!

Moses died outside the land (34:5-8)

These verses describe the events that surrounded Moses' death, but they do more. They capture both the sadness and the significance of Moses' death for the people of Israel. Moses was one of Israel's greatest leaders and his death brought an end to his unique ministry. He served in many different capacities. He fulfilled the functions of a prophet, a priest and a king, yet he was appointed to none of these offices. He is best known as a law-giver, but his role was much wider.

In 34:5 he is referred to simply as 'Moses the servant of the LORD'. This is how he was often described in the Old Testament Scriptures (see Josh. 1:1, 7; 2 Kings 21:8; Ps. 105:26; Mal.4:4). The title 'servant of the Lord' was frequently given to the prophets, to King David, to the nation of Israel and to the suffering servant of Isaiah 53. The point of this designation is that servants place a greater importance on the service which they can render than the status which they enjoy. The writer to the Hebrews characterised Moses as such a servant. 'Moses was faithful as a servant in all God's house' (Heb. 3:5). The implication here in this final chapter of Deuteronomy is that this is how Moses would have wanted to be remembered. He was a servant, not a master in Israel. He pointed people to God, not to himself. That, too, is how Paul came to see himself. 'What, after all, is Apollos? And what is Paul? Only servants, through whom you came to believe' (1 Cor. 3:5).

Having acknowledged this, the death of a faithful servant of God is a blow to the people of God. The death of Moses was no exception. In 34:5-8 we are told that Moses died, was buried, and was mourned.

We are told about his *death* in 34:5. He *'died there in Moab, as the LORD had said.'* Moses was like every other fallen human being, in that he died because of Adam's sin. God's decree in Genesis 2:17 was that Adam would die if he ate from the tree of the knowledge of good and evil. Through that act of disobedience sin and death came upon all mankind (Rom. 5:12, 14), including Moses. Yet the circumstances of Moses' death were peculiar to him. His death did not come at the end of a period of physical decline. He was a remarkably fit man when he died (34:7). *'Moses was a hundred and twenty years old when he died, yet his eyes were not weak nor his strength gone.'* He looked and acted like a man many years his junior when he died. It may have looked as though Moses had discovered the secret of everlasting youth, but he hadn't. The Lord preserved him in a remarkably good condition until his work was completed. Then death removed him just as God had said.

God had said that Moses would die outside the land of Canaan because of his sinful actions (see Num. 20:11-12). Moses was reminded of this in 32:48-52. Yet it was also true that the folly of the Israelites played a role in God's reasoning (see 1:37; 3:26-27; 4:21-22). Moses was both a sinner who suffered the consequences of his actions and a mediator who bore the penalty due to others. Yet nowhere do we read of Moses complaining about his lot. Nowhere does he charge God with injustice or treating him unfairly. Like the psalmist in Psalm 51:4 he acknowledged, 'Against you, you only, have I sinned and done what is evil in your sight, so that you are proved right when you speak and justified when you judge'. Like Abraham in Genesis 18:25, he acknowledged that Jehovah was a just God who could do no wrong. 'Will not the Judge of all the earth do right?'

We are told about his *burial* in 34:6. The burial of our physical bodies is a pointed reminder that we are human and mortal. Our father Adam was created from the dust of the earth, and when he sinned he was reminded that his body would dissolve into the earth.

> Cursed is the ground because of you ...
> until you return to the ground,
> since from it you were taken;
> for dust you are
> and to dust you will return.
> (Gen. 3:17-19)

The ritual of burial is a God-given reminder of our origins in Adam.

This was especially so in the case of Moses for *'He buried him in Moab'*. This refers to an action of God. It was a mysterious and supernatural action with no human involvement. Those who saw Moses ascend the mountain did not see him come down, nor did they see where he was buried. *'To this day no-one knows where his grave is.'* Clearly, God did not want the grave of Moses to become a place of pilgrimage. If the bronze serpent that Moses had made for the healing of the people could become a focus for idolatrous worship (see 2 Kings 18:4), how much more might the place of his burial. God did not allow that to happen. In the gospel accounts of the death of the Lord Jesus we are also told about the burial of his body (see Matt. 27:59-61; Mark 15:46-47; Luke 23:50-55; John 19:38-42). The burial of Jesus is not an incidental detail of gospel history. Paul describes its significance in 1 Corinthians 15:4. It forces us to come to terms with the historical reality of his death. As well as being the Son of God, he became a man. His burial is a reminder that he truly became a man. Many in the early church needed to hear that message. Perhaps some Israelites needed to be reminded that Moses was only a man. His death and burial would have demonstrated that fact beyond all doubt.

We are told about the *mourning* of the Israelites in 34:8. '*The Israelites grieved for Moses in the plains of Moab thirty days, until the time of weeping and mourning was over.*' The death of every child of God is a moment to pause and reflect on both the tragedy of death (see John 11:35) and the hope of everlasting life (see John 11:25-26; Rom. 6:23). The death of an outstanding leader of God's people is a great loss and deserves special recognition. King David exhorted the people of Israel to acknowledge the loss they had suffered through the deaths of his predecessor King Saul and his son Jonathan (2 Sam. 1:17-27); and also the cruel murder of Saul's general Abner (2 Sam. 3:38). 'Do you not realise that a prince and a great man has fallen in Israel this day?'

Moses was a great leader of the Israelites. He was honoured with a period of national mourning which lasted for a month. A similar period of time was devoted to mourning the death of Aaron (see Num. 20:29). Only one other figure in the Old Testament was mourned for a longer period. That was Jacob, the father of the nation. He was mourned for a period of seventy days (see Gen. 50:3). Yet the period of mourning did not last for ever. The people of Israel had lost one leader, but God continued to provide for all their needs. Another leader was waiting in the wings to take over from Moses. He would step forward to lead the people into the land of promise.

Moses laid hands on his successor (34:9-12)

'The king is dead. Long like the king.' Such is the traditional proclamation that the monarch has died. Yet it signals the continuity of the monarchy. There is no interregnum, for the king's successor immediately ascends the throne. Although Moses was emphatically not Israel's king, when he died his successor was at hand ready and able to take the lead. Many years earlier Moses had taken Joshua as his assistant and confidant (Exod. 33:11; Deut. 1:38). Over the next forty years he was trained to take over from Moses. Moses was instructed to make sure that everyone knew who his successor was to be. 'So the LORD said to Moses, "Take Joshua son of Nun, a man in whom is the spirit, and lay your hand on him. Have him stand before Eleazar the priest and the entire assembly and commission him in their presence"' (Num. 27:18-19). So when Moses died, Joshua was both equipped and authorised to lead the Israelites into Canaan.

In 34:9 we are told how Joshua was *equipped* to lead the Israelites. *'Now Joshua son of Nun was filled with the spirit of wisdom because Moses had laid his hands upon him.'* In Numbers 27:18 we are told that Joshua already possessed the Spirit of God when Moses laid his hands upon him. Yet he received an even greater measure of that same Spirit when Moses laid his hands upon him. In particular, he received the wisdom that only God's Spirit can give, the wisdom that enables men to know and do God's will. This is the kind of wisdom which the Lord gave to Bezalel son of Uri so that he might fashion the tabernacle according to the pattern of God's design (Exod. 31:2-3). This is the wisdom that King Solomon sought in order to rule the people of Israel, and in particular to know how to distinguish between right and wrong (1 Kings 3:9-11). Those who shepherd God's people need this wisdom every day, in all the decisions they make (Ps. 78:72). We are all invited to pray for it. 'If any of you lacks wisdom, he should ask God, who gives generously to all without finding fault, and it will be given to him' (James 1:5).

Joshua was *authorised* to lead the Israelites. The Lord had told Moses to give Joshua some of the authority which he had exercised. 'Give him some of your authority so the whole Israelite community will obey him... At his command he and the entire community of the Israelites will go out, and at his command they will come in' (Num. 27:20-21). The result of this grant of authority is described in 34:9b. *'So the Israelites listened to him and did what the LORD had commanded Moses.'* Joshua was able to speak with the authority of one appointed by God to lead the people. This was an awesome privilege and he would have the terrible responsibility of making many life and death decisions over the years. Only with the certain knowledge that God was leading him could he bear this responsibility.

Yet Joshua was not another Moses. The final verses of Deuteronomy, 34:10-12, make that clear. The succession ceremony described in 34:9 clearly took place before the death and burial of Moses described in 34:5-6. The break in chronological sequence is deliberate. Deuteronomy ends not with Moses' death, but with Moses' successor. Joshua was his immediate successor, but not his ultimate successor. In fact we are told that *'since then, no prophet has risen in Israel like Moses'.* Over the years, many prophets would arise in Israel. King David would say, 'The Spirit of the LORD spoke through me; his word was on my tongue' (2 Sam. 23:1-2). It would be said of Elijah, 'You are a man of God and ... the word of the LORD from your mouth is the truth' (1 Kings 17:24). The Lord himself reached out to touch the mouth of Jeremiah and say, 'Now, I have put my words in your mouth' (Jer. 1:9). Yet none of these men would be in the same league as Moses. The final verses of Deuteronomy tell us what made Moses unique in the history of Israel.

i. Moses was unique because *the Lord knew him face to face* (34:10). *'Since then, no prophet has risen in Israel like Moses, whom the LORD knew face to face.'* This was an awesome privilege. When God invited the leaders of Israel to the top of Mount Sinai to confirm his covenant with them, he told Aaron, his sons and the seventy elders to 'worship at a distance' (see Exod. 24:1-2). Moses alone was to approach the Lord. Only Moses entered the cloud and stayed on the mountain for forty days and nights (Exod. 24:18). What Moses saw there is beyond description. It was more awesome even than the throne of God on a pavement of sapphire, which Aaron, Nadab and Abihu and the seventy elders saw in Exodus 24:9-11. Moses saw the unseeable, for 'the LORD knew (him) face to face'. Moses saw 'heavenly things' of which the tabernacle was but a copy and shadow (see Heb. 8:5; 9:23).

This was not something that happened only once, for in Numbers 12:6-8a Jehovah described the recurring nature of his fellowship with Moses.

> When a prophet of the LORD is among you,
> I reveal myself to him in visions,
> I speak to him in dreams.
> But this is not true of my servant Moses;
> he is faithful in all my house.
> With him I speak face to face,
> clearly and not in riddles;
> he sees the form of the LORD.

Moses was the mediator of the old covenant between Jehovah and Israel, and as such had an ongoing fellowship with both. This close fellowship was something that God desired.

ii. Moses was unique because *he performed mighty miracles* (34:11-12). No prophet *'did all those miraculous signs and wonders the LORD sent him to do in Egypt—to Pharaoh and to all his officials and to his whole land*'. Nor did any other man do the miracles which Moses had so visibly done. '*For no-one has ever shown the mighty power or performed the awesome deeds that Moses did in the sight of all Israel.*' Not only are the miracles of the Exodus in view here, but also the miracles performed for Israel's protection and provision over the following forty years. These miracles demonstrated that God was working in and through Moses.

These miracles of the exodus and the wilderness period point to the miraculous work of redemption which has been accomplished for us through the life, death and resurrection of the Lord Jesus. When, on the day of Pentecost, Peter explained the significance of the Lord Jesus, he drew a parallel between Jesus and Moses at this point. 'Men of Israel, listen to this: Jesus of Nazareth was a man accredited by God to you by miracles, wonders and signs, which God did among you through him' (Acts 2:22). The writer to the Hebrews describes the way in which this salvation was announced by the Lord. 'God also testified to it by signs, wonders and various miracles, and gifts of the Holy Spirit distributed according to his will' (Heb. 2:4).

Although we are told in 34:10-12 that no prophet – indeed no person – like Moses had arisen in Israel, we are told in 18:15-18 that such a prophet *would* arise. Moses own prophecy was confirmed by the promise of Jehovah to Moses. 'I will raise up for them a prophet like you from among their brothers; I will put my words in his mouth, and he will tell them everything I command him.' The book of Deuteronomy concluded with that hope, as yet, unfulfilled.

The one to whom Deuteronomy looked would have, in even greater measure, all the unique characteristics of Moses. He would know God and enjoy face to face fellowship with Him. He would perform the mighty miracles of salvation which no man could do. In the opening verses of John's gospel, the Lord

God's treasured possession

Jesus appears as one who is greater even than Moses. 'For the law was given through Moses; grace and truth came through Jesus Christ. No-one has ever seen God, but God the One and Only, who is at the Father's side, has made him known' (John 1:17-18). His greatest miracle was to rise from the dead so that he might deliver his new Israel from the dominion of darkness and lead them into the kingdom of light.